To the Editor

A CENTURY OF LETTERS

OTTAWA CITIZEN

Edited by Doug Fischer

Designed by Ralph Willsey

Published in 2000 by
The Ottawa Citizen
1101 Baxter Road
Box 5020
Ottawa, Ontario
K2C 3M4
613-829-9100

Canadian Cataloguing in Publication Data

Main entry under title:
To The Editor: A Century of Letters to the Ottawa Citizen
ISBN 0-9698908-4-2

Proceeds benefit the Ottawa Citizen Literacy Foundation

Design: Ralph Willsey

Printed and bound in Canada by M.O.M. Printing, Ottawa, Ontario

CONTENTS

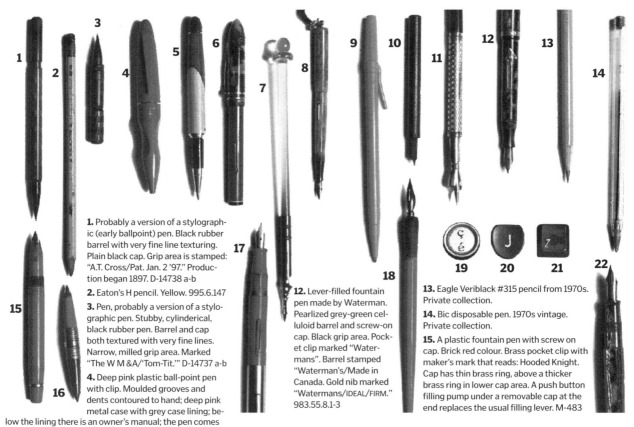

1. Probably a version of a stylographic (early ballpoint) pen. Black rubber barrel with very fine line texturing. Plain black cap. Grip area is stamped: "A.T. Cross/Pat. Jan. 2 '97." Production began 1897. D-14738 a-b

2. Eaton's H pencil. Yellow. 995.6.147

3. Pen, probably a version of a stylographic pen. Stubby, cylinderical, black rubber pen. Barrel and cap both textured with very fine lines. Narrow, milled grip area. Marked "The W M &A/'Tom-Tit.'" D-14737 a-b

4. Deep pink plastic ball-point pen with clip. Moulded grooves and dents contoured to hand; deep pink metal case with grey case lining; below the lining there is an owner's manual; the pen comes with an ink compartment replacement which has a white tube covering the end. On case is the notation: "Luis Gonzalez by Tombow." 1996.39.6 a-f

5. Wood ballpoint pen, fine tipped. Black soft plastic open ended case, with flap. Dark and light woods laminated to form continuous sine wave at top and bottom of barrel. Gold metal decoration and clip. "Crown Multi Roller Refill 0.5 53.11 Korea" on refill. Wide gold band around snap-off cap. 1996.42.2 a-e

6. Fountain pen. Bright medium blue plastic barrel. Mottled light and dark blue screw-on cap. Gold pocket clip stamped with: "Arcadia." D-14736

7. Dip pen with thin glass shaft with end heat manipulated to form a "newel post" finial. Shaft fitted into brass tang which holds a fine steel nib shaped like a stylized Eiffel ? tower (nib is marked "No. 324/VA EXTRA/E"). Narrow black paper-covered box with black velvet lining in base. Lid stamped in gold with a circular symbol and "ABRAXAS." 96-139

8. Miniature pen, mottled amber/tortoise shell barrel and screw-on cap. Cap has gold metal loop for hanging from ribbon or chain. Gold filling lever marked "SB" [Salz Brothers Inc.] and "Peter Pan." Narrow black corded ribbon attached to loop. Production start 1930 c. D-15886

9. Pink felt-tip pen. 1980s. "USA" moulded into end of barrel. Private collection.

10. Straight pen or dip pen. Short, cylinderical wood barrel stained black and impressed: "His Nibs by Brattleboro." Medium broad nib. D-14733

11. Gold and black dip (straight) pen, likely of bakelite. Cylinderical shaft. More than one-half the length is gold, with a fine, engraved, checkerboard pattern. Remainder of shaft is black bakelite-type plastic with a small white metal dot inlaid near the end. Long "tang" holds gold nib in the shape of a pointing right hand, with the forefinger forming the nib. Narrow, dark leather-covered case with purple velvet lining in the base and white fabric in the lid. Stamped on the lid in gold, inside an oval is: "Edward Todd & Co./Gold Pens/New York." 1999.98.19 a-b

12. Lever-filled fountain pen made by Waterman. Pearlized grey-green celluloid barrel and screw-on cap. Black grip area. Pocket clip marked "Watermans". Barrel stamped "Waterman's/Made in Canada. Gold nib marked "Watermans/IDEAL/FIRM." 983.55.8.1-3

13. Eagle Veriblack #315 pencil from 1970s. Private collection.

14. Bic disposable pen. 1970s vintage. Private collection.

15. A plastic fountain pen with screw on cap. Brick red colour. Brass pocket clip with maker's mark that reads: Hooded Knight. Cap has thin brass ring, above a thicker brass ring in lower cap area. A push button filling pump under a removable cap at the end replaces the usual filling lever. M-483

About those pens on the cover:

Along with samples of keys from typing devices, they represent the many kinds of writing instruments used by the countless hands that addressed comments to the *Ottawa Citizen* during the Twentieth Century. Most are from the Canadian Museum of Civilization collections, and several of those were to appear in a Postal Museum exhibit in spring of 2000.

Special thanks go to Isabel Jones of the Museum of Civilization's Historical Division for her tireless search for information on these objects. We are also grateful to Bianca Gendreau of the Museum's postal collection for this preview of her exhibit of pens.

Museum catalogue numbers follow the descriptions (except for the objects from private collections).

Photographed by Ralph Willsey

16. Short-barrelled ball-point pen; one end blue plastic, with gold metal point, the other, red, joined with a central gold metal joint. The central band of the joint forms part of the exterior decoration when a gold metal cap for each end is in place. Interchangeable caps are friction fit, with only one having a pocket clip. 2000.14.45 a-b

17. A red plastic fountain pen with brass or gold plated friction fit cap. Pocket clip marked "National." Gold coloured metal filling lever on side. M-484

18. Wood straight pen, painted red, with cork grip area. F-9706

19. Manual typewriter; black enamel heavy metal frame; wooden space bar; red-and-black ribbon; French accent keys; front of frame has gold lettering: "L.C. Smith & Bros." A decal in the shape of a red seal reading: Typewriters/Sales/Gerard Poulin/Tel. 3-2622/Service/Quebec." Also on the centre of the platen is: "Ottawa Typewriter Co., Ltd./Ottawa, Ont." 981.35.238

20. Underwood 5. Considered by many the ultimate manual typewriter; only an electric would provide greater ease of typing.

21. IMac computer, 1999 model. Ready for all forms of digital communication — including e-mail to the editor — "right out of the box."

22. OMAS celluloid pearlized brown-and-cream fountain pen, marked "1993." (OMAS is the acronym for Officina meccanica Armando Simoni. According to information on various websites, the colour of this pen is named "Arco" by the manufacturer and is described as "a shade of variegated yellow-ochre.") 1996.133.1 a-e

The need to speak freely

After nearly 10 years as the man who looks after the *Ottawa Citizen's* letters-to-the-editor pages, I've started playing a little guessing game with myself. Each morning as I read the newspaper over breakfast, I try to predict which of that day's news items is most likely to fire up our readers. Sometimes I'm right. But even with a decade of practice, most times I'm not.

Let's take the naming of animals at Ottawa's Central Experimental Farm as an example. In October 1999, the *Citizen* carried an item noting that bureaucrats had decided the farm's animals were to be given numbers rather than names to avoid offending their human namesakes. Now, I know that animal stories attract letters, but this one didn't involve cruelty or courage, and so I placed it well down on my scale of expectation.

Holy cow, was I wrong. Before the morning was over, enough e-mail to fill a newspaper page had rolled in. Soon there was enough to fill two pages. Recognizing we were on to something, editor-in-chief Neil Reynolds said we should do just that. And so, on two side-by-side pages, we let our readers, ahem, milk the subject for all it was worth in 48 letters. The overwhelming view was that cows need names, and the Experimental Farm responded by rescinding the order and even inviting the public to help name the next batch of calves. All was right with the world.

Then, early in 2000, along came the story of the bungled billion. Ah, this will bring in the letters, I told myself as I envisioned days of pages laden with anti-government vitriol. Sure enough, there was reaction — but far less, and with far less emotion, than might be expected for a story about the mismanagement of $1 billion in federal jobs funds, and a story the media was portraying as a major scandal.

Why the light reaction? Maybe the numbers were just too big to understand, or maybe the bungling came as no surprise to those who know government. In this town, that's a lot of people. It's also possible the public servants who knew what went wrong were reluctant to speak out for fear of repercussions. After all, whistle blowers still lose their jobs in Canada.

At any rate, mark it down as another bad prediction. But it's probably just that unpredictable nature that keeps the letters pages from becoming dull. Perhaps it's not so much the issue that matters to people as the principle. Take a look at the letters from the past 100 years that make up this book and you'll see a deep need on the part of citizens to right a wrong, to set the record straight, to point out potential solutions. Make no mistake, writing a letter also carries a strong therapeutic value — many a writer has admitted feeling better just by putting his or her thoughts on paper, even knowing they might never be published.

Of all the places in a newspaper, perhaps nothing better represents the special bond between a reader and the paper than the letters page. It offers a feeling of a joint ownership, and a forum where the ordinary citizen is given a voice that carries the same resonance as the rich and powerful. In short, it fulfils the human need to speak freely.

A decade in this job has taught me that letter-writers fall into four main categories: the once-in-a lifetime contributor; the regular who is ready to comment on anything; the lobbyist pushing a particular cause; and the knowledgeable retiree who finally has the time to expound on issues close to his or her heart. I've also discovered that the national capital, because of its special place in the Canadian scheme of things, is home to experts on just about everything — science, the arts, government, justice, sports, religion or the military.

Whatever their expertise, readers are not shy about expressing their opinions. In a year, we receive about 20,000 letters and publish nearly 6,000 on topics ranging from the need for dogs to run free to the place of God in a modern society. For those who like lists, the Top 10 topics of '99 were: the war in Kosovo (214 letters published); the Ottawa Senators (160); Alexei Yashin's salary (120); Ontario election (113); one-tier municipal government (99); religion (95); shootings (80); dogs (78); brain drain (68) and cows (48).

In this age of high-technology and fast-paced video games, it's gratifying to know many schools are still encouraging the art of writing to the newspaper. I know, because every so often a parcel of 30 or 40 letters from a class arrives in the mail. It usually means pupils have been asked to read the paper, pick a topic and write a letter commenting on the news. Those letters might not get into print all that often, but they bode well for the future.

As we embark on that future in a new century, it seems suitable that we should look back at the 100 years just ended through these fascinating personal glimpses into the history of Canada's capital.

But don't take it from me. Turn the pages and read them for yourself.

— Brian Sarjeant

Preface

A letter, like a photograph, acts as a sort of time capsule. It permits us to look back in history, freeze a moment in time and imagine ourselves as part of the past. Through it, we are allowed to relive a great event, or ordinary life, in exquisite detail.

And, like a photograph, a letter more often than not gives us an unvarnished glimpse of its creator's heart. Whether an expression of pain or a paean of thanks, a political screed or a satirical punch, a letter is an intimate affair that can show us the way its author thinks, and talks, and learns — and feels.

Multiply a letter by thousands, publish the results over 100 years, and those many private expressions become a public diary of a century in time. And when they're collected from one place, those expressions become a kind of grassroots chronicle of a community — in this instance, Ottawa in the 1900s.

That type of social-history-with-heart was what *Ottawa Citizen* senior editor Lynn McAuley had in mind in late 1998 when she first pitched the idea of telling the story of Ottawa's 20th century through letters to the editor. As the city's only English-language daily publishing when the 1900s dawned and still at it when they ended, the *Citizen* possessed a unique record of the century, McAuley noted.

Initially, the plans called for a coffee table-style book combining photographs and 200 or 300 of the best letters published between 1900 and 1999. But over time, it was agreed the letters would have a much wider readership — and we would be able to reprint many hundreds more of them — if they were presented as a series in the newspaper. The result was 100 pages of letters, one for every year of the century, published over the final 100 days of 1999.

The response from readers was more than anyone anticipated. Hundreds called and wrote, the vast majority expressing delight and sharing nostalgia. But many of those same people were also dismayed that their collection of 100 years would be left incomplete because of winter vacations in Florida or out-of-town trips over Christmas. Package and preserve them in a book, they told us. And so we have.

Even for readers familiar with the newspaper series, a bit of background on how we picked the letters is probably in order. It's difficult to be precise, but the *Citizen* published at least 250,000 letters during the 1900s. And while most of them were reviewed for this project, they weren't always easy to find. Until newspapers were archived in computerized data banks in the mid-1980s, the *Citizen* stored its letters — and the rest of its content — on microfilm. From the early 1920s onward, that didn't present much of a problem; the quality of microfilm copies was good, and our collection was relatively complete.

The microfilm from the first two decades of the century, however, was a different matter. It contained many unreadable pages, and to make matters worse, it was full of gaps — including a few missing years — that we eventually were able to fill elsewhere, most notably at the National Library of Canada.

Throughout the spring and early summer of 1999, the letters were collected and sorted into two- or three-year bundles and passed out to editors, reporters, columnists and newsroom managers, each of whom was asked to reduce thousands of letters to the best 50 or so from each year.

Their instructions were straightforward: look for letters as full of vitality and interest today as the day they were penned — writing that captures the flavour, drama, enthusiasm and emotion of life in the capital as it emerged from a rough-and-tumble provincial lumber town into a sophisticated international centre of technology. As a general rule, we preferred letters from individuals over those from interest groups, but thoughtful or telling missives from organizations were not automatically eliminated.

Eventually, about 5,000 letters were handed back, and they in turn were culled to the 1,200 letters — and nearly 300,000 words — published in the *Citizen* during the autumn of 1999 and collected, with a few additions and some new photographs, in the pages ahead.

We have taken considerable care to reprint the letters as they were first published. Some have been shortened in the interest of focus, and, in a few instances, punctuation and spelling have been altered to improve readability. But the flourish and flair of the originals remain largely intact.

For the most part, the letters are left to tell their own

stories. Sometimes, though, we've tacked on an editor's note to provide the outcome of an event or debate, or to offer context to a long-forgotten issue. These always appear in italics at the end of a letter. Original editor's notes — those that accompanied letters when they were first published — are clearly identified. And round brackets appearing in letters were there originally; square brackets have been added as clarification for the contemporary reader.

The letters are arranged chronologically and broken into decades for convenience. To offer an extra bit of context, each year's selection of letters is preceded by a brief summary of that year's news highlights and a list of notable births and deaths.

Readers will notice that for the first 21 years of the century, the *Citizen* did not require correspondents to sign their letters, and that *noms de plumes* were commonplace. For most of the century, though, the newspaper insisted on real names and took pains to verify the authenticity of letters, a practice that continues today.

What hasn't changed much in the past century are the issues on the public's mind. The battle of the sexes, children and families, sickness and health, crime, winter, bad drivers, French-English relations, disreputable politicians, lousy phone and mail service, pets, schools, faith, drinking, romantic gossip, the environment, hockey and patriotism were as much discussed in the early 1900s as they are today.

Our wish is that these links to the past might prompt you to reflect on how a well-functioning democratic community debates with itself, and help you get to know the people who worked and walked in the streets of this city in the distant past and who left for us the fascinating and sometimes frustrating place we call home today.

— Doug Fischer,
February 2000

Acknowledgements

Many people played a part in the production of this book.

Ottawa Citizen publisher Russ Mills, editor-in-chief Neil Reynolds and executive editor Don Butler should be acknowledged for their encouragement and for clearing the space and the time to properly collect, edit, research and publish the letters.

Tina Spencer, editor of the editorial pages, is owed thanks for turning over 100 pages of her precious real estate so readers might have their daily helping of polemics from the past and, through their interest, tell us these letters also belonged in a book.

Research help came from many quarters, although Liisa Tuominen of the *Citizen* library and Serge Barbe at the City of Ottawa Archives deserve special mention. Other researchers who made notable contributions include Louie Weidemann, Ron Tysick, Jim Scheer, Bruce Deachman, Jim McAuley, Martin Cleary, Tom Casey, Charlene Ruberry, Lois Kirkup, Drew Fischer and Chris Lacroix.

Editing support came from Kurt Johnson, Brian Sarjeant, John Robson and Bob Reade of the *Citizen's* editorial pages department and proof-reading was provided by Linda Mondoux.

Appreciation is extended to the 25 newsroom employees who put in many late nights working on the initial sort of the letters. Among them, Lynn McAuley, editor of *The Citizen's Weekly*, should be singled out for coming up with the idea in the first place and for devising a strategy to deal with the volume of letters.

Ralph Willsey deserves special thanks for designing the book and its cover, which he photographed and researched, and for his advice. A big debt is also owed to Danielle Gauthier for collecting and collating the majority of the letters under the stress of unreasonable deadlines.

And, finally, our largest measure of gratitude goes to the thousands of readers whose thoughts and ideas — eloquent and raw, generous and narrow-minded, inspired and practical, satirical and earnest, pained and joyous — have been combined to create this unique memoir of a century in the life of a city.

"It is not uncertain prophecy but sound deduction that the year 2000 will come on Canada with a population of eighty (80) million."

— February 18, 1905

1900-1909

1900

Local: The Great Fire of Ottawa-Hull kills seven, destroys 3,000 buildings and leaves 8,500 homeless (April); Eastern Ontario experiences one of the coolest early summers in history, with temperatures dipping below freezing in late June

National: The first Canadian troops ever sent overseas arrive in South Africa as part of British contingent fighting the Boer War (February); Canada marks the arrival of a new century with what is believed to be the first fireworks display on Parliament Hill (December)

World: British working men form the Labour Representation Committee, a trade union alliance which eventually becomes the Labour party (February); About 100,000 foreigners are massacred across China in the so-called Boxer Rebellion, an outgrowth of traditional anti-foreign sentiment combined with animosity toward Christian missionaries (July)

Births: Governor general Roland Michener; jazz legend Louis Armstrong; Newfoundland premier Joey Smallwood; film star Spencer Tracy; British war hero Lord Mountbatten

Deaths: German philosopher Friedrich Nietzsche; British playwright Oscar Wilde; composer Arthur Sullivan

CITY OF OTTAWA ARCHIVES

**Ottawa Fire Chief
Peter Provost**

DID NOT DANCE

JANUARY 26, 1900

A recent publication of your newspaper erroneously stated that Cameron Lodge, I.O.G.T., had wound up its meeting with a hop. I have been requested by resolution of the lodge to call attention to said error and to assure its many friends that Cameron Lodge will in the future, as in the past, adhere to the constitution of the order, which forbids dancing parties in connection with any of its meetings, or in any hall controlled by the lodge. Will you kindly give space for this correction in order to remove any false impression which may have been created by said report.

J. Eagleson,
Lodge deputy

Editor's note: In the late 1800s and early 1900s, the I.O.G.T. (International Order of Good Templars) was the world's largest temperance organization. In some ways, it was a progressive body, permitting women and the poor to serve as executives. By the '20s, however, the order had lost influence and credibility amid a debate over whether to allow blacks and Jews as members. It is not known when the Ottawa lodge was disbanded.

ODE TO THE ABSENT-MINDED EDITOR

FEBRUARY 17, 1900

When you've seized the daily paper, and ejaculated
"Wow!"
As you read the columns cabled from the south;
When you've finished cussing Buller, and have quite decided how
You could manage mighty armies — with your mouth;
Just cast your optics lower, where the efforts of the bard
Are inserted (when the printer fails to "pl" 'em).
By an Absent-minded Editor, who has to work so hard

That he lets a lot of little rhymes slip by him.
Lame rhyme, tame rhyme, worse than a rhubarb pill; —
Fifty thousand blooming bards scribbling beastly verse —
Each of them copying Kipling's ode (and doesn't this make you ill?)
Tear up the sheet — you're caught again
And curse, curse, curse!

E.T.B.G.

Editor's note: Letters in the form of poetry were a common, and sly, way to get unpopular opinion printed in newspapers in the early years of the century. The reference to Buller in the above jibe at the Citizen's editor is to Gen. Sir Redvers Buller, commander of Britain's forces in the Boer War, whose refusal to use modern war methods led to bloody losses and his dismissal a few weeks before the poem was published.

STAY THIS VANDALISM

MARCH 17, 1900

The excellent scheme of the Ontario government to set aside two million acres of forest land as a forest reserve and provincial park, containing within its borders the matchless lakes of Temagaming, Lady Evelyn and Diamond, besides others of lesser note, seems likely to receive a black eye at its very inception, unless sufficient influence is brought to bear to counteract the malign agency at work to utterly destroy the beauty of the park.

It appears that an application is before the commissioner of Crown lands, Hon. E.J. Davis, from the Sturgeon Falls Pulp Company, for permission to construct two dams, one near Temagami Falls, the other at Sharp Rock Portage, the southern and northern outlets respectively of Lake Temagaming, thereby to ensure an extra supply of water during the dry months in summer.

The pulp company's intentions were ostensibly subject to government permission, but before receiving it, they sent out gangs of men and actually commenced work on the dams, and the government had to send out law officers to enjoin them to stop work, although the pulp company had more than once in response to governmental inquiries stated that no work was being done pending the government's decision.

The effect of damming this lake and raising its level will be to ruin the appearance of the park; the action of the raised water kills a fringe of trees along every shore, and only those who have seen the once beautiful Lake Kippewa can realize what a desolation can be created by the seemingly innocent raising of the water level.

It is apparent from the Sturgeon Falls company's action so far, that they intend to ruin this park unless adequate protective measures are adopted.

A hearing is to take place before Hon. E. J. Davis, at which all points at issue will be gone into thoroughly. I hope all friends of the park scheme will be present in force and defeat the intended vandalism.

Yours truly,
A worried onlooker

Editor's note: The two dams were eventually approved and plans for the park radically scaled back. To save face and offset the losses, the Ontario government expanded the boundaries of the province's first park, Algonquin Park, making it the largest provincially operated park in Canada.

AN AXE BRIGADE
MAY 5, 1900

In this morning's edition of your paper I read an article entitled "The Bucket Brigade." Having been present all Thursday afternoon, at different sections, during the conflagration and having noticed many places where the fire might have been arrested by the pulling or chopping down of a few old sheds or wooden houses, I would suggest that you add to your volunteer bucket brigade a volunteer axe brigade. The two working together would have saved property to the amount of many thousands.

A sufferer

Editor's note: This letter refers to the Great Fire of Ottawa-Hull, which began mid-morning on Thursday, April 26, when a small chimney fire in Hull was spread by winds across the Ottawa River, burning the Chaudière Bridge, several lumberyards and most of the homes in the area now known as LeBreton Flats. By the time the fire burned out at midnight, seven people were dead, 3,000 buildings were destroyed and 8,500 people were homeless. No action was taken on the writer's suggestion for a volunteer axe brigade.

HONOUR THE WOMEN
MAY 10, 1900

Will you allow space for this editorial note, clipped from *The Bowmanville Statesman* — a deserved tribute to noble women, who have good reason to fear the licensed barroom:

"All honour to the noble wives and mothers who signed the requisition to the license commissioners against granting licenses in Newtonville and Orono [towns just north of Lake Ontario and east of Toronto]. In some cases, husbands and brothers signed the counter petition. It was a grand victory they won, too. No new licenses were granted. The amazing problem to us is that so many professedly Christian people could be found who would put their names on a petition that a license should be granted. Surely their conscience must have chided them hotly for smothering their principles to please the man who wanted to be legally permitted to assist in ruining the youth, and others who chose to drink the liquor that makes inebriates of all who indulge. Had they seriously considered the nature of their action, we think they would not have lent the power of their name to the would-be liquor seller."

It has been said that women should have the franchise. Perhaps they should. But this instance illustrates the power which they now possess and can exert to protect their homes.

The Women's Christian Temperance Union

STREET WATERING
MAY 15, 1900

Your editorial of yesterday in respect to the watering of our streets is timely and calls for immediate action. By the system in force, the asphalt pavements are so deluged by water that the surface is nearly always covered with a slime, unsightly and dangerous. One of the great causes of this deluge is the size of the openings of the sprinkler, which are so large that the cart does not sprinkle the street — it floods it. If the city engineer would cast away these sprinklers and get smaller ones pierced with holes not larger than an ordinary pin, the carts would gently lay the dust and not make a flood of water and dirt.

A Citizen

DOWN ON DOGS
MAY 29, 1900

I see by the papers that "Acting Police Court Clerk Ross is issuing summons against parties owning dogs without licenses."

When I read that item of news to a party of ladies and gentlemen sitting on the veranda of a certain Lower Town hospital, there was a loud derisive laugh; and not without reason either, for the neighbourhood is fairly polluted with yelping, barking, howling and fighting mongrels of no breed in particular, but making up for their lack of pedigree is noise, filth and bad manners generally.

The idea that the dog tax is paid by the owners of these pests is preposterous: No man with money to burn would give one dollar a year to keep such beasts around his neighbour's house unless the said neighbour were one and all, his bitter enemies.

What right has a man to keep an unclean, noisy and often dangerous animal on the street, impeding travel, defiling lawns, flowers, door-steps — in fact everything in sight? Would such nuisances be endured from human beings?

Yet the depredations committed by those dogs are more unspeakable than anything a human being could do. Besides, dogs are unnecessary in a city where police protection is paid for and furnished. Therefore, if people are bound to make themselves disagreeable in a community, let them pay for it, make the tax prohibitive. In conclusion, why not have dog trappers like other large cities?

Heavy Dog Tax

A FRIEND OF BIRDS

JUNE 28, 1900

I have always been a lover of birds; they are the welcomed messengers of spring and I have always taken great interest in protecting them.

It has been my duty three or four times this spring to remonstrate with boys for shooting spring birds. It seems to me that they do not know there is a closed season for the birds to breed; they think they can shoot them at any period of the year. Should there not be notices in our city papers every spring to warn people to not kill or destroy our welcomed songsters?

Every person should do all he can to protect our spring birds or they will soon be extinct. I notice that there are various breeds of birds that are absent from this section already. I also notice that the crow kills. It is a great enemy of the young of smaller birds, which it feeds to its own young.

Thomas Nicholson
Ottawa

AS A WEATHER PROPHET

JULY 5, 1900

The newspaper yesterday gave Professor Wiggins a great puff and quoted from his weather predictions as follows: "The last days of June will be very warm, but July will come to us with a cloak on her shoulders."

The very reverse to what we have experienced, from the 17th to the 30th June was cold, with high winds and since the 1st we have had it very warm. Yesterday during all the rain it was very warm and today is hot enough for any Christian.

What object the papers can have in stating what it knows to be the opposite to the truth is more than I can understand.

Thomas Powell

THE FLAG ON CITY HALL

JULY 14, 1900

After reading the Flag Incident in this morning's *Citizen*, I feel somewhat in a quandary to understand how any person professing British citizenship could object to the displaying of the national emblem from the turret of a public building in British territory on any day in the year, or imagine that the grand old Union Jack could be offensive to any loyal son of Britain.

Were it an alien flag, such as the tri-color of France, the sun burst of Irish rebels or the existing Boer emblem, there might be some cause to find fault. But the Union Jack!

Had it been an Orange or society flag or banner, I myself would object to its display on a public building on such an occasion. In conclusion, I would call Mayor Payment's at-

EVERYMAN'S HERITAGE

Canadian soldiers started arriving in South Africa in February to support the British troops in the Boer War.

tention to the standing order in the United States: "If any man hauls down the flag, shoot him on the spot."

A. W. Lang

Editor's note: To defuse a potentially volatile altercation between members of Orange Lodge and Irish Catholic patriots on July 12, the anniversary of the defeat of the Irish Catholics by British Protestants led by William of Orange in 1690, Mayor Thomas Payment of Ottawa ruled that no flag would fly from City Hall on that day.

TREATMENT OF CRIMINALS

AUGUST 4, 1900

Six cases of insanity are reported to have been developed at Auburn Prison, New York State, in two days. A girl of sixteen, a child, preferred to jump off a moving train (and was killed) rather than return to a Chicago house of correction. In the jail at Montreal will be found men imprisoned for debt, through legal tricks, although imprisonment for debt is supposed to be done away with.

These examples demonstrate that the crime of the century is our callousness towards criminals sentenced for minor offences. The death penalty is practically enforced today in many cases for which the law provides only gentle punishment.

So far as a state is concerned, the object of the law is, first, to protect the law-abiding; secondly, to reclaim the law-breaker. In the scheme of punishment, vengeance has no part; yet it is only too apparent that the uneducated and callous men who have in their hands the administration of justice of the land are devoid of sympathy.

In most instances, the criminal is mentally a sick person. When the world shall have advanced a little further, we will find many relegated to asylums instead of jails. Those who are hopelessly atrophied, however small be their crime, shall be prevented from transmitting their defects to posterity. Those of fine fiber, who have erred through the temptation of the moment, whose natural instincts are for the uplifting of the people, will be treated more decently than they are.

Our system of legal punishment is as empiric as that of a quack doctor. There is nothing more cruel for which this century will be held to account by the next than the way it made "the punishment meet the crime." In this one thing we are still not much farther advanced than our ancestors were in the dark ages.

Who will set things right? Here is the opportunity for Canada to instruct the world.

Reformer

THE NET-WAIST GIRL

SEPTEMBER 4, 1900

I was rather struck with the article on the Net-Waist Girl, which appeared in a recent issue. Surely we can wear what we like! I think there are many worse things going than the net-waist girl. Honi soit qui mal y pense. I am surprised that even "net" was worn during the heat we have had and all the newspaper talk in the world will not prevent a woman from wearing what she wants to.

Eva

Editor's note: The "net" in question was probably a lace undergarment worn for decorative effect outside a corset, which in these Victorian times would have rarely been seen in public.

CHRONICLE OF THE 20TH CENTURY
Corsets were rarely shown in public, even in ads.

THE UNMARKED GRAVE

OCTOBER 4, 1900

As one who assisted in a small way in the production of the book *The Women of Canada*, I was glad to read your well-written editorial of September 20th. As one of her old pupils, I was pleased to see the appreciation of the good work done by Margretta Graddon (Mrs. Gibbs) years ago, and notice of which was a regretful omission from the book. If any of her old pupils will join me, or some of our wealthy citizens will help, the reproach will be wiped out "that she fills an unmarked grave."

Mary McKay Scott

SHOULD A MAN TELL?

DECEMBER 8, 1900

About a month ago a lady called at my office and asked me to do her a small favor. Her request was a perfectly legitimate one and I complied with it as I should have done had it come from a casual acquaintance.

Years ago there had been a brief and tender episode between the woman and myself of which she was the heroine and I perhaps the fool. The incident had been definitely closed long before I met the sweet girl who is my wife and the only queen of my heart.

While courting I made the mistake — or I did the right thing — in telling my wife of all my former flirtations, including the one with the lady previously referred to. Women are intuitive, and my wife has frequently told me

in confidence that she was only jealous of the memory I might carry in my heart of this one woman.

I did not tell my wife of the lady's call because I know how sensitive she is and because — to confess the truth — I have all of a man's dread of a woman's tears and reproaches.

But someone else did tell my wife that the woman had been to see me. And as a result the peace of a happy household is destroyed. My wife is wretched and insists that, as I have deceived her in this matter, I have been leading a double or treble life.

Our marriage has been an extremely happy one. We have three lovely children, and it is a positive fact that for the one sin of omission which I have related to you, our home bids fair to become a veritable Hades.

Now I want the opinion of your readers. If I had not in the first place made a clean breast of my past, which was neither better or worse than that of the average young man, would I not today be happier?

Inquirer

A MAN SHOULD TELL ALL

DECEMBER 10, 1900

Replying to Inquirer's question, I should say, Yes, by all means a man should be candid with his wife, and he should be so consistently.

The mistake Inquirer made was this, that at the very point where, in consistency, he should have been thoroughly honest with his wife, he failed to tell the facts on the strength of which alone she could have formed a better or truer opinion of him, and he himself could avoid the appearance of secretiveness.

Now the only thing for Inquirer to do is to beg his wife's pardon, putting her completely in possession of all the details of the other lady's call. If she is of a generous disposition and at all worthy of being a true man's wife, she will be able to see through it all at once and be ready to judge more favorably the whole incident. All that Inquirer needs is the courage to carry out the principle that honesty is the best policy.

Hoping that all will be well in the end, I am yours and his, very truly,

Frank Freeman

THE MEN DARE NOT

DECEMBER 13, 1900

In reply to your correspondent, Frank Freeman, who said "a man should tell his wife everything," we, the undersigned, oppose that proposition with all the power of a thousand Samsons.

Why, if such a thing as that should become general, millions of men would have to take to the woods and run like jackrabbits for their future existence. Why, sir, broomsticks, pokers and bric-a-brac would quadruple in price in consequence of their continual use. I, a moral man, would have to take an underground railroad to Siberia.

Mr. Freeman's desire seemingly is to frighten 99 per cent of the married men out of their boots. He ought to know this:

> Wives tongues are little but, O, how strong;
> They're only about three inches long
> Hot when jealousy their rage supply,
> Woe to the man that is six feet high

If Mr. Freeman will just wait until I get my airship built before he agitates that question any more he will confer an everlasting favour on ...

Millions of Married Men

A BACHELOR'S OPINION
DECEMBER 14, 1900

Whether or not a man should tell his wife everything depends on what he has to tell. Women are sensitive creatures and most wives would be shocked into hysterics by the revelations some husbands might make of their doings.

When a man does anything he ought not to do, he ought to be decent enough to keep it from his wife. Why should she be troubled by his moral aberrations?

A bachelor

SHOULD WORK BOTH WAYS
DECEMBER 14, 1900

If husbands must tell all their secrets to their wives, shouldn't wives tell all their secrets to their husbands? It's a poor rule that won't work both ways.

Of course, few women have any secrets worth telling, but some have, and if we are not to have a double standard of matrimonial propriety, the wife must take hubby into her confidence.

Fair Play

TWENTIETH CENTURY WELCOME
DECEMBER 21, 1900

You have asked for suggestions as to how to suitably observe the moment that marks the advent of the twentieth century. History furnishes the incident of the millions of the West Indies slaves welcoming the hour of freedom, which was reached as the clock marked the midnight by a concerted singing of the doxology:

> "Praise God from whom all blessings flow,
> Praise Him all creatures here below,
> Praise Him above ye heavenly host,
> Praise Father, Son and Holy Ghost."

And it was fitting that they should thus recognize that their freedom was won by the triumph of the spirit of Christ. The same spirit has blessed the present generation of Canadians even more richly.

Why, then, should not they, in concert, sing the doxology, as expressive of their gratitude for the birth of a new century?

Old Hundredth

1901

Local: The Duke and Duchess of Cornwall and York, the future King George V and Queen Mary, cap a visit to Ottawa with a run down the timber slide at LeBreton Flats (September); Bessie Blair, daughter of the federal minister of railways, and a companion, are drowned after falling through the thinning Ottawa River ice at a skating party hosted by the governor general (December)
National: About 350 people are rescued after the passenger liner *Lusitania* is wrecked off the coast of Cape Ballard, Newfoundland (June); Marconi receives the first transatlantic radio message at St. John's (December)
World: Queen Victoria's amazing 64-year reign ends with her death at age 82 (January); U.S. president William McKinley dies eight days after being felled by an assassin's bullet in Buffalo. Vice-president Theodore Roosevelt assumes the top job (September)
Births: Anastasia, daughter of Russia's czar Nicholas; Walt Disney; American polling pioneer George Gallup; anthropologist Margaret Mead
Deaths: French painters Toulouse-Lautrec and Jacques-Joseph Tissot

NO SMALLPOX THERE
MARCH 26, 1901

I notice in the *Citizen* of March 21st that Dr. Bryce cites a new case of smallpox at Barry's Bay. That is a mistake. There has been no case of the disease in our village yet, nor is there any within 13 miles of us. You will therefore put this right as we are free from smallpox.

A resident,
Barry's Bay

A DESERVING CASE
APRIL 5, 1901

An old man devoid of one arm and unable to support himself has been literally on the streets for the past few years. The law did not allow him any damage for the injury received in the employ of a railway company many years ago, by which he was deprived of his arm just above the elbow. He generally goes by the name of "old McDonald," although his nationality may prove a puzzle for the census man.

In the summer he travels in the country from Skead's Mills [south of Ottawa on the Rideau River] to Manotick and through Nepean and round about on his annual circuit, peddling fly paper and other funny things that give the country lasses odd occasions for innocent amusement, but even then he doesn't make his porridge. In the winter, he has been on the streets and is getting into the habit of calling daily at places for meals which are not infrequently denied him.

I beg to call the attention of the charitable societies of the city to his case, or will the city avoid coroner's expense by looking after him in time. It is becoming a very serious matter for the poor old one-armed man.

Enumerator

SPITTING IN STREET CARS
MAY 23, 1901

Have you observed that a Montreal magistrate has just sentenced a man to pay a fine of five dollars with the option of going to jail for a month for spitting in a street car?

The general verdict everywhere on this action will be "well done." Too long have human brutes been allowed to make nuisances of themselves in this respect, and it would be well if similar action were taken here in Ottawa, where, like Montreal and elsewhere, delicate women and children have to run the risk, every day, of contracting disease, owing to this beastly and disgusting habit.

The electric railway should display a notice that any person caught in the act, hereafter, will be expelled from the cars, promptly.

There should also be a regulation prohibiting the transportation of drunken men. Indeed, with many, the last named constitutes a nuisance even more intolerable than the other.

Purity, Ottawa

THE GYPSY NUISANCE
MAY 31, 1901

The spring has made its appearance again and the gypsies have settled in their old position. When are we to get quit of this nuisance?

The government sold the property where they are camped to get rid of them last summer but they take possession just as though the place was their own. The property in the vicinity has gone down in value as people do not like to build where this nuisance exists.

These gypsies have money and could afford to rent places to carry on their business. The men doctor up old horses and the women go around hawking trinkets from door to door.

Last summer, they had a horse here running at large that was condemned as suffering from glanders. When the camp broke up last fall, two or three dead horses were left behind and the stench was unbearable at times. The shoes and hides of these old brutes were taken off and the carcasses left for the dogs.

These gypsies are a menace to this neighbourhood and have been for some time. I hope the nuisance will soon be

Gypsies, like this woman preparing a meal at a squatters' camp, are a menace to the neighbourhood, a Rideauville resident wrote.

abated. It is a disgrace to see such a pretty place infested with such people.

A Disgusted Resident of Rideauville

Editor's note: Rideauville encompassed part of the area now known as Ottawa South. It is believed the land occupied by the "gypsies" was somewhere in the area where Lees Avenue, Main Street and the Hurdman Bridge are located today.

THE ZAZA WALK
JUNE 15, 1901

It was with the greatest pleasure that I read your editorial on the apparently "up-to-date" walk that some young ladies here have adopted with the impression that it is the proper thing. I was also more than glad to see that you entered both into explaining how it originated and also who adopts it.

I don't know why it is, but it seems so easy nowadays for girls to cultivate all the dashy conspicuous mannerisms in dress and behaviour without ever a consideration of how they look or how others may criticize them.

I am sure if some of the young ladies who effect this walk had seen Mrs. Leslie Carter and noticed how much and how conspicuous a part "that walk" played in her drama of *Zaza*, they would never have allowed themselves to think of it, much less to have adopted it.

My greatest disappointment last night at Cissie Loftus [a society event] was that Mrs. Leslie Carter was not invited, for I went hoping so sincerely that an exaggerated and emphasised view of that awful walk might have made an impression beneficial as well as lasting to so many of "our girls" of the capital who are ruining their graceful figures for a fad both abominable and unsightly.

A Mother

Editor's note: Mrs. Leslie Carter was a musical actress who worked on Broadway and in early films from the mid-1890s until about 1910. It is not clear whether she actually visited Ottawa in 1901, setting off a series of letters and edi-

torials about the Zaza, the term given to a seductive, sashaying walk inspired by a musical of the same name, or whether the fuss was created by a movie shown in Ottawa. The letter writer's reference to Mrs. Carter's failure to appear at a local society event might well have been sarcasm.

PROTECTING THE FLAG
JULY 5, 1901

If Canadians would show a little of the same spirit displayed in the Skagway flag incident, it would be all the better. I could never understand why Canadians are so willing to let Americans flaunt their flag in all parts of Canada, nor why Canadians are so anxious to couple the stars and stripes with the Union Jack on many public occasions.

Is it because they feel so small and helpless beside this country that they seem so anxious to cater to this country's good will? If the Union Jack should ever be displayed in this country as often as the stars and stripes is in Canada, 99 times out of 100 it would be torn down, and I know what I am writing about, as I have spent 10 years in all parts of this country.

A Canadian from Ottawa,
Baltimore

Editor's note: The Skagway flag incident, part of a simmering Canada-U.S. border dispute over the Alaska Territory, occurred when defiant Canadians raised a Union Jack over territory claimed by Americans. U.S. citizens tried to pull down the flag, which was successfully defended by the Canadians. Similar incidents took place until 1903, when an international tribunal settled the boundary row in favour of the U.S.

DONATIONS ACKNOWLEDGED
JULY 8, 1901

Please acknowledge through your columns the following amounts contributed to the relief fund for fire sufferers of Cache Bay:

Edward Lloyds Limited, Sturgeon Falls	$250.00
City of Toronto	200.00
Town of North Bay	150.00
City of Ottawa	100.00
Traders Bank of Canada	100.00
A.E. Campeon, Sturgeon Falls	50.00
Town of Orillia	50.00
The Davidson-Hay Company Limited, Toronto	25.00
A.G. Browning, North Bay	20.00
Town of Renfrew	35.00
Town of Sturgeon Falls	35.00
F.E. Rutland	23.00
Total	$1,020.00
Also Marsh Liniment Co	2.00
New total	$1,022.00

Thank you very much for your offer to raise a public subscription for the sufferers.

A. J. Young, Cache Bay, Ontario

Editor's note: In late June, a forest fire engulfed most of Cache Bay, a community 40 kilometres west of North Bay, claiming several lives and leaving dozens homeless. News of the fire prompted donations from across Ontario.

A WORKING GIRL'S COMPLAINT
JULY 10, 1901

The working girls of Ottawa have a complaint to make in regards to the way the streets are deluged with water every morning. I think if the mayor or some of the aldermen would take a walk down Rideau Street between half-past seven and eight o'clock, they would see that we have good reason for our complaint. Between shop-keepers and street sprinklers we are very much in the position of the dove which Noah sent out to see whether the flood had gone down — we can find no dry land.

I mention Rideau Street because that is the way I have to come to work, but I believe the other streets are just the same. One shopkeeper on Sussex Street near Rideau takes great delight in making a small river in front of his place every morning. If he would leave the side of the road dry people could step out there till they got past his place. But no, he is not content till he has flooded half across the street. I think the city should raise the water rates on people like that.

A Working Girl

SMOKING ON CARS
JULY 18, 1901

There is a grievance, not to say a positive nuisance, pertaining to the otherwise excellent street car service of this city, which the management would do well to have abated, to wit, the latitude allowed to smokers on the cars.

I am a somewhat heavy user of the weed myself, but claim to be possessed of sufficient decency to avoid puffing tobacco, cigar and cigarette smoke in the faces of my fellow passengers. On the Britannia line last evening, the sensibilities of a number of ladies were so shocked at the ordeal they had to endure and the jibes bandied at their expense by a gang of ill-mannered young men (I had almost said "gentlemen") that they decided then and there never to take the trip again.

On the Aylmer line, a few evenings ago, the puffing was pursued, unmolestedly, on a seat near the centre of the car. Cannot something be done to keep the nuisance, for such at best it is, within endurable bounds?

Decrying Decency, Ottawa

GOOD SUGGESTIONS
NOVEMBER 14, 1901

I observe in your issue of Tuesday an interview with the health officer regarding the proposed contagious hospital. Will you give me sufficient space to ask a question or two and to offer a suggestion?

In the event of Porter's Island being selected as a site for a contagious hospital, is it proposed to provide for smallpox patients on the island as well as for other contagious patients? If not, where is it proposed to provide a suitable habitat for smallpox patients in the future?

The suggestion I have to offer is this: Let the municipal council of the city of Ottawa make a formal demand on the provincial board of health to select a site within the municipal limits of this corporation where this city can erect a hospital for contagious disease that will not be within 450 feet of any inhabited dwelling.

Ask them also to state definitely in an official opinion whether this corporation can house scarlatina patients and diphtheria patients in one building without any risk whatever to the patients. If such patients cannot be absolutely isolated under one roof with one staff of servants and of nurses, will it be necessary to erect more than one building? If such be required, will the buildings have to be 450 feet from one another. If not, why not?

Ask them also if they or any of their officers gave permission to anybody to erect the present St. Anne's Hospital for contagious diseases. Ask them if that hospital is 450 feet from any inhabited dwelling. If it is not, ask them why it was allowed to be erected.

Ask them the date of its erection and ask them if their opinion was ever sought, or if they approved of the plans.

Ask them finally to state in an official opinion if the striking distance of any contagious disease is 450 feet.

Yours, R.W. Powell, M.D.

Editor's note: A small hospital for smallpox sufferers was eventually built on Porter's Island, which is in the Rideau River just off St. Patrick Street, east of King Edward Avenue. The hospital was abandoned and eventually torn down to make way for a senior citizens' lodge in the 1960s.

1902

Local: Spectators line Hull's Main Street to watch the hanging of logger Stanislaus Lacroix, who killed his wife and a neighbour in a drunken, jealous rage (March); Two British cannons that saw action in Peking are mounted on Parliament Hill, where they remain today (November)
National: Results of the federal census show 5.5 per cent of the Canadian population is 65 years or older. Today, the number is nearly 13 per cent (June); Federal government appoints a royal commission to overhaul obsolete public statutes passed over the years (November)
World: The Boer War ends with British victory and South Africa's inclusion in the Empire (May); U.S. Congress approves spending $40 million to build the Panama Canal (June)
Births: Pilot Charles Lindbergh; writer John Steinbeck; composer Richard Rodgers
Deaths: Cecil Rhodes, architect of British empire; French novelist Emile Zola; British satirist Samuel Butler

THE SAWDUST NUISANCE AGAIN

APRIL 29, 1902

As you are aware, the Dominion government prosecuted Mr. J.R. Booth (an Ottawa lumber baron) last summer for dumping sawdust and mill refuse into our beautiful river in defiance of the law. But instead of continuing the prosecutions until the law was respected, further action was deferred on the solemn assurance of Mr. Booth that with the close of milling operations last fall, active steps would be taken to provide for the disposal of such refuse by burning, etc.

What do we find today? The river littered with sawdust and navigation at the foot of the locks almost completely prevented. It appears to me that your editorial columns could not be used to better advantage for the good of that part of our population which takes an interest in the fisheries, to say nothing of the beauty of our river, than by opening a crusade against the government officers who permit this flagrant defiance of the law to continue.

Friend of the Ottawa River

DELAYED MAIL MATTER

MAY 14, 1902

What do you think of its taking twenty-seven and a half years minus two days for a post card mailed at West Winchester, 12 November 1874, ordering one case of Eddy's Telegraph matches, to reach here?

The post card reads as follows: "West Winchester, 12 November 1874. Dear Sir: Send one case of Eddy's Telegraph matches with goods ordered yesterday. —Wm.

Bow." We don't mean to say that it is the fault of the present postal authorities that this card has been so long reaching us, but we just mention it as an item of interest.

Yours truly,
W.H. Rowely, the E.B. Eddy Co. Limited

Editor's note: William Bow, the man who ordered the matches, ran a general store in West Winchester (known simply as Winchester today), a village 50 kilometres southeast of Ottawa.

LET IN THE LIGHT

MAY 17, 1902

By all means let us see the inside of the Grit machine. There is something terrible there, or they would not be in such an awful state for fear we would see it. The federal government must be much interested also, when Premier Laurier makes his majestic threat to resign.

What position would Premier Laurier have the Dominion in today if there had not been a Conservative majority in the Senate since he reached power? They will now soon have that body also and with his dear friend Ross in power in Ontario, he could quickly put his Dominion in the same position of indebtedness which is prevailing in the province of Quebec today.

Besides, he would have such autocratic control that no one could, or would, be entitled to question his actions for all future time. He would rule this Dominion according to his own sweet will.

Ontario has a duty to perform at the present provincial

election. We must take no chances but send a strong Conservative government to Toronto after the 29th. Anything else would be a national calamity for the whole Dominion. A chance has come. Let Ontario grasp the opportunity.

The Grits used to govern for the good of the party, but for a long time back their government is only for the good of the heelers, and the most unprincipled of them at that. They have got to such a pass now that they stop at nothing, from manipulating a local whisky license to pull for a foreign combine in the great northern forests, when the hard cash is required for election purposes.

Ontario Elector

Editor's note: The 1902 Ontario election was won by the Liberals under Sir George William Ross. Three years later, however, the Conservatives crushed the Liberals amid a lingering financial scandal involving several of Ross's ministers.

THE DUST NUISANCE
MAY 22, 1902

Now that the dust nuisance is once more upon us, in even a more intensified form than last season, might I be allowed, through the medium of the *Citizen*, to invite the attention of our rulers in council to the improved method of watering the streets, which is being followed in Toronto and other up-to-date communities?

I refer to the utilisation of the street railway for the purpose. When in Toronto some years ago I saw one of these electric tank cars at work in front of the Queen's Hotel and can, therefore, speak from personal knowledge of the superiority of that system of watering over the slow, inefficient, one-horse method followed in Ottawa.

Of all trials and evils incident to the summer season, perhaps the daily, blinding whirl of dust is the most vexatious and damaging. It penetrates everywhere, and to the shopkeeper and householder must be a source of constant trouble and injury. This being the case, the city council should be quick to remedy the evil insofar as they are able to do so.

Why not give the tank car a trial? Which of our city fathers will be the first to earn the grateful thanks of a crying community in the premises?

Old Timer

CANADIANS STAY AT HOME
AUGUST 8, 1902

Will you kindly allow me the privilege of your columns to offer a few words of advice to the young men and women of Canada who contemplate coming to the United States for the purpose of procuring employment.

As president of the Canadian Club of Boston for several years, I came in contact with many who came here with the idea that work was to be easily obtained and that wages were much higher than in Canada. They were from all walks in life: labourers, men and women with trades and even professional men. They came with the most buoyant hopes of bettering their lot, only to find after weeks of vain seeking that their anticipations were doomed to disappointment.

The industrial condition of the United States is not what it was 20 or even 10 years ago. In those days there were ample opportunities for all who wanted work. At the present time nearly all branches of business are centralized, the great trusts are in control, labour-saving machinery has displaced hand work, wages have been cut down, and thousands of men and women are now walking the streets of the great cities who would, if they could, eagerly embrace the opportunity to earn a few dollars a week to keep the wolf from the door.

The enormous immigration from Europe, especially from the southern part, has glutted the labour market and been a powerful factor in lowering wages. These people can live in luxury on wages that would drive an American to the poorhouse.

My advice to the young men and women of Canada is: Stay at home! Opportunities are better there at the present time than they are here. If the young people of the eastern provinces are not satisfied with home conditions, let them try the Canadian Northwest. That is practically a new country where the chances of success are excellent for those who are willing to work.

Robert H. Upham

"CHALETS DE CONVENIANCE"
SEPTEMBER 8, 1902

I see that the Montreal authorities are about to establish in their streets and squares "*chalets de conveniance*," similar to those which have existed for some years in London and Paris. This is a step in the right direction, and one which might very advantageously be imitated in our own city. Certainly the establishment of half a dozen of these "conveniences" within the business centres of the city, would while adding not a little to the cleanliness of the streets, do away with many disgusting and offensive sights and odours which should not be seen or found at the National Capital.

Old Timer

Editor's note: Ottawa's first public washrooms were installed in 1907.

A SERIOUS CHARGE
SEPTEMBER 13, 1902

The admissions made by those connected with the Contagious Diseases Hospital as to the contraction of disease in the institution itself would seem to clearly prove a most disgraceful and outrageous state of affairs.

That a diphtheria patient should be huddled into a room with scarlet fever through lack of knowledge in diagnosing the disease is bad enough, but when such a thing is knowingly done because the hospital is crowded, it becomes criminal. These institutions are established and maintained to prevent the spread of contagion and right-thinking citizens are encouraged to send their children there for their own and the public good. And these children do not go as pauper patients, the demand of $2.50 per week being made for the maintenance of each in addition to the private doctors bill.

It is to be hoped, Mr. Editor, that when the new hospital is opened it will be run with some kind of system or the board of health may rest assured it will have an ever increasing number of cases of infectious diseases hidden away and a consequently greater danger of an epidemic. As one who has had three years experience in London hospitals, I consequently know something whereof I speak. I consider this a matter of the most serious consequence to the city.

A.D. Ramage

BUSH TEACHERS WANTED

OCTOBER 30, 1902

With the co-operation of the employers, the provincial government and the general public, the Reading Camp Association has opened a number of reading rooms at lumbering camps in Ontario. Instruction has been found to be feasible and very desirable in these camps during the long winter evenings and on rainy days; but as no appropriation has as yet been made by the legislature, the association wishes to make the following suggestion and offer:

Men are scarce in the woods and wages run from $25 to $30 per month, with board, according to the ability of a man to handle an axe, saw, or drive a team. Through the kindness of employers, the association is able to place a dozen good men at from $25 to $30 per month. To school teachers or college graduates who are out of employment and who do not mind roughing it a little, who are willing to do manual labor during the day and spend their evenings conducting classes, the association will pay from $10 to $20 per month additional.

The association guarantees this for five months only, but will try to get work for these teachers in the summer months on drives, at saw mills, in mines and on railway

THE CANADIAN PRESS

Sir Sanford Fleming was the first to send a cable message around the world, a reader contended.

construction, and hopes to be able to extend this offer. Candidates who speak French are preferred.

A. Fitzpatrick,
Nairn Centre, Ontario

CANADA FIRST

DECEMBER 1, 1902

The United States journals are glorifying themselves and their nation by asserting that the first cable message around the world via the Pacific Cable was sent by an American, Mr. Charles J. Glidden of Boston. The message as given by the New York Electrician was as follows:

"Boston, November 1st. Glidden, Boston; Mass., via Vancouver British Cable to Australia around the world." It left Boston at 9:15 a.m. and arrived at Boston November 2nd at 12:35 p.m., having made the journey in 39 hours and 20 minutes. As received, the message read: "Glidden, Boston, Mass. Armund the world."

A message sent by Sir Sandford Fleming was dispatched from Ottawa on October 30 at 10 p.m. It crossed the Atlantic ocean to England thence to South Africa, across the Indian Ocean to Australia, thence to Vancouver across the Pacific Ocean and through Canada, reaching the city of Ottawa early on Saturday, November 1st., before Mr. Glidden's message.

The Ottawa message took 29 hours, less time to go round the world than the Boston message. Moreover, every one of the 39 words of the Ottawa message made the circuit of the globe without the smallest mistake, while the six words of the Boston message had two errors and one word rendered meaningless by error.

Canada was ahead in time, ahead in speed, ahead in accuracy.

G.I.

1903

Local: The Ottawa Silver Seven win their first Stanley Cup. The hockey team successfully defends the trophy nine times before losing it to the Montreal Wanderers in 1906 (March); Mary Ann (O'Connor) Friel, the first white girl born in Bytown, dies at age 76 (June); Ottawa's first city plan to include the ideas of a landscape architect is released. While Frederick Todd's report deals mainly with beautification, he points out the need for a long-range master plan (September)

National: A mysterious explosion blows off the top of Turtle Mountain, near Vancouver, killing 95 (April); In Northern Ontario, hunter Fred Larose throws a hammer at what he believes are fox eyes and hits the world's richest vein of silver (September)

World: After years of tinkering with horseless carriages, Henry Ford decides to form an auto company (June); Baseball's first World Series is played between Boston of the upstart American League and Pittsburgh of the National League. Boston prevails five games to three (October)

Births: British writers George Orwell and Evelyn Waugh; comedian Bob Hope

Deaths: French painters Paul Gauguin and Camille Pisarro; Richard Gatling, inventor of rapid-fire Gatling gun; U.S. painter James Whistler

A MISLEADING TIMEPIECE

FEBRUARY 11, 1903

Would you kindly draw the attention of the post office people to their clock. It is never correct. At present it is 10 minutes slow. They should either fix it or stop it as it is now causing much inconvenience and loss to the public. The writer missed two trains by relying on it.

E.S.

Editor's note: The clock was stopped for three years after a January fired gutted the post office at Sparks and Canal streets where Confederation Square is located today. The building reopened in 1907 with the clock in fine working order.

A PROTEST

MARCH 17, 1903

A deputation of civil servants waited on Sir Wilfrid Laurier to ask that St. Patrick's Day be made a departmental holiday. He positively refused, on the ground that he could not "interfere with the wishes of his different ministers." I would like to ask why Sir Wilfrid Laurier took another view of things on St. Jean Baptiste Day — 24th June last. On the latter day, flags were flying and a general holiday was proclaimed. Evidently there are no votes among the Irish.

Canadian

DOWN WITH THE CLOVEN FOOT!

MARCH 27, 1903

A *Citizen* correspondent in Monday's issue says that Canada does not spend enough money on soldiering. Now, sir, what Canada requires is more ploughs and more plough boys. Our martial spirit is at par. The principal point in modern warfare is to shoot straight and our boys are pretty good shots and will rise as one man if the cloven foot of the invader dare to desecrate her soil.

T. Iliffe

THE MEGAPHONE
AS A WEAPON OF DEFENCE

MARCH 31, 1903

When the "cloven foot of the invader" — one hadn't specially apprehended an attack from that quarter but that's a detail — has desecrated Canadian soil and "our boys" with martial spirit at or above par, have risen up to shoot, what does Mr. Iliffe propose that they shall shoot with? Megaphones?

Of modern rifles, as every one is quite aware, there are not anything like enough to go round. Isn't Mr. Iliffe a little apprehensive that if such an event should happen these same boys of ours finding that their rising up has been to no purpose may before sitting down again look around for the individuals of Mr. Iliffe's way of thinking who have neglected to provide them with the necessity of national life, a rope and the nearest lamp post?

A Canadian

THE CANADIAN SABBATH

MAY 1, 1903

In reading my *Citizen* today I find one paragraph stating that a baseball match was played within a short distance of Canada's government buildings on Sunday. Another paragraph said that a ball match was disallowed in Detroit on the same Sabbath. As Canadians, we are apt to hold up our country as an example, from a moral point of view, but in reflecting on the above statement, I think as Canadians we should feel humiliated.

Ithos Iliff

THE CEMETERY NUISANCE

JULY 14, 1908

The thanks of the residents of the Clarence Street end of Wurtemburg Street are due to the *Citizen* for calling attention to the disgraceful conduct so common in this locality, especially on Sundays. The responsibility for the frequent cases of gross misconduct in our neighbourhood rests largely upon the authorities of the Episcopal and Presbyterian churches, by whose neglect their old cemeteries furnish cover during the whole summer for drunkards.

Clarence Street resident

AGAINST THE RULES

JULY 17, 1903

If the city councillors have the power to make a bylaw to prevent lumber piling in the city limits, why don't they enforce it and not allow the lumber kings to have it all their own way and make the council crawl back in their hole and the people they represent criticize them?

When first the aldermen proposed to pass this bylaw, there was only Ald. Enright who kicked against it, because he's Mr. [J.R.] Booth's friend. And now, for some reason or other, they have apparently all backed down except Ald. Payment, who is the only one who has sand enough to stand his own ground, and he deserves credit.

The lumber kings say their piles do not contribute to fire. They are certainly not going to speak against their interests but everybody knows that if there hadn't been so much lumber piled there there wouldn't have been such a big fire and there wouldn't have been such a large number of houses burned [during the Great Fire of Ottawa-Hull in 1900].

A Citizen

A TIP TO CITY FOLK

JULY 23, 1903

A short time ago while visiting in your beautiful city, I was struck by the utter ignorance displayed by pedestrians, bicyclists and drivers of any rule or order in going from place to place. I have often wondered that you never mentioned this in your very clever editorials, which seem always to be written in the interests of the city and of its citizens.

We (in Stittsville) do not have the same necessity for following out the first principles of order as we do not have the same amount of traffic on our streets. But I would be very much surprised to hear of anyone in Stittsville not knowing that, in a crowd, whether walking or wheeling, he should always keep to the right. And in this I consider that we are very much in advance of Ottawans, who seem never to have realized that their city has grown since Bytown days.

It seems miraculous that there are not accidents every day, and as the city is still growing fast, something should be done to save life and limb. Perhaps if you added to your motto, "The lumber piles must go," another motto, "Keep to the right," this might be effected.

Yours truly,
Anti-rural

INDIANS DON'T WANT TO VOTE

JULY 23, 1903

I was desired by my people to ask you to be kind enough to allow us a space in your valuable paper for the purpose of expressing our views in reference to much talk of members of the Dominion House of Parliament in regard to the franchise extended to the Indians of said Dominion.

We, the Indians of the Six Nations, are not afraid to say that a great majority do not desire to be placed on the voters' list for various reasons which are known to ourselves; and we affirmatively agree with the member for South Brant that the Indians do not fully understand the nature of "franchise."

We can assure the lawmakers of Canada, and the readers of your valuable paper, that the Indians are good in many ways. Now, we would say to the member for South

THE ASSOCIATED PRESS

Henry Ford at the wheel of his first production automobile, the 1903 Model A Runabout.

Brant, let him stick to his word on the floor in the House of Commons, that the majority of Indians do not want the franchise.

Yours truly,
Seth Newhouse, Brant County

PROMISES UNFULFILLED

JULY 27, 1903

When the wicked Tories were in power at Ottawa, the so-called Liberals promised all kinds of reform if they could only get into office. They would abolish our protective tariff. Abolish the Senate. Give no aid or countenance to railways. Commit no gerrymander, and do all manner of good things.

Let us see how these promises have been kept. The protective tariff remains practically the same as when the wicked Tories were in power. The Senate is flourishing with an infusion of good Grits. All the railways in the country are asking for assistance and will no doubt obtain it. Why not? A gerrymander is about to be consummated in a most illogical manner in many instances and all the good things promised have come to pass. Probably the government is responsible for good harvests.

Yours truly, B.

THE FLAG THAT FLOATED

DECEMBER 3, 1903

In speaking of Queen Alexandra's birthday yesterday, the *Citizen* said: "Upon the parliament buildings yesterday the national banner of Canada floated proudly in the clear, north breeze, etc., etc."

Strange! I was at the parliament buildings and would surely have seen the national banner had it been there. I saw in the place where the national banner should have floated the flag of the mercantile marine, and thought what a handsome seamen's hospital our government buildings would make.

M. St. J.

CANADIANS HOLD YOUR OWN

DECEMBER 4, 1903

There is a great deal of resentment in Canada against the United States over the Alaskan award, which we Canadians consider to be an unjust one. There is also a strong feeling amongst us that Canada is being discriminated against by a hostile tariff whose wall is twice the height of ours. There is, too, an ineradicable belief that the alien labour law is unfairly operated against Canadians by the United States officials.

And while we neighbourly hoist the stars and stripes alongside the Union Jack on gala days, the sight of a British or Canadian flag flying in Yankee land arouses the anger of howling anti-British mobs, the flag is torn to pieces, and trampled in the dust.

An American will purchase nothing Canadian that he can buy at home. He will spend no money in Canada that he can distribute amongst his own people. He seeks to build up his own land, not to help Canada. We can't change this unfriendly attitude towards us, but we can show the world that we possess an independent spirit, a native pride, and a love of country, and that we will no longer unpatriotically help build up the United States at the expense of Canada.

There are many ways in which this can be done. Take, for instance, the case of Mr. J.J. Hill, the American railway magnate who recently spoke in the most disparaging terms of our Canadian Northwest, belittling its resources and its fertility. He sought to injure the part of Canada in which we all have such great faith.

Well, Mr. Hill's railway has formed a connection with other Canadian and American rails by which travelers to and from the West can be carried through the United States. The money spent by Canadians who travel by this way goes to enrich American railways, to provide wages for American workmen, to increase American trade. These dollars never return to Canada.

This is only one instance. It could be multiplied in hundreds of cases, but it teaches a lesson: Those who believe in building up Canada, who feel that money spent at home is best spent, who wish to maintain industries, who patronize home institutions by buying home-made goods, spend their money at home and act up to their patriotic cry which we hear shouted from Sydney to Victoria, "Canada for the Canadians."

Yours,
For Home and Country

Editor's note: On Oct. 20, an international joint commission led by British counsel Lord Alverstone sided with the Americans in a long-percolating dispute over territory along the Alaska-Yukon border. As a result, the U.S. received several thousand square miles of coastline.

AN OPEN LETTER

DECEMBER 16, 1903.

To the Society of Prevention of Cruelties to Animals: I overheard my master talking about the dog bylaw, which will come into force next year, and that he could not afford to pay the taxes imposed.

Now, sir, what is to become of me? I served my master faithfully and did my best to be a good dog. It is not my fault that I am here. Being a lower animal and there being no hereafter for me, so it is said, I would like to have a good time here. I claim the protection of your society for myself as well as for other friendless dogs.

What has become of our money already paid to the city for taxes? Do you take charge of it or does the city? This ought, I think, to be under your management. Trusting that your honourable body will look after us.

An Old Dog

Editor's note: The dog tax, or annual dog licence fee, referred to by the old fellow above, amounted to $2 a year. It was implemented as planned.

1904

Local: Fire destroys the main post office building at Sparks and Canal streets. Postal workers are recognized for their "splendid work" in saving the mail (January); The Driveway, later the Queen Elizabeth Driveway, is opened from Laurier Street to Dow's Lake. The speed limit is set at seven miles per hour (July)

National: Fire in Toronto's garment district causes $10-million damage (April); The Liberals under Wilfrid Laurier win their third successive majority (November)

World: Japan and Russia go to war after Japan's surprise torpedo attack on Russian fleet in February. The war rages for 18 months before a treaty is signed in September 1905; St. Louis hosts both the World's Fair and the third modern Olympics (August)

Births: CCF-NDP leader Tommy Douglas; American nuclear physicist Robert Oppenheimer; singer Bing Crosby; Russian pianist Vladimir Horowitz

Deaths: Czech composer Anton Dvorak; African explorer Henry Stanley; Russian writer Anton Chekhov

DOG NUISANCE

JANUARY 18, 1904

There is no reason why a dog with a licence tag should be allowed to promenade the streets any more than one without the tag. They are both equally a danger, filthy and useless.

Did we not read in yesterday's *Citizen* that three people died in one family from hydrophobia, two of these from kissing the first sufferer? A dog with a tag is just as liable to bite, to mangle, to produce death as one that has no tag. Is not that a fact?

Besides, dogs with and without tags destroy flowers and shrubs on the lawns. They pollute doorways and goods. They offend persons on the street and at home.

Let us arrest every dog found on the street or, better, shoot them on sight unless they are leashed.

Poor Dog

A KICK FROM A CRANK

JANUARY 18, 1904

We have read some vigorous protests against the suggestion that dress suits should be worn at the meetings of the Canadian Club. It is claimed that such a rule would exclude many who do not own, or if they own, object to wearing, dress suits on such occasions.

But there are many who would be glad to attend the meetings, in dress suits or any other suits, who are excluded by the smoking in which some of the members indulge. I do not suppose that any protest against this evil would have the slightest effect; the average smoker can never understand that the odour which is so fragrant and soothing to him is a disgusting, sickening stench to others.

The fact he is excluding some of his fellow citizens from the club probably seems to him a meritorious act, since it keeps out cranks, but even cranks should have some rights, and one of them is to be allowed to breathe pure air at public meetings.

One of the Cranks

Editor's note: Since their start in Hamilton in 1892, Canadian Club branches have held regular luncheon meetings to listen to distinguished Canadian speakers. The Ottawa chapter was founded in 1903, and still holds monthly luncheons at the Château Laurier Hotel. The clubs were male-only in the beginning (separate female branches began in 1907), but these days they are open to both genders.

THE ETERNAL CANINE

JANUARY 27, 1904

One of your correspondents states that dogs are of no use in the city. Perhaps this might hold good in a modern, up-to-date city, but in an overgrown village like Ottawa where there is no system of scavenging or garbage collection, dogs are indeed useful as scavengers.

I keep two dogs for that purpose. These dogs dispose of a portion of the garbage and the balance I bury in the backyard. If the people who throw their garbage on vacant lots and on the streets kept dogs, it would be better for the health of the community.

I know of people who, during the summer, put their garbage in parcels and at night take it a few blocks from their residence and deposit it among the long grass on the sides of the streets. And this is in Sandy Hill, not 500 yards from the residence of the prime minister of Canada. As a result of this, the odours at times are not pleasant. However, what else can people do who have no dogs and backyards not big enough to bury their garbage?

I was in the Russell [Hotel] a few nights ago and an Ottawa sport referred to Toronto as Hogtown. A Torontonian who was present retorted, "Well, Ottawa is Garbagetown." Hoping this effusion will be of some interest for those entertaining opinions on the dog question and that it may perhaps point a moral.

Yours etc.,
St. George's Ward

Editor's note: Ottawa city council approved a modest form of garbage collection — or scavenging, as it was known at the time — two years after this letter was written. At first, only garbage from businesses was picked up (for a fee) but the practice was gradually expanded to include households by the end of the decade. By 1910, the pickup fee was dropped and the costs covered through general tax revenue.

CLEAR THE SIDEWALKS

APRIL 1, 1904

Ottawa has attained no little fame among the cities of the Dominion for its success in dealing with snow, but it cannot be said to have attained like success in dealing with the streets when that snow is passing away.

The policy of shovelling snow by civic initiative may lighten the load on the householder in winter, but in the spring the said householder should repay the kindness by exerting himself just a little and clearing off his walks. Had this been done we could for the past two weeks have been walking about comparatively dry shod, instead of wading through troughs of slush.

It is to be hoped that during the next two days individuals and institutions, especially churches, will clear off their walks and open channels for water to run away so that things will be somewhat improved for Easter Sunday.

The present condition is, to say the least, not creditable to a city of Ottawa's size, not to speak of the Capital of the Dominion.

Sojourner

THE GOSPEL OF CHEERFULNESS
APRIL 9, 1904

There's a philosophy, I believe Kant's, which teaches that we are not put in this world to be happy. The members of the Lord's Day Alliance apparently agree thoroughly with it and not only welcome the spirit of gloom to their own hearts, but seek to impose it on others.

There seems to be a desire to take us back to the days when curtains were pulled down on the Sabbath to keep God's sunlight out. (I suppose because it was cheerful.) Literature, except of a religious nature, was tabooed and everyone waited in a resigned impatience till the day was over and they could be normal again.

May I ask the Alliance where the harm lies in Sunday excursions? In Germany, whose people are deeply religious, they praise God in the churches in the morning, then go out into the country or on the rivers and praise him again for giving them one day in

THE STORY OF PHILOSOPHY

Immanuel Kant.

the week to enjoy the beautiful gifts he has bestowed upon them, to draw deep breaths of pure air into their lungs and to renew their health and strength to face the trials and work, perhaps sorrow and disaster, of the coming week.

But these other gentlemen say we are not to go into the country for pleasure and since we cannot go on business the inference is we must not go at all. What is it they would have us do?

Let the Lord's Day Alliance build pleasure gardens out in the country where the poor, tired men and women and pale children can go one day in the week, shut their houses or rooms and get out into the sun and air.

If they go to the gardens, give them coffee or tea, give them cheap excursions on the rivers to gardens further away, give them anything to take them out of the cities and towns, so that "having eyes they may see." Let the children run, jump and play, give them music too; in that way the Alliance will more truly make Sunday the Lord's Day than by any law for the Prohibition of Cheerfulness.

Teach people to laugh, we have forgotten how in this day, and though we cannot be happy — I bow to Kant — at least let us be cheerful. Let us praise and worship the loving God who has given us so much, so much more than we deserved when He gave us the great gift, rather than live in joyless shuddering terror of the jealous God, who sits in wrath and whose pleasure is condemnation.

But alas, I fear the Alliancers are a gloomy clan who take their pleasure sadly. I know none of the estimable gentlemen, I judge them by the laws they would pass; but they seem to be shining examples of Lamb's essay on the Pleasures of a Fit of the Blues in Perpetuum.

Yours truly,
An apostle of cheerfulness

Editor's note: The Lord's Day Alliance of Canada was formed in 1888 under the aegis of the Presbyterian Church to fight the increasing secularization of the Sabbath. A male-only group at first, it actively pressured politicians at the local, provincial and federal levels to restrict Sunday activities, including public transit, sporting events and even ice cream parlours. While the alliance was successful in delaying the relaxation of Sunday activity laws well into the 1960s, it has more or less lost the battle since. In 1982, it was renamed the People for Sunday Association, and pretty much dropped out of sight after a series of Sunday shopping losses in the early 1990s.

AN AMUSING EPISODE
APRIL 19, 1904

The East End Methodist Church, like others in the city, seems to be passing through trying experiences. The worthy pastor (Rev. Dr. Hunter) works faithfully and energetically to improve matters, and with considerable success.

It seems, however, open to question to many in the congregation whether the true spirit and teaching of Methodism is not being departed from by the fulsome announcements of orchestral performances and their introduction into the church. If continued, I, my family and others, intend seeking some other church where these practices are not indulged in.

Another trouble appears to be the capricious attendance and entrance of the choir (never on time). This culminated Sunday morning last to something like desperation on the part of the organist who, after the pastor had entered the church, played a short voluntary number, evidently looking anxiously for the appearance of his choir, but none came. So, taking the bull by the horns, as it were, he began the service alone (ten minutes later) accompanying himself on the organ by singing the first line of the *Doxology*: "Praise God, from whom all blessings flow."

During the singing of the second line, the choir appeared and took their places, singing: "Praise Him all creatures here below."

It became a study to see and note the various expressions of character depicted on the faces of the choir. Vexation, amusement and, on several, I was pleased to detect abasement at the ridiculous circumstances surrounding them.

The organist (Mr. Welch) has done much to improve the music of this church and secured a larger attendance in the choir, but would it not be better to insist on him and his choir beginning the service at the proper time, and thus not wasting that of the pastor and congregation.

Tempus Fugit

RIDEAUVILLE BAD BOYS
APRIL 22, 1904

Bombarded with snowballs while driving a balky horse on Bank Street in Rideauville: Nelson Grayburn, postmaster at Billings Bridge, had that unwelcome experience Wednesday evening.

When near Dufferin Street, Mr. Grayburn was having trouble with his steed. Just then a number of soft snowballs flew through the darkness. Several struck the untamed animal and others landed upon Mr. Grayburn and in his vehicle. Getting off, he pursued his hidden assailants but was unable to catch them.

Apparently troubled also by the conduct of the snowball throwers, a "resident" of the southern suburb has asked me to say the following in a letter to the *Citizen*: "A visit of the county constable to the corner of Canal Road and Bank Street would be very much appreciated by the residents of Rideauville for the purpose of putting a stop to the rowdyism of a number of grown up boys who congregate there nightly for the purpose of insulting passers by. Even children are afraid to pass alone. Wednesday evening their conduct was of a disgraceful character, and when pursued they took refuge in the grounds of the Precious Blood Nuns, much to their annoyance. Such conduct should be stopped."

Displeased observers

REPORTING EXECUTIONS
APRIL 30, 1904

It seems to me that Sheriff Hager would have conferred a benefit upon the community if he had resolutely refused to allow the press to be present at the execution of Goyette.

No useful purpose is served by having all the details of a hanging dished up for the public in the columns of a newspaper. How a murderer spent his last night, what he said, what he had for breakfast, and how he met his well-merited demise is surely a matter of little concern to the public.

The description of a hanging in which the murderer by reason of the great prominence given him (and especially if he meets his death bravely) is made to appear almost a hero to many people who, if they were not blinded by the account of the hanging, would recoil from him with abhorrence, is something which in the public interest should be immediately stopped.

The practice followed in England is the proper one and the sooner it is adopted here the better. There, once a man is convicted and sentenced, he passes out of public view forever. All that appears in the newspaper afterwards is three or four lines announcing that the culprit has been executed.

G.H.H.

Editor's note: In fact, Sheriff Hager did try to ban the press from covering the hanging of Clement Goyette, convicted of murdering Daniel Colligan and his son, Thomas, the previous year in a dispute over money. However, the Citizen and the Journal appealed to the federal minister of justice, who forced Hager to open the execution to Ottawa reporters as well as the local papers around L'Orignal, the eastern Ottawa Valley town where the hanging took place.

SOMETHING OMITTED
JULY 30, 1904

I see by your account of the plans for the improvement of Strathcona Park that facilities for bathing and swimming are not included. Why? There is the [Rideau] river, there is the unoccupied land, there is the money at the disposal of the improvement commission. Why do they withhold this simple boon from the people?

One who cannot afford
to leave town

1905

Local: Ottawa Mayor Sam Bingham drowns while helping to break up a log jam on the Gatineau River (June)
National: *The Victorian,* the first turbine steamer to cross the Atlantic, arrives in Halifax (April); Alberta and Saskatchewan become provinces (July)
World: George Bernard Shaw's new play, *Mrs. Warren's Profession,* is described as morally offensive when it opens in New York (July); After a perilous three-year voyage, Norwegian explorer Roald Amundsen finds the magnetic pole (December)
Births: Canadian painter Paul-Emile Borduas; Canadian track star Bobbie Rosenfeld; writers Arthur Koestler and Jean-Paul Sartre; actors Greta Garbo and Henry Fonda
Deaths: French writer Jules Verne; Henry Irving, first British actor ever knighted

CANADA'S CENTURY

FEBRUARY 18, 1905

Who was the originator of the statement: "Last century was the United States' century; the present is Canada's century?" Banqueters and orators all over the country attribute it to Sir Wilfrid Laurier.

Looking over a copy of a paper published in Ottawa called the *Commonwealth* of date January 1901, I found the following paragraph: "Last century was the United States' century. The present is Canada's century. From the rate at which our population advanced during the past century it is not uncertain prophecy but sound deduction that the year 2000 will come on Canada with a population of eighty (80) million. The United States is filling up and Canada has the only great area of land fit for settlement left on this continent. The United States must ere long cease to be a large exporter of farm and pasture produce both because of the increasing home production and of the comparative thinness of the soil."

This was written on the first month of the first year of the new century. The writer of it was Mr. George Johnson, who seems to me to be entitled to coin the phrase.

Scrutator

Editor's note: Laurier did make a reference to Canada's century, but it was not in the way usually thought. Nor did he say it as the century dawned. In 1904, however, the prime minister said: "The Nineteenth Century was the century of the United States. I think we can claim that it is Canada that shall fill the Twentieth Century." Historians generally believe the phrase commonly attributed to Laurier — "the Twentieth Century belongs to Canada" — was first used in a Toronto newspaper editorial on Jan. 1, 1900.

THE DOG NUISANCE

MARCH 1, 1905

Your correspondent E.M., in his admirable letter on the dog nuisance, expressed his opinion that not until they are shocked by some horrible accident resulting from the freedom with which dogs are allowed at large, will the public realize the full extent of the canine pest.

Such an occasion was almost furnished on Friday afternoon last when a lady and two little children crossing Metcalfe Street at Waverley were saved, through what seemed to the onlookers a miracle, from being knocked down by a horse goaded into a furious pace by the onslaught of five collies, a setter, two fox terriers and several others of the dogs infesting that neighbourhood.

No one was near enough to render any help but the lady just managed to drag the children from under the hoofs of the maddened animal. How narrow their escape was may be imagined from the fact that the sled which one of the little ones was drawing was kicked by the horse's front feet.

Heretofore I have always written you over my own name, but as I desire to save myself and my family a repetition of the obscene abuse over the telephone from various anonymous dog-owners which followed a communication on this subject which you were good enough to publish for me last year, I beg to subscribe myself simply,

Dog Tired

FAIR BRITANNIA'S FARE

APRIL 8, 1905

I believe the old idea that a corporation has no soul is now exploded, and that it may not only be punished for its misdemeanours, but may be trained in the ways of righteousness and so become a commendable, though artificial, member of a moral community.

Taking this for granted therefore, I shall, with your kind permission appeal to the soul of the Ottawa Electric Railway company to do justice to the summer residents of Britannia Bay (including many school children) and give them the privilege of reduced fare from May 1st, instead of making them wait until the dog-day season when, for an extra expenditure of five cents, they may share with the casual passenger all the delights and dangers of riding on the foot-board of an over-crowded car to and from Ottawa's leading summer resort.

We readily acknowledge the enterprise of the company

NATIONAL ARCHIVES OF CANADA

Ottawa Electric Railway came under fire for its fares to Britannia.

in supplying us with open cars during the pneumonia season; but we still think that we should enjoy the joint privilege of transportation and refrigeration for a single fare.

Britannia

GIVE HIM WORK

MAY 2, 1905

Two or three days ago you published a report in your paper to the effect that Canadians will not in future give employment to Italians. Now it seems to me that your report must also refer to upright and honest Englishmen because it is three months since I arrived in this city with my wife and little one and have been to all the largest firms in Ottawa and have not succeeded in procuring permanent employment.

I am a private enquiry agent and was employed by Ex-Detective Inspector Richards of Scotland Yard, London, England, who has given me the best reference of character. I have also a good knowledge of photography, bookkeeping, riding and driving, electricity, furniture salesmen, tobacco and confectionary business and the jewelry trade.

You would do me a great kindness by inserting this letter in your valuable paper as it might be the means of procuring a situation for me.

J.C. Mason,
166 Henderson Avenue, Ottawa

The Citizen's editor replied: We had much pleasure in publishing this letter though we charge the native-born the usual rates for advertising. If this man is steady and industrious and is such an all round chap as he says he is there should be a place for him in Canada. Now it is up to somebody to save the reputation of the country. Who will give him a job?

TEN-CENT BLOCK OF ICE

JULY 12, 1905

In common with most Ottawans I have found ice a necessity of life at this time of the year. It costs me $7 for the season, May 1 to Oct 1., or 10 cents a day. I asked the ice-man if he could tell me offhand how large a piece was a 10 cent block. He said 6 inches by 6 inches! I remarked it would require several such pieces to keep milk, butter and meat sweet from Saturday night till Monday morning. "You can get more," he replied, "by paying for it."

I fear the conditions must bear with severity upon a great many worthy but not wealthy families in Ottawa.

Yours truly, Ottawan

THE CEREBRO SPINO EPIDEMIC

JULY 20, 1905

The disease among the children in some localities in Carleton County which seems, in a measure, to baffle the skill of the physicians is an affection of the spine at its connection with the base of the brain evidently produced by impeded circulation of the blood at the nervous centers, causing muscular contractions which culminate in paralysis of the brain, when death ensues.

The main aim in treatment should be to stimulate the

circulation of blood and a diffusion of the nervous forces to produce a reaction before the too-great contractions of the muscular tissues and paralysis sets in.

This may be done effactually by immersion of the patient in warm water, as warm as can possibly be borne, with the clothing of the patient removed. To aid the stimulating effect of the warm water a tablespoonful of mustard may be stirred in and well diffused before immersion of the patient.

Any vessel can be used, large enough to admit the patient in a reclining or sitting posture, allowing the water to rise to the base of the brain. If a regular bathtub is not at hand, an ordinary washtub may be utilized, the patient to be gently moved in the water that the heat may have its full effect. A surplus of water should be kept heated to renew the water in the bath as it cools in order to keep up a continued immersion of at least 45 or 60 minutes.

After an interval of an hour another immersion may be applied and between the applications drafts may be profitably applied to the feet of sliced onions or an equal mixture of mustard and flour. This treatment seldom fails to give relief in all cases of muscular contractions and convulsions if taken in time and is an antidote to fabric tendencies which arise from impeded circulation.

Any peaceful person can apply it and every house should have a box of mustard in the cupboard for emergencies. The teller of this suggestion has known of many cases of relief in the use of the warm water bath where muscular contraction and convulsions resulted from imperfect circulation of the blood which is usually caused by sudden cold and damp conditions of the atmosphere.

L. Foote,
Fourth Ave, Ottawa

Editor's note: Ottawa's newspapers carried several stories on this mysterious children's illnesss during the spring and summer of 1905. To determine what it might have been, the letter was shown in 1999 to neurologists at the Children's Hospital of Eastern Ontario. Based on the few clues provided, they believe the illness was tetanus, epilepsy or encephalitis, but were unable to make a more exact diagnosis.

MATCH FACTORY PERIL

AUGUST 2, 1905

In relation to your article headed the Match Factory Peril, whatever necessity may exist for government inspection elsewhere, there is little or no reason for it in this neighbourhood.

Some years ago I had occasion to investigate the Eddy match factory in Hull on a request from the British government. I found that so great was the care exercised, so completely was the establishment provided with exhaust and supply fans to take away at once and constantly and effectively all fumes that arise in the mixing rooms or in the dipping rooms where phosphorous is used, that no cases of necrosis [tuberculosis] had occurred for eight or 10 years back. There was really complete immunity from the disease. The census of 1901 shows the same total absence of the disease.

If the Detroit match factories referred to in your article want to conserve the health of the girls working in them they could not do better than send persons to learn how to do it from the plans adopted by the Eddy factory.

An examination of the mortuary statistics of the town of Hull for several years failed to reveal a single case of the dread disease among the 450 or more employees. What was still more remarkable, the general health of Hull showed improvement in several classes of disease. Psoriasis had been banished doubtless because of the sulphur. Deaths from throat affections had been reduced in five years — from 89.46 per thousand to 39.19 per thousand.

George Johnson

SAWDUST NUISANCE
AUGUST 22, 1905

Your recent editorial on the dumping of sawdust in our river, and the letters of protest in your columns against the continuation of the same scandal, should be heartily endorsed by every lover of nature.

Why any group of individuals should be allowed to wantonly destroy one of the finest rivers (the Ottawa River) on this continent in the interest of greedy gain is one of those mysteries that baffle solution.

Let a local merchant presume to throw his store sweepings on the public street and the city will lose no time in making an example of him. On the other hand, the government authorities pay no attention to the incessant dumping of slabs and sawdust into the waters of the Ottawa by our lumber kings, a state of things that has been allowed so long that at low water the deposits in several places touch the surface.

What a contrast on the one hand, a little waste paper recklessly thrown on the street means a fine for the offender. Conversely, several millions of tons of timber refuse thrown into the Ottawa means fame for the perpetrator. It seems curious, doesn't it?

X.Y.Z.

CIVIL SERVICE SALARIES
OCTOBER 9, 1905

Since last session of Parliament, it has been expected that the government, after voting an increase of indemnity to the members, giving for a reason the high cost of living, would for the same reason advance the salaries of the officials; but although a few increases were allowed, it is noticeable that they went to those who were already too well remunerated.

It is safe to say that some of the officials are overpaid, while there are some who would indeed show great administrative ability if they could make both ends meet with their present salary. About a year ago a highly educated man who had a position in one of the most important departments died suddenly of paralysis of the brain after worrying for years trying to devise a means to support a family of 10 with a salary of $2 per day.

The maximum salary paid clerks is $3 per day, or $90 per month of 30 days, and $93 for months of 31 days. The following is what I consider a low estimate of the expenditure incurred monthly by a person with a family of seven or eight: Rent, $25 per month; groceries, $15 per month; meat, $15 per month; coal average $6; wood, $3; light, $2; milk, bread, etc., $5. Total $74, leaving a balance of $16 for clothing, doctors bills, life insurance policies and numerous other unforeseen expenditures.

If the cost of living was found sufficient reason to give $1,000 to our legislators who were already receiving $1,500 for their work, which may last from 31 days to 150 days, surely our government should not begrudge an additional dollar per day to employees who work six days in a week for an entire year.

Now that they have looked so well after themselves, let us hope that the members will not forget that the present high cost of living is certainly more of a burden to the officials than it has ever been to themselves.

Yours truly, A

TEACHERS' SALARIES
NOVEMBER 8, 1905

Evidently there is still a remarkable scarcity in Ontario of school teachers possessing the legal professional qualifications and, in consequence, trustees are finding it very difficult to secure the necessary teachers to handle the schools of the province.

The cause of this is not hard to locate. Every thoughtful person knows that it is traceable to the parsimonious salaries paid by school boards and no fault of the teachers or their qualifications.

When one thinks of the importance of the work done by teachers — a work which deals largely with the moral and intellectual phases of our national character, even the very foundation principles of that character — the question arises: Why are teachers so poorly paid?

When members of school boards are questioned on the subject they try to hide behind the old arguments that the hours are short, vacations long and, on the whole, the pedagogues have a very easy time. But this is a miserably poor argument, especially when compared with that advanced in favour of better wages for teachers. It must be remembered that the school day is not, by any means, limited to the hours spent with the classes as very much more time is spent industriously in preparing and examining papers, issuing merit cards, writing up reports, etc., etc.

Think then of $250 to $400, or even, as paid in Ottawa, $560 for a man who had to spend time, money and energy sufficient to secure a provincial normal 2nd class certificate (the minimum grade certificate now granted teachers in Ontario) as compared with salaries paid in other lines of business, many of which do not require nearly so extensive or thorough an educational training. The salaries paid lady teachers are even much less in general.

What wonder that only some four or five young men, and a less number of young women than usual, are attending the Ottawa normal school this session? How can young men hope, under existing conditions, to marry and settle down to housekeeping on the salaries paid to teachers? Yours,

For fair wages

1906

Local: Supported by a $100,000 donation from U.S. philanthropist Andrew Carnegie, the Carnegie Public Library opens on the site of today's main branch of the Ottawa Public Library (May); The automobile replaces the stage coach which has brought the mail from Richmond for 50 years (October)

National: English-only schools are proposed for Winnipeg after revelations that instruction is offered in 13 languages because of a huge jump in immigration to Western Canada (May)

World: The *Dreadnought,* the fastest and largest battleship in the world, is launched by the British Royal Navy (February); Thousands are killed when a severe earthquake jolts San Francisco (April)

Births: Liberal finance minister Walter Gordon; film director John Huston; American singer-dancer Josephine Baker

Deaths: Hull lumber baron E.B. Eddy; Joseph Glidden, the inventor of barbed wire; French painter Paul Cézanne

WESTERN SETTLEMENT IN OTTAWA

JANUARY 30, 1906

I want to enter a respectful but nonetheless emphatic protest against your opinion that the future residential growth of Ottawa must be southward for lack of suitable building land in any other direction.

It is evident that you are not familiar with the locality lying between the Experimental Farm and the village of Hintonburg. There is not anywhere in or near Ottawa any equal area of choice residential property available. It remains unoccupied because it is not accessible by any direct road from the city. The street railway company has a line through a portion of it, but does not use it during the winter months.

The annexation of Hintonburg, Mechanicsville and the above area would bring within the city limits a considerable population and the choicest building land west of Ottawa, and the creation of another western ward might call public attention to the need of an unobstructed street at the west end.

At present there are but three highways leading into the city, not one of them suitable for general traffic. The Merivale Road is not a direct avenue and it has moreover a long, steep grade a little west of the railway crossing. The same objection, in a lesser degree, applies to Somerset Street, and the third highway, the Richmond Road, is for all practical purposes a part of a railway shunting ground.

Some day when a viaduct is constructed to carry the general traffic over the railway tracks at the west end, when the street railway company builds a loop line to pass through or near the Experimental Farm, and when, if ever, the Improvement Commission realizes that there is a west as well as an east end to Ottawa, the area lying between the Richmond Road and the Experimental Farm will become the best residential section of Greater Ottawa.

H., Ottawa.

Editor's note: Hintonburg was part of a 1,500-acre tract of Nepean Township annexed by the city of Ottawa in 1907. All 99 acres of Mechanicsville were annexed from the township in 1911.

THE FAY TEST

MARCH 7, 1906

Allow me to congratulate you on your article concerning Mrs. Fay's mind-reading performance. You have, in my opinion, conclusively demonstrated that the lady in question has failed to fulfill the fair conditions of your challenge. After reading your editorial, the most superstitious ought to be convinced that mind-reading as practised by Mrs. Fay is nothing but a clever fake.

I think you have rendered a great service to the people of Ottawa by exposing this fake for, in my opinion, a paper that courageously combats the agents of superstition is a real benefactor to its readers. I wish, in the interests of enlightenment and civilization, that your good example may be followed by all editors in this country.

Yours sincerely,
W. Lothmann

Editor's note: Mrs. Eva Fay was a member of the Marvellous Fays, a family of entertainers that played at the Russell Theatre on Sparks Street for three nights in early March. After watching Mrs. Fay correctly identify the contents of audience members' pockets on the first night, the Citizen decided to test her authenticity by assigning a reporter to attend on the second night. In his pocket he carried a note asking, "When was I last in Toronto?" Mrs. Fay was not only unable to answer the question, she could not say what was on the note, leading the Citizen to suggest in a subsequent article that she was a "fake," and her previous success was due to accomplices peppered throughout the audience.

THE LIBRARY NAME

MARCH 13, 1906

Regarding various views on the name of the new public library, there are conditions or phases of this business that are being overlooked, although it may be that the present library committee has given them due consideration.

In the first place, there would not have been any money spent on a library at all, on either building or books, had it not been for [U.S. philanthropist Andrew] Carnegie's $100,000. This money has produced this "work of art" on Metcalfe Street (at Laurier), about which so much has been said, so much written, so much yet remains to be said and over which there have been so many heart-burnings and bickerings and so many resignations.

The terms stipulated by Carnegie were reasonable, and Ottawa city has been forced into the position of having to expend at least a minimum of $7,500 per year on literature. The bylaw makes the minimum and the maximum the same amount. This too shows the keen appreciation Ottawa councillors have for a library of any kind.

Surely the man who, by a gift of $100,000 can induce or drive the citizens of the Capital of Canada to perform a public duty for themselves by maintaining such a monument to intelligence and knowledge, as this, deserves well of Ottawa.

Our city was behind the times. Carnegie pushed us into the light. Are we to take his gift and then conceal the fact from posterity? Are we so mean as to benefit by his wealth and not publicly admit it? Let us be men and publicly acknowledge the gift.

Yours, S.

Editor's note: The library, on the site of the present-day main branch, was eventually named the Carnegie Public Library, and a sign was placed in full view.

SAVE OUR BOYS
APRIL 26, 1906

The Dominion Women's Temperance Union has for some years past been endeavouring to induce the Dominion government to pass a stringent measure prohibiting cigarette selling and smoking to boys under a certain age.

It is earnestly hoped by all who are interested in the welfare of our boys that such an act will in the near future be passed. In the states of Vermont, Tennessee, Iowa and Missouri prohibitory laws are now in force.

A leading oculist wrote to me a short time ago stating his strong objections to the habit of smoking cigarettes among boys. He says in his letter: "There is no question but that tobacco, especially the cigarette kind, affects the brain as well as the eyes, and that it weakens the centre of memory and intelligence as well. Trembling of the hand is remarkable in many young men addicted to the cigarette habit. From the experience that has been taught to many medical practitioners, I do not understand why the government of the Dominion does not put tobacco under the same penalty as alcohol. As regards its use among young people, why not forbid the use of tobacco to boys under 19 or 20 years of age and punish severely youngsters caught on the street or anywhere with a cigarette in their mouths, and punish as well — more severely — the dealer selling them cigarettes?"

Now, Mr. Editor, the smoking of cigarettes amongst our boys is steadily on the increase, and sometimes when spoken to about this bad habit they reply, "Oh, my father or my minister smokes, or my priest smokes." Let the fathers of families, ministers and priests practise a little self-denial and give up the habit of smoking for the sake of the boys, and not be stumbling blocks in the way of others.

G.L.P., Ottawa

Editor's note: Two years later, the federal government passed a law prohibiting the sale of tobacco to anyone under 16. An Ontario law restricting tobacco sales to people under 18 had been in place since 1892.

NEWSIES ON THE LAWNS
MAY 23, 1906

While householders are urged to improve their lawns and thus contribute to the beauty of the city, their efforts to co-operate in the good work are being neutralized by the practice of newsboys, delivery men and letter carriers cutting across lawns from house to house instead of keeping to the walks.

The latter practice would entail more work and walking by the newsies and others, but it would serve to keep the lawns in better condition and give heart to the owners to persevere in the good work of beautifying their grounds.

On Cooper Street I have heard that young lads play ball upon the street and frequently race over the lawns in pursuit of the ball, even knocking over plants. "I have borne with this practice as long as I will," a lady of residence there told me, "and the next offenders will be handed over to the police."

The insolence of the lads is complained of. A lady who lately removed from Maclaren Street remonstrated with boys for trespassing upon her lawn and was answered with insolence and reminded that she could not help herself.

If the police would make an example of some of the offenders, it should serve to abate the evil and help the city.

Gloucester Street

ACTED LIKE BOORS
MAY 31, 1906

I am sure your many readers must have been shocked yesterday on reading about the outrageous conduct of some persons smoking last Monday on a Britannia streetcar. There are many people however, who, like myself, think the gentlemen and ladies referred to only got what was coming to them and that if they have no respect for the rights of others, they must be educated on this point.

What are the facts? The Street Railway company allocates three seats at the back of the car for those who may desire to indulge in a smoke, while the gentlemen who don't smoke in the company of ladies, and the ladies who don't enjoy their cigarette in public, have all the rest to themselves.

There are many men who work all day and have neither the time nor the inclination to smoke until after supper, when they can thoroughly enjoy one in the fresh air going to and returning from Britannia, and surely no lady or gentleman would deny them this little comfort, or mild dissipation, if you would call it so. It is no uncommon sight to see a not very bashful looking female and her little beau (better say lady and gentleman) forcing their way into the smoking seats regardless of the rights of those for whom the seats were reserved.

It is about time some people knew they cannot have everything their own way, so let us who enjoy the weed, smoke in the seats reserved for us regardless of the affected ire of such ladies, who at home perhaps, don't complain when the old man and their big brothers are puffing away at French Dogan.

J.B.,
84 Bank Street

SPEED OF CARS

JULY 11, 1906

In reference to the killing of Mr. O'Leary by a streetcar on Somerset Street, is it not about time that action was taken to prevent the Street Railways Company from running the Britannia cars at a faster speed than the law allows?

Numerous are the complaints on Laurier Avenue East of the fast running of the cars, especially after 11 o'clock at night.

If you doubt me, Mr. Editor, go up and have a smoke some night with a friend on Laurier Avenue after 11 o'clock and watch car after car pass in quick succession at an exceedingly rapid rate.

Why so many cars run and at a rate faster than law allows is a mystery as the cars run at that hour practically empty. It would look as if to save themselves the trouble of turning at the corner of Sussex Street, they run around the loop, in most cases empty, and make up for lost time by running at a rapid rate. A large number of people will be obliged to you if you can do anything to stop the nuisance.

A Reader

MR. FISHER EXPLAINS

JULY 30, 1906

Kindly allow me space in your paper to correct an impression that may have gone abroad in reference to an interview with me that appeared in the *Citizen*. The article in question would lead one to believe I was opposed to shorter hours for the retail clerk. This is a wrong impression.

I am in perfect sympathy with any movement that will lessen the hours of the clerk, as it will necessarily shorten the hours of the proprietor. But I do think that the object would be gained by having Wednesday afternoon off during May, June, July, August and September, and closing at five o'clock during these months, and leaving Saturday as it now is, as there is, and always will be, a lot of shopping that can be done at no other time conveniently.

E. R. Fisher

Editor's note: The grandsons of Emerson Richard Fisher

still operate two men's clothing stores in Ottawa: on Sparks Street, in the same block between Metcalfe and O'Connor streets where the first store was established in 1905, and at the Bayshore Shopping Centre. Although his letter is polite in tone, the article to which he refers must have stung Mr. Fisher, an early workers' rights advocate who introduced job sharing as a way to avoid layoffs, long before it became popular in the 1990s. The issue at stake in this letter was a bylaw forcing stores to close Saturdays at 6 p.m. rather than 8 p.m.

NOT HIS SAWDUST

JULY 31, 1906

In your issue of a few days ago, your correspondent makes the following statement re the sawdust nuisance: "That the incinerator erected by Mr. Booth some years ago put an end to the nuisance for a time as it consumed all the products of his mills at the Chaudière, but apparently during the present season the practice of allowing sawdust to escape into the river has been reverted to etc."

I must give the above statement the fullest denial, for at no time since I erected the incinerator has the refuse from my mill been as thoroughly consumed as it has this summer, as I made many improvements last winter to more fully convey everything that was possible to the furnace, which will consume all I can get into it.

I would respectfully ask your correspondent to do me the justice of paying my mill a visit at any time, day or night, and I will be pleased to show him through every part of it; and if he can point out any better way than I have got to collect and convey to the burner the refuse, I will at once adopt it.

Yours truly,
J.R. Booth

THE OTTAWA CITIZEN

J.R. Booth wrote to deny a report that sawdust from his mill was being dumped into the river.

Editor's note: The Citizen took up the lumber baron's offer of a visit to his giant mill at Chaudière Falls, and reported a few weeks later that Booth's company was among the cleanest of its type in operation along the Ottawa River.

1907

Local: About 10,000 tulip, hyacinth and daffodil bulbs from England are planted at various sites selected by the governor general, Earl Grey (October); An outbreak of typhoid fever hits Hull, with several deaths recorded (December)

National: The National Council of Women, a suffragette organization, calls for "equal pay for equal work" (May); Bridge spanning the St. Lawrence River at Montreal collapses, drowning 80 (August)

World: Mohandas Gandhi, a young Indian lawyer living in South Africa, organizes campaign of civil unrest to resist law restricting Asian immigration (March); Finns elect women to Parliament, the first females to win office in Europe (March); Boy Scout movement begins when Sir Robert Baden-Powell recruits 12 upper-class and nine working-class boys for excursion to the woods (July)

Births: Joseph-Armand Bombardier, Canadian inventor of the snowmobile; poet W.H. Auden; actor Laurence Olivier; comedian Milton Berle; actor Burgess Meredith

Deaths: British physicist Lord Kelvin

THE OTTAWA CITIZEN

Governor general Earl Grey selected sites for about 10,000 flower bulbs from Britain to be planted in Ottawa.

THE TOLL ROAD NUISANCE

JANUARY 16, 1907

Regarding the toll roads question, I had occasion to make an early trip on business on the morning of the 9th of January in very severe weather over a portion of the stone road leading to Metcalfe and had not gone far before I was confronted with a toll gate with the bar down.

After spending a good deal of time rousing the only toll keeper by lusty calls, he shouted from within in a foreign tongue, "Pay your money." Then I had to go to the trouble of taking off my shoes and gloves, undoing my coat and wraps, and finally the 10-cent transaction was concluded. I had spent as much time upon it as would have taken me over a mile of road.

In addition to having been chilled with the cold in the negotiations, the young horse I was driving became almost unmanageable, it having been frightened by the raising of the bar.

This is happening daily to the travelling public, and knowing that the *Citizen's* columns are always open to the discussion of matters pertaining to the public benefit, I have placed these things before you hoping that others having had similar experiences will be encouraged to take a stand and wipe out, as western municipalities have done, this toll road system that has outlived its day.

Yours truly,
A traveler

Editor's note: Ottawa and Gloucester assumed control of toll roads and bridges in 1909, eventually phasing out the fees for passing.

A GOOD SUGGESTION

JANUARY 17, 1907

The open-air skating which afforded delightful and healthful recreation to thousands during the early part of the month has been spoiled by the present fall of snow, and with ordinary weather conditions we shall see no more of it until about the break-up of the winter.

May I ask your assistance to promote a plan to ensure open-air skating for Ottawa throughout the season? My proposal, in brief, is to maintain a clear sheet of ice on the canal from Laurier bridge to Hartwell's locks or Hog's Back. This may be regarded as "a large order," but I venture to hope that discussion will show it to be not beyond the bounds of reasonable possibility.

In other cities not nearly so favoured by nature as Ottawa, public money is spent for the maintenance of skating ponds and rinks, and it seems to me that, with the splendid opportunities we have, it would be well worth while to establish a great winter park as one of the attractions of the Capital of Canada.

I have not consulted any who have special information upon this subject, but I should think that "a cheap sluiceway" could be provided to flood the canal with water from above Hog's Back, as occasion might require, thus maintaining glare ice without the expense of the constant sweeping that would be necessary with the frequent snow falls. Of course, if sweeping were found cheaper or more advantageous, there would be no reason against adopting that plan.

Should the scheme prove a feasible one, this great winter park might be made attractive, not only to those who enjoy long-distance skating, but also to fancy skaters, hockeyists and others by the reservation of small rinks at suitable places along the course.

Dow's Lake should be included in the proposition, and here would be a glorious open-air rink, unless it were decided to use it as a winter racing track.

A.C. Campbell

Editor's note: It would be another 64 years before Mr. Campbell's idea for publicly funded skating on the Rideau Canal became reality. Under the guidance of National Capital Commission chairman Douglas Fullerton, the canal was opened to skaters from Wellington Street to the Bronson Avenue bridge in January 1971. It was later expanded to include Dow's Lake and the stretch of canal beside Carleton University, almost as far as Hog's Back.

SUNDAY TRAINS

JANUARY 31, 1907

Last evening's papers brought us the startling news of the sad and sudden death of poor Andrew Starke of Ottawa. Would that he had protested still more strongly against working on the Lord's Day.

It makes one's heart ache to think of the poor fellow, probably with the thought of helping his poor widowed mother, stifling his conviction of the wrong of such Sabbath desecration, going forth, reluctantly to share in it rather than lose his job, and by so doing lost his life.

Who killed Andrew Starke? Is there no law in this country for big corporations?

Though money cannot restore the son to the mother, I hope a good many times the amount of money made by last Sunday's lawlessness may be transferred from the company's coffers to the home of the grief-stricken widow.

James Lawson,
Chelsea

Editor's note: Mr. Starke, a well-liked employee of Canadian Pacific Railway for about six months, was killed after being crushed between the cars of a CPR freight train.

FOREWARNED IS FOREARMED

MARCH 12, 1907

Typhoid fever has been somewhat more prevalent than usual in the Ottawa Valley during the past winter, and it is beyond any reasonable doubt that *bacillus typhus* will find its way into our river water with the coming spring freshets.

Ottawa River water is usually free from disease germs and the large amount of organic matter which it holds in solution is not, in itself, harmful or dangerous. But we cannot deny that this character is favourable to the multiplication of any germs which find entrance to the river, and this fact seems to justify me in calling the attention of citizens to a possible source of danger during the spring months, when the ice is breaking up, and the accumulations of winter are washed into the river.

The simplest way to avoid danger is to use no water without boiling. Filtration is helpful, provided that the filtering material is properly taken care of, but most of the household filters in use are quite unsatisfactory, either from faulty construction, or from carelessness in their management. Do not imagine that the mere clearness and transparency of water is any proof of its purity or safety. Boil the water.

Anthony McGill, Assistant chief analyst,
Department of health and sanitation (Ontario)

ANOTHER DANGER NOTICE

MARCH 13, 1907

Many thanks to Dr. McGill for calling attention to the threatened spread of typhoid fever in our midst owing to disease germs in our river water. At the same time, permit me to invite the attention of the civic authorities to another source of danger to the public health, namely, the dust nuisance in the streets of the Capital.

Last spring, for over a month after the disappearance of the snow, King Dust reigned supreme in Ottawa before any attempt was made to bring out the water-carts. When we consider the composition of the dust, comprising the accumulated impurities of the winter months emanating from man and beast (the man, not infrequently, being worse than the beast), we can form some idea of what the people of Ottawa have been made to endure from this one source of danger.

The subject is too disgusting to enlarge on, and if not remedied, cannot but have an injurious effect on the character of the city for health and cleanliness. Let Ottawa be a Capital in reality as well as in name.

Old Times

DANGER FROM CONTAGIOUS DISEASE

APRIL 17, 1907

We often hear of cases of contagious disease where a doctor was not called in for fear he would report and thus the patient would be forced to go to Contagious Diseases Hospital [in Sandy Hill]. They preferred to treat the disease themselves at home rather than pay the expenses of a long stay at the hospital, thus exposing to danger others who may come into contact with the patient's family.

If the hospital exists for the purpose of protecting the public from the spread of contagious disease, then fees or any other obstacle that would prejudice people against going to the hospital should be removed. Of course, a patient in a private room or ward should pay, but not public ward patients who are ratepayers and as such contribute their share to support the hospital.

I would like you to express an opinion editorially, not in the abstract, but as if it were brought home to you by some of your family catching contagious disease from people who have it in their homes yet mix with the people.

Rate-Payer

SUNDAY RECREATION

APRIL 20, 1907

I was much interested to read a few days ago of the forming of a club in Toronto for the purpose of furthering healthful, instructive and reasonable recreation on Sundays, that is to say that public libraries, museums, etc. should be kept open for the benefit of the very persons they are most needed by.

Could not such an association be started in Ottawa? There are at present hundreds of conservative, selfish people who, having the means to get all they want, try to, and do, restrict their less fortunate fellows who work from 6 a.m. to 6 p.m., or perchance from 6 p.m. to 6 a.m.

Any parties desiring to forward such a movement may address:

P.O. Box 142,
Ottawa

REGRETTABLE TERM

MAY 20, 1907

I saw with regret in this morning's *Citizen* that the word "scab" was applied to non-union men. Surely things have come to a pretty pass when opprobrious terms are applied to a man simply because he does not choose to belong to an organization largely controlled by foreigners and governed by regulations admirably suited to the dominions of the Czar, but by no means in accord with the principles governing an empire which boasts of freedom and equal laws for all.

Fair Play

IF IT SHOULD FALL

MAY 29, 1907

Some four months ago the steel ornament on the steeple of the First Baptist Church, at Laurier Avenue and Elgin Street, took a decided cant to the east in consequence of a heavy wind storm, and there was a promise made at the time that it would be immediately adjusted; but as yet nothing has been done. Now you know this particular piece of architectural jewelry must weigh about a ton, and if it was to fall upon some absent-minded pedestrian, that particular individual would be apt to have a considerable weight on his mind. Doubtless when he was quite dead resolutions would be passed, couched in the most felicitous language, to the effect that it should have been fixed long ago, which would be most consoling and useful to the recipient of the afore-mentioned intellectual incubus.

There are a number of people who have occasion to pass up and down Elgin Street. If it fell upon any of these it wouldn't matter much, but, as you can readily understand, Mr. Editor, the really serious point is, that it might fall and hit me.

Pro Bono Publico

OBJECTS TO COAL DUST

JULY 25, 1907

Will you lend the aid of your valuable columns towards abating a nuisance caused by the present methods of delivering coal in some quarters? At the east end of Slater Street, on the south side, are circular holes in the sidewalk, near which several loads of fine coal, containing a large proportion of dust, have been delivered recently, with the result that an area of about 100 feet by 15 has been indescribably filthy all day long for one or two days.

The coal carts drive right on the sidewalk and dump the loads without any attempt whatever at restricting the space covered. Scores of ladies in light summer dresses and white boots have to walk through the small coal and coal dust. Should not the use of some hopper, chute, or some device be enforced?

Tan Boots

A CIVIL QUESTION

NOVEMBER 12, 1907

At the recent qualifying examinations for the Civil Service, the paper in arithmetic for French candidates contained the following question: "A farmer buys land from B at $60 per acre, and from C at $85 per acre. For the whole land bought he paid $53,215. How many acres did he buy from each?"

That is neither a problem nor even a puzzle, unless the candidates were expected to make a guess at the contents of the examiner's mind. Without entering into a lengthy dissertation on the requirements in the data of a problem with a double unknown, it will suffice to give a short list of possible answers.

Thus the farmer in question may have bought: From B, 877 acres at $60 and from C 7 acres at $85; or from B 860 and from C 19; or from B 843 and from C 31; or from B 826 and from C 43; or from B 809 and from C 55; or from B 367 and from C 367; or from B 350 and from C 379; or from B 61 and from C 588, or from B 44 and from C 595; or from B 27 and from C 607; or from B 10 and from C 619.

The reader may easily test any of these answers. There are 41 other possible answers, and if fractions are allowed — and there is in the data of the problem nothing to forbid their use — the number of possible answers is infinite. The only correct answer, the only one that should have won for the puzzled candidate the full allotted marks, is: "I don't know, and neither do you."

Add to that the ambiguities, obscurities, and mistakes to be found in most of the other questions, and you have an idea of the disadvantages under which labored the French-speaking candidates at the last examination for the Civil Service.

A. Bélanger,
Ottawa

1908

Local: Lansdowne Park is site of Ottawa's first automobile show (September); Greek push-cart peddlers kicked out of town for obstructing street corners (September)
National: Sir Wilfrid Laurier's Liberals elected to their fourth consecutive majority government, a feat unmatched since (October)
World: The first Model-T rolls off the Ford Motor Company production line in Detroit (August); American Jack Johnson becomes the first black to win the world heavyweight boxing championship (December)
Births: Photographer Yousuf Karsh; Ian Fleming, creator of James Bond; American actress Bette Davis
Deaths: Governor general Lord Stanley of Preston; Ottawa lumber baron Gordon Pattee; former U.S. president Grover Cleveland

THE WHISTLING NUISANCE

JANUARY 27, 1908

At a very early hour on Saturday morning a Grand Trunk engine in Ottawa East indulged in the most furious whistling for several minutes. Apparently a semaphore or switch was set against it, and the engineer expressed his irritation by waking up most of the residents for a quarter of a mile around. Such would be bad enough under ordinary circumstances, but when there is sickness in the family and an unfortunate sufferer is awakened from a much needed sleep by such conduct, it becomes an outrage.

Ottawa East

A STABLE NUISANCE

FEBRUARY 15, 1908

The city engineer has advised the renting of a stable in McLeod Street, if possible, for a term of five years, for the purpose of stabling twelve teams of horse for the use of the civic corporation. The residents of this section of the city have very serious objections to the present stable, with its limited number of horses, for several reasons.

Even if the drainage of the stable was not bad, the smell or stench from it which is sometimes amplified by the presence of dirty garbage carts in the yard, renders it almost impossible for the neighbours to use their verandahs on a summer evening.

The kicking of the horses at night, the late stabling of delivery horses, and the loud and abusive language by the drivers renders sleep in the early part of the night an impossibility to those living beside the stable.

For these reasons, which would be magnified if the number of horses were increased, and from the fact that McLeod Street is fast becoming one of the best residential streets in the city, the residents feel justified not only in objecting to the present stable, but in protesting against the city forcing upon us what is bound to prove a detriment to our comfort and health.

Ratepayer

HEATING PUBLIC LIBRARY

FEBRUARY 24, 1908

I have been much amused by the item which has appeared in your paper to the effect that the heating apparatus installed in the Carnegie Library has been condemned by an expert, and that by the installation of a new apparatus, at a cost of $7,500, a saving of $1,500 per annum would be effected.

During the winter of 1905-06, I was the successful tenderer for coal, and an examination of my books discloses the fact that I supplied seventy tons to the library at a total cost of $426.10. Where a saving of $1,400 can come in now I fail to see.

In my humble opinion this matter should receive the very closest attention of the library committee, as the interest on expenditure for the proposed new apparatus at six per cent would amount to almost as much as fuel cost the library during 1905-06.

Yours truly,
W.D. Morris

Editor's note: Built in 1905 at Laurier Avenue and Metcalfe Street, on the same site as the main branch of Ottawa's present-day library, the Carnegie Library was the source of considerable embarrassment for Ottawa city council. Aldermen at first balked at approving money for the new library, but were humiliated into freeing some funds after U.S. philanthropist Andrew Carnegie contributed $100,000 to its construction.

CLEAN BREAD

MARCH 26, 1908

I must congratulate you on your recent editorial on the subject of "clean bread." It is surprising that something has not been done before this to protect the loaves from contamination between the bake shop and the customer.

The present mode of delivery is necessarily filthy and it is made far worse by the carelessness of delivery men. A few years ago a driver for one of the largest concerns in the city, in order to save himself a drive of a block, sent a loaf of bread to my house by my neighbour's furnace man. The latter carried it under his arm, and to make matters worse, it was in a drizzling rain.

Yet when I complained to the bakery they declined even to reprimand their driver, alleging that men were hard to get and that they preferred losing a customer to losing a driver. This will perhaps scarcely be believed, yet it is the literal truth.

At the present time the driver who comes to my house puts the bread into his basket with the dirty gloves with which he has just been driving, and perhaps has been attending to his horse in other ways. He is usually smoking a cigarette and on his way to the back door he spits and drops ashes about him, quite regardless of whether either lights on the bread. In the kitchen he takes off his gloves and piles them on one of the loaves of bread while he takes the tickets or makes change.

With an article of food, like meat, which is cooked before eaten, this would be bad enough, but it must be remembered that the bread comes direct from their hands to the table without change. It is certainly high time that proper bags or some other covering for the bread is adopted. I venture to predict that the Ottawa baker who first solves it will experience a sudden and great increase in his business.

Paterfamilias

Editor's note: By 1910, provincial and federal health rules specified that all delivered baked goods must be packaged in bags. Within the bakery, breads were allowed to sit un-wrapped on shelves.

PLEAS FOR HORSE TROUGH
JULY 10, 1908

Allow me to draw attention to the broken and dried up horse trough in Hull, by the Bank of Montreal corner, whereby the many thirsty, hard-worked, sweat belathered horses, which toil in the sun all day, passing and repassing this dried up fountain which once gave them cool, refreshing drink, while they, parched with thirst, both see, hear and smell the water they so much desire and long for rustling by them in volumes under their very noses.

Can it not without further delay be repaired, now that the summer is fully upon us, and so restore a precious priceless boon to man's most faithful toiling friend?

P.S. My cheque for a small amount may be found at said mentioned bank.

Plea from the horsey

RULES OF THE ROAD
AUGUST 6, 1908

It has been in my mind a long time to address you concerning the Rules of the Road, and now take the opportunity offered by your recent timely article on the Rules of Navigation.

Allow me to say that there is as much danger to life and limb in the streets as on the river or canal, and all from the same cause, criminal ignorance, wilful neglect, and most culpable devil may care driving.

There is absolutely no regard or respect for the rights of others to occupy the centre of the road turning to right or left without any warning, to occupy the wrong side, to jaunt along and suddenly to sail right across the street with a supine indifference and total disregard of the danger to other people, to cut off corners on the near side.

Why, sir, it is safer to ride a wheel in the thickly congested streets of London than here. Indeed, I have had more escapes on my wheel here in Ottawa in one year than during a long life in the old country.

Descending Metcalfe from Sparks the other day there was one of Nixon's carts [a Sparks Street caterer and confectioner] in front of me. It was occupying the middle of the road, and not knowing which way it was going I kept behind.

Passing Queen I decided to overtake it before Albert and according to custom passed on the left. It was well I did, for as I came abreast the driver, suddenly and without any warning whatsoever, turned to the right into some

stables, and had I, as is often done in such cases, tried to pass on the inside I should have been utterly smeared.

It is time some attention was given to this matter, especially as motor traffic is increasing together with the motorcycle.

Ernest O. Way,
Ottawa East

UNSANITARY PREMISES
AUGUST 17, 1908

I beg leave to call your attention, or rather that of the health department through your columns as it is useless to protest to that body politic, of the very unsanitary condition existing on Laurier Avenue west between Lyon and Bay streets.

There are at least five houses tenanted by about forty people without any form of sewage — nothing — but outdoor closets. This, as anyone will admit, is a menace to the health of all the neighbourhood. Mr. W.J. Campbell has two rows of houses, six each, next to these dens of disease. The fact is during the last month there have been two cases of fever in those houses and I think anyone standing around this street at night would call it miraculous that the number was not twenty.

This case has been reported to the health authorities some time ago, but as yet there is no improvement. Thanking you, Mr. Editor, in advance, I am,

One sincerely disgusted

A CORRECTION
AUGUST 25, 1908

In your issue of the 20th you say: "Will Metcalfe Street become a Chinatown? It is understood that the former Oxford Hotel at Metcalfe and Albert streets is being made ready to be used as a big Chinese boarding house. The entire building, it is said, is to be occupied by Chinese and will be the first real semblance of a Chinatown in the capital." The writer then continues in a similar strain, the whole article tending to greatly prejudice the incoming tenant of the premises in question.

Had the writer of the article taken the trouble to make inquiries he would have learned the facts and there would have been no occasion whatever for such unfair comment. I have rented the premises above mentioned for a definite term of years and hope to obtain permission to transfer my restaurant business there from my present quarters, 67 Metcalfe Street.

This is rendered necessary for the purpose of accommodating the large number of business men who regularly patronize my restaurant at midday and 6 o'clock. A portion of the said premises is being renovated and remodeled by the landlord and when completed will be a thoroughly sanitary and modern restaurant. The remaining portion of the building will be sublet for business purposes.

There is no intention whatever of establishing a "Chinatown" in the capital. As a citizen and taxpayer of Ottawa, I consider it extremely unfair that my business should be injured by such comments as appear in the article above quoted. I also trust that in fairness to the Chinamen of Ottawa, who are responsible businessmen, you will kindly give this letter the same prominence that you did the article which appeared in your issue of the 20th.

Yours truly, Thomas Hamilton,
67 Metcalfe Street

NOISY CARS

SEPTEMBER 2, 1908

I am a frequent visitor to your city, and I must say that in comparison with other cities of the Dominion as to beauty, brightness and cleanliness it stands well in the front; but there are two things in this city which always impress themselves forcibly upon me every time I visit it.

First, Mr. Editor, I cannot understand how the citizens of Ottawa can stand the unearthly racket made by the streetcars on Sparks Street. The "thump, thump" of those cars haunts me for hours after I leave the city.

The cause is very simple. An examination of the rails will show that the beginning of practically every rail between Bank Street and the canal has been flattened down about half an inch, which means half an inch thump at every joint caused by the wheel dropping from one rail to the next one.

And now, Mr. Editor, I come to the next object of this letter. The next time you come within sight of the city hall, kindly take a glance at the flag staff and see what a beautiful specimen of the Union Jack floats therefrom, "the flag that braved a thousands years," etc.

Although I had my doubts once about that legend, now I fully believe it.

In my humble estimation it is simply disgraceful to have a ragged flag like that one flying from the city hall of the fair capital of this great Dominion.

Thanking you for the space in your valued paper, I am,

A Canadian

HOODLUMISM

NOVEMBER 7, 1908

I would like to draw attention to an element of hoodlumism that to my mind is most detrimental to the fair name of this city, most disgusting to any respectful and law-abiding citizen, and most likely to prove ruinous to the rising youth of this city.

I refer to what is called the "Collegiate bunch" stopping and holding up the streetcars by interfering with the conductor in the discharge of his duties. This sort of hoodlumism has been a thing of repeated occurrence in the past, we believe, but last evening was the first time that we have been pained to behold with our own eyes.

At the close of the entertainment given by the choir from Sheffield, England, this "bunch" met the streetcars at the corner of Elgin and Laurier and there they "played" with the cars, holding up each in turn, delaying the service much to the annoyance of the public.

At the same time several hundred delegates from all over Canada were just emanating from a convocation at the Baptist church and surely they will be able to carry to their respective homes and churches a most glowing account of the law-abiding citizens of the capital of Canada.

Every one of the culprits who took part in the shameful "disport" last evening has merited the penalty of the police cell and should be run in. A twenty-four hour rest there would be a healthy tonic for this city and the sooner this "bunch" finds out it cannot do as it likes, the better for all concerned.

A Citizen

Women were already playing the rough game of hockey. Now they wanted to mix it up in the polling booth, too.

THE SUFFRAGETTE MOVEMENT

NOVEMBER 7, 1908

I attended the meeting to form a branch of the Canadian Woman's Suffrage Association and I was particularly impressed by the ability with which the meeting was conducted and by the harmony and good feeling which prevailed.

I was also greatly pleased with the little speech made by [Ottawa barrister] Mr. A. E. Fripp, at the solicitation of the ladies. He came out squarely in favour of the suffrage for women and was manly and direct in the expression of his opinion and in the advice he gave them as to how they should proceed to attain their object.

However, it has always seemed to me to be the very violence of egotism, the very quintessence of absurdity, for men to assume to say whether women have the right to vote.

When did women ever give men the right to say they should or should not vote, and if women did give them this right, where in the name of common sense did they get it? And where, indeed, did the men themselves get the right to vote?

A gentleman solemnly balancing the question as to whether he shall accord his mother and his wife and his sister and his daughters the right to exercise an opinion which counts in public affair, a right enjoyed by every man not actually in the asylum or penitentiary, strikes me as a figure for high comedy.

Why should society voluntarily deprive itself of the intelligence of its most refined and aspiring members? For that is what women are. If the democratic principle be love, if it be conceded that the thought of all the people upon a given matter is on the whole and in the long run more likely to be right than the thought of a few, however highly cultivated, what a pity then to barbarously shut out the thought of one-half the human race!

It is to deny ourselves one-half the light which might come to us. No wonder we go about in semi-darkness. As the chairwoman of the meeting so truly said on Saturday, men will never fully be free until women are also free. As Tennyson puts it in his fine lines in *The Princess*:

The woman's cause is man's; they rise or sink
Together, dwarfed or God-like, bound or free.

J.H.B.

Editor's note: Although the wives, mothers and sisters of enlisted men were allowed to vote in the 1917 federal election, it was not until the 1921 election that all women were able to vote.

1909

Local: Ottawa now has 297 outside toilets in Centretown, about 1,000 in all of the city (July); Trucks are used for the first time to pick up milk and cream from the Ottawa Dairy Co., the city's largest (October)

National: Rather than accede to a British request to contribute to an expansion of the Royal Navy, Prime Minister Wilfrid Laurier creates a Canadian Navy (May); The first Grey Cup game is won by the University of Toronto (October)

World: A Denver chemist claims he's found a cure for cancer — limburger cheese (October); The U.S. selects Pearl Harbour in the Hawaiian Islands as its principal naval base in the Pacific (November)

Births: Canadian painter Jack Bush; writer Malcolm Lowry; British philosopher Sir Isaiah Berlin; jazz musician Lester Young

Deaths: Canadian astronomer Simon Newcomb; Apache leader Geronimo; Napthall Herz, poet, author of Zionist national hymn

PROPOSED NEW MARKET

JANUARY 4, 1909

The plan for improving the farmer's market as laid before a meeting of ratepayers in the Byward Market hall last evening has a great deal of merit and is well worthy of careful consideration. The paving of the market square is a necessity in the interest of cleanliness and convenience and in any event will always be required as a permanent street improvement.

On the other hand, when the Dominion government tears down, as proposed, the old buildings on the west side of Sussex Street and replaces them with a magnificent departmental block, a farmer's market as it at present exists on York Street will be as much out of place as it would be in front of Parliament square.

It is just possible, however, that in the near future farm produce will be sold at the farms to merchants or dealers, who will have it brought from waystations to their warehouses by a system of electric railways — much more conveniently and economically than it can be brought to the market by the farmers themselves and sold direct to the consumer.

With such a possibility in view, it is wisdom on the part of the ratepayers to consider the question carefully before committing the city to an expenditure that is estimated at from two hundred thousand to a quarter of a million dollars without, if possible, interesting the Dominion government in the project.

Yours for Progress

Editor's note: A scaled-back version of the plan for Byward Market improvements went ahead, and included paving of the main square on York Street at the north end of the main market building. No federal money was involved.

BEAUTIFY THIS CITY

MARCH 9, 1909

While reading in a recent issue the intimation that the Street Car company contemplated laying new rails on Sparks Street this summer, the thought occurred to me that it would greatly add to the beauty of the Capital if Sparks Street was without car rails, the rails being laid permanently on Wellington Street, which is a much wider avenue and with much less traffic.

I think that you will agree that with 3,000 auto cars passing through busy Sparks Street per day, there is a great risk to life or limb of the pedestrians who wish to cross the street to enter into or exit from streetcars. There is no doubt but that as the city grows it will be 4,000 auto cars per day.

The distance from Wellington to Sparks is very short, and the blocks are frequent. I am of the opinion that Wellington Street is an ideal route for streetcars. Horse carriages could draw up to the store doors along Sparks with less fear of accident, and ladies could cross the street in safety.

No doubt there must be some objection to the route, otherwise it would surely have been chosen long ago, but perhaps those objections could be waived in the interests of the many notable people and representatives of the whole country who remain in the Capital for several months every year, and who are no farther off from accidents than the permanent residents. Such a change, if it could be made, would be in the interests of humanity. I am,

Yours truly, Reader

Editor's note: Central Ottawa's main east-west rails remained along Sparks Street until streetcars were taken out of service in 1959.

PROFANE LANGUAGE
JUNE 11, 1909

Of late we see many accounts calling attention to how profane and bad language is increasing among boys. The truth of this cannot be denied by any one who happens to come in contact with the groups of boys who congregate in public places and on the streets.

This is really a sad state of affairs, because if such a low habit is to be allowed to continue and become a fixed one among the coming youths, it cannot do otherwise than eventually lead us to become a very irreverent and disrespectful race. The class of youths who seem to become most addicted to this habit are those ranging in ages from 12 to 20, who seem to believe bad language makes them appear more manly.

What is the most shocking of all is the way in which they can be heard calling on the name of "Jesus" or "Jesus Christ," or calling upon God to "damn" everything. Blasphemous language has become very common of late, not only among the lower classes, but also among those in the higher walks of life, which seems almost incredible, seeing that such a low habit as profanity answers no good purpose and can only be an indication that the people who use it are naturally inclined to fall into low and degrading habits.

It has been stated that the schools might assist greatly in checking this hostile habit, but I do not believe that they can accomplish very much without its use being discontinued by the older people and by their parents in their homes.

Yours truly,
George Wright

CIVIL SERVICE HOURS
JUNE 15, 1909

Until recently, the daily working hours of the Civil Service as defined by order in council were from 9:30 a.m. till 4 p.m., although in some of the working departments the staffs did not stop work until 4:30 and 5 p.m. Unfortunately, a few of the departments were allowed to ignore the order in council, and to make the hours from 10 to 4, thereby giving rise to the prevalent impression that the Civil Service as a whole enjoyed kindergarten hours.

This impression was of course most unjust to the service as a whole, but its existence was unavoidable when such ridiculously short hours were allowed to persist. To remedy this abuse, and to meet public opinion, ill informed though it was, the government recently adopted an order in council making the hours of duty from 9 a.m. till 5 p.m., exempting only from its operation the staffs of the Senate, House of Commons and the Library of Parliament.

In these circumstances it seems incredible, but it is nevertheless true, that some of the ministers have up to the present ignored their own order in council and are jogging along as before. Surely it is up to the prime minister to see that all his colleagues respect an order in council that has been passed in solemn form, whether it has their individual approval or not. If it is to be a dead letter in some departments, there will be undoubtedly grave dissatisfaction in the other departments and a rankling sense of injustice as well.

Let us have uniform hours throughout the service, and let all employees be treated alike and the country will receive better value for its money than it has hitherto done.

Fair Play

THE DRIVEWAY
ON MAJOR HILL PARK
JULY 27, 1909

Here, Sir, are a few of the reasons why Major Hill Park should be kept solely for the people and not open to automobiling and driving:

Do you think mothers will keep coming with their children to Major Hill Park when they are much more exposed to be run down by the indifferent aristocratic swell set than in the city streets where children will have to go to be safe?

Where will the thousands of employees lunching in town go for their short rest and quiet smoke after their noon meal if you drive them out of this adopted spot? Moreover, Major Hill is already too small for the throngs that go there in the evening; what will it be when you have taken away a fifty-foot strip from it, and danger is lurking at every turn?

But the main objection is that this driveway affair is becoming shamefully exaggerated. The great majority of the people does not own and never will own either horses or automobiles. Its wants in the matters of parks and fresh air must necessarily be looked after as well as those of the richer class. The latter already rules supreme on Parliament Hill and the prettiest spots around town, and now the object seems to be to chase the people from Major Hill Park to make room for the few.

But, Sir, Major Hill Park is a place where the people's fancy is deeply rooted, and hence it should not be dislodged before long thought is given as to where it shall go after. And, mind you, Sir, the driveway will follow the edge of the hill, so that the people will have to take back seats and be deprived of the best view of the river, making way for the select few.

This driveway business symbolizes the crushing of the toiler under the pomposity of the plutocracy. It represents an idea which is repugnant to our democratic institutions. It is the synthesis of puffism which should not be encouraged in our midst.

Those who drive can cover ground and are well able to get away from centretown. Let vehicles drive out, and leave the poor two-legged animal roam in peace within reach of his strength and his working place.

A Workingman

Editor's note: The driveway, called Lady Grey Drive, was eventually built between 1910 and 1912, extending from Mackenzie Avenue along the east side of the park and eastern edge of Nepean Point to the Ottawa River and then skirting the cliffs along the river behind the present day War Museum. Parts of the original road still exist, in crumbling condition, behind the museum and further eastward along the river. The park's correct name, then, as now, was Major's Hill Park, a tribute to Major Daniel Boulton, who succeeded Col. John By as chief engineer of the Rideau Canal in 1832. Then, as now, the park was often, and mistakenly, referred to as either Major Hill Park or Major Hill's Park.

THE DAYLIGHT ROBBERY CASE

AUGUST 4, 1909

Public opinion in this city seems to be aroused over the farce which was enacted last week in the police court when a pair of audacious daylight robbers, with probably long criminal records behind them, and who had stolen goods from at least one other store in the city, were sentenced to one year in the central prison, instead of to at least seven years in the Kingston penitentiary.

The action of the deputy magistrate in having a medical examination made of the prisoners prior to sentencing them shows that he was looking round to see if he could find an excuse for imposing a light sentence. It was no business of his in the circumstances what the state of their health was. That would have been looked after subsequently by the proper authorities.

But it was his business to inflict a punishment commensurate with the boldness of the crime, and such as would have been sure to act as a determent to others. This he has most signally failed to do, and the people of Ottawa may soon expect to hear of an equally daring and perhaps more successful attempt being made upon some other of our establishments, by reason of the encouragement magisterially given.

Is there no remedy for this deplorable state of affairs?

Fair Flat

DISTURBING THE SABBATH

OCTOBER 5, 1909

May I ask your indulgence in regard to the disturbing and unnecessary amount of bell-ringing in Sandy Hill district, in the early part of the day?

Any individual who desires, or finds it necessary, to rise before 6:30 a.m., can procure an alarm clock for 50 cents. Then why, in the name of common sense, should the entire community be tormented by the clanging of bells in the early hours?

Then, on Sunday morning especially, when all, and more particularly those closely confined to duty during the week, wish to enjoy an hour longer of sleep and rest and nothing in God's beautiful world is of more importance than a necessary amount of sleep and rest in this strenuous age, it is found impossible on account of the steady disturbing clanging of bells from 5 to 10 a.m.

The quiet of the Sabbath has become part of our nature, so in the name of comfort and happiness let those in authority aid in preserving the quiet Sabbath by stopping this altogether unnecessary clanging of bells.

A Sufferer

OFFENSIVE POSTCARDS

NOVEMBER 6, 1909

Regarding the indecent postcards and photographs which have been boldly circulated throughout Canada and the United States in the past few years, we notice of late there have been many engaged in the business who have been arrested and severely punished, but apparently this does not stop the circulation of them.

The reason for this might be placed to the large profit that is made from their sales. The vendors are willing to take great chances in selling them because these profits enable them to pay the fine, and they continue to do business which can show a great defeat in the law.

The vendors do not seem to know where to draw the line at decency in regard to the sale of the cards, as you still can see them displayed openly in stores in most all cities and towns on most suggestive and vulgar lines; these they claim to be amusing, but instead they are simply depicting rudeness among girls and men.

The only way to drive out immoral cards and other things on these lines is to have stringent laws made that will punish people who are found carrying them, as well as those who have them for sale.

A Canadian

"There is a lilt, a painfulness in the high notes, a poignancy in the very impossibility of singing it that makes *O Canada* a real battle hymn. If no one in Canada knew our Anthem before the War, the Overseas men all know it now."

— January 3, 1917

1910-1919

1910

Local: Commission condemns landlords for slum conditions (January); Thousands of lumberyard employees laid off due to strike by Grand Trunk Railway workers (July)
National: 1,000 farmers travel to Ottawa to demand an end to price-fixing by eastern industrialists (October); Alberta introduces workmen's compensation, leaving Prince Edward Island as the only province without such a program (November)
World: In Paris, a cold rain falls for more than a week, flooding streets and homes and causing $200-million damage (January); About 50,000 British dockworkers lose their jobs when their strike backfires (September)
Births: Canadian civil servant Robert Bryce; William Shockley, U.S. inventor of the transistor, French oceanographer Jacques Cousteau
Deaths: American writers Mark Twain and O. Henry; Russian writer Leo Tolstoy; King Edward VII of Britain; Jean Henri Dunant, founder of the Red Cross

ILLUMINATING EXPERIENCE

MARCH 16, 1910

Having noticed with much pleasure the splendid stand the *Citizen* has taken in regard to patent medicine advertisements, I beg to add a few words of commendation and hearty approval to this worthy home paper, for the magnanimous step it has taken in its refusal at a necessarily great financial loss, to insert in its columns these very elusive ads, which are at once repulsive to the eye, obnoxious and nauseating to the senses.

Permit me to give a little personal experience in one of those same fake ads. A few years ago, while suffering from ill health, I read one of these fascinating positive-cure ads and decided to give it a trial; purchased a bottle of same, adhering strictly to directions. Many bottles followed the first until I was forced to realize this grand elixir of life had failed in its mission and that I was, if possible, worse than before.

At this stage I wrote to the physician of this firm, receiving the very encouraging reply to persevere, as failure to cure was an impossibility. Being of an optimistic nature, I decided to give it one more chance, consequently threw away another hard earned dollar.

When this bottle was about half consumed, I chanced to see in a certain newspaper the testimonial and photograph of a well-known and supposedly reputable citizen who had been snatched from the very jaws of some dreadful disease by the same wonderful remedy. Knowing the original of the photograph, at my first opportunity I took the liberty of enquiring the nature of the cure and his opinion of the patent medicine.

ELECTRIC BEANS

Stand supreme as a blood and nerve tonic

They are unequalled for Biliousness, Sick Headache, Constipation, Heart Palpitation, Indigestion and Anaemia. Those who are in a position to know what is best use "Electric Beans."

Write for Free Sample
50c. a Box at all Dealers or upon receipt of price from
THE ELECTRIC BEAN CHEMICAL CO. Ltd.
OTTAWA

OTTAWA CITIZEN
A writer doubted claims made for patent medicines.

To my surprise and indignation he smilingly asserted that he had never taken a dose of the stuff in his life; that so far as he was concerned his photo and testimonial were simply a business transaction. There was what I had always believed to be a sworn testimonial for perfect health restored through the medium of this patent medicine, when in reality health in this case had never been impaired.

The spirit of combativeness which the *Citizen* is putting forth to stamp out this manner of evil should receive the highest endorsation of the general public; not only for its efforts to protect the unsuspecting but in eliminating from its pages undesirable reading matter.

A Sympathizer

TASTE IN GOVT. BUILDINGS

APRIL 27, 1910

The *Citizen* with commendable enterprise, published, a few days ago, a cut representing the exterior plan of the public building to be erected on the Mackenzie Avenue side of Major Hill Park. The government has shown good sense in determining to gather in the officials now occupying offices in abandoned religious halls and wholesale stores and housing them in a government-owned building.

I have nothing to say against the ability of the architect who designed the intended structure of long unbroken walls and window openings, carrying uniformity to excess, but there is room for criticism of his taste.

Someone has said that consideration should be given to stability, utility and beauty in designing public buildings. The proposed edifice may have the two first elements, but the future beholder will be as silent as the statues on Parliament Hill about its beauty. The abodes of the cliff-dwellers had stability and openings for use but nature provided them with projections and recesses that gave them picturesqueness wanting in the plan of the modern fabric in question.

If designs were indeed for models, there are jails in the country with all the required stability but with far more grandeur. If utility was the ambition of the designer of the new building, then there are factories and paper mills symmetrical in contrast with the general form of the design approved. The beautiful Parliament Buildings will blush when this new structure raises its roofless outline and claims to be included among the attractions of the capital.

Why the choice of battlements as a finish to the walls and a flat roof? Are they for the convenience of the government employees who may desire, in their leisure moments, to exercise themselves by shooting arrows over the tall hotel (the Russell, where the War Memorial now stands) on the other side of the park, or are they to remind us of the rude constructions of the barons, minus the taste they displayed in selecting suitable sites on towering rocks?

I am one of those greatly pleased with the intention of the government to add another capacious block to those already standing, and of which we are proud. I believe the government architect is capable of designing a handsome edifice, but has had the misfortune to hit upon a design, in his desire for variety, devoid of beauty.

Let him take his plan and look on the Parliament Buildings, and the Langevin Block, and if he cannot see the contrast then his taste for the aesthetic has departed.

A builder

Editor's note: The Connaught Building, constructed initially as the headquarters for the Department of Revenue, still houses the customs and excise division of Revenue Canada. The Château Laurier Hotel, which stands between the building and Parliament Hill, was constructed about the same time. Both opened in 1912.

MOVING PICTURE SHOWS
JUNE 28, 1910

In your recent editorial on "moving picture shows" you say that, "It isn't much of an argument against moving picture shows that a few cases have been reported wherein young boys have committed thefts to secure money to attend these places."

Such cases are not however confined to a few isolated instances but are on the contrary of frequent occurrence, and if they do not constitute an argument against moving picture shows they certainly do against permitting children to attend them indiscriminately.

The class of picture shows should, as you say, be supervised. There should be provision for the inspection of every film before it is exhibited. But such a provision would leave still unimpaired the worst part of the evil to the children of these exhibitions — the demoralizing effect on the nerves and character of the children brought about by the excitement of constantly attending them.

In this respect they are comparable to the cigarette habit; and, as in the case of the latter, the boy or girl who is addicted to constantly attending these performances is usually to be found, sooner or later, in the ranks of the delinquents. There are few more potent causes of truancy than the attraction of the cheap theatres, and little girls in particular, meet at these places the worst possible companions and the resultant evils cannot be exaggerated.

Many quotations may be given, but I shall confine myself to a report of the Child Labour Committee of the Ontario legislature appointed in 1907: "In cities like Toronto hundreds of boys from nine to sixteen are frequent attendants of cheap shows. The late hours, nervous excitement and moral deterioration resulting from the practice are injurious to character. This, with the reading of dime novels, smoking cigarettes, etc., frequently prevents boys from settling down to a trade or to regular employment, and lead to idleness, theft and vicious habits. Half the men in our prisons had, prior to conviction, never learned a trade. We, therefore, recommend that the attendance of children of either sex under fourteen years of age at theatrical and kindred performances when given by professionals should be prohibited, unless they are accompanied by parents or guardians."

Unfortunately this recommendation has not so far been carried out; yet in its adoption lies the solution of the difficulty.

W. L. Scott,
President, Children's Aid Society of Ottawa

NUMBERING STREETS
OCTOBER 4, 1910

Only a few days ago a large delegation of Glebe residents appeared before the board of control to state their reasons why the name Muchmore Street should be changed to Fifth Avenue.

Without going into the various claims for and against the proposed change, would it not be well to look still farther ahead and by copying the layout of some of the most up-to-date American cities commence right uptown at Queen Street, calling it First Street, and continue along Bank Street numbering the cross streets in consecutive order.

Muchmore Street would then be about 27th Street, while Cameron Avenue, which is situated just north of Billings Bridge, would be about 41st Street, and continuing out in the direction of Ridgemont the cross streets would run into the sixties.

Can anyone put forth a reason why such a change would not be directly in the interests of the general public, as well as a progressive move in the shaping of our Greater Ottawa scheme? With all cross streets numbered consecutively from the centre of the city along all the main arteries leading to the country, just fancy the convenience in directing to and reaching a desired destination.

J. Moffat Ross

AUTOMOBILE RACING
OCTOBER 5, 1910

The annual automobile contest for the Vanderbilt Cup

has taken place in the United States and there is the usual record of casualties, this time four persons killed and many more seriously injured.

If these fatalities were confined to the foolhardy daredevils who operate or own the machines the loss would not be serious, but when innocent outsiders and spectators are the victims, as is too often the case, it is high time for legislation to be enacted for the utter and absolute prohibition of automobile racing under any circumstances.

It is also a matter of consideration whether the manufacture and sale to the public of automobiles of high speed capacity should be prohibited. The annual toll of death levied by these machines is such as to call for the most drastic and serious action on the part of our legislators. The only persons to whom such legislation would be a grievance are notoriety hunters and gilded youths with more money and leisure than common sense.

One single life (if it happened to be yours or mine, Mr. Editor) is worth more than all the automobiles in America.

Yours Truly, Bystander

RELIGION ABOVE RELIGIONS
OCTOBER 12, 1910

Please allow me a few observations on your article of the 8th under the above title. It may be resumed in two points:

(1.) That above the different religions, creeds and opinions which divide mankind, there is a religion of unity in which all should meet on equal terms, i.e., that which has for its end "the good and the gladness of us all," and which imposes as duty a common solicitude for the economic and political welfare of the country.

(2.) That if different religions are still thought necessary their value should be proved, not by sterile discussion, but by the estimate of their contribution to the common welfare; and that each religion will be considered true in the measure that it works to that end.

Please allow me now to examine these two principles in the light of philosophy and common sense:

(1.) The precise meaning of the thesis is not too clear. Does the writer wish to convey that the social, civil, political and economic domain is distinct from the religious — that in this free country different creeds may live side by side under one Union Jack — that Catholics and Protestants, keeping their own beliefs, may and ought to be good citizens and give their common support to such campaigns against alcoholism and obscenity?

If so, all well and good. But if it means that religious preoccupations are a mere useless "survival of the past happily outgrown," and that the only real interests of life are economic and social, we would first have to admit that human destiny terminates here below, and that soul survival for eternal life is a childish dream. We would have to condemn all religions — and our decision would be in itself a principle of discord and therefore "essentially irreligious."

We are told that the only true and useful work is that which contributes to human happiness. But what is human happiness if not the complete and balanced fullness of all vital energies? And, if the religious sentiment enters into these energies, man cannot be completely happy in a system from which it is excluded.

Taking the economic and social ground alone it is difficult to find a condition that will realize the well-being of us all, for there as elsewhere will be divergency of views and conflicts of interest.

The common weal cannot be achieved without the sacrifice of personal views and individual interests. What can impose such sacrifices on the individual or collective conscience and will buy the authority of a superior force, the Supreme Being?

(2.) The principle of your second division is avowedly a popular presentation of Pragmatism — "If it works it is true" and therefore morally commendable.

Now, alcoholism works, divorce works, dirty literature, lying and anarchy also work. Are they therefore true and morally good? Is a successful crime or revolution therefore justifiable? Is an unsuccessful crime bad on that account, and would it be good if successful? Typhoid and diphtheria work with a vengeance. Are they a sign of health in the human frame?

We must not forget that there is such a thing as moral health. No, sir: all that works is not true, all that succeeds is not good, all that glitters is not gold. Truth is above work, and right above might — but if the right is to be more than an empty word it must be able to impose itself on the human conscience, individual or collective, on majorities as on minorities.

If it is something real it must come from a super human source and authority superior to the individual or collective conscience — and this real and superior source is the Supreme Being.

There is no way out of the dilemma: either human energy is the first source of right, and we must submit ourselves to the domination of strength and numbers — or the right is superior to man, and thus comes from God. If we find men without a religion who recognize the right and submit thereto it is because they do not follow the logic of their principles.

"Nature is one, human life is one, religion is one." In principle and in right, yes. Why then is the true religion not absolutely universal? Simply because it imposes intellectual and moral renunciation, work, research, sacrifice, and because many are kept from its healthful yoke by egoism and sensuality. Moral and religious truth can only triumph by an intellectual and moral apostolate.

F. Blanchin,
O.M.I.D.D.

Editor's note: Between 1908 and 1914, Rev. Father Blanchin, a Roman Catholic theologian at St. Joseph's University (part of the University of Ottawa), wrote often to the Citizen, not only on matters of morality and theology but as a champion of francophone rights. O.M.I.D.D. stands for Order of Mary Immaculate, Doctor of Divinity.

WANTS WHOLE CANAL CLOSED

NOVEMBER 4, 1910

I see in your issue of October 27 that you are in favour of closing the part of the Rideau Canal that passes through the city.

There was a time when the said canal was of some use. But that day is past. The residents who live along or near the Rideau from Ottawa to Kingston know that the canal is a useless expensive disease breeder of no use to anyone except a few duck hunters.

The farmers from Ottawa to Kingston would be very pleased to do away with it knowing that it is of no use to them and only a nuisance. Anyone passing up and down the said canal may see the thousands of acres of drowned land along its banks.

No, do not close part of the Rideau Canal but close it all.

An Old Resident

1911

Local: Typhoid epidemic sweeps Ottawa area, killing 56 (January-April); Many horses are frightened by the noise of the city's new six-cycle, 80-horsepower fire engine (June); Work begins on city's first garbage incinerator

National: *Busy Man's Magazine* renamed *Maclean's* (March). The Conservatives under Robert Borden end Wilfrid Laurier's 15-year hold on power, defeating the Liberals on the issue of reciprocity with the U.S. (September)

World: An estimated 60,000 supporters of women's suffrage march in a five-mile procession through London (June); It must be the work of a madman, say French police, after the *Mona Lisa* is stolen from the Louvre. It is recovered, undamaged, two years later (August)

Births: Canadian media theorist Marshal McLuhan; U.S. president Ronald Reagan; British author William Golding

Deaths: British Dr. Joseph Bell, the model used by Arthur Conan Doyle for Sherlock Holmes

SMOKING AT THE ARENA

JANUARY 9, 1911

Kindly allow me sufficient space in your valuable pages to register a kick against smoking at the arena. Saturday evening at the ice hockey contest capped the climax. There was not the slightest visible move made to suppress smoking — why, even some of the ushers were smoking!

The writer, who is a smoker himself, had his daughter with him. There was a young man sitting below us, right opposite, smoking, the smoke rising right up in our faces, almost blinding us. The writer leaned forward and asked the party using the weed if he would be kind enough to discontinue smoking. He said certainly, but instead he kept right on. I then went and spoke to an usher re the matter. He asked the fellow to stop it. He still did not.

I thought that some officer made the statement through your columns last week that the ban would be put on smoking in the future, and that the law would be rightly enforced.

Citizen

Editor's note: Although he occasionally vowed action against smoking to placate public complaints, Edwin Peter Dey, owner of Dey's Arena, built in 1907 at Laurier and the Rideau Canal on the site of present-day Confederation Park, rarely did anything beyond make promises. In fact, he was known to hand out cigars to reporters covering Ottawa Senators games as a way of cultivating their favour. There were no municipal laws against smoking at the time.

DIVORCE BY ACT OF PARLIAMENT

JANUARY 23, 1911

Scarcely a session of the Canadian parliament draws to a close without some member calling attention to the necessity of establishing a Dominion court of petitions for divorce instead of continuing the system of granting relief by act of parliament. That some change will have to be made in the near future will be readily admitted by anyone who takes the trouble to analyse the record of divorces granted since Confederation.

The total number up to the end of last session of parliament was 160. Of this number Ontario is credited with 105, Quebec 30, British Columbia 2, Manitoba 11, Alberta 2, Northwest Territory 7, Saskatchewan 3. Of course the list does not include the divorces granted in the provinces where divorce courts are already established (New Brunswick, Nova Scotia, Prince Edward Island).

The accord shows that applications for divorce are increasing with great rapidity. Dividing the years from 1867 to 1907 inclusive, into periods of ten years, the record is as follows:

1867 to 1877	7 divorces
1877 to 1887	16
1887 to 1897	36
1897 to 1907	57

In the three years since 1907, the number granted was 44. For the present session there will be 32. If the increase continues in progressive ratio, the present system must become wholly inadequate to handle the business.

In private conversation nearly every senator and member of the commons will admit that divorce proceedings would be more conveniently administered by a civil court constituted for the purpose; but the objection raised by Quebec to any change that would facilitate the granting of divorce seems to stand in the way of a necessary reform. Unless a change is made the divorce committee of parliamentarians will have to be increased in number and then divided into sub-committee involving extra-short-hand reporters, typewriters, clerks and messengers to permit of the divorce cases being disposed of during an ordinary session of parliament.

Observer

Editor's note: Until the 1960s, Canada had the lowest divorce rate in the Western world. Respectable opinion — articulated by social and religious leaders, especially from Catholic Quebec — condemned divorce as a threat to the family, and the power of this opinion prevented any profound relaxation of divorce laws until 1968. As a result, for most of Canada's first century, adultery was the only ground for divorce and, before the First World War, only three provinces had divorce courts, although Alberta, Saskatchewan and Ontario created them shortly after. In provinces without access to judicial divorce, the only legal alternative was an appeal to Parliament for a statutory divorce, an expensive process that limited relief to the wealthy.

THE VACANT JUDGESHIP
JANUARY 23, 1911

French Canadians of Ontario find it rather peculiar that whenever a vacancy occurs upon the bench or a public position of any description is to be filled by a government, there seems to be a singular disposition to prevent a French Canadian aspiring to obtain that which in all justice they have an inherent right to.

In Ontario particularly, all well posted will admit that from many a standpoint French Canadians have the British fair play right to be judged by judges who can understand the language which they generally speak.

The *Citizen* recently admitted the right of minorities and this portrayed a well known feeling generously held by the majority in Quebec, where the English population is less than one-sixth of the total population and nevertheless about one third of the judges are English speaking. I do not remember one instance in the sister province when French Canadians were not foremost in proclaiming the right of the English minority.

This view is invariably held by those who are found to favour broadness of view and a laudable spirit of tolerance, and who approach all such questions upon the liberal and generous plane of a conciliatory attitude with a view of promoting the upbuilding of a great and united Canada.

C.S.O. Boudreault

HAT PLUME CRUELTIES
MARCH 4, 1911

In the *Journal* recently there was published a picture of some hats, trimmed heavily with aigrette plumes, with the statement that there was no cruelty in wearing them, as they were dropped in the moulting season, and simply picked up. I know that was sheer nonsense, as it would be impossible to supply the market for them in that way. Naturalists as well as hunters say that when the birds shed the plumes they are so frayed and scattered as not to be worth collecting.

I think I can safely say there is not one woman in ten

REMEMBER YESTERDAY: A CENTURY OF PHOTOGRAPHS

Thousands of birds lost their feathers to the fashion tastes of women.

thousand who would wear these plumes did she know the torture and unspeakable cruelty the taking of the feathers entails, and could such plume tell its own sad story of the little family that all day long suffered, cold and starving, and with every rustle of the leaf and sound of the trees opened their mouths in anticipation of the food their parents would bring them, but never did because they were cold and lifeless in the hands of the hunter.

Aigrette plumes constitute the wedding dress of the several species of white herons or egrets and are only worn during the nesting season. One solitary plume hunter told that with two or three assistants he had killed three hundred egrets in one afternoon, and another boasted that he and his party had killed 130,000 birds during one season. In Florida they are almost exterminated.

Bird life is most interesting and their industry and devotion to their mates and young most touching, in great contrast to some of the human race, who have to have children's aid societies and laws to protect them from each other and cruelly neglect their young.

This being Lent, when probably a little more time can be spared to things of a serious nature, it would be a good thing to take into consideration the cruelty of the destruction of birds for millinery, and when Easter comes, perhaps, there will not be seen in the churches at least, on hats, and bonnets, aigrette plumes called "the white badge of cruelty," nor the distorted skin so suggestive of the death of some poor humming bird or warbler, probably torn from its bleeding and quivering body alive that it may retain more brilliancy.

It is very depressing to have to write and think about these things but being a member of the Audubon Society I felt called upon to do so.

Bessie Kirby Veith

NEGRO IMMIGRATION

APRIL 6, 1911

I notice that Hon. Mr. Oliver, in replying in the House of Commons to a question by Mr. Thoburn concerning an influx of negroes into the Northwestern provinces, took the ground that such an emergency had been unforeseen, and is reported as saying: "There is no provision to prevent negroes coming into Canada, and until parliament makes such provision it will not be possible for the government to take action."

This is not true. Provisions were made in the present Immigration Act to meet just such a contingency as this alleged organized negro influx into the Northwest. As to the giving away of free homesteads in the Northwest, which is said to be causing the present negro influx, the principles of the Immigration Act might very properly be applied to the Dominion Land Act to prevent any danger of having the free lands of Canada swamped by low-grade immigrants.

But any such danger is to be feared rather from Europe than from the United States. Any American negro who can survive in the Northwest will have to work; and any American negro who will work is a better industrial and military asset to Canada than the original slum-breeding Latin now coming unrestrictedly into Canada from Southern Europe.

T.R.E. McInnes

THE NEGRO QUESTION

APRIL 8, 1911

I am in agreement with the views of the *Citizen* on most matters, but your opinion as regards this question is one on which I do not agree with you.

When you state that it is entirely a case of prejudice and sentiment on account of the negro's colour, and that it is due to ignorance, you attribute to the Southern States characteristics which will be certainly denied by those who know them. The sjambok (leather whip) of the Boer, and the more strenuous weapons of the Southerner have only been called into requisition when all other methods proved fruitless, and were the outcome of many years of vain attempt to moralize and educate the native to European ideals, and to get him to do an honest day's work.

In your (editorial) you state: "That the white people in negro communities are almost entirely responsible for much of the bitterness and trouble which arise all over the country is now beginning to be appreciated." Certainly, if you want to know a man you've got to live with him, and this is the only satisfactory way of getting first hand information; consequently, if those practical people in

"negro communities" resent his presence so strongly, you can bet there is something wrong with him.

You say further that "British methods in the treatment of the negro have never been those of the United States" and that the negro has been treated fair in all the British possessions. The negroes who work in the mines of Kimberley and Johannesburg are compelled to live in compounds outside of the cities, and judicious measures are taken, where there is a white population, to keep them as much apart as possible. This is something the same as the system in Canada in relation to the Indians, who are placed on reserves, and have their own villages and live as much as possible according to their own ideas.

The negro is not possessed of the same feelings or sentiments of the civilized white, and all colonials' who have to come into contact with him daily will tell you this, and experience should be the best teacher on this question.

P.J.B.

COLONIAL PECULIARITIES

APRIL 26, 1911

Are Canadians a loose-living people? Is the matrimonial state an exception? Is it singular for parents to both bear the same surname?

I am moved to these enquiries by the insistent way in which, when the doings of the younger set in what is evidently your "high society" are chronicled, the full names of both parents are given. Thus, in the case of a wedding, for instance, we are informed by the society reporters that on such and such a date such and such a church was crowded by a most fashionable gathering to witness the nuptials of Miss Ethelinda, daughter of Mr. J. de Tomkyns Smythe, etc., the natural inference from which is that there would not have been anything unusual had Miss Ethelinda been the daughter of Mr. Tomkyns Smythe and Mrs. Johnson de Buggins or some other lady whose name was not that of the paternal parent.

It is a curious thing, too, that you don't seem to have any "homes." I don't mean orphans' homes or old men's homes, or that sort of thing, but family homes, where father, mother and children live together, like we have in the Old Country, don't ya know. Your children, judging from the announcement in the columns under the head of "Society": when they go away to school in other places, lose their homes altogether as, when they come back for holidays at Christmas or Easter some such announcement as this appears: Miss Belinda de Snooks, who is attending school in Toronto, is spending a few days in town, "the guest" of her parents, Mr. H. de Snooks and Mrs. de Snooks (note the care taken here also to make it clear that the maternal parent's name is the same as that of the father).

Really, some of your colonial customs are awfully funny. What!

Englishman

LET US HAVE PEACE

MAY 5, 1911

The letter from "Englishman" may seem witty to him and

a certain class of Englishmen, but to well bred Canadians and intelligent people in general, it is inexpressibly vulgar.

Englishmen and other emigrants are not compelled to love and admire Canada and its customs, but surely the country which provides them with comfortable homes is entitled to respect at least. I have no objection whatever to the sensible Englishman who makes it a point to mind his own affairs, be he rich or poor, but I do thoroughly detest that specimen who comes over here and straightaway assumes that superior air, "don't you know." He invariably makes himself obnoxious wherever he goes.

It has been my good fortune to meet English emigrants with whom it was a pleasure to associate, but there are others, and lots of them, who must surely come from the backwoods of England. Such people are found everywhere, of course, but they seem to be especially common among the emigrants.

My ancestors, descendants of a good old French family, came to this country so many years ago, that I consider myself a thoroughbred Canadian. Of one thing I am certain, however, if by any chance it became necessary for me to go to England for a livelihood, I would take conditions as I found them and not look down upon the country and its customs.

Canadian, and proud of it

REGULATION OF TRAFFIC
MAY 22, 1911

Can anyone conceive a worse muddle of things than now exists regarding the regulation of traffic upon the streets of Ottawa?

Apart from the two prominent street intersections, viz, Sparks and Bank and Sparks and Elgin, no attempt is made at regulation. Even at these points drivers do not know what it's all about, and think the policemen are crazy. Elsewhere in the city drivers turn corners any and every way, take any side of the street they happen to come to first, and generally go as they please.

Ottawa should get out of its jay and callow days of the Bytown period, and realize that it's a city, and that others than Bytowners are looking on and saying things.

Civis

1912

Local: Ottawa has roughly 400 automotive vehicles, according to the local motor car club (January); Château Laurier opens (June); A train bound for Gatineau is held up by an infestation of tent caterpillars (June)
National: Coca-Cola and 200 other products from around the world are being made in Canada 60,000 Canadians are involved in railway construction, making it the country's second largest employer behind agriculture
World: A demonstration of bravado turns sour when amateur parachute inventor Franz Reichalt plunges like a rock to his death from the Eiffel Tower (February); Nearly 1,600 are drowned when a iceberg sinks the "unsinkable" *Titanic* (April)
Births: Canadian writer and literary analyst Northrop Frye; U.S. economist Milton Friedman
Deaths: Charles Hays, president of the Grand Trunk Railroad; Dracula author Bram Stoker; U.S. aviation pioneer Wilbur Wright; British surgeon Joseph Lister, first man to use antiseptics for infection

SALARIES OF TEACHERS
FEBRUARY 7, 1912

I noticed in Friday's *Citizen* in quite large letters the words, "Salary Increase for Teachers;" I was delighted, but upon reading what came below this glowing headline, my surprise was great to find it should have read, "Large Salary Increase For the Inspector, For His Assistants in the Office and For All Male Teachers in the City."

The article does say something about first-class lady teachers reaching the maximum of $1,000, but it is understood that has been their maximum for the past two years. But what about the second-class lady teacher who bears the brunt of the day and fray? I find that her increase is — nothing.

Let us compare the salaries of the different classes of teachers: Before these last large increases men received an average salary of $1,736 yearly, while the ladies received $636. In the last ten years the salary of principals has increased sixty per cent; kindergarten teachers, fifty-nine per cent; male assistants, fifty-four per cent; and lady assistants only thirty-five per cent.

In my opinion, "The large salary increase for teachers" means simply this: $500 more for the inspector, making his maximum $3,600; maximum for principals, $2,200; first-class male assistants, maximum, $1,600; first-class lady assistants, maximum, $1,000; second-class male assistants, maximum, $1,400; second-class lady assistants, maximum, $900.

Of course, everyone is aware that it is the world's time-honoured custom to pay men greater salaries than it does ladies: but is there not too great a difference in Ottawa, where the lady teachers render as good, as efficient and as faithful service as the men?

Interested

ANTI-VACCINATION
FEBRUARY 22, 1912

In reading the proposed Vaccination Act of Ontario, one is led to ask if we are really living in a British possession, and, if so, where does the British fair play wherein each individual is guaranteed freedom of conscience come in?

If the people against their will and without their consent, also without the consent of their direct representatives, are compelled to submit to having their blood poisoned with vaccine, suffer the consequences and pay the cost, where is British freedom?

If vaccination with all the years of trial had been proven to have been beneficial, surely there would be more people singing its praises, one never hears of anyone submitting to it because they personally know it to be a preventative, but rather because they fear not to.

Let us have freedom of conscience, clean homes, clean streets and clean back yards — and then smallpox, as well as other diseases, will soon disappear.

One of the Sufferers

OTTAWA CITIZEN FILES

The quality of education was a topic of debate in 1912, as it is now.

PUBLIC SCHOOLS

MARCH 16, 1912

We began some years ago to tell each other that our Ontario public schools were the finest in the world. Even if we did not believe it at the time we kept right on saying it until we did believe it.

And though they were perfect twenty-five years ago they have improved under new governments and ministers of education until today they are far beyond perfection. In fact they are so good that, to a plain man, they come perilously near to being good for nothing.

I am asking you, Mr. Editor, to have one of your bright young men visit some of the schools in the city and check up the number of hours the scholars are really working at such studies as young Canadians who have to go out early in life to make a living should be working at. I think it will surprise you.

This is not a kick by a fond and foolish parent whose wooden headed hopeful is not getting on as fast as his inherited smartness would warrant. Nor is it intended as a reflection on our hard working, and generally underpaid, teachers. It is a protest against the system, and I would prefer that you look at it with your own eyes rather than mine.

But I might mention one incident. At last examination one of my boys passed away up between ninety-five and one hundred on some subjects, on others he fell down badly, but still high enough to pass.

The subjects he passed high on he had not received instruction in at school at all; why they were on the papers the teachers did not know. He made his high marks through his home reading. The ones he fell down on were the ones he was supposed to receive instruction on in school. And these were the most important of all, writing and arithmetic.

It was gratifying, of course, to have him score so high on subjects that he had not been instructed in; but these are not the things he can use in making his living, and no matter how beautiful abstract knowledge may be, we must be alive to enjoy it, so the first thing we want is the means of making a living.

The system would not be so bad if each scholar had fifteen years to spend at school, and would eventually enter one of the higher professions. But as only one per cent of them does this, it does seem tough that the ninety-nine should suffer for the sake of the one.

E.J.M.

CONFLICTING STATEMENTS ON TITANIC

APRIL 25, 1912

Have you compared the statements of Major Peuchen and Bruce Ismay, survivors of the ill-fated *Titanic*?

Major Peuchen, a privileged passenger, says in your paper of the 22nd that he was helping in the loading and lowering of the boats with Capt. Smith on the port side; Bruce Ismay, the ship's owner, says he was helping the captain on the starboard side, while other survivors say that the captain remained on the bridge until the boat sank.

After reading all the statements made by survivors, I have not seen one, with the exception of Major Peuchen's, that called another man a coward in face of such a heartrendering scene, and also to infer that the man had been drinking. I refer to the quartermaster of the *Titanic*, who was in the same lifeboat, and also Major Peuchen stoops so low as to say that if the captain of the *Carpathia* [the rescue ship] had been commanding the *Titanic*, the foundering would not have happened.

According to Major Peuchen and his self-recommendation he must have been the bravest and cleverest man aboard; probably he was when he got on dry land. Also self-recommendation asserts itself again when he says he was taking a great risk in swinging out on the rope, holding on with both hands, curling his legs around, and springing out in the darkness — not quite so risky as remaining on the *Titanic*.

Now, Dear Editor, review the statements of the survivors and draw your conclusions. In general, people that criticize others in such happenings as what occurred are fully as bad themselves. Just think of a man condemning a great sailor like Captain Smith, nearly all his life on the seas; it brings tears to the strongest to hear such condemnation.

A Britisher

Editor's note: The sinking of the Titanic had an interesting Ottawa connection. Charles Melville Hays, president of the Grand Trunk Railroad and the man chiefly responsible for construction of the Château Laurier Hotel and the magnificent railway station across Rideau Street, was an invited guest of Bruce Ismay aboard the Titanic on its fateful voyage. Testimony at a subsequent inquiry showed that just hours before the ship hit an iceberg, Mr. Hays had expressed doubts about the wisdom of luxury liners crossing the Atlantic at such high speeds. Mr. Hays' body was found, still floating, two days after the ship went down, and the Château Laurier opened for business without him on June 1. His wife, Clara, her daughter and their maid were rescued.

A PROTEST
APRIL 27, 1912

In a recent news article there was an attempt to explain the action of the Civil Service Commission in refusing even to read the examination papers of women candidates for general work. The following reasons were suggested:

(1) Sufficient women already occupy posts in the lower grades of the service;

(2) These women might qualify themselves by examination for headships of departments;

(3) Women might possibly not be able to exercise the necessary authority over a staff of men;

(4) Women usually have only themselves to support, some women work merely for pocket money and not for subsistence; whereas some men have wives and families to provide for.

Now, if examinations are to be the test of efficiency, there should be no favouritism shown to any class or sex; the best papers should be admitted to the service. And if on the other hand personality is to count, why should women be excluded from an equal footing with men along these lines?

We can sympathize with the Commission in their attempt to choose people with capacity for enforcing discipline and order, rather than those who have mere examination skill; but we cannot approve their action in disqualifying half the candidates merely on the grounds of sex. It is quite as sensible to argue that women might possess the necessary qualities in a high degree as to say they might lack them.

The so-called "economical" reason is amazing. Why should we presume that women need money less than men? We hear that women should be protected. What is a greater protection than money? Good work surely deserves good pay, whether the worker needs a livelihood or pocket money; or does the Commission really mean to be consistent enough to pay bachelors less than married men?

D. Acapo

FATHER BLANCHIN EXPLAINS
OCTOBER 26, 1912

Your article on "Bilingual or French Schools" contains a fundamental error as to its interpretation of the word "bilingual."

A country is certainly not bilingual by the fact that its Government, legally recognizing but one language official, tolerates the speech of a minority within its border and allows the said speech to be taught in the schools as "foreign." A country is really and truly bilingual when by right or privilege it officially recognises two languages, i.e. those of two distinct nationalities federated in one people.

From the moment that such recognition takes place, each has an undeniable right to be perpetuated by education and should therefore have its own schools, colleges and universities, with separate professors and courses of study, plus the common obligation of learning the second language of the country.

Bilingual education for French Canadians would therefore require recognition of their right to a complete scholastic organization comprising the teaching of French in its integrity and of English as a necessary though not primary adjunct. The question of rights would, if this country be truly bilingual, require a like teaching of French in English schools. It is therefore a fundamental error to apply the word "bilingual" to a school system in which English is the sole official or usual language; and in which French is tolerated for two years as a stepping stone to English.

To resume, the question comes to this: Do the French Canadians, according to rights of privileges of the constitution, form an integral part of this country's people on the same footing as English Canadians: or are they to be considered as immigrants or naturalized foreigners? Is the French language officially recognised by the same rights or privileges; or is it a "foreign language" on the same footing as German or Russian?

More concretely: is Canada French in the Province of Quebec only and English everywhere else; or is it a confederation of the two nationalities throughout the Dominion, Franco-English in Quebec, and Anglo-French elsewhere without prejudice to rights of minority in their case?

The question thus presented can, I think, present no great difficulty to any man free from bigotry and racial fanaticism that blind so many in our midst.

Rev. Father F. Blanchin

Editor's note: Rev. Father Blanchin, a Roman Catholic theologian at St. Joseph's University (part of the University of Ottawa), was for many years an outspoken advocate of francophone rights.

AN ANTI-SUFFRAGISTS' VIEW
OCTOBER 31, 1912

I am principally opposed to woman suffrage because it has not been clearly shown how we or our country are going to benefit by it.

In a great many homes where husband and wife think alike, it would not make any difference. In others it would cause quarreling and unhappiness, for you must remember that we women cannot look upon questions in the calm detached way that men can.

Kipling never wrote truer words than, "The female of

the species is more deadly than the male." Why women should wish to enter the turmoil of political life, endangering their already highly-strung and supersensitive minds and bodies, adding extra burden to their country in the shape of increased election expenses when they are able to accomplish so much without, is something which passes understanding.

By steady self-respecting effort we have made men recognize that they are no longer our lords and masters; that our level, though different, is equal in its way to theirs. They have recognized this fact and acted upon it. They have repealed or amended laws unjust to us, and are ready, if necessary, to amend others if properly organized effort be made to have such amended.

I believe that the power of wives and mothers is greater now, though latent, than it would be under real suffrage.

Anti-Suffrage,
Nepean Township

CONNAUGHT NATIONAL PARK
NOVEMBER 20, 1912

I have observed with much interest that a new national park has been proposed for the province of Quebec, in the area between the Gatineau and Coulonge rivers, and I cannot resist the temptation to express the desire and hope that this excellent plan may be consummated at an early date.

During the last year, I have had occasion to make a reasonably careful survey of the condition of wildlife throughout the United States, Alaska and Southern Canada. When I began that inquiry, conditions did not seem to me anything like as alarming as they now appear to be.

I wish to draw your attention to the fact that throughout the whole continent of North America — excepting the particularly remote and inaccessible wilderness regions of Canada and Alaska — the best and most valuable wildlife of the continent is being rapidly exterminated — according to law. Our system of game protection is, in some essential particulars, terribly weak and faulty. Everywhere, without a single exception, the gunners are

entirely too numerous, the laws are entirely too liberal toward the killers of wildlife and the bag limits are too high.

Throughout the United States and Canada, nine-tenths of the laws affecting the pursuit of everything called "game" have been dictated by the men who desire to kill the game. The preservers of wild life who do not kill at all have had very little to say. The result is that the sportsmen and gunners have had everything their own way and have been careful to preserve to themselves the right to kill clear down to the point of total extermination.

These statements may seem to you very sweeping, and in need of details and confirmation. In order to demonstrate the present appalling situation, I shall publish, in December, a volume in which facts are set forth in substantiation of the views I have expressed. I think you will be profoundly disturbed by the showing.

There are many thoughtful sportsmen who now sincerely believe that fifty years hence there will be no game left alive in the United States, outside of well-protected game preserves.

In view of the urgencies of the wildlife situation, in view of the appalling destruction of our best wild life that now is furiously proceeding throughout all the well settled portions of North America, and in view of the value of our wild birds and mammals as a national asset, I sincerely hope that the proposition to create a new national park in western Quebec will be curried into effect at an early date.

Respectfully submitted,
W. T. Hornaday, New York Zoological Park

Editor's note: The extensive national park mentioned in Mr. Hornaday's letter never became reality, mostly due to years of intense struggles between landowners and the government. However, through the Federal Development Commission and its successor, the National Capital Commission, the government began to purchase land north of Ottawa in 1934, eventually accumulating the 88,000 acres contained in today's Gatineau Park.

1913

Local: The price of gasoline rises to 24 cents a gallon, or 5.3 cents a litre (January); City council rejects a proposal to remove disabled people and beggars from street corners (February)
National: Immigration of Sikhs from India causes rioting in Vancouver (July); French banned from Ontario schools beyond Grade 1 (August); Toronto mayor H.C. Hocken introduces sweeping and controversial reforms, including Canada's first minimum wage for municipal workers ($15 a week), new recreation, sewage and filtration facilities and public housing for the poor (November)
World: U.S. athlete Jim Thorpe stripped of the four medals he won at the 1912 Olympics after admitting he played professional baseball (January); U.S. president Wilson pushes a button in Washington that ignites eight tons of dynamite, opening the last segment of the Panama Canal and joining the Atlantic and Pacific oceans (October)
Births: Canadian writer Robertson Davies; governor general Jules Léger; French existentialist writer Albert Camus; U.S. actor Burt Lancaster; U.S. president Gerald Ford
Deaths: Burton Baker, inventor of the X-ray machine; Wall Street tycoon J.P. Morgan

THE SMOKING NUISANCE

JANUARY 29, 1913

"Whatsoever you would that men should do to you do you even so to them." This advice is not only the foundation of Christian ethics but is in the highest sense the charter of a lady and gentlemen. Neither would willingly or deliberately disregard it, in fact they could not and hold the rank.

In a recent issue you lectured on very disgusting habits, but after all they affected a very small percentage of the people, for it is only a fragment that goes to the theatre or the hockey match. You were quite right; so I hope you will add another: "The tobacco volcano going up and down the streets" — puffing his vile smoke and tobacco-soaked breath into everybody's face and clothes.

I see men who pretend to be gentlemen and Christians coming out of church, even smoking with delicate women by their side, who must object to being smothered and have their clothes saturated with tobacco smoke. These men and boys puff their smoke, not only into the faces of the women they are with but into that of every other man and woman they meet.

It is the greatest exhibition of selfishness. The surest wrecking of the claim of gentlemen and a most violent sundering of the Golden Rule we have any record of.

G.H. Fawcett

PERSECUTING CHINAMEN

FEBRUARY 24, 1913

I was so pleased to see in the *Citizen* your defence of the Chinaman. I have been intending to write on that subject but always put it off thinking I had not time.

One Saturday night over two years ago as I was coming up Bank Street I saw a Chinaman walking in front in his usual quiet, reflective way. Two other men got up to him in a swaggering way one on each side and at once

began to annoy him. You know how shallow minded people tease and try to irritate others. The Chinaman never looked at them but kept on quietly. They kept at it and even jostled him until I said to them if they didn't leave him alone I would call the police. I never saw them before or since. They put in a step and turned the first corner.

One very cold Sunday I had gone out for a sharp walk. Two Chinamen — at least I think they were — came up Bank Street in a rig, when trying to cross the car lines the horse was a bit awkward owing to the ice. A number of young men stopped on the pavement to look on and sneer at them. The Chinamen said nothing but got away all right.

One other time some boys were amusing themselves with a stick with a long cord on it on one of the streets off

Attitudes toward Chinese immigrants were questioned.

Bank Street, a Chinaman came along, and one of them swung the thing lasso fashion as he was passing them. I was glad for my country's sake that they missed. The man never looked up.

I do not go about looking for that or any sort of thing but I can't help noticing what is passing around me where I am. I have been jostled oftener than I care about, on the pavement — and I am not big — by the white face men and women, overgrown school boys and girls, especially girls with armsfull of books, the effects of which, surely if they studied aright, would be seen instead of felt, as is the case, unless one takes the outside of the pavement to allow three and four of them to pass in a line.

I never yet could see anything wrong with a Chinaman's manners on the street or elsewhere and I have read that "Manners make the man," or woman.

Missionaries go to China to "convert" them. I earnestly trust they will never be converted into some of the ways of our country — the country they came to — in all likelihood expecting to see in practice what they had heard in precept.

H.I.F.

PUBLIC DRINKING FOUNTAINS
APRIL 30, 1913

Kindly allow me a small space in your valuable paper to express a thought that has come to me in regard to the free use of drinking water, which our city at the present time is supplying the public with.

I have noticed so many workingmen of all descriptions stop at the water wagon which is stationed on Argyle Avenue and help themselves to the greatest blessing under the sun — a cup of cold water.

I have thought what a great blessing it would be to humanity if our fair city had a few public drinking taps stationed on the busy corners for the many human beings that have to be out in the hot sun all day long. And how much more it would mean to so many of us to see our neighbours getting a drink of cold water than to see them quenching their thirst in the bar rooms.

E.F.B.

RIDICULOUS SPEED LIMIT
JULY 3, 1913

I see by the Ottawa papers that the local Improvement Commission are still prosecuting the owners of motor cars who do not or are unable to keep the rate of their car down to the absurdly low speed of seven miles an hour.

Although I have toured and driven my own car nearly 60,000 miles, during which time I have visited England, Scotland, Holland, Belgium, Germany, France, Italy, Spain, Switzerland and Egypt, I have never been asked to crawl at the rate of seven miles an hour. Here in Switzerland, the regulations are said to be more severe than anywhere in Europe; yet one is never asked to go slower than ten miles an hour and that only through the small, crowded villages, with very narrow streets.

Yesterday I motored around the Lake of Thum. Owing to the narrowness of the road and the dangerous curves, the Swiss Government, who own and control all the roads, have only opened this road to motor cars this year for the first time; although it is still closed on Sundays and holidays.

As you enter this pass you are stopped by a guard who gives you a ticket on which the date, hour, number of your car and your name is entered. You are given just so much time to reach the next control, five miles further on. Here your card is checked and if you have exceeded your time allowance: "I am sorry for you!" If not then you are passed on to the next control and so on until the lake is circled at all about 40 miles.

Although at times you are hundreds of feet up on a narrow ledge, at no place are you asked to go slower than 15 miles an hour. I admit that at times you are compelled to go slower than this; however, that is left to the intelligence of the driver.

My object in mentioning this is to show that throughout Europe, where motor transit has been given the most careful thought and consideration, it has been deemed advisable or necessary to limit the speed to that insisted upon by the Improvement Commission and I know from experience that it is much safer and easier to control a car when driving fifteen miles an hour than it is at seven miles an hour; unless in congested traffic where your car is generally on a lower gear.

Let the Improvement Commission punish the reckless drivers by a severe fine or temporary cancellation of their license, but allow the considerate owners the pleasures of the driveway.

E.C. Grant,
Interlaken, Switzerland

USING CHILDREN AS DEBT AGENTS
JULY 11, 1913

You are to be highly commended for bringing to the attention of the public the barbarous manner in which our City Isolation Hospital is conducted and Ald. [William] Macdonald should be publicly thanked for the manly manner he addressed the council and exposed such disgraceful proceedings as the hospital authorities retaining children just recovered from disease for weeks till their poor parents pay up their hospital bills.

If they think these people have the money and are trying not to pay their debts let them be sued like all creditors are. Judging by hospital Controller [Rufus] Parent, who had the audacity to say it was a good system to get the money, just keep the children there for weeks till their poor parents produce the cash, no matter if it's got to be borrowed to do so, it's so easy nowadays to get $100. And then his worship the mayor actually agrees with him.

Does Dr. Parent treat his own patients in the hospital the same way? It's time some of our public men who take an interest in municipal matters called a public meeting, then probably the citizens would be told more about this Medical Health Department's proceedings than they at present know.

One of the Sufferers

Editor's note: Strathcona Isolation Hospital, built in Sandy Hill in 1902 where Strathcona Park is now located, was operated by municipal council through an arm's length arrangement. A few weeks after this letter was written, public outcry and strong editorial opposition from both the Citizen and Ottawa Journal led to an end to the practice of keeping children in the facility until bills were settled.

AN ACT OF KINDNESS
JULY 12, 1913

With your permission I would like to bring to public notice an act of kindness performed yesterday in the city, which is noticeable on account of its rarity.

During the noon-hour two civic labourers working on Slater Street took the liberty of eating their lunch on the lawn of a palatial residence on the north-west corner of Slater and Lyon streets. They had just got comfortably placed, and were opening their dinner pails, when they heard someone tapping on the window.

Past experiences made them prepare for a speedy departure, but before they could make their get-away — they were both up in years — the window was raised and a sweet-faced old lady asked them in the kindest tones if they "would care for a drop of tea."

Overcome by her beauty and kindliness, they muttered an embarrassed acceptance and she had them sit down again while she procured two cups and saucers, spoons, sugar, etc., a pitcher of luscious cream, and a great teapot full of the most delicious tea, and they had what they called "a labourers' tea party."

They decided finally to tell the whole city about it, and in this way to express their appreciation of a beautiful deed done in a quiet, kindly way.

So many sects, so many creeds,
So many paths that wind and wind;
When just the art of being kind
Is all that this sad world needs.

E.W.W.

BEAST OF BURDEN
JULY 26, 1913

May I through the medium of your well read paper ask if it is possible for the humane authorities to pay more attention to the condition of the horses used by the majority of junk dealers in Ottawa?

Passing along Elgin Street this afternoon I met three rigs driven by junk dealers, and from what I know of animals, and from the appearance of the horses attached, I am of opinion they should have been destroyed some years ago. They were so thin and scraggy, bones showed prominently all over their bodies, and one in particular seemed to have the greatest difficulty in drawing his load, stopping about every fifty yards and straining hard to restart it.

I consider it would be a charity to have these poor beasts humanely destroyed, and should like, if possible, to know if any of your readers have had their attention drawn to this matter.

Lover of animals

GARBAGE AGAIN
OCTOBER 4, 1913

The *Citizen* has always proved so public spirited that I am writing to know if you will kindly try to explain a subject that affects us all vitally — namely, the garbage system.

The neglect our garbage receives is positively shameful. I have utilized every receptacle in the house, even unto the wash boiler, to hold garbage because the collectors come so infrequently. Our backyard is a hot bed of fever and flies. And this neglect is not because we live at a distance — we live in one of Ottawa's principal streets where all our neighbours receive like treatment.

Surely somebody is neglecting his duty. If the garbage people are unable or unwilling to handle the subject properly, it seems to me it ought to be done municipally. Other cities do it successfully, so why not Ottawa?

We read about the Improvement Commission that is going to beautify Ottawa. To be beautiful any object must first be clean. If one-tenth of the time, money and brains of the Commission were focused on the garbage question, we would soon have good service.

Won't the *Citizen* agitate this question and get something done?

A subscriber

SOME PEOPLE NEVER SATISFIED
NOVEMBER 25, 1913

In your interesting society column, the Social Whirl, I am occasionally disappointed that in some cases where teas are described full details are not given. Quite often you mention the names of the ladies who cut the ices, pour the tea and coffee and serve the punch, but sometimes you do not.

It is this occasional omission that grieves me. Nothing can so unfit a man for business as to be obliged to begin his day's work without this information.

It would also be desirable to state in every case whether the table decorations are Lawson carnations or just plain every-day carnations. The fact that a Lawson carnation is not recognizable from the other kind does not lessen one's desire to be informed, before starting on the joyous and trifling duties of a business day, just which kind were on the tables of the previous day's teas and whether they were "centred in a large cut glass bowl" or were just standing around loose-and-careless-like in uncut glass vases.

Also would you please always describe the hostess's gown. Of course it is often "chartreuse" but when it is not I think it is only fair to your eager readers to say just what it is.

If the hyphenated names of the guests present could be grouped apart from the ordinary unhyphenated, it would help. If footnotes could be furnished, giving dates upon which the names became of the hyphenated kind, it would be just lovely, and would assist old residents of Ottawa to know old friends in their new aristocratic guise.

J. Hillsden-Willoughby

TEMPORARY WATER SUPPLY MOST IMPORTANT
DECEMBER 13, 1913

When will this pure water supply question be at an end? There are many of us who have stomach trouble brought on by the filthy condition of dope being put into our supply (from the Ottawa River) to render, as much as possible a dead liquid, the life-giving qualities being killed, all I can call it is wet, with the dead germs, and the poison that killed them thrown in.

This state of affairs is known far and near and puts our city in a most unenviable position. We do not question the quality of water from the (Gatineau) hills. Oh, no, judging from the reports it is all that could be desired, but years will elapse before we can quench our thirst with it.

I would suggest that something of a temporary nature be done at once. Lake Deschênes is much better water than is supplied to us at present and I have no doubt there are sand beds at lake level, and in close proximity to the same where a miniature lake might be formed, water soaking through sand would be much improved. With wooden pipes and no land cost, surely this water is available.

I believe there has been money spent on water trouble up till now, which would have defrayed a considerable amount of the expenses connected from the above named source. If gold were found in Ottawa and the nearest available water to wash it, Deschênes Lake, we would count the time by hours when it would be here, surely our health is of more consequence than our money making industries.

R.S. Reid

1914

Local: Ottawa's first police woman begins her duty (January); Strong earthquake centred 200 miles north of Ottawa rocks city, causing slight damage to buildings. No one injured (February)
National: About 1,400 lives lost in 14 minutes when the Canadian Pacific ship *Empress of Ireland* sinks in the St. Lawrence River after being rammed (May); Canada is automatically at war with Germany when Britain declares war on Aug. 4. First Canadian troops leave for Britain in October

World: Archduke Franz Ferdinand, heir to Austrian throne, is assassinated by Serbian nationalists in Sarajevo, setting off events that lead to First World War (June); German army rolls through Belgium but is halted at Marne, France in its assault on Paris (September)
Births: Baseball star Joe DiMaggio, poet Dylan Thomas; British actor Sir Alec Guiness; boxer Joe Louis
Deaths: Governors general John Campbell (Marquess of Lorne) and Gilbert Eliot (Lord Minto); Sir William Van Horne, first president of CPR; Alphonse Bertillon, fingerprinting pioneer; George Westinghouse, inventor or 400 electrical appliances

WELFARE OF THE HORSE

APRIL 2, 1914

In yesterday's paper I noticed a letter entitled, "A Plea for the Horse," and the writer terms himself "an old teamster." If you will allow me a little space I will endeavor to explain the cause of most of this cruelty.

I only term myself a coachman, but I have handled all kinds from the plough or cart horse to a coach-and-four. Needless to say, I have worked for all kinds of people right in this town, and my experience has been this: I admit there are exceptions, not only in the case of butchers, bakers, transfer men and wood dealers, but in the majority of cases where horsemen of any kind are employed — people cannot or will not offer a man decent wages.

Therefore, for the lowest wage they will employ boys or half-witted men who know nothing whatever about horses except to lash and jerk their heads from side to side. And I may truthfully say there are many good horses, not only run down, but who have learned to balk and be disagreeable to such drivers.

A few weeks ago I noticed one of these drivers delivering a load of four-foot wood on Somerset Street for a well-known firm on Catherine Street. The sleighing was not very good, but the horse was getting along at a fair gait when the driver began to curse and shout, and then, pulling a stick from the load, he struck the horse two or three times on the hip, then jumped off, and, by running up, multiplied his blows by two on the ribs.

Now, I know for a fact that this firm, like many others, will not pay men the average wage even in the good days, although men are expected to be up and doing every minute of ten hours. Then as soon as winter sets in and certain mills and works shut down, the men are laid off or their pay cut down almost one half.

Now, I ask any fair-minded reader, is this not enough to discourage good men to look for work or take an interest in the welfare of those folk?

Coachman, Ottawa

DOCTORS CONSIDERATE OF POOR

APRIL 3, 1914

I would be ungrateful indeed did I not accept the opportunity of endorsing with the heartiest goodwill a letter in Tuesday's Citizen signed C.N., and entitled "In Defence of Doctor's Fees."

I have had considerable to do with doctors in Ottawa — three of my children were born here; one has died; they have had whooping cough, measles, chicken pox, along with their share, I presume, of accidents, colds, etc. My wife is not strong; and my experience bears but just what C.N. conveys in her letter, i.e., that doctors generally are very humane and sympathetic in their dealings with poor people.

I recall in particular a doctor living in the Glebe who was phoned for by one of the neighbours on one occasion when my wife was stricken down and I was not at home. He came, did what he could, and went away, and to this day he has never asked for a cent in return for his services. He was a complete stranger, too.

Frequently I have been given free medicine for my wife or children by other doctors. A doctor who had charge of the births of two of my children attended to that and whatever other medical services we needed for several years at a rate of about ten dollars a year and waited our convenience in paying that.

I really feel that we owe the lives of some of our children to his kindness and skill. I also feel that our dead child would be alive today but for the fact that we were compelled by adverse circumstances to move to another part of the city, where it became an almost physical impossibility for the doctor to visit us, in consequence of which we yielded to the peculiarly subtle temptation — to poor people — of sending our sick baby to the hospital.

To sum up, I have found the doctors in Ottawa — and elsewhere — very lenient in their charges; also very accommodating in waiting for their pay. It has been my experience that many poor people leave their doctor's bills to the very last in paying their debts.

Yours, John Lyons,
31 Morris Street

WANTS OTTAWANS TO FLY
APRIL 14, 1914

It seems to require the excitement of the summer exhibition season before we hear the hum of the aeroplane, and then the operator is a stranger.

We are pleased to welcome to our city airmen to perform feats of skill and daring, but where are our Ottawa boys? I do not refer to the lads who have neither time to practice nor money to acquire an aeroplane, but there are many who can afford both time and money, but would prefer to enjoy the ease and comfort of the motor car.

The aeroplane is the only machine that could skim over the whirlpool of Niagara, and pick from its treacherous waters a human being ready to be engulfed and lost forever. It is the only machine that could glide over broken field ice and rescue those who are endangered of being crushed by the movement of the flow, and no search boat should go out without being equipped with this most up-to-date life-saving mechanism.

I know many have been killed by aerial machines, but look at how many times we have been so cruelly thrown, and many killed by the horse, and yet how I wish I could afford one. Yes, and if I had time and money (even although I am getting up in years), I would be one to fly over Ottawa by exhibition day 1914.

White Eagle

THE SCAVENGING SYSTEM
MAY 9, 1914

Kindly allow me space in your paper to vent my feelings as well as those of many others, I am quite sure, regarding the scavenging system. Someone said through your paper it was rotten; a rather rough expression, nevertheless true. If there is a worse expression it can truthfully be applied.

Anyone looking up Lewis Street, between Metcalfe and Elgin streets, this morning would have seen the sidewalk littered with dirt and ashes and the road which was cleaned about ten days ago strewn with tin cans, broken glass, bottles, crockery, old wire, etc. It truly was a sight. What is there to encourage one to keep one's place clean and tidy. I regularly have to clean off my lawn and sidewalk in front after the scavenging men pass.

I telephoned this morning to the city hall about this and asked if something could not be done to make these men be more careful and was told they had nothing to do with this. Speak to the contractors. Telephoned the contractor. We will see about it, I am told. So it goes, but we have no improvement.

A visitor to our city last fall said to me, "You certainly have a most beautiful city. I have visited many but never saw dirtier streets, especially the side streets." I was ashamed, but had to admit the truth.

I do wish our mayor would get busy on the scavenging system.

A Tidy Lady

LATE DRIVING SATURDAY
JULY 10, 1914

You are advocating Saturday afternoons off for workers in shop business places and workshops in general.

I would like to draw to your attention the fact that if some of our (delivery) drivers were given Saturday night off there would be happier homes. I am not saying to close by any means; simply let drivers have their last load at a certain time where they would not be out all or half the night. A driver getting his last load Saturday night say at 6:30 or 7 would be through at least about 8:30 or 9.

Could not the public in general be educated to the fact that it is up to them to give in their orders early? Even if a customer wanted any groceries after 7 could they not carry them home? Even if a driver gets through at say 9 he has pretty near an hour's work in the stable afterwards.

A mother

WHISKEY AND LONG LIFE
AUGUST 12, 1914

Some unknown person has sent me a newspaper clipping telling me an Irishman lived to be 108 years old although he was fond of his glass.

Yes, we occasionally hear of men of such wonderful vitality that they can withstand the injurious influence of drink and live to a good old age. When such cases are investigated the facts are almost invariably found to be very sad. Their children, if they have any, are generally condemned to lives of suffering for the ignorance or the selfish indulgence of the parents.

Dr. McNichol, appointed by President [Theodore] Roosevelt to investigate this question from a scientific standpoint, says that for every child of total abstaining parents that dies before it reaches two years of age there are five children of drinking parents that die before that age. Further statistics show that while 82 children of abstaining parents grow up into good useful citizens, only 17 children of drinking parents do so.

I know of a man who lived to be nearly ninety years of age. He was a constant drinker but never was drunk. Out of his family of ten children only three lived to mature life and of these three only one could be said to be fairly healthy. The others were nervous weaklings. That is only one of many such cases that I have known.

How greedily some people pounce on one isolated case where a drinking man has lived to be old but seem to be perfectly blind to the many examples all round them of men who have gone to an early grave or worse through drink.

H. Arnott, M.B., M.C.P.S.
(Member of the College of Physicians and Surgeons)

ONE RECRUIT'S MOTIVE

SEPTEMBER 1, 1914

A recent letter in the *Citizen* headed "Patriots Not All Soldiers" reminds me of an equally relevant truth — that soldiers are not all patriots.

An acquaintance of mine who has volunteered to go to the front explained his action to me as follows: "You see, Jack, my position at home will be kept for me (he is a civil servant). I shall get $60 a month full pay while I am away, and will be able to clear between $40 and $50 a month on the field as a soldier, then if I return as a veteran I'll be fixed for life."

But if you don't return, what then? I inquired. "Well, if I get killed, my mother will get $5,000 (life insurance) which will make her comfortable for the rest of her life."

"But will you really 'shoot to kill?'" I asked. "Oh yes, if I go I'll have to pull the trigger whenever ordered to do so or I'd be shot as a traitor."

"But surely," I said, "you would not deliberately shoot down in cold blood men with whom you have no personal quarrel (he is a member of the local branch of the Socialist Party of Canada and as such, of course, makes no pretensions re patriotism as commonly understood) for any possible material benefit — financial or otherwise — to yourself or your mother?" (He is unmarried.)

"Well, if they're foolish enough to line up in front of me, I'll have to shoot them down. I'm compelled to follow the line of least resistance in the struggle to live."

And so he rambled on until a lump came in my throat and I had to leave him. He is a bright young fellow in his early twenties, good looking and physically perfect, morally clean, and of more than average intelligence; and yet by this time he is on his way, I believe, to almost certain death, determined, no doubt, to sell his life dearly, but hypnotized, for the time being, by the vision of material reward.

John Lyons, Ottawa

LOOKING A GIFT HORSE ...

OCTOBER 29, 1914

Our attention has been called to a reduction in milk prices, and we have considered this reduction a commendable action on the part of the Ottawa Dairy Company.

But a driver for another milk company mentioned to me that this reduction is really being made at the expense of the drivers of the Ottawa Dairy. Some of these drivers

have told this man that their earnings will be reduced as much as five dollars a month in some cases and ten dollars in other cases.

If this is a fact, I am sure the Ottawa people will be glad to know it, that they may feel grateful to the right people! Already the milk drivers of any city earn the gratitude of all who have the comfort of steady and prompt delivery of milk given them, year in and year out, by these "men who work whilst others sleep." If they now have added their five or ten dollars a month, that we may have cheap milk, we should indeed express our gratitude.

A Questioner

Editor's note: The Ottawa Dairy Company, which supplied about 60 per cent of Ottawa's milk in the early years of the century, later admitted to lowering employees' pay in order to reduce milk prices and squeeze the competition. Under public and newspaper pressure, the pay of staff was eventually restored and milk prices returned to former levels.

W.R.SMYTH, LT.COL.
OFFICER COMMANDING

HEADQUARTERS
43 BANK ST. OTTAWA

BUSHMEN AND SAWMILL HANDS
WANTED
JOIN THE
238TH CANADIAN FORESTRY
BATTALION

CANADA: A CELEBRATION OF OUR HERITAGE

Ottawa Valley lumbermen were recruited for the war effort.

SOCKS FOR SOLDIERS

NOVEMBER 14, 1914

Who supplies the socks our soldiers are wearing? Might be a pertinent question at this time; in fact, the public should be informed of the names of all firms furnishing equipment to our soldiers.

Socks would not be considered a very important item to most civilians but bad socks to the soldier are very nearly as hurtful as being wounded by the enemy. It is most important that a soldier have perfect feet. Feet cannot be kept in good shape that are clothed in cheap, inferior socks that wear into heels in a couple of days.

A letter received here from one of the boys at the front declares that the socks served to our soldiers are shockingly bad and that many men are already suffering from sore feet.

Glebite

SHOULD BLAME SYSTEM, NOT BOSS

DECEMBER 12, 1914

I am working in one of Ottawa's most popular hotels. I have been employed here for nearly six months and have done my duty to my employer. And as far as I can see the rest of the help have done the same.

Today we all got a notice in our pay envelopes telling us that our wages are to be cut down 20 per cent, which will mean a lot to me, as well as the rest of my fellow workers. When a person is working for ten dollars per month and his room bill amounts to eight, he hasn't very much left for clothes, without the wages being cut.

We wouldn't mind if the money taken off us was going to help some other poor person through the winter, but it is going to a source of pleasure for the boss and his friends, as he gives them a party every night, Sundays included. I ask if we should not be treated with a little more care in our faithful fulfillment of our duty.

Oppressed

1915

Local: Worried about the threat of a German air attack on the capital, lights are ordered out in Ottawa after dark (February); Perley Home for care of the elderly opens (July)

National: Canadian troops face a gas attack at Ypres, Belgium; Canadian John McCrae writes *In Flanders Fields;* Statistics suggest more than one million immigrants arrived in Canada from 1912 to 1914, bringing the total to three million since 1891

World: German torpedo sinks British liner *Lusitania*, killing more than 1,500 on board (May) Professor Albert Einstein proposes new theory of relativity (December)

Births: Actor-broadcaster Lorne Greene; singers Frank Sinatra, Edith Piaf and Billie Holiday; actors Orson Welles and Ingrid Bergman; writer Saul Bellow; playwright Arthur Miller

Deaths: Prime minister Charles Tupper; Sir Sandford Fleming, designer of CPR rail system; Albert Spalding, founder of first sporting goods empire

UNEMPLOYMENT

JANUARY 2, 1915

Interned Austrians and Germans are fed, clothed, sheltered and paid 25 cents per day, while native-born Canadians — men, women and children — are starving and suffering in these cold winter months, not considered worthy of equal treatment with our enemies.

Five hundred thousand alien army men are stopped from reaching their country's colours today because Britain rules the waves, yet our government will not allow our clients to cross into the United States where this army of their brethren is. We sufferers want to know why.

We are not provided with honest work. We are not allowed to drill for soldiers' pay, and yet we must be good law-abiding citizens.

We say, give us work. Let us drill five hours per day for 75 cents or 80 cents, that we may eat. Let us break stone, saw wood, cut timber, dig holes or anything that our hands can do. We can work, we can fight and die, but we cannot because we are men and if we are not considered as men finally we must live and therefore we must steal.

And who can blame us? It behooves our country to do something for us and not everything for strangers.

Sufferer

BEER KILLS
QUICKER THAN WHISKEY

APRIL 2, 1915

Any one might know that. We all know whiskey drinkers that have lived to be eighty or ninety, but the beer drinkers have all died under or about sixty.

Dr. Burgen of Toledo, a practitioner of thirty-five years experience, says: "My attention was first called to the insidious effects of beer when I began examining for life insurance. I passed five Germans who seemed to be in the best of health and to have superb constitutions. In a few years I was amazed to see the whole five drop off, one after another, with what should have been mild and easily curable diseases. On comparing my experience with that of other physicians I found they were all having similar luck with confirmed beer drinkers, and my practice has since confirmed that experience."

The first organ to be attacked is the kidneys and then comes dropsy and Brights disease certain to end fatally. Any physician will tell you that the beer drinker seems incapable of recovering from mild disorders and injuries not usually regarded as of a grave character.

The beer drinker is much worse off than the whiskey drinker, who seems to have more elasticity and reserve power. He even has delirium tremors but after the fit is gone you will often find a good amount of vitality. But when a beer drinker gets into trouble it is difficult and often impossible to do anything for him. I have talked this for years, and have had abundance of instances to support my opinions.

For a long time we could not tell why beer drinkers should die so much younger than whiskey drinkers, but a celebrated investigator, Dr. Von-Noorden, solved the problem and showed that all fermented liquors contained an acid which is very destructive to the kidneys.

H. Arnott, M.B., M.C.P.S.
(Member of the College of Physicians and Surgeons)

STREETCAR STOPS

APRIL 24, 1915

Regarding the stopping of the streetcars after crossing intersecting streets, there is no doubt but that the advice of the chief of police is quite right.

For a long time now, the car company has been preaching "Safety First;" one would have thought they would want to practice what they preach. How in the name of common sense they cannot see that the near side of the street is the safest for their cars and the passengers inside them is hard to understand.

It is only a few days ago, when going down Elgin Street, I noticed an automobile being driven east on Slater Street. It made no attempt to slow up when crossing Elgin. Just at that moment a streetcar stopped at the near side of Slater, also an auto containing some ladies at the side of it.

Now, Sir, had that streetcar stopped after crossing the

street, I feel certain that a very serious accident would have occurred, as the auto just cleared the fender of the car.

I noticed a very similar occurrence at the intersection of Queen and Metcalfe streets a short time ago. A cabman whose horse was almost beyond his control came down the hill at a dangerous speed. Fortunately a car had just stopped at the church which prevented a collision.

Now that the streetcars are allowed to travel over the crossing before stopping, and are run into and perhaps passengers injured by broken glass or the pole of a wagon, who would be liable for the damages?

There is no doubt but that the general public who continually use the cars are quite aware of the right stopping places. Strangers coming into the city are to be excused. The motormen must expect these little annoyances.

Does it not look as though they are going to increase their troubles, and at the same time endanger the life and limb of their passengers from the causes I refer to? The authorities in the American cities view the matter in the same light and are wise.

J.S.K.

Editor's note: The debate about the safest place for streetcars to stop at intersections in Ottawa rose out of the increase in automobile traffic in the years after 1910. During the early years of streetcar service, from before the turn of the century until some time during the First World War, the cars generally stopped to let passengers on and off after passing through an intersection. But as motor traffic increased, it became clear that the safer method was to stop before an intersection, thereby ensuring streetcars proceeded through intersections at a slow speed.

POLITICS AT THE CITY HALL
APRIL 28, 1915

When will the mayor of Ottawa cease allowing a certain room in the city hall to be used as an employment agency in the interests of the Conservative party in the city?

A certain store-room in the city hall has been converted into an office for the chairman of the St. George's ward Conservatives. His duties seem to be the dispensing of patronage in the way of civic employment with a view, seemingly, of benefiting the party in power on the Hill.

James McGrath, Ottawa

Editor's note: Not much is known about Nelson D. Porter, mayor of Ottawa 1915-16, except that he got into politics, he said, over his frustration with the condition of the city's roads and water supply. Until his election in 1915, he'd never made a speech and had not even been inside city hall. His greatest surprise, he claimed years later, was being hoisted to the shoulders of his supporters on election night. His obituary in 1961 makes no mention of any ties to a political party, so perhaps it was Mr. Porter's political naiveté that allowed the Conservatives to dispense patronage from a city hall storage room. The issue was not reported in the newspapers of the day. He did not run for a second term.

BANK STREET PAVEMENT
MAY 1, 1915

As a property owner on Bank Street and a citizen whose interest in Ottawa is at least twenty times greater than that of the man who threatens to "knock out" the petition signed by over two thirds of the ratepayers on that street in favour of wood block pavement, I protest against the bulldozing methods referred to above.

Those of us who are asking for wood block pavement are doing so because of our personal knowledge of its advantages, and our personal knowledge of the rottenness of asphalt as laid in the city of Ottawa. We have both pavements where we can see them daily.

The wood block on the Plaza [site of present-day Confederation Square] carrying the city's heaviest traffic is in perfect condition. The asphalt on Sparks Street, laid after the city's bitter experience on every other asphalted street, is going to pieces in a hundred places. Look at it near the shop of Mr. R. J. Devlin for example, where there are holes, each large enough to bury a dog.

Ask the ratepayers on Rideau, Wellington, Elgin, etc. what they know about asphalt. Ask us on Bank street. Ask Mr. Alexander Stuart, superintendent of the Ottawa Improvement Commission for his opinion. He has made no mistakes in his roadways; he visits other cities; he is practical; he favours wood block pavement for Bank Street.

Mayor Porter's outspoken stand in favour of wood block is what we expected of him, and the *Citizen*'s support of that form of pavement is what we expected of the *Citizen*.

We now look to the board of control and the city council to agree to what we pay for.

Bank Street Property Owner

Editor's note: After council and the city's board of control approved asphalt for Bank Street, residents of the street petitioned to have the decision overturned, and the road covered instead with wood block, a paving method common before the advent of the automobile, but falling out of favour by 1915. According to a description in the Citizen, wood pavement "consists of a bed of concrete over which are laid wood blocks with the grain vertical. The wood varies from Norway pine, made rot-proof with creosote, to hard wood ... which requires no treatment. This makes a firm, compact pavement which exceeds stone in durability because, instead of splintering under traffic, it is only pounded down and becomes harder the longer it is used." Even so, council stood by its original decision, saying the petition did not have enough signatures and noting the wood blocks installed a few years earlier on York and Chapel streets were already deteriorating. News stories of the day did not mention the relative costs of wood blocks versus asphalt. The man referred to in the letter's first sentence was William Stuart, who clearly opposed the use of wood, but whose identity beyond that has been lost to time.

DESPICABLE PRACTICE
MAY 7, 1915

The idea suggested in your editorial this morning entitled "Backyard Gardens" is an excellent one. The principle of growing vegetables has been in operation in a great many yards in this section of the city and it invariably proves a splendid source of recreation and besides should reduce the household account.

However, there is one serious discouragement confronting the man who would grow a vegetable garden in this part of Ottawa. For three successive years I have labored during my spare time in planting a garden in my backyard. The results in each year were very promising and I had considerable personal pride in the result of my labours.

But when everything was at its best some rascal would make a raid, steal everything matured and practically destroy what was left. This was most successfully and systematically accomplished two years in succession.

In each case the police were notified: most condescendingly an officer appeared on the scene, looked the situation over, confessed to the prevalence of the crime and the difficulty of coping with it, and departed — apparently quite satisfied with the success of his mission. I never heard of anything further being done in the matter of discovering the culprit.

Until we have some protection from these sneak thieves, who are professedly prevalent, there is little inducement for a man to accept your worthy suggestion and raise a vegetable garden.

Glebe

VANISHING CANADA

Poor children suffered while interned Germans were fed, a reader said.

A PROTEST

MAY 17, 1915

I wish to enter a protest against the practice of advertisements after the place has been filled. Women pay out dollar after dollar of hard-earned money in car fare just to hear the words, "We have been suited," or, "The item has been sold."

It seems to me it would not be a hard task to telephone the *Citizen* office to discontinue the ad when the want is met, but this is just one case of woman's inhumanity to woman — mere thoughtlessness on the part of sheltered women in the home — causing endless discouragement to homeless workers.

A Houseworker

SOLDIER'S WIFE'S COMPLAINTS

SEPTEMBER 25, 1915

Seeing your piece in Thursday's paper in regard to the 41st Battalion company D, it is no wonder that men do not enlist in Hull [site of the area's recruitment centre]. What encouragement does the Government offer?

It is two months since my husband left Hull with the above regiment and I have not received five cents from the government during that time. How does the government expect a wife with a family of small children to live a

decent life, and provide food and clothing?

It is no wonder the men desert when they learn that their families are not looked after as was promised them at the time of enlistment.

A Soldier's Wife

"POLICE METHODS"

OCTOBER 1, 1915

On Saturday last, I was on the look out for a certain lady who had gone marketing. In order not to miss her (and be near the streetcar line) I stood for a while on the grass plot against the fence at Waller Street School, this lady always using Waller Street for market purposes.

I had not stood there three minutes when a newly created police sergeant on the beat came up to me. Gist of the conversation:

Sergeant: "What are you doing here, hanging about?" I stated I was merely waiting for a lady to come from the market.

Sergeant: "Did she tell you to wait here for her?" I was asked. "No she did not, but surely a respectable citizen can wait on a piece of grass plot without causing annoyance," I said.

His reply was, "Don't you get so d____d fresh about it. Clear off and take a walk. Pretty sharp about it, too."

I was so astounded by this act of "Kaiserism" that I could not reply. Now, sir, I am a tradesman and well-known; I have been in several parts of this world of ours, but never have I been so grossly insulted by (what I have always considered a fine body of men, viz. the police) such a pompous and lordly personage as this officious sergeant.

Surely the citizens and ratepayers of Ottawa will not stand for such. "Kaiserism" must cease.

Pro Bono Publico

DISGUSTING PRACTICE

OCTOBER 24, 1915

I would like to call your attention and that of your readers to a most objectionable and disgusting habit which many men in this city have of spitting from windows of offices and other upstairs rooms over stores, etc., along the main streets.

Walking along Sparks and Rideau streets today I had to dodge a spit from some upper window no less than three times. One of these occasions I was passing the Russell House, when it escaped me only by a few inches. Some months ago a spit from some window landed on my coat sleeve!

I fully realize that men cannot be stopped from spitting, but surely some measures ought to be taken to prevent them doing it from the windows along public thoroughfares.

W.R.

Local: Fire consumes Centre Block of Parliament Hill, leaving only the library standing (February); National Research Council is founded (September)
National: Nellie McClung persuades Manitoba government to give women the right to vote, a first in Canada (January); Ontario Temperance Act passed, prohibiting the making, importation and selling of liquor (April); Nearly 25,000 Canadian and Newfoundland soldiers killed in the Battle of the Somme in France (July to November)
World: Ford Motor Co. promises its cheapest automobile yet — a $250 touring model to begin rolling off the assembly line in the fall (August); Joined by Italy, Russia and Romania, the Allies begin to push back the Germans on the war's eastern and western fronts (September)
Births: South African leader P.W. Botha; violinist Yehudi Menuhin; French president François Mitterrand
Deaths: Writers Henry James and Jack London; British war secretary Lord Kitchener; Hetty Green, U.S. shipbuilding heiress and world's richest woman; Gregory Rasputin, adviser to Russia's Czarina; Franz Joseph, Austrian emperor for 68 years

THE CENSOR AND THE MOVIES

MARCH 13, 1916

A week or two ago a film was shown in Ottawa called The Rack. It was well produced and well acted. The story was strictly immoral, marital unfaithfulness, seduction and rape being just suggested, then emphasized, then all but noted before one's eyes until the murder of the villain put a stop to his activities.

The great dénouement was a court scene in which the heroine, wrongfully accused of the murder, is mentally tortured by the prosecuting counsel; in order to convey her torture more vividly a momentary glimpse was given of a mediaeval torture chamber in which the nearly nude body of a woman seemed to be suspended from a beam.

Such was the movie as presented in New York. When it arrived in Ottawa, the censor, ever mindful of the conventions, if not of the morals, of the community, cut out the torture chamber scene presumably because of the momentary glimpse of the human figure.

It is fair to suppose therefore that the censor considers that a movie largely given over to sexual criminality is a healthy amusement for the rising generation while a glimpse of the human body, suggesting nothing evil is anathema and must be cut out. This is perhaps a small thing, but it is one of the straws which show why we do not get better movies. If the censors are to be an asset to the community their convictions should be at least as reliable as their courage.

The world is rapidly growing more healthy minded and nowadays artistic photographs of the nude are to be seen in many magazines and are viewed with as much equanimity and appreciation of their beauty as paintings of the same subject have been since time immemorial; the censor therefore might try and keep abreast of the times.

If the movies are to progress, if the beautiful and good things of the world are to be shown us on the screen, then those who have either achieved or had thrust upon them this right of deciding what is good for us might well consider the truism that clothes do not make vice healthy nor does the absence of them necessarily preclude virtue.

Let the censor but free himself from prejudice and learn to see evil when evil is meant and not when it is not meant, and vistas of wonderful productions open up which will take the place of the sordid sexual criminality which is at present the basis of the moving picture drama.

Eric Brown, Ottawa

WELCOMING SOLDIERS

APRIL 5, 1916

I am writing in response to your editorial of this morning headed, "Why No Cheers For the Wounded." This, like innumerable articles one reads in the papers regarding the care and treatment of "our gallant soldiers," betrays an absolute ignorance of the real truth.

The writer has watched by the bedsides of the freshly wounded soldiers removed just from the trenches in France and has seen them, later, transferred tenderly to hospital ships for special "hospitals" in Great Britain, received there and finally passed on to Canadian hospitals.

They are never "lonely in hospitals in a far country," as you state; they are petted, comforted, nursed and given motor drives by England's aristocracy; entertained at country seats, given concerts continually by the cream of the profession from London, till the honest ones admit "Home was never like this, Yip-I-Addy-I-Aye."

There are no "staggering" cases discharged from the convalescent depots in England. I have escorted many home. They are watched and treated with every possible consideration. Some are misfits who have disgraced the uniform; yet it is disloyal on the part of the casual onlookers to voice the opinions one hears, all unfounded on fact.

Arriving at the dock in Canada, one sees a mob on hand "to cheer the returned wounded." They are surrounded by reporters who offer to write up all their feats of arms, their heroism and valour. Then come the Daughters of the Empire with smiles and sympathy and presents for the now absolutely spoiled heroes.

In comfortable coaches, they have excellent meals provided until they reach home. At Quebec they are discharged and dismissed, if fit, with tickets to their place of enlistment, otherwise sent to convalescent homes. Many get permission to visit friends on side trips, none are rejected or abused.

Many are not "easy to please" and want the earth and a throne. Candidly, no sane, practical creature could hope for more.

One Who Is In The Work

WORKINGMEN'S HOUSES

APRIL 12, 1916

I was pleased to read A. E. Johnstone's letter in Saturday's edition about the houses here in Ottawa for working people.

What he says is only too true. I am a working woman and a widow (stranger in city) and I find it impossible to get a house decent to live in under $14 or $16 a month. There is no working man or woman can pay that amount, and the consequences are we are driven to live in the cow sheds they take $10 and $12 a month for, with the ceilings falling on our heads and burst pipes with no water nearly all through the winter which is the case where I am staying at present.

How can one call it a beautiful city? For us poor there is no comfort, sympathy or consideration.

A. Mills

HELP DOGS — AND BOYS

APRIL 19, 1916

Reading the letter entitled, "A Plan for the Horse," in today's *Citizen* moves me to add another plea on behalf of dumb animals, for the dog that is being used by ignorant and thoughtless boys to drag them around in boxes, on wheels or on runners, for amusement — not a very manly kind of sport, for oftentimes it is only a small spaniel, and the boy may be up to 15 or 16 years of age.

Surely there must be something lacking in the home influence, or else in the education of a child, who thinks it a pleasure to be drawn around by a poor little animal, that usually does not even reach up to his knees and that demonstrates plainly the severe effort it is making, by its extended tongue and panting sides?

I have protested in each case coming under my notice, in every language at my command, but the boys only appear surprised at any supposed wrong-doing and continue in their extraordinary ideas of sport and play.

Who is to blame? Are children in the schools given enough instruction in nature study, to arouse a love and sympathy for "all creatures great and small" or are they supposed to pick it up somehow or at some other time? Are those children not learning anything beyond their catechism? Could not some kind sister or father find time to take them on a nature walk this Easter and explain to them the wonders of the resurrection of life in the animal and vegetable kingdom?

It might teach boys to hold more sacred the things that have been given to man for his use, but not abuse. Lame horses and harnessed dogs seem to be more peculiar to Ottawa than to any other city of my experience.

C.V.C.

VANISHING CANADA

Working people couldn't afford housing on meagre wages.

A PERPLEXED VISITOR

MAY 17, 1916

I am a resident of the United States, but have always had a deep interest in Canadian politics. I had the pleasure of being a visitor in the gallery of your House of Commons the other evening; but there was one incident (which may seem trivial), but at the same time, spoiled for me an otherwise enjoyable evening.

I observed, with some surprise, that a few of the honourable members kept their hats on practically the entire evening, only removing them when they addressed the house.

I left the gallery about 11 p.m., and when about ten feet from the exit door, I put my hat on; immediately a corpulent doorkeeper stood up snapped his fingers at me, pointing at my "lid."

I could not suppress a smile, whereupon the doorkeeper snapped his fingers again, this time with such surprising dexterity, and noise, that he was awarded for his pains by having the leader of the opposition and several members look up at him.

Not wishing to be arrested as disorderly, I removed the offending hat, but nevertheless, I would like very much to be enlightened as to the heinous crime, which I had apparently committed.

J.X.B.

Editor's note: Although the letter-writer doesn't say, the session to which he refers must have been held at the Victoria Museum (site of today's Museum of Nature), where Parliament sat after fire destroyed the Centre Block in February 1916.

SAYS DAYLIGHT SAVINGS A FAD

MAY 29, 1916

Please grant me a little of your space in regard to the movement for more daylight.

Having recently come from Detroit, Michigan, one of the movement's victims, I must say it is a failure. It mixed things up in general; trains, boats, shipping, electric car service from outside the city, etc. The travelling public got the brunt of it. Furthermore, one of the large auto factories claimed they lost 25 per cent of their efficiency during the first week.

As a country-wide movement it may be good but as a local affair a failure. Our city council in this case I think is showing good common sense in having nothing to do with the fad. Leave the clock as it is; people that want more daylight should go north for if they get a trial of it they will soon wish it in a place somewhat warmer.

People that keep regular hours know when they are due

to retire regardless of the clock. As for the extra hour I think the majority would spend it in yawning.

Dan O'Hara

Editor's note: Realizing production of weapons could be increased and energy saved if more work were done during the long daylight hours of summer, wartime governments ordered clocks moved an hour ahead. Germany acted first, in 1915, followed by Britain in 1916 and the U.S. in 1918, although some American states and cities acted sooner. In Canada, where time is a provincial jurisdiction, most provinces moved clocks ahead by the end of the war (Ontario did so in 1917). Although Daylight Savings Time was generally abandoned between the wars, most countries went back to the system during the Second World War. Its popularity led a number of U.S. and Canadian jurisdictions to introduce DST during peacetime summers (Ontario adopted the system in the early 1950s). But it wasn't until 1966 that DST was implemented across Canada, with the exception of Saskatchewan, which still operates on standard time year-round.

PROTESTS BOORISHNESS
JUNE 1, 1916

I wish to call attention to a state of affairs at Britannia which should not be tolerated for an instant further.

I have seen nearly every day good-sized fellows undressing and going in bathing entirely naked in the bay. Often they go in close to a nearby cottage to the annoyance of the residents or close to where a party of ladies are sitting, obliging them to leave.

Also I have seen fellows in the same condition come out of the water and deliberately show themselves and make fun of ladies while walking up the track to their cottages, or paddling on the lake.

The attention of the proper authorities is drawn to this with the hope that they will do their duty. Posters and a few examples would do much towards remedying the evil.

Let's Hope

Editor's note: Complaints about nude swimming at Britannia Bay, the Rideau River and elsewhere in the Ottawa area were printed regularly in the letters columns of the Ottawa Citizen during the early years of the century. Although the practice violated municipal law, it only occasionally drew the attention of police and rarely resulted in arrest. Judging by the date of the above complaint, Ottawa must have enjoyed a warm spring in 1916.

JOY RIDING TO AYLMER
JUNE 14, 1916

Having gazed at the beauties of the north shore of the Ottawa River from the Britannia streetcar line for several weeks, I set out on Saturday afternoon to visit Aylmer.

As I took my seat, shortly before 5 o'clock, in car 54 at Ottawa, a notice caught my eye — "Do not speak to the motorman." I didn't have a chance. The conductor talked to him all the way to Deschenes and about the on-

ly times the motorman's hands had any proximity to the machinery of motion was when he banged the whistle cord as cars passed in the other direction on the city-ward track.

What with wondering what was to happen at the next curve, admiring the motorman's skill in being able to drive without hands and eyes and incidentally holding on to the seat, I am afraid I did not see much of the scenery.

Safety First

NURSES AND SOLDIERS
JUNE 28, 1916

I have been informed that the nurses at Rideau Street Protestant Hospital have been forbidden to appear on the streets in the company of soldiers. My information comes from a most authoritative source and, if correct, should be communicated at once to the governors of the hospital to whom presumably it will be news.

The order is tantamount to saying that when a man enlists to serve his country he is donning the garb of disrepute and becomes at once an object of suspicion and aversion. It is not merely a reflection on the men who have enlisted and an insult to the king's uniform but a distinct restraint upon those who have arrived at the stage of giving serious consideration to their duty.

There would be some sense and more justice to the order if it had placed civilians and not soldiers under the ban. Trusting that you will bring this matter to the attention of the public.

An Unwilling Civilian

THE MOTOR PROCESSION
AUGUST 28, 1916

Standing on the corner of Albert and Bank streets at nine o'clock of a weekday morning I saw an endless line of automobiles whose sole occupant was the driver trailing behind a street car.

"What procession is this, or is it a funeral?" I queried of a bystander. And the reply received furnished the subject for this letter. "These are business men living within four blocks and all the way to Ottawa South and the West-End going to their respective places of business," he said.

"And what of the automobile?" I asked. "Oh, it is left standing all day on Queen street in a scorching sun and all sorts of inclement weather."

Well, Mr. Editor, is not this encroaching on public economy in more ways than one?

In the first place, the lifetime of the paint on the automobile, which is a big item, must of necessity be very short under such usage. Hence so many shabby cars are interspersed in the procession.

Would it not be much pleasanter for the short distance man to walk to his work, especially those of sedentary occupations?

And it would be cheaper for the long distance man to use the streetcar, which, in Ottawa is an up-to-date conveyance with very little to complain of.

Moreover, leaving the car in the garage would give the

wife and daughter an opportunity to go out an hour or two during the day. This would produce more lady drivers, which is very desirable as it is known to the Motor League that the hand that "rocks the cradle" is steadier on the driving wheel of an automobile than the average man's.

Finally, every added automobile crowded into a much-needed space is another menace to public safety, especially children and aged people who often have to scramble beyond their strength to get out of the road of the pesky thing.

Oscar Nordenfeldt

1917

Local: Ottawa Senators charter members of the new National Hockey League, founded in November with Frank Calder as first president.

National: Income tax introduced as a "temporary" wartime measure (July); Prime minister Borden takes conscription to voters in 1917 election, winning the country but losing Quebec — and creating deep divisions between the province and the rest of Canada (December); Explosion of a munitions ship in Halifax Harbour wipes out two square miles, killing 2,000 and injuring 9,000 (December)

World: U.S. Congress votes to enter war in Europe, changing the course of the conflict in favour of the Allies within months (April); Canadians capture Passchendaele, Belgium in one of the war's worst battles. Of 20,000 Canadians sent into the two-week battle, more than 15,000 are killed or wounded (November); Bolsheviks seize power in Russian coup d'état (November)

Births: Privy council clerk Gordon Robertson; jazz trumpeter Dizzy Gillespie; U.S. president John Kennedy; British writer Anthony Burgess.

Deaths: Prime minister Mackenzie Bowell; governor general Albert George (Earl Grey); Canadian painter Tom Thomson; Isabel Mackenzie King, mother of prime minister William Lyon Mackenzie King; chocolate maker Gilbert Ganong; ragtime composer Scott Joplin; William F. Cody, better known as frontier showman Buffalo Bill; Mata Hari, Dutch dancer and adventuress (executed for treason)

THE ILLUSTRATED HISTORY OF CANADA

With so many men off to war, women filled the gaps in the farm labour force.

OPPOSES EQUAL SUFFRAGE

JANUARY 2, 1917

Is it advisable and expedient that the voting franchise should be given to women? Will it better the conditions of home and state to do so? I surmise that it would be an improvement in some cases; but in sixty per cent of cases it is detrimental, and in, I shall not here state the appalling percentage, the ruination of the home.

God created woman as the companion of man — not as his inferior or superior. He gave to us His Ten Commandments to follow and the humble earthly home of his son in Nazareth to look to for example. Then take today's matrimonial altar and examine the sworn pledge torn into

shreds as a "scrap of paper" by the parties concerned. I fear it is, in only too many cases, apparently forgotten, once signed — like the sworn treaties of Germany and other nations.

I fear that men who are encouraging women to enter the political arena are lacking in fidelity. Surely, after this awful war, men will be purified to, at least, direct our political affairs without dragging women into the mire of politics.

Women of this wartime are, as far as they are able, performing manual labour: but, believe me, it is more than their vital strength can long endure. The outcome of it will be the physical wrecking of woman-kind and they will go back to their homes mentally, as well as physically, maimed.

Men of today, it is in your hands to protect the home and not desecrate it or its motherhood. Slam the door against defamity and then woman will be content to do her share in the path preordained for her to follow. Lead her not into the temptation of the political arena, but deliver her from the curse of immorality so rife at the present time.

Margaret J. Howard

THE NATIONAL HYMN OF CANADA

JANUARY 3, 1917

Will you kindly grant me some space in the columns of your valuable paper for the insertion of the enclosed extract from a letter written by Sapper R. Smith, Canadian Engineers, from "Somewhere in France."

I consider it a very effective answer to the questions set forth so recently by the executive committee of the Ottawa Women's Canadian Club, on the face of which is stated that "the committee feel it to be in the best interests of the club for the preservation of unity and good feeling that no patriotic songs or hymns, other than the National Anthem, should be sung."

Why this subject should be raised, at this time, seems supremely ridiculous, as it must be obvious to all right thinking people that *O Canada* is the only distinctive national hymn a strictly Canadian Club could adopt together with the grand and inspiring anthem *God Save the King*, which binds our heart so closely to the great and glorious Empire over which the sun never sets.

It was with the idea of Canada's growing importance within the Empire and the full realization of the fact that she was no longer a child sleeping in the arms of nature, that impelled Governor General Earl Grey in 1908 to urge the adoption of this beautiful prayer for our Canadian anthem.

If a great Englishman like Earl Grey could love Canada to the extent of deeming her worthy of having her own patriotic hymn at that time, how much more worthy is she now when her sons are doing and dying for the Empire.

Mary J. Lyons

Extract from letter sent Nov. 25, 1916 by Sapper R. Smith, Canadian Engineers, from "Somewhere in France:"

I was hurt and and angry last night when I read an article by Arthur Stringer in *Maclean's* magazine called "Wanted, a National Anthem." I'm afraid Mr. Stringer does not know what he is talking about. He calls *O Canada* dirgelike. He says what is needed is "an Anthem that should send tens of thousands singing to their deaths — a marching song to set men's hearts aflame."

If Mr. Stringer could stand beside the road upon which our troops march to the Somme, and hear company after company stumbling by in the darkness to the lilt of *O Canada* while the whole countryside is a mass of flashes and the thunder of the guns keeps the ground all atremble; and every one of those half-seen figures grotesquely burdened with their overland kit is just an everybody-boy thinking of the morning light and of the home and of the family love he'll probably never again see; then I think Mr. Stringer would forget that dirge stuff.

There is a lilt, a painfulness in the high notes, a poignancy in the very impossibility of singing it that makes *O Canada* a real battle hymn. Mr. Stringer needn't worry. If no one in Canada knew our Anthem before the War, the Overseas men all know it now.

THE CANADIAN NATIONAL ANTHEM
JANUARY 6, 1917

I am unaware how *God Save the King* became the national anthem, but it could never have acquired its posi-

tion by merit. The tune is of a very mediocre order and cannot for a moment be compared to the Russian or Austrian national anthems.

Of the words I am little judge, but it is obvious that the first three lines could have been expressed as easily and as nobly in one line as in three, and the words of another verse are so repugnant to many people that they flatly refuse to sing them.

In my humble opinion, the time is ripe for a new imperial National Anthem — one worthy of the immortality which awaits it and looks for its coming.

But when we come to *O Canada* we are in a more musicianly atmosphere altogether, for in it we have a tune at once worthy of Canada and the Canadian people. Its harmonic progressions are majestic in their tread, its stately and limited melody is eminently suitable for being sung by the "people," and, when sung by a large congregation, the emotional effect is as intense as that produced by the singing of the *Marseillaise* or Haydn's *Austria*.

H.S.

Editor's note: Canada's involvement in the war reignited the debate over a national anthem. While O Canada — composed for St. Jean Baptiste Day celebrations in 1880 by Calixa Lavallée, with lyrics by Judge Adolphe-Basile Routhier — had been sung regularly in Quebec for 35 years, it only came to the rest of the country around 1900 and was viewed with suspicion by some English-Canadians as a song extolling the sentiments of Quebec nationalism. Indeed, arguments over O Canada's lyrics continue to this day, two decades after its official adoption as the national anthem in 1980. During the First World War, the debate was mainly focused on which of the many English translations was best, and whether there was a need for more clearly patriotic lyrics. The following two letters reflect both of these elements.

O Canada was written by Calixa Lavallée, a French Canadian who served as a bugler in the Union army during the U.S. Civil War.

A NEW 'O CANADA'
JANUARY 13, 1917

What follows are proposed words to *O Canada* by Dr. A.D. Watson of Toronto, which I heartily endorse.

> Lord of the lands, beneath Thy bending skies,
> On field and flood, where'er our banner flies,
> Thy people lift their hearts to Thee,
> Their grateful voices raise:
> May our Dominion ever be
> A temple to Thy praise.
> Thy will alone, let all enthrone;
> Lord of the lands, make Canada Thine own.

Almighty Love, by Thy mysterious power,
In wisdom guide, with faith and freedom dower;
Be ours a nation evermore
That no oppression blights,
Where justice rules from shore to shore,
From Lakes to Northern Lights.
May Love alone for wrong atone;
Lord of the lands, make Canada Thine Own!

Lord of the worlds, with strong eternal hand,
Hold us in honour, truth and self-command;
The loyal heart, the constant mind,
The courage to be true,
Our far-extending Empire bind
And all the earth renew.
Thy name be known through every zone;
Lord of the worlds, make all the lands Thine own!

Yours, Herbert Sanders, Ottawa

ANOTHER 'O CANADA'

JANUARY 16, 1917

In Saturday's issue you published the latest addition to the multitudinous versions of *O Canada* by Dr. Watson of Toronto, sent you by Herbert Sanders of Ottawa. Therefore I ask you to publish the enclosed verses by T.B. Richardson (which if I mistake not, was the first translation).

O Canada, our father land of old
Thy brow is crowned with leaves of red and gold.
Beneath the shade of the Holy Cross
Thy children own their birth.
No stains thy glorious annals gloss
Since valour shields thy hearth.
Almighty God! on thee we call
Defend our rights, forfend this nation's thrall.
Defend our rights, forfend this nation's thrall.

Altar and throne, command our sacred love.
And mankind to us shall ever brothers prove.
O King of Kings, with Thy mighty breath
All our sons do Thou inspire
May no craven terror of life or death
Ere damp the patriots fire —
Our mighty call — loudly shall ring
As in the days of old "For Christ and the King."
As in the days of old "For Christ and the King."

Yours, Harry Allan

NEVER HEARD OF GEORGE

FEBRUARY 18, 1917

We have prohibited the Hearst newspapers from entering Canada, yet we are undoubtedly becoming 'Americanized' in our press. Last evening I entered a Bank Street book store and said to the gentleman in charge: "Has *The Globe* come in yet?" "Yes," he replied, and handed me a paper.

As I walked out I happened to glance at it. Shades of Hon. George Brown! It was the *Utica Globe*. I started back into the store to explain to the young man that *The Globe* in Canada meant etc., etc.; but what was the use?

Lachrymus

Editor's note: Newspapers from the Hearst chain, at the time the largest in the U.S., were kept out of Canada during the war years because of their stiff editorial stance against American involvement in the European conflict, which Canadian authorities thought might undermine support for the war north of the border. The ban was not lifted until after the war. (George Brown was the founder of The Globe, forerunner of today's Globe and Mail, and a Father of Confederation.)

A PLEA FOR THE SLACKER

FEBRUARY 24, 1917

I would like the opportunity to say a few words on behalf of a class of men who for some time have been the subject of bitter and scathing condemnation from pulpit, press and platform. I refer to the so-called "slacker" or "shirker" — that is to say the man of military age and fitness who does not feel it to be his duty to enlist for service overseas.

It appears to be universally assumed that the only motive actuating them is rank cowardice. The idea that a man may be deterred by principle from setting forth to slaughter men with whom he had no quarrel, in a war which his country had no voice in making, never seems to enter the heads of the hot-gospellers, pen-valiant scribes or bulldozing recruiters.

Settlers came in bygone days to Canada largely actuated with the view of escaping the evils of European militarism, and the entanglements and complications of secret diplomacy. Had it ever been supposed possible that they or their children would have been dragged into a European war, the stream of immigration would have been diverted to the United States.

The Imperialist doctrine that Canadians, either of native or British birth, are under any sort of obligation to render military service to the Empire abroad is of very recent origin. It was repudiated even by such staunch Conservatives as Sir John Macdonald and Sir Charles Tupper.

To force men to enlist for such service either by conscription or the process of moral compulsion now being carried on, is nothing less than a flagrant and insidious breach of faith.

I can respect and honour any man who enlists, sincerely believing it to be his duty to fight for the Empire, though I do not share his opinion. But neither he, nor the stay-at-homes and patriots-by-proxy who, immune themselves by age, position or infirmity, seeks to shine with a reflected glory, have any right to heap abuse and contumely on men who may be just as brave and conscientious as any soldier.

Phillip Thompson,
Oakville, Ont.

THE OTHER FELLOW'S DUTY

MARCH 10, 1917

This morning at about 9 a.m., a crowd of approximately 200 young men were assembled on the north side of Sparks Street, between O'Connor and Metcalfe. At first glance, it appeared as though the "Bantams," who have a recruiting office in this block, were assembling a party of recruits, for clothing or some other purpose.

Had this been the case it would have been the best bunch of recruits for a long time; but it was not so, they were only a party of slackers, waiting to buy tickets for the evening's hockey match.

What are our recruiting offices doing? Here we have an assembly of at least 150 men, of the required age for enlisting, who without shame can stand in line on our most public street, jostling and pushing for what? To obtain a ticket for a hockey match, when their friends and relatives are calling them to come over and help.

The fact that these men could loiter on the street after 9 a.m. proves that their work was not of such an important nature as to be used as an excuse for shirking their duty to their families and their country.

R.E.

CRITICAL LACK OF FARM LABOUR

APRIL 17, 1917

Much has already been said or written with regard to the alarming decrease of cultivators in Canada. However, as we are, or very soon will be, face to face with a national calamity we need offer no apology to discuss this grave question.

When the war broke out, Canada was called upon to go to the aid of England. The minister of militia as well as the prime minister promised 100,000 men. There was a quick response by legions of men who for various reasons enlisted. Elated by the first response, the Canadian authorities promised the British government as many more. After a short time, the number was raised to 500,000. If anyone raised a voice in protest, at such extravagance, at the time, he would have been accused of treason.

We fear that now it is almost too late to call a halt to the process that has brought Canada to the verge of ruin.

Apart altogether from the base number of troops that have been taken from the country, thousands of young men have been lured from the farms into the munitions factories.

The result of this is an appalling dearth of workers for the farm lands. If the present conditions last for another six months, even with help from female farm volunteers from the cities, then we shall face a severe food crisis during the present year.

To remedy a condition that is leading to national ruin, drastic steps should be taken. It is urgent that many, if not all, the munition factories be closed, and the workers released for civilized labour. Release all the farmer boys wherever possible.

The Allies do not need troops or munitions now, but food. Canadians could help the Allies better, if not as bravely, by tilling the soil, than in carrying a rifle or lying in trenches.

George O'Toole, Cantley, P.Q.

CHANCE FOR THE GIRLS

OCTOBER 12, 1917

I am a homesteader and am quite sincere in what I have to say. I am English, Protestant, age 30 next birthday, 5 feet 8 inches tall, 155 lbs. weight, dark hair, brown eyes, healthy, strong, ambitious: never drank, never smoked and don't intend to.

My homestead of 100 acres is about one day's journey from Ottawa on the C.P.R. and only four miles from a railway station and small village. I am logging in a camp here for the winter and will go back to my homestead in spring.

In the meantime I must appeal for a wife, a good sensible girl, no school girl will do, mind you. Must like simple life and be of an affectionate disposition and kind; a good cook essential, passing fair, between 20 and 30 years of age, but not to a year either way. Must be sweethearts till next summer.

P.S. Any photos sent must have stamps to return if need be.

Thanking you, Mr. Editor, for your kindness,
George W. Brown, in care of Hope Lumber Co.,
Dean Lake, Ont.

1918

Local: Roy Brown, an airman from Carleton Place, shoots down famous German flying ace Manfred von Richthofen, better known as the Red Baron (April); Ottawa receives its first delivery of airmail. It comes from Toronto (August); Board of Health closes theatres, schools in effort to control flu outbreak (October); An estimated 25,000 people and 1,000 automobiles pour onto the streets to celebrate the end of the war (November); First live radio broadcast of music is sent from Montreal to Château Laurier Hotel (November)

National: Canadian soldiers break through German trenches at Amiens, a day celebrated as "the black day for the German army" (July)

World: Amid civil unrest, the Bolsheviks execute czar Nicholas II and his family (July); Germany signs the armistice to end four years of conflict that claimed more than 10 million lives (November)

Births: Canadian political economist George Grant; jazz singer Ella Fitzgerald; baseball great Ted Williams; conductor Leonard Bernstein; writer Alexander Solzhenitsyn

Deaths: French composer Claude Debussy

IN DEFENCE OF QUEBEC

JANUARY 16, 1918

A great deal of comment and criticism has been published in the Ontario papers about the resolution of Mr. Francoeur which is to this purpose: If the other provinces are not satisfied with Quebec, this province is willing to go out of Confederation.

In the eyes of many critics, this simple proposition, which has been suggested as an answer to the wild insults hurled at Quebec as a result of the conscription matter, smacks of high treason. I do not approve of it, but why should it be attacked in such strong language?

I am always amazed to see people forget their history so quickly. Perhaps that forgetfulness is not very sincere, because it seems to me that newspapermen who are pretty well up on Canadian history should not lose sight of the fact that a present member of Parliament [William S. Fielding], a strong Unionist, proposed in 1886 a series of resolutions in the legislative assembly of Nova Scotia, concluding in the following words: "The government deem it absolutely necessary to ask permission from the Imperial parliament to withdraw from the union with Canada."

With this platform, Honourable Mr. Fielding swept the province at the next general election. Surely, Mr. Editor, the enemies of the Province of Quebec will agree with me that this resolution goes far beyond the timid expression of opinion of Mr. Francoeur.

Have the same men also forgotten that, at the general election of 1867, the province of Nova Scotia returned a unanimous verdict, save one vote, against Confederation? It is very strange to have to remark that what is a mortal sin in Quebec is not even a venial one in other provinces.

We have not forgotten the harsh words directed against Quebec because that province voted against conscription, and still nothing was said against Prince Edward Island, Nova Scotia and Australia, who have condemned the same system of raising soldiers.

Is it a wonder, considering all this, that Quebec feels annoyed at the attitude of some of our partners in confederation?

St. George Le Moine, Montreal

Editor's note: In early 1917, as it became clear voluntary recruitment could no longer keep pace with the First World War's high casualty rates, Prime Minister Robert Borden was forced to consider conscription to draft soldiers into the army. He took the question to voters in December of that year, unleashing one of the most bitterly fought campaigns in Canadian history. In Quebec, Premier Henri Bourassa rallied anti-conscription forces and argued Canada had done enough to help Britain. In Ontario, Borden's supporters condemned these anti-conscriptionists as traitors. In the election, Borden won the country but lost in Quebec, setting in motion an acrid national debate of the type suggested in the above letter. (The Francoeur mentioned in the letter was Joseph Napoleon Francoeur, a Liberal member of the Quebec National Assembly and a staunch Quebec nationalist.)

DR. DERBY ON 'THE HIDDEN HAND'

APRIL 10, 1918

During the present unpleasantness in Quebec over the conscription issue, the temptation to be intemperate in the other provinces has proven almost irresistible. The *Kingston Standard* advises "To Shoot Them Down." This is unfortunate: it is also unwise for other newspapers to copy it and thus give the idea further publicity.

As matters develop and facts become public, confidence in the wisdom of our leaders returns. Sir Robert Borden's recent speech shows plainly that the government has the situation well in hand, and that the vapourings of a few malcontents is not going to stampede the equanimity of the people of this country.

Sir Sam Hughes [the minister of war], who has never at any time lacked the courage of his convictions, got down to business in a very few words when he said the trouble in Quebec was due to "the Hidden Hand." As no one for a moment missed his meaning, my sins can scarcely be dyed any deeper scarlet if I say in plain language that the teaching and influence of the clergy of the Roman Catholic church, with a few honourable exceptions, has been pro-German propaganda. And of this, this squabble in Quebec is the logical conclusion.

That the people of the province of Quebec, after all these years of appeals to prejudice and passion by those posing as their spiritual leaders, should give such a slight response to this vicious teaching, shows that they are a people well worthy of our best efforts to cultivate a better understanding with them.

As thousands of us who have intimately known the

French-Canadian have for long years contended, beneath the surface in French Canada there is a strong current of common sense and honesty of purpose. Today there are thousands of right-minded men in the ranks of the French-Canadians who are praying that their English fellow-countrymen, strong in the strength of Union, will not give texts for future sermons to their clergy, whose gospel has always been one of distrust and hatred.

Yes, the ambition of the French Catholic clergy has always been to drive a wedge of suspicion and ill-feeling between their people and the English. Even when the English-speaking are Roman Catholics in religion, they have not always escaped from this form of persecution.

Yet, in sum, the situation in Canada is not a critical one. The majority who are loyal to British ideals are united as one man against Quebec; Quebec lies helpless at their feet. Will the rest of Canada wreak a vengeance on Quebec because of the venomous teaching of her clergy? They will if they wish to play into "The Hidden Hand."

There is not in Canada today a well-informed man who does not know that the clergy are the head and front of this offending; but how many are there who will take their lives in their hands and say so?

Dr. W.J. Derby,
Plantagenet, Ont.

SOME MESSENGER BOYS
MAY 18, 1918

Permit me to bring a serious question to the notice of your readers, a matter which concerns practically every business house in the city here, and relates to the class of boys obtainable for the delivery of parcels, etc.

The last three boys we engaged are now in the hands of the police, and in talking this matter over with other storekeepers and also with the police officials, they deplore the unsatisfactory methods in dealing with juvenile offenders, which seem to have done nothing but develop a class of boy which it is unsafe to employ in a store.

On a recent occasion I attended the juvenile court myself in connection with one of our lads, and became convinced that this court holds no fears for the juvenile offenders. In fact, to have been through the court seems to be to them a matter of pride.

We would suggest the time is ripe for something to be done to improve this state of things, as really the character of the majority of the boys is something which is a disgrace to any city.

This is not a reflection on the better class of boy, but if the lads in question are to be saved from becoming hardened criminals, more drastic action will have to be taken than is at present followed.

In school, a boy found guilty of what, compared with stealing, is a really minor offence is sent to the headmaster for castigation, whilst a boy who steals and comes up before the juvenile court is told to either bring the goods or the value of same and is allowed to go free, and the representatives of different societies do all they can to get the boy off with as little punishment as possible.

Is not this system one which tends to develop criminals instead of preventing crime?

A.J. Ames, Managing Director,
E.R. Watts and Son, Canada Ltd.

Editor's note: E.R. Watts was a London-based maker of mapping equipment and engineering instruments.

RIDEAU RIVER CONTAMINATION
MAY 29, 1918

It is one of the frailties of human nature that what we can't see doesn't worry us. We will scour our houses until they shine, rush for a swatter at the buzz of every fly, sterilize every drink, and inspect with rigour the food we eat — we go so far as to advertise a clean-up week, offer ourselves up for reproof to the Boy Scouts and submit to the dispersal of our pet piles of fertilizer obtained at much labour and expense.

But when it comes to making an open sewer of the Rideau River, we regard it as the other fellows business, and go on swatting flies, wondering why they come so fast. Well, they come because they are breeding in the thousands at the foot of each street in Ottawa South, where pipes are discharging their filth into the river. They pour forth their contents at the foot of our lawns, by the side of our boat docks, into the sluggish channel which flows through the heart of our residence district.

Yet in this river groups of boys go swimming; from this river in the winter, our ice is cut. It would be well for us, before the 90-degree weather strikes, to reflect upon certain typhus epidemics known to this city in the past to apprehend that struggle of science against infantile paralysis.

Cleanliness for our city is a matter of individual effort. The sanction of the provincial board of health has nothing to do with it.

A. K. C.

UNPLEASANT MARRIAGES
JULY 3, 1918

Do you think that you would enjoy a married life if your husband were spending his idle hours away from home, in places that were not fit for any decent man to be?

Often, while sitting alone with my family, I have thought of my mismated life. I wondered what the future would bring, having a desire for a better life, not only for myself, but the family also. The one that has made my life miserable, not being satisfied by spending his idle hours in places of immorality, bringing home diseases that would land one in the hospital — that would not only land me in the hospital, but would be inherited by the children. I often think it is no wonder that there are so many puny, sickly, diseased children. If married life was honestly lived by both parties, I am sure we would see healthier children and happier ones.

Why is it that provision is not made in parliament by those in power to liberate the unhappy and mismated people? Surely there should be a way for a woman out of this tangle. Why is a woman bound to support and protect her family, and the father running at large? Are there no rights for a woman in a mismated life like this?

I ask, is it a square deal to leave a woman to support and protect her family, all because she would not allow herself to be sent to the hospital by an unclean and brutal husband?

One Who Loves a Good Home

CAMOUFLAGE CHIVALRY
JULY 24, 1918

I would like to relate an incident which happened in our fair city some time ago: two elderly ladies who got on a crowded street car were not offered seats by any of the gentlemen (?) on the car.

After the car had gone a few blocks, two short-skirted maidens, with camouflage complexions, got on and immediately men popped up and were quite eager to dispose of their seats.

Would they be called chivalrous young men? Perhaps — in the opinion of the young ladies. But in the opinion of the elderly ladies, it was a case of camouflage chivalry.

M.B.

THEY ARE SURELY "IT"
SEPTEMBER 7, 1918

To every man who loves womanhood there comes an unconscious protest every time he hears the enemy nation spoken of as "she." The Prussian nation has forfeited the right to this noble appellation and a world-wide movement to stop the practice might help to bring an erring people to their senses.

Neither does that nation deserve the pronoun of manliness, but should be spoken of as "it" — a thing unlovely — a Frankenstein — a mad gorilla.

So let us alter our terminology: Call Prussia "It." Call Germany "It." Call the Kaiser "it." Call the Crown Prince "it." In the case of the last two, the thought is that the Kaiser is not a man, but a title, and his son a sub-title — hence the lower case 'i.'

These suggestions are made, not in a spirit of hatred for an unfortunate, hypnotized nation, but in a spirit of love for womanhood, and defence of her prerogatives.

If all editors in all Allied nations would, by common consent, adopt the neuter pronouns, as suggested, the note of scorn in these jarring pronouns might have far-reaching reflex action on minds benumbed for generations by false teachings of school and press and pulpit.

Let's call Germany "It."

Christopher North, Jr.

P.S.: An unnecessary addition on my part is the reminder that Germany is never referred to as the "Motherland." What a significant comment on "Its" estimate of womanhood.

CULVER PICTURES
Terminology in reference to Germany should be changed, and even the Kaiser should be referred to as "it," a letter said.

DOING AS DONE BY
NOVEMBER 22, 1918

For four years, the Germans have been inflicting on Belgium and France every cruelty that a devilish mind could invent: starvation, murder, rape, arson, robbery, all kinds of fiendish torture. They revelled in their brutality, wallowing in their filthy crimes to women and children, and boasting of their power to do these things.

Now that Bolshevism and anarchy threaten them, they squeal to their late victims to protect them from similar horrors. I say, let the grovelling, sneaking cowards protect themselves, they deserve neither help nor sympathy; it would be a just retribution if they suffered all that they have inflicted on others, and it is to be hoped that the Allies will not lift a hand to save them

Nemesis

OBJECTS TO PAYING FOR DAY OFF
NOVEMBER 23, 1918

The employees of the American Bank Note Co. were sure a disappointed crowd when they opened their pay envelopes and found they were docked for the day they celebrated peace.

Could you imagine such a dishonourable thing after such a percentage of their boys sacrificed so much for the shareholders who have reaped a good harvest during the war? Last week they actually pleaded with their employees to boost the Victory Bond so that they might become the winners of the honour flag which they sure succeeded in. And to think they took the advantage of one day's pay after professing to be so patriotic.

One Who Knows

OUT WITH GERMAN STREET NAMES
NOVEMBER 28, 1918

Is it not time the city fathers considered the desirability of changing the name of Wurtemberg Street to some name a little less German? To many of the citizens living in the vicinity it is a source of daily annoyance to have Germany so forcibly thrust upon them.

Permit me to suggest names a little more appropriate for the name of the street on which our highly esteemed premier [Robert Borden] lives when he is in Ottawa. Such names as Foch, Haig or Currie might be used without any chance of causing ill-feeling to anyone called upon to use the name regularly.

R.W.

Editor's note: The name was not changed — in fact, it remains Wurtemberg Street today — likely because it was named in honour of Princess Charlotte of Britain, who became Charlotte of Wurttemberg (note the two ts) after her 1797 marriage to Prince Frederick, heir to the throne of the

German kingdom of Wurttemberg. Charlotte Street, which is nearby, was likely named in her honour, too.

A WIDOW'S LAMENT

NOVEMBER 30, 1918

I am a soldier's widow, with five children, and I have given up my best, except my children — a good and true husband, to protect the country, who is numbered with the dead.

This is what we get in return for the great sacrifice we have made: We are paid $48 for ourself and $3 for each child, no matter how the ages run. There is no mother, no matter how thrifty she may be, who can for those amounts provide clothing and food for a child, keep it clean, warm, and make a home for it; it must be lacking in something.

Well, I suppose the month we clothe the child we haven't got to feed it, for if we buy 1 pair of boots and 1 pair of stockings, two sets of underwear, then the $3 is gone. Now, I have four children going to school, the youngest I take with me to work, where I go washing and cleaning by the day, a thing I haven't done for years until the present.

I have to sit up every night until 11 and 12 to do my own work and I feel if the wheel of fortune doesn't soon turn, my health will give way.

I have tried many times for a position in the civil service, but am always put off with the excuse that there is no vacancy — yet I know there are so many other widows working there who have no children and just work to pass the time.

It is true the widows are not having a square deal and I think it is time someone took an interest to try and provide a little more for the fallen heroes' children and give Honour to whom Honour is Due.

A soldier's widow

1919

Local: Ottawa gets its first motorized ambulance (January); Influenza epidemic claims more than 500 lives in Ottawa region (January to March)
National: More than 10,000 brave Ottawa's winter cold to watch funeral cortege for Sir Wilfrid Laurier (February); General strike paralyses Winnipeg, where an armed assault by the RCMP kills one person and injures 30 (June)
World: U.S. Congress passes alcohol prohibition law, making it part of the Constitution (January); Briton John Alcock and American Arthur Brown make first non-stop flight over the Atlantic Ocean, flying from Newfoundland to Ireland (June)
Births: Prime minister Pierre Trudeau; Russian spy Igor Gouzenko; Alabama governor George Wallace; writers Doris Lessing and William Burroughs; folksinger Pete Seeger
Deaths: Canadian physician William Osler; French impressionist painter Pierre Renoir; Frank Baum, author of Oz books

CIVIL SERVANTS' LUNCH HOUR

JANUARY 24, 1919

Whosoever is a civil servant shall lunch between the hours of 12:30 p.m. and 2:00 p.m. Such is the command issued to thousands of Ottawa workers by the recent order-in-council of the Dominion cabinet.

I wonder if those gentlemen assembled at the table of the state stopped to think of the inconvenience and expense which their act would cause to a very great number of households, and whether they considered the extra work they thereby imposed on hundreds, if not thousands, of already overworked mothers and wives.

In the past, civil servants usually selected their lunch hour to conform with that of the rest of the household, thereby lessening the labours of the mother or wife by partaking of lunch "en famille." How many mothers already have reason to complain because the children lunch at 12, hubby at 12:30 pm., cousin John at one, and sister Jeanne at 1:30 p.m., and they have to keep the food warm for an hour and a half every day, thereby consuming extra fuel? Now the new order will greatly increase the number of such cases.

In commercial establishments it is often necessary for business reasons to create a spread in the lunch hour; however, such is not the case, with rare exceptions, in the civil service, and I cannot see that the efficiency of the staffs will be increased by such an order.

If the government desires to make certain that its employees do not leave their work for more than an hour and a half for lunch, why not let everyone choose his or her hour of departure and check the time of their absence by time recorders or otherwise.

S.A.J.

Editor's note: Strictly prescribed lunch hours for public servants continued in one form or another until today, although they are not as closely monitored now as they were at the time of this letter. Today's lunch break is usually an hour, and the work day generally runs from 9 a.m. to 4:30 p.m. Until the 1950s, when the civil service work week was cut from 5½ to five days, a typical work day began at 9 a.m. and ended at 4 p.m. (Monday to Friday) and from 9 a.m. to noon (Saturday).

TELEPHONE SERVICE

FEBRUARY 22, 1919

The war has taught me to put up with any inconvenience without grumbling; however, now that we are returning to normal conditions why should we be compelled to endure a most inefficient telephone service.

There is not a day that I could not with good reason register a complaint; however, even doing this seems to gain no relief. I am compelled to use the telephone quite frequently. As often as not there is a delay in answering my call, a wrong number given, nothing doing after my call is given, a cut off during conversation, or some equally annoying result. I know that mine is not an isolated case, as I hear the same complaints on every hand.

If the Bell Telephone Company, instead of trying to make the public pay a higher charge for a poor service, would use some of their large profits in bringing their service up to a better standard, it would be very much more to the point.

A subscriber

PROTEST VACCINATION
MARCH 22, 1919

In trying to enforce the medical fetish of vaccination on an unwilling public it seems to me that the germ-huns owe it to the public to give a definition of what vaccination really is.

Unfortunately, no medical man has ever had the candour to give such a definition — for obvious reasons, for the only truthful definition is about as follows: "Vaccination is the inoculation of the pure blood of a healthy individual with the filth obtained from the festering sore on a diseased calf, with the object of preventing a possible but altogether improbable disease, viz. smallpox."

There are many people who fail to realize the seriousness of this apparently trivial operation. A vaccination is only "successful" when the victim's blood has been thoroughly contaminated with the virus. It is this contamination which is supposed to protect against smallpox, and the "protection" only lasts as long as the blood remains polluted, according to the theory. One might think that the doctors had precise knowledge of what they were doing when they interfere with the established order of nature, but sad to relate, such is not the case — as the following facts will show:

No doctor knows the composition of the vaccine virus.

No doctor knows what the effect is on the blood.

No bacteriologist can guarantee that any given lot of virus will not communicate syphilis, or lockjaw — or result in death.

No doctor can guarantee his vaccinated victim against smallpox.

No doctor can say how long the supposed protection will last.

I invite your Dr. [Robert] Law [Ottawa's medical officer of health] to come out and say wherein any of these statements are inaccurate — and prove it. I understand the Anti-Vaccination League of America will pay him $1,000.00 if he can do so.

There is no reliable evidence that vaccination prevents smallpox, or ever saved a single life. On the other hand, a world experience of 130 years proves that vaccination is utterly useless as a prophylactic, and that it has been, and is, the cause of untold disease, suffering and death, and a probable large factor in the dissemination of syphilis, cancer, tuberculosis, leprosy, and the degeneration of the human race.

Health is the only preventive of smallpox; let us fight for it. Those who have no faith in health can get vaccinated — and leave us alone.

S.L. Macbean,
57 Victoria Street, Montreal

Editor's note: S.L. (Stephen) Macbean was for a time the head of the Canadian branch of the Anti-Vaccination League of America. Despite vociferous protests over several decades, the league's efforts ultimately failed and vaccination became the principal weapon in the battle against contagious disease throughout North America and Europe.

A SIX-HOUR DAY
MAY 10, 1919

Lord Leverhulme, chairman of Lever Bros. Limited of Great Britain, outlined at the company's last annual meeting his plan for a six-hour work day, which was adopted. His speech was as follows:

"Now I come to . . . the proposed adoption of a six-hour working day. We have worked out our scheme, and I may tell you that all the trade unions consulted are most anxious to make the scheme workable and satisfactory, and that the government, as far as the state of the law will permit, are equally anxious. It is anticipated that the consent of the Home Office will be given to the draft proposals which have now been submitted to them.

"The general feature of the scheme is, with regard to day-workers and piece-workers, that we shall work in two shifts — six hours each shift. The morning shift will commence at 7 o'clock, and, after a break of a quarter of an hour from 8.45 for some light refreshment, they will continue to work until 1.15 p.m. At 1.15 the morning-shift work for the day will be over. They will not return to their work until 7 o'clock the next morning. This makes a total of six working hours per day, with fifteen minutes break for a meal, for six days in the week — Monday to Saturday included.

"When we come to consider the afternoon shift, there is a strong feeling and desire to retain the Saturday afternoon half-holiday; and to meet this wish the afternoon shift will only work five afternoons, the average being seven hours 12 minutes each afternoon, instead of six afternoons of six hours. Therefore, the afternoon shift will commence at a quarter-past one (there will be a break of half-an-hour for refreshment from 4.45 to 5.15 p.m.) and will stop at 9 p.m., but on Friday work will stop at a quarter of an hour earlier at 8.45 so that the weekly average is thirty-six hours.

"For each shift, the rate of wages will be exactly the same for a 36-hours week as for a 48-hours week. In addition, wages will be paid by cheque, and each employee will choose his own bank for deposit, not the firm's bank."

This experiment, both as to solving labour unrest, and at the same time maintaining production at a standard that gives a just reward to both capital and labour, will be watched with great interest in Canada.

H., Ottawa

WHAT IS DRUNK?

MAY 31, 1919

When a man is drunk every cell in his body is drunk. The body is composed of millions of living cells each having its own particular work to do. When a cell is drunk it cannot perform its function efficiently. Likewise, when a man is drunk he is neither efficient nor capable of doing his work properly.

One duty of the red blood cells is to carry oxygen. The duty of the white blood cells is to fight the disease germs. When the oxygen carriers are drunk the system is poisoned by waste matters that should have been burnt up by oxygen. When the destroyers of disease germs are drunk, infection is liable to occur.

The British War Office is authority for the statement that animals that are immune to certain diseases; that is, cannot be infected even by inoculation, lose that immunity and are easily infected if given a dose of whiskey 24 hours before inoculation. Drinkers are more liable to disease than abstainers, and when ill they have a much poorer chance of recovery.

When these facts are generally known there will be few who will indulge in alcohol in any form, or in any dose. A great effort must be made to spread this truth. We must stir ourselves or run the risk of losing what we have gained by years of hard work.

H. Arnott, M.D., M.C.P.S.,
[Medical Doctor; Member, College of Physicians and Surgeons]
Department of Social Service, Toronto

EMANCIPATION OF WOMAN

JUNE 21, 1919

I agree to a certain extent that only for women's assistance in the war it would have gone against us; but now the soldiers are being discharged from the army to find a lot of work they can do is being done by women who won't give it up.

Women who, because they worked in factories and made a lot of money, may think they have done their bit in winning the war, but the war-worn soldier has done a lot more. They have undergone trials that not a woman in a thousand could endure, surely after they have fought and hungered and thirsted, bled and suffered so that our women could live in security, surely they deserve some consideration when they are seeking work.

I appeal to all women to see that discharged soldiers are not kept out of a job by a woman. Few women have any conception of what these soldiers, most of them, have gone through. It is not easy to tell, these soldiers say — it was Hell! It is difficult to conceive what that hell of noise, of wounds, of wet and misery, of sleepless nights and constant peril can be like. If any one woman thinks she knows, then let her be sure that the actuality was a hundred times worse than she believes it to be, and let her be merciful to the fellows who need the work.

If I am not right in this, ask the soldiers themselves. I know that lots of women do not understand the situation, but now that I have told them, I hope they will combine

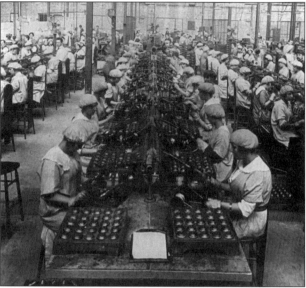

CANADA: A CELEBRATION OF OUR HERITAGE

Women who have been working to help the war effort should ensure that soldiers being discharged are not kept out of a job, a writer argued.

their efforts to help our wounded and discharged men to secure employment.

H. Lévesque

HULL'S LITTLE JOKE

AUGUST 29, 1919

Our neighbors in Hull are not without a sense of humour. They have erected pretty signs at various points advising the public that the speed limit is 16 miles per hour, and requesting visitors who have braved the perils of Hull's roadways to come again.

A Joke Lover

Editor's note: Ottawa's speed limit was still 10 miles per hour in 1919.

FAVOURS NEW POLITICAL PARTY

NOVEMBER 5, 1919

It is quite noticeable by your recent editorial that you consider the present government to have outgrown its usefulness. No one who has taken any interest in the present political situation can doubt that opinion is the opinion of the country.

Now, Mr. Editor, I think that the time is ripe for the formation of an entirely new party for, as can be seen, the opposition's only policy is flat rejection of all the government proposes.

What is needed in my humble opinion is a party that represents all classes and there is only one body in Canada today who can do that — and that is the returned soldiers. They represent all walks of life, all trades and professions and when it is taken into consideration all they have done, it is only reasonable to suppose that they would make as good a job of governing the country as they did in saving it.

G.W. Forster, Westboro

SAYS THINKING IS NOT ENOUGH

NOVEMBER 12, 1919

You publish in the November 10 issue a bulletin signed by "Geo. E. Foster, Acting Prime Minister," in which we are asked to devote two whole minutes to concentrated thought in reverence to the dead, and in appreciation of the sacrifices of the living who fought the long fight for freedom, etc., etc.

Does the honourable acting prime minister and the rest of his cabinet imagine for the brief space of those two minutes that they will have shown their appreciation of the sacrifices of the living? The government policy as far as the returned men are concerned would lead one to believe that they are over-estimating the thought period by something quite a little over a minute and a half.

When we run them from office we will give the honourable ministers something to think about that will require more than two minutes thought, so if they have a second or two to spare tomorrow at eleven o'clock after paying due respect, let them also bear in mind that returned men are entitled to just a little bit more in the way of substantial appreciation rather than the suggested form of this "stop and think for two minutes" business, which, in the words of one of the comic strip artists — "doesn't mean anything."

Unsigned, Ottawa

MOTOR TRAFFIC ON SPARKS STREET

DECEMBER 3, 1919

I would be strongly opposed to the proposed scheme to divert motor traffic from Sparks Street. As remarked by some of our prominent businessmen, "Ottawa is no country town," but the carrying out of this project would certainly put this city in a much lower category, and, in fact, would make it a genuine laughing stock.

Sparks Street is the principal business street because it is the direct connecting link between upper and lower town and it is on account of the traffic that the great volume of business is attracted to shops and stores on that thoroughfare.

By switching the traffic you would switch business. Shops and stores on Sparks Street have high values, rentals, taxes, etc., because of their location in the traffic area. Merchants should not be made to suffer, by loss of traffic, for what can only be termed negligence on the part of either the general public or the public bodies.

The "automobile menace," as it is called, should not be very great in this city when it is considered that Ottawa has fewer cars for its size than most cities and towns in North America; and yet it is doubtful if any one can be found where regulations exist that would parallel this proposed scheme.

No, the proper solution would be to enforce our present regulations, and to do so we should have an increase in the traffic squad and an increase in their activities. Offenders against these regulations should be heavily punished, especially those breaking speed-limit and street-crossing rules. The inadequacies of traffic control are indirectly responsible for many of the accidents caused by the reckless driving of automobiles, because many drivers seem to think that they are entitled to do just as they please and vie with each other in carelessness and recklessness.

Pedestrians should not be permitted to cross the principal streets at points other than the intersections and safety would be practically assured if those intersections were controlled by traffic police.

A.M. McKay,
Manager, Ottawa Motor Transport

Editor's note: Ottawa Motor Transport was a local association of automobile owners. Sparks Street was not transformed into a pedestrian mall until the 1960s.

"For mercy sake, ye rulers, awaken your conscience and safeguard the public by making the maximum for autos on highway not more than fifteen miles per hour, and less than five miles per hour upon city streets, or society must fall by its own inertia!"

— September 29, 1928

1920-1929

1920

Local: Ottawans crowd into Château Laurier ballroom to hear first local radio transmission of live concert from Montreal (May); Cornerstone laid for new Civic Hospital on Carling Avenue (December)

National: Canada becomes a founding member of the League of Nations, forerunner of the United Nations (January); Winnipeg Falcons win hockey title at the first Winter Olympics in Belgium (March); Robert Borden resigns as Conservative prime minister because of poor health; he is succeeded by Arthur Meighen (July)

World: Boston Red Sox sell Babe Ruth to the New York Yankees for $125,000 (January); American women win right to vote (August)

Births: Jazz legends Charlie Parker and Thelonius Monk; writer Pierre Berton; boxer Sugar Ray Robinson; science fiction writers Isaac Asimov and Ray Bradbury

Deaths: Alphonse Désjardins, founder of Caisse Populaire; Arctic explorer Robert Peary

INCREASE IN CITY HALL SALARIES

FEBRUARY 18, 1920

As a citizen of Ottawa, I am thoroughly dissatisfied with the increase in salary given to the mayor and the city controllers and the way and time of doing it. Why was the advance not made before the [December] municipal election? Why were we not told before the election that such was contemplated? Was it not a sad want of straightforwardness?

It will be said that the increase won't be much when spread over the whole city. Every little helps to make the whole so large that it grinds the poor who pay their taxes with difficulty. There are not a few of those who have their taxes increased by that advance who are unable to procure sufficient meat, potatoes, milk, and butter for themselves and children — eggs are not to be thought of. Could not the council have waited till the price of food got lower?

Your newspaper has done a great deal of good work in advocating reforms; but I am greatly dissatisfied that you did not publish a few strong editorials on this subject. You could, I think, have prevented this increase. Two strong letters appeared in your columns, but I failed to see a word from your editor, so I must assume you were in favour of the raise or you did not think it good policy to speak.

When the mayor and controllers ran for office and were very anxious to be elected it was a silent assent that they were willing to serve for what was then the salary. If this is not now breaking faith with the people, what do you call it? And those whose fidelity is found wanting are not, I am afraid, morally qualified to municipally govern our city.

A Voter

Editor's note: The salary increases, approved with only one dissenting vote, raised the mayor's pay by $1,500 a year to $5,000 and controllers' stipend by $1,000 to $2,500, a whopping 67-per-cent hike. The mayor and controllers likely earned additional money at other jobs, since their elected posts were not considered full-time positions. By comparison, the average salary in Ontario in 1920 was about $1,200.

IN VOGUE: 75 YEARS OF STYLE

Women's clothes were improper and immodest, according to one official.

WOMEN'S DRESS

FEBRUARY 23, 1920

The world has been reading in its newspapers the opinions of prominent New York women on the prevailing style of female dress. About this, Miss Laura M. Riegalman, M.D., chief of the Bureau of Child Hygiene in Brooklyn, is reported as saying:

"Emphatically, I consider the present models in women's clothing improper and immodest. Skirts too short and too narrow. Five or six inches from the ground is sufficient to secure comfort and short enough for all sanitary purposes. The slit skirt is vulgar, and fabrics such as chiffon, georgette crepe and net should never be worn without a proper lining.

"The modern evening gown is greatly to be condemned. It is cut too low both in front and in back and offers bare shoulders. These gowns are worn by women of fashion and social standing, and young girls point them out as examples of good taste to old-fashioned mothers who rightly object to their daughter's evening costumes.

"For the past three years I have been a lecturer on social diseases, and in the course of my work have visited cantonments [lodgings for troops] where men have confessed to me their transgressions of the moral law. In so many cases they placed the blame on the lack of sexual knowledge in dress on the part of their women friends.

"You doubtless think I am speaking very strongly, but I assure you that if the women who wear the fashionable clothes could hear the tales of tragedy that have been encountered by the social service workers during the last two years, they would be surprised and aggrieved."

A reader

MARRIAGE TOO COSTLY

MARCH 6, 1920

To get a suitable house for his family nowadays, a man must pay from thirty to forty dollars a month. Potatoes are selling for four dollars a bag, sugar at eighteen cents a pound, coal at fourteen dollars a ton, meat is almost out of reach and flour at fourteen dollars a barrel. I could mention numerous other articles that are required for the up-keep of a household which are sky high.

So I would like to know how a man such as myself earning twenty dollars a week is going to get married and expect to make a home and make the woman he marries happy? I am a single man and I am not a coward — I have seen service in France for three and a half years. No, marriage is not too dangerous. It is too costly.

E.W. Brunette

A CRITICAL VISITOR

MARCH 8, 1920

Being a visitor to this capital of Canada, I cannot help noticing the disgusting state of your streets, especially all your good boulevards or avenues, with dirty garbage boxes and parcels standing alongside the houses. Some I have noticed for days at a time, and the streets are a disgrace.

Where are your city councillors or those whose interest it should be to keep the city clean? What a bad garbage collection you have.

Unsigned

A VISITOR'S OPINION

MARCH 19, 1920

Coming as an American to Ottawa from New York City to live in Canada for the first time in this winter, I have wanted for some time to find a means of congratulating the city upon its possession of so splendid a civic institution as the recreation grounds at Rockcliffe.

I have seen nothing of which I think the city can be so justly proud — not even the admirable new Parliament Buildings — for the provision of a wholesome location for the recreation for the young people of a growing city is one of the most difficult and important problems with which every community is faced.

The idea that having achieved the well-nigh impossible, the social worker's Utopian dream, the community should then allow a group of misguided religious dogmatics to close the place up on the one day when the working people of the city can all use it, is a horrifying conception. What wouldn't New York City give to have Rockcliffe so near to its center.

I do not know whether Mr. McKay in his recent letter expresses views representing the general thought of the Lord's Day Alliance. If he does, that organization must possess an odd wind-twisted soul. There is a large group of splendid men and women in the States, and they happen to be largely church people, too, who in connection with the National Board of Moving Picture Censors are trying not to suppress "movie houses," but to promote the production of more and more clean and decent, but not prudishly dull, films. They are instigated for one thing by recognition of the fact that the moving picture house is the one successful rival of the saloon.

However, there is no use arguing with minds who turn to Christianity and the Bible only for such authority of suppression as they can find worded therein. What I should like to find out is whether there is any organization or group of citizens in Ottawa that is working to make it legally impossible for such a blow to be struck at the physical and moral welfare of the community as is accomplished in the closing of the Rockcliffe slide on Sundays. For this sort of suppression the city in the long run has to pay a heavy price.

Sincerely yours,
Corolyn Bulley Cox

Editor's note: The ban on the use of city parks and recreation facilities for Sunday amateur sports continued only until the mid-1920s, when it was deemed too difficult to monitor. However, a ban on Sunday professional sports — and sports facilities with commercial potential, such as bowling alleys and pool halls — remained in effect in Ottawa until 1965, when the third plebiscite on the issue in six years finally ended the prohibition. Even so, the rules for Sunday sports were strict. For instance, football, soccer, baseball, hockey and lacrosse could only be played between 1 p.m. and 6 p.m. Interestingly, Ottawa lost a chance for a Triple-A baseball franchise in 1960 when the city refused to relax its Sunday ban on pro sports.

COMMENDS FIRM'S THOUGHTFULNESS

AUGUST 14, 1920

In these days of so much labour trouble and strife, when large interests of all kinds are being subjected to so much interference through strikes, etc., it is only fair that someone ought to give credit where credit is due.

Having been employed by the American Bank Note Co. for a number of years, I think I am in a position to let the public know how well we are treated. I have never known of a strike to occur in our factory and all difficulties have been settled between ourselves and the management with the greatest harmony, and I believe we have the most up-to-date and best-paid factory in Canada.

In the first place we have the insurance scheme, which insures every employee according to length of service, amounting to as much as $4,000 for the men and $1,000 for the girls; and it must be remembered that we do not pay one cent for the above policy.

Next we have a system of holidays for the employees by which anyone not having been more than five minutes late in any month is entitled to one day's holiday with full pay. Many let these holidays run for over a year and are then due two weeks holidays with full pay during the summer months.

Then we have our sick benefits which, should any of us be so unfortunate as to fall sick, entitles us to $10 per week for the men and $5 per week for the girls; also, as far as I know, all of the above business is negotiated and transacted during the company's time.

Next we have our first aid room, with bed and full equipment, to take care of any accident that may occur, and the best nurse available. She has served overseas for quite a number of years and was mentioned in the despatches of [British commander-in-chief] Gen. Douglas Haig. She has lots of work to do and handles it with the greatest skill and attention.

Every employee, when starting with the company, receives a locker and key to keep their clothes in good order; also soap and clean towels, hot and cold water, shower baths in every department; every place is bright and clean, and the sanitation is the very best.

Last but not least, every employee with over three years service received a handsome bonus last Christmas. I do not know whether it is the intention of the company to give this every year, but at any rate we are very thankful for what we received last Christmas.

In conclusion I might say that I am not very good at letter writing, and I left off doing this for quite a long time thinking that some of the employees might take the opportunity, as I have, to thank the company for all they've done for us. Now that I have made the break you will have to excuse any grammatical errors that have occurred.

A Well Satisfied Employee

Editor's note: In 1897, the U.S.-based American Bank Note Co. was awarded a controversial contract by the Dominion government to supply postage stamps and paper money on condition it built a printing plant in Ottawa. The firm fulfilled its obligation by erecting a fireproof four-storey building on Wellington Street (near the site of today's Bank of Canada) in an amazing 13 weeks. In 1922, just after the above letter was written, the company was renamed the Canadian Bank Note Co. to dampen continuing criticism of a U.S. company printing Canadian stamps and money. However, it retained its U.S. ownership until foreign investment laws forced its sale to Canadians in the '70s. In recent years, operating as the Canadian Bank Note Co. on Richmond Road, it hasn't always been the happy shop described by the letter-writer in 1920. In 1998, for instance, the company was hit by a bitter strike over pay equity.

BAITING THE MENTALLY AFFLICTED

SEPTEMBER 8, 1920

In your article on "The Village Idiot" you very properly point out the danger from persons of unsound mind who are not adequately cared for either in institutions or in their own homes. Such persons, though ordinarily harmless, may become dangerous when their peculiar delusions are touched, or when they are teased or provoked into a rage.

Unfortunately, the teasing or provoking of half-witted people is in too many places a popular amusement. Either the press and the governments might do a good deal to educate people into sounder and kinder views on this question. The human being who is intellectually weak ought to be treated with the same consideration that is extended to the blind, the deaf and the lame.

The baiting to which I refer is due in part to a streak of cruelty which is too common, but also largely to more thoughtlessness and a sort of initiative mob spirit. I have some recollection that in my own boyhood days I was not guiltless in the matter. I remember two excellent teachers who talked to their pupils on the duty of kindness and consideration toward the mentally afflicted, and the example is one that ought to be followed by teachers, preachers and editors.

A reader

EXTRAVAGANCE AND WASTE

SEPTEMBER 13, 1920

A prominent lady visitor a few days ago was reported in the press to have stated that what impressed her most of all in Canada was the lavish and extravagant manner in which food was served.

It is probable that conditions differ somewhat according to one's financial circumstances. I have, however, during the past week or so been seeking evidences of such lavishness and extravagance, but in vain. It is true that I do not take my meals at the Château Laurier, but rather at such places as are frequented by the majority of people.

Having to exist on a limited income, I find it necessary to spend no more than forty cents or so on a meal, and sir, I can assure you that on many occasions I have felt very much like Oliver Twist, but have been, perforce, compelled to resist the temptation to spend another ten cents or so. The gist of which is that very little waste or extravagance is seen in places as are patronized, from dire necessity, by the majority of both the washed and the unwashed proletariat.

It is, I know, quite true that one can obtain a good meal, so far as quantity goes, for the price of forty cents or so at the average Chinese restaurant, but my insular upbringing, perhaps, makes me wary of such places. And, in passing, I pause to wonder how it is that the restaurant business of the Capital of the Dominion is mainly in the hands of the Celestial. No, Chinese restaurants and chop suey are not for me, and the field is consequently narrowed down very considerably.

And finally, sir, I have to confess that so far as the catch-as-catch-can variety of restaurants, better known as quick-lunches, are concerned, the public are largely to blame for their existence, as they patronize them and bolt their food as though they were being pursued by a plague of demons. A habit is difficult to break, but I am thankful to give my humble testimony that I have succeeded, though am somewhat like Dfogenes and am still seeking for fair value for my very limited supply of cash.

Epicure

A LITTLE GIRL'S PET

OCTOBER 23, 1920

"I am having a lovely birthday, but I would be really happy if Peggy would come back: I would rather have no presents at all and have my little kitten back."

Our little girl was seven years of age today. On Monday evening her kitten strayed from the yard and was poisoned by one of those human fiends who delight in giving pain to others. So Peggy will not come back.

On Tuesday night two other cats were poisoned by a certain individual who lives in the block between MacLaren and Gilmour on the east side of Bank Street. If those whose pets are missing would like to know the name of this individual I shall be only too glad to supply the information.

It is high time that this sort of thing were stopped and a concerted move on the part of animal lovers would make poisoners extremely wary, as such wretches are by nature despicable and cowardly.

Dr. M. LeBourdais

THE EMPIRE'S TRIBUTE
NOVEMBER 6, 1920

On Thursday next there will occur an act without precedent in the history of our Empire, if not in the history of the world. A procession will pass through the streets of London heading towards Westminster Abbey, a long procession of field marshals and generals and admirals and great ones of the nation, with stately and solemn tread, will walk behind a gun carriage on which will lie a coffin covered by the Union Jack. Right behind as the chief mourner will walk the King.

It is indeed a marvellous thing, when you think of it. For in that coffin will not lie the body of some member of the Royal Family, some great leader, some noble hero of international fame, but simply the body of an unknown soldier who laid down his life for the Empire's honour and lay in a nameless grave somewhere in France or Flanders.

Think of it! The glory of it! There is something in this so unique and splendid that one wishes that every anti-British Irish or American heart could be made to see the glamour of this tribute made by the Emperor-King to this anonymous and unidentified warrior. And to think of his having a place in Westminster Abbey, that great temple of reconciliation and silence where the enmities of twenty generations lie buried and where the illustrious sons and daughters of England, kings and princes, queens and princesses, dukes and lords and statesmen and poets lie crossed together in venerable graves.

Verily we can thank God as Canadians today that we belong to an Empire that has imagination as well as heart, that has sentiment as well as justice.

Dyson Hague, Toronto

1921

Local: Smallpox outbreak forces train travellers from Ottawa to show vaccination certificates (January); The first air-photo map of Ottawa is completed (February)
National: The Dominion government authorizes five-cent nickel coin (February); A provincial plebiscite upholds Ontario's 1916 ban on the making, importation and selling of liquor (April)
World: Italian fascist leader Benito Mussolini declares himself Il Duce (November); British and Irish officials sign treaty creating the Irish Free State, leaving Northern Ireland in British hands (December)
Births: Hockey great Maurice (Rocket) Richard; Prince Philip; Canadian journalist Doris Anderson; astronaut John Glenn
Deaths: Tenor Enrico Caruso; French composer Camille Saint-Saens; Lady Randolph (Jennie) Churchill, U.S.-born mother of Winston Churchill

SIDEWALK SLIDES
JANUARY 3, 1921

For several years past I have attempted to draw the attention of the powers that be to the danger of not only thoughtless children but many young men and women making slides on the sidewalks of our city.

If not too much absorbed in thought with family or business worries, one can easily avoid these slides when seen. But how is such possible when they are covered with a light coating of soft snow, or on a badly lighted street at night?

I have previously suggested that the police department issue a public notice that sliding on footpaths is a punishable offence; also that they ask the public school board to have teachers explain to the children the dangers and possible injury such may cause to others, perhaps their own parents.

Looking at the practice of sidewalk slides from every point of view, one can only conclude that it is nothing short of criminal stupidity. Our city authorities have a heavy job making the sidewalks fit to travel on during winter. Why should they be subjected to the risk of damages for injury from this cause? Live and let live should be the motto of all.

J.S. Kingston, Ottawa

SAYS SANITATION NEEDED
JANUARY 18, 1921

Without going into the merits or otherwise of vaccination, may I point out how disease is being spread. In Ottawa South, in that section between Seneca Street and Bronson, Cameron and Pansy avenues, a condition exists that is a menace not only to those who live close by, but to the whole city of Ottawa.

For some time garbage and refuse has been dumped all along Bronson, and on the lower ends of Sunnyside, Hopewell, and Glen avenues. This garbage comes from Ottawa homes, whether infected with smallpox or not, and is dumped for filling but really to propagate a menace to everybody.

What infection is not spread by the winds of Heaven will be carried by melting snow and rains into the swampy places, and next summer the myriad mosquitoes and flies that breed there, will doubtless be busy doing their share to carry infection around. The drainage and other seepings from the houses in this section also finds its way into these swamps, as the citizens in this locality have been denied sewers and sanitation for a number of years.

The primary duty of our board of health is to see that disease cannot be bred or hatched — for if no disease prevails, no care is needed; but possibly I may have a mistaken idea about that.

J. Rothwell

Editor's note: The public debate over mandatory vaccination was waged for many years after the First World War, often becoming heated during outbreaks of diseases such as smallpox, which claimed dozens of lives in Ottawa early in 1921. That outbreak was bad enough to require the vaccination of anyone wishing to board a train leaving Ottawa. In general, the arguments against vaccination were twofold: that it was dangerous, and probably unethical, to inject a healthy person with a small dose of a disease in order to develop immunity; and that forcing inoculations on schoolchildren and others violated individual rights. The medical community, on the other hand, argued that vaccination was the long-awaited key to ridding the world of deadly disease. As the following letter shows, the debate was often muddied by misinformation and fear over related medical developments such as the Wassermann analysis, an uneven diagnostic test for syphilis, in which a blood sample was taken. The Salvarsan treatment for syphilis, also mentioned in the next letter, involved a series of minute injections of arsenic. It was linked to many deaths and was eventually discontinued in the 1930s. By the 1940s, syphilis was treated with penicillin.

SIGNIFICANT IF CORRECT

JANUARY 22, 1921

The recent inquest here on the death of Miss Monica Kenney may have an important bearing on the question of vaccination, as well as on the uncertainty of the Wassermann test and the danger of the Salvarsan treatment for syphilis.

Miss Kenney, of 597 Palmerston Ave. in Toronto, was one of the two women who died almost immediately after Salvarsan injections at the office of Dr. J.H. McConnell, January 9th.

Naturally, stories have been circulated throughout the city about Miss Kenney. As she seems to have been highly thought of in her neighbourhood and among the people of St. Peter's church, we started inquiries. Two brothers and the mother have given me signed statements, paraphrased in substance as follows:

Miss Kenney vaccinated February 4th, 1920, by Dr. McMahon, of St. George Street, Toronto, while at the residence of a cousin named Cummins, on Tyndall Ave., where she lived while her younger brother was recovering from smallpox. Previous to vaccination she had perfect health, her last illness being when she was fifteen years of age, when she suffered from quinsy [a throat infection related to tonsillitis].

Miss Kenny was 21 years of age when vaccinated in the left arm. Became very sick, symptoms severe. Was examined at the City Hall a day or two later by a nurse who put on some lotion. Arm was very sore for three and one half months, never healed properly.

Boils appeared on the face, beginning with one on the left cheek about seven weeks after vaccination, then around the eye and in both ears, which became worse in the summer. Dr. Harrington treated the boils in July and August. Said it was a dirty skin disease brought back by the soldiers.

Dr. McConnell treated with medicine from about September 1st. Took a blood test (Wassermann) about the beginning of December, which resulting positive, he began the Salvarsan treatment, the fatal injection of January 9th being the third.

The above facts are supported by C.R. Kenney, the older brother; Harry C. Kenney, the younger brother, and Anne Kenney, the mother.

The danger from Salvarsan treatment was recently brought out in a report from an English health officer in *The Abolitionist*, London, in which were cited cases showing that either immediate death or severe arsenic poisoning were not uncommon from the use of Salvarsan.

Sincerely yours,
A.B. Farmer, Toronto

OPPOSES COMPULSION

JANUARY 26, 1921

I saw in the *Evening Citizen* of Jan. 24th that Mr. Louis Cousineau, mayor of Hull, was opposed to compulsory vaccination, and I also understand that Mr. [Frank] Plant, mayor of Ottawa, is against it with all his will.

With those gentlemen I am taking my stand against such a criminal practice, and it is time that the fathers and mothers of the city children should rise up and stamp out this wholesale mutilation of innocent children.

It is a well known fact that vaccination has left in its wake imbeciles, suffering and death. No doctors will give a certificate that there will be no complications of disease setting in after vaccination, and until the day comes that all doctors give such certificates, vaccinations should be used the same as you would a snake in the grass or as a one-sided money proposition.

George Daly,
123 Boulevard St. Joseph, Hull

A SKATER'S COMPLAINT

MARCH 2, 1921

Many tickets have been sold this winter for the Gladstone Avenue rink on which the following extract be inscribed: "Band Every Night and Saturday Afternoon."

Well, sir, there has not been a band for several weeks although it has been extensively advertised at the professional hockey matches and throughout the city, and skaters have gone to the rink only to be disappointed on finding there was no band. For instance, a band was advertised for Saturday afternoon and evening of the 12th, and although the weather was ideal for skating, there was no accompanying band.

Occasionally season ticket holders have not been allowed to skate as the rink has been given over to hockey for an entire evening. Is this not accepting money under false pretenses?

A Season Ticket Holder

A PLEA FOR WOMEN AS HIGH EXECUTIVES

MARCH 15, 1921

It is a matter of looking back but a short period to mark the time when the majority of women were not in favour of receiving the right to vote, the right to enter the professions and even objected to the right to publicly express themselves.

Although through the ages individual women did — ignoring what was looked upon as the barrier of the sex — become factors in politically and socially shaping great events, it is only within the last half century that by united efforts a number of devoted and progressive women so exerted themselves that women have been recognized as being entitled to the full rights of citizens on practically the same footing as men.

The last stronghold to stand out against the demand of women is the higher executive and administrative posts in the governments of all countries. In Great Britain an agitation is afoot to cause all positions in the civil service to be thrown open to women without reservation; in the United States similar action is contemplated. In Canada, the proved worth of women both as administrators and executives during the war was so evident that it will be quite difficult for the state to ignore demands that all posts in the government be open to both sexes.

There are but few positions in the civil service today that could not be successfully filled by women. They have in the lower positions the same training and work as the men; in all but a few instances their work is performed in every way as satisfactorily; but in no known instance has there been promotion to any position higher than secretary to an executive or head clerk, and it would be interesting to know what number have reached even this stage.

Many of the brightest, most efficient personalities in the service today are women. Why do these never reach the same offices as men? Of course the excuse was once that the major-proportion of women are only in the service for a brief period before they marry and that the civil service is only a stop gap to their marrying stage. This may be true as regards a small number, but women today enter the service and take their duties very seriously — they enter for a livelihood.

The days of arguing that because a woman works "she's doing a man out of a position," or that "she gets too much for a woman," are past — and a woman with equal ability is entitled to the same opportunity as a man.

There are women today in Canada who might even make good ministers — to write now of a woman secretary of state, president of the council or minister of public works, etc., might not be treated seriously, but with woman taking her political rights earnestly, which it is evident she is doing the world over, such a thing within the next few years is within the realms of possibility.

Janetta Grant,
Editor, The Civilian

Editor's note: It would be another 45 years — when Jean Sutherland Boggs was named director of the National Gallery in 1966 — before a woman reached the rank of deputy minister in the Canadian government. Nine years earlier, in 1957, Ellen Fairclough had become Canada's first female federal cabinet minister with her appointment as secretary of state. In 1994, Jocelyne Bourgon became the first female Clerk of the Privy Council, the highest position in the public service. The Civilian was a journal devoted to civil service issues. It was published every two weeks between May 1908 and June 1921.

CONFESSION BY A SMOKER

APRIL 5, 1921

The habit of smoking is one easy to acquire, but most difficult to break. I remember when as a boy of 16 or 17 years buying a pipe and puffing it with more or less trepidation; but with what gusto I thought myself a man. Had I been told at that time that it was a sign of weakness rather than of strength of character, I should probably have eschewed the act before it had become a habit.

Like many other habits, however, it had its birth surreptitiously. I have since smoked more or less regularly and so the habit has gained a stronger and stronger hold upon me, until now it has me in its grip, luring me on with a temporary feeling of restfulness and quiet, only later to permit its baneful effects to result in a reaction of lassitude.

Cigarets are often singled out and held up to scorn, and undoubtedly they exercise a strong and pernicious hold upon many, particularly latterly upon girls and women. Pipe and cigar smoking, however, are just as bad. So many men comfort themselves with the thought that they are not cigaret smokers; but, as a pipe smoker, I must confess that the fumes from a foul pipe (and all pipes are more or less foul) or the spent fumes from a cigar are just as obnoxious as those from a cigaret.

My advice to any young man (or woman) would be to shun smoking upon the ground that it is a selfish, unclean and useless habit. Those who have made a close study of it are agreed that it lessens one's power of endurance, stunts growth, shortens the wind, produces catarrh [colds] and is the stepping stone to other bad habits.

At the same time it is questionable whether prohibitory measures would be successful in materially lessening the evil. The solution lies rather in educating the young to the dangers of smoking and in parents setting the necessary example, remembering that example is better than precept.

Fiat Lux

SPEEDING ON THE DRIVEWAY

APRIL 18, 1921

The season's first serious accident has already occurred on the Driveway and it is to be hoped the Improvement Commission will take steps to prevent as large a number of accidents as took place last year.

One of the most dangerous points is where Waverley Street joins the Driveway. The writer knows of at least six motor accidents at this point last year. In every case save one, the accident was due to excessive speed in rounding the curve there. In one instance, a fine new car just out of the shops and driven by two young men, in attempt to round the curve at a terrible rate of speed, ran into a tree six inches in diameter, uprooted it and ran over it, only stopping a little short of going over the embankment into the canal, and making scrap iron of the car. One of the occupants was hurried through the windshield and was considerably cut up by the glass. Only a few moments before a group of children had been playing on the lawn where the accident occurred.

The driver, who was said to be under the influence of liquor, announced in the newspaper that the accident occurred because he was trying to avoid colliding with a lady motorist who was driving very erratically. Several people witnessed the accident and there was no car save his own in sight when it occurred.

If the new speed limit of 15 miles an hour were enforced by the commission it would eliminate nearly all of these accidents. It is difficult to do away with speeding entirely but those living on or making frequent use of the Driveway know that adequate steps are not being taken to enforce the present regulations.

There appears to be only one uniformed officer who patrols the Driveway on a bicycle. What is needed is a number of plainclothes men with stop watches and, above all, prosecution of offenders.

A Driveway resident

GERMAN LADIES WANT HUSBANDS
APRIL 20, 1921

On account of the unhappy war, in which more than 1,800,000 young Germans lost their lives, a still greater number of young German ladies are deprived of the opportunity to find a husband. This calamity, if I dare call it thus, is still increased by the fact that, owing to the extraordinary dearness of household furniture and the scarcity of apartments, matrimony has become a luxury and a privilege of the rich in this country.

In their distress our young ladies look over to America in the hope of finding there the conjugal happiness for which reason they appeal to all American bachelors who cannot find a match over there, and who are desirous to contract matrimony with a well bred young German lady, to approach them on this behalf. The linguistic difficulties should be no obstacle as our ladies are mostly acquainted with the English language.

The German ladies asked me to be their interpreter in assisting them to find an American husband, for which reason applicants are requested to apply to my address below.

Very faithfully yours,
J. Stahl, 14 Realschulstrasse, Dulsburg, Germany

AN INSULT TO WOMENKIND
OCTOBER 26, 1921

I wish to call your attention to a very vulgar advertisement inserted in your morning paper Oct. 20th regarding Russian domestics claiming sisterhood to Mlle. Pavlowa.

To make my complaint short, there is one passage in the advert which says this was the fashion for slaveys and caused so much annoyance to the famous Russian dancer.

There is one thing I wish to make clear, that domestic servants, such as waitresses, chambermaids or kitchen maids, whom the advert calls dishwashers, are no more slaveys than the troubled and aggravated Mlle. Pavlowa. The expression slavey goes to show the low, uncultured and vulgar person the author of this advert is.

The slavey, as this advert calls the domestic servant, is just as much entitled to honour and respect as is the famous Russian dancer. No matter what his or her nationality may be, there is no more honourable calling than domestic work. It is disgusting to think that because a person earns his or her living as a domestic, they must be branded as slaveys.

For my own part I would sooner be a dishwasher than fifty famous dancers.

I will ask you and the community at large which is the most honourable title, slavey or dancer? All I can say, whoever the author of the advert is, he should take a course of domestic or slavey's work, as he calls it, and I vouch he will know how to conduct himself as a gentleman.

Mrs. Murphy, Smiths Falls

Editor's note: Although the advertisement chastised by the letter-writer was unsigned, it seems to have been placed by promoters of Anna Pavlowa's appearance at Ottawa's Russell Theatre in 1921. The ad was likely designed to discourage domestics from claiming to be the Russian ballerina's long-lost sister, a practice that appears to have followed Mlle Pavlowa on her tour of North America. A few weeks before her Ottawa appearance, she sought the help of the Russian consul-general in Chicago to put an end to the stories, claiming she never had a sister. In any event, her stop in Ottawa caused a stir that can only be compared to a modern-day visit by a superstar such as Céline Dion. During her stay, Mlle Pavlowa made appearances at several local businesses — Devlin's furs, the Studebaker dealer, a hat shop, photo studio and beauty parlour — to promote their products, and, presumably, to earn some extra cash or gifts.

Russian ballerina Anna Pavlowa made appearances at several local businesses, including a Studebaker dealer, during her visit to Ottawa.

1922

Local: A confrontation between 10,000 Orangemen and a gathering of Irish Catholics is narrowly averted when police persuade the groups to go their separate ways (July); Ontario Motor League erects signposts for roads and villages throughout Ottawa Valley (August)
National: B.C. drivers join rest of Canada on the right side of roads (January); Researchers Frederick Banting and Charles Best announce discovery of insulin in Toronto (February); Snowmobile invented by Quebec's Joseph-Armand Bombardier (November)

World: British colonial court sentences Mohandas Gandhi to six years in prison in India for civil disobedience (March); The tomb of King Tutankhamen is found in Egypt (November)
Births: Quebec premier René Lévesque; governor general Jeanne Sauvé; Canadian book publisher Jack McClelland; jazz bassist Charles Mingus; British novelist Kingsley Amis; singer-actress Judy Garland; fashion designer Pierre Cardin; Israeli soldier and politician Yitzhak Rabin
Deaths: French novelist Marcel Proust; globe-trotting U.S. news reporter Nellie Bly

A WOMAN'S VIEW

APRIL 5, 1922

You must be getting tired of receiving letters regarding daylight saving, but it is right, I think, to discuss it, as it is something that affects us all.

Those who oppose it have, it seems to me, the best arguments to use, though I do not think anyone is really opposed to real daylight saving. What we are opposed to is putting the clock on an hour, and making it tell a lie in order to do so. The mothers and little children certainly suffer the most in convenience from it, and our adult young people did not seem to get to bed any sooner for it, but continued to stay up half the night and cheat themselves of their much needed rest.

A correspondent in Saturday's paper tried to show us that the country people who have always practised early rising were the better for it. Does he not know that these same people who have always practised daylight saving are the ones who most strongly objected to pushing on the clock, and complained of the confusion it caused when they came to town?

Another good reason against it is that those who are in the habit of attending Sunday evening service during the hot weather find it rather trying to start out in the blazing sun and I have wondered why our ministers have not seen fit to have the service begin an hour later (even with standard time). We might have better attendance.

This daylight saving measure was adopted in Great Britain and the Empire during the war, and no doubt served a good purpose then. But why should we continue a thing that only brings confusion all over the country?

Mrs. J.B.K., Ottawa

"GOD'S TIME" — SO CALLED

APRIL 14, 1922

Will the people who object to daylight saving because the children suffer explain to an anxious inquirer in what respect the children of Ottawa differ from those of Edmonton, say, where it is daylight during the summer months up till 10 o'clock? If the mothers from whom we are constantly hearing this complaint were to get on to a fast train and travel due north for half a day, they would find the same condition without the necessity to alter the clock time.

One of your correspondents lately remonstrated against "giving the clocks the lie." Does he imagine that standard time is settled by Divine ordinance, any more than is "summer time"? Another, in today's issue, hopes that "the wee tots in their mothers arms" will grow up to make the advocate of summer time "satisfied with God's own time."

What is God's own time? Why is the time fixed by the government as "standard time" and more "God's time" than the time fixed by the government as "summer time?" Would these mothers, if they lived near the Arctic Circle, think it necessary to keep their children out of bed during the summer months, and in bed during the winter because one was nothing but daylight during one part of the year and nothing but darkness during another.

If the government can decree that "Eastern time" shall change to "Central time" at Fort William, as it does, what is there in God's ordinance to prevent or forbid, the same government decreeing that "standard time" shall change to "summer time" on any given date, and vice versa? Most of the opponents of daylight saving argue as if they imagined that the sun set at the same time the world over.

The whole business is, of course, a matter of the greatest convenience to the greatest number. We cannot change the time of the rising and setting of the sun, but it is a simple matter to change the time of the clock, which is arranged today, under present regulations by man for the benefit of the greatest number of the population of Canada, and I have never heard that the Lowland farmers of Scotland suffered because the sun rose and set during the summer months at about the same time by the clock as it does in Ottawa, by "daylight saving" time.

R.J. Snell, Aylmer

MAN AND MONKEYS

APRIL 26, 1922

In reading the discussion about Darwin, I cannot understand why Darwin and his believers did not, and why they do not now, put his conclusions to the test, with everything in their favor as compared to what the monkeys had when they were evolving into man.

Take now the breeders of Holstein or Ayrshire cattle, or along any such line — horses and so forth. In a very few years, with these breeders' evolved monkey-man wisdom, they get very good results along certain lines, chiefly more milk and greater size. In using "evolved monkey-man," of course, I refer to the view of the Darwinites.

As for myself, I don't believe any such stuff. My reason tells me man, if anything, has degenerated instead of advancing. Sin always degenerates, and we can observe in our own day those who completely give themselves away to sin and wickedness. What happens? They generally end a complete physical and mental wreck. And man as a whole has been sinful — some more, some less.

But these people trying to evolve man from monkeys simply do not believe their own doctrine. I wonder what the present monkey race evolved from or did they just stand still during man's evolution and since?

According to some Darwinites, there never were any miracles from God. For myself I consider all life more or less a miracle. The reason we don't regard it as such is because we have seen it all our lives and it has become commonplace to us, and we take it as a matter of course. Take the trees that grow and the food we live on — what else are they but chiefly stored up sun's rays put in that form by the miracles of God.

THE CANADIAN PRESS

The followers of Charles Darwin cannot believe in both evolution of man and heaven, a reader said.

But Darwinites cannot both believe in evolution of man and in heaven. Do they think God would prepare heaven for monkeys? I suppose they would have it that God waited till man's evolution from the monkeys. Now I think they will agree with me that monkeys have no doubt or knowledge of God or heaven. They do no know any more along that line than a cow, horse or any such.

Now had man evolved from monkey, he would not know there was a God or have any knowledge whatever of God or heaven and how was he to learn? According to their doctrine there could be no such thing as miracles of God conveying it to him in a supernatural way. Then, how was a man to get his conception of God as he had it long ago and at the present time? I consider, according to their arguments, it would be impossible.

Now we are told that most all men have a belief in a Higher Being and I believe that men knew there was a God after his creation by God (according to the Bible) in His image and that through sin they degenerated and fell away from Him to their past and present state.

When the Darwinites go to an animal show they must be proud when they look on their "relatives." It surely must be elevating to them. For myself I want to think I spring from something higher and more Divine.

A. B. McPherson,
Williamsburg

WHY MEN DON'T MARRY

MAY 17, 1922

Why does a young man not marry? Is it because he does not want to? No, many a young man would like to get married and have a home of his own.

But he doesn't, and here is one reason: The wages of today are not sufficient for a young man to live on. It is very often the case that the girl is better salaried. Would it be fair of him to ask her to quit her position and exist with him in a second-rate housekeeping room on a salary of $45 per month, which is considered his earning capacity after having given for the cause of the country three, four or five years of the prime of his life?

Is it getting better or worse? When a young man applies for a position today, what are the chief questions asked? As a rule, as follows: Have you been overseas? Yes. Are you married? No. Well, we prefer a married man.

Consequently, it is necessary in order to get work at all, first to marry, and then to wait until someone takes pity on him, providing he is not a stranger wherever he may happen to live.

Here is how some men spend their hard-earned (monthly) salaries:

Salary and bonus	$72.88
Rent for a room	15.00
Meals	30.00
Laundry	5.00
Toilet soap	.75
Shaving soap	.10
Tooth paste	.25
Maintenance of clothes	1.00
Amusements	1.00
Carfare	1.50
Tobacco	4.50
Daily paper	.60
Haircut, etc.	1.00
Shoe repairs	2.50
Recreation	1.25
Insurance policy	2.34
Total	$66.79

Balance for clothing, stationery, postage, etc. $6.09

A. Petersen,
Ottawa

QUESTIONS FOR "SPORTING" PUBLIC

MAY 31, 1922

The report, if true, that Jack Dempsey, the pugilist, since visiting England has affected a monocle, calls for the following questionary communication which may prove an interesting study to large numbers of ex-service men, and women.

Heroes of the ring versus the trenches: Of these two classes of heroes, if one may term a pugilist a hero, which cultivates and attracts the greater amount of public patronage and attention? Compared, for instance, with the tremendous sums awarded the pugilist Dempsey, commonly termed a "slacker," i.e. an evader of military or naval service, what sums have been awarded maimed, blinded and shell-shocked ex-combatants from the fields of past European warfare?

Compared with Dempsey's reception in France and England, but not Berlin, what forms of reception were anon bestowed upon units and straggling fragments of brigades, divisions, etc. returning to this continent from German prisons, and hospitals in the Motherland?

Compared with bets made at the ringside during the recent Dempsey-Carpentier match at Jersey City, and the huge sums paid there to pugilists to shuffle, clinch, and feint over a roped area in the midst of a fascinated, wildly delighted concourse of professedly civilized and war veteran loving men, women and girls, what bets are being laid and huge sums guaranteed by Canadians present at that match for, or against, the probable success of the venture of "General" Macdonald and his veteran band of demonstrators [to get improved benefits for veterans]?

Finally, compared with the salaries and profits of ring contest promoters, managers, trainers, "fans," etc. etc. what shall it profit an ex-service man, or woman, upon this continent to believe otherwise that the primeval attractions of the prize ring far exceed those afforded in favor of those who fought, bled, and suffered agony and woe to preserve their countries from the aggressions of a mad Kaiser, now happily dethroned?

I beg to suggest the introduction of a form of a bill to the legislature for limiting, at least, sums paid as prizes to professional pugilists, if not for the suppression of ring contests which in late years have largely contributed towards the moral corruptions of numberless women and girls, no longer able to arouse even respect for their sex in the breasts of true sensible men.

A.E. Venn,
77 O'Connor St., Ottawa

THE SALES TAX

MAY 31, 1922

When the sales tax was first proposed I protested in the public press on behalf of the consumers in so far as they are organized in this movement. As it is the traditional policy of the Liberal party that the incidence of taxation should be in proportion to the capacity of the people to bear it, I was hoping that the present government would abolish the tax altogether. Instead they are increasing it by one half.

In these days of intensive organization of almost every definite and special interest in the country, equity does not prevail on questions of public taxation, legislation or administration. Governments find themselves compelled to come along the line of the least resistance.

In the old land [Britain], the government has to take into account that about five million householders, representing with their families nearly half the people, are organized as consumers. It is not long ago that a governmental taxation proposal oppressive to them was defeated in the British house of commons.

The consuming public is the largest interest in Canada, being co-extensive with the people, but of all interests it is the least organized. Its back is broad even though at the present time it is not strong. It is compelled to accept, almost without demur, every burden imposed upon it.

In our fiscal policies it has long been accepted as an axiom that the man who dares to raise a family ought to be taxed through the protective tariff on almost every dollar he finds it necessary to spend for its support. In consequence we cannot rely upon natural increase to do justice to our land and mineral resources. We have to depend almost entirely upon immigration.

The principle of taxation upon consumption is iniquitous. It taxes a man in proportion to his obligations and not to his capacity to pay. The wage-earning class on short time, and with diminished earnings even when on full time, are going to have the purchasing power of their slender sort of dollars further decreased by taxation. When people find it difficult to make both ends meet, even on a bare subsistence level, extra taxation on consumption means not only serious physical discomfort but impairment of the health of the rising generation.

When it was decided to impose the tax at the source of production rather than at the point of final distribution, I pointed out that the burden was greatly increased to the advantage of private interests. Virtually, the manufacturer and the distributing intermediaries act as tax collectors, charging on the tax at each point of transmission the usual ratio of profit of each on the commodity.

It is likely that by the time the consumer pays he does so to the extent of from $1.50 to $2.00 for every dollar which goes into the national treasury. Imposed in this way, it is natural the organized trading interests have no particular objection to the sales tax.

The war left a heavy legacy of debt as well as of woe. The people have to face this fact and make heavy sacrifices to liquidate it. I appreciate they should do so as cheerfully as they can.

The finance minister is entitled to sympathy and co-operation in his efforts to solve the grave problems which confront him.

Nevertheless, I suggest that this country, in a manner which, in these depressed times, will seriously reduce the standard of living, is making a mistake. It is no doubt raising money, but eventually it must defeat its own object. If wealth is to be produced in abundance to meet abnormal national expenditure and obligations, the first necessity to that end is to see that the actual wealth producers are well-fed, well-clothed and well-housed.

It is to be hoped that the electors will make representations to their legislators against any increase in the tax on consumption.

George Keen, General Secretary
Co-operative Union of Canada,
Brantford, Ontario

Editor's note: Faced with a large war debt, the Dominion government began to look at new ways to raise money. In 1920, uneasy about increasing the income tax it had implemented during the war as a "temporary" measure, Finance Minister Sir Henry Drayton tried a one-per-cent excise tax on a range of products, including tobacco, gasoline and cars. It proved unsatisfactory as a revenue generator, however, and was replaced in 1921 with a one-per-cent sales tax on goods (food and coal were exempted) sold by manufacturers to wholesalers and another one-per-cent levy when those goods were passed on to retailers. After more tinkering, Drayton decided on a flat system of three per cent in late 1921 and then raised it again to 4.5 per cent in his May 1922 budget. That's the increase mentioned at the end of the letter writer's opening paragraph. By 1924, the tax was officially installed as the Manufacturers Sales Tax, which was lowered and raised over the years, ending its life at 13.5 per cent in 1990 when it was replaced by today's Goods and Services Tax. The letter writer's employer, the Co-operative Union of Canada, was an umbrella group representing various co-ops, most involved in agriculture.

1923

Local: Ottawa Senators win the Stanley Cup (April); As part of his vision for the future, Mayor Frank Plant proposes a new east-west driveway, a zoo and city-owned golf course (July)
National: New Canadian Chinese Immigration Act virtually bars entry of Chinese into country (January); Foster Hewitt makes his debut as hockey broadcaster from Toronto (March)
World: More than 30,000 die when earthquake levels Tokyo and Yokohama (September); Adolf Hitler arrested after his attempt to overthrow German government fails (November)

Births: Bertha Wilson, first female Supreme Court of Canada judge; abortionist Dr. Henry Morgentaler; U.S. writers Norman Mailer and Joseph Heller; actor Charlton Heston; developer Robert Campeau
Deaths: U.S. president Warren Harding

WIVES IN GOVERNMENT EMPLOYMENT

FEBRUARY 10, 1923

No doubt many married women secured employment with the government during the war, owing to the lack of male help, and many are no doubt still retaining their positions.

Perhaps many war widows and girls have married and are still working unknown to those in authority over them. Naturally, these last few years there are not so many vacancies and whatever vacancies might occur can easily be filled by returned men and widows who must work. However, those who are not entitled to the different positions (particularly married women), should resign or be dismissed immediately and make way for those who must work.

Out of 300 or more women office cleaners employed by the char staff alone of the Public Works department, it can be proved that more than 120 are married. There may, of course, be a few deserving cases amongst this number, but upon sufficient honest proof being given by the party concerned this obstacle can be overcome.

Because a husband might be intemperate or lazy or have a slight attack of rheumatism should not be accepted as excuses for deserving work, as no pity is shown towards a widow, not even if she is ready to collapse from over-exhaustion.

We quite understand that the head of the Public Works department may not be aware of such conditions and we would like to see legislation enacted prohibiting the employment of married women. Also, some punishment could be imposed on married women who obtain work under false pretenses, not only in government buildings but in the various shops, firms and factories throughout the city and country.

The Union of Federal Office Cleaners, Local No. 67, which is affiliated with the Associated Federal Employees of Canada, will be pleased to co-operate with the government in every way possible to eliminate such injustice without bringing hardship to any one party.

Mrs. M. Stanyar, Ottawa

GETTING A BIT BACK

MARCH 7, 1923

The other day a jockey was bitten by a racehorse. That is an incident which, I should have thought, would pass unnoticed, except perhaps by the jockey. But the newspapers made as much of it as if Mr. Bernard Shaw's beard had been caught in a circular saw.

It seems that jockey-biting by racehorses is a rare occupation. I am surprised. I should have thought it would have happened every day or oftener.

Think of the life of a racehorse. It is true that he has good food and lives in a stable in which many a man would be glad to keep his wife and family. But the poor thing never knows when its branmash is going to be doped. It never can be certain whether it is going to have its toilet performed with a brush or comb or hypodermic syringe.

This alone is calculated to wear any average racehorse to catmeat. But there is much more. How very trying to the temper to be brought in seventh time after time, when, if the jockey had only let you run in your own way, you could have romped home first, with leisure to look round and nod to your friends en route!

And how would you like, I wonder, to endure the low-bred laughter of farm horses at the sight of your sock and the coarse chaff of butchers' cart-horses at your taste in fancy waistcoats — the ones with the large holes for the eyes? And it must be remembered that a racehorse gets very thin-skinned through constant grooming.

The life of a racehorse, believe me, is a dog's life: and since a jockey is generally more easily accessible than a trainer or an owner, I cannot marvel that it is the jockey who gets bitten. The only reason I can suggest for the infrequency with which the racehorse seeks this relief is that to its pampered palate, the flavour of jockey is repellent.

P.H.

DOMESTIC CAT CONTROL
JUNE 13, 1923

Everyone whose heart is gladdened by the lilt of the song-sparrow, the chatter of the house-wren, or the gossip of the tree-swallow must feel a touch of remorse to think that these little optimists are singing in the face of death from the crawling, sneaking, murderous cat.

Ottawa public schoolboys are making from 700 to 1,000 bird-houses annually and are having the best possible luck getting tenants. Often a house will be occupied within 24 hours after it is up — to the great joy of the boy and his family, who are forever after champions of bird life.

What a reward for his efforts to find that a half dozen prowling, angry cats sneak up the post at night and reach a paw into the house and kill and eat the inmates!

How can we fight the cat? You can't train a cat not to touch birds except while you are watching it. Try it on your canary. In the city, one cannot use firearms. There are hundreds of homeless cats in Ottawa which live by robbing garbage pails and by killing birds. There are numerous birds which by nature nest in the grass and thus fall easy victims to these thieves. The majority of bird houses are easily accessible and there isn't a particle of doubt that the birds live in constant fear of attack.

To all who love the birds, to all who would have their boys and girls grow up as bird-lovers, and to those who have seen what a blessing even a few birds are in the garden, I would say, destroy all the cats you can.

G.T. Rowe, Ottawa

DEFENCE OF THE CAT
JUNE 20, 1923

Your paper seems to be utilized of late by a few cat-haters to work up a campaign against pussy and, as is usual with overly enthusiastic propagandists, extreme argument is resorted to and unfair assertions made.

I am not disposed to defend the prowling "barnyard" variety of cat, but certainly think when it comes to being a nuisance some varieties of birds have left the cat a long way in the rear. I have watched bird life more or less closely in the past two or three years and noted that when a beautiful oriole and his mate appeared among the apple-trees, they were immediately attacked by

sparrows in massed formation and absolutely prevented from adding the joy of their presence to the locality.

I have never seen a cat interfering with a bird-house, but have noted the more belligerent type of feathered animal make prey on his fellow bird. I venture the statement that more young are taken from nests and devoured by those bird cannibals known as blackbirds, in a week, than are destroyed by cats in five years.

A well fed, properly cared for cat will not devote much time to the birds, even though by nature he is a hunter. The Ottawa Cat Club was formed for the purpose of assisting in the prevention of cruelty to all dumb animals and aims at the extinction of the "mangy backyard" variety by encouraging in the breeding of high class animals such as the Persian, which instead of being a nuisance as described by your correspondents, are greatly cherished household pets.

As between a sparrow, or blackbird, and a good well bred cat — well, give me the cat every time.

M.D. Cumming,
President, Ottawa Cat Club

PUT A CARILLON IN TOWER
JULY 21, 1923

As the time for the completion of the central tower of the new parliament buildings draws near, many Canadians who take a keen interest in music and the development of the musical sense in the rising generation of Canadians look forward to the completion of the tower as a unique opportunity for the installation of a carillon of bells.

Everyone who has heard the wonderfully beautiful carillon placed last year in the tower of the Metropolitan Church, Toronto, will appreciate what it would mean to turn this beautiful tower from a dumb monument into a speaking exponent of national sentiment.

Surely, the belfry of the new parliament buildings when finished will not be allowed to remain silent when for such a comparatively small expenditure a world-renowned carillon of forty or fifty bells would complete it, capable of sprinkling their music over the capital and the surrounding country, crashing out national airs on history-making occasions, leading community singing, marking the time of day, tolling at times of national mourning, and in fact making the tower a real part of our national life.

George McCann,
Secretary, Music Committee,
Metropolitan Church, Toronto

Editor's note: In the early 1920s, as reconstruction of the centre block of the Parliament buildings was under way after the 1916 fire, Senator George Bradbury first suggested a carillon for the new tower. The idea caught on, and in 1923, the government proceeded with the project. The 53-bell carillon arrived from England four years later, in time to be inaugurated on July 1, 1927 as part of Canada's Diamond Jubilee celebrations. The tower itself, initially known as the Victory Memorial Tower, was officially christened the Peace Tower in 1933.

OXFORD COMPANION TO CANADIAN THEATRE

Canadian playwrights such as Merrill Denison did not get their just due of praise, said a writer. The Weather Breeder about an Ontario backwoods farmer and his daughter was staged at Hart House Theatre.

CANADIAN DRAMA

JULY 26, 1923

Your editorial on Canadian drama is provocative to a belligerent mind. "There is real need for Canadian plays at the present time," you say.

Well, sir, there is more need for a decent chance of hearing when they are written. We are suffering from an inferiority complex and the tyranny of commercialization in all things literary, but especially in drama.

Merrill Denison's plays should create as much interest here as the work of the neo-Celtics in Ireland — Lady Gregory, Yeats, Synge and the rest. They are just as racy of the soil, just as true to the comedy-tragedy of Canadian life. Somebody will discover this — when he is dead.

If the playwright were making sausages or paint, he would almost certainly be famous, or if he were a Mohawk Indian or got himself killed or some railway magnate or *The Times of London* critic said he was good.

If a Canadian playwright could get a cast, he should have the use of the Little Theater to try out his play because it is impossible to tell how a play will act until it has been staged. He would be quite content with such audience as was interested in experimental Canadian drama — or with none.

The commercial theater wants names or sensations, and if anyone needs to know how bad it is, he has only to read the columns of the "Best Plays of the Year" which have appeared in the United States. Their badness is incredible — speaking of the majority, Canada would be better off than this if it really had no drama.

Considering the little expense of production at the Little Theater, its aim should be to experiment in Canadian drama. It is not out to make money. It should be out to give a hearing to Canadian drama, whether it has audiences or not. It should have some curiosity about the Canadian dramatists who have been snubbed by commercial publishers, managers and timid critics who do not believe that anything dramatically good can come out of Canada.

The playwrights would ask simply for fair field and public judgment and they would ask for no favours because they happened to be working in Canada. Yes, there is Canadian drama, but it can't get a hearing.

Alfred Buckley, Ottawa

Editor's note: It would be another 75 years before Merrill Denison's controversial 1923 play, Marsh Hay, the story of unmarried pregnancy, poverty and twisted justice in the Ottawa Valley, was produced professionally, when the Shaw Festival staged it in 1998. Wrote Shaw artistic director Christopher Newton in the playbill: "Too provocative? Too strange? Too close to home? Perhaps it's only now we can recognize this fine and moving play as it comes towards us."

AN APPEAL FOR HELP

AUGUST 8, 1923

This is no doubt a heart-breaking case I am about to put in your paper with the hope that some person of means will be kind enough to come forward and offer this man a position, as the city's grant of $3.20 weekly will not keep him and his wife and kiddies. I think any society that offers a man that pathetic sum of money who is willing to work ought to be ashamed of itself, especially in the circumstances that this person is in.

This man, when war was on, answered the call of his country, and the great hue and cry was, "Go and nothing will be too good for you when you return." When he returns he finds that he cannot do any hard work because of an inward trouble.

I ask, is there anyone who can live on ten dollars a month? No, well why should this man with a family to keep, starve when we have, or are supposed to have, what we call a Great War Veterans' Association and a City Relief Fund?

This particular man was in hospital and discharged and came home and to his sorrow finds his seven-month-old baby had died through lack of nourishment, and he did not have the means to pay for the infant's burial.

It seems a shame to think that this kind of thing is coming to the public's eye every day and that nothing is being done to rectify matters and to have some help provided, as goodness knows we are paying enough taxes which I think could be used to proper sources besides building civic baths, etc., when the city is in great need of relief in every way. Surely we have enough land in the cemetery to give this child a respectable burial.

O, where are these good Samaritans of Ottawa who are supposed to give freely?

R.H. Dale, Ottawa

THE CONDEMNED ESKIMOS

OCTOBER 27, 1923

Allow me to compliment you on your October 23 editorial on the condemned Eskimos. It is a most timely and fair representation of the case in which a verdict has been made, which, if carried out, might well stain the good name of Canada in the eyes of the world.

As I have lived for two years among the Eskimos in the

Coronation Gulf region where the murders were committed, I should like to mention certain elements entering into a fair treatment of the case not referred to in your editorial.

It is first of all necessary to consider the case from the Eskimo point of view, and as the accused cannot speak English nor express themselves in writing, it devolved upon the judge and jury at least to make themselves acquainted with Eskimo psychology and conceptions of morality, and not be content with their personal impressions and the services of an interpreter. Apparently the court has not considered this, in spite of the fact the Dominion government employs half a dozen highly-trained scientific men for the express purpose of studying the native tribes of Canada in a most comprehensive way, and these impartial scientists have shown by their writings that they probably understand more of their psychology than all the lawyers in Canada combined, not one of them has been asked for an opinion in the matter. This is a most serious mistake, and for that reason alone should the execution be postponed.

It should not be forgotten that the Eskimos are people who, as far as their civilization and material culture is concerned, live in a stone age, and that as far as their mentality is concerned, they are largely as children, with the irresponsibility, ignorance and emotional character typical of children.

The Dominion government has long ago recognized this by making the Indians and Eskimos wards of the federal state allowing them largely to live their own primitive life and when they came in conflict with the law, a careful and impartial investigation of the causes for each crime committed was made, and the result of this, together with a consideration of their complete lack of understanding of white man's principles, entered into the verdict and determined the severity of the latter.

In this case, the murder of [Northwest Mounted Police corporal] Doak seems to have been a matter of the desperate attempt of the prisoner to regain his liberty; but was perhaps more akin to the acts of a cornered savage or wild animal.

There is no quality more essential in dealing with Eskimos than patience, supported by firmness, self-control and irreproachable morality, and mighty few of the white men who have come into contact with the Eskimos possess these qualities. When one thinks of the dregs of humanity carried into the Arctic by whaling-ships from the Pacific coast and certain private traders who have entered the Arctic, and the crimes committed by them against the Eskimos, and the disease they brought with them which wiped out whole communities of natives, one may well understand why it is that the Eskimos fear the white man, whoever he may be.

I have had opportunities of observing personally in Hudson's Bay the qualities of the Eskimo: He is cheerful, capable and fearless both on land and sea, helpful and considerate, and stands by his word. He is a marvel in the line of making a living and using the supplies of nature in regions where others, similarly situated, would starve or freeze to death. He supports his wife and family without any outside help, and even children-waifs, infirm and old people are taken care of by their own community.

In our days when bank-robbers, burglars and highwaymen receive life sentences or less for just as serious crimes, it seems absolutely wrong to condemn two young, able-bodied Eskimos to death for a crime the seriousness of which they do not understand. No sensible person would condemn to death irresponsible children, even if they committed murder.

This letter must not be understood as a criticism of the persons who have reached their verdict after a, no doubt, careful consideration of all judicial evidence. I merely want to call attention to the psychological element, apparently overlooked, but which explains everything to me and many others; and to do what I can to prevent the government of a part of the British Empire, which has always been fair in its dealing with the primitive races subjected to it, from taking the life of an Eskimo for the first time in history.

Frits Johansen, Ottawa

Editor's note: Alikomiak and Tatanagma, the two Inuit men convicted for a series of killings in the summer of 1923, were eventually hanged. But not before their case sparked a national debate and was even appealed to the Dominion cabinet, which refused to stop the executions. There never was any question about whether the men did the killings, which occurred after Otto Binder, a Hudson's Bay Co. employee, seized Alikomiak's young wife. A feud arose among the Inuit concerning the affair, and six were killed during the melee that followed. Binder fled. Alikomiak and Tatanagma were arrested by Cpl. Doak, but Alikomiak escaped, killing Doak in the process, and later tracking and killing Binder. A judicial party from Edmonton travelled to the western Arctic to try the men. A jury trial was held and the two sentenced to death. According to the Oct. 23 Citizen editorial, the case was worthy of attention because of several factors: "One is that it was through the lust of white man that the trouble originated. Another is that the Eskimos belong to a remote region which has lived by its own primitive laws and knows little of 'the stern justice of the white man.' Lastly, the jury consisted of white men — not 'peers' of the accused — and the trial was joked through by the two prisoners, who themselves unwittingly gave the evidence which brought about their convictions."

A COMMERCIALIZED SANTA CLAUS
DECEMBER 19, 1923

No doubt the idea of Santa Claus arose out of the endeavour to give a tangible embodiment to the spirit of generosity and goodwill which is supposed to prevail at the Christmas season.

How inappropriate, then, it is for shopkeepers throughout the land to represent the bounteous, good-natured old self as presiding over their stock of Christmas wares which are being doled out in terms of dollars and cents! What a cold, selfish, ungenerous figure Santa Claus must be in the minds of many poor children as they walk along the streets and gaze at his effigy through shop windows and notice his broad, fatherly smile transformed into a business grin which says: "You shall not have toys unless you have shekels!"

If Christmas has the significance which Christians would attach to it, why contaminate the symbol of Divine beneficence presented to the childish mind by associating this symbol with the miserable dollar?

Sell goods for what they are; gather all the coin you can but do not undo the imagination of childhood by bringing poor old Santa Claus into the circle of "money-grabbers."

P. Drohan,
Roseathal, Ont.

1924

Local: Two new civic baths open and are named after ex-mayor Frank Plant and acting mayor Napoleon Champagne (May); New Civic Hospital opens on its present day site on Carling Avenue (December)

National: The Canadian Red Ensign becomes the country's official flag and the Royal Canadian Air Force is established (January); Ottawa Senators' forward Frank Nighbor is the first recipient of the Hart Trophy as the NHL's most valuable player (April); Methodists, Presbyterians and Congregationalists join to form United Church of Canada (November)

World: Vladimir Ilyich Lenin, mastermind of Russian revolution, dies, leaving papers saying Joseph Stalin should be removed as Communist party secretary (January); Major Hollywood film studios merge to form Metro-Goldwyn-Mayer Corp., which as MGM will become a movie powerhouse for decades to come (April)

Births: Actors Marlon Brando and Lauren Bacall; U.S. writers William Styron and Truman Capote; U.S. president Jimmy Carter

Deaths: Writers Franz Kafka and Joseph Conrad; U.S. president Woodrow Wilson; composer Giacomo Puccini; U.S. labour boss Samuel Gompers

SENSUAL DANCING

JANUARY 5, 1924

Surely all lovers of decency must rejoice to read the pronouncement of Cardinal Bégin of Montreal against popular indecencies of today.

Though we may differ from our Roman Catholic neighbours in Quebec in some respects, yet now we should be glad that there is enough sincerity, seriousness, and courage in their authorities to plainly and openly denounce vice, and to warn all that those who persist in practising or in countenancing vice cannot shield themselves under the name of Christ, but must be treated as rebels against His word and His spirit.

The advertising pictures allowed in this city without protest from anybody proclaim with loud voice how low the sense of decency and the sense of duty in fighting against indecency have become, both in private individuals and in authorities of church and state. If the action of Cardinal Bégin fails to arouse us to corresponding efforts it will be to our exceeding shame and guilt.

S.D. Hague, Ottawa

OTTAWA SWIMMING BATHS

JANUARY 5, 1924

At a meeting of the executive of the Eastern Ontario section of the Canadian Amateur Swimming Association held on Wednesday last, the undersigned were authorized to inform the citizens of Ottawa through your columns as to the importance of having the two new indoor civic swimming pools put in operation at the earliest possible date; and also to give those who have not had the opportunity of first-hand knowledge of the use to which these buildings will be put, a suggested mode of operation and an explanation of the benefit to be derived by the community from the knowledge and practice of swimming, diving and life-saving methods.

The new Ottawa swimming tanks are lined with white tile and the water will be filtered and clarified so as to make it clear and pure. The water will circulate through the filters continuously. The teaching of swimming and life saving will be greatly facilitated and the pupil will have greater confidence knowing the actual depth of the water at a given point in the pool. The carrying on of instruction will not be handicapped by the climactic conditions affecting outdoor swimming.

It is considered that a supervisor with an assistant for each swimming pool, one woman for every day in the week and an additional woman for Saturday if needed, is all the staff required. The supervisor or assistant should hold papers necessary to comply with the law regarding the boiler and one, or both of them, be able to make necessary minor repairs. A knowledge of swimming and life-saving would be an advantage as a qualification for supervisor; and also that he be a married man.

It is suggested that the use of these pools be divided off for the following groups: Plant Bath — Monday, mixed (men and women); Tuesday, women only; Wednesday, men only; Thursday, women only; Friday, men only; Saturday, family.

Champagne Bath — Mon., women only; Tues. men only; Wed. mixed (men and women); Thurs. men only; Fri., women only; Sat. family.

The school authorities should be consulted as to hours required for their classes in the morning and afternoons, under their supervision. The baths to be open to children without special supervision after school hours. The baths to be open for adults between 1 and 6 p.m., and 7 to 9 p.m.

Admission: Family tickets, to be used on family swimming day, entitle the parents purchasing them and their dependent children, in charge of one or both parents, to at least four swims in the month. These tickets to be issued at 50 cents per month.

General tickets, sixteen swims for 50 cents. Regular admission, at hours not made free, to be five cents. School children to use the baths free on Saturday mornings. After regular hours at night, say after 9 o'clock, to be reserved for swimming clubs and a suitable fee charged for the use of the baths.

Cleanliness of swimmers. The dressing rooms of the baths will be operated by the locker system and it will be duty of the supervisors to insist that each person before entering the tank shall take a shower with soap and hot water.

The experience of other cities such as Montreal, has been that in the building and putting into operation of their first indoor swimming pool they have passed through exactly the same conditions as Ottawa is doing now: that is to say, politicians have made capital of the lack of knowledge of the citizens in general as to the great benefit to be derived by the community from the indoor swimming tanks in an endeavour to secure votes. Montreal now has eleven civic indoor swimming pools and eleven or twelve club pools, a total of twenty-two for the city.

A.E. Smail, President,
Ernest R. Williams, Secretary

Editor's note: The Champagne Bath, on King Edward Avenue, is still in operation. The Plant Bath, on Preston Street, was closed in 1998 to save money.

FLOWER THIEVES ACTIVE

MAY 3, 1924

Any person who goes along Elgin Street can hardly fail to notice the lawn and flower beds in front of the Normal School. Yesterday, the flowers came into bloom again and there were several dozen large daffodils which had opened out fully and would have been in bloom for more than a week had not some sneak thief systematically cut every flower.

Systematically, I say, because every plant was cut by someone who knew how. They even took so many leaves to each flower to give a bouquet effect. I do not know for what purpose they were taken but with daffodils selling at a dollar per dozen it does not seem as if they were taken for any other purpose than that of selling them.

It is very discouraging for a man to spend hours of time preparing flowers for the sake of beautifying these premises only to have his work snuffed out in one evening by a sneak thief or thieves who think nothing of beautiful flowers in public places but only think of furthering their own ends by dishonest means.

H. Pearce, gardener,
Normal School

THE ENGLISH "JOHNNIE"

MAY 14, 1924

Years ago several types of humour were common on the music hall stage, and were later designated "Vodville."

I refer to the Irish, Jewish and German comedians, all of which in turn were the accepted means of amusing the public. The English Johnnie was another means of raising a laugh and also caricaturing the English race as a whole. Each of these types have had their day and are now seldom seen.

The English Johnnie, however, refuses to die. A night ago I called at a local theatre and saw one of these ridiculed by his partner for his perfectly good English to the great merriment of a Canadian audience, and to further increase the disgrace, tweaked the Englishman's nose, pulled around his hat and generally made a monkey of him.

Most of this may be very acceptable in the States, but here in Canada it is about time theatre managers made enquiries of their artists as to what their show consisted of, and also laid down rules governing them. I doubt if any of our boys who went overseas to defend the Empire ever met such a cowardly individual as the public here are expected to believe could for one moment be regarded as an Englishman.

M. Powell, Britannia Bay

THE VAGARIES OF SCIENTISTS

MAY 21, 1924

A series of entertaining articles on the Darwinian Evolution have been running in the Saturday evening editions of *The Citizen*. The writer seemed convinced of the truth of the whole theory from the original ooze to highest order of development.

Like many careless people, he has, however, put imagination to work in his deductions from the facts presented. All that he has shown is that there is a general similarity of forms and that different species approach each other very nearly in structure. All else, beyond that, is pure imagination.

I am not a biologist and do not claim to be an expert geologist, but in the course of preparation for mining business a general knowledge of the latter science was acquired. In geology there is nothing to prove the Darwinian theory. We see types in one age, disappearing in succeeding ages. It seems quite as rational to claim that the older forms died out, and the new ones were created as to say the new types were the product of evolution.

There is an axiom in nature, and science: "Like produces like." Another saying equally true: "A river cannot rise higher than its source." That seems to leave no room for Darwinian Evolution.

In ancient Egyptian tombs there are some wonderfully accurate paintings. Among them some of the red-legged goose of the country. Pictures 5,000 years ago have depicted the bird exactly as it is today, after thousands of generations of bird life. It has not become a swan: it is still the same goose of old. Why has the evolution not gone on?

There is an evolution, but a different thing from the Darwinian. It may be called natural evolution. It is this evolution that has made so many varieties of one species. The dog, for instance, was without a doubt, created in one type. Just what sort of an animal is now not known: but it is safe to say it was a true dog, in every respect, and not some other animal. This natural evolution has given the varieties we have today, from the huge St. Bernard, to the tiny lap dog.

The claim that all life proceeds by evolution through millions of years, from half-inanimate primordial germs, is just asking a river to rise higher than its source. At most, life has had varied forms from the earliest times, which seem to die out and be replaced by new creations, just as the biblical prophets say.

N.B., Ottawa

OTHER PEOPLE'S FREEDOM
AUGUST 27, 1924

I would like to protest against the drunks on the street-cars. On Saturday evening a white-haired old lady had to give up her seat and stand in a crowded aisle because the drunken fellow on the same seat began to splutter and swear. A clean-looking young athlete was prepared to have him pulled him off, but the old lady said, "Don't touch him, some poor thing is waiting for him."

God help and pity the poor wives and children of such "men." But they should know no law demands them to be tied up to a drunkard, not even love, as the love they get is only filth after the "ladies" that got their living from such have finished with them.

Why are the drunken lot allowed on streetcars anyway? One will say it is a free country and they have as much right to the street cars as anyone else. Quite so, but it is also a free country for decent people, and they have a right to ride on the street cars without being poisoned by fumes from the breath and clothes of the drunks.

H.J. Bailey, Ottawa

CHOOSING A NAME
SEPTEMBER 13, 1924

I have got a new-born sister,
I was nigh the first that kissed her;
When the nursing lady brought her
To papa, his infant daughter,
How papa's (dear) eyes did glisten!
She will shortly be to christen;
And papa has made the offer
I shall have the naming of her.

Now I wonder what would please her
Charlotte, Julia, or Louisa;
Ann and Mary, they're too common;
Joan's too formal for a woman;
Jane's a prettier name beside;
But we had a Jane that died.
They would pry, if 'twas Rebecca;
That she was a little Quaker.

Edith's pretty, but that looks
Better in old English books;
Ellen's left off long ago;
Blanche is out of fashion now.
None that I have named as yet

Are so good as Margaret.
Emily is neat and fine;
What do you think of Caroline?

How I'm puzzled and perplexed
What to choose or think of next!
I am in a little fever
Lest the name that I should give her
Should disgrace her or defame her;
I will leave papa to name her.

Ernest R. James, Ottawa

BOOZE AGAINST TEMPERANCE
OCTOBER 22, 1924

Thursday next will be a momentous day in Ontario. "Booze" and "Temperance" will be fighting for supremacy, and the vital question is: Which will win?

It all depends on the voters, each of whom should ask this question: "Which side has done the most good in the world?" If he faced this questions fairly, he would have no hesitation voting on the side of temperance.

There is not one single word to say in favour of booze; it blasts, blights and injures not only individuals but whole communities. Booze is the father of nearly every vice. No, booze never has been, never can be, and never will be, any good.

The moderationists try to prove that booze is a good thing for everybody. Whoever heard of a drunkard being reformed by giving him the opportunity to get more booze?

They say also that prohibition interferes with a man's liberty, and they would give him the liberty to get more drink so that he may the more often beat up his wife and children and do a lot more mischief in addition.

Which does the policeman have to watch more, the sober man or the one filled with booze? Does the street car conductor trouble about the man who boards his car sober, pays his fare and quietly takes his seat? But he worries good and hard when he sees a gentleman from Hull loaded up to the neck get on his car.

Opponents of the O.T.A. [Ontario Temperance Act] are whining, "Don't rob the working man of his beer!" That used to be the cry in England, so they let the poor working man have his beer, with the result that the drink bill every year is enormous and the poor working man still remains poor.

Fred Bateman, Sr.,
Ottawa East

Editor's note: By a margin of 40,368, Ontario voted to retain the Ontario Temperance Act, which since 1916 had banned the making, importation and sale of alcohol. Ottawa voters, however, ignored the advice of the Citizen and cast their ballots in favour of ending the prohibition. Indeed, voters in the province's three largest communities — Toronto, Hamilton and Ottawa — preferred the establishment of government-controlled liquor stores. In the end, though, the province's rural vote carried the day.

AGAINST DEER HUNTING
NOVEMBER 5, 1924

Saturday's paper states that hunting is starting in Quebec and that sportsmen of Ottawa and Hull are on their way up the Gatineau with hounds. To every person who thinks this over must come a feeling of pain.

People are constantly boasting about civilization being in an advanced stage; there are clubs and lodges and institutes in the interests of social, political and moral welfare — there are humane societies and protection acts and a hundred and one other similar futile attempts to regulate human action.

Daily we read of some one being fined for driving a lame horse or a horse with a sore back. These are sights which people will not permit. They are offences against the law.

But consider the case of the deer, harmless beautiful creature of the wild woods. The sight of one delights the heart. Yet these beautiful creatures are chased by hounds in packs for days at a stretch. They are forced to swim lakes, climb hills and thread ravines at break-neck speed, forever confronted by fresh hounds or by the human scent. Scarcely can they get a bite of grass or a drink of water while the season lasts. They run till their tender hearts break from the terror of the hounds.

You call them sportsmen who go out with hounds, they who lie in wait behind a truck or boulder to try their luck with high power rifles, who congratulate themselves if they can only hit a breathless fugitive. Seldom are they killed outright but with broken bones or punctured lungs they drag their weary bodies along until they must give up.

We who speak with horror of the Spaniard with his bullfights, who consider cock-fighting beyond the pale of the law, who fine a man for driving a lame horse, we permit by legislation the heartless, beastly slaughter of the innocent children of the forests.

What a thin veneer is civilization when opportunity and $2 will license the sportsman to act like a savage. Surely the world belongs to more worthy representatives of civilization and humanity.

G.F. Rowe,
Ottawa

THE OTTAWA CITIZEN

Hospital authorities prohibited nurses from wearing the bobbed hair style such as worn by screen star Colleen Moore.

HOSPITAL TRUSTEES AND BOBBED HAIR
DECEMBER 12, 1924

I feel that some measure of reflection will be cast upon the intelligence of Ottawa's citizens, if they take no account of this absurdly prejudiced and irrelevant attitude on the part of the trustees of the new Civic Hospital.

I refer, of course, to their attitude towards nurses with bobbed hair. What, in heaven's name, has the length of a woman's hair to do with her efficiency in nursing?

Granting for the sake of argument (and in perfect opposition to my own opinions), that short hair is unsightly — are we paying taxes to maintain a palace of beauty, a Dream of Fair Women, or are we expecting to secure the best possible professional service at a time of physical distress?

The agitation over bobbed hair is so stupid a crusade that one finds it is difficult to defend it intelligently. It is rather like throwing bulwarks of steel against a fog. One can see the implication behind the term "bobbed hair": one is brought to the realization that it is fallaciously regarded as a hoydenish mode welcomed by flappers and suited to the very young. This, I submit, is an unconsidered view to take.

Granting again, for the sake of argument, that dignity and age are measured by a woman's hair, it is not at all necessary to adopt the original mode of coiffure — one which looked in many cases like a surprised feather bed. There are as many modest ways of dressing short hair as long. It is not, as so many people seem to think, unnatural to a woman, nor does it proclaim her a godless creature, careless alike of her morals and her person.

It is a great convenience, bobbed hair! Easy to keep tidy, and a revelation to women who have struggled with ounces of mutinous hair. It offers relief to those whose brain-fatigue is largely the result of carrying a top-heavy superstructure. It has so many advantages over long hair that there is not room to set them forth.

If only a tenth of all this flurry were made over the state of people's teeth!

Alice Howat, Ottawa

Editor's note: Although the hospital board said it preferred longer hair that could be neatly pulled back into a bun, in early 1925 it lifted its restriction on nurses wearing bobbed hair, which was associated with loose morals and fun-loving women such as film star Colleen Moore.

1925

Local: Arches crack in the Victoria Museum and other buildings are damaged as Ottawa is rocked by its most severe earthquake since 1753 (March); The Russell Hotel, centre of Ottawa's social life for four decades, closes its doors, the victim of lost business to Château Laurier (October)
National: 12,000 coal workers begin five-month strike in Nova Scotia (March); Canadian Senator Raoul Dandurand is elected president of the Assembly of the League of Nations (September)
World: Out of prison just two months, Adolf Hitler reorganizes his banned party and releases *Mein Kampf*, the Nazi blueprint he wrote in jail (February); In a celebrated trial, John T. Scopes is convicted of teaching evolution in his Tennessee classroom (July)
Births: Canadian jazz pianist Oscar Peterson; New Brunswick premier Louis Robichaud; black militant Malcolm X; U.S. senator Robert F. Kennedy; actor Paul Newman; U.S. journalist William F. Buckley Jr.; bluesman B.B. King
Deaths: Baseball star Christy Mathewson; Elwood Haynes, inventor of first automobile; poet Amy Lowell; hydro-electricity pioneer Adam Beck; Charles Ebbetts, owner of Brooklyn Dodgers baseball team

THE GLEBE POSTAL SERVICE

JANUARY 10, 1925

Two years ago, a sense of justice impelled me to write a letter to *The Citizen* regarding the unfailing kindness and courtesy of the employees of the central post office, Ottawa, during the rush season of Christmas and New Year.

This year once more, in the Glebe post office, working amidst conditions which naturally tended to test one's spirit, the officials struggled calmly, heroically, and efficiently, morning, noon and night, to answer all the questions and meet all the demands, day after day, of an inconsiderate public.

I am simply amazed that the physical strength of those who so faithfully serve us is capable of enduring the terrible strain for so long a period; and I certainly believe that the people of Canada are most willing to furnish them with the best working conditions and extra help under extra circumstances.

L.M. Weeks, Ottawa

Editor's note: A month after this letter was written, employees of the post office — a branch of the Dominion government — were for the first time brought under the same regulations as other civil servants. That meant a raise in pay, but also slightly longer working hours. Some critics predicted this would be the end of the unfailing service referred to in the above letter.

A STRANGE PREDICAMENT

JANUARY 10, 1925

I was in rather a strange predicament today while having my lunch. There was a lady sitting at a nearby table, and judging by her fur coat, I should imagine that she was the mother, feeding her child with a knife.

The child was not old enough to feed itself, therefore not old enough to approve of such a daring action or the cold thrills others must have received from the performance. I did not know whether to rescue the baby or to warn the lady of the danger of cutting the child's mouth. Seeing as it was none of my business, I hurried up and got out before any further excitement.

Again, I doubt that being fed at such a high speed could be good for a child so young. She would shovel three knifefuls into the child's tiny mouth, to her own once. I am sure that this lady was fond of her child, and that it was an action that she had learnt from somebody else which is too great a risk to try on a child.

Victor Bernard, Ottawa

OLD TIME CONDITIONS

JANUARY 17, 1925

No doubt, some like myself have listened to the patriarchs of old as in a reminiscent mood they waxed enthusiastic about the good old days. The days when a person in receipt of eight dollars weekly lived in clover and when office clerks receiving a salary of $500 annually had a place in the sun.

The rank and file of course had small wages but, bless your life, they kept out of debt, very different from some of the present generation, who receive $1,000 or more yearly. Some of the old stock actually believe that even in these days a householder with a salary of the above dimension should be in a position to feed, clothe and educate his numerous infantile group and have a margin left to spend on real estate.

They seemingly are unconscious of the passing years, and that the cost of living has advanced four fold during the last twenty five years. We have all heard how in those old days, eggs were sold at three dozen for 25 cents, chickens at 60 cents a pair, front and hind quarters of beef for a mere song, apples at 75 cents a barrel. And in respect to the winter fuel, one could fill their shed or cellar for a matter of $10. Instead of paying rent, many people bought their happy homes in the same way that many in the present time purchase kitchen cabinets and pianos, on the installment system.

Remembering these old times and comparing the purchasing power of the almighty dollar, one might well realize that the present day householder in receipt of double the wages paid in former days will, if he is not very careful, to use a common expression, be as fast as a dog in dough.

We are living in a progressive age and in days of efficiency, where there is little room for sentiment and where it is not good form to have many children.

J. R. Wilkinson, Ottawa

RADIO TASTES DIFFER

JANUARY 31, 1925

The purpose of this letter is to suggest that the *Citizen* work up public opinion to demand that all radio stations in Canada broadcasting jazz programs be compelled by the government to broadcast at the same hour, say from 12 midnight onwards, and further, that if they broadcast jazz before this time they shall be suspended from the airwaves for ten years, and that any goof caught writing or phoning to a broadcasting station in favor of the aforesaid negroid noises shall be placed in a large squirrel cage for two hours a day for six months, and compelled to perform in the public parks.

This is sumptuary legislation with a vengeance, but worth trying.

Charles B. Hoby, Ottawa

WHY THE BAD SIDEWALKS

FEBRUARY 18, 1925

Much fuss has been made about the streets last week being in a bad state; but the streets were not the most important thing, it was the condition of the sidewalks.

The real cause of the terrible condition of the sidewalks last week was owing to the non-removal of the snow, which caused their great height with a ridge in the center, owing to the Indian-like way pedestrians had to travel in the fresh snow. This would not have happened had the snow been removed, as it fell, but this was not done, many times this winter the plough never appearing, but the snow allowed to be tramped down by foot traffic.

The next mistake was committed by shoving the road snow to the curb and over the grates and drains line, causing them to block the first thaw. This was done at the behest of a few auto faddists to the great disadvantage of the vast majority of those who use the sidewalks.

Allowing the snow to pile up at the curb was the secret of the flooded sidewalks when the rain came.

Joseph Firth, 232 Lisgar Street

ON STREET TREE DISTANCES

APRIL 22, 1925

In a delightful travelogue of Ottawa gardens, Mr. George Simpson, president of the Ontario Horticultural Association, recently showed among other Ottawa views, a picture of Clemow avenue.

The scene was used to demonstrate particularly the value of the uniform planting of trees. Mr. Simpson told his audience that the trees stood thirty feet apart, and expressed the opinion that they would have been much more effective had they been fifty feet apart in the row.

Mr. Simpson was followed by Mr. A.H. MacLennan, professor of horticulture of the Ontario Agricultural College, who approved of the wider planting of the Clemow avenue trees but recommended the still greater width of sixty feet, which would in a few years have made the avenue a delightful one. The trouble with our tree planters, he said, was that they often failed to take into account the growth that the trees would make if given reasonable opportunity.

Ottawa is regarded as one of the beautiful cities of this continent and the Horticultural Society in bringing out the suggestions that their speakers express in these educational courses will, I feel sure, be helpful to our repre-

JAZZ; AMERICA'S CLASSICAL MUSIC

Reader wanted "negroid noises," as made by the likes of Louis Armstrong, limited to radio air time after midnight.

sentatives at the City Hall as well as to the Ottawa Improvement Commission in their continued efforts to beautify the city.

J.B. Spencer, Ottawa

SOMEONE SHOULD SAY THIS IN THE SENATE

MAY 23, 1925

You ask, "Who should be senator?" I think that we would easily agree that as the Senate is at present constituted to appoint political friends to vacancies, only men of high character should be so appointed — men whose efforts in the Senate should be religiously made for the greatest good of the greater number of all Canadian citizens, not one's mere political friends.

If the soul of the Senate was imbued with the simple desire to work for the general good instead of for various class interests, there would be no necessity for criticism of senators; but, unfortunately, we find it almost impossible to believe that senators are moved by noble motives, for their actions in the past have proved to us that the rights of democracy have not been served by the political friends whom ruling governments have appointed to review the acts of elected representatives of Canadians in parliament.

If our Senate was elective, instead of appointed, might we expect that the general good of all our people would receive more careful treatment? It seems to me that men relying upon the good will of voters would be careful to retain that good will, knowing that their re-election depended upon it, whereas present senators, nominated for life, are not required to render account of their services.

Patronage has been abolished in the civil service, but the highest class of civil servants, senators, are still wrongfully subjects of the very system which the whole people of Canada have abolished after decades of effort. It is my opinion that those who serve or those who govern are the servants of the people, and that both should hold power to serve or govern only by passing competitive examinations or by the lawful votes of the adult people.

An elective senate might not be perfect, but we would at least have the power by our votes to change it, and, just at present, I do not see a better way to bring it into being than by popular vote.

Garrett O'Connor,
Bridgeburg, Niagara River

VERY MUCH SHOCKED

JUNE 10, 1925

I want to draw the attention of the authorities to a very deplorable state of things which happens every year during the swimming season. And what I mean is — denuded swimmers in public places, such as a certain spot in particular, on the shores of the Canal, behind the Pure Food Show building at the Exhibition Grounds.

Every day, several youngsters ranging from ten to fifteen years old, have the nerve and seem to be tolerated to have their daily dip without a bathing suit of any kind. I mention "tolerated," as it certainly must be known; this is not a deserted place, it is right here in the heart of the city, and the R.C.M.P. barracks are not so far away.

The result of this is that respectable people who are quietly yachting or canoeing along the Canal are scandalized by the demoralizing scene, which are unavoidable to the eye, and in most cases, especially canoeists of the fair sex, are insulted by these ill-breds who do not know the consequence of their act, but should be watched more carefully and given a good lesson.

This should not exist in a civilized country, and especially in a city which boasts of having a good reputation. It is a disgrace, and its prevention is urgent.

Frank Baker, Ottawa

THE LIBRARY AND THE CHILD

AUGUST 15, 1925

In a recent issue of the *Citizen,* there appeared an editorial which began by mentioning the flocks of boys and girls who use the children's department of the public library, and went on to speak in a disparaging tone of the books these boys and girls borrow. The writer finds fault with these borrowed books, saying: "In far too many cases, they are school stories or adventure stories" of little literary value.

I do not think he knows, or possibly can know, what children in Ottawa read. He ignores altogether non-fiction, or the whole popular group of books on scouting, camp-lore and woodcraft; or books on how to make things, such as "The Amateur Electrician's Handbook", which has been borrowed ten times since May 26th; or collections such as John Drinkwater's "Way of Poetry" which has been out ten times during the last half year. Examples such as these, enlarged a hundredfold, give a rather good defence of the children's department.

But why in any case should one speak superciliously of school or adventure stories? What is wrong with "Tom Brown", "The Hill" or even "For the Honour of the School?" If it comes to adventure stories what fault is to be found with "Two Years Before the Mast", "The Cruise of the Cachalot", "Captains Courageous", or the humbler but wholesome tales of Henty or R.M. Ballantyne?

Nothing more fully betrays the writer's lack of grasp of the subject than his reference to children's books as "light, romantic fiction with its sugar-sweet endings." Presumably he has in mind the kind of novel written many years ago by E.P. Roe. This has nothing to do with children's fiction, which is very rarely romantic.

If by "sugar-sweet endings" is meant the married-and-lived-happily-ever-afterwards type, they are exceedingly rare among books for boys and girls. Perhaps the most common happy endings in school stories are those which tell of the winning of a prize or of a game, or the successful entrance to college life or to some occupation. It would be a marked misuse of language to call these "sugar-sweet."

There are, however, some things in this article with which one must agree. The writer properly emphasizes the function of the public library in supplementing the work of the schools. He rightly insists on the place of fairy tales and legends in children's reading.

But when he proposes to do away altogether with the children's department of the public library and to substitute for it a collection of the best books from all ages, he is surely going too far. We fear his perfect library would have to wait for the perfect child. In children's books, as in other things, perfection is rarely found; one must often be content to accept dross if one gets gold in paying quantities. It is all a question of judgement — where to draw the line.

In summary, the writer appears to be irritated because there is nothing morally wrong with children's books. Is he looking for cases of infidelity or for the hackneyed triangle even among books for children? From such a contingency Good Lord deliver us!

W. J. Sykes, Librarian,
Ottawa Public Library

CRITICISM OF HUMANE SOCIETY

SEPTEMBER 25, 1925

The Humane Society of Ottawa has done so much good work that it cannot but grieve any true lover of kindness to criticize it adversely. But above our duty to animals there is our duty to mankind — when an organization dependent upon public support and sufferance, but directed by the rich, becomes a mere instrument of oppression for the poor.

And yet it is very, very often the human who should have the pity. I know human nature and I know the poor. I know that many a poor man under the awful grind of poverty, many a woman under the unavoidable power of coercion, has envied the privileges and immunities of the animal.

A few weeks ago a Humane Society officer summarily shot the horse of a woman vendor on Byward market. His contention was that the horse could not eat hay. In vain did the woman alone with a wagonful of produce and many miles from home, plead that the horse did not need to eat hay as the grass in her pasture was knee high and that she fed him mash and crushed oats; in vain did she make clear her helplessness and dependence upon the horse; in vain did she beg for the privilege of bringing an independent veterinary to testify that the horse was fit to live and labour. The officer was adamant.

Commenting upon the case to me, the officer said: "If the woman had brought a hundred vets it would have made no difference. If I want to shoot a horse I have absolute authority. So to shorten the argument, I shot hers before she could bring anyone at all."

And this in Canada — where British justice, British fair play, is supposed to obtain!

The woman of whom I write, English and a newcomer to this country and to the land, handicapped by a total lack of financial resources and with a couple of babies, is fighting desperately hard to obtain a foothold. She hauls and sells the vegetables so that her husband, an ex-soldier, may have the time to grow them.

Is there a single member of the Humane Society who knows what it means to grow and sell, at the present heart-breaking prices, sufficient vegetables to pay the rent, taxes, market stall and fees, stabling of horses and food for horses and vendor, and have sufficient left to maintain a family? Cruelty to animals! We can never be as cruel to animals as life is to the poor and as we are to one another!

Mrs. W.E. Hopkins,
Ottawa

HUMANE SOCIETY ANSWERS
OCTOBER 3, 1925

With regard to the letter of Mrs. Hopkins criticizing my action in destroying the horse belonging to a neighbour of hers, I may say that the horse in question was absolutely unfit for any work, otherwise it would not have been destroyed. The horse was examined by two veterinarians before any action was taken.

Surely the public will not believe that we are heartless enough to destroy animals without just and sufficient reasons for doing so.

L. Mulligan, Inspector,
Humane Society of Ottawa

Local: Ten years after fire destroys the centre block of Parliament Hill, the Peace Tower, called the Victory Memorial Tower until 1933, is finished (February); Ottawa celebrates the centenary of its founding as Bytown in 1826 (August)

National: Scandal forces resignation of Liberal government in June, and Tory leader Arthur Meighen is installed as prime minister. His defeat a few days later leads to September re-election of Liberals under Mackenzie King; Ontario voters decide in favour of government control of liquor, ending a decade of prohibition (December)

World: Scottish inventor M. John Baird unveils a new wireless machine that transmits moving pictures. He calls it a television (January); Buried Mayan city is found in Mexico's Yucatan province (February)

Births: Canadian novelist Margaret Laurence; actress Marilyn Monroe; Queen Elizabeth II; Canadian director Norman Jewison; poet Allen Ginsburg; jazz musician Miles Davis

Deaths: Film star Rudolph Valentino; French painter Claude Monet; sharpshooting cowgirl Annie Oakley

ON POLITICS
JANUARY 2, 1926

In your editorial taking aim at the thirty thousand voters who did not vote in the last municipal election, they being too indifferent to vote, I think they are discouraged knowing the way their majority vote can be twisted by the members they elect to suit themselves, as in the case of the amendment to the Ontario Temperance Act.

These elected members set aside the majority vote and worked on the minority vote in favour of the wine and beer bibers; and threaten to go farther at the next session of the Ontario legislature — thus violating their promise that the majority vote should stand.

Also, of the unbalanced budget, they show a deficit of $4,905,293, and voted an appropriation for their own use of $68,000 extra sessional indemnity, which may be Canadian law, voting away the people's money without consulting the taxpayers, but it may not be British justice.

Why could not the electorate devise ways and means to defend themselves and stop all voting away their money, boosting salaries to suit themselves without consulting people? Generally speaking in law the principals are responsible for their agents' doings. In the case of the electorate electing M.P.'s as their agents, to act for their interests, and the prosperity of the country, do they vote away all their authority to protect themselves?

Our national debt is high and out of all proportion, through politics, for a young country like Canada full of wealth and promise. We have in sight waiting for development, our mines, forests, lands, fisheries and deep waterways. These can be developed with the help of our army of unemployed, but we lack the men with efficiency to manage successfully the affairs of this great country.

I am well aware I carry no weight in these matters, but there can be no harm done in advising as I see it. Trying to govern a young country like Canada with its untold wealth through political governing is futile. Get wisdom, and with all your getting, get understanding — and adopt a platform of industry and progressiveness coupled with common sense and goodwill, and have no fear of the results in our Home of the Maple, and save Canada for Canadians.

The time to put this into action is now, the present moment.

Burt Harum, Ottawa

Editor's note: Although Ontario had voted in 1925 to retain the Ontario Temperance Act, the province went ahead and made beer and wine available, on a trial basis, through government-controlled outlets. That appeared to ease fears sufficiently to sway a majority to vote in favour of a full lifting of Prohibition in another plebiscite in December 1926.

THE DOMINION ARCHIVIST

JANUARY 9, 1926

The danger of losing our Dominion Archivist, Dr. Doughty, naturally leads those who care for Canada, and whose horizon is not bounded entirely by dollars and cents, to ask again what is the value to the country of our collection of historical records, and what has Dr. Doughty done, and what is he doing for the Archives?

Moreover, it raises the question whether the government would be wise to allow a larger corporation, even one so old and honourable as the Hudson Bay Company, to take him away from the service of this country. It should be possible, and it would appear to be the beginning of wisdom, for the country to retain a good servant when it knows it has one.

Each year, the Dominion Archives are being more widely used by writers and teachers of history. To illustrate, three of the outstanding books of the year in Canadian history are practically founded on the material obtained from the Archives: Professor Trotter's "Canadian Federation," General Cruikshank's three volumes of the "Simcoe Papers," and Senator Andrew Haydon's "Pioneer Sketches of Bathurst."

Each summer, more teachers of history in our schools and colleges come to Ottawa to pursue some line of research. This summer, a school of history is to be conducted under the auspices of the Archives. Should anyone object, "What has this to do with the masses of the people?" the reply is obvious. It is the result of historical research as seen in such books, and as taught in the universities, that filters down through our high schools, and public schools, so that the truth about this country's history may reach in some degree every boy and girl in the land.

Under the direction of Dr. Doughty, the Archives have been not only much enlarged but transformed. He has secured in Canada, in England, and in France, a vast deal of material connected with, or forming the basis of the history of our country; he has had it arranged and classified, and made available for study. Students who have pursued their researches in various capitals of the western world bear testimony to the Archives in Ottawa as being one of the best managed. From my own observation this summer in Paris and London I can testify to the activity of branches of the Canadian Archives in securing material in Europe.

But perhaps one of the chief services Dr. Doughty has rendered to Canada is the securing of certain very valuable collections as gifts through his personal influence. Examples of this are the magnificent Wolfe collection given by the late Lord Northcliffe, and the great Durham collection. I do not think there is anyone else in Canada whose personal influence in England and France would result in such great acquisitions to our Archives.

LYNN BALL, THE OTTAWA CITIZEN

Dr. Arthur George Doughty, who developed the National Archives of Canada, is the only public servant who was honoured with a statue.

I think it is still possible to retain the services of Dr. Doughty for the Dominion Archives. It may be that the government is doing all it can in this direction. If so, it should, in this matter, have the support of every enlightened citizen and member of parliament.

W.J. Sykes,
Ottawa Public Library

Editor's note: Despite an attractive offer from the Hudson's Bay Co. to write the firm's history, Dr. Arthur George Doughty was persuaded by prime minister Mackenzie King — and his own sense of duty — to stay with the Archives, where he remained chief archivist until retiring in 1935. Six decades later, Doughty is still considered one of the finest public servants in Canadian history. For 31 years beginning in 1904, he developed the Archives into a significant cultural institution through his genius for searching out crucial historical materials and his determination to make the Archives accessible to the public as well as academics. He was awarded a knighthood in 1935, and the statue erected in his honour behind the Archives is the only such tribute ever bestowed on a public servant.

WHERE CHAMPLAIN STOOD

FEBRUARY 1, 1926

As an old-time resident of Ottawa, I venture to express the hope that the writers of poems, on what is sailed with somewhat doubtful propriety the centenary celebration of the foundation of the city, will endeavour to be more accurate than the author of an effusion which has appeared in your columns.

There is not the slightest ground for the statement that

Champlain ever stood on Nepean Point — on either the true geographical point of the township, or upon the bluff to which ignorance of the precise location of "The Point" and careless usage during nearly fifty years have irrevocably, I fear, transferred that storied name.

I should like also to correct the popular error that Champlain's observations of latitude was made at the Chaudière Falls. That opinion is based on a misconception of his narrative coupled with a disregard of the character and location of the portages of the Chaudière. These were three in number, the first by the Falls, the second by what is known as the Little Chaudière Rapids, and the third by the Rapides Des Chênes. The rapids did not render a portage or even a decharge necessary, but were difficult to ascend.

After passing the first portage by "about a quarter of a league" — his distances are merely estimates and not always accurate — Champlain had taken to the water again, as was usual at a point where a large pulp mill now stands at the east end of the viaduct over Brewery Creek.

Then, "We had," he says, "to land a second time and go about 300 paces" — to pass undoubtedly the Little Chaudière Rapids — "after which we got into the water to get our canoes over sharp rocks, the trouble of which can be imagined, I took the altitude (hauteur) of this place and found it to be 48 degrees 38 minutes of latitude."

After passing the second portage of the Chaudière the only place where there would be trouble in getting the canoes over sharp rocks was at the Rapides Des Chênes. There and not elsewhere the observation was made. Some day I trust the point projecting into these rapids will be marked with a memorial to the great explorer and the first astronomical observation made beside the grand River of the Algonquin.

F. R. Latchford, Toronto

Editor's note: In the years since Mr. Latchford — a Supreme Court justice and amateur historian — wrote his letter, little fresh evidence has emerged to justify the placement of Samuel de Champlain's statue at Nepean Point (it was put there in 1915). In fact, most historians would agree with Mr. Latchford's suggestion that any Ottawa area memorial to the French explorer should be erected above the Deschênes Rapids at a spot just east of Aylmer, which is probably where Champlain's party rested after its final portage of the rapids.

DISABLED SOLDIER'S QUESTION
FEBRUARY 12, 1926

I am a returned disabled veteran, originally enlisted in the 77th unit, and served in France with the 12th C.R.T., where I was disabled.

Before enlistment I never knew what it was to be sick in any way and never had to be attended by a physician; but since being injured on active service, I have been operated on in France and since my return to Ottawa I have received five more operations, which I can prove by a statement of my hospital record.

I have a medical certificate from some of the leading physicians of this city recommending me for disability pension from 50 per cent to 100 per cent, and after endeavouring for about two years to be awarded a pension, as I am unable to earn my living as I did before enlisting, the Pension Commission awarded me a pension of $5 a month.

I have been receiving city relief this past month and as my wife, who is not in good health, is working trying to help and earning $23 a month, they deduct the amount she earns from the amount of relief I would get if she was not working. I find it impossible to buy clothes or other necessities as it takes up the actual cash my wife earns to pay for insurance, electricity and other small items, which must be kept up.

Do you think I have been treated fairly? I was fit in every way when I enlisted, and had always done hard work, but when I came back and tried to do the work I was accustomed to do, I found it was not only impossible for me to do so, but could not do lighter work which was offered me. I have a certificate from my former employer to that effect.

Peter Ouellette, Ottawa

Editor's note: Such complaints were common in the years after the First World War, and many ended up in the letters columns of the Citizen. Although details are unclear, it appears that after writing the above letter and receiving published support from other veterans, Mr. Ouellette was given an unspecified pension increase.

ON WOMAN'S HALL OF FAME
FEBRUARY 24, 1926

I understand there is a scheme on foot to erect a woman's hall of fame at Nepean Point. This edifice is to be built by the woman's club of Ottawa.

Well, Mr. Editor, the public are weary of these campaigns for institutions and in times like these each household requires every dollar for the upkeep of their own homes.

Just what is the object of this woman's club? We have one club — the Canadian Club for Women — why have two? Why not economize by using one club house for all purposes?

I understand there are to be several rooms in this famous proposed hall, and anyone can purchase fame by giving $25 and have their names upon the walls. I never heard of fame bought for so low a figure — it is even less than a bargain. How can $25 make anyone famous? Just how the gathering of $25, by selling cakes and pies, giving teas in private houses at an entrance fee of 50 cents, creates an opportunity to have names places upon the walls of fame where intellect and heroism only should enable one to hold a seat with the mighty, is beyond me.

Our purses have been drained enough, and we sicken at this scheme. The raising of money from the public for this kind of notoriety is simply a nuisance.

It is the pioneers of Canada, women who have suffered hardships in the building of our nation, who have left footprints in the sand of time, who have passed to the great beyond, whose memory will remain green. These are the women who ought to occupy a prominent place upon the walls of Canada — not bridge ladies, or afternoon ladies, or those who sell the largest number of tickets for a concert or a tea. These methods are not sufficient to have her name engraved upon a hall of fame.

Now if these ladies would only turn their attention to the servant question and train them to become proficient minds. We cannot secure faithful, trustworthy girls who are proficient in every way, like we had years ago. They ask the highest wages and are not worth it. They do not want to work or even do their duty to their employer. They are so full of jazz to do their work properly.

This, Mr. Editor, is work for women. If they would enter into this it would be a great help to the young mother, by giving her a useful experienced servant who would co-operate with the mother, give her more time for training and upbringing of the future youth of Canada.

This would be something achieved, instead of building up brick and mortar their own vain glory, such as a hall of fame for women.

Ethel Topley, Ottawa

Editor's note: The women's hall of fame was never built.

DO THEY CATCH MUCH?
APRIL 28, 1926

While enjoying a walk in the vicinity of Hog's Back I have noticed on many occasions men fishing in the Rideau Canal; with large nets attached to wooden poles. After watching this method of fishing one comes to the conclusion that it is certainly an easy and quick way to obtain results.

Those of us who are familiar with the canal know it is the "fishing grounds" for the boys of our city. What effect then has this net fishing on the efforts of our boys who use the stick and line, and who are not out for any selfish motive of their own, but there simply to enjoy themselves at this healthy pastime?

The answer is clear. A boy thinks he is a very poor fisherman, gives it up as hopeless, and finds amusement elsewhere, usually in some undesirable place.

City life has its snares and disadvantages for the boys of our land. We should therefore do all we can to encourage out-door life for our boys. By putting an end to this net fishing we will have gone a step in that direction.

David McCausland, Ottawa

MIXED BATHING
MAY 29, 1926

The very clever little prophecy regarding mixed bathing which appeared in your columns this morning is worthy of comment.

I am one who has not as yet lost my timidity for deep water, and the one strong inducement to go to the Plant baths this past and present season was the existence of mixed bathing on club nights, when my husband could swim with me, giving me more confidence and helping me lose fear of the water, and thus accomplish the art of the glorious sport of swimming and diving.

I know I am expressing the opinion of all the ladies of our swimming club. Club members represent citizens of Ottawa, and even though "mixed bathing" is prohibited in general, we are thankful that swimming clubs can still exist and each lady may be permitted to swim with her husband, her brother or her father as the case may be. Let's be broadminded.

Elizabeth Spencer Bullis, Ottawa

1927

Local: Cornerstone laid for Confederation Block, the largest government building in Ottawa, still standing today at Bank and Wellington streets (July); First airmail from U.S. arrives in Ottawa (October)
National: U.S. places quota on number of Canadians looking for work south of border (April); Transatlantic telephone service between Canada and Britain begins (October)
World: Charles Lindbergh first to cross Atlantic Ocean in solo, non-stop flight (May); Babe Ruth hits 60 home runs, a new single-season baseball record (September)
Births: "Mr. Dressup" Ernie Coombs; Canadian financier Paul Desmarais; Cuban leader Fidel Castro; Canadian philanthropist Phyllis Lambert; Inuit painter Kenajvak Ashevak; actress Gina Lollabrigida; writer Gunther Grass; governor general Roméo Leblanc
Deaths: Dancer Isadora Duncan; Spanish cubist painter Juan Gris; governor general Henry Petty-Fitzmaurice (Marquess of Lansdowne)

WHY BRING CHINESE IN?
JANUARY 29, 1927

You recently reported a suggestion made by Professor W. W. Goforth of McGill College. No doubt this learned gentleman knows his business, and far be it from me to show him what he should do. Being only a labourer, my education is limited, in fact very limited.

But sometimes education is not all, and a little common sense and knowledge by personal experience goes a great deal further.

The professor suggests that labour be brought from China to work at road-building and opening the province [British Columbia] for settlement; I have no doubt, Mr. Editor, that you are a fair-minded man and a good and upright Canadian citizen, with patriotic ideals, and not looking forward to have foreign decorations pinned on your breast for helping foreign governments relieve their congested countries, and making a dumping ground of this fair Dominion of ours.

The wage proposed by this professor is 25¢ per day with board, and with an agreement signed for three to five years. This wage should be for half an hour's work instead of one day. Why bring Chinese to do labouring work when there are thousands of unemployed Canadians waiting for such work to start, and very glad to get a chance; but at a living wage, so that a man can walk with his head up knowing that he is one of the spokes of this mighty wheel, getting a living wage for a day's work instead of having him going around like a whipped dog for the want of food and other necessities of life; or having to beg for them?

Why bring Chinese or others when Canadians are out of work, especially when our white man is worth 20 Chinese at any time? The white race cannot live at the wage suggested by the professor, but they can certainly give satisfactory work for decent wages which will enable them to live like men and good Canadian citizens.

We must never forget that Canadians stood the grind and came out smiling in years from 1914 to 1918, so why try to deprive them of an honest living and give it to Chinese?

Joseph Mirabelli

ILL-PAID PROFESSIONAL WORKERS
FEBRUARY 16, 1927

Professional workers form less than four per cent of the whole civil service, and they are comprised of engineers, technical agriculturalists, chemists, biologists, etc. Although comparatively few in number, they are of vital importance to the welfare of the people of the Dominion, and the results of their researches have been of inestimable value in the development of Canada, particularly in the basic industry, namely, agriculture.

One of the first requirements of a man aspiring to a professional position is that he shall have graduated from a university of recognized standing. This implies that he has spent several expensive years of hard study, and, in addition, he is expected to have perfect health, good address, research ability and a number of other acquired virtues.

For this, the magnificent salary of $1,500 is usually offered — in some cases it is less — truly a splendid inducement to ambitious young men; and then, if the applicant is successful, after many years of hard unremitting service devoted to the welfare of humanity, he may, if he is fortunate, attain to the top of his profession, which often means a salary of less than $3,000.

Consequently, a considerable percentage of the best men graduating from our universities seek better-paid positions in the United States, while many of our own junior professional positions are filled by men who do not really measure up. This situation, if it continues, will prove very serious, because the men who fill the junior positions today will fill the senior positions in the future.

On present salaries it is very difficult for professional civil servants to maintain a decent social standard, and at the same time raise a family. This is the chief reason why they usually confine their children to one, or two, rarely more. It is only reasonable that they should wish to give their children the same cultural and educational advantages that they themselves enjoyed, and to do this they must strictly limit the size of their families. Thus Canada is denied many potential citizens of the very finest type.

Pro Bono Publico

A TRIBUTE TO THE CITIZEN
APRIL 27, 1927

A pure press goes a long way towards making a pure people. One is glad to know that on the whole the Canadian press is moral and uplifting in tone; and in this respect, and I know I am voicing the opinion of scores of others, the *Citizen* stands second to none.

The churches are usually only opened for public worship one day in seven. On that one day the people hear the scriptures read, and also listen to one, maybe two, sermons. On these they have to feed the rest of the week.

And here it is where the *Citizen* fills the gap. Every day in the week — six of them — the reader is brought face to face with the inspired words of "Holy Writ in A Bible Message For the Day," while the mind is further deeply impressed by the inspiration "The Greatest Story in the World" ably portrays in pictures.

While a bitter controversy is being waged between science and religion on the one hand, and modernism and fundamentalism on the other, the Bible still remains undisturbed and unshaken, and the *Citizen* is doing fine work in the community by keeping to the front the glories and beauty of the Old Book in word and picture.

It sometimes seems the fashion to indulge in diatribes against the press. We have heard sweeping statements from the pulpit, without qualification or discrimination, that newspapers delight to publish sensational stories and discuss unwholesome subjects, and encourage unworthy things.

Let us be fair and discriminating, and recognize the good things that are provided in the press and the evident desire of many editors to maintain a high standard.

Fred Bateman, Ottawa

Editor's note: For several decades until the 1940s, the Citizen published Scriptures daily on Page 1 and Bible stories, in picture form, elsewhere in the paper. From the late '40s until the mid-'60s, the paper routinely published Bible verses on its editorial page.

HARD ON HORSES
MARCH 2, 1927

Our honourable municipal politicians and engineers sit in their cushioned chairs, while the men under them absolutely murder poor old Dobbin by allowing five or six good big storms to pile up our streets and then come along with their tractor and pile it up more.

After all this, they get one team of horses, put them on the city's walkway plow and plunge them day in and day out up to their ears in snow piled mountains high. There should be three teams on this plow instead of one, in such soft weather when this snow is so hard to move.

If some poor fellow was stuck with a load, through his horse being a little balky, and not willing to draw, and was compelled to give him a few lashes of the whip, there would be a woman in every door and window going to have him arrested for cruelty. Yet these very same women will play bridge and gaze through the windows while some poor man is compelled to murder his horses for the city of Ottawa to clean several piled storms when they should be moved after every storm.

I would like to see the mechanical tractor we have spent thousands of dollars to buy try to move what the city was trying to move with one team. It would be there until the sun thawed it out next summer.

John Haley,
Dalhousie Ward

ST. PATRICK'S HOME WORTHY CAUSE

MARCH 5, 1927

Many worthy causes have made appeals to the people of Ottawa but none it seems to me more deserving than that which will be brought to the attention of the charitable on what is known as Shamrock Day. It is on behalf of the indigent, whose misery and whose helplessness must touch every human heart — the orphan children.

There are 272 of these helpless ones in residence at St. Patrick's Asylum at the date of writing. They stretch out pathetic hands to all the kind of heart as well as to those who hear the Divine Master's words, "What ye do to the least of these ye do unto Me."

In remodeling the old building of St. Patrick's Home, special attention was given to sanitation. The health of the children is safeguarded in every way under the supervision of prominent physicians who give their services to the cause. The results are most gratifying. There was not a single death.

Through the kindness of several well-known dentists, a clinic was established at St. Patrick's Home and a number of volunteer nurses assist in this work.

Classes for children in the lower grades are in the charge of experienced teachers amongst the Sisters of the Grey Nuns. A number of boys and girls passed the entrance class last year, while others are continuing their education in secondary schools. It is the aim of the sisters to furnish these little ones with an intellectual training which shall safeguard their future and make these native-born Canadians good citizens who may successfully vie with the best of the immigrants coming to these shores.

Giving motherly care to these poor victims of misfortune, watching over the little ones, is the noble mission at St. Patrick's Home, and it makes but one appeal yearly to the general public by the sale of shamrocks. It is hoped then that the generous people of Ottawa will give freely for this mostly worthy cause.

Anna T. Sadler, Ottawa

Editor's note: The Grey Sisters opened their first home for orphans in the 1860s in a Lowertown home, moving in 1873 to Kent Street and Laurier Avenue, where they cared for orphans — and later the aged — until 1956, when the government decided to place children in foster homes. Since 1963, St. Patrick's Home has provided care to about 200 elderly residents in a complex on Riverside Drive.

PARKING MATTERS

MAY 7, 1927

Judging from the promiscuous and haphazard manner in which motor cars are permitted to park on the main thoroughfares, the man on the street would, I think, be perfectly justified in concluding that either no regulations exist or that, if they do, very little effort is made to enforce them.

I am not referring to places or length of time parking may be permitted. What I wish to refer to, and what, I believe, would tend materially to improve both parking and traffic conditions, is the manner or method of parking. That is, parking too far from curb (often from one to six feet); parking at an angle; parking on both sides of narrow streets; parking too close to street corners, making turning of corners very dangerous to all traffic; parking opposite water hydrants; taking up too much space — frequently sufficient for the parking of two or three cars; and, in short, parking in about every place and position imaginable that can present the greatest elements of inconvenience and danger to traffic.

The driver of a car who has to be constantly on the watch, not only for other vehicles, but for pedestrians and cyclists who seem determined upon a speedy and messy termination of their existence, and who can neither travel nor see in four different directions at the same time, may often merit allowance being made for minor infractions of the traffic regulations.

The person, however, who parks his car without regard to the rights or safety of others is either ignorant, careless, or selfish — and probably all three.

I submit that a brief campaign of education and supervision would quickly remedy this condition to a very material degree. Yes, I know all about the Police Department being undermanned; I make all due allowance for this situation.

What I venture to state is that one active intelligent individual could in from one to two weeks improve parking "manners" 90 per cent, and without the necessity of wholesale fines or summonses. A moderate campaign of control and instruction, coupled with the knowledge that a few wide-awake men are "on the job" all the time, would prove many times more effective than the periodic and spasmodic "drives" which are forgotten as suddenly as they end.

F.S. Graham,
Britannia

JACK MINER FOR CANADA GOOSE

JUNE 4, 1927

In reply to the many requests as to my opinion of the white-throated sparrow as our Canadian national bird, I will say that the white-throat is a lovely bird, but not a bit more so than the white-crowned sparrow, bluebird or some of the warblers, or yet the rose-breasted grosbeak. My, what a beautiful, lovely, musical variety we have to select from!

And, I say, by all means let us have a Canadian national bird, but let it be the Canada goose, the noblest creature that ever lived on land, in the air, or on the water — yes, or on the ice or snow where he is also perfectly at home.

I was born under the protection of the eagle's wing, and I respect that great bird as much as it is necessary for any man to, but our Canada goose is far superior.

When in captivity he will wash himself up and keep clean and respectable, and in about three years, with his mate, will settle down to raise a family of from four to eight, as all Canadians should.

Wild geese pair off for life. I never know them to even make an application for divorce. The male guards his mate on the nest. As soon as the young hatch, he protects them from the opposite side of the mother, keeping the babies between the parents. He will leave his family for her, and for her only, but he will die in the front ranks for any of them.

When travelling in the air, the male Canada goose leads the way, breaking the air for his sweetheart, who is quartering behind him, and his family travels next to her. In brief, he is one of the most self-sacrificing godly-principled leaders the human eye ever beheld, and to know him is to love and admire him.

There is not a human being on earth so good but what personal acquaintance with our noble Canada goose will give him a desire to live better.

Jack Miner, Kingsville, Ont.

Editor's note: Despite endorsements from eminent ornithologists like Mr. Miner, Canada has never adopted a national bird, although every province has one (Ontario's is the loon). The American-born Miner became one of Canada's best known bird experts after establishing a sanctuary near Windsor, Ont., in the early 1900s. The sanctuary and a museum still operate outside Kingsville.

PAINTING BY ROBERT HAUTMAN OF PLYMOUTH, MINNESOTA

If Canada needs a national bird, let it be the Canada goose, the noblest creature on land, in the air, or on water, wrote Jack Miner.

NOISY SHOWS ON QUIET STREETS

JULY 13, 1927

Much as the splendid work of Orange Lodges and kindred associations is to be commended, it appears to me that the method of raising finances by means of inflicting midway shows on unoffending citizens is hardly in keeping with their dignity, or with Christian doctrine, in that the ancient injunction to treat your neighbour as yourself, appears to have been lost sight of.

I think that any fair-minded citizen of Ottawa will agree that to have your garage driveways blocked, your lawn a litter of raucous youth and debris, your flowers stolen, your doorstep a gathering place for borrowers of trifles and souls athirst for city water, the ears of your children assailed by language, which I am sure would be frowned upon in any lodge meeting, and your family driven to distraction by the blare of alleged music and other show noises from noon till 11 p.m., and for some period after that by the honking of the horns of impatient motorists, and the brass mouthed advances of modern youths to ladies, who are shrilly receptive or otherwise, is an infringement of the personal liberties, from which they should be protected by the city.

I might draw your attention that at Bronson and Powell avenues, where such a show is now being placed, the housewives are in most cases alone all day, and imagination can easily depict the sufferings of any who are at all nervous or sick in this hot weather.

The "Brighter Ottawa" we all wish for will not be gained until recognition is given the fact that such shows, whilst all right in their place, are now out of place in the midst of a quiet-loving and respectable residential district.

R.C. Bowen,
652 Bronson Ave.

1928

Local: The Russell Hotel, closed in 1925, burns weeks before it is slated for demolition to make way for Confederation Square (April); Champlain Bridge opens, becoming the area's westernmost span across the Ottawa River (October)

National: Eileen Vollick is the first Canadian woman granted pilot's licence (March); Supreme Court rules women are not "qualified persons" and therefore ineligible to become senators (April)

World: An 80-foot wall of water created by a dam break kills 400 outside Los Angeles (March); Joseph Stalin unveils the Soviet Union's first five-year economic plan (October)

Births: Ottawa mayor Marion Dewar; Quebec chanteur Gilles Vigneault; actress Shirley Temple; artist Andy Warhol; Cuban revolutionary Che Guevara; film director Stanley Kubrick

Deaths: British writer Thomas Hardy; polar explorer Roald Amundsen; U.S. auto pioneer James Packar

FLOGGING

JANUARY 7, 1928

If an individual was to tie up a dog and lash him with a cat o' nine tails he would be arrested and fined for cruelty to animals. Yet a judge will callously hand out this kind of punishment to a human being.

The progressively humane administration of penitentiaries is being nullified by cruelty of this nature. Even in Michigan, where banditry is rampant, the legislation refused to insert a flogging penalty in the statutes.

Surely banditry can be cured without resorting to animalism.

A.P. Clark, Kingston

CRIME IN THE NEWS

FEBRUARY 11, 1928

Someone has said that "a clean, decent press makes a clean, decent people."

I believe this to be true. The newspaper that gloats overs its many columns of sordid crime news injures itself, and doubly injures its readers. Personally, I very seldom read a crime story through. It is generally too revolting and nauseating.

But many of our boys and girls, and especially the former, seem to revel in this class of news, much to their moral disadvantage. Crime news, as news, is valueless and should be eliminated from newspapers as much as possible. It is but pandering to the lowest in human nature.

What we need is a press in our city that is much bigger and better.

Fred Bateman, Ottawa East

Editor's note: Readers might remember that Mr. Bateman also wrote to the newspaper in 1927, effusively praising the Citizen for its moral, Christian tone.

RADIO ADVERTISING

FEBRUARY 18, 1928

A great deal of criticism has been made of advertising done over the radio from the United States. There is great consolation in the fact the listener does not pay for that advertising.

In Canada, we have radio advertising 10 times as monotonous and prolonged beyond comparison and we pay for it. I am speaking of the CNR stations, the upkeep of which is borne by the people of Canada.

The line is not reached or even approached when the president of the railroad gives his regular marathon speech on the merits of the CNR; but when a banquet or concert is broadcast, and must have a "yell" for the CNR given at frequent intervals, and after ever song or selection, no matter how minute, the world must know CNR is broadcasting.

The people of Canada are evidently willing to pay for advertising to themselves yet raise a howl when they get it free from across the border.

H. Stuart, Ottawa

Editor's note: The originator of public broadcasting in Canada was CNR president Sir Henry Thornton, who opened a radio broadcasting service for train travellers, hotel guests and CNR employees in 1923. While most of Canada's stations were privately owned and used U.S. material, the CNR service occasionally employed Canadians for concerts, lectures and other programming. It also used the airways to promote CNR train and hotel services, and regular aired speeches by Thornton. The radio service was discontinued in 1932 with the creation of the CBC.

CANNED FOODS

MARCH 7, 1928

Prejudice against canned foods is happily passing. "Canned," as applied to many minds, is a condition of inferiority; but it is now safe to infer that those who still hold a prejudice against these foods have been unfortunately at the mercy of an indifferent purchaser of the diet of the household.

Canned foods are now standardised according to their quality and one has but to read the label to understand accurately what the can contains.

In the administration of the Meat and Canned Foods Act, the Dominion Department of Agriculture sees to it that the canning that goes on in the 136 operating plants throughout Canada is done with due regard not only to the quality of the products, but also to modern sanitary conceptions.

J.B. Spencer, director of publicity,
Department of Agriculture, Ottawa

A LIVING MEMORIAL

MARCH 24, 1928

In a news item published in today's issue of your valuable paper, I note that it is proposed to make Ottawa's memorial to its heroic dead in the Great War a cenotaph which is to be erected in Confederation Square.

As a citizen of Ottawa, and as a returned man, may I be permitted to express the opinion that I do not believe it is the wish of ex-soldiers that "memorials" in the form of cenotaphs should be erected, when the money subscribed for this worthy object could be used to far greater service in helping those returned men who through no fault of their own are practically destitute.

Here in Ottawa there appears to be a great need for a "Soldiers Home," where men whose health has broken down so that they are not fitted for the labour market could spend their days in comfort. Some of these are in receipt of small pensions which are not adequate enough to pay for their board, etc. outside an institution. But if a home were provided, they could be paying guests as far as it were possible on their pensions.

I am of the opinion that sufficient money could be raised in Ottawa to purchase a medium sized house that could serve as a "home" for these poor fellows I speak of; and that a small grant from the city council would take care of the overhead charges each year.

As I pen these few lines on the above subject I am reminded of those immortal lines from In Flanders Field: "To you from falling hands we throw the torch; be yours to hold it high."

What would our dead comrades say of a Cenotaph Memorial if they could but speak? I venture to suggest their answer would be as one. "Take care of the living."

Our dead comrades are at peace in yonder Flanders Fields, but there are those in our midst who hunger for bread and a comfortable place to rest their war torn bodies. Will you give them a stone?

Douglas Thompson, Ottawa

Editor's note: Although the National War Memorial, a 70-foot-high granite arch designed by British sculptor Vernon March and shipped from England in 35 crates, was erected as proposed in Confederation Square, it wasn't completed until 1939, when it was dedicated by King George VI and Queen Elizabeth. It cost roughly $400,000. A soldiers' refuge was not built until the Rideau Veterans' Home went up in the mid-1940s.

ALIEN IMMIGRATION

MAY 16, 1928.

In discussing immigration into Canada it has been the habit of many speakers to add the number from the United States to those from the British Isles and then compare that total with the total from continental countries in order to arrive at a conclusion as to the amount of foreignization going on in Canada.

Table XIV of the government report for the year ending March 31, 1927, gives the influx into Canada from the United States as 21,025. Of these nearly 10,000 had their racial origin in no less than 30 foreign countries, some of them anything but "preferred."

Many of these people are not desirable immigrants even when they come directly to Canada, but after they have been Chicago-ized they are, well, even less desirable than before.

Perhaps the best way would be to class the whole stream of immigrants into British and non-British, adding one half the U.S. influx to the British side and one half to the non-British. Worked out in this way table one of the government report would give us for the year ending March 31st, 1927: of British racial origin 61,403 and of non-British origin 82,588.

George Exton Lloyd,
Bishop of Saskatchewan (Anglican),
Prince Albert, Sask.

Editor's note: At a Anglican synod held in Kingston in 1927, bishops drafted a proposal calling on the government to slow the pace of non-British immigration and find ways to encourage more Britons to come to Canada. The proposal sparked much public debate, including many thinly veiled attacks on Eastern Europeans, who made up the majority of "non-British" immigration.

THE KING'S BIRTHDAY

JUNE 2, 1928

Upon the eve of the birthday of our gracious and noble King, this sonnet should have especial emphasis, and I have often wished that it might be universally accepted as inseparable from the National Anthem:

Long Live the King! Who hath for his own
The strongest sceptre the world has known;
The richest crown, and the highest throne,
The staunchest hearts, and the heritage
Of a glorious past, whose every page
Reads: Loyalty, greatness, valour, might,
Peace with honour, or stubborn fight!
And a Flag that will never cease to be,
So long as it waves o'er land and sea,
The emblem of Truth and Liberty!
Britons! Britons! the wide world o'er,
Long Live the King! we cry once more:
LONG LIVE THE KING!

George A.S. Gillespie, Hull

Editor's note: This sonnet, with its overweening adoration of the King, was written by Ontario-born poet Jean Blewett (1872-1932), whose work is considered the most conspicuous Canadian example of a late 19th century class of writers who attempted to raise the ideals and moral standards of ordinary people. Mrs. Blewett published several volumes of poetry, and remained one of Canada's most popular poets from the 1890s until the 1920s. For part of that time, she was Domestic Editor of the Toronto Globe.

AIR DISTURBERS OF THE PEACE

JULY 7, 1928

Why do we have to have airplanes? Is there to be no refuge from these pests? Our early morning slumbers are made wretched by the horrible noise. Children are killed by poor landings; pilots by mistakes and passengers fall out.

If there are any practical uses, do they compensate for these tragedies? Is time so essential that we, the multitude, should suffer?

The country which used to be our happy haven is no longer safe, either. In the remote region of the Gatineau these pests swarm noisily over our heads and all make pleasure on the water a terror for fear of the poor landings of the hydroplanes.

Have we others no rights to peace and quiet?

Helene Viets, Ottawa

EX-SERVICE MAN'S PLEA

JULY 18, 1928

I think I have been badly treated after my service towards my country and king, serving 26 years ago in the Boer War, and in Egypt in 1898. I also went through the last war and have received the D.C.M [distinguished service medal].

I have lost my wife now and have got five children. Have been out of work all winter. I belong to Australia — from Sydney, N.S. Wales — and came here 12 months last September.

Could you give me advice as to where my son and I can get work? I am a cook by trade. My son is 16 and knows French and English.

Sir, I should like the public to know what has been done to me. I lost my left eye and have got nothing and must tramp the roads. My son and I have had a hard time since we have been in Canada. Can you find us a job?

John Lavigne, D.C.M., Ottawa

THE CANADIAN RACE

JULY 19, 1928

In an otherwise commendable letter in a recent issue, Mr. John Brown, of Westboro, states that the only true native-born Canadians are the aboriginal Indians. This makes me ask, In what state of the development of a country is nationality or race achieved?

Following the Conquest, England was populated by Normans and Saxons and certain other established races. Their intermarriage gave rise to what are now known as Englishmen. When did they cease to be known as Norman and Saxon? When was the English race first accepted as such? How many generations of birth and environment does it take to establish an individual race?

Most of the younger generation of those born in Canada are of mixed racial origin including the best strains of English, French, Scotch, Irish, Welsh, German and other stocks. In many cases it would be somewhat difficult to determine accurately just what was the preponderant race in a child's make-up. If a boy born in Canada of parents and grand-parents also born in Canada is not a Canadian, what is he?

As time goes on, it will become increasingly difficult to determine the racial origin of people born in this country, and eventually it will be necessary to admit the existence of a Canadian race.

Why not start now? Racial characteristics, due to the accident of birth, have always been greatly exaggerated and are tending to disappear under modern civilization and intercommunication.

A true Canadian is one with true Canadian ideals which he may have assimilated after three or four generations of Canadian birth or which he may have adopted the day he landed from Jugo-Slavia. If he is made of the right stuff the immigrant soon becomes a good Canadian no matter what his birth may have been. His children, in spite of Mr. Brown, of Westboro, will be native-born Canadians.

R.G. Lewis, Ottawa

IS SOCIALISM INEVITABLE?

AUGUST 29, 1928.

Referring to your recent editorial headed "Socialistic Anti-Socialists," in which you mention some of the triumphs of Socialism achieved by the anti-socialistic governments of Canada, one is reminded of Byron's line: "And saying she would ne'er consent, consented."

I think it was Herbert Spencer who once gave it as his opinion that Socialism in the Twentieth Century is as inevitable as Christianity in the Fourth Century. It is in the air we breathe. All the activities which differentiate civilized society from savages are socialistic — police, fire, sanitation, streets, parks, public buildings, railways and canals.

Every year the world is becoming more socialistic and less individualistic, and as we progress from the anarchy of private trading towards co-operation, such as the Canadian Wheat Pool, we are increasing our efficiency and progressing in civilization.

In the above connection, the following extract from G.B. Shaw's new book, *The Intelligent Woman's Guide to Socialism and Capitalism*, may prove interesting to your readers. Under the heading, "Sending Capital out of the Country," this passage occurs:

"Capitalism has no home, or rather, it is at home everywhere. It is a quaint fact that though professed Socialists and Communists call themselves Internationalists, and carry a red flag which is the flag of the workers of all nations, and though most capitalists are boastfully national, and wave the Union Jack on every possible occasion, yet when you come down from the cries and catchwords to the facts, you find that every practical measure advocated by British Socialists would have the effect of keeping British capital in Britain to be spent on improving the condition of their native country, whilst the British capitalists are sending British capital out of Britain to the ends of the earth by hundreds of millions every year.

"If, with all our British spare money in their hands, they were compelled to spend it in the British Isles, or were patriotic or public spirited or insular enough to do so without being compelled, they could at least call themselves patriots with some show of plausibility. Unfortunately, we allow them to spend it where they please; and their only preference, as we have seen, is for the country in which it will yield them the largest income."

In striking illustration of the truth of the above statement, the *London Graphic* for July 14th prints the following evidence:

"A large Boston department store sold over 3,500 pairs of ladies' shoes in one day at a trifle under twelve shillings (say $3) a pair. It was plain that those shoes could not have been produced in America at that price. Inquiries were made, and it was found that the shoes had been manufactured in an American factory established in Czechoslovakia, with money advanced by Boston banks."

Surely these Boston capitalists cannot complain if we have serious doubts as to the practical genuineness of their patriotism, when they use their capital to employ cheap labour in a foreign country to undersell the product of their own home factories.

It is also an example of how capitalism gets round the "quota laws" designed to protect the American workman from being swamped by the immigration of cheap foreign labour. Unable to import it direct, they export capital to the country where the cheap labour is.

That their action results in still further demoralizing the market for labour, and the fruits of labour in their own country, does not enter into their calculations.

C.E. Benedict,
Westmount, P.Q.,

THE ASSOCIATED PRESS
Reader quotes G. B. Shaw's guide to socialism to support argument.

FOR FIFTEEN-MILE SPEED LIMIT

SEPTEMBER 29, 1928

"Public safety is the highest law," about which who can doubt? But where is that safety today when autos are allowed to travel 35 miles an hour, and 100 is often reached?

Such is encouraging crime to pile Olympus-high upon crime, when in 1866 the railways upon guarded tracks didn't travel more than twenty miles an hour in Canada. In that year, when travelling from Point Levis to Montreal a herd of cattle feeding alongside the rack outran our train!

Now "men are lovers of pleasure more than God," as the prophet describes; but the craze for speed has overtaken even this, the most decadent age since history's dawn.

"In a good man's breast is a God — his conscience," and if this be asleep the future is dark and dreary. For mercy sake, ye rulers, awaken this conscience and safeguard the public by making the maximum for autos on highway not more than fifteen miles per hour, and less than five miles per hour upon city or town streets or society must fall by its own inertia!

W.H. Compton,
Justice of the Peace, Kingston

1929

Local: Experimental filtration plant, Ottawa's first, begins operation on Lemieux Island (February); Driveway extension from Laurier Avenue north to Sparks Street opens (July)
National: Canadian schooner carrying 2,800 cases of liquor is sunk by U.S. Coast Guard off the Louisiana coast. Captain and crew arrested on suspicion of smuggling, but eventually released after protests from Canada (March)
World: The movie Wings wins the first Academy Award for best picture. Janet Gaynor is best actress, Emil Jannings best actor (May); Financial world descends into chaos after stock market crash (October)
Births: Prime minister John Turner; Ontario premier Bill Davis; Canadian writers Antonine Maillet and Peter C. Newman; civil rights leader Martin Luther King Jr.; Jewish refugee Anne Frank; jazz pianist Bill Evans; businessman-environmentalist Maurice Strong; actresses Audrey Hepburn and Grace Kelly; golfer Arnold Palmer
Deaths: U.S. frontier lawman Wyatt Earp; actress Lillie Langtry; auto pioneers Carl Benz and David Buick; Ottawa organist and composer C.A.E. Harriss

HAIL THE KING'S RECOVERY

FEBRUARY 1, 1929

Everyone should urge upon the government of Canada that a day be appointed for observance throughout the Dominion as one of thanksgiving and praise to God for so mercifully restoring His Majesty the King.

Never in the world's history have so many prayers been offered up to the King of Kings for the recovery of any earthly king, from the humblest poor old woman at the gates of Buckingham Palace to the most exalted to walk this Earth. The miraculous recovery of His Majesty from the very valley of the shadow of death is the answer to these millions of supplications.

Should such a day of thanksgiving be ap-

CHRONICLE OF THE ROYAL FAMILY
King George V's chain-smoking harmed the British monarch's health. He nearly died in 1929 but survived to live until 1936.

pointed, the hearts of all Canadians, indeed of the whole world, will go out, not only to His Majesty for the devotion to duty he has exhibited throughout this long and trying illness, but also to Britain's most beloved Queen Mary and all other members of the Royal Family.

Frank J.D. Barnjum, Montreal

Editor's note: After several years of suffering from a chronic bronchial condition — likely aggravated by chain-smoking — and septicemia, a form of blood poisoning, King George V slipped into a feverish coma in December 1928. When x-rays failed to identify the source of the problem, chief royal physician Lord Dawson de-

cided on drastic action — he plunged a syringe into the king's chest and drew off 16 ounces of fluid from the lungs. Within hours, the king was on the road to recovery. He stayed in relatively good health until his death from heart failure in 1936.

A CANADIAN —
YET NOT A CANADIAN

FEBRUARY 25, 1929

My grandparents were all born in Canada; my parents were born in Canada; I was born in Canada. But what am I? I would like to say I was a Canadian, but evidently there are no such people.

Four of my great-grandparents were born in Canada. Of the remaining four, one came from Scotland, one from England, one from Ireland and one from Germany.

On the card I received on which to register my baby, I read, "Do not say you are a Canadian." So I wrote down on the card that I was born in Carleton county and was pure Irish. My husband preferred to be Scotch. He wouldn't spend time working it out logically, as I did. I was spared being asked what the child was.

Every father and mother in Canada have to sign these cards. I wonder if many of them see the humour of it, as I do. But I would like to know why our government will not allow us to acknowledge ourselves Canadians?

(Mrs.) Ross McDougall, Maxville

Editor's note: It wasn't until the late 1940s that the government officially laid out the conditions needed to be Canadian. As a result, those born in Canada or those who successfully applied for citizenship were finally able to formally think of themselves as Canadian.

CANADA'S FLAG

MAY 25, 1929

Occasions arise when Canada, within our British Commonwealth of Nations, would signalize herself as a national unit by some flag or banner.

This legitimate desire implies no loosening of our Imperial cohesion. On the contrary, the wish would be to proclaim British citizenship coincident with Canadian identity. Heretofore the Union Jack, with the "arms" of the several provinces grouped upon a shield in the "fly," has served. But it seems an incongruous make-shift.

We all loyally accept the Union Jack as our British Imperial emblem. Canadians as a racial fact are not English, Scottish, Irish, French, Swedes, Italians or any other separate people. They, or their ancestors, left their old homes across the water as such. Today they are Canadians; and as such and as part of the Empire, are, in its widest sense, "British."

To signify this Canadian amalgam, a virgin emblem must appear. And with our Union Jack in proper place, none would have more significance than a green maple leaf in the "fly" of that Imperial flag.

However, it seems essential that parliament should authorize such a flag, before it can lawfully be flown by Canadian citizens.

H. Percy Blanchard, Ellershouse, N.S.

Editor's note: The maple leaf has served as a symbol of Canada since 1700, and was first used on a national flag in 1924 when it was made part of the "fly" of a revamped Red Ensign. It did not become the dominant part of a flag until today's flag was adopted in 1965.

MORE ON QUIBBLING

JUNE 15, 1929

Mr. Charles Benedict, in a letter in today's *Citizen*, gives further proof of his expertness in the genial art of quibbling. If there is any "applesauce" in our letters, Mr. Benedict can rightly be credited with furnishing a very generous quantity of spice. And if your readers are not informed, well, they shall at least be entertained.

Mr. Benedict admits that our present economic system is "rotten," yet is ever ready to sing its praises. He seems obsessed with the idea that "by feeling in a man's pocket you can tell what is in his head." The rich, in his estimation, are all "exceptionally bright and good people," so thoughtful of and helpful to the poor (whom he seems to consider as generally envious, dull, vicious, degenerate — a worthless lot as a whole), giving them not only work but wages, or, as he puts it, placing their wealth where "it helps to pay their wages."

Is he not aware that the workers themselves produce the wealth that "pays their wages," and that they do not get paid until they do? The workers are continually loaning or advancing wealth to their employers. More than that, in the case of Mr. Henry Ford, whom Mr. Benedict extols, his employees have presented him with possibly the largest individual fortune in the world today.

Furthermore, government ownership of the CNR is not an instance of "pure Socialism," for the simple reason that the CNR employees are exploited to the same extent as are the employees of the CPR. The freight and passenger rates on the CNR are not Socialistic labels by any means, but, like those of the CPR, are arranged according to "what the traffic will stand."

Our streets, sidewalks, water-works, sewers, schools, etc., also our country roads and national highways, are used more or less in a Socialistic manner — but the workers concerned in their creation, upkeep and operation, are exploited to the limit as a rule.

It will never do for us to fold our arms and rely on the "inevitability" of Socialism, no matter what Herbert Spencer said. Nor must we let clever triflers like Mr. Benedict cajole us into thinking "Socialism is making rapid headway" anywhere but in Russia.

John Lyons, Ottawa

APPEAL TO AN AUTO DRIVER

JULY 12, 1929

I wish to protest against the recklessness of an automobile driver who killed a pet dog on this street today. I would appeal to him still to make some statement regarding this perhaps minor tragedy.

It affected not only the life of the little dog, but greatly grieved the small children who saw what happened. The dog was not unaccompanied, but had been taken out by an adult. The driver may have felt that he was not to blame, but surely he could have left his name or done something to identify himself.

Mrs. J.R. Leader, Chapel Street

EPISODE
JULY 24, 1929

During the evening of the 11th July, about 7:30 o'clock, in a city of the province of Quebec I entered a hotel to obtain and consume a draught of an amber coloured liquor called beer. By this confession one may gather that I am not a member of a temperance organization.

Immediately opposite the small square table upon which was deposited my order, two men at a similar table and over similar liquor to mine I saw engaged in animated conversation. One of them upon his right knee was nursing a youngster of about the age of three years; evidently at that age already a tipster, upon two occasions eagerly quaffing the liquor offered him, (or her) with a relish apparently born of a somewhat lengthy habit.

It was merely a "side glance" that I took of the trio, nor was I shocked or amazed at the spectacle of a child drinking beer. My past acquaintance as a police officer of pre-Great War days of public houses and liquor consuming kiddies in the underworld of a vast metropolis, having inured me to such incidents and spectacles, which in my day in the period referred to were common everyday occurrences.

But the irony of it all, the time, the place, the child, in connection with the hubbub occasioned by North American prohibition activities, and child welfare movements, smote me with peculiar and grim force and emphasis.

A.E. Venn, Ottawa

FROM AN AUTHORITY
JULY 27, 1929

Permit me to commend to city newspapermen generally, and also to the lady journalists, a picture showing at a local theater entitled *Gentlemen of the Press*. Not since Upton Sinclair wrote the book *Money Writes* has there been presented to the public so damning an indictment of modern journalism.

Here, the *Gentlemen of the Press* are portrayed in their true colours, from the highly efficient newsmonger, with his flair for a good story, loyalty, self-sacrifice, etc., to the weakling who drinks to excess, sleeps at his post, and whose vows are written in water.

Possibly there is no profession extant today — apart from modern warfare — in which its devotees are so quickly exploited, burnt out, and cast on the scrap heap, as in connection with the great city dailies. The workers engaged therein have to deny themselves the joy of friendship, the ecstasies of love, the delight of reading good literature, the charm of home life, music, art, and all the essentials of modern culture.

They live and have their being at the very center of things, but, without actual contacts. The salt of life has indeed lost its savour insofar as they are concerned.

This of course does not apply to the proprietors, or to the high salaried editorial writers — although there is a special poison prepared for them as well. Despite the immense fortunes of the owners of our modern city dailies, also the high salaries and political plums received by the editorial writers, they never know the day they may be made the laughingstock of the people in general.

In any case riches generally corrupt the owners, while the editorial writers are denied the privilege of the lowliest toiler, or that of the tramp on the highway, i.e. the blood-bought right of self-expression. *Gentlemen of the Press* ignores both owners and editorial writers, possibly because the author felt he could not conscientiously designate either as "gentlemen."

J.L., Ottawa

THE WORDSMITH WRITES
AUGUST 3, 1929

May I be permitted to thank your correspondent, Mr. J.H. Ogden of Ottawa, for a very interesting and amusing letter. It is the type of letter that one expects to get from persons who ask, "How many words do you know?" and, "How many words are there in the English language?"

Mr. Ogden says the recognized vocabulary of the language has never grown by the frequency with which words in it were used. Alas, that he should be so mistaken. In the days when William Shakespeare walked the earth, the dictionaries of the time contained not more than five to seven thousand words, notwithstanding the fact that Shakespeare himself had a command of a vocabulary of 21,000 words.

Not until Nathan Bailey undertook to make a dictionary did the bulk of these find place in a printed record of our speech. Ever since then, the vocabulary has increased apace. The dictionary with which I have been closely associated for forty years next spring, prints, within its covers, a vocabulary of 455,000 terms, but in doing so, it by no means exhausts the terminology of our mother tongue.

There are at least another 200,000 that must be considered before a new edition of our book is issued, excluding the vast vocabulary of scientific terms never required outside of technical books, and the vocabularies of the different grades of the underworld and subnormal conditions, which are restricted to works that are specifically devoted to them. Nowadays when publishers issue a dictionary, they always cater to the home and the needs of the respectable elements of society.

The linguistic democracy under which dictionaries are developed do not take into consideration scientific technology. It takes into consideration the present conditions under which we live, in which every Tom, Dick and Harry, as your correspondent calls them, has assumed the right to coin whatever word he wishes to use, or to twist the meanings of words that already exist so as to give them meanings that do violence to their original, hoping to get away with it.

Frank H. Vizetelly,
Managing Editor,
Funk and Wagnalls Dictionary, New York

SUMMER SHOPPING HOURS

SEPTEMBER 7, 1929

May we express through your paper our great appreciation of the kindness your readers have shown us this summer? Their support of the movement for shorter summer shopping hours has made this innovation a success and has contributed in no small measure to the health and happiness of a large part of the community.

The attitude of the press, too, is deserving of praise and of our sincere thanks.

Wm. Newland Stephens, Ottawa
(On behalf of the Murphy-Gamble staff)

Editor's note: In the 1920s and '30s, it was routine for Ottawa retailers to remain open until 8 p.m. or 9 p.m. on Saturdays. In 1929, store employees pushing for earlier summer closing times ran into resistance from many shop owners, who feared business losses. But supported by Ottawa's newspapers, the workers managed to convince much of the public to shop earlier. As a result, many store owners agreed to earlier closing times.

THIS BEDLAM

OCTOBER 5, 1929

I quite agree with the sentiments expressed by Mr. John Brown in his letter about the ringing of the bells, particularly in the early morning, being a terrible nuisance.

But how would Mr. Brown like to have to work in an office totalling columns of figures all day, and have a bell clanging in his ears every ten minutes or so, as do those employed in the old lumber factory at present occupied by the Dominion Bureau of Statistics in New Edinburgh? Is it any wonder mistakes occur?

The bell I speak of is one that has been installed to warn of the approach of street cars and its horrible din is something which has to be experienced for a day or two to be appreciated.

Really, I think one way and another we are living in a veritable Bedlam these days.

Winnie White, Ottawa

THE COMFORT STATIONS

OCTOBER 12, 1929

If there is economy in the proposed elimination of O'Connor street comfort stations; if the space is needed for a bank or other revenue bearing institutions, not many should object. But if said space should revert to parking of automobiles, as this correspondent irreverently suspects, well, that is another story.

In any event, these stations should not be removed until other conveniences are provided. They are a public necessity. Anyone with only half an eye can see it; in fact, there should be a number of such squatting catacombs scattered in different places in a city of this size.

This has nothing to do with tourist traffic or travellers in general, who stay at their respective hotels, but it appeals more especially to the man in the street and the "stranger within thy gates."

It may surprise readers to know that similar public conveniences have been in use in Scandinavian cities for more than a century and are generally found at the entrance to public parks.

Oscar Nordenfeldt, Ottawa

Editor's note: The debate over public washrooms created a bit of stink several times during the first three or four decades of the century. On one side of the argument were those who considered comfort stations an indelicate eyesore, especially for visitors (as a result, some washrooms were located underground). On the other side were those holding the view of the letter-writer. In this case, it seems the O'Connor street washrooms were razed to make way for new businesses. There's no mention of whether they were replaced elsewhere.

UNIFORMS AND BOSSES

DECEMBER 31, 1929

Ottawa seems to have become a city of uniforms. I saw blue uniforms, two different shades of grey, brown, black and one green uniform.

On a recent visit, in a public place, I was accosted by an important-looking man in a blue uniform. I happen to belong to the class called the Great Unwashed, and this nobleman took a dislike to me, and told me so and also told me the Union Station was no place for the likes of me.

I also encountered a man in a black uniform, a round-collared dignitary. He had me somewhat at his mercy, and took advantage of it. He told me my views of life were all wrong, and his views were all right and when I contradicted him, he became angry and abusive.

What a world! Instead of wanting to be fair and equal with one another, we all want to be boss and domineer somebody. Especially is this so with certain types of religionists who would deny an honest opinion to all who disagree with them. Then we have Liberals, Socialists, Communists, etc., who profess they would free us from these bosses and tyrants, but who would actually like to be big bosses themselves.

We have a word in the British language — Honesty — and at present it is entirely out of place almost everywhere. If it ever does come back into its own, religions, uniforms, and bosses will have disappeared from the face of the earth and 'twill be a great deal better place to live in.

Frank Jennings,
Toronto

"I am declaring that this business of putting men
to work for twenty cents a day is no good in this rich
Dominion. It makes the boys go 'Red,' and no wonder,
for they can see no way ahead."

— June 11, 1934

1930-1939

1930

Local: Britain buys the historic Earnscliffe mansion on Sussex Drive as a residence for its high commissioner (February); British airship R-100 flies over Ottawa (August)
National: All federal civil servants are included under new Fair Wages and Eight-Hour Day Act (May); Carine Wilson named Canada's first female senator (May); Conservatives under R.B. Bennett topple Mackenzie King's Liberals from power (July)
World: Joseph Stalin begins collectivization of Soviet agriculture (January); Accompanied by a growing group of followers, Mohandes Gandhi stages his famous Salt March in symbolic defiance of British rule of India (March)
Births: U.S. astronauts Neil Armstrong, Buzz Aldrin and Michael Collins; jazz saxmen Ornette Coleman and Sonny Rollins; German chancellor Helmut Kohl; actors Sean Connery and Clint Eastwood
Deaths: British writer D.H. Lawrence; actor Lon Chaney; British prime minister Arthur Balfour

A HOCKEY SUPPORTER

JANUARY 4, 1930

Being a great outside supporter of the Ottawa Senators hockey team, I thought I would drop a line in respect to the knocks that are continually being thrown at the Senators by Ottawa hockey followers.

By all accounts, the public in Ottawa is very hard to please. It is true that when the Senators were winning games, nothing could be too good for them. With the same team now in a losing streak, all these fake supporters are casting their knocks at the very same team that was winning just a few weeks ago.

I was listening in on the Ottawa-Rangers game in Atlantic City, and I tell you it was a tough one to lose, for if the announcer was broadcasting right, which I believe he was, it was just tough hard luck that the Senators had.

Fancy casting jeers at [goalie Alex] Connell. If the jeerers had been listening in at the recent Ottawa-Montreal game which ended 2-3, then I think these fellows must be talking just to hear themselves speak — either that or they don't know the first thing about hockey.

I only wish that I lived in Ottawa. I would attend every game. But instead, I just have to take a chance and wait until a game is broadcast.

Now, Mr. Editor, I think this is all the space you will allow me but I shall ever be a supporter of the Ottawa Senators, no matter if they lose every game. And here's hoping that these knockers will in future turn to boosters and wishing my favourite "King" Clancy and all the Senators the best of luck in New York, also the management, and that we will see Ottawa in the playoffs.

George Atkins, Brockville

Editor's note: Ottawa did make the Stanley Cup playoffs that year, finishing the season in second place in the Canadian Division, but losing 6-3 to the New York Rangers in a two-game, total goal series. It would be the last season in Ottawa for the legendary Francis Michael (King) Clancy, the team's most popular player and a Senators mainstay since 1921. In October, the Ottawa-born Hall of Fame defenceman was traded to the hated Toronto Maple Leafs for two journeymen players and $35,000.

Ottawa-born Hall of Fame defenceman King Clancy was traded to the Toronto Maple Leafs for two journeymen players and $35,000.

THE CULTURE OF MINORITIES

FEBRUARY 7, 1930

I have much pleasure in congratulating you for your remarks on the condition of foreign minorities in Canada as represented in this instance by the Hellenic Educational Association of which a branch has just been organized in this city.

You were right in saying that the citizens of Greek origin contribute much toward enrichment of our community life. You say further of the residents from other countries that they are an asset to Canada and that they should be encouraged to keep alive the best traditions, particularly of art, literature and culture, of the countries whence they came. That is the right spirit, and a better formula could not be found on which all patriotic men could agree.

I don't suppose, though, that in penning it you merely meant to utter a pious platitude. Surely you will admit, sir, that the only means and place to conserve the culture of any great nation is in the school, public or private. But to give such a commendable acknowledgement all its value it should be followed up with some kind of public recognition and support.

If it be true — and we all know it is — that the cultural contribution of some of our foreign colonies is an enrichment to the life of Canada, this country should extend due consideration for such a contribution. They do it in Quebec. The Montreal school boards maintains special classes not only for Greek children but also for Italian, Jewish, Polish, Ruthenian [Russian], Syrian, Hungarian and even Chinese children.

That is what you see in French Canada, a province which is itself a minority in the Confederation. There you could even argue Quebec's interest as such should be to turn as quickly as possible its foreign immigration into the French-Canadian melting pot, as they do in the United States and elsewhere.

But that is not the Canuck's way. He may be wrong. As a matter of fact, in Quebec they take a practical view of what they think to be their obligation to their fellow citizens of foreign origins.

Sir, you profess to share those views and no doubt you would support any move to extend to other parts of the Dominion the good understanding that you notice and commend between majorities and minorities in this portion of our big country.

Don't you think that the school boards in the different regions, including Ottawa, should be prevailed upon to take cognizance of the wishes of important minorities in towns and districts? If they lack the necessary powers to satisfy those wishes, then they could address themselves to the proper authorities and have a general rule adopted after consultation in an interprovincial conference.

W. Gascon, Ottawa

MECHANICAL MELODY

MARCH 3, 1930

With the advent of the phonograph and machine-made sound, many of us have been striving valiantly to maintain and preserve the art of living music. It has developed into a battle — a great battle — in which the makers of mechanical music are sweeping along to victory. Their supremacy seems inevitable.

Why? Because although there are organizations, clubs, etc., doing everything in their power to put the musician back in his rightful place, there still remains a great number of people who are heedlessly whizzing through life to the clatter of this infernal machine.

Perhaps this is because they have not actually grasped the situation. What encouragement is there for the would-be musicians of today? Certainly the movietone theatre has no use for him. You might argue that there is still the ballroom to attract him, but may I prophesy that if we keep flocking to the theatre the way we have in the past and are doing at present, the day is not far off when dancing masters, realizing the swollen box-office receipts of movietone houses, will have their ballrooms wired and we will glide over the floor to the strains of synchronized music.

The art of real music, to my mind, is the most glorious and most beautiful gift this world has been blessed with and nothing can ever take its place — not even synchronization.

Lewis C. Hill, Ottawa

FOR NATIONAL BROADCASTING

MARCH 8, 1930

No nation is worthy to be called a nation unless it has a patriotic literature (poetry and prose) and song. These are the signs which point to the birth of a nation's soul. Give a nation literature and national songs, and there follows immediately a strong, healthy, national patriotism.

Tune in your radio, and study the phenomenon which is there displayed every day. In a cadence true and strong, there comes up north lightly the songs of a country. You hear the sweet notes of *Carry Me Back to Old Virginia, Come West, Little Girl, Come West,* and *Old Man River,* scores of songs, in fact. You hear dramas depicting famous incidents and scenes in American life and history.

One realizes that this is a great national phenomenon, and the more so when you realize that these broadcasts are penetrating into the sacred precincts of hundreds of thousands of American homes. Never a night goes by but the American home hears songs, dramas and stories that create pride in country and love for their spots of beauty and romance.

Then what a contrast. Tune in on Canadian stations and listen for such a phenomenon, and never a song will you hear glorifying the magic of Canada's beauty spots. No one is singing of the witchery of our lovely lakes and streams; no one is telling stories of Canadian import and tradition.

The greatest home penetrator on earth is busy, but not one song will you hear that will create pride in Canada. You will hear masterpieces of famous foreigners, but not one original Canadian song, story or drama, not one glorification of Canada's wonderlands.

Tens of thousands of dollars are spent annually on advertising publicity. Surely if these expenditures have been efficient one rightfully might conclude that the phenomenon which is so pronounced in American broadcasting should at least appear in some form in Canada.

Under a system such as we have in Canada, we will never be able to achieve such a desirable condition. Study Canadian broadcasting thoroughly, and you will see that from a national standpoint it is not achieving the national results that one would expect. Our broadcasting is not national, and it is not difficult to understand why it is not.

The conclusion is that to gain national aims and ideals there is only one way to do so, and that is by nationalizing the radio broadcasting system. Nationalize the radio and immediately the whole situation is changed in Canada, our country.

Canada, the land of opportunity, the land of witchery and magic beauty, the land of history, romance and song will then find its rightful place. Our poets and writers, our singers and dramatists will then find the field for the exploitation of their wares.

Never will this be obtained under the present hotchpotch system, uncontrolled and directed by diverging ideas and aspirations.

There must be a common directing force, a wise and strong directing bond to achieve national results and unified thought.

I know I want to have more and more of Canada and less and less of the beauties and wonders of a foreign country. The radio can play an important part under the national system — building Canada.

Duncan Johnson, Ottawa

Editor's note: A publicly funded national radio broadcast-

er to keep Canada from being swamped by American culture had been recommended in 1929 by a royal commission. However, the idea was pushed aside by that year's financial crisis and the July 1930 federal election, won by R.B. Bennett's Conservatives. In 1932, Bennett created the Canadian Radio Broadcasting Commission, the forerunner of the CBC, and gave it a mandate to generate pride in Canada.

CNRO PROGRAMS
JUNE 2, 1930.

Would it be out of the way to suggest that until the radio-music public has, as a whole, reached the evolutionary stage when it will demand at least the better class of music as its principal fare, the "cheaper" kind of music (?), or American jazz, be largely eliminated from the CNRO programs during the noon hour, and also during the hour after four o'clock in the afternoon at least?

This would no doubt help to some extent in saving the taste of the younger generation, which is especially prone upon leaving school to indulge in what requires the least conscious effort, whether it be constructive or the reverse.

It may be that what is offered the public in this sphere depends partly, as in other spheres of activity, upon the type of public spirit and the discrimination possessed by those directly responsible.

A. Suzor Greaves, Ottawa

FASHION RIGHTS FOR MEN
JUNE 28, 1930

"Put on your coat, or leave" was the notice given to me at a well known local establishment, advertising a pleasant evening's informal dancing.

The women don't object: why should the men? Why cannot men have the right to be cool and comfortable by removing their coats? What crime is committed by dancing without a coat, sleeves rolled down — or up, for that matter?

Women have to fight for their rights, but mere man is evidently afraid to do so. Here's one who will not be uncomfortable. Who else?

L.R. Adair, Ottawa

LET EVERYTHING BE SETTLED
SEPTEMBER 20, 1930

At present, the subject of employment seems to be a matter of world-wide concern.

It is common knowledge that wealth and employment are inadequately distributed. For instance, one man had a salary of (we'll say) $1,000 for working five and one-half days a week, and uses the other day and a half filling another position paying him approximately the same yearly stipend.

We could infer from this that this man is doing two men's work while someone else, capable of the same work — or at least of filling one of the positions — is "out of a job."

Then again, we have the knowledge of daughters of wealthy parents filling positions of trust and drawing good salaries which they use to further their amusement and vanity while many another girl — or man — needs the work and the resultant salary to feed and clothe a rising family for the betterment of the nation.

A recommendation is that employment be given only to those women and girls who really have to support themselves and one or more dependents, but not to those whose parents have enough to support them at home.

As girls seldom have anyone but themselves to keep, it is unfair to the man who has a family to raise to place these girls on the same salary basis as the family man. No man can raise a family and keep up with the national standard of living who has to compete with the lassie who has no more need of the work than to buy powder for her nose.

There is something radically wrong about the distribution of the burden of taxation between the married and the single men. The latter pay a small income tax on all over a certain salary. The married man has a greater exemption in income tax but has a family to raise and educate, a home to keep up and many other responsibilities which make his salary — in comparison to that of his single brother — dwindle to the vanishing point.

As a suggestion for the assistance of the "out-of-works," let the government proceed with all the proposed public works immediately. Let our authorities insist that all industries operating in Canada employ Canadians. Let Ottawa insist that most of those she aids be *bona fide* residents of the city. There will be time enough to bring in immigrants when our own surplus labour is all employed at full-time work.

If immigration is allowed, let the immigrants be of such physical and mental standard as can stand the rigours of our climate and the requirements of our conditions of labour. Let us have the agriculture and real workers — regardless of creed — debarring only the Asiatics, who are more parasitical in nature, and the bolshevistic Russians, who do more to degrade Canada than to elevate her morals and manners.

(Mrs.) Jessie E. Carter, Ottawa

ON "RUSSIA'S FARM EXPERIMENT"
OCTOBER 22, 1930

Your selection from the *Christian Science Monitor* of an article entitled "Russian Farm Experiment" affords to a casual reader suggestions for other similar treatises which might grace yours and the pages of that "Christian" paper.

In Russia alone could be found numerous subjects for such articles. For instance: the Soviets' War on God; How religion is being extirpated under Soviet rule; How Russia's churches are being turned into barracks, stables, dance halls and theatres.

If the imaginations of the *Monitor* writer runs short on Soviet Russia's benefactions to humanity, he might turn to other fields and regale us with an essay on The philanthropy of bandits. The esthetic sense of some international bootleggers. A famous criminal's taste for art. The happy family life of notorious murderers.

Does *The Citizen* and its twin brother — the *Christian Science Monitor* — condone and abet Soviet Russia in its satanic warfare on religion?

If so, what guarantee have we that if some mad revolutionaries here in North America were to get in control of our governments (not an impossibility), that these twin sheets and their satellites would not abet them in their desecration of the churches, murder of priests and ministers, and confiscation of property, set aside and built up by the sacrifice of the clergy and the people for religious and educational purposes, the perversion of children — because of more of your pet social theories?

Having read *The Citizen* at different times during 15 or more years, I have noted that your paper invariably abetted revolutionary movements, whose main plank was warfare on religion and particularly on Christianity.

In the present case, by presenting to your readers the fairest side of a hideous monster, you are true to form, and so is the *Christian Science Monitor*. The latter should at least throw aside its hypocritical mask and dub itself — the *Soviet Science Mouthpiece*.

George W. O'Toole,
Pakenham

1931

Local: Spectacular fire destroys St-Jean-Baptiste Roman Catholic Church and the adjacent Dominican monastery (February)

National: Census puts Canada's population above 10 million for first time. Ontario leads the way with 3,431,000 residents (June); Maple Leaf Gardens opens (November); British Parliament passes Statute of Westminster, establishing complete equality between parliaments of Britain and Canada and in essence granting Canada full legislative independence (December)

World: Depression begins to take hold as unemployment reaches record levels in North America and Europe (January); Empire State Building, at 86 storeys the world's tallest building, officially opened by president Hoover (May)

Births: Baseball greats Willie Mays and Mickey Mantle; Soviet leader Mikhail Gorbachev; newspaper magnate Rupert Murdoch; actors James Dean and Joanne Woodward; TV personality Barbara Walters

Deaths: Cornetist Buddy Bolden, generally considered first jazz musician; Russian dancer Anna Pavlowa; British tea magnate Sir Thomas Lipton

SPELLING, WRITING, GRAMMAR

JANUARY 7, 1931

Dr. Campbell Laidlaw hit the nail on the head when he recently blamed current and general bad spelling to phonetic teaching. That is my observation and I fail to see how it can be otherwise, when speech, by most of us, is little short of atrocious.

To illustrate, a child of ten had to write a story about "Our Home" and, believe it or not, the child wrote, "are" home. Asked how to spell "our," the reply repeatedly came "are" — the evils of phonetics. If anyone would blame the child, let them consider how often they hear the phrase, "Come to 'are' house."

Grammar should correct both the above fearful errors, but in the case of the child, she did not know that "are" was a verb and "our" a pronoun. Ten years of age — five years at school and no knowledge whatever of the parts of speech.

Thoroughness, accuracy, not to mention scholarship, are entirely sacrificed to facility. This is also apparent in the art of writing, apparently no longer an art. But why children should be trained to scribble instead of "write" is beyond comprehension in these days of shorthand and the typewriter. My observation is that hardly a child today can write slowly, carefully, neatly, and naturally.

In justice, it must be said it is not the teacher's fault. Unlike the Centurion, they are men and women under authority and too often labour valiantly under the handicaps imposed on them.

E.O. Way,
Ottawa

FOR MADE-IN-CANADA GOVERNOR

JANUARY 12, 1931

It is not my intention now to nominate a governor-general but as the subject is *sub judice*, with many wild guesses on both sides of the Atlantic, I would ask permission to take a stand.

The suggestion of [constitutional lawyer] Mr. J. S. Ewart to appoint a Canadian for the governor-generalship and half-heartedly concurred in by Sir Robert Borden when he said that "the accident of birth and residence was of minor importance" was the sanest and most daring suggestion that could be made.

For why in heck should we have to go outside of Canada when we ourselves have so much competent and worthy material to gracefully fill that office? It may have been necessary a hundred years ago when the country was more unsettled for the King to keep his ears to the ground but that condition does not obtain now.

If it is from fear of secession then it seems so much more stupid. Canada knows her own mind, and when the time comes to secede, if ever, any governor-general cannot prevent it and it will come about with the King's consent. Apart from the novelty of being governor-general, a foreigner spends most of his term to get his bearing and to understand the vastness of the country.

It would be a step in the right direction to have a native Canadian grace the office at Rideau Hall, one who needed the job and one who is conversant with every phase of Canadian consciousness.

Oscar Nordenfeldt,
Ottawa

Editor's note: Vincent Massey became the first native-born governor general with his appointment in 1952.

NATIONAL BIRTH
OF BROADCASTING
FEBRUARY 7, 1931

The country faces a serious and critical decision as to the future of broadcasting, whether it shall be primarily commercial or primarily a public utility, ministering education and amusement to all the people.

During the last few weeks several addresses have been delivered by outstanding publicists enabling American citizens to make the great mental adjustments rendered necessary by the success, or partial success, of the Soviet "Five Year Plan." To the best of my belief, none of these were made accessible to Canadian listeners through the hook-up of our Canadian stations, which in many cases drove out the distant stations.

Justice demands recognition of the real service rendered by our stations in giving us the London broadcast every Sunday noon, but the orderly development of our national life requires a fuller acquaintance with living currents of thought than is now possible under a commercial system of broadcasting.

As a churchman, I would suggest that broadcasting should be used in the field of religion, not primarily for the advantage of any particular congregation or group, but primarily to minister to fundamental and universal religious needs; representative advisory committees could select speakers who are likely to have some message of real value to large numbers of people, many of whom for various causes are isolated from congregational worship.

It is claimed that this presentation of elemental Christian faith and life by competent persons inspired by rich sympathy and deep insight may be of great value to thousands of people. Surely the Christian Church would wish that this public utility should promote eternal values rather than local or sectional strifes.

For these and other reasons I strongly advocate the adoption of some national control which, while leaving every listener free to avail himself of stations, commercial and otherwise, all over this continent, will minimize the clamourous advertising, and make accessible great events — Canadian and foreign, now beyond our reach.

Ernest Thomas, field secretary,
Board of Evangelism and Social Service,
United Church of Canada, Toronto.

Editor's note: The Canadian Radio Broadcasting Commission, a publicly funded forerunner to the CBC, was created in 1932. Although its principal mandate was to generate pride in Canada, it did carry a range of religious programming designed to represent the country's major denominations.

STREET BEGGING
APRIL 27, 1931

Street begging as a practice was supposed to be peculiar to Oriental people, particularly in countries dominated by Turkish misrule, but now it has become a daily custom in the Capital of our Dominion.

Is it not a fact that Ottawa has welfare associations handling considerable sums of money which are expended in relief? Did not an emergency Parliament a few months ago pass a relief measure authorizing the expenditure of 20 million dollars to meet the necessities of the unemployed? And yet there are unemployed members of the community who apparently live by begging.

It would seem to be a situation surely worthy the serious attention of the city authorities.

Malcolm Cameron, Ottawa

WORKLESS WORSE OFF
MAY 9, 1931

Hon. Mr. Stevens' sympathies are stirred by "the strain and self-sacrifice imposed upon the Russian workers by the Five-Year Plan."

But what about the strain and sacrifices imposed upon Canadian workers by the lack of intelligent direction of a much better economic machine than Russia yet possesses? At least the Russian workers have something to look forward to, while the prospect for Canadian workers is one of increasing insecurity.

Then Mr. Stevens is disconsolate that the average wage of Russian workers is only $600 a year. In Canada's principal industry, according to the Monthly Bulletin of Agricultural Statistics for February, the average remuneration of male farm workers during 1930 was $326 plus $233 for board — a yearly wage of $559 — while for female workers the average was $409 for the year.

R. Campbell, Ottawa

Editor's note: The letter-writer is likely referring to Henry H. Stevens, who was minister of trade and commerce in the Conservative government of R.B. Bennett.

RICH MEN
JUNE 20, 1931

Some years ago you published an article from my pen in which I endeavoured to show that enormously rich men were a danger to the state and suggested that they should be compelled at their death, not to leave their wealth to only one or two heirs, but to distribute it to many heirs or legalees.

I would again draw attention to the fact that very rich men are a danger to the state because wealth concentrated in the hands of a few is the cause of Socialism, Bolshevism, Communism and revolution.

It would therefore appear to be reasonable that legislation should be [adopted] to encourage every man to be rich yet to prevent him from becoming too rich. The income tax can be made a medium to help towards this end. After a rich man has spent all he reasonably can in his necessities and pleasures he has absolutely no use for the surplus of his income but to invest it and so make himself still richer. The income tax instead of taking only twenty-five per cent of this surplus should take at least seventy-five per cent.

I believe that the majority of rich men, being aware of the danger and of the fact that the burden on poorer men would be considerably relieved, would be patriotic enough to pay the tax without hesitation. Such a tax would disarm any attempt that might be made by Socialists, etc., etc.

Samuel Bray, Ottawa

TRYING IT OUT

JUNE 30, 1931

The people are now indulging themselves in a big experiment. They have a regular "pile-driver" protectionist at the helm of the state in Premier Bennett.

He believes and acts on the principle that trade is a bad thing, that the man who has something to sell that we want is our enemy, and that we should put as many obstacles in the way of his selling to us, and we buying of him, as possible, and that such a policy, carried out on a national scale, will cure unemployment, lift the depression, and make the people rich and prosperous.

On the other hand, the friends of freedom believe protection to be a bad policy — bad morally, bad socially, bad politically — founded upon injustice, and that it is sure to bring on

NATIONAL ARCHIVES

PrimeMinister R.B. Bennett was seen as a "pile driver" protectionist by W.D. Lamb.

any people as many evils as plagued Egypt. They believe it to be class legislation, producing a vicious distribution of the wealth that labor creates, causes unemployment, depresses business, and a policy, if continued long enough will make a nation of thieves out of any people, however honest they may be at the beginning of such a policy.

So, which of these two policies is right, best for the people, beset for everybody, is the big thing the people are going to find out by having put Mr. Bennett at the head of the government.

W.D. Lamb, Plumas, Manitoba

WAR AND YOUTH

SEPTEMBER 4, 1931

Some days ago you published a letter over the signature of Hart M. Devenney, who refers to economic planning, disarmament, and the elimination of racial prejudices, and throws down a challenge to the youth of today to help eliminate war.

What beats me is how any body of men can delude themselves into thinking that they can abolish war as an instrument for settling international disputes. No sane person wants wars; that is a recognized fact, but we have them just the same. No one wants jails, hospitals, insane asylums, murders, robberies, etc.; but we have them just the same.

Why? Well, in my opinion it can be given in just two words — human nature, a condition which is the same to-

day as it was when Noah built the Ark, as it was when Julius Caesar enlarged the Roman Empire, and as it was when the Princess Pats marched down Bank Street, many years ago, on their way overseas.

Those of us who were living during the last war, and have given the matter any thought at all, realize that war truly is a catastrophe. It is brought home to us more strongly because we have had a direct connection with it.

But, how will the people feel twenty-five, fifty, or seventy-five years from now? They will read in their history books of the glorious armies of the past, of the strategy used by former famous leaders, of the heroic dead who gave their lives for a great cause, and the aftermath will be forgotten — the maimed, the blind, the blighted ambitions of thousands of young men, the hospitals that are still full of what was once men but are now physical and mental wrecks.

That will all be submerged under the achievements of the victors, and the mistakes of the conquered. It was like that before the last war and it will be the same before the next.

Yes, the youth of today and tomorrow will be like the youth of yesterday. They will let the older hands hold the reins, they will let the famous statesmen drive the wagon of state, and when it gets stuck in the mire, they will come forward and lend a hand to pull it out.

G. H. Giles, Ottawa

A 'STAGGERING' HEADLINE

SEPTEMBER 12, 1931

I was alarmed on opening my yesterday's *Citizen* to find a glaring headline: "Staggering New Tax Burdens for Britain." On reading down, I found that one penny per pint had been added on beer.

The heading was a gem and I must congratulate the writer for his subtlety.

Mark Powell, Ottawa

THIS VITAMIN BUSINESS

OCTOBER 2, 1931

This vitamin business — and surely it is a business as far as advertising is concerned — has gone far enough in my opinion. They speak of vitamins by many of the letters of the alphabet but what will they do after the letters of the alphabet are exhausted? We hear of the "Sunshine Vitamin" and so on, but only the United States, let us suppose, has the "Moonshine Vitamin."

I would rather read in our press today articles dealing with the minute particles of matter in our foods which are harmful, and will coin the word "Mortamins" to describe these death-dealing particles, than all this advertising matter re vitamins. These benevolent vitamins cannot be seen with the naked eye, but many harmful pests in our foodstuffs can be seen.

The fresh and clean foods that nature has given us contain all that is good for us, so why buy special advertised foods which are said to contain all the vitamins necessary to health, when nature's own from the farm direct has all that is good in it?

Visit any of the good old farms of Ontario today, and see the children there who have been fed only on what the farm supplies, and then come back to the city and weep!

Arthur Browett, Ottawa

HE WANTS CROMWELL

OCTOBER 24, 1931

I went into a shop the other day to buy a sweater. I was shown a number of all-wool sweaters, and told that they were each worth six dollars. At my request the salesman weighed one, and found that it weighed two pounds.

At the present price that the farmers are receiving, the wool in the sweater was worth ten cents. The dye and the making made the sweater sixty times the price of the wool in it. I suggested that the profit on wool was similar to that on milk. The farmer receives two cents a quart while the milk sells for twelve cents a quart in the city.

The salesman astonished me by saying, "It is all the fault of the farmer. He should tell the government about it. That is the only power that can set things right." At first, I thought it was a joke but saw later that he was serious.

What is the use of telling! The government are not for us; they are against us. We have lost all the faith in them that we once had. They are sitting smug on their fat salaries, while we are suffering. They think we are stupid enough to believe them, when they tell us that there is overproduction. Do we not know about the poor starving millions?

What we need in this country is an Oliver Cromwell, who will step up and say: "Here, take away this bauble." We need men like Cromwell who desire to see the people, not their purses, prosper. Our country will continue to suffer until men of that type replace the "bauble," which is not on the Hill.

W. Hall, Osgoode

THE SMOKE NUISANCE

NOVEMBER 13, 1931

The season of soot and smoke is upon us. With the advent of the wintry blasts, the firing of furnaces sends smoke curling around the corners and over the housetops, while soot spatters the apparel of the citizen, eddies into the doorways, sweeps into the open windows, to say nothing of handicapping the man or woman on his or her way to and from work. Not only this, every person inhales the poisonous gases from semi-combustion, lessening the activity and vigour of the breather.

The cleanliness of the whole city is affected. Many a building, once vying with the snow in whiteness, bows before the onslaught of smoke and its resultant dirt. It does not seem to me that any of this is necessary. Large manufacturing plants are continually making studies of this ever prevalent menace and many of them have solved the problem in several ways.

Could not our city prepare and pass necessary legislation that would at least bring this nuisance to a minimum? Other cities have done it. Why not Ottawa?

M. N. Playfair, Ottawa

1932

Local: About 7,500 unemployed workers demonstrate on Parliament Hill (March); New filtration plant opens on Lemieux Island in Ottawa River (May)

National: League of Social Reconstruction is founded, eventually leading to the formation of the CCF (January); Dominion government sets up relief camps for transient unemployed men. Up to 20,000 men use the camps, run by the military, and receive 20 cents a day (March); Parliament establishes Canadian Radio Broadcasting Commission, forerunner of the CBC (May)

World: Infant son of Charles Lindbergh is kidnapped in March. Body is found two months later; Promising a return to prosperity, Franklin Roosevelt wins landslide victory in U.S. presidential election (November)

Births: Pianist Glenn Gould; developer Bill Teron; Canadian industrialist Frank Stronach; native painter Norval Morrisseau; actress Elizabeth Taylor; U.S. senator Edward Kennedy; writer V.S. Naipaul

Deaths: André Maginot, French minister of war; Kodak founder George Eastman; canine actor Rin Tin Tin

WHISTLE AND LIGHTS

JANUARY 26, 1932

As one who has taken a very active interest in traffic conditions, I was very greatly pleased when I came down Sparks Street this morning and saw and heard the new device now operating at the O'Connor Street corner. Everyone on the scene was of the opinion that the traffic lights were a great safeguard to the lives and bodies of pedestrians, and an assistance to the autoists in avoiding traffic disasters.

The whistle operating in conjunction with the lights makes the traffic warning and signal service complete and makes the crossing of autoists and pedestrians 100 per cent secure. The whistle blows on the amber light and gives a positive and sure warning of the certain arrival of a green or red light. There is no fooling here, the whistle, shrill and policeman-like in its command, says — "Stop! Look!"

I am sure this is an epoch-making change in our traffic protection system and that the clever brains which devised it have hit upon a traffic safety idea that will mean the saving of hundreds of lives each year.

D. Johnson, Ottawa

BUY OUT THE DEPRESSION

JANUARY 29, 1932

I am just a working man, but even I am about fed up with the parrot talk of the supposed brains of our society regarding the sources of our economic depression, and so will give you the impression of one of the common herd.

In 1929 a panic started among the gambling fraternity in Wall Street, for they are gamblers — not producers. A panic starts easily. This condition spread to the business heads, and they in their panic started to economize by firing their employees. These employees, their earning power cut off, could not buy the goods produced by other workers. These workers in turn are let out because demand has fallen off.

How can one conclude any theory except that these business men are acting like a cat chasing its tail; getting no place but more exhausted all the time; lying down and hoping for an "act of God" to bring back business?

How much better it would have been for the business men to have taken a loss, kept the wheels of industry turning and men working. I believe the condition would have righted itself in six months instead of dragging its weary way for three years, causing untold misery and ruination for thousands, instead of hundreds.

The way to help now is for the people who have steady employment and bank accounts to just buy, buy, buy. If you have the money to buy a car, a radio — somebody has to make another one for every one you purchase. This depression can be ended only when people learn to buy.

D. Fielding, Ottawa

ON SWIM SUIT MORALS

FEBRUARY 11, 1932

I was anxious to see if in this morning's *Citizen* there was a reply to yesterday's article bearing the heading "The New Swim Suits," and I was pleased not to find it, for it does not deserve a direct answer, particularly if the article in question was meant as an advertisement in favour of the coming indecent fashion.

Yet, may I take the opportunity to point out how subversive was that article and how burdensome is the responsibility of those who have allowed its publication.

For to say that "morals are just a matter of custom and not a fixed law" is equivalent to saying that God did not lay down any commandment to govern man's conduct and life. Hence, blasphemy, adultery, murder, theft and so on are not sinful according to God's law, but only so by common estimation, which, of course, may change according to fashion.

What then of these words of St. Paul: "Know you not that the unjust shall not possess the kingdom of God? Do not err: neither fornicators, nor idolators, nor adulterers, nor the effeminate, nor liars with mankind, nor thieves, nor covetous, nor drunkards, nor railers, nor extortioners, shall possess the kingdom of God." (1 Cor. VI, 9, 10).

Let it, then, be said that, alas! man gets used even to sin and is not ashamed of it.

Father Fortunatus,
Ottawa

VOGUE: 75 YEARS OF FASHION

The swimming suit styles of the 1930s raised concern about public morals.

The Citizen replied: Taken apart from the subject of clothing, under discussion in the editorial, it would indeed be an extreme statement to say that "morals are just a matter of custom and not a fixed law." Our writer intended to say "the morals *of clothing* are just a matter of custom..."

CASUALTIES OF CAPITALISM

MARCH 23, 1932

Again we have seen a king leave his vast domain in this world and go to the next. The Swedish match king, Ivar Kreuger, committed suicide in Paris. His undertakings in organizing and financing great concerns were on a scale so tremendous that they caused men to wonder, even in our age. To the ordinary mind, undertakings of so vast a scope seem to be beyond human control and the failure of many of the greatest organizers when it came to managing their creations leaves room for doubt as to the possibility of doing this at all, if profit is the only object.

Seeing the results of such failures, ruination of thousands of investors, thousands and thousands of labourers thrown out of work, and sometimes finally destruction and death to the promoter himself, no longer able to handle the monster he has created, life becomes a grim spectacle, a game with only a few participants playing with the life and welfare of millions, the fate and destiny of nations, and to what end?

It is surely about time for the people and their elected

representatives to consider seriously if economic life shall continue to be controlled by leaders aiming only at profit and seemingly often guided by their gambling instincts only. Let us have leaders who have the welfare of the people in mind, leaders who think of mankind instead of glorifying themselves by building great corporations which cannot be safely controlled but only cause danger to civilization.

John Ingvar Jensen, Ottawa

GALLOWS PUBLICITY RESTRAINED
APRIL 9, 1932

The absence of headlines, editorials, and comments previous to the execution of Austin Cassidy in Hull has certainly not passed unnoticed. This action on the part of the Ottawa dailies deserves compliment and consideration. Though interesting as these columns might have been, no one will lose or suffer from not having been informed of the actions and preparedness of a murderer about to be strangled to death.

Christian charity and sound human sense are two great factors that will eventually be used to eliminate the injurious publicity given to happenings of this nature. Space for good wholesome reading can certainly be found to replace descriptions of atrocities which, rather than interest, serve to disgust and throw sorrow into a community.

Society may want a man to pay his debt to them by dying, but surely society does not want to expose their anticipated revenge or broadcast events intimating its supposed satisfaction.

Rudolph A. Potvin, Ottawa

PARLIAMENT HILL RABBITS
APRIL 20, 1932

In his recent encounter with six rabbits, was the Speaker of the House of Commons breaking the law in firing a revolver at them, and if so, what law?

There is a city bylaw against using firearms within the city limits, but personally, I think someone should be charged with conspiracy to deceive the public.

I, for one, refuse to believe: (a) that there were any rabbits; (b) if there were, that Mr. Black could hit them with a .22 caliber revolver; (c) if he did hit them, that it would kill them; and (d) if he did kill them, that he would eat them in a stew. Surely the honourable member would prefer rabbit pie.

John MacDonell, Ottawa

Editor's note: In a front page story on April 13, the Evening Citizen *reported that Capt. George Black, described as a "colourful figure of the Yukon gold rush," traded his gavel for a gun after spotting wild rabbits feasting on the bark of evergreens outside his Parliament Hill office. Said Speaker Black: "You can go out and see the damage they had done before I bagged 'em with a .22-caliber target pistol." Added the* Citizen: *"The cotton tails hung last night in the Speaker's apartment, undergoing the usual seasoning before being transformed into a prime rabbit stew." No other articles were published, leaving the veracity of Mr. Black's story up in the air.*

YOUTH AND GREATNESS
APRIL 30, 1932

Mr. Winston Churchill notes with regret that the young Englishmen nowadays go in for politics while the best of American young manhood goes in for business.

While this may look very sad to Mr. Churchill, who may have his own reasons for being disgusted with politics, there are, however, some who see some hope and brightness in the fact that youth now is becoming more interested in how society should be governed. The young men of England, many of them belonging to the finest families, deserve thanks for showing the way.

Let the sons of Uncle Sam go in for salesmanship and end up as great financiers, chain store czars, stock brokers and movie magnates, and let us hope they all reach their high and shining ideals. But let us not despise the young Englishman because, as an aristocrat or as an idealist, he has the idea that he might serve his people and his country as a member of Parliament. Let us not blame him for thinking that the finest and most gentlemanly qualifications should be required for the nation's leaders, and these leaders naturally should have their place in Parliament.

Perhaps the thinking youth of today and tomorrow will come to recognize other standards for "greatness" than those that were current yesterday. Perhaps before long the ideals of Mr. Churchill and his generation will have vanished for others more suitable to the needs of human society today, and strange to say, when we see them, we shall probably all have a faint idea of having heard of them before somewhere long, long ago.

John I. Jensen, Ottawa

MOVING DAY
MAY 6, 1932

I wonder when we in Canada will get away from making the first of May the most unpleasant day of the year. Would it not be better if we did not sign leases that ended on this one day? Why not sign a lease from the day you move in, regardless of the day or month it happened to be?

The first of May is a most hectic day. Often the incoming tenants have to wait in front of a house with their van, while the out-going tenants rush frantically about trying to get theirs moved away.

Some people leave their houses in a most deplorable condition. The new tenants have no alternative but to move their goods in and have no opportunity to remedy this condition. I sympathize with them because I have seen some filthy places. Even the decorator has no chance to do any necessary decorating with heaps of furniture stacked in every room. The moving contractor is fortunate if he gets his work done by midnight.

D. Fielding, Ottawa

Editor's note: Although leases no longer begin and end on May 1 as a matter of common practice, moving companies still report May 1 as their busiest day, especially in Quebec, with its higher proportion of renters.

THE ANIMAL SHELTER

JUNE 20, 1932

When so many humans have practically no shelter or means of subsistence apart from charity, it is not surprising that popular sentiment is unfavourable to the building of a $10,000 animal shelter. Especially when that shelter will have to be maintained by popular and civic subscription.

In this time of general unemployment and dire poverty, there should be no need for an expensive shelter in a city of this size: more particularly if, as you say, there are already a dozen kennels operating for private gain. It would surely be much cheaper for the Humane Society to make occasional use of those private shelters and, incidentally, help their owners make a living, than to build, and maintain a lavish edifice of their own.

If this summer is to be like the last, when hundreds of starving men, and even some women, had their habitat on the dumps of the city, we would surely die of shame to have our stray dogs and cats in a $10,000 shelter.

Mrs. W. E. Hopkins, Ottawa

Editor's note: The shelter in question was not built until after the Second World War.

PLIGHT OF COLOURED CITIZENS

AUGUST 20, 1932

We do not wish to bore our governmental heads with details of the King settlement established in the township of Raleigh in the County of Kent, Ontario, around the year 1847 by the Rev. Wm. King, nor the struggles of those settlers up to the present time; but we would like to draw attention to the effect of the present depression on the survivors of that settlement.

We do not claim to be a peculiar people from the average Canadian citizen, yet we know from experience that our customs work to a great disadvantage to our people from an economic point of view. We do not feel we are any better to lose the few remaining farms in that settlement than other people in the present crisis but we do say when those farms are gone our settlement is gone, and what have the coloured people of Canada to look to as in an individual way to maintain self-respect and self-reliance?

We do not complain if financial and commercial institutions desire to employ labour of their own, but we do say if the sons and grandsons of those old settlers, who were born in Canada and who helped develop those settlements, can not have some advantage in a financial way, our hope is lost, we sink and are in a worse condition than we were in the beginning.

Some help in the re-arranging of our credits, a little here and a little there, and our settlement would be saved. The debts of our people are often brought to our attention at the present time; but it should be remembered, quite a few of those settlers brought money to this country with them and that money was spent in this country.

We believe this is the first consideration of consequence the coloured people of Canada have asked, and we pray we may find thoughtful consideration of our request. We have made our mistakes but on the whole I believe we can be classed as a law-abiding people.

Flavius G. Shadd, Chatham, Ont.

CLASSICAL MUSIC AND JAZZ

AUGUST 31, 1932

I really think it would be just as foolish to attempt to compare Edgar Wallace [British author of popular fiction] with William Shakespeare as to compare classical music with jazz. When we want real music of great depth which stirs the soul it is to the classical we must turn.

Edgar Wallace and jazz is perfectly all right for light, relaxing entertainment; in fact, it is quite beneficial in that respect. But it should not be taken seriously. It is for the classical we must reserve a little serious thought and great appreciation.

Ernest Barnes, Ottawa

AN "AMAZING PROPOSAL"

SEPTEMBER 7, 1932

Isn't it about time that our city fathers took a definite stand on this business of cutting down trees that belong to the citizens at large, simply to provide further parking space for those privileged to own automobiles?

The latest proposal in this connection is so outrageous that it approaches the confines of the grotesque. The city traffic committee — presumed to be a body of intelligent and responsible men — is prepared to sacrifice some 25 fine trees located in one of the most attractive sections of center town (along Mackenzie Avenue behind the Château Laurier) simply to provide further free storage space for automobiles!

I am glad to see that this amazing proposal has been definitely turned down by our Dominion government. But that it should ever have been made is, to my way of thinking, disgraceful. It can only be a very few years before this fact is recognized by the absolute prohibition of street parking, in the business districts, at least.

G. R. L. Potter, Ottawa

A FARMER'S GRATITUDE

OCTOBER 3, 1932

It is still a good old world — when trouble comes such a spirit of neighbourly thoughtfulness is manifest.

In the early morning hours of August 30, my farm home in City View fell prey to the flames. The night previous I had made plans to have eight men on hand that morning to help with the threshing. The machine was already on the place. When word of the fire got about, sixteen men instead of eight men turned up for work. I had plenty to look after just then, they said, they would see the job through without my help.

There were nine in my household. We escaped in scanty attire, but from far and near apparel and shoes came to cover us until we had time to procure new clothing. All this kindness was not enough, however. We were later given a surprise party which completely furnished our kitchen — and a farm kitchen needs some furnishing!

One's faith and belief in human goodness is immensely strengthened by such acts as these.

A. W. Swan, City View

Editor's note: City View was an area of farms located where the suburb of the same name now exists southwest of Merivale Road and Meadowlands Drive.

ON JEWISH YOUTH

DECEMBER 15, 1932

As one who has been, for the greatest part of her life, in constant contact with Jewish youth — and also with those closely allied with their education and religious guidance — it is a pleasure and a privilege to be able to state that, in these contacts, I have found a healthy, wholesome interest in the ideals pertaining to their religious belief, and enthusiastic co-operation in any effort pertaining to the study and development of a purely Jewish culture.

The right-thinking, intelligent Jew has no need to worry about what his Gentile neighbour will think of him — as the right-thinking, intelligent Gentile neighbour will accept the intelligent Jew at his proper value; and if a Jew does point out, with pardonable pride, to the accomplishment of his co-religionist in the world of literature, music, art, drama, politics, the medical or legal professions, sci-ence, architecture, industry or any other field of endeavor, surely this does not denote that he is possessed of an inferiority complex!

Where the will to learn and to study has existed, regardless of lack of opportunity, regardless of obstacles raised — and this, not always by the Gentile neighbour — and please mark that well — Jewish youth has lived up to his heritage.

Anna Wolfe Margosches, Ottawa

Editor's note: Anna Wolfe Margosches was probably the first Jewish woman of influence in Ottawa's history. Born in New York in 1883, and educated in New York and Toronto, she came to Ottawa with her family (her father was a furrier) around the turn of the century. An accomplished "dramatic soprano," Ms. Margosches performed at recitals under the patronage of the city's elite, including several governors general and prime minister R.B. Bennett, company generally not available to Jews during that era. Ms. Margosches also busied herself with social work — she was the first president of Ottawa Daughters of Zion, a group that helped the poor — and as a writer — she penned How to Honour the Flag, *an authoritative guide to flag etiquette. She is best remembered today for a history of Jewish life in early Ottawa written in 1934 for the Ottawa Hebrew News. She died in 1952. Another of her letter appears in April 1933.*

1933

Local: Census shows 11,405 dwelling houses in Ottawa (January)
National: New state-funded national radio network begins broadcasting in English and French from Montreal (May); CCF adopts Regina Manifesto, calling for nationalization of banks, railways, insurance companies and public utilities (June); Unemployment rate hits 23 per cent, the highest since statistics were first collected in late 1800s (July)
World: Adolf Hitler becomes German chancellor in January. Before the year is over, he outlaws all political parties except the Nazis, breaks up unions, bans thousands of books and begins sending Jews to prison camps; U.S. president Franklin Roosevelt introduces industrial recovery act, the main plank in his New Deal plan to reduce unemployment (June)
Births: Canadian cable TV magnate Ted Rogers; U.S. criminal lawyer F. Lee Bailey; filmmaker Roman Polanski
Deaths: Canadian military commander Arthur Currie; Canadian feminist reformer Emily Murphy; U.S. president Calvin Coolidge

CASH ON DEMAND

JANUARY 7, 1933

I have been reading over the address delivered by the president of the Bank of Montreal to the shareholders and have found a wholly unexpected vein of humour, for he cannot have been serious in his remarks concerning the evils of issuing unredeemable paper money.

I have before me a five dollar bill issued by the Bank of Montreal. It is, of course, absolutely sound money. It is, in fact, redeemable. Across the face of this impressive document are written the words: "Will pay to bearer on demand Five Dollars." Consoling, isn't it?

I decide to collect forthwith. I walk into a local branch of the bank and push my precious bill through the bars of the teller's cage, saying, "I'd like my Five Dollars please." He looks stunned for a moment, then answers, "But sir, this is Five Dollars."

"No, no!" I say pityingly, "See, it says 'Will pay the bearer on demand.' I'm the bearer. I want my Five Dollars."

"How do you want it?" he asks.

I suggest gold, hesitatingly. "Oh, no!" he fairly shouts. "It doesn't say gold and it doesn't mean gold. We haven't dealt in gold currency for years. Now exactly what is it that you want?"

"I don't know," I answer. "What have you got?"

He pushes the bill back to me with the advice, "See here, that's a perfectly good Five Dollar bill. If you don't want it, leave it here and I'll put it in the Red Cross box."

"But I only want to know what that means," I plead.

"You should worry what it means," he retorts. "You gave Five Dollars worth of something to get that bill, and you'll get Five Dollars' of something in return when you spend it. So long as everybody accepts it in payment, what difference does it make?"

I readily admit it makes no difference at all. I only want to know what provision the bank has made for the redemption of this piece of paper. "I don't know," says the teller. "Better ask the president."

I won't ask the president. He doesn't know the answer because there isn't any answer.

But, of course, the Bank of Montreal only issues good redeemable money.

J.R.K. Main, Ottawa

Editor's note: Until the creation of the Bank of Canada in 1935, all Canadian currency was issued through private banks, although regulated by the Dominion government. Between 1935 and 1950, the private banks slowly got out of the currency business, leaving the central bank liable for all notes.

FOR MORE PUBLIC OWNERSHIP
JANUARY 11, 1933

During these trying times, we hear and read many solutions to end the depression, but none appear to the writer to go far enough. Public ownership or control of all banks, water power, all big industrial concerns, railways, etc., seems to be the only true and permanent solution.

Money, the medium of exchange, appears to have got into too few hands. These hands control the banks, half our railways, all our big industrial concerns and most of our natural resources. Our governments, from municipal to federal, dance to their commands.

These big interests were allowed to gobble up our natural resources for a mere pittance, develop them with the life savings of many of our best citizens, who today are unemployed, giving them in return watered stock, which was never, at the best of times, worth ten per cent of its face value.

Another of their tentacles are the banks. Take, for instance, a small industrial firm that not long ago was forced into liquidation by a bank. This firm employed 75 to 100 men, had paid good wages, and when the depression hit, were doing their best to carry on keeping as many men as possible.

Financing became difficult and the bank refused to co-operate and forced this solvent company to assign. The custodian is now in control of plant and equipment that could not be replaced for $150,000, for which at present there is no sale, and will be lucky if he realizes ten per cent of its value. The bank will be looked after by a secured claim; but what about the other creditors, and the 75 to 100 men placed on the unemployed list?

Had this bank been owned or controlled by the government, the writer feels the human element would have been considered, and with careful co-operation would have weathered the

OTTAWA HUNT CLUB

Harry Towlson was Ottawa Hunt Club's first golf professional, a sport that was attacked and defended by letter-writers.

storm and kept these men from being forced to ask for charity.

The writer is far from being a Communist, but fears that, unless the government progresses more quickly in the right direction, Soviet propaganda that has been flooding Canada will begin to bear fruit.

C. Douglas Wright, Wrightville, Que.

WHILE LITTLE ONES STARVE
JANUARY 28, 1933

In today's issue of *The Citizen* is printed an editorial under the heading of "Larger Golf Holes." Nothing could be more directly designed to inflame the public mind in these times of harrowing distress.

Nero's fiddling while Rome was burning has for two thousand odd years been held as an example of the most callous disregard of human distress. Bad as Nero's music may have sounded amid the crashing holocaust along the Tiber, it would be certainly much more comforting than a dissertation on golf holes just now.

Golf holes? Ye gods! Is that a true reflex of your unburdened mind? Do you not know that to ninety per cent of the people golf is an anathema, not a game — a social disease, a reflex athletic inferiority. Very rarely a top-notch athlete will stoop to golf. Nearly all golf votaries are social climbers bluffing at athletics and the most annoying result is the after-chatter (of the game) in public places.

When a labourer or would-be labourer passes a golf course and sees the flanneled Willies lugging about more impediments than a Roman soldier, all to tend the spanking of a poor innocent wee ball, he sees and thinks in many colours.

"What are you swearing at daddy?" quoth his little son. "Oh! at those goats over there!" "Why those are not goats, daddy. They are people." "Alas! yes, but that pasture would serve a much better background for goats." "Gee daddy, I wish they were goats so we could get nice rich milk and would not be so terribly hungry."

Ninety per cent of the people think with the boy. Mr. Editor, allow me to modernize for you Tennyson's advice to Lady Clara Vere de Vere:

Go help the orphan boy to feed;
Go help the orphan girl also.
Pray heaven for a humbler heart.
And let the goofy golfers go.

M. F. Cross, Ottawa

CROSS PURPOSES

FEBRUARY 1, 1933

I noticed in a recent *Citizen* a tirade on golf by Mr. M. F. Cross. His attitude to the grand old game may be explained by the old saying, "Where ignorance is bliss, it is folly to be wise."

He imagines that the public mind is "mortified and inflamed by the white trousers" seen on the golf courses. If this be so then those poor minds must be sorely distressed in many places during our hot summers. Is he not aware of the hundreds of thousands employed by golf clubs all over the world, of the money that is put into circulation by them and of the enhanced beauty of the countryside where these courses are?

His statement that "a top notch athlete will very rarely stoop to golf" can even be disproved in Ottawa where I know of numbers, some of them holding Canadian championships, who are very keen exponents of the game. If he cares to look up the records of the world's greatest players, he will find that most of them excelled in other sports as well.

Instead of sneering at the devotees of this game, whom he would class as "flanneled Willies and goats," he should realize that these are the ones that subscribe freely to all calls for aid, who give their time willingly in welfare work and other charitable organizations. Nearly all the executive on the Ottawa unemployment relief fund are keen golfers.

E.C. Grant, Ottawa

ON THE NAZI TERROR

APRIL 19, 1933

A recent letter appearing in your newspaper, signed by George Herman Bayer, would be laughable did it not pertain to conditions that are too utterly tragic to deal with lightly.

His presumption in drawing a comparison between the distinguished leaders of the two great political parties in Canada and the upstart fanatic Hitler is an insult to the intelligence of the citizens of Canada, who know that the methods Mr. Bayer attributes to the Fuhrer in "his beloved fatherland," have never been put into practice in the history of Canada, or any decently governed country.

What credentials has this correspondent to show he has been authorized to speak "in the name of 500,000 Canadian Germans; 1,000,000 German New Yorkers and 25,000,000 Germans living abroad" (who, incidentally, are being permitted in their respective adopted countries to live in peace and equal rights of citizenship, and to pursue their various vocations and professions without interference)?

No country can prosper which persecutes innocent victims of its prejudices. History proves that, as does the holy judgment of God, the Almighty Father of all mankind, regardless of which form of religious affiliation is professed. "With whatsoever measure ye mete, so shall it be meted unto you" — never fails.

May the day speedily dawn when sanity will prevail in that unfortunate country, and when those blinded with the lust for power will realize that any disgrace that has defamed the fair name of Germany, has resulted, entirely, from their own acts in defiance of civilization and justice!

Anna Wolfe Margosches, Ottawa

WHAT DOES IT ELIMINATE?

MAY 6, 1933

During the last two or three weeks, thousands of Ottawa citizens have purchased a device selling for 20 cents which claims to be "an aerial eliminator." So great has been the local demand for this commodity that new supplies have had to be ordered. This is perhaps natural in view of the present unsatisfactory radio reception in the Ottawa district.

The device consists of three wire terminals, coloured red, green and brown, enclosed in a discarded tube base filled with sealing wax. On the outside is a gold label instructing that the red wire be connected with the aerial post, the green to the ground post and the brown to a radiator or water pipe.

Those who break apart the sealing wax will get an eye opener; they will discover absolutely nothing inside except that the red and brown terminals are joined (why the different colours?) and that the green wire leads nowhere! Moreover, into the two spare holes of the discarded tube base is looped a small piece of the brown covered wire whose ends hang loose inside.

A copy of this letter is being mailed to the Federal Radio Commission to alert them to this fraud.

G.H. Parry,
Ottawa

THE WORKLESS MARRIED MAN

JULY 15, 1933

Now that we have passed into a state of "glorified slavery," and our governments are about to put into place another scheme to alleviate unemployment, and place more single men into relief camps, what about us poor married men with families?

I am one, homeless about every three months, out bag and baggage, six of us in the family. Landlords want to see dollars and cents, not a scrap of paper. We are forced to beggary, to ask for this, to ask for that. Why not give a man with a family a chance to work on the highways? I would labour for the old army pay — $1.10 a day, and an allowance for the family. I could grow enough to keep six of us.

I am voicing the opinion of many, sick and tired, week in, week out, who never see money. One almost thinks he never will see any again. Now I get $3.50 a week to live on, not an existence.

I say, take married men, physically fit, with families, place them in camps, at $1.10 a day, with allowance for the children, and proper supervision, and a pick and shovel, and we'd feel like living. Anything is better than the present system. Give our children a chance, if we can't have it.

Let's hear some other unemployed married men with a

family voice an opinion on this letter. Winter's coming fellows!

Charles E. Gray, Eastview, Ont.

Editor's note: With unemployment approaching 25 per cent, the Dominion and provincial governments established relief camps, often in remote areas, where men would travel to build highways and bridges, clear forests and engage in other public works. At first, the camps were open only to single men to save the expense of caring for families, and in the hope the exodus of single men to the camps would open jobs for married men in the cities. Eventually, some camps permitted married men, without their families, and during the Depression's later years, a few were outfitted to handle women and children. Relief projects were also established near urban centres, allowing men to return to their families in the evening.

A MOTHER IN DESPAIR
AUGUST 12, 1933

I have ten children who are in unfit condition through under-feeding and ranging from nineteen years to eleven months, with one child of four and a half who is blind in one eye and delicate. I have tried everything possible to make both ends meet, but without success.

My husband is not fit for hard work although he has been to the Civic Hospital clinic and had an X-ray examination when they could not find anything the matter with him. He was advised to go to the clinic by the Welfare Bureau investigators. I think he is not well because he cannot get enough to eat. But after the X-ray did not show anything wrong, they told him he would receive forty-five cents an hour in relief if he worked.

And so my husband has to work eighteen hours in a week. He says that if he works for the relief he should be able to receive enough to feed his family; but we do not. For twelve persons for one week we receive 22 loaves of bread, sixteen quarts of milk, four pounds of butter, seven meat tickets and $3.15 of groceries, and I try and get oranges and arrowroot bisquits specially for my baby. And we are not getting any relief for our rent or taxes.

I would like to know how twelve persons can live and eat on $8.31 a week, which is the value of the order we receive. I cannot do it. I do not know what to do for I am so discouraged. If I steal I will be arrested and if I beg, the same.

I hope someone will be able to help us. I hope someone will stick up for us. Anyone who wants to investigate my case could call at my home.

Mrs. Rose Goyer,
22 Adeline Street, Ottawa

SUPPORT FROM SMITHS FALLS
AUGUST 23, 1933

I read in your Wednesday issue a speech given in Saskatchewan by [Opposition leader] Mackenzie King, that if he got in again he would appoint a royal commission to work with the Red Cross and other welfare societies in an effort to care for the unemployed, as well as solve the problem.

Let me say this, from one that is sorely affected, that his statement is indeed sickening, as well as discouraging. He is going to make the unemployed a national charity group as well as copy Mr. Bennett in his commission fad.

I do not know much of the C.C.F., but thank goodness they have some plans that give hope to the downtrodden people. My husband and I have heard them in Smiths Falls and we are going to vote for their candidate when next there is an election.

Mrs. W.R. Whyte, Smiths Falls

WORLD DAY FOR ANIMALS
SEPTEMBER 23, 1933

Oct. 4th (the day dedicated to St. Francis of Assisi) is celebrated in many countries as the "World Day for Animals."

Its object is threefold: Firstly, it aims to direct attention to the wrongs inflicted on birds and animals for sport, commercialism, and so-called science; secondly, it plans to focus thought on the proper means to abolish such soul-degrading cruelty; and, thirdly, it hopes to inspire action for correction of ignorant and thoughtless persons who perpetrate such and sympathy for the creatures who are at the mercy of man and cannot speak for themselves.

As ministers and churches are responsible for the spiritual welfare of the people, an earnest appeal is being made to them by the Ontario S.P.C.A. to emphasize the spiritual aspect of animal cruelty in one of the services on October 1st, the Sunday nearest to "World Day."

Cruelty, which causes suffering whether it is supposed to be in the interests of mankind or not, is a serious offense to God and his living creatures as it deadens the spiritual qualities of love, justice and mercy in the persons who perpetrate and consciously encourage it; therefore, it is a stumbling block whereby our sisters and brothers are being made weak by that sin.

E. Clifford Pratt,
Scarborough Bluffs, Ontario

MAKE WAY FOR THE INSECTS
OCTOBER 16, 1933

Today we are told that there is going to be another great war of our beloved humanity. If it should be so — which I sincerely hope not — then the flies and insects and parasites will come in to their own.

Bayonets and bombs are nasty and painful instruments to use in these modern days — in fact they are too much antiquated. Would it not be much nicer if we could use a perfumated laughing gas and then we could all laugh ourselves away?

We are blessed with considerable intelligence — yet we oftentimes act with a great degree of lunacy. Many of us mutilate and destroy each other with our dear little toys called automobiles and aeroplanes, etc. Multitudes of us swarm around cities like ants and millions of acres of good land is crying out for company.

Sometimes a person warns us that the world is coming to an end and we may become stricken with fear, running to and fro in terror of our own shadows. If we do not check our speed, we shall surely become bowlegged or knock-kneed.

We believe everything we hear or read and do not try and think for ourselves. Is it any wonder that so many of us act sub-normal or abnormal?

We humans take a delight at playing tricks on each other — one favourite game is bluffy-bluffy-crooky-crooky. It is not nice to play tricks on each other. We should try and help each other more instead of living like greedy misers. After all, we humans are only on this earth walking around for a few years and then away we go for a long, long time. Many of us are walking around to save funeral expenses and many of us would gladly go any time if our minds were at ease.

If we would go in for an orgy of spending and giving, the depression would vanish overnight. If we would give away the money which does not belong to us and practise common horse sense, then the bogey-bogey cries of war and famine and disease would disappear.

Alexander Factor,
Ottawa

THE DANISH EXAMPLE
DECEMBER 23, 1933

It has been stated in the press that due to the system of Dominion government inspection, residents in Canada and tourists need have little fear of being served bad eggs in any form.

The new grading of eggs now consists of Grades A-1; A; B; C, in place of Specials, Extras, Firsts and Seconds. It is further stated that C grade consists of all eggs below A and B, but which are fit for human consumption. I venture to say that the majority of people would be rather skeptical to eat the C grade egg from the shell.

Some years ago a certain gentleman was asked to state the various grades of eggs. He stated as follows: First of all we have the Newly Laid or Strictly Fresh egg, secondly we have the Shop egg, and thirdly, Egg.

In Denmark, I believe new laid eggs are stamped with a dated stamp on the eggs at the time they are laid as a protection to the public. This might be a good suggestion for the Canadian Department of Agriculture to consider.

F.W. Brander,
Ottawa

1934

Local: First 10 fighter planes are delivered to Royal Canadian Air Force in Ottawa (August)
National: Annette, Emilie, Yvonne, Cecile and Marie Dionne, the first surviving quintuplets in history, are born outside North Bay (May)
World: American outlaws Bonnie Parker and Clyde Barrow killed in police ambush (May); German chancellor Adolf Hitler adds presidency to his power, thereby assuming total control of country (August)

Births: Prime minister Jean Chrétien; governor general Ramon Hnatyshyn; broadcaster Peter Gzowski; native architect Douglas Cardinal; hockey commentator Don Cherry; home run king Hank Aaron; U.S. consumer advocate Ralph Nader; actresses Brigitte Bardot and Sophia Loren; Yuri Gargarin, first man in orbit
Deaths: French physicist Marie Curie; British composers Sir Edward Elgar and Frederick Delius; gangster John Dillinger; legendary baseball manager John McGraw; governor general John Campbell Gordon (Earl of Aberdeen)

LANSDOWNE PARK
JANUARY 6, 1934

The proposal to sell Lansdowne Park in order to provide money for a new City Hall is not likely to become a live issue for some time. But should it ever appear in practical politics, I hope people of progressive mind will be ready to make a substantial master plan.

It would be little less than a crime in this age to sell such a public property. If it is not to be kept as a park and playground, but is to be cut up into lots, the land should be handled in modern style. First the area should be carefully planned and proper terms of occupancy decided upon. Then lots should be leased at rentals to be re-assessed from time to time in accordance with their value.

This would yield a revenue which would increase with the growth and prosperity of the country and of this capital city.

A. C. Campbell, Ottawa

WHY MAKE ANY CHANGE?
FEBRUARY 3, 1934

A lady member of the large deputation from the churches requesting Premier Henry not to increase facilities for sale of alcoholic beverages asked this brief but pointed question: "Mr. Premier, why make any change?"

Whatever protestations are offered about hoping to aid temperance by selling more beer, as though the way to keep dry is to go out in the rain, the real answer to the lady's timely question is:

1) The drinkers want more drink.

2) The brewers want more profit.

3) The government wants more revenue, more votes and perhaps some campaign funds, too.

What an indication of intelligence is a democracy when, after four years of cruel depression, a government takes as an election slogan: "Return us to power: we promise beer parlours." William Cowper might have had 1934 Ontario in mind when he wrote one hundred and fifty years ago:

> Drink and be mad, then: 'tis your country bids!
> Her cause demands the assistance of your throats.
> Ye all can swallow, and she asks no more.

Come into my beer parlours, the Ontario government

spider is going to say to its electoral flies. By ballots, the invitation may be declined. Vote as you drink.

George A. Little, Toronto

Editor's note: The Conservative government of Premier George Henry lost the July 10 election to Mitch Hepburn's Liberals, who made no immediate changes to the province's liquor laws.

IDLE HANDS AND IDLE LANDS
MARCH 3, 1934

I note in your issue of Feb. 26 that a plan to settle 40,000 workless British families in Canada is under consideration. How strange that the British Isles should realize the value of Canada to absorb their unemployed, when Canada herself is blind to see the value of our "empty acres" for our own unemployed.

R.S. Reid, Ottawa

TENANTS ON RELIEF
MARCH 7, 1934

After residing in my house for the past thirteen years, I am told to vacate the premises by the end of March, with no reason provided, so I start looking around for a house. Then I begin to realize the difficulties that beset the person on relief.

Everybody is very courteous at first, but when you state that you are on relief, you will meet with all kinds of rebuffs that are anything but complimentary, and you will begin to wonder what makes your position so humiliating. You are willing to work, you don't want to be on relief, yet there is no other way out at present, so what else can one do?

Only this evening I got in touch with a gentleman who had a house to let. I asked him if he was willing to accept two families, my own and another, which would cover the rent he was asking. He told me he had several houses with two families on relief but he would have to tell them to get out soon, as Mayor [Patrick] Nolan stated a short time back that the city would not be responsible to help the landlords who had relief tenants in the very near future.

There will be hundreds of families in Ottawa looking for houses in the next few weeks, and if they encounter the experiences I have, they will be amazed at what I would term man's inhumanity to man.

Joseph Fitzpatrick, Ottawa

THE KING ON THE NICKEL
MARCH 10, 1934

The public find it difficult to distinguish the Canadian nickel five-cent piece from the Canadian 25-cent piece. There is great complaint about this matter because people frequently put down a nickel as a 25-cent piece in making a purchase.

The two pieces are of about the same size and on account of the King's head on each coin being of the same design, it is hard to tell which is which when the head side of the coin is turned up and when the nickel and quarter are seen separately.

Might I suggest that a smaller King's head than the present one be put on the nickel and under it a beaver? As it is well known that King George is a hard worker, this Canadian emblem appearing beneath the King's head could be regarded as a compliment to the King as well as serving to distinguish the nickel from the quarter.

L.M. Fetterly, Cornwall

OTTAWA SYMPHONY ORCHESTRA APPEAL
MARCH 14, 1934

In an effort to raise a comparatively small sum to insure that the Ottawa Symphony Orchestra may continue to function for at least another year, the undersigned have mailed an appeal to a few hundred music lovers in Ottawa.

While the invitation to give is not, of course, confined to those to whom these letters have been sent, we wish to point out to all interested that large individual subscriptions are not expected though, of course, they will be welcome.

The total which it is hoped to raise and which, indeed, is needed if the Ottawa Symphony Orchestra is to continue — one thousand dollars — will be secured if each friend of the orchestra will contribute two dollars. Donations may be sent to Mrs. H.S. Southam, Casa Loma, Rockcliffe Park.

Lilias Southam, C.G. Cowan

Editor's note: Mrs. Southam, a well-known Ottawa socialite and philanthropist, was the wife of Citizen publisher Harry Stevenson Southam. Despite tough economic times, her appeal for donations brought in more than $1,000.

FOR GENERAL PRIVATION
MARCH 22, 1934

The civil service are the servants of the country, charged with administering certain affairs for the nation; consequently, their lot is one that should be in harmony with the rest of the citizens of the country.

And yet you, Mr. Editor, write day after day, through news or editorials, urging the restoration of the salaries of these people to the standard that prevailed during prosperous times. Rather you should write to urge that these salaries be lowered a great deal more than they are already lowered.

The conditions that prevail among the first-producers of Canada are such that the incomes of these people are on the whole not more than one-quarter to one-third of what they were in prosperous times; and without these workers in agriculture, lumbering, mining and fishing, our cities would die. Yet in the cities you wish to continue large wages and salaries out of all proportion with the non-urban population.

It is hard to understand why you do not see the injustice you are perpetrating; even worse, the cruelty you are perpetrating towards the people upon whom the cities live. These matters require to be seen with a larger vision than that which is furnished by the interests of centers that are government-supported or tariff-propped.

James Taylor, Eganville, Ont.

A STOWAWAY'S EXPERIENCE

MARCH 26, 1934

I see by this evening's *Citizen* that Miss Catherine Carr, Irish girl, who stowed away on a freighter from Belfast to Halifax, has been ordered by immigration officials to leave Canada.

As one who has also made an Atlantic crossing as a stowaway, I can sympathize with Miss Carr, and believe me, any girl who has the courage to make a trip like that in a freighter's lifeboat, deserves all the sympathy and help she can get.

If some of the immigration officials who are so anxious to deport her had suffered as much as Miss Carr must have, they might feel a little more inclined to apply the Golden Rule.

W.M. Angus, Kinburn, Ont.

RELIEF CAMP REFLECTIONS

JUNE 11, 1934

Owing to a stroke of luck and the kind consideration of friends, I have managed to escape the depressing life in the Rockcliffe relief camp — at least for the time being.

I am now enjoying myself — and working — as a free citizen in Canada's gay and fascinating metropolis, cosmopolitan Montreal; quite different, as you can imagine, to swinging pick and shovel at the rate of twenty cents a day — plus "grub" and "flop" and, let us not forget, some pretty strong tobacco.

I promised the boys not to forget them if I again wrote to you. So here I am declaring that this business of putting men to work for twenty cents a day is no good in this rich Dominion. It makes the boys go "Red," and no wonder, for they can see no way ahead: they go only further in the hole, losing their time.

Most of them would quit the camps tomorrow if they had only a few dollars to pay their way for a few days. And, by the way, why is there not any employment service established in connection with these camps full of able-bodied men anxious to get out into real life again?

I understand that my frequent letters to you on behalf of the working people and less favoured citizens (some call

them the underdogs) have procured me a socialistic reputation amongst my more distinguished and successful friends. Some of my compatriots are afraid I am the living proof of "something rotten in Denmark." However, I am no agent for Russia — Canada can breed "Reds" herself, evidently.

John Ingvar Jensen, Montreal

BRITISH FASCISM

AUGUST 11, 1934

Much has been written recently of disturbances in London, allegedly created by Fascists. It is not generally known that there are two organizations of Fascists in Great Britain, namely, the Imperial Fascist League and the British Union of Fascists.

The former has been in existence for many years and is a genuinely patriotic body of men and women who stand for the good of the state. The aim of the league is to replace the present outworn democratic method of government by the adoption of a Fascist constitution headed by the monarchy.

The principles of statecraft which they would follow include the provision of adequate protective forces to secure the safety of the Empire, the elimination of evil alien influences, deliverance from the gold standard, federation for the Empire, protection for our industries and compulsory arbitration in industrial disputes and cessation of industrial civil war.

The slogan of the league is, "All Within the State, None Against the State," and is particularly interesting to Empire lovers the world over, more especially in these days of "welfare."

John Campbell, Ottawa

ACCORDING TO THE DICTIONARY

AUGUST 22, 1934

Beverage room, is that not a lousy name? I bet that over half of the local proprietors can't even spell or correctly pronounce "beverage." The dictionary gives its meaning, "a drink of any description."

Well, there may be some different varieties of beer sold there, but there's only one description, so why not cut out the hooey and call them beer rooms?

J. A. Murray, Ottawa

PUFFBALL CHALLENGE

OCTOBER 13, 1934

It appears from the Ottawa newspapers that the prize puffball in this area weighed eighteen pounds and was found near the Montreal road. I can report that this now has been bettered by a puffball fifty-eight inches in circumference and weighing nineteen and three-quarters pounds when it was weighed four days after picking.

It was found by Hubert Smith in company with Eyre Holmes, both of Ottawa. The location of the find was on an island in the Paquette Rapids of the Ottawa River.

This mammoth puffball had a twin growing out of an indenture. The twin weighed eight pounds, which we ate. The large one we kept in the auto to bring home as proof. It also was in a perfect edible condition. If we had

NATIONAL ARCHIVES

Through a stroke of luck and help of friends, a reader said he managed to escape the depressing life in the Rockcliffe relief camp.

weighed them immediately their weight and size would have been much more, as they must have shrunk a few inches in the four days before departure.

Eyre Holmes, Ottawa

DAD AND JOHNNY
NOVEMBER 19, 1934

When I read in your paper of man's "evolution from something lower than an ape," the lobes of my brain began to hop from place to place, for that idea was new to me, having hitherto thought that man began his existence at the ape and not lower down the line.

Thinking now that he may have originated in a reptile, fifty million years ago, I went into a slumber room in my subconsciousness and found the following dialogue between Daddy and Johnny.

Johnny: What's that you're reading, Dad?

Dad: Something about the origin of man.

Johnny: O! I can tell you all about that, Dad. About 50,000, or perhaps 1,000,000 years ago, a female baboon had twins, a little baby boy, and a tiny baby girl. Or it may be the baby boy was born in one year, and the baby girl the next year. Or maybe the boy was born of a gorilla mother and the little girl of a she monkey. I have been thinking, Dad, that maybe these kids were not born in the same patch of woods, but very far away from each other and I am wondering how they were cared for in their infancy, and whether they were hairy, and had tails like a monkey, and if they were born of different mothers far away from each other, how they came to meet each other when they had grown up, and with what language they greeted each other, and a heap of other things, Dad, I'm thinking about. There's a chap in my class at school named Jimmy Irish, and he says his father told him it was the Irish language Adam and Eve spoke.

Dad: And where did you learn all that you've told me, Johnny?

Johnny: In one of my school books, Dad.

Dad: And where did the writer get this information?

Johnny: They found some bits o' bones, you know, here and there all over the world, and they patch up the gaps with soft clay and let it bake in the sun, and they found some molars too and they made lots of photographs. Haven't you heard of the Broken Hill Skull, and the Pilt-Down Remains and the skull of an ancient Galilean, and the Neanderthal Man, and the Dune Dwellers of Shabbaerack Ussu?

At this point, Dad looked bewildered, but the dialogue is too long for any further quotation.

E.P. Hurley, Ottawa

WAR TRAINING FOR UNEMPLOYED
DECEMBER 19, 1934

As we walk the busy streets of Ottawa we see a surging mass of humanity going hither and thither — some going to their daily occupations, others not so lucky, walk casually along without any particular goal in sight.

It is to the latter class I would refer, whose ranks are chiefly made up of young men ranging in age from 18 to 35 years and who possess a clean, neat appearance, and a bright, intelligent manner. These young men, many of whom belong to our Capital's well-to-do families for some unforeseen reason are unable to obtain employment.

Would it not be better to educate these young men and give them a military training instead of incurring the expense on the nation of building long lines of highway — highways we may never need? In this work a wage could be given the homeless and needy and to those who wish to enlist for training. Military training aids the physical side of the individual as it is proper exercise that keeps the body sound.

To many, military training is scorned and considered as a disadvantage to the youth. Many think it an invitation to war. On the other hand, it is an advantage and something that will be useful to the country in case of invasion. Let us hope for the best and prepare for the worst.

Jessie E. Carter,
Ottawa

1935

Local: Thousands of unemployed workers from across Canada converge on Ottawa by train (August)

National: Bank of Canada, charged with issuing currency and regulating money supply, begins operation (March); William Aberhart leads Social Credit party to election win in Alberta (August); Liberals under Mackenzie King return to power with landslide victory over the ruling Conservatives (October)

World: Nazis pass laws stripping Jews of German citizenship and banning them from politics (September); Italian fascist leader Benito Mussolini orders invasion of Ethiopia (October)

Births: Elvis Presley; labour leader Bob White; U.S. writer Ken Kesey; U.S. black activist Eldridge Cleaver; governor general Ed Schreyer

Deaths: Colonel T.E. Lawrence (Lawrence of Arabia); French auto pioneer André Citroën; New York Times publisher Adolph Ochs; governor general Julian George (Lord Byng of Vimy)

TO UPHOLD FREE SPEECH

JANUARY 12, 1935

As my name has been prominently connected in this morning's *Citizen* with the rental of the Little Theatre for the cancelled meeting which was to have been addressed by Mr. Tim Buck, general secretary of the Communist Party of Canada, I feel in justice to myself your paper should be willing to allow me to make my connection with this matter perfectly clear to the public.

May I say at the outset that I am not a member of the Communist Party, the Canadian Labour Defence League or any other organization of this nature. I am interested in a business which arranges lectures, concerts, tours, and things of that description, known as Sponsors, located at 504-505 Hope Chambers, 63 Sparks Street.

Some days ago, I was approached by the Canadian Labour Defence League to find a hall for the purpose of presenting Mr. Buck to the citizens of Ottawa. On January 8th, I was successful in securing the use of the Little Theatre for this purpose.

The following day at noon, I was informed by the treasurer of the Ottawa Drama League that, although I had secured sanction for the use of the theatre, and had, furthermore, paid a deposit on account of the rental for my clients, something had happened to make the directors of the Drama League wish to reconsider their decision as to the use of the theatre. At 5:30 p.m. that same evening he telephoned to me again to inform that everything was in order and my clients could make their final arrangements for advertising, printing, etc.

Then at 4 p.m. on January 10th, I was again asked to visit the treasurer of the Drama League, who informed me that another re-canvass of the directors had been made by telephone, and that this telephonic directors' meeting had been detrimental to my clients' interests. I was advised that I had better visit [drama league chairman] Mr. J.A. Aylen for a final decision.

The rest of the story is now public property. Mr. Aylen informed me the directors had now decided not to allow the use of the Little Theatre for the Tim Buck meeting. I

CITIZEN-UPI

Communist leader Tim Buck was denied use of the Little Theatre for a speech, which he gave outdoors at a nearby site.

could secure no reason, Mr. Aylen definitely stating that he wished to give none.

Well, Sir, I have always been led to believe that I am a free and independent British citizen of Canada, for which country I served four years overseas helping — as I was then persuaded — to save the world for democracy. As a British subject I have prided myself on those hardly won and dearly bought liberties for which my Scottish ancestors have always stood and often fought, chief among which is the free and unfettered right of every man to express his views whether one agreed with him or not.

Undoubtedly pressure had been brought to bear upon the directors of the Drama League from highly placed official sources, with the obvious intention of stifling freedom of speech. I intend to take a very definite stand in this Tim Buck matter irrespective of any attitude assumed by my erstwhile clients, the Canadian Labour Defence League.

I am going to appeal for the support of those fair-minded Canadians, who still have an ounce of the red fighting blood of our pioneer forefathers left in their veins, to make this matter a national Canadian issue. I am taking it upon myself to form a Free Speech Fund, the proceeds of which will be used to bring Mr. Buck back to this Capital City of Canada to speak in the largest hall which can be secured. Donations of this purpose may be forwarded to Sponsors at the address previously provided, and will be acknowledged by receipt.

It's about time freeborn Canadians showed these autocrats their proper place in the scheme of things.

A.T. McFarlane, Ottawa

Editor's note: After the Drama League turned Mr. Buck away, the Canadian Labour Defence League sought and received police approval for the Communist leader to speak outdoors at a site near the Little Theatre. Nearly 1,200 people braved sub-zero weather to hear his firebrand oratory, defiantly delivered from the theatre's front steps on the same night he was to have spoken inside. Mr. Buck, a founder of the Canadian Communist party in 1929 and its leader for the next 32 years, remained an apologist for Josef Stalin and the brutal excesses of Soviet communism until his death in 1973. In 1971, he was given the Order of the Great October Revolution by Soviet president Leonid Brezhnev.

HEATING ELECTRICALLY
FEBRUARY 13, 1935

I was interested to read your article on "Heating Houses Electrically" and would state that I installed the English system of tubular electric heaters in a church at Shawinigan Falls in 1932, which has proved to be very satisfactory in every way during the sub-zero weather which prevails in the St. Maurice Valley during the winter season.

The actual cost of the installation was 30 per cent less than any other modern system of heating, and the floor space in the basement that would ordinarily be required for boilers and coal storage was used as a school room.

Such an installation is only practical when surplus electric power is available and can be procured at a low cost compared with coal or fuel oil. Actual costs taken over a period of two years in Shawinigan Falls show that electric power at six mills per K.W.H. compares favourably with coal at $12 per ton or fuel oil at 11 cents per gallon.

The simplicity of the design and application of the tubular electric heaters is a great factor; they can be placed horizontally, vertically or at any angle at all, which in the case of a church building allows of them being placed along the roof rafters thus cutting the cold down-draughts so common in lofty buildings. They can be placed under the seats and along the walls thus giving a uniform heat in every part of the church.

The above installation was controlled by thermostats installed in the main body of the church, in the basement and in the vestry, so that any part of the building could be used at any time without heating the other, thus making the system flexible and efficient.

G. Claxton, Ottawa

AT THE CIVIC HOSPITAL
FEBRUARY 27, 1935

Kindly allow me space in your valuable paper to express my appreciation and most sincere thanks to all those who had anything to do with my case while I was a patient in the Ottawa Civic Hospital.

The remarkable part of it was the great kindness of the doctors, nurses and orderlies; it was indeed service with a smile, I was in West 2, a public ward, and paying only $1.50 per day. Had I been in a private ward and paying $10 a day I could not have received better treatment, nor could any of the others, all were treated alike.

John W. Curran, Ottawa

WOULD KEEP DESTITUTE OUT
MARCH 28, 1935

The Women's Municipal Association of Ottawa intend to carry on a publicity campaign through the press and individually to prevent so many people from outside districts moving into the city in order to go on relief.

If property-owners would refuse to rent their houses to these newcomers, and this be publicly known, many would remain where they are now. We also feel that all men on relief who are supposed to work for their rent be forced to do so. One member stated that in a city in Western Canada men on relief who refused to work were publicly punished. This sounded drastic, but proved very effective and saved the city a lot of trouble.

We, therefore, hope that our city fathers act in whatever manner necessary to safeguard the taxpayers of the city.

Cecilia E. Hesser, president;
Adelaide Lemire, corresponding secretary,
Women's Municipal Association of Ottawa

Editor's note: Although many Canadian cities implemented rules trying to ban outsiders from collecting relief, no such prohibition was employed in Ottawa. The following letter deals with the matter of working for rent.

REPLY TO WOMEN'S ASSOCIATION
MARCH 30, 1935

After reading the letter from the Women's Municipal Association, I feel I cannot let it pass by without a reply. They state that all men who are supposed to work for their rent should be forced to do so.

I am astonished at the ignorance of this body of women. If they would only take the time to inquire they would find that the Welfare Board see to it that every man must work before his rent slip is stamped and sent on to the finance commissioner for payment. Only those who are absolutely unfit for work are exempt; and they must be examined by a doctor every month or so.

These women, many of them who will call a man in to do some decorating for them this spring and offer him a miserly 25 cents per hour, are not very anxious to take men off relief. I know, as I have had experience with them, and still they rant about the poor taxpayer and the burden he has to bear.

I will say this much for the man who is in real need, he is only too anxious to work. I personally am open to take any work at my trade, painting and decorating, these women can put my way at the recognized trade rates. And I would like to see how anxious they are to help at least one man to get off relief.

Ed E. Kesterton, Ottawa

CHILDREN FOR CANNON FODDER
APRIL 6, 1935

Women bring children into the world much the same as farmers raise turkeys — for the Christmas trade. In Italy and Germany it is "bigger and better families for bigger and better (!) armies." They have baby clinics, child welfare societies, society for the prevention of cruelty to children, medical inspection of schools, health officers, etc. for — the successful cultivation of cannon fodder!

Christendom! Christianity! They call it so with upraised head and unblushing cheek. If Christ is responsible for what is happening we wonder what they think the devil could do. Blasphemy indeed, and soon to be avenged.

Really, it requires but the average amount of intelligence to realize that the world is in the grip of fanatical fiends and homicidal maniacs with the clergy kowtowing to both while the devil pulls the strings.

Edna Snider, Westboro

ON HANGING WOMEN
APRIL 24, 1935

In your recent issue appears Thomas L. Church, Toronto East (Conservative), giving notice in the House of Commons of his bill to amend the Criminal Code, abolishing capital punishment for women. From my observation this is sure a sign of weakness — but if we are to abolish capital punishment, let it be for all murderers.

For what specific reason should a woman murderer be exempt, any more than a man, I fail to understand. If one follows crime in the cities of larger and older countries than Canada, one will find women are the leading brains and far superior to the man criminal. When a woman leads she leads, therefore if a woman is a cold-blooded murderer, I do not see why she should escape capital punishment.

Leo N. Keyzer, Ottawa

Editor's note: Capital punishment, for men and women, was banned by Parliament in 1976 (although under the National Defence Act, execution can still be used for cowardice, desertion, unlawful surrender or spying). The last hanging in Canada took place in 1962.

'FISHING NOT RECOMMENDED'
JUNE 19, 1935

Apropos the very fine article in your Saturday issue regarding the wonderful playground to the north of Ottawa, the attached may be of some interest to you, and will demonstrate that there is at least one honest advertiser in the country. This chap is located on one of the best trout lakes in the Ottawa Valley district, namely, Lac Simon, on the Nation River.

We have planted in this lake since 1922 roughly three and a half million speckled and gray trout, but due to wholesale netting, spearing, and night lines, the lake is cleaned of trout. Some intelligent official of the Singer Sewing Co. planted bass in a little lake just off Lac Simon and draining into it, with the result that bass are now in the lake.

But unless the local populace change their ways there will be little use in planting any fish in this lake, and this applies to the Lievre, Gatineau and Pontiac districts. A local druggist (Ottawa) recently caught 600 pounds of brook and speckled trout, and sold four hundred pounds, these from a series of lakes and little streams that we had restocked two years ago.

In your future articles on this district, please make it clear to people that it is up to them to protect their own country, and if they do not they need not expect sportsmen and visitors to come here. We have on hand many inquiries from very prominent sportsmen in the U.S. who wish to come here for good speckled trout fishing, but outside of getting the privileges of some private club, I do not know where to send them where I feel sure they will get some sport.

James McCuaig,
Secretary-treasurer,
Fish and Game Protective Association, Hull

The Citizen added the following postscript to Mr. Mc-Cuaig's letter: The writer encloses a folder issued by the manager of a camp on Lac Simon, describing the many attractions of his establishment. The paragraph on fishing reads: "Not recommended. The local populace, through lack of educational work by the authorities, have just about fished out the lake by illegal means."

OFF TO ITALY
JULY 10, 1935

I read in your paper a few days ago that a group of young Italians of Ottawa have left to visit Italy, and it was stated that "the group are all members of the Italian organization of Ottawa."

What it did not say is what organization they are members of. The four boys and the four girls who have left for Italy were attending Dante school last winter to learn Italian, a scheme promoted in Canada by the Italian government. But the real objective was to teach them Fascist doctrine and Fascist songs, and early last spring it formed a young Fascist organization, to which all the members of the group belong.

Although they are born Canadian citizens, they all took the oath of allegiance to Italy, and now they are travelling attired in Fascist uniforms.

Michele Trentadue, Ottawa

GARDENS, YARDS AND RATS
JULY 26, 1935

"Of the dwellings visited, over 19 per cent were found to be rat-infested, and over 17 per cent were found to be vermin-infested." What a truly pathetic report from your July 20th issue concerning this fair city, the capital of the Dominion of Canada.

Once a year, and once a year only, we are appealed to by the city hall authorities to use the broom on our backyards, and make a clean sweep of the rubbish. But for the remaining 51 weeks, year in and year out, let the rubbish pile up until the yards take on, more and more, the appearance of miniature municipal dump-heaps.

On my returning to Ottawa, after an absence abroad of many years, my mind is carried back to the days when each house had a well-cared for "garden" and when the nomenclature of "yard" was applied to our farming fraternity.

Only recently when discussing with a gentleman high up in government circles, this very question of "dump-heaps in yards" even in the center of the city, and unsuitable garbage containers which are left uncovered at backdoors, he made some very caustic remarks, and he ventured to predict that, given another year of two, there will be such a plague of rats in this city, that our old friend the

Pied Piper of Hamelin will appear to have been a mere neophyte.

E.A. Reynolds, Ottawa

MILK ON SUNDAYS
AUGUST 1, 1935

Since the recent arrest of milk drivers for delivering on Sunday, I have been expecting to see your editorial criticism but to date have been disappointed to find nothing.

In this city there are several hundred families on relief, who have young babies. These families live in places where it is impossible to keep milk over Sunday without souring. They have no money to buy emergency requirements and many are beyond reach of the dairy who supplies them.

It has been the custom of the dairies to make special deliveries on Sunday to people whose supply has gone sour, and this action of the police has been the cause of the cessation of this service.

Now, I ask, what is to become of these infants? The handicap against these children is quite sufficient without starvation for one day every week. The fact that they can get only pasteurized milk in this city is bad enough, it being a well-recognized fact that pasteurization destroys the greater amount of vitamins in milk.

Right here, let me remark that aldermen who have advocated a city pasteurization plant would be spending their efforts to much better effect if they advocated a certified, unpasteurized milk depot, where infants and invalids might be served milk that has superior food content.

C. Vermilyea, Ottawa

1936

Local: Federal government decides to demolish main Post Office to make room for National War Memorial on Confederation Square (August); First dial telephones installed in Ottawa homes (November)
National: More than 200 deaths blamed on worst heat wave in Canadian history, which scorches southern Ontario for 10 days (July); Union Nationale, led by Maurice Duplessis, wins Quebec election (August)
World: King George V dies in January and is succeeded by Edward VIII, who abdicates the throne in December to marry a divorced American woman; Civil war erupts in Spain as Fascist leader Francisco Franco vows to topple Republican government (July); American Jesse Owens is star of Berlin Olympics (August)
Births: Environmentalist David Suzuki; basketball star Wilt Chamberlain; designer Yves St. Laurent; actress Ursula Andress
Deaths: British writer G.K. Chesterton; German philosopher Oswald Spengler

HEARING THE KING ON SUNDAY
FEBRUARY 26, 1936

The news that the first message from King Edward VIII to his people will be broadcast next Sunday morning has, no doubt, created a lot of interest among us all. Due to the fact that it is on Sunday morning, would it not be a great opportunity for all the churches of all creeds to make some arrangements whereby all the people connected with the various churches could hear His Majesty speak to us, on this, his first public message?

I understand some are already planning to install radios in their churches, and would it not be a kindly act if all churches placed this privilege at the disposal of all the classes of people? For many have not, and cannot afford radios, but if their nearest church provided the same, I am sure that this would be a great pleasure for them.

Probably some churches would object to the use of the church, but could this not be overcome by using the basement or church hall before the morning service?

Let everyone have the opportunity of hearing our King in this, his first message, to his loyal subjects.

A.H. Jarvis, Ottawa

ART GALLERY SUNDAY CONCERTS
FEBRUARY 28, 1936

I want to draw the attention of the public to the experiment which is being tried out at the National Art Gallery, Victoria Museum, in the form of radio concerts.

Edward VIII makes his first radio broadcast. A reader said churches should have installed radios so that everyone could have heard it.

Every Sunday afternoon the wonderful concerts of the world-famous New York Symphony Orchestra, commencing at three o'clock, may be heard on the ground floor of the Museum building, in the sculpture rooms, where many chairs are provided for those who care to be seated.

It is most fitting that the arts, which are all closely related (music being one of the fine arts), should be brought together and centralized, so to speak, in one building; and as painting and sculpture are already presented in the two sections of the Victoria Museum, together with other forms of artistry, a further extension of the idea is therefore being made, as is done in other cities.

Whether these concerts will be continued depends upon how well they are appreciated and patronized by the public, however, and I appeal to those who value the fostering and thriving of art to give this gesture of the Art Gallery their encouragement.

A. Suzor Greaves, Ottawa

ON RECIPROCITY
MARCH 4, 1936

A better bargain for whom? On February 10, the Hon. R.B. Bennett, in his four-hour speech, spoke scornfully of the Liberals' tariffs agreement with the United States: "No man could negotiate a treaty in 24 hours or 72 hours and if he did he was properly trimmed."

Let Mr. Bennett turn back to 1911 when the Conservatives carried the country against reciprocity. It was not six months after being elected until they tried to negotiate with the United States but were repulsed. Ever since, those who supported reciprocity have been waiting for some measure of better relations between the two neighbours.

What are the facts? Mr. Bennett says, "We were offered the same proposals but would not accept." Every thinking farmer knows that his government would not accept. Instead they laid such heavy burden on the farmer that thousands of farmers are suffering the results of high tariff and Bennett's sound money policy.

He says, "Business interests will suffer." Had he looked to the business interests of the farmer whom he ignored, the business interests to which he refers would be in a better condition.

He talks of ridicule in different places of the treaty. Look at the thousands of farms mortgaged since his government took over the reins of power! Surely the Conservatives should be held up for both ridicule and censure.

Ellen A.A. Wallace, Bells Corners

Editor's note: Within weeks of toppling R.B. Bennett's Conservatives in the 1935 election, Mackenzie King's Liberals signed a series of reciprocal trade agreements that lowered the duty on many exports between Canada and the United States.

ECONOMIST AND HUMOURIST
APRIL 29, 1936

Perhaps my good friend, Mr. John Jensen, in his next letter to the *Evening Citizen,* will tell your readers just what Professor Stephen Leacock, whom he eulogizes beyond reason as "writer, philosopher, humourist, speaker, observer, thinker, artist, poet man, lover, Canadian and strange economist who irritates the Marxists and bewilders the distinguished orthodox economists," has to offer as a solution of our present economic problems?

At any rate, Professor Leacock's seven-thousand-word essay, entitled, "Economic Analysis of Industrial Depression," which he read to those in attendance at the annual meeting of the Canadian Political Science Association held in the Château Laurier in May, 1933, was, to those earnestly desirous of finding a way out of the depression, as sounding brass or a tinkling cymbal.

Both Professor Leacock's economic theories and his humour have always proven shadowy and elusive to many Canadians, despite his standing at McGill University as an economist and the number of his literary achievements. It was difficult to take the former seriously or to really enjoy the latter.

To describe him as "the first Canadian" is not only to do him a great injustice, but constitutes a very serious indictment of our best citizens.

Mr. Jensen's letter, with your leading editorial on the same page, "The Next Five Years," brings to mind the great lack of constructive thought and effort to solve our economic problems.

Apart from the Communist solution, the untried and somewhat discredited Social Credit theory, the diluted and inapplicable Socialism of the C.C.F., what have we? Nothing but a flogging of dead horses, chaff blown by a whirlwind, words, words, words!

And every day brings war or revolution a step nearer. Do we want chaos or comfort?

John Lyons, Ottawa

COMMUNIST CRITIC ANSWERED
MAY 11, 1936

Mr. John Lyons' fulminations provoked by my "eulogizing beyond reason" of Professor Leacock, the lack of constructive thought in my letter and your editorial make most entertaining reading. It is evident that the old McGill professor is a pretty small potato seen through Communist glasses.

But I hope that my old friend realizes that it takes more than his most heroic display of debunking fireworks to convince discriminating people that his adversary is no good and that his theories are just so much bunk. Some of the class-war Fuhrers have rather grandiose conceptions of their own importance and intellectual capacity. A little self-criticism and soberness might not harm the movement in its present stage.

When one looks a little closer at the parrot lingo of Mr. Lyons and his like, their mock heroics, and abuse, their intolerance towards their "friends" and all who dare question their creed, or deviate from the class-war path — or "sound money principles" — then it becomes a little more comprehensible why sensible people hesitate to join the Leftists organizations in this country — and this despite five years of depression with the old systems falling to pieces all over the world.

When a Communist candidate in a city of Ottawa's size with a liberal-minded and intellectually awake electorate gets only about two hundred votes, then I think the candidate ought to scrutinize his own methods, and personality, instead of "flogging dead horses" of other parties or cry for constructive economic thinking in a letter dealing with the national consciousness of a Canadian writer.

John Ingvar Jensen, Ottawa

"SMIRKERS OF THE WORLD UNITE!"

JUNE 1, 1936

Your correspondent, Mr. McFarlane, wants the people to "own" Canada, and says that not until they do can we all share in the nation's wealth.

That hoary gospel was born in 1848 — and it will be 2048 before there is the slightest hope of it being realized according to the medieval technique espoused by Mr. McFarlane.

The people want goods *now* — and they know there is, at present, no particular virtue in the ownership of the means of production. Eventually, perhaps. But the first, the most vital step, is ownership of the means of making money.

To Mr. McFarlane and the rest of the Tory Reds — Smirkers of the world unite, you have nothing to lose but your brains!

S.J. Collett, Ottawa

NIGHTGOWNS OR PYJAMAS?

JUNE 19, 1936

It has been my privilege to meet a young man from the Land of Evangeline who is at present in our midst, and who asserts that the wearing of pyjamas is only a "style," and a habit that decent people have acquired from the "movies."

He claims that the habit or style of his people in general is to sleep in their underwear in all seasons of the year, because it is more comfortable, just as healthy and less trouble.

I wonder if L.M. "Doc" Davis from Ottawa, Illinois, who is quoted in your paper, belongs to this clan or cult, whether he means that the three great statesmen he mentions belonged to that class of people, or did they and does he wear nightgowns?

W.A. Fuller, Jr., Ottawa

Editor's note: Nothing shedding light on this quirky and enjoyable letter was found in the Citizen's files. We leave its signficance to your imagination.

ALL IN THE LIFE OF A TRAMP

JUNE 24, 1936

Half the world doesn't know how the other half lives, and may be interested to know how I exist without working.

Perhaps there may be a few readers unfortunate enough to be going on tramp who might like a few tips about it, and there may be some readers fortunate enough in the material world to enable them to change a tramp into a good material citizen if they choose to do so.

It could easily be done: find enough employment to enable me to get the necessary comforts of life, and instead of a short while, I might yet enjoy ten or 15 more years on this planet.

But I don't think that the sordid details of a tramp's existence would interest many readers. There is no glamour about extreme poverty and hardship, and only those who have actually experienced it can understand it or sympathize. Welfare and newspaper investigators and religious experimenters don't understand it: they have homes and

salaries and rich organizations behind them — they never know actual poverty.

Your correspondent says he can't understand a penniless tramp with aches and pains enjoying the beauties of Nature. 'Tis true I have bad teeth, only four of them meet and two of them are rotten, but they don't ache. What plagues me is neuritis in the thighs. That's impure blood from faulty digestion, caused by the improper food a tramp has to eat, and imperfect chewing. Were I able to buy food that suits, my neuritis would soon be gone.

I have known several other paupers who enjoyed Nature's beauties, and a great many who enjoyed other things: drinkers, dope fiends, card players, musicians, singers, some who were interested in nothing but horse racing and sport, some crazy about politics and some religious maniacs.

I have little or no taste for such things, not even the humble pipe or tobacco in any form. But the beauties of Nature always delight me, the mysteries of space fascinate me, and the idiotic insanities of me and my fellow-beings sicken me.

I wonder how many aeons of time stretch before us until man has developed enough intelligence to properly handle the riches of this beautiful planet the Great Creator has given us.

F. Jennings, Toronto

Editor's note: Not a lot is known about F. Jennings, except that he emigrated from Britain and for several years during the Depression wrote dozens of letters to Ontario newspapers describing his experiences as a hobo, using them to expound on his philosophy on a wide range of subjects, especially those close to his heart — wealth and poverty, greed and generosity. Whoever he was, his articulate writing suggested a good education, or at least a well-developed intellectual curiousity, and his wry wisdom triggered responses from readers whenever the Citizen published one of his letters. Other Jennings letters appear further on in this book.

NINE CHILDREN SINCE 1930

AUGUST 21, 1936

Both my husband and myself have of late become very interested in the publicity given Mr. and Mrs. Dionne and their quintuplets.

I avail myself of this opportunity to place my own case before you for your consideration, trusting you can find it convenient to reserve a little corner in your valuable paper and give us a little bit of publicity. It may help things along, as at present we are in very humble circumstances, brought along to us through the depression.

My husband is a thoroughly trained landscape gardener and a horticulturist, but has been unemployed for the past four years. He is very anxious to find employment with some nursery firm requiring a good man. I am 40 years of age, and the mother of 15 children, the eldest of which is only 13 years old. In reading your paper, I notice Mrs. Graziano has nine children born since October 1926. Very good indeed, but I can go one better than this — I have given birth to nine children since February, 1930, four pairs of twins and one single birth. My latest pair were born on July 4th last.

I think if I were living in Toronto I might have some show in the stork race [a multi-birth contest sponsored by a Toronto newspaper]. As for this Prescott of ours, where highways, railways and waterways meet, I don't think there will ever be any such races run.

Mrs. J.E. McLaughlin,
Prescott

MORE QUINTS
AUGUST 26, 1936

The regularity with which things are produced in fives in this country leads to the suspicion that there must be something in the air.

Mrs. Henry Mohns uprooted quintuplet carrots from her vegetable garden in Petawawa and sends the curious specimens to the *Evening Citizen*. In passing may I say that Mrs. Mohns sends best wishes to the *Citizen* and its staff. On behalf of my friend Mrs. Mohns, I beg to remain, etc.

(Miss) Louise Dugal,
Petawawa

The Citizen replied: Receipt is acknowledged of Mrs. Mohns' "quintuplet" carrots, which by now have entered an old-fashioned Irish stew.

LEARN FROM GERMANY AND ITALY
OCTOBER 24, 1936

Why can't other nations copy Italy's and Germany's ways and do what they have been doing in the last year?

Many officials of both nations have been travelling into each other's countries. From Italy came Ciano's wife, who is Mussolini's daughter, Agriculture Minister Edmondo Rossi, Propaganda Minister Dino Alfieri and Air Under-Secretary Giuseppe Valle. From Germany came Propaganda Minister Goebbels, Justice Minister Hans Frank and Air Under-Secretary Erhard Milch. Heinrich Himmler, head of the Gestapo, also is in Italy at present.

Instead of fortifying borders, why not fortify plans for peace and co-operation among nations?

Giovanni Nunzio,
Ottawa

LOYALTY TO THE KING'S IDEALS
DECEMBER 9, 1936

As I write this, millions of British subjects are awaiting some official word regarding His Majesty's momentous decision. Is it possible that thinking men and women the world over are still unable to see beyond the obviously transparent excuse for ousting the King from his throne, to the real and far-reaching issues at stake?

Apparently no steps were taken to end the King's friendship for the lady of his choice until His Majesty's recent pointed remarks as to unemployment and want in certain portions of his kingdom; and his deliberate attack on the negative attitude of those in whose hands some remedy lies.

The "crisis" has been cleverly engineered; and the lever that has been used, having the support of both Toryism and the church, could not have been more aptly chosen for its effect upon public sentiment.

That "the dominions would not consent" to such a union as His Majesty contemplates has been heard repeatedly. I think this should be revised to read, as regards Canada, "those on Parliament Hill would not consent."

Unfortunate as the circumstances may be, and as much as we should like to see a less married lady take her place as the King's consort, I hope and believe that the mass of the people, the King's loyal subjects, would rather have Edward VIII as their ruler (despite unconstitutional desires on his part for a mate), than to see him abdicate at this time of general chaos and anxiety in world affairs.

Whatever His Majesty's decision may be, and we can only pray that he will be guided by the deepest wisdom, may our loyalty to him and to his ideals concerning the betterment of those less fortunate, be steadfast and unswerving. We shall, in any case, have learned that even in this so-called civilized era, money power stops at nothing, not even the removal of a monarch who has the cause of the people at heart.

Roxanna Bond,
Ottawa

Editor's note: Two days after this letter was published, Edward VIII stepped down as king in order to marry Wallis Simpson, a divorced American woman. He was succeeded by George VI.

1937

Local: Federal cabinet approves money for construction of new Supreme Court building and terminal for new Ottawa airport (May)

National: Joseph-Armand Bombardier patents a seven-passenger snow machine costing $7,500. He calls it a snowmobile (June); First regular flight of Trans-Canada Air Lines, forerunner of Air Canada, travels from Montreal to Toronto (September); After meeting Adolf Hitler in Berlin, prime minister Mackenzie King describes the German fuhrer as "a simple sort of peasant" who presents no danger to the world (October)

World: Amelia Earhart lost at sea in bid to fly solo around the world (July); Adolf Hitler reviews parade of 600,000 soldiers in powerful display of might at Nuremberg (September)

Births: CBC broadcaster Barbara Frum; actors Jane Fonda and Dustin Hoffman

Deaths: Prime minister Robert Borden; Canadian writer Ralph Connor; jazz pioneer Jelly Roll Morton; composer George Gershwin; Canadian wheat scientist Charles Saunders; appliance inventor Frederick Maytag

FROM AN ANSWERER OF 'ADS'

JANUARY 23, 1937

"With reference to your advertisement in today's *Citizen*..."

Gentlemen, I am a mumbler. A business-letter mumbler. In my sleep, smudged papers, wrong dates, mis-spelled words pass in quick procession before my eyes. Limping, incomplete sentences leer at me. Life is miserable.

So I write today to soothe my ruffled feelings, reinstate my hurt pride and clear the venom from my shocked system. I hope I am cured. I hope I will lose that haunted look that simply screams, "I am an ad-answerer"!

Consider the facts, you gentlemen who seek stenographers, filing clerks, etc. You make us go through hours of torture, composing letters with painstaking care. We state our qualifications, giving *verbatim et literatim*, our school history. We mention who we are, what we are, and what we could be, if given half a chance. (Some of us must get a chance. But who? Can't we all play?)

And what does it all give us? You don't believe us. Oh, you are indeed our *bête noir*.

Maybe I overrate myself; perhaps I wrong you. Possibly my vision has become so blurred by embittered thoughts that I cannot see that the blame lies with me. Let us say that I once had faith in myself. Now, what self-esteem I had has perished from exposure and starvation.

I come to this conclusion: Having no experience, no office-training, having nothing except a diploma or two, I find that a keen desire to work and a stout heart are not sufficient requisites to entitle me to a chance in the big game.

Or the alternative, that I am nothing more than a moron. Either my usual application-letter bears this out so cruelly that my fate is decided upon without the favour of an interview, or else I get the interviews, but my face confesses such blatant proof of my childishly naive stupidity that I am, after a few curt, well-chosen words, dismissed. Quickly, unconditionally and irrevocably.

Occasionally, of course, interviews have taken concrete form. I concede that you can't climb from the top. But the microscopic munificence of those up high is sometimes staggering!

B. Chevrier, Ottawa

A MORBID EXHIBITION

MARCH 1, 1937

I read in your paper about the hanging in Hull, and about the executioner cutting the rope into lengths of two inches for souvenirs.

Well, being an old sailor, I have seen lots of rough stuff pulled off and heard lots of it, but cutting this rope into lengths of two inches for souvenirs after a man paying the penalty beats all. May I say it is a disgrace for a civilised country like the Dominion of Canada.

John Graham, Ottawa

A LESSON FOR CANADA

MARCH 6, 1937

The terrific floods that recently roared down the populous Ohio and Mississippi valleys to the Gulf, taking a toll of some 500 lives and half-a-billion dollars in property loss, are a profound object lesson on the nemesis which is following the sweeping away of the forest cover on this continent.

This whole question of floods, droughts, erosion and worn-out soils, as related to the forest cover, is a problem of the farm, the city, the county, the province or state and the entire nation concerned; for after all, the watershed problem is more of a public responsibility than any other aspect of conservation.

One vitally important factor in the case of such a severe flood as this last one is the heavy burden of eroded top-soil being carried along in the turbid, rushing torrent. In this connection be it remembered that if the speed of a stream be increased three times it can carry eight times as much fine soil in suspension and can roll along on it stream-bed at least 750 times as great a weight of sediment!

It is true that the vast basin of the Ohio system is still well-dotted with farm woodlots, but the general and destructive habits of woodlot grazing and ruthless cutting have so robbed these woodlands of humus, litter, underbrush — in a word, their water-holding power — that they retain today very little more than if they were bare land.

In all this there is surely a great lesson for us in Canada. True, our soil erosion and flood problems are on a small scale, but nonetheless of vital import. A 1934 Ontario assessment reveals that 27 townships have now less than one per cent of forest cover; 113 more have a mere one to five per cent; while 113 more have only five to 10 per cent. By contrast, even densely-populated Germany finds it advisable to retain nearly one-third of its land surface in forest.

Let us not forget that an adequate forest cover has many uses, values and far-reaching benefits. It may indeed be regarded as an indispensable foundation of local and national safety and prosperity.

J.R. Dickson, Ottawa

HIGH FLYING SOCIETY NEWS
APRIL 21, 1937

The many friends of Captain Joe and Lady Martin will be pleased to learn that they have returned from the South where they have spent the winter. They arrived by air line this morning, the 19th, and reached their old home at 1000 Somerset Street at 6 a.m.

They served notice on the landlord that they and their friends wish to occupy the beautiful mansion with twenty-four apartments, all with strictly private entrances and large landing floors.

Mrs. Joe was much interested in the mirror set in the wall on one of the verandahs, and after assuring herself that the beautiful Martins which she saw in the mirror, every time she looked, were neither in the apartment nor yet round the corner, after looking again and again, she seemed to get an idea and settled down and proceeded to adjust her "make-up." After powdering her nose, she announced to Joe that she was ready and they started off to round up the rest of the colony.

They will be at home to their many friends about the 25th, and will remain till about the first week of August. Owing to wind and weather conditions they arrived four days late this year.

Landlord S. Breadner, Ottawa

Editor's note: For those who missed the joke, landlord Breadner's "Martins" were birds of the same name.

ON ADVERTISING GOOD DEEDS
MAY 31, 1937

At 5.30 this a.m., I was sitting in a large railroad station. The place was practically deserted. Presently down the aisle appeared a peculiar looking aged woman. Clad in long voluminous skirts and carrying two long roped satchels, and peering through thick-lensed glasses, she stumped labouriously along on unbending legs that seemed to be of wood or metal. Every few steps she stopped and looked all around.

Then she came straight over and sat beside me. Producing a cigaret she lit up and puffed vigorously. I detest tobacco and moved away from her; she immediately arose and stumped away.

Looking around I saw she had left a small purse and opening it, I counted the contents, $4.60. I don't know how many begging tramps would have felt inclined to restore this to the owner, but I certainly felt like that. Then I thought of the cursed cigaret and I paused. But a remembrance of my aged grandmother at her lace-pillow, puffing away at a clay pipe, decided for me.

I found the old lady at the ticket counter, peering into the wickets as if looking for clerks who had not yet appeared. At the fourth wicket she stopped and pulling up her skirts she fumbled at a long stocking. I paused, half expecting to see her produce some money, but two officious men appeared so I delayed no longer.

"Did you lose your purse?" I inquired. "By God, yes," she replied, and grabbed it roughly from my hand without a word of thanks.

'Tis said we should never tell about our good deeds, but in these greedy, selfish hard times, I don't think a little advertising is a sin. Moreover, it seems to be fashionable. When begging meals from women, the most of them who entertain me prefer to feed me on the doorsteps or verandah where everyone can see the good work. I have turned down many a meal because of this, for I hate to be stared at; but sheer hunger, or the need to satisfy a good-natured woman, has often caused me to make an exhibition of myself.

In a small town recently, I approached a good-looking house but a bad-looking woman who turned me down very roughly and said, "Don't go to that other house for that woman never gave away a meal in her life."

On the step of the other house was a sign with the name Murphy. Most Murphys I've known were impressionable, and this one was no exception. I told her my need and what her neighbour had said. A grim look came over her face, and taking me in the front room and clearing the bay window, she placed therein a table and chair in full view of her neighbours and on the table she spread a meal that would have filled the hungriest tramp alive.

Most people like their good deeds to be known in some way. Millionaires and business men who donate to charities, etc., are generally made much of in the newspapers; that seems to be good business. But apart from this vanity and greed of ours there is surely that mysterious law and the great unknown power that ever always rewards good deeds, however small.

And whilst there are some good-natured people who take to heart that passage that says, "Let not one hand know the good the other does," I find that the majority like to exhibit their goodness, and probably there's no harm in that.

F. Jennings, Toronto

TRAMP CORRESPONDENT ON MONEY
SEPTEMBER 25, 1937

Yesterday I passed through a district that I had not seen for some time, and I failed to recognize it. Not so many years ago it was a district of shady woodlands and cool, quiet lanes. Gone is all this; gone even are the ice-cold little creeks that had quenched many a thirst. Now it is a brazen, blaring place of paved streets and aristocratic buildings.

It was around noon and although I was hungry enough to beg a dinner from Satan himself, I had a most uncanny conviction that I was on hostile ground and amongst Philistines, and 'twas so. Never have I encountered harsher Jezebels, or more unkind bullying men. Although I begged at 28 doors, I did not receive a crust of bread, and I was glad to leave the district behind me. A wayside notice told me the place was known as Kingsway. God help the poor king if he ever passes that way as a tramp begging for a meal!

Four hours later I was in downtown Toronto and once more rested my weary body in the bums' sitting ground, the rear of St. James' church. Here I was accosted by an eccentric old character called Farmer Jack, who told me he had met a man who said that either he or someone in his office had some money for me.

Farmer Jack is truthful and I hope this stranger is, too. For all I know he may be my forty-second cousin of . . . who I understand is a millionaire who could easily hand a few dimes to a man in my circumstances.

I have no use for money itself but only for the good things it buys, juicy steaks, pork chops, ham and eggs, etc, which, with four teeth and a temperamental digestion, I generally manage to digest to the good of myself and all others concerned.

To me, it seems there can be no easier take than giving or paying away money, unless it is talking about it.

F. Jennings, Toronto

ON THE LETTERS OF A TRAMP
SEPTEMBER 29, 1937

For some time past there have been appearing, every now and then, letters to your newspaper signed by F. Jennings. Are not "letters to the editor" selected with the aim of being of general interest to the public?

Now will anyone kindly inform me just why anyone would be interested in the wanderings of a tramp and a self-confessed loafer, who seems to consider it not only his privilege but his right to expect a good meal wherever he happens to call, when he is hungry, and if he can find a housewife, foolish enough, to encourage him, to continue being a loafer, by giving him a meal?

Mr. Editor, this type of citizen has no place in Canada and should have been deported long ago. Here's hoping the next dog that chases him will have good sharp teeth.

Mrs. E. Hayes, Ottawa

EVEN THE SPARROWS ARE FED
OCTOBER 2, 1937

I have read the letter signed by Mrs. E. Hayes relative to correspondence signed by F. Jennings. Mrs. Hayes must either be a very critical person or else she has never experienced hunger or privation in any form.

The letters by Mr. Jennings depict very accurately indeed the conditions confronting those who, through circumstances, are unable to live a proper life. It seems unfair to say that Mr. Jennings is a self-confessed loafer as he no doubt would, if given the opportunity, accept a job of any sort rather than continue to go about begging alms from door to door.

I only wish it was in my power to offer this unfortunate man a job and he would, I know, prove that he is desirous of earning a decent living as are a great many other men in his category.

It is a pity that Mrs. Hayes should go so far as to say that it is foolish to give a tramp a meal, as I know that anyone who does this will certainly be amply rewarded at the proper time. There is surely one thing definite, and that is, if anyone in need should read Mrs. Hayes'

letters, she will not be troubled by being asked for assistance.

There are many worse ways of obtaining help than by begging as is noted from daily reports of robberies, etc., and it is to the credit of Mr. Jennings and a lot more of his kind that they have followed the straight and narrow path rather than end up in criminal institutions where they would at least be assured of three meals a day.

Last spring I noticed a note in the paper encouraging all citizens of Ottawa to leave bread and scraps within the reach of birds who were finding it difficult to exist on what vegetation then was present. I am wondering now if Mrs. Hayes could have found it in her heart to heed that.

John K. Steele, Ottawa

A TRAMP'S PROGRESS
OCTOBER 9, 1937

In spite of Premier Hitler's — I mean Hepburn's — boastings, Ontario is still full of tramps. Probably Wilson [another letter writer] will deport them all, and in my opinion all who wish it should be deported. But they should not be sent away empty-handed: when I landed here I had a good outfit of clothes and over £10 in my pocket; that at least should be restored to me.

Another recent correspondent quotes the text about getting bread by the sweat of our labour. Few thoughtful people with good feeling would care to quote that, for if it were lived rigidly too many of our best friends and probably half the country would starve.

I used to do muscle racking labour that strained my body and tore my stomach, and for a long time I suffered torture from a rupture. During the many years since I quit doing hard work, that has gradually grown together, and now bothers me little. I have worked night shifts on straining jobs; and in the small morning hours when the body is at its lowest, I have felt as if the shadows of death were upon me.

I have shoveled coal until the dust and sweat and the great scoops which bosses forced their men to use, have caused me to stagger with exhaustion. I have pitched long hay on hot days until the sweat has poured from my chest and back and dripped from the seat of my overalls. But I'll do no more of it; anything that brings me my living now must be of a kind that strains neither body nor mind. Failing to get that I'll do no work at all.

And for this I am called an undesirable. But that bothers me little — I have long concluded the only desirables are slaves and rogues.

Another correspondent, a kindly spoken one, speaks of those who have fallen. My fall was not great; experience shows that morally and spiritually I am as good as 99 out of every hundred people I meet. Neither was my material fall great. I was born in the direst poverty and in my most prosperous days I got a shelter and a bite and a few shillings for other of life's barest necessities.

Nay, my greatest trouble was not a fall, but that I did not rise. How I have envied those who were fortunate enough to enter the brain training institutions of the land! What would I have given to have studied with such masters as

CANADIAN PRESS

While tramps went from door to door looking for a meal or just a crust of bread, others settled for a meal at the Montreal soup kitchen.

[astronomer Arthur] Eddington, [economist John Maynard] Keynes and [physicist Albert] Einstein! And as I often sit with their books before me, contorting my brain to see through problems that seem second nature to them, I realize that if they know little about the universe around us, that little seems a mighty lot to me.

Another woman correspondent speaks of the lucky woman who didn't marry me. Well, I am sure about that, but apparently there are women I'm lucky I never married or even met. But when I think of that dark-eyed trusty girl I passed by and wonder had I taken her seriously, there might have been one tramp less in Ontario and these wailing epistles in the *Citizen* would never have appeared. But back in that crowded Old Land might have been a little

home and about 12 or 16 more Jennings, all in good circumstances and a credit and comfort to us and the community.

F. Jennings, Toronto

REQUEST TO SANTA

DECEMBER 9, 1937

A day or two ago I witnessed an incident that would make anyone's heart feel faint. In one of the large stores of this city "Santa Claus" was seated in a golden chair, meeting a steady stream of little folk, and listening to their requests that he deliver to them on Christmas eve, the toys of their choice. To all he promised to bring what they had requested.

Just in front of me and my little laddie was a little girl about seven, very shabbily dressed, with thin shoes, much-darned stockings, shabby coat and old and very dirty once-white woolen hat. Her request was not for dolls, skates, etc. She asked the good St. Nicholas for just one gift — a pair of overshoes — and that in a pleading manner, and she did not forget the "please." He promised to do that, and she left with a big smile on her face.

Reconstructing the story, one can see where the little girlie, slipping down to where she knew she would see the King of Toyland, unbeknown to her mother, to ask for what she needed most — something to keep her tiny feet warm.

Later, one will see, on December 25th in early morning, the despair when this same little lass finds out that Santa Claus is not all that he is cracked up to be.

It took a little while for the whole story to sink in to me, but I have thought that this is an excellent place for a social worker to stand by, and the little folks of that class may be questioned, their address ascertained, and if it be found out that their case warrants, the new overshoes, or mitts, or coat, or shoes, or underwear, and maybe one or two little toys could be delivered on Christmas, thereby doing a real service and maybe restoring a little confidence in the lives of these poor little kiddies who, through no fault of their own, are forced to stand by while others are more fortunate, and to be satisfied with toys that are separated from them by heavy plate-glass window.

Jas. R. Fraser,
Ottawa

1938

Local: Automobile parkway proposed for Gatineau Hills (February)
National: No one hurt when Honeymoon Bridge at Niagara Falls collapses after being crushed by ice (January); Toronto Daily Star publishes the first Superman comic, created by Canadian Joe Shuster (June); Canadian doctor Norman Bethune joins Chinese communist army and forms world's first mobile medical unit (August)
World: Europe on brink of war as triumphant Adolf Hitler takes control in Austria and Czechoslovakia; Orson Welles panics the American public with radio broadcast of War of the Worlds (October)
Births: Ottawa-born comedian Rich Little; Quebec premier Lucien Bouchard; Russian dancer Rudolf Nureyev; basketball legend Jerry West
Deaths: American novelist Thomas Wolfe; U.S. criminal lawyer Clarence Darrow; jazz pioneer King Oliver; governor general Victor Cavendish (Duke of Devonshire)

GRIM SIDE OF RELIEF IN OTTAWA

MAY 7, 1938

Case 23. A lady came in great distress on Saturday and told a sad tale: She is separated from her husband and as she has no work, and is not receiving relief, she depends upon friends to give herself and her six-year-old boy meals at odd times to keep them alive.

However, her last misfortune seems to be the last straw, it being her eviction from her room at the (name withheld) apartments. It so happens the female who presides over the apartment building literally kicked this poor woman into the street, and kept not only her furniture, but all her clothing and the little boy's also.

She owns just what clothes they both wear, which seems most unjust. The woman stated the landlady could have the furniture for the two months' rent owing, but she did want to get her personal effects.

So, having an idea that all policemen were big-hearted, kindly souls, we made our way to ye olde police station No. 1. We finally located a uniformed official sitting behind a desk, and outlined our case. He simply smirked at us, and did not seem disposed either to be helpful or courteous.

We had to pry information from him, in bits, and we learned the truth of the statement that "possession is nine points of the law." The woman had no recourse whereby she could get back her personal effects.

Our patience was exhausted. The police desk official manifested impatience, too, and as the cells are somewhere down there, I believe, I thought the best place was outside, and I got myself there. Maybe this man was somebody of importance, but if he had been, I think he would have been more courteous, and then again he might not. I note the "pavement-pounders" are gentlemen beside this person, so enough said.

This gets us right back to the little woman and her eviction, and the fact that the landlady still has her clothing. What a funny thing law is! Is it just?

Tenants are warned to read their leases before signing. In small letters on some of these leases are words that say that the landlord may possess personal effects as well as furniture, so beware.

Jean Graham Low, Ottawa

Editor's note: Ms. Low, a volunteer with a relief agency that helped young women, wrote regularly to the Citizen to draw attention to some of the hard-luck cases encountered in her work. Another of her letters, with a happy outcome, appears later in the 1938 section.

MORE ABOUT POOR JEWS IN WARSAW

MAY 30, 1938

I wish I had the means and the necessary time to go with Mr. Austin Cross [a well-known *Citizen* reporter] on his next visit to Poland, and, if he prefers, pay particular attention to Warsaw itself. But the visit would of necessity have to be longer than Mr. Cross's usual one hour as I am sure that he would condemn himself for jumping to conclusions, altogether without foundation and misleading to the average Canadian reader.

As a native of Poland, I had an ample opportunity to observe conditions of the poor Jews. Picture, Mr. Average Reader, a small room, the walls black with moisture that is penetrating them and dripping gently onto the floor. There are three beds, situated in three corners of the room, and in the fourth corner there is a kitchen stove.

Two families, in some cases three, occupy this dingy hovel. In this age of enlightenment and modern conveniences, this Jewish home, and there are hundreds of similar homes in Warsaw, has no toilet or hot water, and a naphtha lamp is the only means of illumination. There is hardly any furniture; the cupboard which used to adorn most of Jewish homes has disappeared, because in Poland you pay tax for such a luxury.

What a different picture to the beautiful apartments so vividly described by Mr. Cross, and the sumptuous food adorning the table of first-class hotels where a great deal of his information has been gathered. Mine is a true picture of one who has lived and seen these conditions for 15 years, and not one hour in a taxicab.

Is there any wonder why the Jew is considered "dirty" when he lives in such inhuman conditions? The Jew in Poland is being persecuted with the avowed knowledge of the Polish government, although the Jew fought in the first ranks for Polish independence and gave his life for Polish freedom — which turned out to be Polish ruthlessness to its loyal minority.

Mr. Cross implies that the Polish government had tried patiently to uplift the Jewish residents of Warsaw, but persecution and withdrawal of all means of earning a livelihood is a very poor medicine indeed.

C. Levine,
Ottawa

AGAINST PARKING METERS

JUNE 8, 1938

It is surprising to many people that our Ottawa newspapers have taken so passive a stand with regard to the installation of parking meters on our city streets. It would appear these iron standards are to be accepted with no more protest than is occasioned when the tax rate is increased one-tenth of a mill.

If our citizens could visualize our main thoroughfares lined with hundreds of aluminum-painted monstrosities, many of which soon enough will lean and sag, become chipped and weary looking, then we would hear strong protests from our merchants and others.

Already our main streets, such as Sparks, Rideau, Bank, Queen, Elgin and Albert, are unsightly by reason of many telegraph poles, wire-hung street lights, untold wires, "no parking" signs and billboards, and now we are expected to tolerate the planting in concrete of hundreds of unwelcome and unlovely iron standards.

The $100,000 annual revenue looks good to the city fathers, yet we might contrast this income with the annoyance caused thousands of already over-taxed motorists, who now bear too heavy a burden of provincial taxation. Picture the scene: a busy man feeling for a nickel, then requesting a constable to please change a quarter.

Remember, once we have the meters they are with us for a long time.

Stanley Petrie, Ottawa

Editor's note: City councillors managed to resist the lure of parking meter revenue for another 20 years. And even when about 1,000 meters were finally installed in April 1958, there were howls of protest.

A LESSON IN ECONOMICS

JULY 4, 1938

I note on the first page of a recent issue that Mrs. Annie Middleton of Windsor, Ont., a 40-year-old mother of five children, offers to sell to any blind person the cornea of one of her eyes for $6,000, claiming that her husband has lost his business, and she "can't see any point in raising a family of undernourished children."

Just fancy the sacrifice this mother is prepared to offer in order to properly feed those depending on her. What a difference between this woman and those "leaders" in Canada who for years have promised to put the unemployed back to work and to find prosperity, which should not be a difficulty in a country of plenty.

What a pity that our people should suffer and their children be undernourished just for want of proper use of our unused natural resources, which we have in abundance. But if those in power refuse to listen to the fact that the expense of keeping the unemployed in idleness drags down and retards the wheels of industry, then we must continue to suffer from this man-made condition of unemployment, which it is possible to rectify, provided, we get together and consider the cause of our present lack of purchasing power and act according to reason. We will then be able to give the world a lesson in economics.

Our present-day condition proves that we have politicians, but are lacking for the want of statesmen.

R.S. Reid, Ottawa

ANOTHER SIDE OF RELIEF

JULY 20, 1938

May I report that through the *Citizen* and the fine co-operation of interested readers, Case 38 is now the happy possessor of a good job. She started work already this morning. Quick results indeed, because her case appeared in your pages only two days ago. Also, she received enough clothing to do her for a considerable time.

Many calls came in for this case, and offers of work, mostly, it is true, with very low wages, or just the offer of food and clothing, in exchange for her services; but, the offers were kindly proffered and accepted in the same spirit. These people will understand why the girl did not call on them as she has now a job with good pay.

Another woman has received work also, and a few more will be placed just as soon as I can get to them to advise them where to apply.

It is most gratifying to be able to bring assistance to people, but it is doubly gratifying to get them placed in employment so that they will be able to help themselves.

Jean Graham Low, Ottawa

DOES NATIONALITY COUNT?

JULY 21, 1938

Being a married man with five children who ran an appeal for work in your paper last fall, I would like to state that after receiving employment only 10 days ago to help construct the War Memorial at the Plaza through my own efforts, I was discharged along with three others. If our work had been unsatisfactory we were never told so, and there was no reason for a lay-off mentioned.

Going back the next morning to see if I could get put back to work, I find while standing there that four French workers have been put in our place. Why? It seems a little out of place that English-speaking labour should be let go and nearly all French labour employed.

Around the construction job, which is the undertaking of a Montreal company, there is a high wooden fence, and one has no chance to get in to see if there is any work to be got. It seems to me that if there is a vacancy, the French workers receive the preference.

Born and raised in Canada, I cannot see why French should be given the preference on a government job in Ottawa. Something should be done about it!

H. Pennett, Westboro

Editor's note: Eight days later and still looking for work, Mr. Pennett wrote his fourth letter.

DOWN BUT NOT OUT

JULY 29, 1938

There are times in every man's life, I surmise, that he can come forward and tell of one experience that stands out above all others. I can truthfully say mine has just occurred.

After three letters in the *Citizen* begging and pleading for employment to fulfill one's province towards the loving, cherishing and caring for one's family, I have to admit I have met with defeat. I never as much as received a letter of condolence, or a letter of encouragement, that would have let me know if there was still a chance things might take a turn for the better.

I will admit there are a lot like myself out of work and on relief, and some of these men are quite satisfied to go on living under such conditions; but I am not, and will not rest until I have steady employment. If the general public who have read my letters are under the impression this is a publicity stunt, they are quite mistaken. I have taken this means after everything else has failed to let them know that a man's entire family and livelihood are to be considered.

I am not on relief and I can say it is a poor proposition to offer a man, yet at the same time accepting relief is the only means to keep from starving to death. It puts a man in poor standing when it comes to applying for work; you can imagine being asked where you were last employed and having to answer that for the past three or four years you've been on relief. You might just as well have answered that you had just finished a jail term.

I do not relish the idea of going on day after day not knowing how it all is going to end. If anyone who has been reading my letters should later on see my name and character all over the paper for something that I had done to get results, he would say, Well I guess he was no good anyway; or he would say, There's a fellow who must have been sincere in what he has been writing — it is just too bad someone didn't give him employment and this wouldn't have happened.

I don't want all I've ever accomplished in the past few years torn apart in a few minutes through some misunderstanding. I hope someone will consider my circumstances and give me a chance to prove myself a trustworthy, efficient and reliable person and capable of holding a good position.

H. Pennett, Westboro

Editor's note: Mr. Pennett wrote two more letters to the Citizen, the last in mid-August when, still without work, he listed his experience as a chauffeur, gardener, truck driver, painter, rough carpenter, cement mix operator, roofer, driller and dynamiter and again pleaded for a job. Because he was not heard from again in the Citizen's letters columns, his fate remains a mystery.

TO CRITICS OF MR. CHAMBERLAIN
SEPTEMBER 27, 1938

I have read the letter of Mr. John Archer in your recent issue putting questions to Mr. Neville Chamberlain. If Mr. Lloyd George or Winston Churchill were at the helm, is it possible that the situation might now be quite different? Better or worse? Some of the avenues by which Mr. Chamberlain is seeking peace might remain unexplored.

But Mr. Chamberlain happens to be the statesman whom the British people have placed in command. It

CHRONICLE OF THE 20TH CENTURY

Swastikas and Sudetens greeted the Nazis as they marched unhindered into a Czech city, a situation that inspired some letters about British prime minister Neville Chamberlain.

would be very easy for him to lead the people into war. Anybody could do that. With a better conception of what war means than is displayed by his critics, Mr. Chamberlain is seeking to avoid it if possible; and it is not right to say that he is forcing "ignominy on all the British peoples," or that he "will not fight at any price."

In any case, it is too soon to pass condemnation on Mr. Chamberlain's course; nor will it be fair to blame him if he meets with failure, as unfortunately seems not at all improbable. It may turn out that the critics will get all the fighting they want.

E. Byers, Ottawa

Editor's note: A few days before this letter was published, British prime minister Neville Chamberlain, without Czech input, agreed not to stand in the way of Adolf Hitler's plan to annex part of Czechoslovakia. His policy of appeasement was designed to avert a war, but within a few months Hitler had trampled on the deal by overrunning the rest of Czechoslovakia. By September 1939, after the Nazis rolled into Poland, Britain and Germany were at war.

HITLER'S MARCH OF CONQUEST
SEPTEMBER 27, 1938

The heart feels like condemning Chamberlain. The blood boils for the wrong done to the helpless Czechs. France and England are 100 per cent guilty of the present situation. They have blundered in the past but, in my opinion, this is their largest blunder.

For five years, the Fuehrer has been preparing. They permitted him to walk into the Rhineland and then Austria; now Czechoslovakia and next Hungary and Rumania. Not only did they permit him, but indirectly they helped him.

At present he calls it *Der Drang nach Osten.* Who knows what will be tomorrow, when he will control the Mediterranean, the Black Sea, the Adriatic and the Baltic? Who will rule the waves then?

Max Feller,
Ottawa

AN ADMIRER OF HITLER
OCTOBER 19, 1938

The world seems to be disappointed, judging by the press, that Chancellor Hitler did not ignite the powder keg. This goes to show how stupid the world is after all.

It is really sickening to see how few are the people who have taken the lesson of 1914-18 to heart. It makes us blush with shame to see the great majority of our statesmen the world over are as stupid as ever they were. We can thank our lucky stars that Premier Neville Chamberlain of Britain is on hand; he is practically alone among the so-called democracies, and he is a realist and a statesman combined.

If Chamberlain is swept away by his political adversaries, sure as the rising sun the mad orgy of 1914-18 will be repeated in all its glory. Millions of lives will be hurled into eternity by gas and smoke and murder.

The victors, immediately after the 1918 armistice, got together and planted the seeds of another Great War. The way they stripped the vanquished, confiscated its territories and signed treaties and made pledges to keep it down in the mud for ever, all these were bound to lead to discontent.

I am not an Austrian by nationality or by descent — I am a Briton 100 per cent. But I do admire this Austrian, Adolf Hitler. He is like a beautiful spot in the desert, all eyes admire it, except the biased and the distorted mind. He is a man who stays by his guns for the sake of, and in the cause of, peace.

I am a democratic man like my forefathers were, but I should ask my Creator to annihilate me if I were guilty of calling Hitler a liar and a fool when the man has the purest and noblest intents in his mind and heart. Nothing will destroy the British Empire as surely and as quickly as stubbornness of mind and policy. Follow Chamberlain, I say.

J.C. Jones,
Montreal

THE WINDSOR UNIFORM
DECEMBER 7, 1938

Once again the *Citizen* helps — in a boxed, front-page item — to perpetuate the hoary fallacy that the Windsor uniform has some connection with Canadian official life. How this extraordinary idea ever got its start, probably no one can now say, but surely it might be decently buried before our royal visitors arrive.

Here, in slightly condensed form, are the official particulars:

WINDSOR UNIFORM

Worn only at Windsor Castle and worn by the Royal Family and certain officers of the household, etc. It consists of:

Evening dress coat of blue cloth, with collars and cuffs of scarlet cloth;

Buttons, gilt, mounted, garter star within garter, surmounted by Imperial Crown;

Waistcoat, white, with gilt buttons;

Trousers, plain black evening dress material;

Breeches, plain black evening dress material, or stockinet;

Hose, black silk;

Shoes, plain court, with bows, no buckles;

White bow necktie and white gloves.

These particulars are taken from the official publication, *Dress Worn at Court,* published with the authority of the Lord Chamberlain. The publication may, I believe, be consulted in the Library of Parliament; perhaps our local scribes might note accordingly.

Two other points might be mentioned. I have been told that the Windsor uniform is now seldom worn. And, from the description above, it is difficult to see how such a sum as "$1,000 to $1,500" could be charged by even the most rapacious court outfitter. Perhaps, this is the price per dozen.

G.R.L. Potter, Ottawa

Editor's note: It seems that only the six cabinet ministers who already owned Windsor uniforms — including prime minister Mackenzie King and transportation minister C.D. Howe — wore them to a state banquet honouring the 1939 visit of George VI and Queen Elizabeth. The rest of the cabinet had to make do with the usual formal wear.

1939

Local: Russian composer-pianist Sergei Rachmaninoff performs in Ottawa (January); King George VI and Queen Elizabeth arrive for state visit, and unveil the National War Memorial in Confederation Square (May)

National: National Film Board is created and sets up in Ottawa, where it remains until the late 1950s (May); Ten days after the Nazis roll into Poland, Canada joins Britain and France in declaring war on Germany (September)

World: Francisco Franco's Facist troops seize control of Madrid, ending the Spanish Civil War (March)

Births: Canadian writer Margaret Atwood; prime ministers Brian Mulroney and Joe Clark; feminist Germaine Greer; Canadian neo-nazi Ernst Zündel; race car driver Jackie Stewart; governor general Adrienne Clarkson

Deaths: Sigmund Freud; Irish poet W.B. Yeats; Canadian financier Joseph Flavelle; U.S. writer Zane Grey; French novelist Ford Madox Ford

MODERN MIRACLE MAKERS

FEBRUARY 15, 1939

The miracles of the New Testament will fade into insignificance beside those to be shortly performed in Ottawa when Controllers Putman and Ford instruct the parents on relief how to equip a child for public school on 70 cents per month.

And when this is reduced to 40 cents per month, will these intrepid men perform even more astounding miracles? The only alternative appears to be the establishment of nudist colonies, but then there are the exigencies of our climate and the objections of our morality squad to consider.

Or could the example of our first parents be followed? As we lack fig leaves, we might employ maple leaves, and such nice colourful dress could be obtained.

Sarcasm aside, you can cut down father's pants for junior but not the smartest mother can make over a pair of boots.

Emmie J. Barnes, Ottawa

BICYCLE MENACE IN OTTAWA

FEBRUARY 20, 1939

I would like to call your attention to the ever-increasing hazard of delivery boys riding their bicycles over slippery and snow-covered streets with huge parcels on the handle-bars. On one occasion I noticed one carrying a bag of potatoes.

This practice will continue until a fatality occurs. In other cities it frequently happens. Montreal prohibits these dangerous machines from the streets during the months of December, January and February.

Only a short time ago, Mayor Lewis issued precautions to motorists and the public generally to avoid accidents and exercise more care. This was, I understood, the inauguration of a safety campaign in Ottawa. The first item on the program in my opinion would be to bar these bicycles in winter.

R. B. Anderson, Ottawa

IN DEFENCE OF DELIVERY BOYS

FEBRUARY 23, 1939

The delivery boys of our city are a very hard-working class, and it is both unfortunate and true there are a great number of storekeepers who insist on having these boys carry bags of potatoes on the handlebars of their bicycles; that is, an 80-pound bag or more.

But, the unfortunate boy has no other alternative than to accept this form of slave work and to prove his ability to be able to take it under the circumstances. I have seen many a pitiful-looking delivery boy who is unable to wheel his bicycle along through many places, but has shown wonderful courage in accepting many insults from motorists, because he happens to be noticed pushing a bicycle on the roadway with his heavy load.

In defence of these boys, I ask fair play and kind consideration, because they are doing a wonderful service to our community, whether it be bringing the newspaper to our door, or being called upon to drive 12 blocks to deliver an 8-cent can of tomato juice. I pray you remember this:

If you don't like a bicycle, please like the lad.
He is doing his best for his Mother and Dad
He'll deliver the goods, whether cold or mild
And after all, he's somebody's child.

H. A. Sheehan, Ottawa

BIBLICAL PICTURES

MARCH 15, 1939

Doubtless this letter will seem unusual in the daily paper, but I have often been astonished at the incongruity of painters in portraying the likeness of Jesus.

Years ago when a young girl, I would look at a picture of an old man of 60 or more, with grizzled features and white hair, and wonder: for the Scriptures distinctly tell us He was only 33 years of age when He had finished His life work, which He was sent of God to do, namely, the redemption of the world.

The picture which so greatly impresses me now is on my Scripture calendar for 1939. It is of Jesus in Pilate's judgment hall in a long white robe, the like of which I am sure He never wore, with much cloth swirling about His feet like a modern prima donna; but the hands impress me most, delicately white with tapering fingers, and His hair in twisty curls much like a modern mother curls her child's.

One wonders if the authors of these pictures have ever studied the life of Jesus, a carpenter whose hands would not be so white or delicate. I deem the picture an insult to our Blessed Lord, Who in every way lived and suffered as a strong man.

I have met several men in my life-time who remind me of Jesus, strong, yet gentle. Their very presence gives me pleasure: men who enjoy a good joke, but pure of heart, and merry as a child, and with hands that remind us of the hands of Jesus.

I am sure if painters studied this subject more as they do others, they would get a proper mental view of the Man before making a picture.

L. E. Merifield, Ottawa

DR. PUTMAN AND THE BEES

JUNE 19, 1939

I note by today's paper that Dr. Putman thinks that Italian bees are "long, graceful, golden-yellow and peaceful." Surely he knows better. Italian bees are known by their small stature, dark complexion, their thieving nature and the daggers they carry in their tails.

Dr. Putman also complains that his bees tried to swarm away from him many times. He should examine his own conduct at the time. Bees will seek out a godly and Christian home. I am sure they resented his Sunday experiments. I, too, have kept bees and I know.

W. L. Wilson, Ottawa

HOW TO ACQUIRE BEES

JUNE 21, 1939

I know why Dr. Putman was so unlucky with his bees. Just look how he got them. By importation. The best way to get bees is to find a swarm and give them a home. Bees always work hard for a kind master.

I won't sell bees but anyone is welcome to come visit my yard at night and take what he wants. He had better leave a generous price on the stand where the skeps [beehive] stood, because the bees will come back the next day to see what reparation has been made for the crime of the night before. If the thief has not been fair with me, they will all be likely to come back to me of their own accord. At any rate, they will do him no good.

My boy is going to college and he was reading in Latin last year about how Vergillius Maro Publius kept bees; I copied this from his notebook (he is not at home now).

"But if a bee-master has lost his whole stock at once and has no source from which he may derive a new generation, it is time to tell by what method the corrupted gore of slaughtered oxen has often before now produced a stock of bees.

First, a confined space is chosen and further hemmed in with walls and tile roof. Toward the four winds build four windows. Now search out a two-year old bullock. Stop up his nostrils and mouth, then slay him with blows crushing in his whole body but not breaking his skin. Leave the body in the closed room with broken branches of thyme and fresh cassia flowers. As the corpse ferments many wondrous forms of life swarm till like a summer flower the bees burst forth."

Do you remember how in the Bible Samson killed a lion and out of its skeleton Samson later got honey? Without doubt other animals than oxen may be used but people don't use those ways now.

Dennis McCarthy,
Hawkesbury

A DOG'S LIFE ENDS AT THE POUND

JUNE 28, 1939

A little more than a week ago, a young black dog with a small spot of white on its chest strayed here and adopted some neighbours who fed it and let it sleep there.

It seemed to be part spaniel and some larger dog, the head and feet being similar to the spaniel. We have a picture of a Labrador retriever and Irish settler in our *Everybody's Dog* book, and I think eventually it would have looked like one or the other of these dogs.

It was a nice dog, so anxious to please, so very appealing in so many ways. It would have made a fine children's dog or farm dog. It was clean; never ran away. In fact, the young lady of the house took it to town, hoping it would find its way back to its former home, but on her return it was on the doorstep.

Although the people it had adopted (the best way I can describe its being there) felt they could not keep it, they were going to try and get it a home. But it would go and play with another dog, a neighbour's, which was tied up, and that owner thinking of it as just being a "stray," what a pitiful word, phoned the police and it was taken to the pound.

When I knew it was to go, I got my daughter to phone there and plead for them to keep it, if possible, past the allotted time in case the home we all hoped to procure would be forthcoming. She was spoken to very nicely and informed that often dogs were kept there till homes were secured.

She was also told something we did not know; that had we or the people who had fed the dog secured it a home, we could have been fined. Had we not been told this I doubt if it would have ever reached the pound. However, to make a long story short, it was put out before 48 hours which we had been told was the time they were kept.

How ironic that if we had found it a home where it could be still alive and happy, we could have been fined. Yet by obeying the law it was sent to its death. Surely there is something wrong here. I do not wish to criticize, for without the Humane Society there would be so much more suffering among dogs and other animals, yet this particular case does seem to be the opposite of humane.

Alice Goodyear Watts, Ottawa

YOUTH SPEAKS FOR ALL

JULY 10, 1939

This is neither a personal confession nor an autobiography, but an attempt to review existing conditions as seen in the minds of many of our young people.

I am around 21 years of age, that mysterious period arbitrarily set aside when the male of the species is supposed to attain something that has not existed before in his life. The biological urge has functioned for quite a few years, and it has culminated in an overpowering desire to set up housekeeping with the choice of my heart to be a husband and a father, to fulfill the natural requirements of a mature citizen.

There is nothing exceptional about me. I am not clever either mentally or physically, if that phrase may be used.

How I have lived up to the present is one of those mysteries that cannot be solved; probably my parents could be made to divulge something of the secret but for the purpose of this story it is not important; it is sufficient to say that I have become aware that there is more to life than just living.

What to do and how, are the burning questions that present themselves to me. It is useless to tell me that I should have prepared myself for this development. I haven't and there are thousands like me. Besides, would a foreknowledge have availed anything? Willing to do anything, physically fit and mentally sound, not specially trained but anxious, so that it hurts, to play our parts in the world of affairs.

So I make the weary rounds. The highly mechanized industrial plants ask the question: "Have you any experience?" The farmers ask the same question. An odd job here and there. Where is the security? Where may I live and how?

The stupid sophistry, "the world doesn't owe you a living," doesn't help me. I want nothing given. I'll give, and all I've got, mind and body. In return, I expect sufficient to establish a home, the most desirable thing for myself and the country of which I am a citizen. This has been dinned into my ears since I was knee high to a grasshopper, by teachers, preachers, social uplifters, politicians, my next-door neighbours and my natural instincts.

Well, I'm ready to do my part. What is stopping us? The sacrosanct money temple may not be invaded. The god, Mammom, must not be disturbed! He is thinking, or is he? With his idle hands placidly resting and his unseeing eyes looking off into space, Buddha-like. He knows or cares nothing of what is happening to flesh and blood, and his satellites, equally unconscious, calmly allow the seething cauldron of injustice to brew, until the poison concoction will deprive the person and state of life.

Work must be provided. If private enterprise is not equal to the task, then the people's representatives must be held responsible to find a way out of the impasse. A readjustment of the monetary system is overdue and is retarded only by a blind adherence to the belief that money is of paramount importance.

"God made man and gave him dominion." Was the reference to man collectively? If the latter, where is my share of the power and right vested in me?

Swallowed up in paying tribute to Caesar, whose superscription is on the coinage? No! Not even as fair as that, but in paying an endless tribute to some, through whose hands the coins have passed.

To sum up, all I want is contained in the words of a popular song of today: "I love life, I want to live."

How long can this continue? Until patience breaks down or the standard of living is lowered and free men become slaves in fact, as they are in practice, or will some bright genius arise and prove to us that our idol (money) has feet of clay and that it (money) should be the servant?

This is not meant to be a "soak the rich" appeal but a call to the simple application of the principle of "love thy neighbour as thyself," by providing a broader distinction of the means of exchange, so that a larger number may become consumers, therefore purchasers, hence producers — the natural circuit — instead of the treadmill of useless effort, that serves only to keep a minimum of the people in contented security.

John Pratt, Simcoe, Ont.

ONE FOX TERRIER
AUGUST 23, 1939

In a bailiff's sale notice in tonight's paper, I happened to see among the itemized rugs, lamps, etc., the following — "one fox terrier."

Surely such an affair is distressing enough to the main participants without their dog being included. I do not know the people in question and I'm not a sentimentalist in such things, but it seems to me if the dog's owners are as fond of it as most owners are, the seizure of the animal is unnecessary and cruel. A little kindness and imagination should solve the problem.

Kathleen Harris, Ottawa

GETTING HITLER GROGGY
AUGUST 30, 1939

We should now have no fear of war. Mr. Chamberlain has involved Herr Hitler in the receiving of notes and the replying to notes — and if there is one thing at which British diplomats are excellent, it is the writing of notes. After centuries in the art of "compromise," Herr Hitler hasn't the ghost of a chance of standing up to British diplomacy.

Herr Hitler has himself said that the conference table is his weak point — that he is only happy when he is on the rostrum from which he can work on the passions, emotions and prejudices of the people. So, if the British diplomats can get him at the conference table, he is finished.

E.M. Hoben, Ottawa

CONSCRIPTION
SEPTEMBER 12, 1939

Conscription is essential, not only of manpower, but of the entire resources of the country for the duration of the war. The crisis is as great, if not greater, than in 1914; we have that experience to guide us, and there should be no half-measures this time, but let us get together and get this beastly thing over with as quickly as possible.

The voluntary system is wrong from every angle, particularly from the point of view of eugenics. However, Canada is not so much concerned with the physical standards, though they are important, as with the spiritual standards of future generations, and men lacking in patriotism, and the love of freedom and the courage to be willing to die for them will produce a generation lacking in the same qualities.

The leaders, therefore, should see to it that conscription is put into effect as quickly as possible and ensure that the future generations shall consist of people inheriting the true qualities of greatness.

The aftermath of the last Great War leaves no doubt in the minds of most of us that conscription of all our resources is essential, so that no man, or group of men, shall profit by the sacrifices of the men who fall in their interests. Ghouls is the only name to apply to war profiteers who fatten on the dead bodies of their countrymen.

Men do not hesitate to sacrifice their lives for the right, but all should be called on to make sacrifices. One of the conditions of the conscriptions bill should be that when the war is over the men who return shall find their jobs waiting for them with no loss of seniority.

Howell Smith, Toronto

JEWISH EXODUS
OCTOBER 5, 1939

"Jews must leave their homes in perfect condition." That is the order given to Poles of my faith who today are being evicted and dispossessed of property. Throughout Poland, all resources, all means of earning are taken from Jews; winter is here and privation will destroy many.

My father was so killed. He sent me to Canada four years ago, because he feared Hitler and Hitler's fearful hatred of Jews. Once we had many friends who were not Jews: but no longer did they dare to be friends because of the Nazis.

The black S.S. Guards are the worst. They are young and Hitler crazy. The S.A. Storm Troopers are pretty crazy too; but they are older men and know that Jews are like Christians and often good people. Both S.S. and S.A. make Germans hate and break windows and hurt and rob and kill Jews. I know two S.S. who should die for the brutal things they did.

At first, most Germans did not wish to rob and hurt Jews whom they knew. They wanted to live, work, earn and be happy with their own families and would let the Jews do so too. But Germans do not think of more than one thing at a time and they believe what they are told, even if it is lies. So many of them believe the Guards who say bad things about Jews: and even kindly German folk become like the Guards and hate, rob and are very rough to Jews.

Though we are oppressed, we shall endure. Egypt and Babylon enslaved Israel yet today Israel's children are strong, in every land. Yes, even in Germany, we are strong and we shall still flourish there when Hitler is forgotten.

Our genius and our industry are our strength: in every exodus, they are with us and give us our promised land.

Hans Bethein, Montreal

A TRAMP'S CHRISTMAS CAROL
DECEMBER 27, 1939

Yesterday morning I felt irritable and un-Christmaslike: traffic was in my way, great trucks blocked crossings, cars swung viciously around corners on the left, bicycle boys rode on the sidewalk and missed me by inches, Salvation

THE OXFORD COMPANION TO WORLD WAR TWO

A German photograph of Jews forced from their homes in Warsaw.

Army beggars on every corner irritated me, pedestrians were in my way and jostled me all around.

So I took refuge in a library. Whilst there I happened upon a Christmas poem describing my condition, its cause and cure. The cause: I was too self-centered; and the cure was to forget myself and give somebody a Christmas box.

In my pockets were just my rent and the price of a few meager meals; it really seemed that 'twas I who needed a Christmas box. But on my neck was a scarf and that morning a penniless friend with neuralgia had bemoaned to me his need of a scarf. The writer of the poem was a literary genius worth millions, so he must be right. Therefore I hurried away and gave my scarf to my suffering friend with a good Catholic lie that I had another.

But instead of better, I felt worse. I have a long thin neck and the bitter wind gripped it unmercifully. I was growling along to myself with my eyes looking into the gutter when I spied something unusual, and stooping, I picked up a very dirty two dollar bill. A Christmas box from God! Immediately I felt better — traffic was all right, so were the buffetings of the pedestrians. I gave two cents to the Salvation Army and went and bought a 25-cent scarf.

Editors and publishers all seem to prefer beautiful unrealities and ideals. Well, it's just as easy to print that as anything else, but favour us this time, Mr. Editor, and print this little bit of true life.

F. Jennings, Toronto

"The trouble, I think, is that people back home think of this war as a big romantic show of heroes and medals. It is no such thing! It is a hard, dirty, and filthy war with no holds barred."

— July 8, 1944

1940-1949

GEORGE KENNETH BELL

1940

Local: One of the world's first wind tunnels, designed to test airplane strength, opens at Ottawa's National Research Council (August)

National: Mackenzie King's Liberals sweep to large majority government in election (January); Jehovah's Witnesses, along with fascist and communist groups, are outlawed in Canada (July)

World: Germany expands its grip on Europe to include Denmark, France, Belgium and the Netherlands; bombing of Britain begins (January-May); Winston Churchill becomes British prime minister (May); Japan joins the German-Italian Axis, and promptly invades Indochina (September)

Births: Canadian harness racer Hervé Filion; golfer Jack Nicklaus; Brazilian soccer star Pele; Canadian business lobbiest Thomas d'Aquino; auto racer Mario Andretti

Deaths: American writer F. Scott Fitzgerald; Russian bolshevik Leon Trotsky; German painter Paul Klee; British prime minister Neville Chamberlain; U.S. auto tycoon William Chrysler; governor general John Buchan (Lord Tweedsmuir)

EVEN AS THE SPARROWS

JANUARY 3, 1940

With reference to the decrease in the number of birds which were discovered by the Field Naturalists Society recently, may I be permitted to offer some observations?

This decrease was said to be a possible result of the recent inclement weather. I am, at present, residing at the McKellar Townsite [the area around today's Carlingwood Shopping Centre] and noted weeks ago that the birds had disappeared. Other winters they came in dozens about the house daily, looking in the windows and waiting about for their rations of bread-crumbs, etc.

There have been none for many days now. I mentioned the fact to members of the household, stating that I thought it strangely significant. May we not believe that He "Whose eyes is on the sparrow" conveyed to them, in some way, a warning concerning the impending war menace, and that many heeded it and took flight?

Shall we be less intelligent than the birds? Can we not see on every hand, signs of impending danger? Have we not, to a great extent, forgotten God? Of how many of us may it truly be said, "God is not in all his thoughts?" Let us take with us words, and turn to the Lord our God! Let us flee to the Rock of Ages!

M.B. Kirke, Ottawa

ON CHRISTMAS CARDS

JANUARY 9, 1940

I wonder how many people have noticed the type of Christmas cards on display during the season just past in the various stores of the city.

I searched a great many stores for a Christmas card — I mean one significant of the great feast of the Nativity — but alas dogs, cats, etc., were pictured instead, even jingles were used to take the grace out of that hallowed message of ages ago.

I think the Christmas card that omits reference to the great central feast of Christianity hardly conforms to the Christian ideal of gladsome Christmas greetings. Here's hoping Christmas in 1940 will bring a change in this regard.

(Mrs.) F. Brennan,
Hurdman's Bridge, Ontario

MEMORIES OF TRAMPING

JANUARY 10, 1940

Recently your letter column calling me a tramp was read by some friends of mine and indignation flared. How dare an editor call me a tramp! Scandalous, an apology should be called for.

All the years they had known me I was just a quiet, respectable, inoffensive man, etc. Dear, thick-headed old English folks they are, so very respectable. To them a tramp is something between a snake and a murderer.

It was no use me telling them that a tramp is a man who walks, for they wouldn't have it. Maybe they are right, but so am I, for I've tramped. My first long tramp was in Olde Englande from Holloway to St. Albana and back, a 38-mile all-night hike for a wager, done after a hard day's work and finished in time to start work again at 8 a.m.

My first Canadian tramp was away from a half-civilized farmer near Renfrew who refused to pay me what he owed me, and I walked to Ottawa broke and took shelter in the old mission on George Street. Another well-remembered tramp was an 11-week hike between the shafts of a hand truck in the C.P.R. freight sheds at Fort William; three five-hour shifts every day including Sunday, returning to Winnipeg with a $400 stake to keep me in comfort all winter.

Another notable tramp was during the war, for a Markham farmer who was unable to hire help. Three hours every day, wet or fine, hard or soft, for three months I tramped behind a walking plow, and plowed all the arable land on a 250-acre farm. I'm not an expert or even a well-experienced plowman, but with the aid of two wheels I did neat work. He paid me one and a quarter dollars an acre, and except a few days when the ground was too hard, each day I stepped out two acres and finished before night. I didn't kill horses for I had eight good ones to choose from and never worked the same pair a succeeding day.

But that's all done! The glamour of those days is just a memory, I no longer like or am able to do long tramps. I am feeling old, laggy and cranky, stiff jointed and troubled with age pains. And my toothless gums (for I haven't a tooth left) can no longer gnaw tough beef and crusts.

We oldsters are finished, and I'm sure that when the hour comes we should not regret leaving this troubled, tortured world for a peaceful rest in the ground or a happier land where tramping is not necessary.

F. Jennings,
122 King Street E., Toronto

Parcels are checked at the Canadian Forces Post Office in London while at home, a soldier's wife found the mailing costs abominable.

A PARCEL FOR A SOLDIER

JANUARY 15, 1940

With reference to sending foodstuffs, etc., to England for our Canadian soldiers, I beg to say as much as we would like to do so, we are not at liberty due to the fact that the cost of mailing is more expensive than the products and woolens we are interested in sending.

I recently endeavoured to send my husband three pairs of socks, one box of cigarets, and chocolates; and candidly the rates for mailing were not only unreasonable but abominable.

Naturally we Canadian women, interested in the soldiers' welfare overseas, would like to know if there will be any change in the cost of mailing, otherwise we will be very much disappointed.

Mrs. H. Gagnon, Ottawa

Editor's note: Packages and letters destined for overseas soldiers were sent by regular mail to a central depot in Ottawa, where they were coded, bagged and forwarded to a military dispatch building in London. From there, they were sent to soldiers in the field. Within Canada, letters were mailed at regular domestic rates. The parcel rate was determined by distance between point of mailing and Ottawa. There is no evidence the government ever implemented a special rate for overseas parcels, as suggested by the letter writer.

A CORNWALL CRITIC OF COSMETICS

JANUARY 16, 1940

The other day I read an article in your paper where a business man refused to employ women who painted their finger-nails and spread lip-stick freely over their dials. It's a pity there are not more men like him.

To my mind, women who paint their finger-nails or use red shoe polish, are detestable. It not only detracts from their natural beauty, but causes them to look like cold, calculating, crab-like creatures.

J.E. Morgan, Cornwall, Ont.

LADYLIKE LIPSTICK

JANUARY 19, 1940

With reference to a recent letter regarding girls wearing lipstick and nail polish, I wish to ask exactly what Mr. Morgan means by women using *red shoe* polish?

I have been living in Ottawa, among civilized people, for the last 25 years and I have yet to see that. This is not 1890 and a woman nowadays uses cosmetics in order to look attractive and she still is called a lady.

In Cornwall women may spread lipstick freely over their "dials" but here in Ottawa we use cosmetics with discretion and we are far from looking like "cold, calculating, crab-like creatures."

So don't be an old sour puss, Mr. Rip Van Winkle. Wake up and move with the times. It's 1940.

Lillian Morrow, Ottawa.

ONE HOUSEWIFE REBELS

FEBRUARY 10, 1940

Why do we have to put up with the rise in the price of milk? Milk has been used lavishly in our household, for drinking, in milk soups and desserts. Now I shall substitute fruit juices from fruits canned during the past summer, and gelatines in place of blanc-manges. Ice creams made at home have now become sherbets.

Formerly I used a quart of whipping cream a week, now I shall use no cream, and a minimum of milk for drinking. Old people, children and invalids must have the milk, but there are many places where substitutions can be made. Let the housewife make them.

The public has been assured there would be no rise in the price of sugar. Look at it now, and watch what happens during the coming months, and watch some of the other commodities.

I feel imposed upon. In fact I think I am becoming infuriated. I daresay many other homemakers feel the same.

Naomi E. Bradley, Ottawa

HE USED TO BE SOCIETY'S IDOL

FEBRUARY 22, 1940

Today the whole civilized world mourns the loss of a dearly beloved and honoured public servant of the British Empire. Tomorrow the Dominion of Canada will need some able, loyal and understanding person to fill the high office of Governor General left vacant by the death of Lord Tweedsmuir.

I honestly believe that the only man in these trying and troubled times that should occupy Rideau Hall as the personal representative of His Majesty the King is the Duke of Windsor, his brother.

I sincerely believe that King George VI, by such an appointment, will receive not only the warm and whole-hearted thanks of the people of Canada in particular, but of the whole British Commonwealth of Nations; and I also believe it would be looked on as a fine gesture of friendship by the United States of America.

Ex-King Edward VIII has all the qualities necessary for the greatest office in Canada that it is in the power of the King to confer. Furthermore, he is still a young man in his forties and should be able to devote many years of good and beneficial public service.

To the social duties of this high office he would be able to bring all the worldly and royal graces that I feel would be greatly appreciated on Parliament Hill. Throughout Canada the Duke of Windsor has — like his father and grandfather before him — manifested the deepest interest and keenest enthusiasm; during his many visits while Prince of Wales he won the acclaim of the whole nation.

I feel certain that if the Duke of Windsor were appointed, he would not be a mere figurehead and a tool in the hands of political parties, but that he would miss no opportunity of getting into intimate touch with all classes and their problems: political and social, economic and spiritual.

He is further needed to help Canada assist the Mother Country in the holy war it is waging against dictators and their medieval creeds — surnamed Naziism, Fascism and Communism.

Morris Goodman, Montreal

Editor's note: The letter-writer may have believed the Duke of Windsor was just what Canada needed to fight fascism, but that was not the view of the Dominion cabinet, which worried privately about the former king's publicly stated sympathy for Adolf Hitler. The British government had the same worry, and assigned the Duke to a post well away from the European war theatre — Governor of the Bahamas. The job of Canada's governor general went to the Earl of Athlone, another solid blueblood and husband of Queen Victoria's granddaughter. He served at Rideau Hall from 1940-46.

VOTES FOR WOMEN
MARCH 20, 1940

The press recently reported that Cardinal Villeneuve of Quebec does not approve of votes for women.

Of course, everybody knows the Cardinal is quite right. Indeed, it is very doubtful whether women should be given a blessed thing. The awful truth is they help themselves to everything in any event, whether it is firmly nailed down or loose.

Now I can remember when I thought my trousers were safe to help me adorn my person, but look at what has happened. She stole them long ago, and not content with that she tore off all the buttons for her own use and put that awful thing called a zipper on them.

Frequently I have to take several looks to find out who and what it is that is approaching. I soon see a creature with painted finger nails and tobacco-smelling breath — some choice brand of Fior de Cabbage leaves probably — and I ask myself once more why do I keep trying to live any way that is not perfectly clear that the world is going to the bow-wows? Votes for women, indeed! Why it only encourages them to think for themselves!

Charles Walkden, Victoria, B.C.

Editor's note: After a raucous debate, Quebec women were given the right to vote and run in provincial elections in April 1940.

BLITZKRIEG FISH STORY
MAY 1, 1940

Suppression of free speech in Germany and German-controlled countries has given birth to lots of quips and jokes about Hitler, some of which have escaped the concentration camps.

A very popular one that is current along the Maginot Line is a fishing story which tells how Hitler and [former French premier Edouard] Daladier were plying rod and line somewhere on the Rhine. Daladier was filling his creel, and Hitler counting the last of his bait. "How is it," said the Fuehrer impatiently, "that you catch lots of fish, while I can't even get a bite?" "Eh bien!" drawled Daladier, "I give them time to open their mouths."

Dr. W. J. E. Scott, Ottawa

SADNESS IN FRANCE
Editor's note: The following letter was sent from Dijon, France in May 1940 and published June 15, 1940. It is likely that Hannes, to whom the letter was addressed, lived in Ottawa and passed it on to the Citizen for publication.

Dear Hannes,

Give me great courage, I am in need of undying courage; my brother, Marcell, has just been killed in battle. My sister, Marguerite, in order to inform me of his death, has come to Tonnerre where I had been put in charge of the care for refugees of which there are millions, Belgian and French.

Now I have to leave at once for Annecy (French town on the Swiss-Italian border) to announce my brother's death to my parents who are actually staying down there to help my sister, Geneviève.

I am waiting in a coffee house for the departure of the train; there are a lot of young fellows, young officers. I think of Marcell, I recall him. I am very, very sad to know his beautiful life is annihilated, and his beautiful character; his courage, his ardor, and his untiring optimism.

I must write you all this, I simply must. It is horrible to be persecuted by this idea: Marcell is killed — and to be alone. And to be obliged to announce his death to father and mother who had brought him into this world. Mama had already been so worried when she wrote to me last time.

There is an enormous amount of misery in our country, but of courage just as much. Today is the eleventh day that a flood of people keeps pouring through Tonnerre, people who have abandoned everything; some of them have been on their way for more than two weeks, walking, riding bicycles, on carts and on horseback; whole families in big horse-drawn carriages have left their homes.

These people give us the example of courage. Often they have lost some members of their families; but they are hopeful still. This morning I had been hopeful myself; hopeful that one day good news will arrive from our Marcell; and then my sister, Marguerite, has come . . .

Continue to write to me often; I need it badly; it will do me good.

Yours, ever,

Françoise

CAREFUL TRUCK DRIVING

JULY 10, 1940

We hear so much of war and sorrow, you may enjoy the following small happening.

The other day while walking along Echo Drive where it is narrow and winding, I saw a perky black squirrel scramble down a tree, then dash out on the pavement. When half-way across he saw a huge red truck coming around the bend. Just as some humans do, he turned, started to come back, then seemed to change his mind and started for the opposite side again.

I held my breath as he could not possibly make either side in time. The boys in the truck, though had seen him, too. They stopped, giving the wee thing time to cross; which he did in great hurry, scampering up a tree, voicing his fright and indignation in no uncertain terms.

The boys went on their way grinning broadly. I went mine grinning, too, but with deep thankfulness of having seen this act of kindness, and feeling our cause of freedom is safe in the hands of just such lads.

G.C.C. Ward, Ottawa

OLD AGE LIMIT

SEPTEMBER 5, 1940

Because a man happens to be over what is called the age limit (65) should he be considered useless?

The Dominion government requires the services of some thousands of men as accountants for the duration of the war, and thousands of "over-agemen" can do this work, better and more efficiently than the younger ones just out of school, for the reason that they have had practical experience and know how.

Why not give them a chance? Henry Ford once said that his best men for mechanical work were from 50 to 65 years because of their experience. The same would more than apply for clerical work because of less physical strain.

I am 60 and can turn a hand-spring yet, put up two 56-pound weights over my head. I can go on a hunting trip and walk 10 or 15 miles a day over hills, bush and swamps. A man is not old or useless until he is dead from old age.

G.P. Spittal, Ottawa

LITTER IN THE STREETS

NOVEMBER 4, 1940

Can you tell me why the citizens of Ottawa take so much delight in littering the streets with paper and other muck? The Capital City sometimes looks like a hick town.

Can't the streets be cleaned and flushed at night? And some folks talk about Ottawa becoming the Capital of the British Empire! *Absolvi meam animam.*

Eulalila Lance, Ottawa

GIFT PUPPIES

DECEMBER 26, 1940

Whether a puppy is a nuisance or a pleasure in a home depends largely on the first care it receives in its new home. The advice in this article is intended to help those who have a new dog given to them at Christmas.

A small puppy that has just left its mother and brothers and sisters is naturally strange and lonesome. Be prepared for it to keep the household awake for the first night or two. Have a special bed for the puppy and teach from the first that it has to sleep there. If, however, it cries, be kind, patient and firm. Do not whip or scold it, talk to it often and show that it is welcome in the home.

House-breaking a puppy needs time and patience but with method and regularity it will soon learn. Put a small puppy out very frequently either onto a newspaper, outside or into the basement, always just before meals, almost immediately after meals and last thing at night and first thing in the morning. Do not expect a small puppy to go all night without soiling.

If possible put your dog to sleep in a cool place, off the floor and out of a draught. If it is a long-haired dog that will later on sleep outside put it to sleep in a warm kennel or box in a porch, stable or garage but not right outside till it is full grown. Try to avoid extreme changes of temperature for the small puppy. By no means bath a puppy till it is six months old.

Remember that a small puppy is like a small child and needs plenty of rest and sleep.

Scraps from the household table will usually provide ample food for the average dog with extra milk when it is very small. Feed a puppy at least four times a day and leave it milk and a dry crust or biscuit at night and clean fresh water at least twice a day and where it can always get it.

A dog of the big breeds needs extra raw meat, bones, cod liver oil and eggs. Never give a dog bones from chicken, rabbit, turkey, goose, etc., but a good big bone should be given once or twice a week.

If a dog has to be kept confined and a small fenced yard is not possible, attach it by a light chain to a ring and put this ring onto a wire pulled tight between two posts, this will enable the dog to obtain more freedom and exercise than if tied to a stationary post or kennel. Take the dog for exercise at least three times a day.

If you are not willing to do this and to give the dog care and consideration, do not keep one.

Mercedes Gibson, Carlington, Ont.

1941

Local: The Second World War upsets life in Ottawa. Blackouts a regular occurrence, temporary buildings are erected around town to accommodate the war effort and an air raid system is implemented.; Census sets Ottawa's population at 149,881 (September)

National: Unemployment Insurance Act comes into effect; CBC introduces it own national news service with Lorne Greene as first announcer (January); In wake of German invasion of Soviet Union, Canada signs Anglo-Soviet treaty and allies itself with U.S.S.R. (July); Winston Churchill speaks to Canadian Parliament, is photographed by Yousuf Karsh (December)

World: After successful invasion of Greece and Yugoslavia, Germany launches massive invasion of Soviet Union (June); Japanese attack U.S. naval base at Pearl Harbor, bringing the U.S. into the war. Canada also declares war on Japan (December); Nearly 300 Canadians killed in Japanese siege of British-controlled Hong Kong (December)

Births: Ottawa-born singer Paul Anka; Senators' owner Rod Bryden; folksinger Joan Baez; U.S. black activist Jesse Jackson; soul singer Otis Redding

Deaths: Frederick Banting, Canadian co-discoverer of insulin; Lord Baden-Powell, founder of Boy Scouts; baseball great Lou Gehrig; jazz pioneer Jelly Roll Morton; kaiser Wilhelm II; governor general Freeman Freeman-Thomas (Viscount Willingdon)

VETERAN OF THIS WAR JOBLESS

JANUARY 2, 1941

I am a father of eight children and at present unemployed. I also served eleven months in this present war, besides forfeiting a pension of $40 a month in order that I might serve.

Not long after I was discharged in 1940 for medical reasons I was given a job through the employment office to work for the Department of National Defence. After four months I was laid off with the pretext of reduction in staff for which I am sure there was no need. The officer in charge gave me only one consideration — a letter of reference. Yet at the same time there were young, single men and others that are not returned men, kept.

The reason I write you this letter is to back up the words of the Canadian Legion in a recent article in your valuable paper, and in which it was said by a certain government official that he knew of no hardships among men who have been let out of the army.

Well, I am one of them, and I can bring you evidence of what I say. I say this not because I want to publish this letter: it's more of a matter of record. I have tried in vain to get back on some job from the government, but it's no use.

I don't want charity — it's work: otherwise, in the near future, if there is not something done by the government for me they will have a wife and eight children to keep because I am liable to take flight. It's not because I would like to, but before I'll accept relief that's what I'll do.

Raymond Morris, Ottawa

ANOTHER GAEL REPLIES

JANUARY 9, 1941

From time to time I have read with interest letters protesting the action of the board of censors banning the use of the Gaelic language over the Canadian telegraph services.

This action by our censors may seem harsh but no doubt not without just reason for they could not sanction something they did not understand. If our Gaelic-speaking friends in Nova Scotia who wish to send a Gaelic message, a personal greeting or greetings from one society to another, were to attach a true copy of the message in the English or French language, no doubt it would be sent. This method was at least suggested by someone in authority about one year ago.

Your recent issue instead contained a letter under the heading of "A Gael Replies," and signed by Donald Mac-Shimidh. If he is understood correctly, he concurs with the New Glasgow *Eastern Chronicle* calling the banning all nonsense. This we question. True, he has a right to his own opinion but that does not say the opinion given is correct. The question deserves full consideration by the proper authority.

(I note that the P.S. to the Donald MacShimidh letter informs the censor that MacShimidh is the Gaelic family name of the Frasers. The Frasers in Gaelic is "Frisealach," MacShimidh is the Gaelic for "Simon's Son or Sons." Simon Fraser (Shimidh Frisealach), the first head of the Fraser clan, was put to death by Edward I in 1103.)

John A. Gillies, Past President,
Gaelic Society of Ottawa

Editor's note: Using the War Measures Act, the Dominion government prohibited the use of any language except English and French over telegraph wires, fearing other languages could be used to transmit coded messages to or from the enemy. The ban was lifted in 1946.

WOMAN'S PLACE IN A NEW WORLD

JANUARY 15, 1941

In your report of a recent meeting of the City Council regarding appointments to the various civic boards, Alderman Nelson Lacasse is said to have opposed the appointment of a woman as a Civic Hospital trustee in the following words: "It would be a great favour to the women to leave them at home. That's the place for them."

Now I know that if Ald. Lacasse dared to tell the men of this city to mind their own business and leave the public business to him, he would soon cease to be alderman. Women also must, for the sake of their children as well as themselves, begin to make their influence felt in the management of their country.

Our daughters have as much right to the full exercise of their citizenship as have our sons. This cannot be longer denied them. Women realize quite as well as men the needs of the day and are determined that their children shall have something better to look forward to than they have had in the past.

Labour has nothing to fear from the onward march of women: the right of each citizen to develop his faculties and talents to the full must be admitted and no one must be allowed to dictate to others and set a limit to their achievements. The principle of equal pay for equal work will prevent labour's exploitation by the greedy, who now use helpless unorganized women as a means to enslave the working man.

The new world must be a co-operative effort if we are to achieve a better way of living.

Lillian Kennedy, Ottawa

BETTER BOOKS FOR BOYS WANTED
FEBRUARY 20, 1941

In the course of my work I have visited the Detention Home for juvenile delinquents, and was shocked to find that they have no library worth the name: indeed, very few books that would serve to improve knowledge or character. They have any amount of popular "funnies" and "Western Story" magazines.

Such trash, I was told, is brought to the home by parents of the children. There is something radically wrong with the mentality of parents who do not see that this sort of literature is harmful to their children and is a contributive influence to their being led into crime.

The matron told me that sometimes she has had to burn some of this cheap literature featuring immodest illustrations. After a viewing of the collection, I advised even a more thorough "conflagration." Consequently, anyone who could send to this institution some educational books for boys between twelve and sixteen years of age would be helping to supply an immediate need.

Those in charge of this institution are working under a serious handicap. The public should demand that an experienced teacher be employed: one trained in child psychology, who could help these young offenders to become good, useful, citizens.

Social problems should not be overlooked just because we are so busily engaged in war activity. Is it right to deal with the enemy without and allow a greater enemy within to spread such deadly work?

David N. Mitchell, C.A.
Assistant Pastor, St. Margaret's [Anglican] Church

TEA FOR BRITAIN
APRIL 3, 1941

I read in the news there was a shortage of tea in Britain, and that Mr. Churchill has stated this might be the deciding factor in winning the war.

We who have not suffered from raids over here cannot realize what a godsend a hot cup of tea must be to those who have come through a raid, and have, perhaps, lost homes and possessions and worst of all, their loved ones and members of their families. We all know how welcome and bracing a cup of tea is after having been through some trying ordeal.

I thought perhaps each person in Canada might be willing to give up their cup of tea at one meal during the day, and would like to donate that tea to be sent to Britain.

YOUSUF KARSH

Winston Churchill, photographed by Yousuf Karsh during a visit to Ottawa in 1941, was said to be concerned about a British tea shortage.

There might be some who would desire to give up tea altogether for the duration of the war and donate all they use. This would rest with the individual. I feel each person would think he was making some small sacrifice to help those heroic people who are fighting our battle for freedom and democracy.

F. Gorman, Kemptville, Ont.

COCKNEY CONFIDENCE
APRIL 19, 1941

As a humble Cockney-Canadian still undismayed and still confident we British are going to beat the Germans, I give to your readers the following, which in part gives me that confidence:

William Pitt, prime minister during the worst period of the Napoleonic War, consulted with King George III on the finances of the country which were at their lowest ebb, and also about the terrific shipping losses caused by the hundreds of privateers licensed by France and the countries dominated by France.

The prime minister told the King the treasury was so low he intended authorizing "war" lotteries with prizes ranging from a moderate sum up to £40,000 sterling. This was done. Much money was raised but much scandal was raised, too. It was intended by Pitt that the public should pay £10 per share, but in their anxiety to fill the treasury the government sold blocks of shares to wealthy speculators at £17 per share who, creating a false scarcity, sold them to the public at £22 per share.

The shipping position was as serious then as it is now, and Pitt reported to His Majesty that notwithstanding our losses, the country would ultimately capture or build two to every one enemy ship, and the country did.

If in George the III's time we could trim Napoleon by methods such as these, we can in George VI's time, with American aid, trim Hitler.

George Bull, Westboro

FOR ADULTS ONLY
APRIL 24, 1941

I am a mother of three small children, two in their first year of school, the youngest just toddling. They are just ordinary children, of ordinary parents. As a rule, they are well behaved, accustomed to strict discipline in regard to personal behaviour, as well as in respect of other people's property. They are clean and healthy. My husband has a steady job, with a good salary. We pay our rent regularly, and are always willing to do minor re-decorating when necessary.

Yet, in spite of all this, we are forced to live in a lower standard neighbourhood under crowded conditions because some landlords, capitalizing on the serious housing problem in Ottawa and district, raise the rent five dollars or more if you have children. And some are doing even worse by putting up a notice, "Adults Only."

We have been searching Ottawa and district for three months now to find a house suitable for our family. Child psychologists tell us that home environment is the key factor in a child's becoming a good citizen.

Granted that houses are scarce because of the war work in the city, but must landlords — the selfish ones I mean — completely forget our responsibility to the future generations of Canada? Were not these landlords children at one time? Have they forgotten those days of happy, carefree childhood? Home comforts, room to play outdoors, comfortable rooms in which to sleep, pleasant companionship? Or have they memories of cold, cramped quarters, four sleeping in one room, no yard to play, and very poor companionship?

This is a mother's urgent appeal to all landlords. Give the kids a break. Don't think more of your property than the future citizens of Canada.

Mrs. A. Green, Ottawa

PROPAGANDA IN PENCIL SHARPENER
APRIL 26, 1941

I have just received a pencil sharpener as a gift. This was purchased on Sparks Street for a few cents, and it is in the form of a globe atlas, a miniature of such as are used for instruction in many of our schools.

On closer examination I find it was made in Japan, and is distinctly not for the instruction of any, save Axis progeny. The British Isles, Eire and Ireland are shown as belonging to Adolf's idea of a United Europe, which includes all Europe, even Turkey, Spain and Portugal.

Japan is shown as in control of Australia, New Zealand, Singapore, the Dutch islands and all the western Pacific. The Americas are left with Greenland, apparently.

It would be interesting to know how these little articles from Japan are on sale in Ottawa and what bearing they have on Canada's war effort.

C.J. Pasley, Ottawa

A LESSON IN TRAFFIC CONTROL
MAY 3, 1941

A headline in today's *Citizen* says I had the traffic court puzzled when I appeared and pleaded "not guilty" to a charge of "placing a motor vehicle within less than six feet of a fire hydrant." Your headline places this rather trivial incident in the wrong perspective, because instead of trying to fool the court officials, I was fooled in three ways:

(1) I thought I knew enough English to understand the meaning of the words "less than six feet." I have found out that this may mean as much as fifteen feet, or more, according to the location of the hydrant.

(2) In common with the majority of motorists, I thought the first pink ticket received in a given license year could be considered as a warning. I was wrong.

(3) After living for six years at the same address and seeing right under my window, without any notice being taken of it by anyone, cars parked day in and day out at the very same spot that has meant for me a conviction of illegal parking, I had gained the foolish notion that I was entitled to the same consideration as every one else.

So, Mr. Editor, if anybody was puzzled, it was I. And it cost me $5 as a fine for conviction.

A.H. Beaubien, Ottawa

FRENCH-SPEAKING
AND CANADA'S POSITION
JUNE 27, 1941

An Open Letter to French-speaking Canadian leaders:

My words, deliberately considered, may have the bite of hard and stubborn conclusions. They will have, at least, the merit of being plain, square-faced language. I know of no other way to write.

Have we really, truly realized what's going on "over there"? Day in and day out, all around the clock, Britain's people live under the shadow of sudden death. Do we ever pause and think what it must mean to those weary, nerve-racked folks to listen to the threatening whine overhead, interspersed with the bursting of bombs, the bark of the anti-aircraft guns, the splatter of shrapnel and the machine gun bullets on the roofs and against the windows? Not even the dead can rest in peace, for cemeteries have been torn up by blasting bombs.

Have our eyes been closed to the rape from the skies of thousands of children, women and men, mercilessly bombed and slaughtered by ruthless raiders flying high and hurling death as carelessly as small boys tossing pebbles into a well? What's burning "over there" is much more than a city. What's burning is Christianity and civilization, both being consumed in flames and reduced to ashes.

You may ask, what can we do about it? To pretend we do not know is the language of cowardice. I suggest you try this experiment:

(1) Place a cease and desist order on the constant trickle that Quebec is entitled to some sort of priority over the concerns of the rest of the country. This has resulted in a heavy burden to the country.

(2) Drop our twenty-five years' imaginary grudge which we have been taught to hang on to like a bulldog grips a tramp's ankle.

(3) Let us cease being brothers in oratory merely to add a lot of meaningless verbiage to the repertoire of Quebec's loyalty and patriotism, for it does strike one as rather sinister that many of those making these voluble, high-sounding speeches, pretentious as the sweep of a peacock's train, in reality, shallow as pie-plates, flat as dish-water, would really prefer playing political games in Canada than fight the enemy overseas.

(4) Let us talk less about the denial of tiny privileges and talk more about the single privilege that we have of being Canadians.

Do these things and you will prove to all Canadians there is no sacrifice too great to make — none that could be too appalling to be accepted by French-speaking Canadians as other than a sacred duty to God and the nation.

J. A. Martineau, Rockland, Ont.

Editor's note: As the threat of war grew more acute in the late 1930s, the question of military conscription again sparked a spirited debate in Quebec. Sensitive to strong francophone feelings held over from the First World War, the federal Liberals pledged not to use compulsory enlistment for overseas service. War broke out in September 1939 and by the next spring, the government adopted an act calling for enlistment for home defence. But by 1941, as voluntary overseas recruitment began to slow, voices were raised for conscription in English Canada. Prime minister Mackenzie King decided to hold a referendum asking Canadians to release the government from its anti-conscription vow. The result echoed the 1917 referendum — 73 per cent of Quebecers voted against conscription, 80 per cent of the rest of Canada cast ballots in favour. Quebecers continued to fight against conscription, however, setting the stage for the ugly debate over patriotism and cowardice that continued for the rest of the war.

BETTER THAN "MORAL" SUASION

JUNE 28, 1941

Well, Mr. Editor, I had a birthday last week. I was (let us say) 90. So, of course now I am in favour of conscription for everybody up to 89.

Beecher Parkhouse, Fergus, Ont.

SLICED AND WRAPPED BREAD

AUGUST 9, 1941

The Wartime Prices Board has made a ruling that bread may not be wrapped in double waxed paper and may not be sold sliced after next Monday. Surely it would have been simpler and have caused less friction to have allowed the bakers to have two prices — one for the single wrapped unsliced and another, at say, a one cent increase, for sliced double-wrapped.

There are very many busy people who find the sliced loaf a great convenience. This applies especially to women who are working, many of whom must make sandwiches before leaving in the morning — both for themselves and the children left at home. Also, the double wrapper keeps the bread good for a day longer, thus eliminating waste for one who must watch the pennies. These and others would gladly pay one cent extra for these services.

A few public-spirited women — good housewives who have raised families — sitting on the Wartime Prices Board would be a step in the right direction.

L. Kennedy, Ottawa

LAST POST FOR AN AIRMAN

OCTOBER 18, 1941

"One of our brothers failed to return." I was present today at one of the most moving spectacles I have ever seen. It did not matter who the individual airman was. He was the symbol of all his race — those who are giving their young lives in the sky to save us on earth. His name is Glorious — the unknown airman — and he will live forever in all our lives.

The gray blue of his brothers' tunics fitted in with the autumn colouring of blue sky and golden trees, and their slim, straight figures kept a perfect line before and after the gun carriage on which he lay shrouded in his Union Jack. There was no black or visible sign of mourning to spoil the perfect beauty of the scene. It was youth mourning youth, and as the bugle played the *Last Post*, the notes floated across the land he had loved so well.

Elsbeth Dimsdale, Ottawa

1942

Local: On visit to capital, Dutch Queen Wilhelmina is offered Ottawa as a refuge for her pregnant daughter, Princess Juliana (August); Beginning with rationed sugar, Ottawa faces food shortages because of war demands (September)
National: With Canada at war with Japan, government rounds up Japanese living in coastal B.C. and takes them to internment camps in the interior (February); Canadians suffer terrible casualties in raid on French port of Dieppe (August)
World: Allies begin to batter Japanese navy as war in Pacific intensifies; Allies estimate more than quarter million Jews have been executed by Nazis (September)
Births: Boxer Muhammad Ali; singers Barbra Streisand and Aretha Franklin; writer John Irving; Canadian Olympic Association official Richard Pound; Nepean mayor Ben Franklin
Deaths: Canadian writer Lucy Maud Montgomery; U.S. actor John Barrymore; governor general Arthur Albert (Duke of Connaught)

THE HUMANE WAY

JANUARY 2, 1942

Living in a district where so many cases of neglect and abuse of animals comes to my attention, it is a pleasure to have had brought to my personal attention a different side of the picture.

This week a man aged eighty-four years, a hard worker all his life, had humanely destroyed a mare 25 years old that he had himself owned for twenty years. Two years ago he refused to sell her to a pedlar though he could have used the money to advantage. With tears in his eyes he said: "When I lose old Nellie I have lost all interest in life," and the splendid condition of that animal showed the case she had had.

What a pity it is that all of us having had an animal serve us faithfully for many years do not see to it that it is humanely destroyed rather than for the sake of a few dollars, sell it to end its life from overwork and perhaps neglect!

Mercedes Gibson,
Carlington, Ont.

A DAY TO REMEMBER

JANUARY 3, 1942

Jammed in a mass of eager, straining humanity, all with only one purpose in mind — to see that man from across the sea, Winston Churchill — I waited patiently and wondered whether it was worth it. Curiosity had taken me from my work to the Parliament Buildings grounds.

At the first glimpse of that solid, determined figure and those very familiar features, I was heartily glad I had come. Here was no stranger. To most of us, he was as close as our own best friend. At his every gesture of acknowledgement, a spontaneous hurrah rolled through the assembled masses, a cheer of welcome, of confidence, of hope, and I soon became a lusty part of it.

A page of history had been written at our own front doors. In the better years to come, I can say with pride, "I was there and I saw it happen."

L. Lipson,
Ottawa.

TEA WITHOUT SUGAR

JANUARY 28, 1942

To consume less sugar, let anyone try tea without sugar, five or six times, and they will like it much better. You get the real flavour without sugar.

(Mrs.) E. Mills, Ottawa

A CANADIAN MOTHER'S VIEW

FEBRUARY 4, 1942

I am a mother who feels very strongly that the proposed plebiscite regarding conscription is an unworthy measure and that if it takes place Canada as a nation will earn the contempt of all its Allies. What our enemies will think of us is too distressing to contemplate.

The plebiscite, as I see it, is a case of Heads I Win, Tails You Lose. Even if the vote is affirmative, the government is not bound to bring in a measure for conscription. The public is and will be confused. Many people think they will be asked to vote for or against conscription; instead they will be only voting to release the government from its non-conscription pledge.

Conscription of manpower is no more shameful than conscription of money, and the government is conscripting money when it levies taxes. Conscription is the only fair means of distributing the burden of war. The unfairness of clinging to a non-conscription pledge and at the same time allowing the heavy load of voluntary enlistment to fall on the back and hearts of a few responsibility-conscious citizens is too obvious to need stressing.

I (and thousands of others) resent being placed in the position of having to state publicly that I am for total war effort. The government should assume that every Canadian is for total war effort, and act accordingly before it is too late. Our actions are dangerously parallel to those of pre-war France. It is quite conceivable that our *shilly-shallying* will have the same result!

No people, however peace-loving and loyal, has the right to permit its government to jeopardize the fate of the nation or betray the heroic men and women who are trying to hold a thin front line against an enemy 100 per cent conscripted and organized for total war.

It is my profound belief that without prompt action on the part of our leaders, without adequate reinforcements and supplies, our valiant soldiers will be needlessly wasted and we may as well prepare for existence under the Nazi heel.

Madge Macbeth, Ottawa

AN OPEN LETTER TO MR. KING

FEBRUARY 4, 1942

Dear Hon. W.L.M. King

This is Canada's most humiliating hour. Britain to whom we owe everything is faced with invasion, but we are going to have a plebiscite. Australia is menaced every hour with an invasion.

To equal Australia's army we ought to have ready a million men according to population of both countries, but we are going to have a plebiscite. Singapore and the Far East are in grave danger, but Canada is going to have a plebiscite. Canada's West coast is now threatened and along the East coast ships and many previous lives have been lost but we are to have a plebiscite to see what can be done about it.

Precious time, precious money and more precious lives will be sacrificed, Sir, while you call for a plebiscite to release you from a political pledge which was gratifying to Quebec. The world is on fire, and Canada has already been scorched by the flames. Yet you desire a plebiscite to learn if it is in order to go ahead to call out all the fire equipment to fight the flames.

I beg of you to rise to the occasion. Go to the microphone and tell Canada that you were mistaken in making such a promise to have no conscription, then go to the House, not fearing the religious and political power of certain elements, and call upon your government to give us all out conscription legislation.

Only such action will convince us that you no longer place party and position above people. You did not ask for a plebiscite or referendum for the declaration of war, which is a more momentous step than conscription of manpower.

Sir, for the sake of our boys in England and Hong Kong, for the sake and comfort of their loved ones, for the sake of Canada's honour and dignity among the other Allied nations, for the sake of our God-given British Empire which has given us democracy and religious liberties, I beseech you, Mr. King, to give us all-out conscription. I want to serve so I have offered myself to my country.

(Rev.) Robt. E. J. Blackstone,
Ottawa

APPROVAL OF MR. KING
FEBRUARY 13, 1942

Just because a few of the men that no doubt found living at home unbearable ran to join up in a worse place is no reason at all why everyone else should be compelled against their better judgement to do the same thing. Because one jumps into the river can't be a reason why all the country should jump in too. Let our government go to the country on this measure.

Mr. King might just as well spend the money this way as Britain spending thousands of dollars on golf courses for their officers, while the everyday soldier goes without and gets $1.30 per day.

Right now, Churchill's footing is none too sure, and you know it. Mr. King has kept his word right along and we trust him 100 per cent.

(Mrs.) George Perry, Arnprior, Ont.

PRO LIBRIS
FEBRUARY 27, 1942

Cut down on our Library? Might as well shut down the vital sunlight. Banish the mental and spiritual pleasures of hundreds of readers who are constantly streaming in and out of the Library doors?

Surely none of our intelligent municipal leaders could harbour such a lamentable negation for even the suggestion of a second in time; surely no civic administrator would wish himself influenced to the point of allowing this city of knowledge, enlightenment, advancement; this leading city of Canada to think of itself as a city without a library?

For what is a library? Is it a church, a hospital, a bank, a travelling bureau, a bureau of general and specific information, a kind of mental forum, a citadel of refuge for those rather weary of heavy materialism? It is each and all of these; the library is every socially benevolent institution "rolled into one." The library is a place where the ill-at-ease may rest at ease; and, in time, become completely cured.

And the children? What do they think of the library? Children are the unacknowledged legislators decreeing: "Keep the library open." What have we more important than the children?

A.P. Nicholas, Ottawa

Editor's note: The letter-writer was responding to a suggestion from an alderman to reduce or even eliminate library spending and use the savings to help fund the war. The idea never got off the ground — public opinion and newspaper editorials were strongly opposed — although the library's budget was frozen until after the war.

IN THE PATRONAGE PRIZE RING
MARCH 14, 1942

Indeed I was shocked upon reading in the *Evening Citizen* that the member of Parliament for East Ottawa was severely beaten in a fight with the private secretary to the minister of public works. It is a disgrace that such a thing could occur in the Parliament Buildings, especially in the present time when the government is striving for national unity and the full prosecution of the war.

It would be in the public interest to know why it is that the East Ottawa member is not getting fair treatment in the allotment of departmental jobs, and how it is that preference is given to other members. The Civil Service Act distinctly states that it is positively unlawful to use political pull to obtain appointment, promotion or increase of salary within the service. Any person found directly or indirectly violating the act is liable to prosecution or dismissal from a position.

Such action as that of the secretary is enough to make anyone wonder what is wrong with high officials. There was no need to tell the M.P. that it was none of his business to ask a question, or give him the "move along" order. All members of Parliament have a right to ask questions or find out certain facts within the departments.

If all private secretaries took the same attitude, then it would mean that we do not need a House of Commons as they would appoint themselves as being qualified to handle all affairs of the country and no one would have a right to know what is going on behind the doors.

Surely the proper authorities will see to it that in the future, a member of Parliament may walk in to a minister's office without being treated in an unspeakable manner.

Raymond A. Pierce,
Wrightville, Que.

Editor's note: Joseph Albert Pinard, the Liberal MP for Ottawa East, suffered a bruised face, swollen lip and cut forehead in his fight with the private secretary to the public works minister. But the altercation appears to have paid dividends for his constituents. In exchange for agreeing not to press charges, several government projects were awarded to Ottawa East in the next few months.

THE APPAREL WAR IS ON
MARCH 19, 1942

As a war economy measure I hear that trouser cuffs are to disappear. This is all to the good. They are only dirt catchers: sometimes convenient ash trays.

But, Mr. Editor, would you urge the government (can you be friends with them for once?) to go one step farther? Let us do away with collars and ties. They are only bottlenecks which make us too warm in summer, and embarrass us at Christmas. We should be more healthy for the wearing of nice open neck sports shirts, and I'd plump for the short shirt sleeve, too.

If you will not take up the cudgels for the benefit of mankind, I shall write to the editor of the *Journal*.

R.T. Bowmans, Ottawa

ON PERFORMING ANIMALS
JUNE 29, 1942

Referring to the report of the school board in your recent issue of the harmful effect of the visiting circuses on the children's school work, this may be an opportune moment to make one more plea for the performing animals.

As a supporter of the "Friends of Dumb Animals," may I suggest that if the children in the schools were given a vivid picture of the suffering involved: first, when the animals are caught and kept at the distributing points; then the appalling tortures of their training; then the thirst, discomfort and terror while travelling about, it would arouse the better natures of our young people and they would find no pleasure in watching the undignified antics of our dumb friends.

In these times of unprecedented horror and suffering for millions of human beings it may seem a small thing that the lower order of creation should be ill-treated, but it is only a short step from cruelty to animals to bullying and ill-treating weaker children and our fellow-men.

Surely we have grown beyond circuses as a form of entertainment.

Alice M. Fellows, Ottawa

NAZI PERSECUTION OF THE JEWS
SEPTEMBER 2, 1942

May we draw the attention of your readers to the further plight of the Jews in this war?

We have been the victims of Nazi sadism since 1933. All this time, we repeatedly warned the world that the barbaric cruelty unleashed upon us would not stop with us but would engulf all nations. But the conscience of the world was so dulled that the only response consisted in some kind words of sympathy and protest. The inevitable happened; finally Hitler's legions marched against the rest; the awakening began.

Our martyrdom, including the Spanish inquisition and the massacre of Petlura's hordes during the Russian civil war, was merely the shadow of the mass-murder committed by the Nazi beasts in the occupied countries. We know that physical extermination, whether by starvation, disease or the Gestapo, faces us wherever Hitler triumphs. Our enemy knows no mercy — that is no "Aryan" virtue but a "Jewish" weakness! — and we don't expect it.

But may we not expect some word of condemnation, some act of sympathy on the part of our friends? If Lidice, where about 1,500 innocent Czechs were slain in cold blood, could, justly, arouse such horror and world-wide protest, why could not the slaughter of 700,000 Jews in Poland merit more than a news item?

But the civilized world is silent, leaving the hundreds of thousands of helpless victims to the mercy of Nazi murderers, bleeding away and desperate — instead of raising a storm of protest and warning the Nazi bandits that their people will have to pay with their blood for the killing of civilians in the occupied lands. To keep silent in face of this butchery is a crime itself!

We wonder if this silence may not give the Nazis themselves the genuine impression that Jewish blood is of no account — even "abroad," as their propaganda asserts.

The cry of the thousands of victims must be heard, public opinion in the Allied and neutral countries must be aroused. The most horrible tragedy of the long-suffering Jewish people must alarm the conscience of the civilised world! An urgent appeal should be sent to the governments of the Allied Nations to take all necessary measures to stop the Nazi cannibals in their attempt to exterminate the entire Jewish population in Europe.

S. Small, secretary,
Labour Zionist party, Ottawa

Editor's note: Canada's record in accepting Jewish refugees during the Second World War was far from exemplary. During the years of Nazi persecution from 1933 to 1945, Canada accepted only about 5,000 Jews — proportionally fewer than any other western nation, and just one-third of the number accepted by tiny Bolivia. The most visible example of Canada's reluctance to provide shelter came in 1939 when a ship carrying 907 German Jews was denied entry and forced to return to Europe, where most of the passengers eventually died in the Holocaust.

HOW TO SAVE CURRENT
SEPTEMBER 19, 1942

If the powers that be are sincere in their endeavour to save electric power, then let them ban so called "Soap Operas." If they cut these sob sister programs, thousands of radios would not be turned on during the daytime with an immense saving.

C. Ostrom, Alexandria, Ont.

NATIONAL ARCHIVES OF CANADA PA-116063

Women working in factories to help the war effort, like these Hamilton munitions employees, should be proud to wear their overalls, even in the street, said a female war worker.

SHACKLES AND COSMETICS
OCTOBER 14, 1942

I've often heard the remark, from various quarters, that Canadians will not really wake up until they have experienced a good bombing. Personally I think that if the thought of their own, in chains in Germany, doesn't rouse them to spartan sacrifice, fanatic working speed, fighting-mad spirit, then nothing will. The churches aren't the only offenders in spreading the gospel of self-centredness at home.

I heard a man recently from a local radio station telling Canadian women not to get careless about their appearance as they would be if they didn't use lipstick, etc! He held forth about the Russian girl sharp-shooter (recently in the news) and her reply when asked why she didn't use make-up that "there were other things to think about at the front." I should think so indeed. Other things to do with a vengeance.

Instead of telling Canadian women to be as sensible as that wonderful Russian lieutenant and forget themselves, the radio speaker urged them to waste more time and money painting their faces. It's a funny age we live in when a girl is considered "careless" for omitting cosmetics which at one time were regarded as extremely bad taste.

H. Gillanders, Ottawa

WAR WORKERS' OVERALLS
OCTOBER 30, 1942

I am a female war worker, employed in a factory in Ottawa making a vital contribution to Canada's war effort. For this work I wear the regulation dress of navy blue overalls, and for convenience I walk to and from work in these slacks.

Yesterday, while returning along Bank Street I was surprised to be accosted by a woman who demanded if I were not ashamed to be seen walking out in such clothes. I replied that I was proud to be wearing them, and to be working in a war factory for my country.

This is the first time that disapproval has been so openly expressed, but on many other occasions I, together with others of my fellow women workers, have noticed passersby who look askance at our dress.

This is surely a strange attitude to adopt towards women here and everywhere in Canada who are doing their part in helping to win the war.

B. Quesnel, Hull

THREE BLIND MICE
NOVEMBER 7, 1942

Three blind mice,
The Jap, the Wop, the Hun.
They all came after Britannia's life,
They put up a terrible killing strife,
They struck from inside with a treacherous knife,
The three blind mice.

Three blind mice,
Three blind mice.
They nibbled away in many lands,
Till they thought they had them in their hands,
They gained a footing on foreign strands,
The three blind mice.

Three blind mice.
Now see how they run, just see how they run.
Rommel is caught in a fearful jam,
We've captured his leading aide-de-camp,
Our boys have landed right on his lam,
Now ain't that nice!

Three blind mice,
The Jap, the Wop, the Hun.
From now till the end of this gruesome strife,
We'll pummel them all till they whine for life,
But they'll get theirs, you can bet your life,
The three blind mice!

F.R. McKechnie, Ottawa

1943

Local: Dutch Princess Juliana, using Ottawa as safe haven from the war, gives birth to daughter, Margriet, at Civic Hospital (January); Ottawa Car and Aircraft Co. adds 600 women to workforce to meet war demands (March); Franklin Roosevelt arrives in Ottawa for first visit by U.S. president to Canada's capital (August)

National: Ernest Manning succeeds William Aberhart as Social Credit premier of Alberta (May); Churchill, Roosevelt and King meet for war conference in Quebec City (August); Canadian troops begin famed Battle of Ortona, eventually forcing German retreat from Italian town (December)

World: Desperate Jewish uprising in Warsaw ghetto is brutally put down by Nazis (May); Germans pushed back on Russian front (July)

Births: Corel Corp. president Michael Cowpland; Ontario premier David Peterson; U.S. chess champion Bobby Fischer; Polish Solidarity leader Lech Walesa; U.S. tennis stars Arthur Ashe and Billie Jean King; French skier Jean-Claude Killy; actress Catherine Deneuve

Deaths: Russian composer Sergei Rachmaninoff; black educator George Washington Carver; Edsel Ford, president of Ford Motor Co.

JOURNALESE

JANUARY 20, 1943

I learned shorthand as a boy, and still love it. I thought in those days I'd like to be a reporter. But, gosh, what a bad one I'd make! I could never do the "stories" some of the cult seem to revel in.

Take that column of ballyhoo under the heading of "Royal Child to be Born by Holland Ave." I declare, it reconciled me to the butter rationing; what I mean, it put me off my feed. Quote: "The Princess wants no fuss, and indeed, would throw a modest quiet over the whole event, except that privacy at such a time is not the privilege of royalty."

I don't quite connect with that "except," but anyhow, the storyist makes it quite clear that what Her Royal Highness wants and what is being dished up to her are different. "Privacy at such a time?" Fat chance!

The raw vulgar fact is that the lady is being put in a spot. If the baby unfortunately — should I say unfortunately? Yes, that seems to be the word indicated in the "story" — turns out to be only a girl, well then, what to do? Will the Princess have to apologize?

The exuberance of the "story" writer just about puts it up to her Royal Highness not to disappoint with a baby girl. And he sort of quotes classic precedent for the whole campaign: "The fierce glare that beats upon royalty at such a time," he calls it. A Tennysonian phrase? Well, pretty near. "Glare" is more modern anyhow; the Victorian laureate, of course, would not be so familiar with that word. He never had occasion to say, "Darn that guy, I wish he would dim his glare headlights."

For that matter, the Princess can't say it either; they are not supposed to swear, the royalty aren't. They are supposed to be "able to take it," although I am told they have feelings the same as other people. It must be just as hard for them as for you and me to be focused in the searchlight of target spotters.

Meanwhile, where is all this Canadian hospitality we boast about. Is this the way to treat a guest? Reasonable press comment would be O.K. But couldn't it be, sort of, rationed?

So, you see, I wouldn't do for a reporter.

E. Byers, Ottawa

Editor's note: Dutch Princess Juliana and her daughters.

A reader complained about the press treatment that Dutch Princess Juliana, seen here with her husband, Prince Bernhard, and daughters, Beatrix, left, Irene and baby Margriet, received when she was preparing for the baby's birth at the Civic Hospital.

Irene and Beatrix, spent the dark days of the Nazi occupation of Holland living at Stornaway in Rockcliffe Park. In 1943, amid much fanfare and media attention, she gave birth to a third daughter, Margriet, at the Civic Hospital. To ensure the child would be Dutch, the Dominion parliament unanimously enacted a special bill declaring extraterritorial the area where the princess was born. On the day of her birth, the Dutch flag flew from the Peace Tower. Until Holland's liberation in 1945, the Dutch royal family remained separated — except for a few visits, Juliana's husband, Prince Bernhard, spent the war years in London with his mother-in-law, Queen Wilhelmina, and the Dutch government.

LANGUAGE IN HEAVEN

FEBRUARY 15, 1943

One of your correspondents advocating universal bilingualism for Canada apparently considers the French language a world unifying medium. Citing Adam and Eve, and also Heaven, as his basis for the French-language idea, he reminds us of a west-coast Irish lady who said in our hearing: "Gaelic is the language of Odin. Adam and Eve spoke it in the garden and the Lord spoke it back to them, so the Irish must be God's own people."

Now, Sir, with Gaelic claiming Edenic sanction, French surely would be out in Heaven. Therefore, to avoid a clash of ideas up there in the ultimate, why not commence down here to avoid catastrophe by adopting one language and one "national idealism" in Canada?

W.R. Mackay, Ottawa

MORE LANGUAGE IN HEAVEN
FEBRUARY 20, 1943

The letter telling the story of Gaelic being spoken in the Garden of Eden was very amusing although not altogether new. The early Church fathers disagreed about what language the Bible was first written in. Some claimed it was Hebrew, others said it was Greek.

We find a similar dispute about the language of Adam and Eve in Paradise. Andrew Kempe published a book in 1569 wherein he maintained that God spoke to Adam in Swedish and Adam answered back in Danish while the serpent spoke in French. A book published in Antwerp by one named Goropius in 1580 said the language in Eden was plain Holland Dutch. The Spaniard Erro who published a work in Madrid claimed the language in Eden was Basque.

I have never been able to trace or find any dispute as to the language spoken by Balaam's ass [a prophet's donkey given a voice by God]. The ass being a kicker it may have been Irish.

Peter Leckie, Ottawa

REBUKES THE CITIZEN
MARCH 13, 1943

I am writing to ask what standard of honour, duty and dignity we are seeking to develop in the womanhood of this land, and what would be the judgment of any person reading tonight's edition of a paper that most of us respect greatly.

Tucked away on page 5, down in under a two column wedding cut, is a two by three inch cut of Squadron Officer Willa Walker, and a few lines reporting, without commendation or comment, her appointment as senior officer of the Women's Division of the R.C.A.F., a position that places this competent young Canadian, who has sacrificed and achieved greatly in this war, in charge of over 10,000 of our women in the W.D., and of a projected force of probably 20,000.

Then, on the front page of your second section you have a double column display, four inches by six, of an airwoman who, having broken every rule of the service to follow a purely selfish purpose, is reported to be rewarded by the high privilege of overseas duty at R.C.A.F. headquarters.

Women are asking equality of treatment these days. What would be done in the case of an airman, who, knowing the probable grave danger to bomber, crew, precious mail cargo, and the whole flight, stowed away for his own reasons in a plane of the Ferry Command bound over the Atlantic?

Nothing was allowed to matter, no consideration of possible consequences of her sudden discovery in a moment of dangerous flying etc., no regard for her oath and service when this young woman's personal interests came to the fore.

It passes my understanding how Canada can expect duty, obedience and honour from the thousands of women in the services when such conduct is commended — and the boon every service woman seeks, posting overseas, is its reward.

What example or spur to honour, duty and ambition can anyone offer to young women in Ottawa, in Canada, to youngsters in the schools, when the *Citizen*, with its fine standards of integrity, far from questioning the fundamentals involved in this whole regrettable occurrence, so plays up the airwoman who broke all her responsibilities to duty, and relegates to an inner page a quite young Canadian woman, who is an honour to her sex and service and, at a remarkably early age, promoted to the highest post within it?

Charlotte Whitton, Ottawa

Editor's note: This appears to be the first of many public dustups that came to characterize future mayor Whitton's relations with Ottawa's newspapers. Combative and energetic, and one of the century's most colourful and controversial women, Ms. Whitton was elected Ottawa's mayor four times in the 1950s and '60s, and was a central player in municipal politics for a quarter century. As a social worker prior to her entry into politics in the late 1940s, Ms. Whitton was an outspoken crusader for the care of neglected and poor children. Throughout her life, she championed women's equality in politics, the workplace and under the law. After the Citizen responded to the above letter by saying readers should leave news decisions to journalists, Ms. Whitton sent the following reply:

ALL SQUARE
MARCH 17, 1943

Fair enough! You tell me that judgment in news priority is your business and suggest that my concern over the ethics involved in the bomber-stowaway incident is another matter.

But you opened your columns to my opinion thereon — frankness and equity well in keeping with the *Citizen* tradition. I have no complaint.

Charlotte Whitton, Ottawa

FOR SUITABLE OPERA HOUSE
MAY 19, 1943

I'm hoping this letter will arouse an interest in a postwar plan for a suitable theater or auditorium where we can hear such artists as Jeanette MacDonald in comfort and in keeping with the event.

I personally think that it is a disgrace and a shame to expect such artists as Grace Moore, Miss MacDonald and her co-stars to appear in a place with boys yelling, "ice cold drinks," and during a most impressive part of the opera to have someone kick a soft drink bottle which could be heard in every part of the auditorium.

Then, too, it's bad enough to have to pay top notch prices for seats that are so horribly uncomfortable, but to have ladies sit in front of you with hats on which they refuse to take off, is certainly adding insult to injury.

When you think that Ottawa is the capital city of the Dominion of Canada, and we are without a suitable place for such events, it is time we commence to think about such plans. Someone once suggested the city square taking in Wellington St., Lyon St., and Sparks St., as a suitable place for the new city hall, fire station and auditorium. This would give us access to streetcar, parking space and taxi service without congesting city traffic.

Why not make this a post-war plan, so that we can do things becoming the capital city? It is a most urgent need, and could be planned in a way that it would soon pay for itself. Let's get busy, Ottawa.

Edmund J. Bullis, Ottawa

Editor's note: Ottawa did not get a formal home for classical music and dance until the National Arts Centre opened in 1969.

JUSTICE AND RESTITUTION
JULY 28, 1943

On the night of May 6, three Quebec gentlemen, of military age, entered my yard, and stripped my car of tires, wheels, rugs, and almost everything else removable. Two other cars in this area were left in similar condition on the same night.

Early next morning I notified the local provincial police, giving numbers of tires and other particulars. That afternoon the thieves were overtaken, and arrested at Vaudreuil, P.Q., and their huge load of stolen goods taken on to Montreal. The following week a trial was held and the three sentenced to eighteen months.

A week went by, and I wrote our provincial member, complaining about the delay in return of tires, as it was a great inconvenience for me and involved much effort getting to and from my school — a six mile drive each day. He replied, expressing his sympathy and willingness to assist.

Toward the end of June I wrote provincial headquarters, Toronto, again stating the facts. The reply from there stated that Ontario authorities have no jurisdiction over property found in possession of any person in Quebec and that such property was at the disposal of the Quebec authorities.

Not yet convinced that the quest was hopeless, I wrote our federal member and sought to enlist his help. He, in turn, got in touch with the Minister of Justice, Mr. St. Laurent. Finally the R.C.M.P. took a hand.

About the first of July we received notice that our property was in Alexandria ready for delivery. When we arrived there, the other two gentlemen and I each were given only two tires, minus tubes, and *nothing more*.

The incident now seems closed. What sort of justice prevails in our country?

Mrs. Rossie MacDougall, Maxville

MERIT IN CIVIL SERVICE
SEPTEMBER 6, 1943

Among the real bits of service the *Citizen* occasionally renders is that of calling attention to the worthy work being done by some of the men and women in the humbler ranks of the public service. In their qualifications for the office they hold, and in their unselfish devotion to the interests of any who may need them, they are worthy of all recognition and praise. And yet, perhaps because they themselves are not adept at advertising, or the place they hold is not in the public eye, they go along, quiet and faithful, without reward, of either promotion or financial reimbursement.

So, I was especially gratified when I saw your recent appreciation of the services rendered by Mr. Hardy, at present acting in charge of the Parliamentary Library. I have had in my experience a rather extended contact with books and reading, and with libraries, parliamentary and otherwise, in the cities and provinces in which I have been serving.

Without being unnecessarily fulsome I can say sincerely that I have very seldom met one in charge as pre-eminently fitted and as gracious in his service as Mr. Hardy. Time and time again I have wondered at the comprehensiveness of his knowledge of the stock under his charge as well as his minute remembrance of the subjects and methods of treatment.

Furthermore, with his exceptional executive capacity and a special gift for meeting the public, Mr. Hardy is a gifted servant. Surely the powers that be recognize ability enough, and will do the right thing by appointing Mr. Hardy to the position in a permanent capacity. [Prime minister] King himself is scholar enough to see the appropriateness and value of such a worthy appointment.

Robert Milliken, Ottawa

Editor's note: The government agreed with the letter-writer and appointed Francis A. Hardy chief Parliamentary Librarian in 1944, a post he held until 1959.

SLOW WAIT AT QUICK LUNCH
SEPTEMBER 18, 1943

My friend Samuel has one hour for lunch. To get a quick bite he goes to a well-known Bank Street drug-store. It is close to work. The drug-store is crowded. Samuel is a patient man. He knows, too, that the waitresses are doing their best. He admires their efficiency under such duress.

He opens *The Citizen* and covertly watches for a seat. Samuel spots two women who are about finished. He slyly approaches. On the plates in front of the ladies there is a quarter-cut of a sandwich. In the glass there is one inch of milk. Mentally, Samuel rubs his hands in anticipation. What a break! In two minutes he will have a place.

While Samuel pretends to read, one of the ladies, the dark-haired one, turns to the other, a semi-blonde. "I've just bought the darlingest lipstick," says the dark one. "Let me see it! Let me see it!" exclaims the blonde.

The dark one slowly opens her enormous purse and plunges a well-manicured hand in the cavernous maw. The hand fishes for two minutes. It comes up. "Oh! darn! It's the old one. Wait a minute." The hand dives in again. Samuel holds his breath in anticipation. A minute crawls by. The hand comes up. "Here it is."

"Oh, do let me try it," pleads the blonde. The lipstick changes hands. The blonde opens her arm-pit travelling bag and an equally well-manicured hand is sunk in search. A minute almost limps by when the hand comes up with a small mirror.

Samuel has now completely forgotten his *Citizen*. Samuel is hungry. The stare he sends in the ladies' direction is becoming glassy.

The blonde performs the application. The performance is slow and studied. Finally both ladies shake their heads negatively. "No, I guess not," says the blonde. "I guess not," says the dark-haired one.

The mirror is replaced in the vast deep. The lipstick is buried in Dante's Inferno. The quarter-cut is nibbled at. Samuel sways. Samuel is awful hungry.

Time hobbles on. The milk is drunk. "Flip you for the eats," says the blonde. "Ah, no, not today," says the dark one. "Oh, come on," says the blonde.

"Oh, all right," says the dark one.

They flip. The nickel rolls to the floor. The dark one says, "Watch my seat" and gropes for the money. She returns. The ladies begin to gather their things.

Samuel hopefully staggers nearer. The blonde hesitates. "Let's have another sandwich." "O.K." says the dark one.

Samuel slumps to the floor in a faint. The end.

Sgt. J. Colucci, Ottawa

THE ROBE
OCTOBER 23, 1943

In your issue of Oct. 9, you report that the best-selling fiction in Canada is *The Robe*, Rev. Lloyd Douglas' newest work, it having sold 40,000 copies since publication.

That statement set me to enquire as to how extensively read those 40,000 volumes would be. Among my friends I know six who own copies of this book, and on enquiry I find that those volumes have been read by at least sixty-four people, an average of nearly eleven readers for each book: and if like figures prevail concerning every copy, then 425,000 people in Canada will have read this book.

I find *The Robe* universally commended and in that commendation I thoroughly concur. I would not change a paragraph in it, for it is a sane and basically correct presentation of the doctrines and practices that come from belief in Jesus Christ. In the domain of recognition of Christ's miracles it might have gone further, but in the department of Christian doctrine nothing could improve on the following extract from p. 478 of the text I read:

"'This was my master's robe,' Stephanos announced in confident tones, as if delivering a public address. 'He wore it when He healed the sick and comforted the sorrowing. He wore it when He spoke to the multitude as no man has ever spoken. He wore it when He went to the Cross to die — for me a humble weaver.' Stephanos boldly scorched Marallus' astonished face. 'And for you a wealthy tribune!' He turned towards Demetrius. 'And for you, a slave!'"

Should not the press of Canada secure rights to publish this book as a serial? It is miles ahead of most of those that are being published as serials.

James Taylor, Arnprior

A QUESTION OF DESTRUCTION
NOVEMBER 17, 1943

With reference to numerous editorials in your paper and others would you kindly explain how, with:

449,580,000 people under the British flag;

122,775,400 under the U.S.A. flag;

65,366,500 under the Japanese flag;

63,312,460 under the German flag;

and with the world to draw on for our supplies, both mechanic and vegetable, this holocaust of destruction is carried on.

T.G. Brigham, Ottawa

TOYS OF UNHAPPY ORIGIN
DECEMBER 27, 1943

Last week at a local store, I bought for my son two small toys made of tin, one a boat, and the other a modern armoured car. On the boat are the words, "made in Germany," and on the armoured car is clearly marked "Germany." After being nearly 4½ years at war with Germany, I am very anxious to get a full explanation as to how these toys are brought into Canada.

B.C. Mallett, Woodroffe

FOR LONG DISTANCE CALLS
DECEMBER 31, 1943

I have noticed in an American paper, it is being made possible for men in the armed forces to converse with dear ones in the New Year. As a father whose children are away, I derive great pleasure when they call us. I should be glad to contribute to a fund to help to pay long-distance calls for absent relatives in uniform.

Max Feller,
Ottawa

1944

Local: Blackouts lifted in Ottawa as prospects for victory improve in the war (October)
Opera comes to Ottawa with performances of *Aida* and *Carmen* at the old auditorium on site of present-day downtown YMCA (November)
National: Canada gets its first socialist government when the CCF, led by Tommy Douglas, wins the Saskatchewan election (June); First Canadian army liberates Dieppe from the Nazis (September)
World: War deaths mount on both sides, but overall fortunes improve for Allies in Europe and the Pacific; Franklin Roosevelt wins an unprecedented fourth straight term as U.S. president (November)
Births: Media baron Conrad Black; U.S. writer Alice Walker
Deaths: Humourist Stephen Leacock; French pilot and writer Antoine de Saint-Exupery; painters Edvard Munch and Pieter Mondrian; U.S. band leader Glenn Miller

OTTAWA MARKET

FEBRUARY 3, 1944

I wish to call attention to the disgraceful condition of the so-called market place. The same old conditions that existed in the times of our forefathers still prevail at the Byward Market.

In all weather, hot or cold, wet or dry, normal or subnormal, no protection whatever is made for the buyer, seller, or their produce. Every seller had to cart along and set up his own stand and other equipment.

All across Canada, many of the smaller towns now have closed-in markets where the public can do their marketing in comfort. Here in the capital city of Canada, we are not even in the horse and buggy days, but in ox and sled times.

So far, I have never heard of any of our political leaders suggesting any change or improvements in this backwoods system. It remains for someone to take over from these complacent do-nothings, and introduce many needed up-to-date measures. This market is a disgrace to even a one-horse town. Even in backwards India, they have many closed-in markets, and no zero weather to provide for.

We hear a lot about giving the poor farmers a better deal, but a trip around the present market gives abundant evidence that the poor farmer, who comes to the Ottawa market, is still the "forgotten man."

Alex Nugent, Ottawa

FOR CANADIAN UNITY

MARCH 8, 1944

The subject of Canadian unity — referring, of course, to unity between the people of Quebec and the rest of Canada — has been discussed pro and con in your columns many times. Numerous recipes and panaceas have been brought forward, but there is one solution that has been entirely neglected, and it reflects a far more intimate relation between our two races than has yet to be mentioned.

No one can walk the streets of Ottawa and not be impressed with the prevalence of the French language spoken by the multitude of pretty, well dressed, vivacious, and chic French girls. They have a style and manner reminiscent of New York. They are both distracting and alluring.

So alluring are they that five young English-speaking men of my acquaintance have each married a pretty demoiselle, and are living in a state of ecstatic bliss. If a certain dour Scotchman can talk the way I hear him, and still be in his right senses, then this kind of unity is what we want. If the young men of Ontario and Quebec could spend their vacations in the other's province, I am convinced the question of unity would be settled in short order!

Seriously, however, to travel and to study at first hand the customs, manners and home life of a different race is the one sure way of having our own prejudices softened, and gradually reduced to understanding and appreciation of one another.

To understand a people or another race one has to *know* them, and that can only be done by personal contact and with an open mind, not hampered by blind prejudice and ignorance.

E.M. Hoben, Ottawa

SECRET WEAPON

MARCH 11, 1944

Having read several articles on the secret weapons of this war, I have often wondered if our loved ones at home realize that we also possess a secret weapon.

We of the 1st Canadian Division here in Italy have a secret weapon which is far greater than any which our enemies might produce. A weapon which is so powerful that Germany's best troops have been beaten by it. This weapon made it possible for us to stay in the line longer than any other division in the 8th Army. A weapon that when one of our infantry regiments ran out of ammo, they charged the enemy and drove him back at the point of the bayonet.

This same weapon enabled one of our tank regiments to travel all night over treacherous mountain roads, then engage a German panzer division at Termolie in the morning and thoroughly beat them.

A padre once told us he had read a book written by a German general where he had said that a few well disciplined and determined men could hold a town against twice their number. This was partly true in the case of Ortona. Partly so, because the Germans didn't hold it.

The reason they didn't hold it was because of our secret weapon: a weapon without which we could never have accomplished what we have, both in Sicily and here; a weapon that every man who has been in the strife has.

The weapon? Faith — the faith that what we are fighting for is right, the faith in ourselves that we can do the job we have undertaken, the faith in God, knowing that He is beside us always.

Time after time many of us have had "close-shaves" and called it luck. But when we begin to think about it seriously, could luck alone have gotten us out of that one? I think not.

Corporal Kenneth Barland, Somewhere in Italy.

Editor's note: Cpl, Barland wrote regularly to the Citizen from Europe during the war. His final dispatch appears later in 1944.

ON BEING SLIGHTLY FAT

JUNE 24, 1944

Thank you, Mr. Thistle, for restoring my confidence. I read your article in Wednesday's *Citizen*, and as one of this world's slightly tubby inhabitants, I think you deserve the thanks of the rotund.

I intend to "pin up" your article in my bedroom where it can be read by the critical members of my household. Possibly the rowing machine, which was given to me ostensibly as a Christmas gift, will be taken from the den where it has stood against the wall for some time now and be placed under your article — without comment.

Some awful things can happen to the pleasingly plump when they try to reduce. I have known some men who were concerned because the snap buttons on their pyjamas wouldn't meet and they resorted to a diet. Fat men on diets rapidly become cross-strained and irritable, and I find that even my best stories evoke no laughter from them...

I profess a fondness for a man whose "tummy" shakes when he laughs. I know then that he really got the point of the joke. Now take the case of my friend Mr. X, who resided in Lachine. He was a tall, portly fellow with a host of friends and a great capacity for laughter. True, his tummy did protrude somewhat — but then if he needed to see his shoes he could always look at them when he took them off.

One of those lean fellows, Mr. Y I'll call him, whose spine was bent east instead of west, talked Mr. X into the purchase of a rowing machine with the double purpose of causing deflation and proving a mathematical problem.

The problem stated in algebra was: Let X plus a rowing machine equal Y.

As a result, my erstwhile happy friend has become a cantankerous counterpart of Mr. Y, and all the joy has gone out of his life, thusly:

> There is a tall man in Lachine,
> Who'se temper is vicious and mean,
> 'Cos he lost all his lard
> By working too hard
> To reduce with a rowing machine.

Ronald Sharp, Ottawa

LAST MESSAGE TO CANADA

JULY 8, 1944

An Ottawa boy, Corporal K.C. Barland, wrote the following letter in Italy to *The Citizen* just four weeks ago. Last Tuesday his mother, residing in Woodroffe, received word that he had been killed in action, June 26, 1944. — Editor

Again I am writing to you, this time because of having read a recent press survey which reported that one civilian in four believes the bombing of German cities will shorten the war. It also stated that some people feel sorry for "the poor German" civilian.

Why is this? Now that Victory is so close are we to become "soft" and fight according to specified rules? Nazi Germany was going to bomb England off the map, once, but now that they are getting a sample of their own treatment back, people who have never seen war feel sorry for them.

If those same people had seen mothers holding their dead children, or civilians lying torn and mangled in rubble heaps, they would feel glad, as we over here do, that the Germans are suffering the same things now.

The trouble, I think, is that people back home think of this war as a big romantic show of heroes and medals.

It is no such thing!

It is a hard, dirty, and filthy war with no holds barred, and as Germany started it, it is our job to finish them any way we see fit. By bombing them steadily we can break their morale, slow up production and in general impede their progress in the field.

If some civilians are killed while doing so, they are still Nazis and as such our enemy. Germany has waged war on civilians in every country she attacked, so if we want to feel sorry when we hear of 1,000 plane raids on Berlin, let us feel sorry that there weren't 2,000 instead. 'Till Germany is bombed off the map, I remain,

Ken Barland, Somewhere in Italy.

MORE ON WOMEN'S RIGHTS

AUGUST 26, 1944

At the risk of having my head bitten off by the vitriolic pen (watch that metaphor!) of your correspondent Miss Scott, may I offer some further observations of humanity in our street-cars?

I, too, am a daily customer of this Ottawa Electric Railway. During my voyages back and forth, I notice a lot of diverse human behaviour.

First, there is the "battle-axe" type of woman, who mows her way down to a seat, trampling all obstacles. The men merely smile, indulgently, the women — ah! the wonderful, kindly, tender, gentle females — make loud, sarcastic remarks concerning "the nerve of some ignorant people."

I notice, too, the 5:30 shopper who, knowing that quitting time for the workers is due, still persists in squeezing into a street-car crowded with men and women who have been toiling all day and yet are expected to forfeit their seats to this package-laden creature who could easily have shopped earlier in the day.

I am also angered and embarrassed when I notice giggling "young things" making derogatory references to the appearances of every work-harassed male entering into the tram.

Finally, we hear much of the ladies who have been striving, for years, to attain what is loosely termed "equality" with men. Therefore, I personally do not feel that I should relinquish my seat to a perfectly healthy looking girl who's been sitting in the office all day, if I don't do the same to my brothers.

Naturally, if the lady before me appears to be very tired (these are usually middle-aged), I am willing to give up my seat. And, by the way, I have seen men of 65 give up their seat to women of 40, while the "slim young housewives" stared stonily at the soap-ads.

I might mention, before signing off, that, during the Christmas liquor line-ups of last year, the only persons I saw trying to cheat their way up to the clerk were women.

J. Colucci, Ottawa

WHO HAS HAZLITT?

SEPTEMBER 27, 1944

Could I, through the medium of your columns, appeal for the return of my marked copy of Hazlitt's *Spirit of the Age?* It was in the right pocket of my raincoat which someone wrongly took from a Sparks Street tearoom last Thursday evening.

In the left pocket was a pair of scissors. I am not fussy about the return of the scissors. They were not much good anyway. Or even of the raincoat, if it has been of more use to the "borrower" than to me during during this showery period.

But the Hazlitt book to me is priceless. I've only had it 40 years. Originally it cost a shilling. Thanks.

Sydney T. Checkland,
Ottawa

THAT HAZLITT BOOK

OCTOBER 4, 1944

Thanks a lot for printing my letter regarding the loss of my raincoat containing a pair of scissors and Hazlitt's *Spirit of the Age*. Many friends have enquired if either has been returned, and I have had to tell them no. But my entreaty brought the following letter on Saturday in a mean, scrawly handwriting:

"Kindly accept my sympathy in the loss of the overcoat (sic) and scissors. But it seems to me that you should feel relieved of the loss of the book. How in h--- a man can keep his nose in one book for 40 years is beyond me. I assure you that there are many interesting books in circulation for every kind of literary taste. It seems to me that a book than can keep one spellbound for 40 years should be sold in the drug store as an anesthetic.

"If, as you say, you are not fussy, why so fussy about words? Why not say that the articles were d--- well stolen. If the thief needed the coat worse than you he might claim that it was not wrongfully taken. Anyway, he is in danger of a punishment greater than the crime. If that book enthralls him so that he has to keep his nose in it for 40 years, that is surely punishment. But if it takes 40 years to get through the book, your chances of seeing it on this earth are slim. Furthermore, if the thief is a slow reader it might take him a century to read what you did in 40 years.

"Hazlitt's *Spirit of the Age* seems to be more potent than *spirit fermenti* of any age. If a rubby-dub ever got that book he would never part with it. Forty years of enthrallment would beat any liquid . . .

"Well, I hope you do not suffer too much in regard to the loss (?) It is not my right to criticize you, or anyone

CHECKLAND FAMILY PHOTO

Sydney Checkland of Ottawa, front left, got an unusal response when he wrote to plead for the return of a missing book. At right is his wife Fanny ; behind, from left, are their sons Edward, Kenneth and Sydney.

else. I probably do a lot of foolish things that might cause you to laugh. As I am not going to sign my name or address, I will just thank you for the amusement that your letter in the press gave me. I regret the loss of your coat, and even the scissors; but I think that you should thank the thief for taking your nose out of that book. With best regards, X"

Mr. Editor, I should be sorry to rob my anonymous correspondent, or anybody else, of his laugh in these saddening times. But the fact is that, 40 years ago on Christmas, the youngest of my five brothers — all of whom are now dead — said to me: "What do you want for Christmas? I don't know what to get you." I asked: "Well, how far do you want to go?" He replied: "Oh, ten bob." "Fine," I said. "I'll pick out ten of the World's Classics now being published. They'll form the nucleus of a library for me."

Hazlitt's book was one of the ten, which, by the aid of my late wife, our three sons, and a sister has multiplied a hundredfold, so that "the little one has become a thousand" books which form our family library.

Its loss is the first break in the original ten, and I'm sorry to have appeared to be sentimental. But I felt I ought in fairness to let my anonymous correspondent know, in order to relieve his apparent anxiety for me, that it has not been at all necessary for me to pose as a man who can keep his nose in *one book* for 40 years.

His philosophy of thieving I leave to students of ethics and criminology.

Sydney T. Checkland
Ottawa

Editor's note: For those unfamiliar with English essayist and critic William Hazlitt (1778-1830), his Spirit of the Age, written in 1825, is a vigourous analysis of the social significance of the leading thinkers of the early 19th century. As for Mr. Checkland, it appears his cherished copy of the book was never returned. A journalist for both the Citizen and the Journal until his retirement in the early 1940s, Mr. Checkland had his personal library divided among his three sons when he died in 1956. The Hazlitt, it seems, did not go to any of them.

1945

Local: City council votes to build 200 homes for returning soldiers (May); Federal civil servants given 10 days off, with pay, to work on undermanned farms in Ottawa Valley (May)

National: Canada among 50 nations attending San Francisco conference at which United Nations is established (June); Canadian death toll in Second World War is 41,992. Nearly 1.1 million Canadians, including 49,624 women, served in the Forces. Cost of the war to the Canadian treasury is nearly $11.5 billion

World: Gruesome extent of torture and death of Holocaust horrifies world as Nazi death camps liberated (January-March); U.S. president Franklin Roosevelt dies on eve of victory in war; Harry Truman assumes the post (April); Germans surrender to Allies in May, Japanese surrender four months later after U.S. drops atomic bombs on Hiroshima and Nagasaki

Births: Canadian rocker Neil Young; Quebec journalist Lise Bissonnette

Deaths: Canadian painter Emily Carr; Anne Frank; Hungarian composer Bela Bartok; British Liberal party leader Lloyd George

PIONEER SPIRIT FOR STOCKINGS

JANUARY 3, 1945

Why this moan about no stockings? Any shops I've been into had stockings galore displayed on their counters.

In one large store I bought some nice-looking ones made of mixed rayon and mercerized lisle — just right for this time of year indoors with wartime coal-saving in operation. There were hundreds of similar pairs at a very reasonable price for other purchasers. I noticed that most of the women merely tossed the stockings about into a tangled pile and turned up their noses. I've seen plenty of wools stockings, too, for outdoor wear; also cosy underhose, and silk stockings (rayon) for those who like them in winter.

As far as I can gather the moan is going up not because of an actual stocking famine but because of a shortage of the luxury kind. The pampered beauties who plead they must go barelegged in winter if they can't get the diaphanous trifles of gossamer in which they were wont to invite frostbite should give thought to the pioneer women. Probably the latter had to knit their own from coarse yarns or go without and really freeze in those days of no central heating. No doubt they would have been grateful indeed for the wool, lisle, rayon and cotton stockings in the shops today.

A little more of the pioneer spirit of endurance is needed on the home front. Hankering after luxuries during this national emergency of war only delays the longed-for time when the whole world can have a happy new year.

H. Gillanders, Ottawa

PERMISSION TO LIVE

FEBRUARY 26, 1945

"Canada! the land of the free." For the first time in my twenty-four years, I have begun to doubt those six little words that have always meant so much to me. Those are the words I have always lived by. Those are the words I would have fought, and perhaps died, for had not fate intervened.

Today they ceased to mean as much to me as they did five years ago when I joined the army to fight for what they stood for.

For today I received a letter from the Wartime Prices and Trade Board, informing me that my application for a permit to rent public ownership living quarters in Ottawa had been refused. Now, I have heard of some pretty raw things in my life, but I believe that just about takes the cake.

After sacrificing the best four years of my life, plus my health, and yes, my happiness, too, for my country, I should think it would be my privilege to live in that country where I like, and as I like. Over and above that, I have just as important a job here as anyone else; and I cannot for the life of me see the reason why I haven't as much right to live here as the next person.

In closing, I want to point out again, that this law besmirches my favourite words. "Canada! the land of the free." And I'm wondering what our boys in the trenches of Europe would think about this little state of affairs.

Frank Eggens,
Laurentian View, Ottawa,

A FIGHTING MAN'S RETURN

APRIL 3, 1945

On the day after my eighteenth birthday, April 26, 1941, I enlisted in the R.C.A.F. Following training in a ground-track, I remustered to air crew and went overseas as an air gunner.

After completing two of my thirty-five trips over Germany, I married an English girl — who went through the terrible suspense of waiting for my return from each trip. She kept our house and gave me the inspiration to carry on when many times my nerves began to crack.

Like a bolt from the blue, my posting back to Canada came. We were so overjoyed and I am so happy at the thought of bringing my wife home to Ottawa — to good food, freedom from V-bombs.

Upon arrival home I received my commission and the glow of "welcome home" was wonderful. After staying with my mother for a while we applied for a place to live and we were fortunate enough to obtain one, but with the provision we vacate in three months.

In the meantime, I was retired from service and am now serving my apprenticeship as a steel plate printer. Now we find that to our horror, with only a month more to stay in our home, we are met by smugly complacent people who laugh at our predicament.

My wife is expecting our baby in May and so help me I do not know where we can live! Here I am — a life-long resident of Ottawa — which I thought was good enough to fight like hell overseas, and yet — we three, my wife, our unborn child and myself just cannot have any priority at all.

I beg of you, sir, to publish this letter in the hope that someone will have compassion enough to help us. We want an unfurnished apartment because I then can take advantage of my re-establishment credit to buy furniture.

A.M. Duncan, Ottawa

Editor's note: Like the letter-writer, many servicemen found it difficult to find a place to live when they returned from overseas. In part, the situation had arisen from a significant shift in the dynamics of the city during the war years. To fill urban jobs vacated by men leaving for the war, many rural residents came to Ottawa, moving into the homes and rooms left empty by the departing servicemen. The soldiers returned to severe housing shortages. To help alleviate the problem, Ottawa city council voted in May 1945 to build 200 homes, specifically for returning soldiers, in the neighbourhood known today as Carlington, southeast of Clyde and Carling avenues. Most were ready for occupancy by fall.

WAR CRIMINALS
APRIL 25, 1945

Millions of innocents have been directly or indirectly murdered by the Germans; mass punishment of the instigators, perpetrators and accessories of the present crime is therefore essential.

Ordinary legal prosecution of individuals cannot cope with the situation. An international trial of the German people as a whole is suggested.

Ample evidence of atrocities and mass murder is available. Convict the German people, en masse as murderers and or accessories to murder, and subject to sentence of international courts according to the degree of the crime.

Sentence all murderers and instigators to death. Sentence all knowing accessories to various terms at hard labour in the service of their victims' countries. Place the remaining mass of the German people (doubtful or unknowing accessories) on probation.

Absolve Germans who are known to be peace-loving anti-Nazis and probationers who through appeal can prove that they are in this category.

Hold all Germans except those absolved subject to all penalties including death for a period of at least twenty-five years.

Recognize that some innocent Germans may suffer, but consider always the consequences of letting a second Hitler live.

Another war must be averted at all costs.

Hugh G. Ross, Ottawa

MUCH ADO IN SHORT PRAISE
JULY 2, 1945

I was deeply shocked at the article by Betty Cole on the men buying ladies' panties. I'd like to know where she got her information.

My own personal survey did not reveal a single male purchaser of these scant scanties. In other words, I accuse Miss Cole of deliberately fabricating a libel against our sex.

Can she sit at her typewriter and still maintain that the men would much rather confess to a woman? Come, come, we have not yet reached such a feminine millennium. We men still stick together.

Something has bitterly provoked Miss Cole to manufacture such a grave slander. I think I know what it is. She, herself, was unable to obtain these panties. Within her there welled up a sudden resentment against the male administrators of rationing and pricing. She could not see what a big six-foot-hunk of male or perhaps a mild middle-aged must had to do with such typically feminine items as scanties, panties, peekies, sleekies, svelties or skinnies.

Ergo, Miss Cole suddenly began labouring viciously on her Underwood and brought forth a crafty bit of calumny.

The truth: I maintain is that no man bought any panties — at least, no one calling himself a man. And I'm sure Miss Cole will admit it. However, should Miss Cole prove the veracity of her news, does she know where I can get some?

Joseph Colucci, Ottawa

CANADIANS IN HOLLAND
JULY 28, 1945

We have a daughter living in the city of Amsterdam, Holland with her husband and their two daughters. We have recently received three letters from them (the first letters in five years). These letters came after the liberation, and each letter has come to us mainly through the courtesy and assistance of some kindly Canadian serviceman helping them to get it in the mail, so we would get it speedier here.

Now, Sir, according to what they are able to write us, in every letter, they have the highest praise for these Canadian servicemen. My daughter was raised in the States; then married a family-friend in Amsterdam who had a good position there before the war, so they all speak English.

They have all visited with us about ten years ago here;

LIBERATION: THE CANADIANS IN EUROPE

Members of the Canadian 3rd Division were welcomed by the people of Ghent following their liberation from the German occupation.

and now they write us what fine, clean-cut, and jolly, intelligent gentlemen these men are, as they encountered them with the Allied invasion. Some were invited and visited my daughter's home (such as it was, after all their years of hardship and suffering, no gas, no electricity, etc.) and all we read and hear is praise for them!

So please will you accept this writing from us, with a special request to give this as much publicity in your paper as possible, as a real uplift and good morale builder, to the Canadian public, so that relatives and friends of these men may know how fine these boys act over there and how much this is appreciated over there. And also by us here, in the States. Praise them to your public as much as you can.

Mr. and Mrs. William F. Koning,
Cleveland, Ohio, U.S.A.

BATTLE TO BE WON ON HOME FRONT

SEPTEMBER 1, 1945

I fear that while we have won the battle on the foreign field, we are sadly losing it at home. Moral delinquency has increased among our young people as high as three and four hundred per cent and is still rising while the members of our parliament are scratching their heads and wondering what is the cause.

Nonsense! Anybody with good eyesight and half a brain can see what it is. What with giant bill-boards displaying in glaring colours almost nude women and pretty girls addicted to their cigaret curse, what with the inside and outside of movie houses plastered with suggestive pictures and bedroom scenes, what with liquor and booze flowing thick and fast, what with modern dance hall and night club, is it any wonder our young people are going the way they are?

In the name of God let us rise up and banish these evils from our land lest God rain down fire from Heaven like on Sodom of old.

May I add that I am not a kill joy or an old crank, but a young man in his early twenties who feels like answering the call of the great General Booth, "For God's sake, do something."

Rev. A. Voteary, Metcalfe

FARMER ON BY WARD MARKET

OCTOBER 1, 1945

I am one of these poor farmers who must stand, sit or lie in rain, shine or snow, cold, hail or blow, with no protection on this wide open space other than my own car. And there we sit or stand, cold or wet, waiting for the consumer to come who may not even turn up.

And you can't blame them. No one cares to walk to By Ward market and purchase wet or frozen, spoiled or half-cooked goods.

A day like Saturday last was enough to turn any farmer against farming after standing on By Ward market that day.

Now we turn back a few pages to July and August, and boy we surely wish that boiling sun would never appear. On York Street at this time one might just as well stand on the Sahara desert, and again there is no protection while farmers stand with a piece of paper shooing flies off their dead fowl and vegetables.

In a recent letter from a Mr. King, he says "We must beautify our city," it being the capital. There is certainly room for it around By Ward market. Why, even towns with far less population than Ottawa have covered markets for their farmers.

To our men in uniform we give due thanks and credit. We read and speak of them daily. All this and more they deserve. We had four brothers who have seen it through. But could we not also spare a word for the farmer who fed them all, instead of letting them freeze, drown or roast on this so-called market of Ottawa.

Surely the farmers are entitled to a little bit better than that.

Bert Eggens, Osgoode, Ont.

WHERE TO DANCE?

OCTOBER 25, 1945

We the young people of Ottawa have come to the conclusion that it is about time a nice dance hall was built. Why is it that every other city has plenty of places to go dance and the capital city of Canada is completely without?

We know there is the Chateau grill; but to the boys who are just getting started and are trying to save a little money, it is rather expensive. What we want is a place to go where only cokes and maybe hot dogs are sold. Even if there isn't an orchestra we would gladly welcome records as long as we had a decent sized hall.

Most of us enjoyed roller skating at the Minto the summer before last but suddenly that fun came to a quick end. Why? We haven't any place to dance and there isn't any place in Ottawa in the summer to roller skate.

What are we supposed to do when we have dates? It gets rather tiresome going to the movies all the time. Our only hope is that some day and we hope soon, some person or persons will realize the need of providing some recreation center or some dance hall for young people to attend.

We want to be proud of what our city offers us by way of entertainment and when young people from other cities visit Ottawa and ask where they can go to dance, we don't want to have to say, "We're sorry, but there just isn't any place in the city."

B.J. Moffat, Ottawa

THOSE WITH TWO COATS

DECEMBER 19, 1945

I know a girl in Ottawa who has two fur coats — one for day and one for evening wear. She won't part with one for those in Europe who have no coat at all. I know another girl who has two, who wears only one of them but won't give the other because her parents don't want her to.

Neither is native Ottawan — but just in case there may be some who are doing the same, let them remember that Jesus urged those who had two coats to give one to someone who had none.

It happens that I know another girl here who gave her one and only ski-suit to the National Clothing Collection.

She still skis, but not so comfortably; but at least she knows that one fewer European victim of the war is in danger of death from exposure this winter. I know a man who gave his only winter overcoat to one clothing collection, along with his only warm sweater, then gave one of his two pairs of pyjamas and one of his two pairs of gloves to the current collection for Spanish refugees from France's terror.

They were not covered by the previous collection. In New York last week a department store advertised mink coats for lapdogs, at prices up to $246. In a civilization where poodles come before children in consideration and sympathy, where girls would rather be stylish than help keep a child alive, anything can happen — and it probably won't be good!

Paul A. Gardner, Ottawa

1946

Local: Dutch Queen Juliana sends 20,000 tulip bulbs to Ottawa as thanks for giving her safe haven during the war (June); Planner Jacques Gréber is hired to design master plan for Ottawa area (October)

National: Royal commission is set up to investigate Igor Gouzenko's allegations a Soviet spy ring is operating in Canada (February); Dominion government buys Canadian section of the Alaska Highway from U.S. for $108 million (April); Canadian Citizenship Act passed, establishing Canadian citizenship as distinct from being a British subject (May); Saskatchewan introduces first program of socialized medicine in Canada (July)

World: United Nations holds its first general assembly in Britain (January); U.S. medical symposium reveals possible link between cancer and smoking (October); Nine Nazi war criminals, including Julius Streicher and Joachim von Ribbentrop, are hanged after Nuremberg trials (October)

Births: U.S. singer Liza Minnelli; German film director Werner Fassbinder; baseball star Reggie Jackson; Ottawa mayor Jim Durrell

Deaths: Economist John Maynard Keynes; Ontario premier Howard Ferguson; film star W.C. Fields; author H.G. Wells; author and arts patron Gertrude Stein

A CURE FOR HOOLIGANISM

JANUARY 16, 1946

I read that at a recent meeting of the Rotary club a judge of the juvenile court said, "There are no such things as bad boys and girls, they are unfortunates who haven't received a square deal."

Surely such a statement from such authority is an encouragement to crime. There should be no such sob sympathy for the young gunmen and strongarm thugs of the present crime wave. They are a vicious danger to all society and should receive drastic punishment when captured.

There is none of the Robin Hood chivalry or consideration in these young hoodlums. To them, labourer, watchmen, struggling shopkeeper or tradesman are victims, and a few hard earned dollars fair loot. They are not facing starvation and destitution. They are well dressed, well nourished, have homes, and are young, strong and well able to work.

Their recent serious crimes show that if not drastically checked they will become more numerous and more dangerous until no resident, storekeeper or pedestrian will be safe from them. We badly need authorities who will exercise ruthless determination to stamp out this lawless danger. Jail terms are not proper punishment for these toughs. Such hard natures quickly naturalize themselves to jail until it becomes little more than an inconvenience and then a kind of jail birds' club, a home from home.

Neither are a few strokes of a strap much of a deterrent to them. What's needed is the old English cat o'nine tails well laid on, and a revival of old time sentences of 40 to 50 lashes. This seems brutal; but this crime situation calls for drastic unusual dealing.

When I was a young boy in London, England, a wave of young hooliganism terrorized our district. Jail terms failed to suppress it but liberal use of the cat o'nine tails quickly stamped it out. It would be just as effective here.

It's regrettable that our present authorities are so lax and negligent in administering it.

F. Jennings, Toronto

Editors note: Readers will remember F. Jennings from earlier letters as the man who wrote so eloquently about his life as a tramp. This appears to be the last letter he sent to the Citizen.

RIGHTS OF A CHINESE CANADIAN

APRIL 1, 1946

Today I was told by Capt. Grant, the head of a naval selection board interviewing officer candidates for technical appointments in the Canadian navy — "Your application will not be successful because you are of Chinese descent."

Here is a situation where a former officer in the Canadian army, who had volunteered for Pacific service, is told bluntly that he cannot become an officer in the Canadian navy because of racial origin, even though he is Canadian-born. Such a statement by a senior officer of a branch of the Canadian armed services to an ex-serviceman deserves closer examination because Hitlerian Germany did not do much better with its — "You have no rights because you are a Jew."

The Canadian navy is recruiting graduate personnel, especially electrical engineers, for specialized work of a scientific and technical nature. This emphasis on technical men is recognition of the important role of engineers and scientists in present-day warfare.

My qualifications are particularly suitable for such an appointment. I am intensely interested in all phases of radio and electronics. I am a graduate electrical engineer from Queen's University, graduating with high honours after an undergraduate career marked by nine scholarships. I was discharged from the Canadian active army with the rank of 2 Lieut. and am at present a member of staff of a Canadian university. I was born in Montreal and am therefore a Canadian by birth.

If my qualifications had fallen short of requirements, I would have had very little to say. But I resent being told that my application will fall primarily because of racial reasons, thereby implying that my technical training counts for nothing.

If this is strictly the personal viewpoint of the officer concerned, he should not be permitted to allow personal bias to influence his professional decision: if this is the viewpoint held by the Canadian naval authorities, it is high time that such a dangerous policy be changed. It violates a fundamental principle of democracy, namely that there shall be no discrimination due to race, colour, or creed.

Such a policy, leading to ill-feeling and dissension, has NO place in a true democracy.

Frank B. Lee, B.Sc.,
Queen's University, Kingston, Ont.

RENTALS "DICTATORSHIP"
MAY 11, 1946

Last August I decided to rent my furnished home to a gentleman, his wife and young daughter. We got together and decided on a rent that we all considered very reasonable.

The home was a six room one, fully furnished with a good furnace, hot water heater installed with heavy wiring, a gas stove and an ice refrigerator besides other electrical appliances, such as an iron and toaster, etc. Fifty dollars was to be the rent.

After drawing up the lease we decided to allow the tenant to collect the rent from a garage which was on the property which brought the rent down to $47.00. The tenant was entirely satisfied and appreciated the deal he was getting.

We wrote the Rentals Administration asking them to send their adjuster to look over the house just to be within the law. All went well until November when I received a letter saying that the rent had been set at $41.00. I was advised that if I was not satisfied with this I could take it to the Rentals Court.

The tenant suggested just carrying on at the pre-arranged rent, but that was out of the question. I am wondering how long this particular state of dictatorship will be allowed to continue.

Mrs. E. Taylor, Ottawa

Editor's note: Rent review administrations were set up in many Canadian cities, including Ottawa, after the war to keep landlords from taking advantage of housing shortages created by returning servicemen.

FILMS FOR SUNDAY SCHOOLS
JUNE 19, 1946

"Protestanism Wanes Over All England." This quotation from your newspaper is, for Protestants, an alarming outline of facts.

The explanation, "a low standard of preaching" and an "inferior clergy," is not convincing. Those who listen to the radio sermons of Roman Catholics and Protestants, will agree that the latter do not suffer in comparison.

There is a psychological reason for the religious atrophy that is emptying Protestant churches in Canada as well as in England. This is a swiftly moving age, brought in by telephone, automobile, radio, aeroplane, television and the lately released atomic energy, the future of which transcends our imagination.

With all this speed, the one organization that still operates with "horse and buggy" gait is the average Protestant church, at least in the matter of religious teaching. Can we expect that youth, fed on thrillers, sex and gangster pictures accompanied, as a rule, by good music and trained voices, and enjoyed in comfortable cushioned seats, will be attracted by the pious talks of, too often, untrained teachers, and inferior music, all listened to in uncomfortable straight backed chairs, in the average Sunday school? Is is any wonder that less than ten per cent of Canadian children get any religious teaching?

Why not face these facts and try to meet the changing need? Unless this is done, the union of any number of churches, I believe, will be futile.

I read that the people of one Ontario city (population about 165,000) spends $2,000,000 annually at the movies. At this rate Canada must spend over $145,000,000 annually for this form of entertainment. What might we get for this enormous sum? If a united demand for carefully censored movies for theatres were made by the churches, Hollywood would meet that demand and the greatest educational force science has revealed would help make a better world.

Then why could we not have in our Sunday schools moving pictures and slides, carefully prepared or directed by Christian educators, presenting Biblical history, literature and geography? Records of music, classical as well as sacred, should be used. These films, slides and records could be produced in Canada and used interchangeably in the provinces, and sublimity, beauty and dramatic interest as well as spiritual truth, might radiate from our Bible.

The Roman Catholic Church, said to be the only one gaining ground, is demonstrating its faith in the power of the cinema. Pictures like "The Keys of the Kingdom," "Going My Way," "St. Francis of Assisi", etc. are clean well acted and outstandingly religious.

Before the "past redemption" point is reached, can we not rally round the standards borne by Wycliffe, Ridley, Latimer, Milton, the Wesleys and the unnumbered hosts of saints and martyrs who have thrown the torch to us to carry on?

Mary Brookfield Lothian,
Niagara Falls, Ont.

CANADIAN PRESS

The attitude of most people toward Japanese-Canadians, seen en route to a B.C. internment camp in 1942, was unbearable, a writer said.

EXPELLING SOME JAPANESE

AUGUST 10, 1946

The attitude of most people toward the expulsion from this country of Canadians of Japanese race is most depressing. It is bad enough that a government should pass such legislation; but that almost an entire people should condone it, is unbearable.

Particularly vexing is the habit of most people and newspapers of talking about sending these people "back home." How can anyone go "home" to a country he has never seen? This thing is not reparation: it is expulsion.

Even *The Citizen*, in a brief editorial of August 3, appears to be using this language; and your closing sentence disgraces your own standard of editorial excellence by seeming to excuse the whole nasty business with this completely irrelevant statement: ". . . but they are the victims of a racial discrimination of the worst kind."

Canadians would do well to stop and ask themselves if expelling some thousands of people from one of the most sparsely populated and most potentially wealthy countries in the world to one of the most heavily populated and poorest countries in the world, is a worthy contribution to world peace.

Wesley McCullough,
Navan, Ont.

Editor's note: Canada's treatment of its ethnic Japanese population during the Second World War was not one of the country's finer moments. Twelve weeks after Japan at-
tacked *Pearl Harbor in December 1941, the Dominion government used the War Measures Act to round up all Japanese-Canadians living within 100 miles of the Pacific Coast and send them to internment camps. Officially, they were removed to protect national security, although the order was opposed by both the Canadian military and police, neither of which saw any reason to fear Japanese-Canadians. In 1945, Japanese-Canadians were forced to choose between deportation to war-wrecked Japan or dispersal east of the Rockies. Most chose the latter, moving to Ontario, Quebec and especially the Prairies. In 1946, the government considered the deportation of 10,000 Japanese-Canadians but was halted by public protest, including letters such as the one above, from all parts of Canada.*

FOR A PRODUCTIVE CANADA

SEPTEMBER 2, 1946

Some of our Members of Parliament in different parts of Canada are just plain rabble rousers. They are just as nationalistic as the most ardent Nazi ever was, all they preach is hate and unessential nonsense.

Our productive capacity is badly curtailed, resulting in a bigger shortage of homes than there should be, and shortages in other essential necessities of life, chiefly caused by strikes. Yet all you hear is what design of a flag Canada should have, should Dominion Day be called Canada Day, war with Russia, and other ridiculously unimportant issues.

To the man on strike, the man unemployed through strikes or through other needless obstacles, the homeless, industry in general, production is the only issue.

If Parliament will put all its efforts and concentrate on settling strikes and remove other obstacles that are retarding productivity and do this with the same vigour and common sense as they created our productive capacity for war, they will be entitled to be called leaders and be worthy of their positions as Members of Parliament.

A productive Canadian with a good week's wages earned each week, with a decent home, and the easy procurement of other necessities and of course the odd luxury is the best defence for Canada against anything that may arise.

S. Ferguson,
Ottawa

ELECTIONS ON SUNDAYS

SEPTEMBER 10, 1946

I see that still another European country holds a Sunday election. I would appreciate it very much if you would supply the names of countries which held elections since the close of the Second World War, and which chose Sunday to do their country's business. By so doing, are they not invoking the patronage of Satan — and according to world news — getting what they want? Should the United Nations continue to recognize such governments?

(Mrs.) Robert M. Lillico, Hawthorne

The Citizen replied: Nearly all countries of Europe have held elections on Sunday for scores of years past. Continental peoples look on Sunday very differently from those of Ottawa or Toronto.

HOME FOR A VETERAN'S FAMILY
OCTOBER 1, 1946

Is there a worthy veteran's family with the little children facing eviction before the coming winter? Little children must not be subjected to cold and suffering.

There is an old farm house south of Ottawa near Manotick station, now empty. It still has a lot of old farm furniture for kitchen, dining room, living room and three bedrooms. The old house can be heated by a kitchen stove so plants do not freeze. It is sturdy.

If a veteran family with small children wish to use this old farm house to shelter them during the coming winter, it will be given to such a worthy family free of rent. There is enough dead wood in the bush to keep them warm, also free for cutting and splitting. The father can use the barn to keep a cow or pigs or chickens. There is a big drive shed, and a little chicken house.

But a word of warning — the borrower will have to put a few shingles on the old weather-beaten roof, and a pane

or so of glass in the windows. There are kind neighbours nearby who will give regular work to the husband during the winter.

If such a needy family comes forward, I will be happy to offer them shelter for the winter months only; it is a good neighbourhood among my friends, the farmers of Carleton county. These kindly farm folk have never yet let a decent neighbour family starve.

George Byran Curran,
Ottawa

BARE-LEGGED IN WINTER
OCTOBER 12, 1946

Would it be possible to enable Civil Servants to obtain their share of silk and nylon stockings after working hours? I would suggest that the sale of nylons be carried on from 5 p.m. until 6 p.m. each evening in every store in order to eliminate standing in line during the lunch hour.

At 9 a.m. these stockings are put on sale. Can we not get some change in the hour, we poor civil servants, or must we go bare-legged this winter?

Doris Williams, Ottawa

1947

Local: City fetes Barbara Ann Scott on her return from the world figure skating championships, where she won the gold medal (March); Ottawa now has four AM radio stations and one low-power FM outlet (May); U.S. president Harry Truman visits Ottawa (June)

National: Supreme Court of Canada made final court of appeal, ending recourse to British Privy Council (January); Big well gushes oil near Leduc, Alta., signalling start of the Alberta oil boom (February); Wartime food rationing officially ends (November)

World: Jackie Robinson becomes first black to play in baseball's major leagues in the modern era (April); U.S. state secretary George Marshall unveils ambitious aid plan to put post-war Europe back on its feet (June); Britain grants independence to India and Pakistan (August); Princess Elizabeth and Prince Philip marry at Westminster Abbey (November)

Births: Prime minister Kim Campbell; Canadian playwright David Fennario; U.S. football legend O.J. Simpson; baseball catcher Johnny Bench

Deaths: Auto pioneer Henry Ford; Chicago gangster Al Capone; Quebec Roman Catholic cardinal Jean-Marie Rodrigue Villeneuve; U.S. novelist Willa Cather; German physicist Max Planck

RADIO ADVERTISING
JANUARY 3, 1947

We are subjected nearly all day to fantastic radio soap operas which claim that their products do all the washing, scouring and numerous other household cleaning chores while the housewife simply sits in a comfortable chair waiting feverishly for the next installment of "—'s Other Wife" or some yarn about the average American or Canadian woman.

Surely these million-dollar soap and chemical companies realize that we are not so stupidly gullible as their semi-effeminate announcers apparently think we are? (We can always turn off the radio).

We are also told that food companies have the health of the people at heart. Yet we find that nearly all of life's essential foods are slowly reaching an all-time high in price. All we can do is moan and pay ridiculously high prices for our daily needs. Yet these big monopolistic food companies continue to make millions yearly which tends to make me believe that their main concern is the annual

SOAP OPERA ENCYCLOPEDIA

The Guiding Light — seen here with Theo Goetz and Charita Bauer in the TV version — began on radio in 1945, one of the soap operas aimed at the gullible, a reader said.

dollar profits, and not the health of the people at all. These tactics are only opening the gates for the "isms" they frown upon so much, and not without reason.

It is high time these profiteering wizards realized, before it is too late, that they are not fooling the people nearly as much as they are apt to think.

Mrs. R. Kinsey, Ottawa

I AM A CANADIAN

JANUARY 8, 1947

I can boast of being a Canadian Citizen. It is with deep gratitude that I would like to extend my thanks to the government for giving me the opportunity to make my home in the land of freedom.

I shall endeavour to maintain its high standards and to help it to advance into the future so that I can proudly say, "I am a Canadian."

Joseph Litvenchuk, Ottawa

Editor's note: The Canadian Citizenship Act took effect Jan. 1, 1947, establishing for the first time Canadian citizenship as distinct and primary to being a British subject. Mr. Litvenchuk was among the first group sworn in as Canadians two days later.

SOFT VOICES IN WOMEN

JANUARY 11, 1947

Your correspondent, Mr. Sydney J. Harris, under the misleading heading "Speak Gently Dear, It's More Becoming," castigates the ladies for the manner in which they speak, the voice in particular coming under criticism as a screech, bray, whine, bleat, moan, snort, yelp, gibber, culminating in "whinny." He further remarks that women talk 95 per cent of the time, and ends his letter with "Now Shut Up!"

Analysis indicates that if this correspondent had been turned face downward over the proverbial checkered apron some decades ago he would have showed more respect for the female of the species. Mr. Harris appears to be oblivious that women have to tolerate, with what patience they can, coughs, whistles, guttural growls, harrumphs, bellows, etc., which men carry on with the slightest provocation or with none at all. As Shakespeare says:

There is no voice so simple but assumes
Some mark of virtue on his outward parts.
How many cowards whose hearts are all as false
As stairs of sand, wear yet upon their chins
The beards of Hercules and frowning Mars.
Who inward searched have livers white as milk
And these assume but valour's excrement
To render them redoubted.

Yours for softer voices, sir, less guttural innuendoes — and, no, we won't Shut Up! Ever!

Laura E. Cram, Ottawa

THOSE WHO CRITICIZE CANADA

JANUARY 15, 1947

Every time I pick up a newspaper or magazine I find Canadians complaining about Canada. Someone "deplores the lack of national consciousness." Someone "regrets" we have no awareness of Canada as a nation. Someone says my country is "mediocre." Someone else says we must "strive" to "emulate" this or that ideal, this or that country.

Well, sir, there is only one thing wrong with Canada and it is this. We have dared to toy with the poisonous premise that all men are not created equal. Such a doctrine leaves room for the two privileges that generate the fear that paralyzes my country.

Canadians of the English language have the privilege of speaking their native tongue everywhere in Canada while they deny that privilege to their brother Canadians of the French language. Among Canadians of the French language a select group has the privilege of educating young Canadians in a way that it has chosen without consultation with the people.

Two basic fears now dominate and paralyze the nation. The Canadian of French language is afraid of losing his language. The Canadian of English language fears the influence of a certain section of the Roman Catholic Church.

All the inequalities and wrongs existing in Canada may be traced directly to these two fears. If we abolish these two privileges and write a constitution based on the premise that all men are created equal we can deal with these gloom-gatherers.

Allan Ronaghan, Ottawa

FIVE KINDS OF BAD DRIVERS

JANUARY 28, 1947

With the icy condition of Ottawa streets and attendant traffic hazards, I find five major classes of objectionable urban drivers:

1. Goofus impedimentius: Straddles crossings when he stops for the red light, forcing pedestrians to detour either to back or front of the car. Answers your "dirty look" with "dead pan."

2. Motorus precipitus: Shoots out like a comet the moment the green light shows, regardless of stragglers. Knows his rights but still classed as obnoxious.

3. Promptor irritabilis: Making right-hand turn sneaks up behind pedestrians calmly crossing the street and then suddenly blares horn. Many a kind disposition ruined by this type.

4. Trepidator stupidus: Motions nervously to pedestrians to go ahead then decides to do same. Stops again, starts again, stops again encouraging pedestrians to do likewise, feeling foolish.

5. Joker practicalus: Comes rushing to the intersection as if to mow you down, then stops on a dime just as your heart misses second beat. Fiendish gleam in driver's eyes. Accursed type.

Careful observation has revealed no less than 17 minor classes. These, however, will be treated in a broader work entitled "Psychology of the Motorist" or "What power assumeth the man behind the wheel."

Albert Potvin, Ottawa

FEEDING THE GERMANS

FEBRUARY 7, 1947

To those of us with sense to understand the terrible Nazi concentration camps, extermination chambers, soap factories and death laboratories, where ghoulish beasts tortured and slaughtered millions of our allies, the present and weak-hearted concern over "starving" Germans is just another proof that the appeasing western bourgeoisie of 10 years ago have learnt nothing and forgotten nothing.

At that time they encouraged and supported the Fascists of Germany, Italy and Japan, as well as Spain and other minor plague-spots, in the murder of democratic peoples all over Europe, Asia, and even parts of Africa.

Now they ignore the misery and starvation in countries like France, Poland, Greece and Yugoslavia, which were our allies, and grow hysterical over a little newly-acquired malnutrition in Germany.

D. Bannister, Ottawa

WHY VETERANS GO SOUTH

MARCH 14, 1947

While I was overseas with the Canadian army I heard many comments on how lucky we Canadians were to have such a vast, rich country. It started me thinking and I resolved when, and if, I came back, to find out for myself what the possibilities were in making a career for myself in the development of such "tremendous mineral potentialities."

Well, I am back in Canada and I have made my study. It has convinced me that by the time our politicians get around to giving the industry a square deal I will be an old man.

It was made clear to me that a small group of politicians representing a small fraction of this country's population — knowing little, and caring less, about the great potential wealth lying under Canadian soil — are effectively curbing the adventurous, ambitious spirit of Canadians.

When this country is blessed with leaders who can realize the tremendous possibilities for prosperity in Canada's mineral wealth and will say, "Go ahead Canadians — develop it — we are behind you," then, only then, will I "go north young man." Right now I'm headed south. First stop U.S.A.

Bruce Young, Ottawa

WOMEN TAXICAB DRIVERS

MAY 3, 1947

Regarding the ban on women taxicab drivers, when the war began I had to learn to drive a car in order to keep our family taxicab business together.

During the six years I have driven over 150,000 miles without an accident and without a fine of any kind. I have had many requests, both from young and old, especially mothers of young children of whom we drive hundreds of customers who ask for us daily for all kinds of appointments. I have driven long hours many, many times, both day and night shifts, when men were not available or did not show up for work, also in all kinds of weather.

The work is made rough and tough often by the taxi-drivers themselves. Many become careless and rude and not dependable and are apt to indulge in too much liquor.

But women drivers have never given the police commission, our insurance company, or our many customers any trouble.

Mrs. W. Baske, Ottawa

Editor's note: In 1947, under pressure from unemployed war veterans, city council proposed banning women from driving taxis to open more jobs for men. The idea never became law.

IN REVOLT AGAINST FASHION

SEPTEMBER 20, 1947

I once told my children, "The world is now too civilized to have another war." In less than two years I was proven wrong. I have also said: "The woman of today is too sensible to fall for silly new fashions; we like neatness and comfort." Maybe I am wrong again.

One thing I do know and can prove — I have often appeared in a dress five and six years old and been complimented very highly. It is not the trend in fashion that counts, it is what suits and flatters each individual.

The new, long dress is definitely "out" for the short woman. It makes her look fat — and cheap. The tall girl can well do with this type of dress as it at least covers her knees. Heaven knows, it is time she did.

A really smartly dressed woman is the one who plans her clothes to camouflage her faults and still looks sophisticated. Regardless of style trends, if you are not completely comfortable in your clothes you cannot achieve that smart look.

So for my money, I shall put it in my own pocket and not the business promoter's.

Olive Poole, Ottawa

STREET CORNER MISBEHAVIOR

SEPTEMBER 26, 1947

The interviews appearing recently in your paper with girls of different ages concerning the fining of boys for whistling and shouting at passing girls, have left a very bad impression of the girls attending the School of Commerce.

We, the girls of Commerce, resent the remarks and would appreciate being recognized as a group who definitely object to be whistled and shouted at by street-corner loiterers. These boys evidently have nothing better to do with their time and minds and as such should be ignored.

We like fun but of a sensible and clean variety.

Janet Taylor, Ottawa

HARDSHIPS OF LIFE IN U.K.

SEPTEMBER 27, 1947

In the *Manchester Guardian* for Sept. 20 there is a report of a speech by Mr. James Gardiner, your Canadian Minister of Agriculture, in the course of which he said that the standard of living in the United Kingdom was higher than at any time since 1936.

I presume that in view of the position he occupies the statements of Mr. Gardiner will receive considerable publicity and will be regarded as accurate. They are, in fact, completely inaccurate and grotesquely distorted. Fearing Canadians may accept them at their face value, I ask you to give publicity to this letter.

May I say in the first place that I am a person of no importance whatever and I have no authority to speak for anyone except myself. I am a middle-aged man with business and domestic responsibilities and I occupy a salary position in the commercial life of Manchester. Occasionally I do a bit of soldiering.

In pre-war days I enjoyed a standard of life which would I presume be described as comfortable middle-class, certainly not luxurious, the result of 35 years' hard work and sustained effort. We had a maid and a car and the usual "trimmings."

Today we have no maid, and my wife, who should be able to take life a little more comfortably, finds herself doing work more menial and arduous than she did 30 years ago — i.e. floor scrubbing, the family wash and so on. To assist her she has one-quarter the amount of soap she requires, and of very poor quality at that. I do not think we have anything here at present — food, clothing or equipment — that is better than third grade.

The car, which was laid up during the war, was brought into use at the end of 1945, and now is to be laid up again owing to the imposition of the petrol ration. As a consequence the family will now become an additional burden on the already overloaded public transport system which is half as efficient, three times as crowded, and twice as dear as pre-war.

Food? We have the barest minimum of monotonous fodder capable of sustaining life. We get as much meat for the week as we used to consume at one meal. It is coarse, hard-grained and tasteless. Two weeks ago the joint was green and slimy when delivered and stank like a manure heap; but we had no remedy, we just did without. Sugar looks as though it had been swept off the floor, bread is dark and repulsive. We get three ounces of butter per person per week; enough to put a thin scraping on your bread for two or three days.

My mother, who is 80, gets half a pint of milk per day: families of six adults have been receiving one pint between them per day. If you go for a walk in the country, it is a crime to call at a farmhouse for a drink of milk; a schoolchild cannot buy a cent's worth of sweets without a ration document. We have not had an egg in the house for a month, and I have not seen a slice of ham or a steak of undercut since 1939. We get sufficient bacon for one breakfast per week.

Clothes? I used to buy three suits per year at $30 or $35. Now I buy one every three years for $100: shoddy material and shoddier workmanship. The elbows shine in three months; the buttonholes and cuffs fray in six months. A short time ago I bought my small boy a pair of rubber-soled shoes for $7; the soles came apart from the uppers after they had been worn five times.

I recently bought a $1 alarm clock for $6 and reckoned I had got a bargain. Cigarettes are three times their pre-war price. And so I could go on: the above came to mind without an effort. I don't want anyone to think I'm whining, but I do complain, and bitterly, about statements such as that which I criticize.

Anyone who says the standard of life is higher now than in 1936 denies the evidence of his own eyes. Except for the absence of bombing, the position is worse now than at any time during the war, and the only things we have more of are restrictions, shortages and scarcities.

I have no opportunity of buying your paper, but if anyone including Mr. Gardner questions the accuracy of this letter perhaps you will let me know and I will deal with any points they raise.

John P. Burd, 35 Moss Lane,
Ashton-On-Mersey, Sale,
Cheshire, England

1948

Local: Ottawa's Barbara Ann Scott wins gold medal at Olympics in St. Moritz, Switzerland (February); Rideau River flooding causes extensive damage in Eastview, now Vanier (March)

National: In a second referendum, a majority of Newfoundlanders vote for union with Canada, which is scheduled for March 31, 1949 (July); After more than 8,000 days in office — a Commonwealth record — Mackenzie King steps down as prime minister. He is succeeded by Louis St. Laurent (October)

World: Mohandes Gandhi, spiritual leader of Indian independence, is assassinated by a Hindu extremist (January); Communists stage coup in Czechoslovakia, extending reach of Soviet Union in Europe (February); U.S. and Britain mount airlift to thwart Soviet blockade aimed at forcing Allies out of Berlin (April); In a portent of things to come, Arab attacks greet establishment of the state of Israel (June)

Births: Margaret Trudeau; Britain's Prince Charles; Russian dancer Mikhail Baryshnikov

Deaths: Aviation pioneer Orville Wright; Russian filmmaker Sergei Eisenstein; French photography pioneer Louis Lumiere

NO! WE HAVE NO BOHEMIA

JANUARY 31, 1948

Regarding the topic discussed by Mr. Carl Weiselberger in a recent *Evening Citizen*, that of Bohemian life in Ottawa, let us be clear that philosophy, the arts, and science are the propulsive forces of man's progress.

All else, politics, sports, religion, either helps or retards. Profound thinking produces the former; Ottawa thinking is concerned with the latter. Rising prices, the latest styles and hockey scores, constitute what counts for the "Bohemian" chatter that ricochets from the walls of Ottawa cafés.

We have no permanent symphony orchestra, only mediocre performances and art galleries that sell calendar art. Thought is culture and Ottawa is the burial ground of thought.

John Donnelly, Ottawa

U.S. WAGES — AND MARGARINE

FEBRUARY 4, 1948

The Chicago Tribune, in a despatch from Ottawa, claims that wages are 50 per cent higher in the United States than in Canada.

I am employed for years by the largest corporation in the world, namely, General Motors. In our division alone there are 9,000 employees. Wages are good but the cost of living is so high that the ones who can afford a little luxury are those whose wives also work here.

In return for the few more dollars that women earn, the children run around and become delinquent. And you should see the lunches the men eat. No self-respecting Canadian would touch them — baloney, sausages and margarine.

I give credit to Canada and its citizens for forbidding the use of such a food-product. Here, butter was so scarce and is now so high in price that in almost every home there is margarine. I had that counterfeit butter on my table for eight years. I doubt if it could be used to grease a wheelbarrow!

Woe to the man in our plant or any other plant in our area who only works 40 hours. How they cry and moan when there is no Saturday work at time and a half! How am I going to live? How will I pay my bills? With long faces they work and keep on moaning.

I have been going to Ottawa on my vacation for a good many years and am now yearning for another trip to the Canadian capital. I know that I will not be served oleomargarine.

L.C. Petrie, Naperville, Illinois

Editor's note: Unfortunately for Mr. Petrie, margarine — or oleomargarine as the butter substitute was then known — was legalized in Canada in the fall of 1948. Invented by Frenchman Hyppolite Mege-Mouries in 1869, margarine was banned from sale in Canada by an 1886 act of Parliament prompted by intense lobbying from the dairy industry. The ban was lifted in 1917 because of wartime butter shortages, but reinstated in 1923. The conflict between farmers and consumers over its legalization continued until 1948, when Parliament referred the matter to the Supreme Court, which lifted the ban. Even so, some provinces continued to restrict the ways in which margaine was sold — insisting, for instance, it must be white and therefore less appetizing than butter.

WOMEN WILL NOT HAVE WAR

MARCH 13, 1948

A father writes in the *Evening Citizen* of March 8 of his willingness to plunge the world into the horror of an atomic war in the hopes of saving his infant son from fighting a war in his generation.

What of this generation? Have the last two world wars settled any issues or brought security? Has this father heard the warning of the scientists: "It is not a question of war or peace, but the choice between peace and total destruction?"

To this father, I would say: Down through the centuries, men have made wars. In early times, war was their life. They gloried in war, and roamed abroad seeking war. As the world became more civilized, man still retained his war-like nature, and governments their war-making powers. As science and education progressed, war weapons became more terrible and destructive, until man has at last reached the atomic age, and with it, the urge to destroy with atomic weapons.

The only way to prevent a war is for every man — every father — to determine wars shall not be. Peace can only be maintained if man can put the worship and love of war out of his system. Only by this means can this father save his son — and the hopes of others.

Down through the centuries, women have borne and reared children, only to see them die in wars. "Men must

CITIZEN FILE PHOTO

The U.S. was conducting atomic tests over Bikini Island in 1947, shortly before a reader warned governments that talk of atomic war should take heed of the second insurrection of women.

fight, and women must weep" was the accepted theory. We no longer believe nor accept that theory. Women today are not weeping. We are furiously aroused, and are determined that governments of nation-states shall be compelled to settle international disputes without resorting to wars.

Today, the broken bodies of children are still lying under the rubble of ruined cities. The living are crying for bread. Long ago, the cry of hunger was heard by the mothers of France, and Carlyle describes it in his "French Revolution" as the insurrection of women.

Let governments take heed when they glibly talk of an atomic war, for the second insurrection of women is yet to be written in history.

(Mrs.) F. Patricia MacCordick, Richmond, Ont.

A VETERAN WITHOUT A HOME
MAY 19, 1948

I am a veteran with wife and two children living in one room since the date of my discharge from the service. Now I have to move from that one room.

I have exhausted every channel for help. I have telephoned and answered all kinds of advertisements for accommodation but the answer is "no children." I can hear it in my sleep.

I could go on forever about the condition of today's living but what's the use? Nobody seems to care. I suffered plenty during the war convoying ships across the sea but I suffered more in the past two years without a home.

Thomas Walsh, Hull

Editor's note: In a letter published a few weeks later, Mr. Walsh reported he had been offered a three-room apartment, at low rent, in Ottawa.

EPISODE AT MR. DREW'S MEETING
MAY 26, 1948

In the course of an address by Premier Drew at a public gathering at Glebe Collegiate on the evening of May 21, a woman three or four rows behind me in the gallery interrupted the speaker. This was the second such interruption.

Since I became involved, perhaps foolishly, in the matter; and because I do not know how many people in that gallery may have recognized me, I wish you would be kind enough to publish this letter.

At the time of the interruption I found myself unable further to stomach the abuse which the Premier heaped on the person responsible. She was a private citizen obviously excited and overwrought. The Premier seemed to be under the impression that a man was the target for his vituperation.

Seeking only to put an end to Mr. Drew's breach of good manners, and content to leave the heckler to the police, I shouted down to him twice: "*She*, Premier," when he used the masculine gender. I was forthwith referred to as a Communist by Mr. Drew: "There's another one of them," he shouted.

Since he had left no doubt whatever that he considered the person who interrupted him to be a Communist, I feel certain that he meant to include me as well. Other people present seemed to take the same meaning. One or two of them took up Mr. Drew's lead and referred to me as "a dirty Communist." Soon, a constable appeared to usher me from my seat in the gallery.

I would like to take this opportunity to state publicly that I am not a Communist, in any sense of the term. Moreover I would like to serve notice that, in future, if any man intimates at a public gathering of this kind that he thinks I, a private citizen who owes no allegiance to any political party, am a Communist, that man will be given an opportunity to prove his contention in court.

This business of pinning indiscriminately the Red label on everyone and anyone who dares to disagree with our present crop of politicos has gone too far already. Much more so when one considers how filthy an object that label has become in the eyes of a generally gullible public.

J. Robt. Hartree, Ottawa

THE HOLE-WATCHERS OF BY WARD
JUNE 19, 1948

As founder and president of the Incorporated Hole-Watchers of By Ward, New Edinburgh and Lindenlea, I note with pleasure the recent granting of space in your columns to my old friend Mr. Jos. Trou, President of the Eastview Hole-Watchers Association.

Mr. Trou and myself have for some years carried on a lengthy correspondence as to the relative merits of the holes on the Montreal Road, and on Sussex Street and Springfield Road. While I am inclined to admit that for sheer age and vitality the holes in Eastview [now Vanier] have few peers, nevertheless, we of the IHWOBWNEAL — as we briefly style ourselves — maintain that for variety and unexpectedness our holes are superior to those on the Montreal Road.

We have lately, for instance, been watching the hole at the east end of the Sussex Street bridges, and have been delighted to find that over a period of close to a month it has defied no less than three efforts on the part of the stalwarts at the city works department to fill it.

As for Springfield Road, we claim that no sportier course for the motorist exists anywhere in the Dominion. And this has been true for at least five years, ever since the last occasion on which over-zealous employees of the works department mistakenly attempted to smooth it out. Here, to the thrill of hole-watching is added the exciting hazard of the O.E.R. [streetcar] tracks, which often rise from two to three inches above the remaining pavement.

Nor does the F.D.C. [Federal Development Commission, forerunner of the National Capital Commission] — according to our watchers — lag behind the city. There is a quintuple washboard effect going west on Lady Grey Drive which for the past six years we have recommended highly as a means of shaking up back-seat drivers. We are happy to report that it is still in excellent condition.

And though Center Town and the West End are not properly within our sphere at the IHWOBWNEAL, we have long admired the superb roller-coaster on Metcalfe Street near Gladstone; while we feel that the middle stretch of Fairmont Avenue is almost as cunningly laid out as the washboard on Lady Grey Drive.

Lately, however, we have noticed that the dear old gentlemen who pour loose earth into holes from the rear of venerable trucks are being replaced, here and there, by younger men who seem familiar with crushed rock, and even hot tar. Such activities could easily have a serious effect on our membership and we view them with considerable alarm.

Mr. Trou and myself have long regretted that such bodies as the Canadian Travel Bureau and the Ottawa Tourist Bureau have not pointed out the excellent facilities for hole-watching which exist throughout the Ottawa area. We feel sure that visitors from the United States, where such facilities are so regrettably absent, would leap at the chance of testing our holes which, we believe, are exceeded in size, depth and frequency only by the new stretch of the Trans Canada Highway between Geraldton and Hearst.

But so long as our street signs remain largely invisible save to seasoned Ottawans, it is probably asking too much to expect Mayor Lewis to consider the above suggestion. We hope, however, that he will act some time during the next seventy years; otherwise the progress of the Greber Plan [a regional planning blueprint] might render such action unnecessary.

J. Percy Pothgite
Founder and President,
Incorporated Hole-Watchers of By Ward,
New Edinburgh and Lindenlea, Ottawa

'WE WUZ ROBBED!'
AUGUST 18, 1948

I'd like to know what happened to the Lower Town Flyers softball team. On Monday, August 9, they were playing the Cilvets a sudden death game when the official umpire got hit by the ball at the start of the seventh inning with Flyers at bat, the score 8-6 with one man out, two men on the bases, three balls one strike on the batter.

By the time the doctor came for the umpire it it was too dark to finish the game. I don't know what kind of sportsmanship that is.

They kept the Lower Town Flyers going from day to day until Friday morning to tell them that they were not going to finish that game, and that they were out and Cilvets were in. I understand that the Lower Town Flyers pay their money to have a square deal, win or lose, and after playing all season and have a deal like that the first game of the play-off.

Maybe that's what they call sportsmanship; I couldn't say. But we want the reason why the Lower Town Flyers were left on the outside looking in. Maybe the Playground Registrar can tell us.

(Mrs.) Margaret O'Meara,
Ottawa

Editor's note: Subsequent editions of the Citizen carried no further news of the dispute.

OTTAWA ON SUNDAY
SEPTEMBER 15, 1948

Again last night, as it has been in the past, for any forms of entertainment which have been shown in Ottawa theaters on Sunday evenings and at the midnight shows, the fact that the Capitol theater was packed to capacity by the people of Ottawa and vicinity to see the concert clearly shows how badly the provincial law of Ontario prohibiting organized entertainment or sports on the Sabbath Day should be abolished. (Of course, this does not apply to the well-to-do people who have their private clubs, gambling places, or can afford the expensive golf courses and clubs of the Aylmer Road, etc., and need not resort to cinemas, concerts or organized sports on Sundays for entertainment.)

Is it not time that a plebiscite be called and have this "hypocrites' law" abolished? Of course, it may be that our provincial government, of past and present, feel it more profitable to prohibit organized entertainments and to draw the liquor sales' tax derived from people who (for the want of something to do) buy bootleg liquor on Sunday or an "extra stock" on Saturday for Sunday.

I would imagine that the Lord would much prefer to see some form of entertainment on Sunday in order to keep a person's mind occupied than have them wondering what to do, or "cross the river for a beer" which is sometimes done with excess, or as in the case of teenagers, to walk the streets looking for pick-ups.

"Keep your mind occupied and it will keep you out of mischief" is at times difficult to do on Sundays in the Province of Ontario.

Harold Butcher,
Ottawa

Editor's note: Through a series of plebiscites over the next two decades, Ottawa retained its puritanical attitude toward Sunday sports and entertainment until the mid-1960s.

1949

Local: Ottawa five times larger after expropriation of areas west and south of the city (December)

National: Newfoundland, with Joey Smallwood as premier, becomes Canada's 10th province (March); Construction begins on Toronto subway, Canada's first (September); British North America Act is changed so that Canada has the power to amend its own Constitution (December)

World: Chinese Communists under Mao Tse-Tung seize control of Peking in January. By year end, China is declared a People's Republic; Allies organize North Atlantic Treaty Organization as a collective defence against the spread of communism in Europe (March); Soviet Union develops atomic bomb (October)

Births: Ontario premier Bob Rae; Canadian pop composer David Foster; Canadian astronaut Marc Garneau; Canadian jockey Sandy Hawley; actress Meryl Streep; golfer Tom Watson

Deaths: Margaret Mitchell, author of Gone With The Wind; dancer Bill (Mr. Bojangles) Robinson; German composer Richard Strauss; U.S. arts patron Solomon Guggenheim

HOCKEY FAN ANTHROPOLOGY

JANUARY 8, 1949

One of the most glaring throwbacks to the caveman era is the still prevalent malpractice of ice-littering during an otherwise enjoyable hockey game.

Why a great majority of fans should be subjected to the idiosyncrasies of lesser fanatics, and why opposing players must submit themselves as vile targets when spectators expect a good game instead of a side-show attraction, is simply beyond comprehension.

Was it mass hysteria or was it some inner symptom of the infamous Black Plague that caused these disturbances? To learn its origin and perhaps an antidote, I delved into some scientific research in anthropology and herewith I list my findings:

1) A certain species of Homo Sapiens is afflicted with a morbid sense of humour;

2) They are more familiarly known as morons and like any other common pests, must be tolerated;

3) Their misbehaviour is one of the strong proofs of the Darwinian theory.

These revelations left me with graver misgivings than before until I was heartened by the past achievements of that noble organization, the Aylmer Cow-Watchers' Society, whose remarkable perceptions of that hitherto shameless creature proved a guiding influence towards its eventual passive resistance in the margarine issue.

I now appeal to them to focus a vigilant eye on the fresh "squirts" who threaten to slow up the fastest sport in the world.

George Ayoub,
Ottawa

EUTHANASIA AND WAR

JANUARY 12, 1949

"Life was given by God and can only be taken by God," says Rev. J.F. Dempster in opposing euthanasia in your pages. "Man has no right to take life except judicially according to the Scriptures."

Did Mr. Dempster declare himself unalterably opposed to World War Two, in which innumerable lives were taken, not by God, but by men in our fighting forces? Did he do his best to dissuade men from enlisting to kill and perhaps be killed by men, non-judicially?

If he didn't, his present position is completely in reverse

of his wartime position. Same goes for your other correspondent, Rabbi Lifschutz.

For the record, I served voluntarily in the war, as a pacifist believing that there are extreme circumstances in which one may have to fight to preserve the hope of genuine peace. I believe in administering a merciful death to an incurable person suffering constant agony, but only after such safeguards as suggested by the 379 Protestant and Jewish ministers in New York State who petitioned that euthanasia be legalized.

I believe it even more important to be humane to human beings than to animals.

Paul A. Gardner,
Ottawa

OUR MORONIC RADIO

JANUARY 15, 1949

After carefully reading your editorial titled as above, I have the impression that you are not familiar with the broadcasting industry in Canada, particularly private radio. I am sure if you were to make a trip across Canada and visit private radio stations, you would not make these unfair criticisms.

May I point out that radio was first introduced to the Canadian public 25 years ago through private enterprise? It was private enterprise that pioneered the broadcasting industry in this country, that developed this medium to its present high standard.

Radio imposes no price of admission to hear Lawrence Tibbett, Lily Pons or Sir Ernest MacMillan. You have a front seat to hear Canadian talent such as is heard on "Singing Stars of Tomorrow" or "The Leslie Bell Singers." Your radio opens the door to talent which has had little or no recognition in the past.

All this is yours on what you call "Our Moronic Radio," and is made possible by sponsors, whether large or small. Furthermore, you will find private radio used constantly in emergencies such as the disastrous floods in the West last year, or the blizzard in Toronto last winter. It would take pages to outline the voluntary services rendered by private radio, in most cases at a loss in revenue.

Less than three weeks ago, right here in Ottawa, 135 needy families received a huge hamper of food Christmas Eve through the unselfish efforts of this private station. Private radio is private enterprise, and private enterprise is the backbone of our country, a guarantee to our democratic way of life.

Before closing, may I add that I am sure many of your readers resent being called morons for listening to their radios. Is a person a moron because he or she listens to news, sports, drama, music, or any other type of entertainment on the air?

I am just wondering how one can describe a person who reads a newspaper crammed with advertising.

Louis E. Leprohon, Manager,
Radio Station CKCO, Limited

Editor's note: The editorial to which Mr. Leprohon responded offered a vigourous endorsement of public radio, and criticized private radio for its juvenile ads, inane chatter and American-oriented programming.

A PLAN FOR THE MARKET

JANUARY 22, 1949

As president of the local Vegetable Growers Association, I feel it my duty to reply to remarks made by Controller Tardif as reported in your paper. In one breath Mr. Tardif says, "The Ottawa market is in a ridiculous condition," and in the next says the 10-cent stall fee should be raised to 25 cents.

He does not sound very logical. Can Mr. Tardif tell us what this 10 cents is collected for? We have always been told it is for the cleaning of the market. Well, sir, one man alone sweeps the market and one truck alone makes one, perhaps two, trips costing very little in comparison to what is collected in fees at 10 cents daily from each stand-holder.

What is done with the rest of the money? The 10-cent fee collected in one day would pay for cleaning the market for a month. And by the way, the stand-holders are requested to draw all carrot tops, cabbage leaves and other refuse home on their trucks. When a stand-holder pays from $55 to $60 a month for his stand, which he only uses about six months in the year, he should not have to pay this 10 cents at all.

I suggest Mr. Tardif get a horse or a used truck and get down to the market with a load of vegetables at four o'-clock in the morning as many do, and be there till six in the evening — be there when it rains or snows all day with no protection from any kind of weather, dirt, dust, wind and everything else, and I feel sure he would soon be exchanging the horse and cart for some more desirable quarters.

And why does Mr. Tardif not get at that white elephant of a market building which was built for stalls for market gardeners, and not for butcher shops, fruit stores, etc. Put two large doors in the front and back of that building so that the gardeners could drive into their stalls, unload and take their trucks out at the other end.

Another thing we need in the worst way is parking space. Our market gardeners haven't half the patronage they used to have due to the fact people go down there with a car and the police are just watching for a chance to put on a ticket. Not a day passes but some get tickets with

THE OTTAWA CITIZEN

Vegetable growers with stalls in the Byward Market said they should not have to pay 10 cents a day to help pay for cleaning the area. They were also unhappy about the parking situation.

the result these drivers never go back. Then Mr. Tardif has the nerve to say the fee should be raised.

Our city fathers had better think it over and use some judgment in these matters instead of leaving it to what one man thinks.

D.B. Craig, President,
Vegetable Growers Association, Ottawa Branch

CANADA'S HOCKEY POLICY

MARCH 16, 1949

May I tell your correspondent Mr. Robert Kinder that he knows as much about hockey conditions as I know about Eskimos, which is about nil. On the other hand, Miss Doreen Smith writes a most sensible letter on the subject, and I suspect the lady's knowledge of the amateur requirements surpasses even those of the learned gentleman.

To send a team from the Intercollegiate League, as Mr. Kinder suggests, is out of the question, since these students cannot afford to take time off their studies. Mr. Kinder thinks it better not to send any good Senior A team, such as the Sudbury Wolves, because of their professionalism. The same therefore goes for any good team at all including any junior team you care to mention. Where, then, would you get better amateurs than the Wolves?

I agree with Miss Smith that there is a choice but of three things: 1) keep on sending inferior players; b) withdraw from competition; or c) have the Olympic Committee change its definition of an amateur so that it corresponds with the Canadian Amateur Hockey Association's.

We will all agree that the first step is out of the question. If the CAHA cannot make the Olympic Committee change its stand, then let us withdraw from competition. Let the governing bodies spend the money on development of juniors instead of spending money which helps give Canada a bad name.

Incidentally, as to that 47-0 score, goal averages often

determine winners; is it poor sportsmanship trying to win?

George Montgomery, Ottawa

Editor's note: Until the 1960s, Canada generally sent the country's best senior hockey team as its representative to world and Olympic championships. Because some senior players received small paycheques for playing, there were frequent debates about their amateur status. But it wasn't until senior teams stopped winning regularly that Mr. Kinder's idea to send a national team made up of purely amateur university players was adopted in the 1960s. Indeed, the Sudbury Wolves, Canada's representatives at the 1949 championships in Sweden, started that losing process when they were beaten by Czechoslovakia and had to settle for the silver medal. In a preliminary round, however, the team trounced Denmark, playing in its first championship, 47-0, a score that still stands as the record for the most lopsided win in tournament history.

A BETTER DEAL FOR WIVES
JUNE 8, 1949

I am particularly interested in the status of wives and mothers in this fair Canada of ours. Our laws regarding such are medieval, and both they and the courts that administer them are long past due for a good overhaul.

In these days of unions and syndicates, of shorter hours and higher pay and better working conditions and holidays with pay, it seems to me that the women who do the hardest and most important job of all — being a mother to her children and keeping a family together — should get a little more consideration according to law.

At present a woman is entitled to nothing more than a roof over her head (and it may be a leaky one) and a bite to eat. She may work half her life for a man and his children and be denied enough to go to the next town if her husband should be disposed to refuse it.

There are women putting up with cruelty that would not be tolerated to an animal because their only alternative is to leave their children to the mercy of strangers and earn their living in some other way.

It is a woman's privilege as well as her duty to care for her own children, and she should not be denied it for the sake of the almighty dollar. If woman's place is in the home, then it should be a place of security to her.

(Mrs.) Clare Johnson
Rideau View

MOTHER ONTARIO MOURNS HER DEAD
JUNE 22, 1949

I'm sitting by the side of my dead boy. The boy that has cost me so much in pain of body and mind and heart. The boy who was such a joy to us both in youth. The boy who did so well in public school; who we thought was going to go to college and make a name for himself.

But now he lies before me — dead. Killed in a motor accident. They had probably stayed too long at a beer parlour. Then, I believe, they had gone to a cocktail bar. Sixty

miles an hour on Yonge street. Trying to buck a streetcar.

Who was responsible for his death?

My eyes are dim as I look at his mangled body. I start. Didn't those eyes shine with joy when they looked at George Drew at that political meeting a year or two back?

I put out my hand and touch that cheek, now so pale and cold. Oh say! Didn't those hands clap with joy at that meeting when Mr. Drew made one of his "points." God! One of his points is piercing through my heart right now.

My fingers are in contact with my darling boy's skin, once so soft and smooth and rosy. Heavens! Didn't those fingers put a cross opposite the name of Drew, George, on that ballot paper?

What did they call him? Mr. Premier? I know what I would call him now. Now, as my dead boy, our dead boy, Canada's dead boy, lies before me.

Now this same man — can I believe my senses? — is trying to climb up into the highest political job in Canada. And, isn't Canada, my country, my dead boy's country, called a democracy? What will it be when the reins of government fall into the liquor-stained hands of Drew.

Drewocracy. Brewocracy. Boozocracy — by far the worst form of autocracy there is. But I must get ready for the funeral.

D.C. Maddox, Ottawa

Editor's note: As compelling as it seems, this letter does not mourn the loss of an actual person, but was part of a province-wide campaign against former premier Drew's relaxation of Ontario's drinking laws. In late 1948, Drew resigned as premier to become leader of the federal Conservatives, which lost the election to Louis St. Laurent's Liberals in June 1949.

SMOKING IN STREET CARS
AUGUST 10, 1949

In recent years letters have appeared in your paper protesting against the smoking nuisance on street cars. You even had an editorial on it remarking that there was something wrong with a person who could not refrain from smoking for the few minutes they were on the car.

This I have always maintained as well. Cigaret fiends are nicotine-drug addicts. Tobacco is a drug injurious to mind and body. Soon it will be found that cigaret fiends are just as great a traffic menace as drunkards, more so, for their condition is not obvious.

I was on the car the other night when a woman got on and sat in a front seat. Presently she was joined by a man smoking, obviously a friend. She drew his attention to the "Please Refrain From Smoking" notice. His answer? "Oh, nobody pays any attention to that!" There should be a straight "No Smoking" notice as on the buses and with teeth, like the "No Spitting" one.

Also, there should be two men on the cars to patrol such rules. There certainly were when the fare was five cents and the patrons not nearly so many. Now, then, Ottawa Transportation Co. executives, do you or do you not intend to do something about this?

E. Earl, Ottawa

"The Hydro and telephone wires are augmented by a low overhead network of streetcar wires. The city should clamp down on the commercial interests that are reducing our streets to such agonizing ugliness. And the business firms should have enough civic pride to vie with one another in negating such a hodge podge of advertising."

— June 28, 1957

1950-1959

1950

Local: Average cost of a new Ottawa home reaches $10,000 (June); Work starts on new Bureau of Statistics building in Tunney's Pasture (September)
National: RCMP ship *St. Roch* becomes first vessel to circumnavigate North America (May); National rail strike creates one of most serious transportation crises in Canadian history (August); Special Canadian military force created to serve with United Nations in Korea lands at Pusan (November)
World: Joseph Stalin and Mao Tse-tung, Communist leaders of Soviet Union and China, sign a secret defence pact (February); RCA announces invention of three-colour TV picture tube (March); Communist North Korea invades the South, drawing Americans, Soviets and Chinese into escalating conflict (June)
Births: Laurie Skreslet, first Canadian to climb Mount Everest; basketball legend Julius Erving
Deaths: Prime ministers Mackenzie King and Arthur Meighen; writers George Orwell and George Bernard Shaw; U.S. singer-actor Al Jolson; Edgar Rice Burroughs, creator of Tarzan books; Russian dancer Vaslav Nijinsky

TRAM FARES IN NEPEAN

JANUARY 7, 1950

I have always been a strong supporter of your newspaper — your editorials, in my opinion are broad-minded, your writers are usually well versed in their subjects, and at no time are the facts distorted merely to prove a point.

My face tinged, however, when I read your editorial headed "OTC Wheels for Nepean Travellers," which discusses the new rates of street car fare for Nepean, and particularly the extra five-cent fare that residents living from McKellar to Britannia will have to pay.

Your editorial passes off this extra fare as being a system of zoning practised in many large cities. This is definitely untrue. No system of zoning now exists whatsoever. The zoning system which originally existed along the Britannia line has been discarded and in its place is one area, a distance of possibly two and one-half miles from McKellar to Britannia.

There has never been another area on any other route set aside and treated in this way by the OTC [Ottawa Transportation Commission] in the whole of the city of Ottawa, nor even into surrounding municipalities such as Rockcliffe, nor even across the river into Hull. Surely, sir, this is the setting up of one zone to be charged an extra five-cent fare, which becomes most discriminative and unfair, whether intentionally or otherwise.

There are two main schools of thought on the fares charged by transportation systems. One maintains that transportation is a common necessity of everyone and therefore everyone should pay a uniform fare regardless of how far one travels. The other school of thought maintains that the further a passenger travels the more he should pay, and accordingly a system of zoning is set up throughout the whole transportation area.

Under this latter system, travellers going long distances to and from outlying points, do pay a higher fare, in consideration of the many miles travelled. This is compensated for by having a lower fare for travelling short distances. In other words those wishing to shop in a downtown area pay an extra fare to do so; but on the other hand, those content with shopping areas close by, pay a relatively lower fare.

Such was formerly the case along the Britannia line. Each zone had a fare of 2 1/2 cents. If people wanted to travel from Britannia to the main shopping center of Ottawa (approximately eight miles) they paid a 12 1/2-cent fare. If they were content to travel to the nearby shopping center of Westboro (approximately three miles) they paid a five-cent fare.

This is how, to my knowledge, a system of zoning works. The residents of Britannia will not have the matter passed off another way. They will not rest until they, now as part the expanded city of Ottawa, are charged the same rates of fare as the rest of the city.

F.L. Smith, Secretary,
Britannia Community Club, Britannia Bay

Editor's note: The OTC eventually relented and imposed a flat fare for travel anywhere on the bus-streetcar system.

THE OTTAWA SPORTS BOOK

The 1948-49 Ottawa Senators, Allan Cup champions.

SENATORS STILL CROWD PULLERS

JANUARY 10, 1950

The remarks contained in Mr. A. Davies' letter headed "Come On, Senators!" contain the impression that attendance at Senators games has declined.

On the contrary, a modest increase in the early part of the season has now consolidated itself into an encouraging upward trend. If Mr. Davies would care to do so he may have this fact proven by the records.

The Senators appreciate the interest of Mr. Davies and other fans who have supported them. However, questions such as are contained in Mr. Davies' letter must be answered by performance on the ice. The highly creditable record they have compiled in the four years since the club was reorganized in the fall of 1945, advancing to the final round of Q.S.H.L. play twice, 1946 and 1947, advancing to the final round of Allan Cup play in 1948 and winning the Allan Cup in 1949, should not be discounted too soon.

The club will give a good account of itself in what promises to be the most interesting Quebec League race in several years. Despite several setbacks the club will not fall back on excuses or alibis when this year's hockey awards are presented at the season's end.

Even Barbara Ann Scott won't be blamed for the schedule which will see them play four games in five days on the road while she takes over the Auditorium with her touring Skating Sensations.

Frank Gorman,
Ottawa Senators Amateur Hockey Club, Inc.

Editor's note: For many years, Frank Gorman and his brother, Joe, managed the old Ottawa Senators for their father, T.P. Gorman, perhaps the most important figure in Ottawa sports history. The senior Gorman was not only a world-class athlete — at 22, he was the youngest member of Canada's 1908 gold medal Olympic lacrosse team — he was one of five men involved in the creation of the NHL in 1917, he owned the original NHL Senators and introduced harness racing and Triple-A baseball to Ottawa. When the original Senators left the NHL in 1934, the team was eventually reorganized as a senior team, playing first in a Montreal-area senior league and then its successor, the Quebec Senior Hockey League. The team was successful on and off the ice until the early 1950s, when attendance began to fall as the team struggled to win. The Senators folded in December 1954, blaming televised NHL games for their demise.

TWILIGHT DOUBTS
JANUARY 19, 1950

Could you tell us what the average man is supposed to do in order to be a good citizen in a "free enterprise" country? For over 40 years I worked hard to provide my children with a good education; scrimped and saved to pay for life insurance and a small government annuity. We did without things we couldn't afford — movies, travel, liquor, and other luxuries, and contributed to all worthy causes.

Now it seems that our provision for old age has been entirely inadequate and we are faced with serious financial problems owing to the high cost of everything. Should we have been thoroughly selfish and refused to contribute to the numerous social, charitable and welfare organizations that appeal for public support? Or should the government have been more alert in preventing profiteering?

The free-enterprise chaps certainly are making it hard for us who are trying to live on superannuation. The steel, lumber, clothing, flour, bread, glass, oil, coal, drug, and other industries are thriving. Free enterprise allows them freedom to lobby for high tariffs, to keep their prices up, or low tariffs, to keep costs down. But who is supposed to protect the ordinary people?

Between 1945 and 1948 the cost of fuel oil just about doubled. Yet, at the end of 1947 the oil companies reported the highest net profit in history!

What can the ordinary "good citizen" do when many of our cabinet ministers can be deceived by certain free-enterprisers. It would seem that even illegal combines can profiteer and increase net earnings regardless of conditions?

Are too many of our Members of Parliament shareholders in our vital industries? I know several who are.

Charles Wilson, Ottawa

OLD-AGE SECURITY
FEBRUARY 2, 1950

The public discussion about the need for pensions prompts the observation that medical science has done a better job of prolonging life than the rest of the community has in providing for the comfort and security of older persons.

In the first half of this century, the number of people over 60 in this country has increased from 7.7 per cent to 11 per cent of the total population. The passing of the horse-and-buggy era has complicated the problem of old age adjustment just at the time when the number of older persons is steadily increasing.

Our society is in the middle of the stream of social change from a rural culture of strong family ties to a highly urbanized, industrial society. Today, the family is only temporary, often breaking up when children are old enough to fend for themselves. As a result, many older persons are left out in the cold as far as the family or community is concerned.

Our present old-age pensions are inadequate, both from the standpoint of coverage and benefits. How can anyone live in a city these days, or anywhere for that matter, on a meagre $40 a month! Fifty dollars is the absolute minimum. Worse still are the age limit of 70 years and the means test to demonstrate need and prove residency. At present, only about 42 per cent of those eligible are participating in the plan. Many persons would rather suffer in poverty than submit to this means test.

The people over 60 are the men and women who did the spade work in making Canada the nation it is today. Yet when they need assistance they are offered a pittance. Elder members of the community who have not been able to provide for their later years, often through no fault of their own, have a right to a decent standard of living.

Contributory old age insurance would enable all to provide for retirement during their working years. Everyone would participate in such a plan and everyone would be entitled to benefits but nothing is accomplished by delaying the introduction of an old age insurance scheme.

Older persons have a definite contribution to make in community life. The experience gained in their triumphs and defeats can blaze the trail for future generations. After all, today's experiments are tomorrow's traditions.

The "sunset years" should and could be happy, useful years. Our senior citizens should not be put out to pasture and treated like "old fogies" who have to be taken care of and are no good for anything but dreaming of the "good old days."

Don Swain, Ottawa

Editor's note: The contributory plan suggested by the writer was not introduced until 1965, when the Canada Pension Plan and Quebec Pension Plan, compulsory programs based on earnings, were introduced, eventually covering more than 90 per cent of the labour force.

MARRIED WOMEN IN JOBS

MARCH 28, 1950

In her letter on married women in jobs, Mrs. Margaret Byrncs seems to have missed a few points.

I agree that in normal circumstances a woman's place is at home tending her children. The high cost of living, and I mention here the extremely high prices of apartments, houses, etc. and food prices, can definitely not be called normal at the moment. In comparison, salaries have gone up but little. For most of our working women it is a bare necessity to hold a job which will enable her family to exist more decently than would be possible without her help.

And don't think we like it so much either! It means working approximately 14-15 hours a day, and this especially in a hot summer is not to be recommended. While women at home may be fortunate enough to spend the best part of the summer on lawns and beaches, we are sitting in the stuffy offices during daytime and come home to housework. No, if it was up to us (ambitious career women exempted) we would all be at home enjoying privileges which are beyond our reach when working.

In a country like Canada there should be every possibility to develop new enterprises so that all the young men could get employment notwithstanding the fact that married women are holding jobs. Besides, most men could not support a family on the salaries we are receiving.

As an afterthought I am glad that my husband is not too narrow-minded to let me assist him financially, otherwise this would mean that we would spend the rest of our lives in two unheated rooms.

(Mrs.) William J. Larocque, Ottawa

AH! MOTHER'S DAY

MAY 17, 1950

Now that the tumult and the shouting are over and we have survived one more Mother's Day, I would like to mount my soapbox for a few moments and open an escape valve — I am sick to death of Mother's Day.

When I was younger, Mother's Day was sensibly observed by the wearing of a white flower as a mark of respect for one's mother. The minister made brief reference to the duty and responsibility that lay in the hands of the mother, and reminded the children that filial respect was the expected behaviour in civilized society. The whole thing was then over and done with, and that was decently that.

But not now, not any more. It's not even just a Day, now: it is Mother's Week at least, if not longer.

Take the radio. Every minute of the day, for days past, it has dripped oozy remarks, sticky with sentiment, about a synthetic creature that I sincerely hope doesn't exist.

But there's one thing I'm sure of: if my husband ever presents me with a gift for Mother's Day — why, my own mother's love will have to follow me to the highest hill, because I swear I'll murder the brute.

Kathleen Gillen, Ottawa

THE GOOD NEIGHBOURS

SEPTEMBER 20, 1950

"A friend in need is a friend indeed." This famous saying, as well as the "good neighbour" policy was again illustrated to me last Sunday.

My wife and I were enjoying the pleasures of motoring on Ottawa's lovely driveways when a tire went flat several miles from any source of aid. I got out and looked. I could flag a car to take my wife into town and send out a tow truck or I could try and make the change myself.

The trouble with the latter plan was that I was dressed in my "Sunday Best" and I didn't know how to change the tire anyway. Now, Sunday is a day of rest and Ottawa drivers must believe this for car after car whizzed by without even slowing down. Finally a car bearing an American license plate pulled to a stop just past us. A handsome head stuck out the window and spoke in a deep Southern drawl.

"Ah you havin' some trouble, suh? Is the-ar somethin' we could do for ya?" I rushed forward and asked if they could take my wife into town so that she would send out a mechanic to change the tire. I had no sooner explained my problem when the two piled out of their car and looking at the wheel exclaimed, "Why suh, we can fix that little thing for yuh!"

In a twinkling they had flipped the old wheel into the trunk and tightened the spare into place. I thanked them profusely and offered to pay them for their kind service. This they flatly refused.

We talked for a few moments about Canada and the United States and I remarked that the goodwill between our nations was wonderful. I asked them if they were visiting Canada.

"We're workin' here in Ottawa." Asked where, they told me they were members of the Ottawa Football Club. "Ah'm John Wagoner and my friend here is Bill Stanton."

I thanked them and they drove off leaving another pair of staunch Rough Riders fans and friends of our Southern Neighbours.

A. R. Manka, Ottawa

Editor's note: John Wagoner was an offensive-defensive lineman who played with the Riders for several years in the late 1940s and early '50s. A tobacco farmer from North Carolina, he was allowed to report late to training camp each year so he could bring in his crops. Bill Stanton, a defensive end and receiver, played for the Riders over roughly the same period as Wagoner (both played for the '51 team that won the Grey Cup). Another southerner, Stanton stayed in Ottawa for several years after his career with the Riders, coaching the football team at Carleton College, the forerunner of the university.

1951

Local: Ottawa's Charlotte Whitton becomes first female mayor of a major Canadian city (September); Princess Elizabeth and Philip, Duke of Edinburgh, visit Ottawa for first time since their marriage (October)

National: Canadian troops defend Kapyong Valley in Korea against Chinese attack, earning a U.S. Presidential Citation for their courage, a first for non-American soldiers (April); Census puts Canada's population at 14,009,429 (June); Report of Massey royal commission urges greater government support for the arts (June)

World: In sensational U.S. espionage trial, Julius and Ethel Rosenberg are convicted of giving wartime atomic bomb secrets to the Soviets. They are executed in June 1953 (March); British voters return Winston Churchill as prime minister after six years out of power (October); November truce ending Korean War is shortlived as fighting resumes along the 38th parallel dividing North and South (December)

Births: Canadian astronaut Roberta Bondar; dancer Karen Kain; Soviet chess champion Anatoly Karpov

Deaths: U.S. newspaper tycoon William Randolph Hearst; Nellie McClung, first Canadian woman elected to office; U.S. writer Sinclair Lewis; Harold Ross, founder of *New Yorker* magazine; composer Arnold Schoenberg; Austrian philosopher Ludwig Wittgenstein; Broadway star Fanny Brice

A TRAILER LIFE FOR ME

JANUARY 31, 1951

We read with interest and then with growing indignation your editorial titled Ottawa's Trailer 'Homes.' You are obviously under the impression that no one could possibly call a trailer a home!

Yet a great many intelligent hard-working people, perhaps possessed of a more self-reliant character than average, live in these trailers from choice, and find all this misinformation about trailer life rather irritating.

Take for example our own trailer camp, comprising 12 trailers. These have cost anywhere between $3,000 and $5,000; i.e. they're not exactly given away with cereal box-tops. They are equipped with every possible modern convenience considering size and price, including refrigerator or ice-box, full-size cooking stove, ample cupboard and storage space, and sleeping accommodation for four to six adults. We have a communal utility building containing bath, showers, toilets and laundry facilities. So much for the "elementary sanitary conditions" you condemn.

The poor housewives do try to make the trailers as attractive as possible, and believe me, it isn't very hard: Twenty minutes with vacuum cleaner and dust cloth and the glass and wood paneling of walls and ceiling mirror, the colourful draperies and bright knick-knacks so dear to the heart of the female, are spotless and sparkling.

The children have plenty of fresh air and sunshine all year round, and are as healthy a bunch of youngsters as you could see anywhere. They are free to play as they please within reason, without the landlord bogey being held over their heads.

All in all, we consider the advantages of trailer life far outweigh those of the city apartment dweller, and we should be able to judge, having lived in both!

Jeanne Miller, Rockland, Ont.

SCALPING, OLD AND NEW

FEBRUARY 6, 1951

Not so many years ago when a Canadian wanted a haircut he simply picked a fine afternoon, strolled into the woods and, in an unguarded moment, some co-operative Iroquois or Huron performed the job quickly, neatly and efficiently.

In those days the service was fast . . . no sitting around for hours waiting your turn . . . and satisfaction was guaranteed. There were never any complaints from the customer. Another advantage of this older, more honoured method was that the job was permanent. You didn't have to come back in a fortnight for a re-tread.

But, like many essential services, the scalp-lightening trade has gone from bad to worse. The old carefree catch-as-catch-can days have gone, replaced by an era of grim, mercenary scissors merchants.

This trend first became evident when barbers adopted the sadistic practice of subjecting their customers to long, harrowing political discussions. In those days there was also the hazard of cunningly-located spittoons which placed themselves underfoot at the most unexpected moment. These devices were replaced in time by such horrors as the crew cut, the facial massage, the scented hair tonic, the dull razor blade and the shoe shine concession.

But these innovations were as nothing compared to the latest trend — higher prices for lowered ears. The new motto seems to be, "A pound of flesh for an ounce of hair." And, judging by recent price history in the barber trade, there seems to be little actual hope that the tonsorial tacticians will hold to the 75-cent price line.

The reaction of most red-blooded men to the threat of higher cost of hair hacking is to swear off haircuts immediately. But the barbers are unafraid. They well know that most red-blooded men's wives will not permit their husbands to do any such thing. They know that business will continue as usual and returns will be higher than ever.

Do you happen to know any Indians?

B.M. Erb, Ottawa

THE FIVE-DAY WEEK

MARCH 24, 1951

A request by the Professional Institute of the Public Service of Canada for a five-day week for all civil servants would appear to be uncalled for.

There is every indication that the great majority of civil servants would be strongly opposed to any further lengthening of the work day in order to make up for the hours lost by eliminating the half day on Saturday.

This Association undoubtedly represents nobody but

themselves. As most of the higher-paid employees are not required to register their attendance, no one but themselves know how many hours they are on duty.

The case of the junior employee is very different. In the case of a five-day week they would work eight hours each day. Their work for the most part is of a monotonous nature, with very little diversion, performed in some cases without even five minute recess during the day.

Moreover, it has been proven that the same degree of efficiency cannot be maintained during an eight-hour day, and certainly not in an atmosphere such as exists in many government offices, where there is an overcrowding and poor ventilation. Also, the staggered hours now in effect would result in many getting out of work at 6 o'clock and 6:15 making it impossible to attend to certain obligations after hours. No, I think this is too big a price to pay for one half day off a week.

It is time that civil servants awakened and elected a truly representative body. The various civil service associations have in the past succeeded in obtaining nothing for the staff except salary increases which were long over due, and which no doubt would have been forthcoming in any event had suitable representations been made by the staff. After two years of negotiating they succeeded in introducing a health plan which offers nothing more than any individual can obtain from an insurance company.

Is it any wonder that the membership has dropped and is continuing to drop?

R. Murphy, Ottawa

Editor's note: In the early 1950s, the vast majority of civil servants put in a 36.5-hour work week — 6.5 hours from Monday to Friday and another four hours Saturday morning. In the summer of 1951, at the request of employees associations — there were no civil service unions until the 1960s — the government agreed to a five-day work week, with no reduction in hours, on a trial basis. It was considered a success, and implemented permanently in 1952 (outside Ottawa) and 1953 (in Ottawa) with one condition — civil servants had to agree to work an extra hour each week in exchange for getting their Saturdays off.

THE LACK OF A RINK
MAY 2, 1951

I am sorry that my recent letter regarding the need for indoor rinks in Ottawa has aroused Charlotte Whitton to such an extent that she is raining abuse on the head of both the editorial department of *The Citizen* and myself for "giving broad circulation to errors."

In my letter I merely stated the fact that an indoor rink in Ottawa was badly needed, and had been for many years now; that every town and village in Ontario and Quebec of any importance had their indoor rinks, and that the capital City of Canada at least should be put on even terms with those. I also stated that a plan for three indoor rinks submitted by the city Playgrounds department had been withdrawn by request of Controller Whitton. Here I quoted the newspapers.

If, as Miss Whitton states, a special study of the matter is to be given "leisurely study" by Board of Control in June or July, then so much the better, that leaves a tiny ray of hope. But I fear that it is only a move to strangle and kill the plans without raising much interest in the matter. It is well known that the people of Ottawa during the summer months show no interest whatever in anything connected with winter sports or activities.

Miss Whitton is guilty of errors when she states that only three or four teams could use the rink each night. Six teams could use the rink each night for games or practice making three games of one hour each, from 7 p.m. to 10 p.m. Besides that there is all day and afternoon for skating and practice.

Controller Whitton's barrage of technicalities is only a smoke-screen designed to obscure the pressing need for one indoor rink in Ottawa, but it does not work. Not with me and not with people connected to sporting activities in Ottawa.

When the top [minor hockey] teams from the city go out to play in the play-offs, they play against teams that all season have practised and played on indoor ice. We cannot invite these teams to Ottawa in a home-and-home game, because there is no ice available.

It has to be sudden death games, which is unfair, especially as the Ottawa teams have had very little practice and experience due to the weather conditions and the outdoor rinks. This is why the championship always goes to Buckingham, Cornwall, Carleton Place or Pembroke, etc., all of whom have the privilege of indoor rinks.

A.O. Olson, Ottawa

Editor's note: In 1951, the city's only indoor rinks were privately owned — the Auditorium on Argyle Street by the Gorman family, and the Minto Arena by the Minto Skating Club. Efforts to convince council to build a publicly owned facility went on until 1958, when construction was approved for an arena on Elmgrove Avenue, near Scott Street in Westboro. Called the Western District Arena when it opened in 1959, it still operates today as the Lion's Arena. As for Charlotte Whitton, the city controller was made mayor by a vote of Board of Control after Mayor Grenville Goodwin died in office in late August.

CANADA'S UNOBSERVED BIRTHDAY
JULY 4, 1951

From Canada's university of democracy — Parliament Hill — there was a ghostly, faith-shattering silence on July 1 because, once again, the so-called statesmen who claim to be the champions of democracy failed to practise what they preach. They urge every Canadian to believe in our free way of life, yet not one of our 262 elected representatives believed our heritage sacred enough to do something about it.

What would be that "something," it may be asked? If the "statesmen" of this great nation were not so stagnated in self-preservation they would have organized some sort of a Parliament Hill celebration to honour the anniversary of the nation's birth.

Can you see Washington, or any city, town or hamlet in

the United States letting July 4 go by with just the raising of a flag? We Canadians are prone to brush aside such U.S. demonstrations of solidarity as so much "ballyhoo" and "national propaganda," but in those same United States today you will find a more fervent patriotism than we have here in Canada.

This, therefore, is a censure for all of Canada's paid representatives for not making something more of July 1 than a day of rest or another holiday to add to their three months respite from wrangling in the green-carpeted chamber. None of them can offer a *bona fide* excuse for this dereliction of duty. They were in Ottawa until late Saturday night, so any one with an iota of gumption could have organized a fitting tribute to the nation's birthday with little trouble.

We rise in righteous wrath when anyone suggests that ours is a "decadent democracy" but we must question if our animosity is sound when we see such an apathetic approval of our freedom as was shown here on July 1.

The gargoyles peering out from the four corners of the clock tower showed more animation than our federal politicians who are sent here by the people to "fight, work, give — make democracy live." Canadian democracy has been given a black eye by the very men who are entrusted with its care.

Don C. Brown, Ottawa

Editor's note: Although Canada's birthday had been celebrated on Parliament Hill during special years — in 1927, for example, 60 years after Confederation — it was a relatively quiet affair most years until 1967. That year, the capital threw a giant 100th birthday party on the Hill, featuring a huge cake, day-long entertainment, an afternoon walkabout by the Queen and Prince Philip and an evening fireworks show. Since then, the July 1 party has become an annual institution on the Hill.

IN FAVOUR OF PARKING METERS
AUGUST 16, 1951

Regarding your editorial, "The Parking Meter As A Tax," I fail to see where and how parking meters installed in Ottawa would impose hardship on any special group, as you state. I am a taxpayer as well as a motorist, and would welcome any source of revenue your City Council could find, other than increasing the over-burdened taxpayers' taxes on property.

Most cities and towns in Ontario have installed parking meters. Motorists from Ottawa are compelled to pay to park on the streets in these places just as do the local motorists. I think it only fair that visiting motorists pay for the use of parking space on our streets.

With the high cost of gasoline, etc., it would cost less to put a few pennies in a meter than to have to drive around a block five or six times looking for a space to park. One motorcycle traffic policeman could check more meters for violation than most of the men now using the back-bending, tire-marking, on-foot method of checking parking violations.

A.G. Ruffo, Ottawa

Editor's note: Using the argument it would diminish tourism, Ottawa resisted the installation of parking meters until April 1958.

THE HOCKEY BROADCASTS
AUGUST 18, 1951

On behalf of the patients of the Royal Ottawa sanatorium this letter is being written to protest the decision of the directors of the Ottawa Senators Hockey Club to discontinue all hockey broadcasts for the coming season.

We wonder if Mr. T.P. Gorman ever considered that there are hundreds of people in the city who would attend the games but are unable to, either through illness or disabilities. During the past two seasons our only means of following the Senators was through the radio broadcasts. It had become our major source of entertainment and we are sure it didn't affect the box-office to the extent that the broadcasts had to be discontinued.

We ourselves cannot imagine someone passing up an opportunity of seeing a hockey game to stay at home and listen to it on the radio. Moreover, the broadcasts certainly must have helped to make the Senators a much more popular hockey club throughout the Ottawa Valley.

So come on! Give us fellows a break! Many of us have played hockey, and we are sure we don't want to be satisfied with just reading about it in the newspaper.

Len McCormick, Ken York, O.L. Bouvier, Ottawa

Editor's note: Despite many such letters and, presumably, other forms of pressure, it appears the hockey broadcasts were not resumed.

FROM AN ARMY WIFE
DECEMBER 5, 1951

It is 8:45 a.m. and I am sitting here in my kitchen , 22 miles from civilization, surrounded by dirty dishes, sandy floors and the assorted socks, sweaters and pants of three under-5-year-olds. To say that I am browned off is putting it mildly.

Now why am I picking your shoulder to weep on? Because you published an article recently by Jack Scott entitled, "You Can Beat It," and I am one of those housewives who, as Mr. Scott so aptly puts it, is "chained to monotony and drudgery."

Mr. Scott recommends that we "Develop fresh interests — learn something new. There are millions of doors out from an enclosed life."

Of these millions of doors, I am trying to think of just one. Here I am enclosed by the confines of a military camp, the mountains, and the barrier of being English in a French-speaking community. Not only that: I am socially enclosed by the military caste system which in an army camp decrees that the sergeant's wife doesn't speak to the corporal's wife.

I am still further enclosed by the demands of a seven-room house plus basement, stairs, hallways and verandas, and the demands also of four children (one at school), to say nothing of the demands, wants and needs of the head of the household who, like all men, (Jack Scott excepted on the strength of his article), think that just being a house-wife all day long and seven nights a week is the ultimate aim and goal of every woman born.

The radio has just announced cheerfully that "it is time to do the dishes." See what I mean? The announcer, of course, is a male just giving the little woman a nudge in case she has decided to linger too long over that extra cup of coffee and cigaret.

For the record, I am an old Ottawa girl and before I moved here to the wilderness I occasionally used to break the monotony of living by getting a job for a few months at a time. I'd get some new clothes, meet new people, get a fresh outlook on life and when I returned to the arms of my family at nights I could even love them all again.

The main purpose of my letter is to congratulate Jack Scott on his sympathetic approach to this modern prob-lem of women and ask him to do another article or two along the same lines. We subscribe to the *Citizen* regular-ly, and I must admit that going for the mail and getting my copy of the paper is the one bright spot in the day for me — my one adventure.

How low can a woman get?

Ruby Baird,
Valcartier Camp, Que.

A CANADIAN FOR GOVERNOR GENERAL

DECEMBER 8, 1951

Although I yield to no one in my respect to the ties that bind Canada to the Old Country, I cannot agree with the letter written by A. Brownlee, who observes "the man best fitted for the position of Governor General is an Eng-lishman."

That sentence seems to argue that no Canadian is fitted to be Governor General of Canada. Such a stand runs counter to the published result of the recent public opin-ion poll on this issue. More than 65 per cent of those ques-tioned across Canada stated that they wished to have a Canadian as our next Governor General, while 24 per cent wished to have one from Great Britain chosen.

The Governor General of Australia is a native son. This goes also for New Zealand, South Africa and Pakistan. Does Mr. Brownlee argue that these distinguished gentle-men are unfitted to represent His Majesty the King? After all, each of them was appointed by the King.

V.M. Baldwin, Ottawa

Editor's note: The majority of Canadians got their wish on Feb. 28, 1952 when Vincent Massey became the first Canadian-born Governor General.

1952

Local: Unhappy that a Canadian has been named governor general, Mayor Charlotte Whitton boycotts installation of Vincent Massey (February); Parliamentary library is badly damaged by fire (August); In municipal elections, Whitton wins mayoralty; plebiscite to allow Sunday sports is soundly defeated (December)

National: Lester Pearson elected president of the UN General Assembly (October); Shakespeare-an Festival Theatre is founded in Stratford (November)

World: King George VI dies and is succeeded by his daughter, Elizabeth (February); Dwight Eisenhower, with Richard Nixon as his running mate, is elected U.S. president; John F. Kennedy is first elected to Senate (November); Korean war appears to be close to truce after visit from president-elect Eisenhower (December)

Births: Tennis star Jimmy Connors; basketball player Bill Walton

Deaths: Canadian economist Harold Innis; Quebec nationalist Henri Bourassa; Argentine heroine Eva Peron; U.S. educator John Dewey; philosopher George Santayana

ROYAL FRUMPERY

FEBRUARY 16, 1952

I read Mr. Adam Bonner's recent letter with an odd mix-ture of wonder and disgust. Can he not see that that which does not progress does not survive?

What possible benefit can come from such long and burdensome titles, i.e. Royal Mail, Dominion, OHMS, etc.? It would appear that that which does not have a title long enough to bog it down completely is not considered satis-factory. Possibly I am unimaginative but I really cannot see what is "magnetic" about OHMS or "proud" about the title "Royal Mail." Why should Canada be so burdened with these gaudy, frumpery designations?

Sweeping with the same broom are those who object to a Canadian Governor General. We should feel proud that a Canadian [Vincent Massey] was considered worthy of this honour. If the protesters are ashamed of Canada and its people, why can't they say this in so many words?

I think that we should be heartily ashamed of such citi-zens. Let them cling to the customs of a distant land if they wish. As Canadians, we should stand square on our own feet; we cannot add to our status as a nation by trampling on all that is Canadian.

So, let us have our own flag, our own national anthem. Let us remain no longer followers of an old leader; we should become leaders ourselves.

In closing, the thought most distant from my mind is that we should break all ties with the Royal Family. Not that! But all other British ties, yes.

Fyffe Cooper, Vankleek Hill, Ont.

A DESPONDENT MOTHER

MARCH 8, 1952

I am raising a family of four girls and one boy, ages 18, 16, 14, 10 and 9 years. I have been living in my present home, in Lower Town, for the past 15 years and during this period have had two very good landlords. But now, much as it hurts my landlord, as well as myself, he was forced to give me notice to vacate in order to get a home for his father-in-law who also must vacate owing to his landlord wanting to make repairs.

Now, when we look for a place we're told, "We don't take children" (as if they were not, themselves, children at one time). Or else the rent is so high we cannot afford to pay it.

We understand the government needs the Rockcliffe and Uplands shelters for the defence of our country, which is a very vital necessity. But could not enough money be scraped up to build similar accommodation elsewhere until this housing crisis is past? I'm sure it would be a very charitable and human act.

Many of us would like to build our own little homes, but with the prices of food, fuel, clothing, building materials, and the restrictions, we cannot.

(Mrs.) Mildred Lajoie, Ottawa

CBC'S 'HORROR' NEWSCASTS
MARCH 12, 1952

I protest that CBC newscasts are valueless in the nourishment of citizenship. They are inimical to the Christian sensibilities of men. Particularly are they a serious menace to the enthusiasm for adventure, and confidence in the inherent rightness of virtue that every youth must have as minimum equipment of the strenuous years of adulthood.

The newsbroadcasts are read without a fault yesterday, today and forever. Disaster piled on horror, and panic polished up with hysteria. Even on a Sunday morning when we might just conceivably expect a change in emphasis, we are given to understand that if anyone thinks being alive offers some inducement to satisfaction he is badly informed.

Agreed that the news content of such broadcasts is "news." But is it necessary or right that I should be left with the impression that such "news" alone is important? Were there no thrilling dramas in the air flights that were successfully completed? Surely someone got on with someone else and in a matter that concerns me? Who recovered by some miracle of healing? Who did something superbly brave? Give me some reasons to lift up my head; to love mercy and to value trust in the almighty power of God — in Whom I still believe, I and hundreds of thousands of other Canadians!

Any adult knows that life is strenuous and that disasters can strike the most innocent and inoffensive. But most of us believe that life is worthwhile, and that no disaster can destroy the valiant Christian spirit. Instinctively men respond to the challenge of good news. Those of us who work so closely with people know that the greatest folly is not in failing to remind experienced adults that disasters happen, but in teaching by implication that they alone are newsworthy.

Of course, we should resent "pollyanna" broadcasts just as strongly as we resent this interminable series of frightfulness. In time we may come to the point at which we shall listen to horrors with complete indifference. That

will be national disaster of the most catastrophic kind. For we shall be sub-Christian.

Macbeth spoke to news broadcasts when in bitterness he wrung his hands and cried: "We do but teach bloody instruction which, being taught, returns to plague the inventor."

(Rev.) Owen G. Barrow,
Marathon, Ont.

TOO MANY PATIENTS,
TOO FEW BEDS
MAY 17, 1952

Dr. J.K.M. Dickie's recent letter dealing with the lack of beds at the Ottawa Civic Hospital was the subject of able editorial comment in the local press in support. It followed an excellent presentation of the facts by the Hospital Trustees to the city Board of Control, who are now regarding it as gross exaggeration.

It would appear that the only way of acquainting the taxpaying public of Ottawa with the ghastly situation that prevails is by statement of irrefutable facts — for which we beg space in your columns. The need for expansion has been increasingly apparent to the medical staff since the end of the war, when it became obvious that the number of patients requiring hospitalization was never going to decrease (owing to increase of population).

The waiting list today is over 1,700, of whom only some 550 are tonsil cases. The hospital has tried to cope with this situation by setting up various emergency procedures. Thus, patients applying for admission have for several years been divided into three categories: elective, urgent and emergency.

a) Elective cases are those in which treatment, while necessary, can be deferred. Examples are hernias, haemorrhoids, prolapses, etc. These uncomfortable, and very often disabling conditions are forced to wait from nine to 15 months for admission.

b) Urgent cases comprise those where treatment which should be immediate has to be deferred on account of lack of beds. Examples, again, of these are chronic haemorrhage, heart disease and possible cancers. These unfortunates have to live and sleep with their worry for two to eight or more weeks before admission.

c) Emergency cases are self-definitive, such as acute appendix, sudden heart attacks, injuries etc. These are treated to the very best of the hospital's ability. While there are no beds specifically available for them, and while it is impossible most of the time to keep any beds vacant for possible emergencies, nevertheless accommodation is arranged if necessary in sunrooms, corridors, etc. In spite of such a makeshift, however, immediate admission is often not possible and a delay of several hours is of frequent occurrence.

As this is a matter of transcendent importance to the community, over one per cent of whom — men, women and children — are at present on the waiting list for admission, we hope that the courtesy of further space may be accorded us in the near future in order that the citizens of Ottawa may come to appreciate the difficulties under

The Ottawa Civic Hospital had to wait another eight years before work on a 260-bed addition was completed, following years of conflict between the Civic and city council.

which their hospital is operating, and the necessity for immediate remedial action.

L.D. Wilson, MD,
Secretary, Publicity Committee,
General Medical Board
Ottawa Civic Hospital

Editor's note: The conflict between the city and the hospital continued for several more years before city council and the provincial and federal governments agreed to construct a new 260-bed building adjacent to the original hospital. The new $5.5-million building was completed in 1960, and featured a large new maternity ward, 12 operating rooms and enlarged emergency facilities. The addition brought the Civic's overall capacity up to 1,200 beds and 125 nursery bassinets.

EPISODE ON THE VELDT
JUNE 28, 1952

I don't presume to suggest any solution to deal with the non-whites of South Africa, but I do believe that the majority of the blacks there are desirous of a racial "uplift," and that if only the national government would pass some legislation that would control but still give them some help to that end the present discord would be greatly reduced.

On the other hand, if they are further subjugated I see no end to the trouble.

I would like to cite an apparently simple episode which happened to me during the Boer War. I was in the Karroo desert on a certain day, and took the opportunity of entering a Kaffir hut, with an eye, I must confess, to getting some of their brown (distinctly so) bread. But when I saw the meager contents of the so-called home, I couldn't do it. The mother was there with two or three children including a little girl about 7, and two or three hens. The father, a goatherder, was on the veldt tending his goats.

The family was a little frightened at first, as, of course, I had a uniform on. I soon reassured them and on leaving gave the little girl a "ticky" — worth about 6 cents. I had not gone very far from the hut when I heard footsteps behind me, and on catching me up the little girl timidly put two hen's eggs in my hands. She would have made right off again but I held her attention for a moment or two, by pretending to eat and enjoy the eggs. I just had time to pat her head, for which I think I got a little smile, and she was off home again.

It all seemed very simple but she was unknowingly helping to fulfill one of the great spiritual precepts. Of course this happened long ago, but I have written it in the hope that there are often strange possibilities in the noble but uphill work of the missionaries.

G.H. Wattsford,
Ottawa

THOSE STREET NAMES
AUGUST 9, 1952

Your proposal for a large-scale re-naming of the streets seems to me a most extraordinary aberration.

Granted, there may be excellent reasons for re-naming a particular street, Laurier is certainly an improvement on Maria, Lisgar on Biddy, and Gladstone on Anne. And where adjoining streets have very similar names as with Lakeview Terrace and Lakeside Avenue the resulting confusion may justify changing one of them.

That the City Fathers apparently can't spell Roseberry, and that a good many inhabitants call Gloucester "Glossesster" might justify changing those, though a little educational work might be more appropriate. There may also be some reason for changing the name of a particular street to commemorate some great man, or woman.

But your "broader program" seems to me just another example of the inexplicable itch to change things merely for the sake of changing them.

Your specific suggestions are not reassuring. Queen Street you single out as one of those whose "names have little meaning." Why? Doesn't it commemorate Queen Victoria, in whose reign Confederation took place, and whose birthday we still celebrate?

You would change it to Queen Elizabeth, and in fifty years someone else, with equal reason (or lack of it) would doubtless want to change it to King Charles (or perhaps, by that time, President What-not; though God forbid!).

I suppose Albert will have to become Duke of Edinburgh? Metcalfe commemorated a Governor who resisted responsible government: presumably that will have to go. Sussex, you suggest, might become Confederation; and Little Sussex, I suppose, Little Confederation?

Commemorating great men is all very well, but there is always the danger of premature decision. In the first flush of rapture after Munich, I recall, there were suggestions that Elgin Street should be re-named Chamberlain Way. This idea probably seems less attractive now. If it had been adopted, by 1940 there would probably have been a demand to change it again, perhaps to Churchill.

By now, somebody might have decided that Borden or Mackenzie King would be even more appropriate.

Your "broader program," once started, might be very hard to stop. There would be a tendency for every fresh City Council to try its hand at re-moulding the street names nearer to its heart's desire.

You feel confident that widespread changes, including such streets as Queen, Bank and Sussex, wouldn't cause any appreciable confusion, because the changes in some of the newly annexed suburbs didn't.

Surely there is a vast difference between changing the name of a small street in, say, Westboro, with a dozen or so houses on it, and changing the names of Bank, Queen and Sussex, with thousands of homes, stores and offices?

Eugene Forsey, Ottawa

Editor's note: Mr. Forsey, an economist, author, constitutional expert and for nine years in the 1970s a senator, was also a prolific writer of letters to the editor. Using his trademark dry, often acidic style, Mr. Forsey wrote hundreds of letters to newspapers across Canada on any subject that made him rankle, or giddy. Many more of his letters appear on the pages ahead.

HOUSEWIVES ON VACATION
AUGUST 30, 1952

A recent article by Jack Scott regarding the trials and tribulations of housewives at summer cottages prompted me to write the enclosed lines (with apologies of course to Longfellow). We don't have a summer cottage and I'm sure now we never will!

Came they to their summer cottage,
To their cabin in the forest,
To their weatherbeaten cabin
With its leaky roof of asphalt,
Saw they that the door was broken,
And the porch was old and shaky,
And the windows streaked and dirty,
All in all, a mess entirely,
While the children went in swimming,
And the father did some fishing,
And the dog went groundhog hunting,
Mother set about the cleaning,
Scrubbed the cottage inside outside,
Made the windows bright and shiny,
Washed the curtains stiff and starchy,
Swept and polished, cleaned and painted,
Chased the mice and fought mosquitoes,

Chopped the wood and hauled the water,
Cooked the meals and washed the dishes,
While the children went in swimming,
And the father did some fishing,
And the dog went groundhog hunting,
So through all the long vacation,
Thus did Mother toil and labour,
Till the summer months were over,
And they headed for the city,
Headed for the dusty city,
To their seventh floor apartment,
With its light and running water,
Electric stove and fridge and iron,
And all the other city comforts,
Thus the long vacation ended,
And the Mother, weak and weary,
Sank into the nearest armchair,
Sank into its cosy cushions,
Heaved a sigh and then she murmured,
"Though it's pretty in the country,
Ain't it heaven in the city?"

Mrs. Barbara Ditmar,
Deep River, Ont.

EIGHT POINTS
NOVEMBER 15, 1952

As civic election day draws near, we hear more and more about the Sunday sports issue. What are the arguments against sport we hear?

1. "Sport but not commercialized sport." Football, hockey and baseball require money for playing fields, equipment and travelling expenses even for amateur teams. If it provides entertainment surely it is not wrong to support the team.

2. "Active participation in sport is to be encouraged but spectator participation, particularly on Sunday, is wrong." It would be nice if more people could actually play in the game. It must be recognized, however, that watching sport is enjoyable even as a Sunday symphony is enjoyed by those in the audience, some of whom are unable to play a musical instrument.

3. "Some people, such as groundskeepers, will be forced to work on Sunday." This is a reasonable objection, provided it can be shown that those affected do, in fact, object to such work on Sunday.

4. "People living near sports parks will be bothered by the large crowds and noise." This is a sound objection, and the people concerned have a real reason to vote against Sunday sport.

5. "Our young people will be led astray." Attendance at a football, hockey or baseball game would seem to be less harmful than some of the alternative activities, such as horse racing, now available to them only a short drive away on Sunday.

6. "Attendance at churches will be reduced." The hours allotted to sport in other parts of Ontario do not seem to conflict with the hours of church services.

7. "Commercialized sport would be first, Sunday movies next, and soon Ottawa would be a wide open town

on Sunday." Surely Ottawa is not a Godless city held in check only by force. The influence of the churches on the community is much greater than is thought by those who advance this argument.

8. "Commercialized sport on Sunday is evil." If this is the case, then it is also evil on Saturday and we should outlaw completely commercialized sport. We have, however, accepted commercialized sport in Ottawa as fine and often outstanding entertainment.

Since we should have only one moral code which applies every day of the week, it follows that if commercial-

ized sport is accepted Monday to Saturday, it should be acceptable on Sunday.

C.R. Crocker,
Ottawa

Editor's note: The question of whether to allow Sunday sports was easily defeated in a municipal referendum in December 1952. The question was put to voters three more times before public opinion finally overturned the Sunday ban on professional sports in 1965.

1953

Local: Golf course at McKellar Park in city's west end is proposed for housing development and a shopping centre, eventually to become Carlingwood (April); Ottawa's first television stations, the CBC-outlet CBOT and its French-language counterpart, CBOFT, begin regular broadcasting (September)

National: National Library of Canada is established in Ottawa (January); Armistice signed to end Korean War. Canadian casualties set at 314 killed, 1,211 wounded, 33 captured (July); Inmate riot at Kingston Penitentiary results in a dozen injuries, destruction of three buildings, $2 million in damages (August)

World: Soviet premier Josef Stalin dies after stroke; Georgi Malenkov is named his successor (March); Dr. Jonas Salk's vaccine against polio is tested successfully on 90 children and adults (March); New Zealand adventurer Edmund Hillary becomes first to scale Mount Everest (June)

Births: Canadian dancer Frank Augustyn; boxer Trevor Berbick

Deaths: Poet Dylan Thomas; U.S. playwright Eugene O'Neill; athlete Jim Thorpe; country singer Hank Williams; Russian composer Sergei Prokofiev; gypsy jazz guitarist Django Reinhardt

CATERING TO THE 'COMMIES'

JANUARY 9, 1953

The Rosenbergs have been tried in an American court of justice on the charge of high treason, and were found guilty and sentenced to die. Behind the iron curtain, people who are charged with spying for foreign powers have a "trial" and are executed within days of its conclusion. The Rosenbergs have had a fair trial and, being found guilty they must die.

To those who say, "What about the Rosenbergs' children?" I say they are better off in a state orphanage.

The people who parade in front of the United States Embassy here in Ottawa are only making fools of themselves. Some may not be "Commies" but they are, in their effort, catering to the Communist party in Canada.

If the Rosenbergs eventually manage to secure complete freedom, I don't doubt that they would continue their spying.

The proper way to control disease insects is to kill them. As insects which endanger the peace of the world the Rosenbergs deserve that treatment.

W. Leonard Stanbrook,
Carlsbad Springs, Ont.

Editor's note: In one of the most highly publicized trials of the time, Julius and Ethel Rosenberg, a husband and wife from New York, were convicted in 1951 of stealing U.S. atomic bomb secrets and giving them to the Soviet Union. They were sentenced to death. The outcome ignited a fierce public debate laced with accusations that the Rosenbergs, who maintained their innocence to the end, were the victims of

THE ASSOCIATED PRESS

Ethel and Julius Rosenberg were executed in 1953 after they were convicted of stealing U.S. atomic bomb secrets. The couple maintained their innocence to the end.

anti-communist fervour and anti-semitism. After years of appeals, and a request for clemency submitted to president Dwight Eisenhower, the Rosenbergs were executed in June 1953. Their two young sons went to live with Mrs. Rosenberg's sister.

UP WITH THE TOWER!

JANUARY 13, 1953

My compliments to Mrs. Mary Wingrove for her timely letter under the caption "TV Tower versus Aerials." When the proposed site of a TV tower on Richmond Road was announced, I felt that Ottawa was finally making some progress towards television transmission. It is with regret that I note Mayor Whitton's objection to the proposed site on the basis that the adjacent Bingham house has historical value.

I say to h___ with the Bingham estate as a place to be pointed out as 100 years old, but hurrah for it as a place from which marvelous entertainment for countless residents could emanate!

We have the distinction of having the oldest street-cars, worst pavements and unfairest property tax on any city in the province. So who is going to worry if we have one of the highest TV towers?

Let's go modern! It can be fun.

J. A. Spencer, Ottawa

Editor's note: The tower was eventually erected, although it was about 25 feet shorter than originally proposed, in deference to Mayor Whitton.

ADVICE ON CIVIL DEFENCE

FEBRUARY 23, 1953

I am writing in reference to the recent letter from Mr. S. J. Gilberg, who is a public-spirited citizen, alive to the awful-possibilities of the hydrogen bomb. Civil defence is everybody's concern. Everybody must share in preparedness or take the consequences.

This correspondent, a former chief of small arms in Canada's Permanent Force, offered his time and knowledge to the city, and was officially snubbed.

General Worthington does a good job as Canada's top atomic "watch dog." The Corps of Commissionaires is a valuable aid in civil defence, but, so far as is known, only Sergeant-Major C. T. E. Coleman and Staff-Sergeant W. G. Comrie are trained in atomic defence.

Yet everybody — ministers, deputies, office boys, bank managers, clerks, controllers, street cleaners, senators, clergy — should have some knowledge of civil defence. Then — when the crash comes — if they can't help others at least they can help themselves.

I am unable to go all the way on "evacuation" as a civil defence measure. Will there be time? Better, if trained, to stay put, stand fast. The bomb or its effects will catch up with you even when running away. A bomb warning may be a couple of moments.

I believe that if Ottawa is a city worth living in, even without civil defence, it is a city worth dying in. Death is a great leveler, with no class distinction.

We must prepare and prepare now! After that, we must trust our airmen to drop a dozen bombs on the enemy for every one he drops on us.

W. K. Walker,
Ottawa

ON SUNDAYS ONLY

MARCH 11, 1953

Open rejoicing and, I gather, even cheering, in local cinemas at the announcement of the death of Josef Stalin hardly befits a civilized, so-called Christian community.

An appreciable percentage of such people no doubt attend church on Sundays, and perhaps in the week also. Can it be that the Ten Commandments are for Sunday observance only?

If such primeval demonstrations are made by the public, how can we expect the politicians to do better in the international field? They are, among other things, merely our representatives. We may secretly hope for an improvement in international relationships, but why rejoice when Georgi Malenkov [Stalin's shortlived successor] is an even greater enigma?

B. H. Atkins, Ottawa

CORONATION CLEAN-UP

APRIL 2, 1953

If we really want to honour the Queen at her Coronation, there is one very simple and inexpensive way to do it: Clean up her Canadian Capital City.

At present, every street in the place looks as if the whole population had been running a paper-chase with cigarette boxes, candy and gum wrappers, and miscellaneous rubbish. Just tidying this mess up would be a far better way of expressing our loyalty than any number of robes, shields and fireworks.

1. The city should get some hundreds of large, strong metal waste-baskets, and plant them on all the main street corners, outside all the schools, and near as many of the candy and soft drink shops as possible.

2. The schools should start a campaign to get the children to put rubbish in waste-baskets, public or private. Until the city provides public ones, the children should be told to take their rubbish home and put it in the family waste-basket. Such a campaign would be a most valuable edition to "social studies" courses.

3. Decent citizens should take a vow not to throw papers on the streets, but to take it home and place it in the waste-basket or garbage-can. Those who find this too much of a strain on their intellects might at least try not to tear up the paper they do throw on the streets. One piece of rubbish torn into 50 pieces doesn't make less mess. It makes a lot more.

4. We might also all take a vow that when we see people throw rubbish on the street, we should pick it up and hand it to them. It's their property, and when they drop it it's only courteous to restore it to them. This would help to cope with the pedestrian litter-strewer. The motorist who flings debris out of his window as he speeds along is a tougher problem. Perhaps we need a special anti-litter by-law to cover him; then we could report his number and let the law take its course.

All this may sound pretty drastic. But will anything less work? It's about time we made up our minds whether Ottawa is a city or a glorified pig-pen.

Eugene Forsey, Ottawa

FLOWERPOT HOLES

MAY 7, 1953

Since the potholes in our Ottawa streets seem to be here to stay, may I suggest that they be put to practical use.

With the annual Tulip Festival coming soon, wouldn't it be a lovely idea to fill these potholes with good Canadian soil and then plant a tulip bulb in them? Canadians, loving flowers as we do, would certainly avoid the pot-holes, and save the wear and tear on our cars.

Besides, the lovely tulips would improve the looks of our shamefully kept streets.

Mrs. Myrtle Stevens, Ottawa

THE "8" EXCHANGE

JUNE 24, 1953

Is there any good reason why the telephone subscribers on the "8" exchange have to suffer the pangs and tortures of the ancient system by which we need an operator to make a connection while other parts of Ottawa have had the dial system for at least 15 years?

Recently I had my telephone changed from a party line to a private one, hoping that the removal of the strong-jawed female on the other half of the line would result in better service (all at extra cost, of course!)

Alas, it seems it just isn't meant to be. Frequently when I call home from a dial telephone I wait and wait and wait and then, suddenly, come the smooth dulcet tones of a "Bell" operator, sweetly asking me what number I was calling. I tell her eagerly, glad of the assistance about to be offered me, and then I am told to hang up and dial the number again!

This sometimes goes on for hours.

The straw that broke, etc., etc., etc., was a few nights ago when through the weird machinations of some electronic gremlin I found myself the middleman in a three-way conversation, nothing of which I knew anything about. My brief role in this triangle ended when one of the women (naturally it was women talking) told me to mind my business and hang up, which I did, blushing furiously to think what they thought of their neighbours.

I'd have phoned you about this beef, Mr. Editor, but wanted you to suggest some remedy this month — not in July!

Tom O. Moore, Ottawa

ACRES OF CONCRETE

SEPTEMBER 5, 1953

You are to be commended on the stand you are taking on behalf of the citizens who are trying to retain the McKellar Golf Club property either as a greenbelt or certainly not less than a restricted area.

One of the features of the proposed shopping centre is a parking lot for 1,350 cars. What this means in traffic is obvious, but perhaps the worst feature is that it means replacing the green areas of McKellar with acres of concrete, and the architect does not live who can make anything other than an eye-sore out of a parking lot, no matter how useful they may be in their place, which is certainly not in the heart of a residential district.

Surely the residents of the McKellar district — long established as a residential area — deserve something better than this.

Arthur May, Ottawa

COMES THE DELUGE!

NOVEMBER 16, 1953

An editorial published in your paper some time ago touching the possibilities of artificial rain-making has been brought to my attention.

Well, sir, for 12 years I have been operating a rain machine of my invention which will produce increased rainfall scientifically. The power of this machine produces an electro-magnetic-gravitational pull on the moon as a medium to draw air-currents, rain clouds and rain from the Pacific Ocean and the Gulf of Mexico to areas in Saskatchewan, Alberta and Manitoba. It is, in principle, applying gravity as a means of power to draw inland the rainfall from its source or origin, the sea.

And it is through the operation of this machine that the record wheat crop of 1952, in Western Canada, was produced — as well as the bumper crops of 1942, 1951 and 1953.

In the past few summers, newsreel men on three different occasions wished to make a film record of the operation of this machine with, of course, the accompanying results — rain. And the following is the usual routine with which they proceed to make the picture record:

(1) Starting on the day of their choice, at about 1 o'clock in the afternoon, with a clear blue sky and the weather forecast "clear and fair," or "sunny." And with no forecast for rain — that would be out.

(2) Now, with the camera trained on my machine, and on the sky in the direction from which I am to draw the clouds, and;

(3) The clouds are coming. Out on a farmer's field on the open prairie you have a good, wide picture of the sky. The clouds are getting closer. And blacker. Then they are coming over-head. It starts to rain. The rain comes heavier, with lightning and thunder.

And here is a moving picture record of actual rain-making that has been shown many times in theaters.

Donald S. Johnston, Regina

1954

Local: National Capital Commission considers moving Central Experimental Farm out of urban area, but relents under public pressure (June); British prime minister Winston Churchill visits Ottawa for first time since war (June); Ottawa's Charlotte Whitton and other area mayors announce plans for east-west expressway across region (October)

National: Marilyn Bell becomes first person to swim across Lake Ontario, a distance of 32 miles (September); Major uranium discovery is made at Elliot Lake, Ont. (September); Hurricane Hazel strikes southern Ontario, killing 83, causing extensive flooding and $250 million in damage (October)

World: Baseball legend Joe DiMaggio marries Marilyn Monroe (January); U.S. Senator Joseph McCarthy expands scope of his hunt for communists from the government and entertainment industry to the military and the White House (February); First rock 'n' roll hit, *Rock Around the Clock,* is recorded (April); U.S. Supreme Court outlaws racial segregation in American public schools (May)

Births: TV personality Oprah Winfrey; singer Dan Hill; actress Kathleen Turner; astronaut Steve MacLean; writer Diane Schoemperlen

Deaths: Artist Henri Matisse; American composer Charles Ives; Canadian war artist Mary Riter Hamilton; actor Lionel Barrymore

LIFELIKE ATTITUDES

FEBRUARY 10, 1954

It was an agreeable sight to watch the clever and enterprising ice sculptor creating a piece of igloo-land outside the police station. Such an endeavour should be warmly praised and encouraged — and extended.

On the lawn in front of the Parliament buildings we might have, for educational purposes, a Senatorial session outlined in ice and snow, demonstrating in chill solemnity their inert functional purpose in the constitution of the realm. Or we might go farther and have our clever snow-carver portray in flouncing and frosty furbelows the mayor of our city in one of her tirades.

Let the Board of Trade capitalize on this accursed climate until the spring flowers come.

M. Dellis, Kingsmere, Que.

SENATOR MCCARTHY'S GOOD WORK

MARCH 31, 1954

Senator Joseph McCarthy's scheduled visit to Toronto has been cancelled, temporarily at least. While many opposed the idea of bringing him to this country, others believed it to be an excellent way of scaring Canadian Communists. I am among the latter.

When we realize the terrible ravages of Communist infiltration in other countries, we ask ourselves: is it right to condemn the work of Senator McCarthy — who thinks more about patriotism than his own political party — in unmasking those whose subversive activities tend to overthrow and destroy our democratic system?

Many people were surprised to hear the mayor of Toronto refused to welcome Senator McCarthy, and he evidently is not obliged to do so. But we wonder why he was in such a hurry to wash his hands of this matter.

While Senator McCarthy may lack diplomacy and tact in his anti-Communist campaign, we must remember that this man has rid the federal government at Washington and other states of many notorious Communists whose sole aim was to establish a reign of revolution in a peaceful country. While agreeing he may sometimes have gone too far, under no circumstances can he be called a traitor to the American nation.

We remember a time not so long ago when Toronto welcomed certain well-known Communists without much official protestation. Among them were the Dean of Canterbury and Paul Robeson, while Tim Buck and members of his Canadian Communist Party are regular visitors in Toronto.

Senator McCarthy may not be free from certain reproaches, but he is to be preferred a hundred times to any Communists or their fellow travellers who take advantage of the liberty accorded every citizen of a free and democratic land to undermine that country's freedom and hard-earned ideals.

Rudolphe A. Potvin, Hull, Que.

U.S. TV PREFERRED

APRIL 28, 1954

I've watched TV for almost one year and the Canadian shows leave much to be desired. Take first the costumes of the Canadian shows and then the U.S.A. shows we see — they can't come anywhere near the shows produced over the border. Then take your cameras — ever see a show from across the line go blurred as they start a close-up?

I'm all for Canadian talent, but you see the same actors and actresses on everything produced in Toronto and Montreal, and not good ones all of them at that. It looks like all the good ones have gone across the border. On the "Hit Parade" you have three former Canadians, and it's been rumoured that Shirley Harmer, the female singing star of "Showtime," has turned down offers from across the line but no mention is made of offers to keep her here.

What have we on Canadian TV? Mostly actors from England where they could have stayed with their accents, and for Canada to get back the ones they got from us.

Canadian TV needs a good overhauling, and if you want real unbuttered opinions go to the schoolyards, or wherever children

FILE PHOTO

Senator Joseph McCarthy is to be preferred 100 times to any Communists, wrote a reader.

gather, then you'll get down-to-earth opinions on Canadian TV.

Henry T. Giekes, Ottawa

THROUGH A NEWCOMER'S EYES
MAY 22, 1954

It is only one week ago that I arrived in Ottawa, via Halifax, direct from Germany. I have never before been in the New World. At the first glimpse it struck me that:

1) The people here are extraordinarily kind and helpful. If on the street you show slight signs of uncertainty where to go, someone will spontaneously tell you, sometimes even open his car to offer you a lift.

2) In spite of the dense traffic, Ottawa is a quiet town in comparison with the big German cities. The strong motors of the American cars are running more noiselessly, there is not so much gear shifting. Drivers over here seldom use their horns. They are, as it seems to me, generally more patient, more self-disciplined, often better trained than German automobilists.

3) Parliament Hill is beautiful beyond all expectations. The building, outside as well as inside, is simply grand. Moreover, I like the way you can come and go freely, make your way to the Senate Chamber, say, or up the Peace Tower, the constables not asking you for your identification, but helping you along, giving explanations. The visitors can regard the Parliament buildings as their very own. And they need not keep off the grass.

4) It is a pity the power line poles and masses of electrical wire blur the view of so many roads. It is likewise a pity hundreds of somewhat shabby looking houses are in sharp contrast to the shiny recent model cars parked in front of them.

5) It must be good to have an auto, so you can go to all the fine places you see when looking around from the top of the Peace Tower — and to some more, for the countryside seems to be abundant of beauties.

6) You need not drive more than a few miles out of the crowded city to feel like Robinson Crusoe. Last Sunday, one of those kind Canadian families invited me to drive 10 or 15 miles along the broadening Ottawa River and then go by boat to one of those dream islands. Were it not for the empty Coke-bottle and small sign that forbids hunting and trapping, I might well have imagined to be the first human being to set foot on the little isle.

7) Apart from the wild untouched nature, which may give the deepest impressions to immigrants from densely populated and cultivated Europe, the Driveway along the Rideau Canal, for instance, can match with Europe's most outstanding built-up beauties.

8) In their manner of dress, particularly in the kind of hats and shoes they wear, the women here do not vary so much as the female back home in one of Western Germany's larger towns; whereas the Canadian men — as the American — like to dress more colourful than the average European.

9) Boys and — even more conspicuously, girls — start smoking cigarets earlier than young Germans.

10) I found a brown grass-hopper, more than an inch long, among the vegetables in one of the city's Chinese restaurants. Being in a Chinese restaurant for the first time in my life, I asked the moon-faced waiter, whether the insect was a casual ingredient or was meant a special delicacy. He gave me no answer, only laughed loud. But from the fact that he did not seem to be embarrassed at all I guess, the grasshopper must have been a planned ingredient.

11) Each Canadian who finds out you are new in this country will ask you most certainly: "How do you like Canada?" So far I have seen pier 17 in Halifax, a few hundred yards on both sides of the railroad to Ottawa and a bit of Canada's attractive capital only. But as sure as the next Canadian whom I meet will ask me how I like Canada, I'm as sure I feel I'll like it.

K.H. Wilsing, Ottawa

THE MAYOR PROTESTS
JUNE 5, 1954

I have consistently refrained from protesting the repeated falsification of fact which marks much of your editorial or news reference to myself as Mayor of Ottawa.

However, I cannot ignore such a mischievous representation which appeared in the 5 o'clock edition of Thursday's *Citizen* to the effect that, "A decidedly angry Mayor Whitton stalked out of an OTC [Ottawa Transportation Commission] meeting this afternoon to tell newsmen the transit commissioners had refused to 'give a bonus' to regular OTC patrons."

I did not stalk out of the meeting; the meeting had adjourned (General Turner had left some ten minutes before); I was on my way to my lunch. *The Citizen* and the *Journal* reporters were in the corridor. I told them the Chairman was waiting to give a statement to the press and that I myself was thoroughly discouraged with the refusal to adopt the recommendation of the Chairman, first made several months ago, to increase transportation on the OTC by a special provision for the constant riders which would likely increase business and could be dropped were it a failure, at the end of three months.

I consider this procedure, followed by *The Citizen*, and not its reporters, of twisting factual news, in the case of nearly every reference to myself, so that a distorted editorial may follow in a few hours or days, is beyond the standards and ethics which at one time characterized the Southam paper in this city.

I intend to refrain from protesting in such continuous misrepresentations that one wastes one's time attempting to correct them, but this is such a gross misstatement of fact that it cannot stand.

Charlotte Whitton, Ottawa

The Citizen replied: The sentence quoted above appears precisely as the reporter wrote it. *The Citizen* did not intend to convey the impression that Mayor Whitton left this particular meeting before it was over — if indeed this impression was conveyed. In all other respects, the account is both unambiguous and accurate. The charge that news is "twisted" in order to provide material for editorials is, of course, absurd.

THREAT TO LIBERTY

JUNE 21, 1954

A few days ago a news report appeared which stated that the government of Guatemala had, by reason of a certain article in its constitution, abolished all the usual guarantees of civil liberty such as free speech, free assembly, freedom of the press, and so on.

No doubt all good Canadians were properly shocked, but I wonder how many of them are aware that both in 1914 and 1939 we did exactly the same. In 1914, the War Measures Act was passed and it remained in operation for the duration of the war. In 1939 it was called into operation again, and again remained in power during the course of the war.

Under the War Measures Act, virtually every single one of our traditional liberties was at the disposal of government. Canada, in other words, was legally just about as close to dictatorship as Guatemala is today. The difference lies in our differing background of traditions. It is hard for us and for our rulers, even with the best will in the world, to live down the tradition of self-government under which we have been brought up.

How long will tradition go on saving us, I wonder? The next time we call the War Measures Act into existence, conditions may be such that it will stay in existence for a very long time, and with it our traditional liberties will continue in a state of suspended animation which may gradually deepen into lifelessness.

If, by some unlikely combination of events, a Guatemalan-style government should come to power in Canada, nothing would be more convenient for it than to find the War Measures Act still on the statute books.

Yet I venture to say there is no public pressure for its removal, and that no administration, whatever the party in power may happen to be, could be induced to remove it!

A.R.M. Lower,
Queen's University, Kingston

Editor's note: Professor Arthur Lower was a well-known historian, author and constitutional scholar.

'DRUNKEN BUMS'

AUGUST 7, 1954

About this T.C. Archer who complains about a "Filthy mess" of litter on Wellington Street near the Parliament Buildings, I would like to know what evidence he has for his statement that "in about ten places on the pavements the drunken bums who beg money on this stretch had been abundantly sick fairly recently."

Now I have worked that stretch myself, and I am certainly not a drunk. There are a lot of people who go along there, often quite late, and how does this T.C. Archer know that the trouble he talks about wasn't caused by some of these newspaper fellows from up on the Hill, or maybe somebody from the East Block? They go to a lot of cocktail parties.

Joe Storcie,
Ottawa

WATER SPEED DEMONS

AUGUST 28, 1954

My husband and myself are lovers of the out-of-doors. We enjoy a Sunday in a boat with our fishing tackle, as do many others.

It has been our habit to go to Innisville for our fishing trips. This summer we spent our vacation in this lovely spot. Unfortunately, this spot on the Mississippi has become very hazardous through people who are of the selfish opinion the waters are theirs to the exclusion of their fellow men.

With the advent of the outboard motor the younger element have made the waters unsafe for the average person. They maintain no courtesies, which I understand are the unwritten law. These speed boats pass close to anchored craft at full speed with reckless abandon.

Added to this are the water skiing crowd. Last Sunday one boat and a skiing enthusiast decided it might be fun to use anchored rowboats as course obstacles. The net result was that we were nearly tipped over by the waves.

City dwellers who appreciate the green of God's country and the sport of fishing should be given some measure of assurance that they can take to the water without being in peril of their lives at the hands of a group of water speed demons who care nothing for the other fellow.

Mrs. Florence Despins, Ottawa

PARKING AT THE 'EX'

AUGUST 31, 1954

The Exhibition is over for another year. I wonder if Ottawans realize what impression the present parking arrangements make on visitors?

Parking arrangements can be of three types. They can be municipally run, with attendants and set charges. They can be voluntary, with the collection boxes of some local charity conveniently displayed. Or, they can be run by children, which is a lot of fun, provided the little terrors don't overcharge.

Whichever of these methods is adopted, *the visitor should be made to feel welcome.*

What then was the picture in the Glebe last week? Quite truthfully, the district resembled a South American seaport, everywhere. Women flapping around like hens; women accosting, screaming at passing cars and often coming to blows with one another. There were middle-aged women leaning against lamp-posts. Burly women, bursting out of blue jeans, leaping in front of speeding automobiles. Old women, croaking "Parking" and swinging home-made signs in the manner of intoxicated croquet players.

The first night I saw it all, I could only stare goggle-eyed. Here indeed was a charming facet of dear old, respectable Ottawa that was new to me. But quite frankly, gentle reader, what sort of impression do you think it made on visitors?

Patrick Arthur Hill, Ottawa

SPEED BOATS AT INNISVILLE

SEPTEMBER 27, 1954

We are lovers of the out-of-doors, who enjoy a Sunday

in a boat with our water-skis, as do many others.

It has been our habit to go to Innisville for our water-skiing trips. This summer we spent our vacation in this lovely spot. Unfortunately, this spot of the Mississippi has become a restricted area through people, who are of the opinion the waters are theirs to the exclusion of their fellow men and women. With the "parking" of so many boats, the waters have been made out of bounds for the average person. So-called courtesies they want, but none will give. These boats will stand still in deep waters so that "speed boats" have to be kept on the beach for emergency calls only.

Added to this are the fishing crowd. Some time ago, a

fishing enthusiast decided it might be courtesy to occupy the area where speed boats would necessarily have to pass. The net result was the letter you received regarding water speed demons.

City dwellers who appreciate the green of God's country and the sport of skiing on water should be given some measure of assurance that they can take to the water without being annoyed by a group of "water angels" who care nothing for the other fellow.

René Lajoie, Lomer Lafortune,
Jacques Charbonneau, Irenée Charbonneau,
Robert Brulé, Ottawa

1955

Local: Aylmer town council passes morality law banning, among other things, swearing, fortune-telling and roller skating (April); Extensive drought destroys crops throughout the Ottawa Valley, and prompts authorities to close Gatineau Park because of fire danger (July); Fluoridation proposed for Ottawa's drinking water (December)

National: Government announces plan to build Canada's first nuclear power station at Des Joachims, Ont. (January); Suspension of Montreal Canadiens star Maurice Richard for the duration of 1954-55 hockey season triggers riot at Montreal Forum (March)

World: Winston Churchill bows to age and retires as British prime minister at age 80 (April); Disneyland opens in Anaheim, California (July)

Births: Canadian writer Neil Bissoondeth; Kevin Sullivan, producer of *Road to Avonlea* TV series; federal cabinet ministers Stéphane Dion and Jane Stewart

Deaths: Physicist Albert Einstein; novelist Thomas Mann; actor James Dean; jazz legend Charlie Parker; baseball greats Honus Wagner and Cy Young; American painter Grandma Moses

UNSUPPORTED ENTERTAINMENT

JANUARY 28, 1955

The departure of the Triple A baseball Athletics and of some other such institutions from Ottawa is not unwarranted. They do not get much encouragement to stay.

What has prompted me to write is the puny number of people who turned out the other evening to see [Swedish film actress] Signe Hasso at the Glebe Cinema. It must be most discouraging to the theater management and the performers. It seems to me the Glebe is attempting to bring excellent entertainment to Ottawa, but unless it is patronized, how can it be successful and remain?

Everyone left the theater with the satisfaction of having spent an excellent evening, but with regret that more people had not found it convenient to attend.

Unless Ottawans support these institutions, they will eventually be forced into living in a city ungarnished with any amusement whatever.

Hill Arson, Ottawa

Editor's note: The Ottawa Giants became the first Triple-A baseball franchise in 53 years to play in the nation's capital when they arrived in 1951. However, the team was not a success on or off the field, finishing seventh in an eight-team league that year and attracting just 132,000 fans to 77 home games at Lansdowne Park. After one season, the team left and was replaced by the Ottawa Athletics, top farm team of the Philadelphia Athletics. After three years, the Athletics also moved on, leaving the capital without Triple-A base-

ball until the arrival of the Ottawa Lynx in 1993. Ottawa actually lost two teams in 1954 — the Ottawa Senators of the Quebec Senior League folded in December because of poor attendance.

DEFENCE THROUGH PEACE

MARCH 2, 1955

In answer to Mr. S. J. Gilberg's letter proposing expanding our civil defences, I would like to refer the writer to the example set by the City of Coventry in England in refusing to continue a civil defence organization because the City Council considered it a waste of time. *Peace News* of Jan. 28 reports that in Canada two cities have abandoned the idea of organizing.

There is no real defence against atomic and hydrogen bombs — except peace — therefore why not spend time, money and energy working for peace? I think your correspondent would find our Ottawa Mayor and Controllers more interested in preparing for peace than for war and the "facade" of civil defence.

Mrs. Edith Holtom, Ottawa

THE TV LOOK

JUNE 15, 1955

Careful study of the microphone technique of the girls who have lately reached the top as singers on television has led me to some disconcerting conclusions.

The way to popularity is not to stand up and sing in a loud, clear voice. That is old fashioned. No, the singer has to know how to put on a yearning look. She must flutter her eyelashes, pout, pucker the brow faintly, wriggle a little and smile a lot.

She must also croon, huskily if possible and soulfully of a certainty, and if she can make her eyes melt with sincerity for the close-ups, her fortune is made.

J. Holland, Ottawa

NOISES IN THE NIGHT
JULY 14, 1955

Periodically there is talk of an anti-noise bylaw coupled with the protest about the abomination of the cross-town tracks in the vicinity of Pretoria Bridge.

Can nothing be done about these hellish noises at night? We hear apathetic reports about removing these ghastly operations to Walkley Road, but nothing happens.

I can honestly say, from experience, that the earth-shaking crash of heavy metal cars is more nerve-wracking than the bombing of London in the last war, while the disturbance to Ottawa residents can and should be eliminated.

Capt. John Skinner (retired)

Editor's note: The rail tracks running alongside the east side of the Rideau Canal were relocated when the central rail terminal was moved from its site across from the Château Laurier in the 1960s.

GOAL POSTS FOR SOUVENIRS
AUGUST 16, 1955

I should like to show my support of the three Calgary football fans who let themselves be carried away in their enthusiasm over their team's victory to the extent of running off with the goal posts. I believe that Ottawa football fans could use a little of the spirit shown by supporters of Western teams, or even those in Toronto and Montreal.

In regards to this being considered theft, it is common practice in college football games for the supporters of the visiting team to attempt to tear down the goal posts at the end of the game. At Varsity Stadium in Toronto, where the loss of goal posts in past years has been exceptionally heavy, the officials have come up with the solution of constructing the uprights of steel pipe, embedded in solid concrete supports in the ground.

Perhaps if the management of Lansdowne Park fears further losses, they could copy this plan. Or are they afraid that football in Ottawa is not here to stay, and therefore the expense would be unwarranted?

A. L. Barry, Ottawa

Editor's note: Although many football fans fondly recall the 1950s as one of the Canadian Football League's golden eras, the Ottawa Rough Riders faced on- and off-field problems during the mid-'50s that were eerily similar to those that eventually led to the team's demise in 1996. After the 1955 season, for instance, there was serious talk that the team would have to fold without a new infusion of community support, and a renewed commitment to winning from management. In the end, a ticket drive and some personnel changes saved the Riders. Here's another letter on the subject:

THE ROUGH RIDERS
OCTOBER 19, 1955

The Ottawa Rough Rider situation will certainly come to a head after the game last Saturday with Hamilton. It was unfortunate that we lost; however, I do not think that I have ever seen a team put so much fight and enthusiasm into a game, as our boys did.

The dismissal of the assistant manager and of some of the players came as a surprise to many of their fans. Was this action necessary? It is my opinion that many mistakes have been made these past few weeks about the management of the team.

Ottawa simply needs more spirit and to get out and support our team, win or lose, for it is the sportsmanship that counts, not the winning of the game. Someone has to lose. Even the best fail sometimes.

We have a good team. With a lot more support from their fans and their management we may yet have a winning team. How about it, Ottawa?

S. P. Carson, Ottawa

WOMEN IN THE CIVIL SERVICE
OCTOBER 24, 1955

In recent articles, *The Citizen* appears pleased to know that the special disabilities under which married women have suffered for many years in the Civil Service have been removed; apparently now they are to be allowed the same opportunities as single women.

Yet the married women are less than thrilled over this information. It will be worth a headline when women are allowed the same opportunities as men.

There are two labour forces in our Civil Service, one male and one female. If a woman with better qualifications than any of the male candidates applies for a promotion, she will be told some of the most fanciful fairy tales imaginable to explain why the position must be occupied by a man.

Some or any of the following requirements are considered in some parts of the Civil Service to make the positions unsuitable for women: traveling, meeting the public, supervising staff, responsibility of any kind, a salary of over $3,000 a year.

The reason I have been given for the last is "a woman doesn't need a good salary." This poses the question — is the civil service supposed to be a charitable institution, salaries being paid according to need: or is it an agency for serving the public, salaries being paid according to the demands of the work involved and the qualifications required in the incumbent?

Some of the departments where these quaint ideas persist allowed a few women in the stress of war-time to do work involving some responsibility, because they couldn't get men of any kind to do it. And if the women happened to be permanent civil servants, the departments could not down-grade these persons as they did the temporary women employees. A few of this type remain in respectable positions, because no fault can be found with their work.

The Comptroller of the Treasury, in whose service I was incarcerated for about 14 years, having escaped only last May, operates quite brazenly according to these 10th century employment principles. Posters advertising promotional competitions for clerks grade three and higher regularly begin with "Open to male applicants." Positions are usually advertised during the Parliamentary recess, possibly to avoid their being seen by female MPs and Senators.

Other parts of the Civil Service have been known to advertise open competitions, and when women appeared on the eligible list so high that they ought to be appointed, they are told that there are no positions suitable for female employees.

You, Mr. Editor, and your readers, are among the taxpayers who are paying for Civil Service work to be done, and have a right to demand that the most capable persons (according to our Constitution, women are persons) be placed in the positions of responsibility that serve you.

I am quite sure that the male or female category of the clerk who checks your income tax return makes no more difference to you than does the colour of the paint on the adding machine used to add it. It simply does not matter, so long as the work is done properly.

L. Gladys Harvey, Ottawa

Editor's note: It wasn't until the 1969 Public Service Employment Act that women were guaranteed the same access to public service jobs as men. In broad terms, though, women did not enjoy equal status with men in the public service until the recent ruling granting them equal pay for work of equal value, and ordering the government to compensate them for years of inequality.

DRIVE ON OBSCENE BOOKS

NOVEMBER 17, 1955

Tuesday morning I was shocked to hear on the eight o'clock newscast from a local radio station a sneering documentary regarding the campaign presently being waged by the Catholic Women's League against obscene literature found on Ontario newsstands. The newscast quoted the writer, Mr. Morley Callaghan, as well as the editor of *Maclean's* magazine, as being fearful of what this campaign of a "pressure group" would lead to!

It amazes me that an author of Mr. Callaghan's stature would exhibit such narrow-mindedness on a problem of such magnitude. And it is a problem, let there be no mistake about that!

Read your daily papers and be appalled, as all decent-thinking people are, by all the crimes committed by teenagers and juveniles. And how often it is reported that their ideas for such shocking behaviour were found between the pages of so-called "comic-books" and pulp magazines!

Monday evening, I was entertained by a delightful TV program saluting the freedom of the press in general, and overseas correspondents in particular. It made one proud,

indeed, to belong to a country where freedom of the press is, thank God, the order of the day.

But like all privileges, it is one that lends itself to abuse; and the abuse is very evident today when one glances over the filth and obscenity that is displayed on the newsstands.

Nobody, least of all the Catholic Women's League, wants to destroy the freedom of the press. But how ridiculous it is to allow this abuse of our much-touted freedom to continue when it is leading to the destruction of the minds and lives of our impressionable adolescents.

Ask yourself, Mr. Callaghan, what type of citizens you want for the Canada of tomorrow? One wonders if our noted Canadian author would be occupying such an exalted position among Canada's intelligentsia if, in his youth, he had been exposed to the type of reading material our young people can pick up today in any corner newsstand.

It has already been stated that the classics and, in fact, any of the widely read books are not now on the list of those being denounced by the CWL. And will anyone, with even a grain of intelligence, explain how comic-books and magazines that glamourize murder, rape, sex and immorality in all its forms, contribute one iota to the good — materially or spiritually — of a city, a province, or a nation?

M. Eunice Lanigan,
RCAF, Rockcliffe

THE TV GUIDE

NOVEMBER 30, 1955

In your last issue of last Saturday's paper was a surprise — a TV guide.

I was wishing for such a thing for a long time and now it has come. It was easy to assemble and the result was an interesting guide for every day of the week. It was a grand idea.

E. Boulay, Ottawa

MR. MARTIN ON THE WORLD STAGE

DECEMBER 10, 1955

Canada now occupies a proud place in the family of nations. Its prestige has been appreciably enhanced during the present sessions of the United Nations, following the constructive leadership given by its eloquent minister of health and welfare, the Hon. Paul Martin.

His suggestions and counsel are of a nature that should make an appeal to the so-called realistic chiefs of the Russian Soviet. His efforts to secure the admission of additional members entitles him not only to their gratitude, but the thanks of the major powers.

Mr. Martin has shown qualities of statesmanship that reflect credit upon his modest self, his fellow citizens and the nation on whose behalf he speaks. With his knowledge of social and economic problems and international relations, he is not only qualified to represent Canada abroad, but hold the highest office in the service of his fellow Canadians.

It would be a signal and deserving tribute on the part of

the members of his party that when the present leader of the government retires or resigns, that he be chosen as his successor.

We Canadians are citizens and, as such, should at no time discriminate because of race or faith. Only merit and qualifications should count. Mr. Martin would make an ideal prime minister.

I nominate Paul Martin, Canada's minister of Health and Welfare, as the Man of the Year!

Bernard Rose, Montreal

Editor's note: Paul Martin, the father of Canada's current finance minister, ran three times for the Liberal leadership, in 1948, 1958 and 1968, losing to three future prime ministers, Louis St. Laurent, Lester Pearson and Pierre Trudeau. As minister of health and welfare in the 1950s, he introduced a national health insurance scheme that was the forerunner of medicare. In the 1960s, he was external affairs minister before ending his 33-year tenure as an MP by accepting a Senate appointment. He died in 1992.

'THE DEVIL HIS DUE'

DECEMBER 24, 1955

"The Mayor," "the City," "the government" are made the target of every trouble from time to time, and presently it's "the Post Office" that is under fire. And as is usual in such cases, a thousand good performances go unnoted to allow a hue and cry over one or two.

I have received over 4,000 personal letters and cards in this past week. I have checked on hundreds of the envelopes; the date of dispatch and receipt are amazing.

I have been keeping in touch with a very ill friend at the West Coast. I have regularly received letters written in Victoria one evening by special delivery here, the next. I wrote to a friend in London on a Sunday, had the answer back here Thursday night of this same week. I mailed hundreds of cards late on Sunday night and Monday and Tuesday yet by Thursday scores of these were reported received.

I can bear witness to a gruelling job being well done here by the Post Office. It's the miss of one inch not the steady measure of the mile at which we bring dispraise and blame.

Give the devil his due. The Post Office has done well.

Charlotte Whitton, Mayor, Ottawa

THE OTTAWA CITIZEN

Charlotte Whitton used her own experience as evidence of Post Office efficiency.

NO STUDENTS ADMITTED

DECEMBER 30, 1955

Students in Eganville were not allowed admission to the movie *Blackboard Jungle* while individuals no longer in school, and much younger than the average student, were.

Personally I did not (could not?) see the picture, nor would I have been free to do so at the time. But as an amateur movie-TV critic, I should like to be free to see and criticize any movie I wish!

The plot, I conclude, was that dealing with juvenile delinquency. But, tell me, did the delinquents win out in the end? Taking the answer to be "no," I should think that this would be a lesson to anyone in the audience with such intent and act as a warning to others.

Our teachers keep harping at us to act like young adults, but why should we (or how can we) if we are not treated as such? If there is something obscene about the picture, I should think that adults should have had no right to see it either.

Orville W. A. Levean, Eganville

1956

Local: Fifteen killed, including 12 nuns, when a military jet crashes into Orléans convent (May); Ottawa gets a new passenger air terminal (June); Charlotte Whitton steps down as mayor, accepts offer to become an *Ottawa Citizen* columnist (December)
National: Using parliamentary closure for the first time in Canadian history, the Liberal government pushes through a bill to provide an $80-million loan to company building the $300-million trans-Canada pipeline (May); Lester Pearson proposes creation of special United Nations police force — the first peacekeepers — to ease rising tensions over Suez Canal (November)
World: Bus boycott in Montgomery, Alabama forces changes to rule forcing blacks to sit at back of buses (April); Elvis Presley sets TV viewership record when he appears for the first time on the *Ed Sullivan Show* (September); Soviet tanks brutally crush anti-Communist uprising in Hungary (November)
Births: Tennis star Bjorn Borg; Cree grand chief Matthew Coon Come; politician Sergio Marchi
Deaths: Pooh creator A.A. Milne; journalist H.L. Mencken; jazz pianist Art Tatum; trombonist Tommy Dorsey; German playwright Bertolt Brecht; legendary baseball manager Connie Mack; Harold Box, Canadian discoverer of cure for gum disease; IBM founder Thomas Watson; governor general Vere Ponsonby (Earl of Bessborough)

AWKWARD LOCATION

FEBRUARY 13, 1956

The site for the new City Hall has been chosen. Too late to change that. But may I vote my disapproval of the choice?

How often does the average Ottawan's business take him down Sussex Drive in the direction of Rockcliffe? How often will the people of Ottawa enjoy the sight of their fine city hall, tucked away as it will be, beyond their daily reach?

Has anyone ever noticed, coming along the Driveway (the finest and most natural approach to the center of town), how impressive a sight is the University of Ottawa's Medical Faculty standing out in full view across the canal? Then beyond it, and as far as Laurier Bridge, what does one see? The dull brick sides of houses at the tag ends of dismal streets!

Since when has the city, or the government, lost the power of expropriating city or government property in the interests of the people at large? Why could not a block of these old houses be expropriated, torn down, and Ottawa's magnificent new city hall erected on a site where it can easily be seen and used by the people of Ottawa and out-of-town visitors?

Must it be necessary to make a special out-of-the-way expedition to see that which should be seen in the ordinary course of affairs?

Charlotte Kindle, Ottawa

FRIDAY NIGHT ON TV

MARCH 7, 1956

I usually uphold the CBC in its choice of television programs, but I must give way to my feelings concerning the change that has been made in the late show on Friday nights.

While I may not be speaking on behalf of some viewers, I think that the majority would rather have the feature film than the variety show, especially with the specimen which acts as master of ceremonies, namely Lister Sinclair. I thought he had disappeared with *Scope*, [a cancelled public affairs program] but apparently not.

I fail to see why a man with his apparent education does not get a job as a teacher in a kindergarten class, or something, for his subjects have no real value to the general public and he could not really be termed a humourist. In my opinion he should be put alongside that dreadful fellow who advertises "Morton's pot pies."

Of course, he may give a far better impression if he shaved off that growth of beard and left the moustache. At least we could see what he may be hiding.

I would usually hurry home on Friday nights, purposely to sit down and enjoy the late movie, but was very disappointed when I saw that it was changed to the type of stuff that was called entertainment.

I think the CBC is really scraping the bottom of the barrel when they make such a drastic change as this. I noticed that one of his final remarks last Friday night was, "You should have turned your sets off long ago." Well, I realized that, too, but I left mine on thinking it could get better. But it did not.

So if the old style movie does not come back, I'm of the opinion that a lot of people will do just what he suggested. At least, they will save power. So give the poor fellow Friday nights off and let him go to bed. I'm sure nobody will cry for him.

A.L. Jones, Ottawa

LOVERS' LANE

JUNE 27, 1956

Now that we are spending $300 million for a silly old pipeline, why don't we spend a few thousand to re-establish Lovers' Lane behind the Parliament Buildings? In spite of its present ramshackle condition, it is still one of the most pleasant walks in Ottawa, when (and if!) you can sneak past the big Mounties at each entrance.

Paul J. Beneteau,
Ottawa

A CASE FOR EGYPT

SEPTEMBER 19, 1956

Egypt nationalized Suez. Britain demands a return to the international status quo of the Canal and Egypt refuses to permit it; both powers are utterly unwilling, in the last analysis, to concede anything to the opposition.

And this is the problem which now confronts the state department of every nation on the face of the earth — how to reconcile two direct and adamant opposites when the issue at stake is world peace.

Egypt remembers only too well the full century of humiliation, the oppression of her national aspirations under British domination. In this memory, she can speak for all the nations of the Near East which have long been humbled by various West European powers.

As an individual, too, she aims at an economic power and prestige that she feels could be hers if she controlled the total resources within her recognized national boundaries. She compares herself to her neighbours of like race who are more wealthy, more influential than she and feels that, of them all, she alone has been unable to claim a rightful economic recognition. Within herself, then, she unites retaliation and ambition.

Britain remembers her centuries of imperial pride and colonial grandeur — and does so, surely, with a certain blindness. In this she is the protagonist of many a European nation which once lorded it over various "native" territories and now sees these same peoples wrenching themselves away from foreign domination. She sees in Egypt an economic threat, a threat to her oil in the Near East; and fears not so much Egypt's possession of the Suez Canal as the example which such a successful venture in nationalization must pose to the oil-rich Arab nations.

These are the cross-purposes and vying ambitions which now cry for a solution.

B.E. Lay,
Ottawa

Editor's note: The solution came from Canadian career diplomat Lester Pearson, then external affairs minister, who proposed the creation of an international police force, under the direction of the United Nations, drawn from countries seen not to have a direct stake in the Suez crisis. Within a few weeks of the outbreak of war in late October, peacekeeping troops from Canada and several other nations had restored peace in the area. Pearson's idea led to the use of UN peacekeepers in dozens of conflicts, and won him the Nobel Peace Prize in 1957. More letters on the topic appear later in this section.

CONSERVATIVE LEADER
OCTOBER 3, 1956

Mr. Sloan's letter reminds me that "Hope springs eternal in the human breast." If, however, Mr. [Donald] Fleming should become leader of the Conservative Party, I am afraid that Mr. Sloan is doomed to live in hope and die in despair.

In my opinion, the electorate of Canada will not follow a leader who resides in Toronto the Good — or, as our parents called it, Hogtown-on-the-Humber. The fact of the matter is that anyone who is backed by the Bay Street bigwigs starts with two strikes against him.

I personally have voted Liberal more often than Conservative, but if Mr. Diefenbaker were leading the Conservatives I am inclined to think I would support him.

A.B. Lawson, Ottawa

Editor's note: John Diefenbaker won the Conservative

Party leadership in 1956, and after wrestling power from the Liberals in the 1957 federal election, appointed Donald Fleming as his finance minister, a post he held until 1962.

INTRUSION OF RIGHTS
OCTOBER 10, 1956

I feel sure that your news item, "Bilingual Signs Protested," will be widely read and discussed by the thousands of English-speaking citizens who have for some time been profoundly alarmed at the encroachment by our French-Canadian citizens in an effort to bilingualize the province of Ontario or indeed all of Canada.

I would like to ask Controller [Paul] Tardif on what page and in what phraseology of the British North American Act is the French language spoken of as an official language of Canada?

Alderman [Raymond] Aubin is a bit more vague when he is reported as saying that as sponsor of the bilingual sign motion in council it would be effective only in Lower Town and at the main highway entrances to the city. May I suggest to Ald. Aubin that Lower Town and the entrances to the city on the south side of Ottawa are in the province of Ontario, where the English language, according to the B.N.A. Act, is the language of communication and instruction.

It might be well at this time to inform Messrs. Tardif and Aubin just what the B.N.A. Act really does cover. Does it not say, as regards the province of Quebec, that the French language shall be the language of communication and instruction in that province, and as a further privilege, but by no means as a right, the members of Parliament may deliver speeches in the French language, but those French-language speeches must be translated into English within 24 hours and so appear in the House of Commons *Hansard*?

In closing, may I sound a note of warning to those bilingualists, and it is this: English-speaking citizens are fast becoming fed up with this intrusion on their rights, and are now ready to rise in their might to defend out language and our right.

Robert Rennick,
Osgoode Station, Ont.

U.N. POLICE FORCE
NOVEMBER 7, 1956

Mr. Pearson has sounded the call to arms for a U.N. force to end the fighting in Egypt. The immediate need for such a force is not in Egypt, where two of the great democrats are looking after the situation very capably, but in Hungary, where heroism is being crushed by Soviet armour. However, our minister has made it clear that Canada will support such a U.N. force.

Surely this is just the sort of situation where our small, well-trained and equipped fighting forces can be used. Here is the chance for Canada to strike a blow for freedom. Let a balanced Canadian force be sent immediately as the vanguard of the U.N. police force.

Our forces in being are sufficient for such an operation, NATO commitments notwithstanding, and would be better utilized in this capacity than in practice drills for Armistice Day parades.

P. Rhodes, Ottawa

MARRIED WOMEN IN EMPLOYMENT
NOVEMBER 17, 1956

Could I call your attention to the tremendous number of married women in the labor force today? These ladies can be found everywhere in offices, behind counters, working as ushers, in fact, in all industries.

Many of them have husbands who hold good positions. They may or may not need the money, but if they want work, they can perform voluntary work which is badly needed now.

It is my opinion that single girls should obtain these posts, thereby helping younger brothers and sisters secure a good education. Sick parents could also be helped by their daughters earning these salaries. Employers should question these persons and make sure they really are in need of wages. If not, they should seek single people who apply, and give them work. This is only fair and just.

I am told many young people are seeking work and cannot obtain much these days. If this condition continues, they will leave for the U.S., which is something we must avoid.

(Mrs.) F. McDougall,
Ottawa

CANADA'S SUEZ POLICY
DECEMBER 4, 1956

When President Wilson was quoted, in World War I, as saying that the Americans were "too proud to fight," our fathers, who had fought from the beginning, treated it with the scorn it deserved. When President Roosevelt, in the Second World War, said they "would not fight to save the British Empire," our brothers treated it with disdain, and fought on alone.

Now it is our government, applauded to a man by its party, who are too proud to fight and will not be a "chore boy to the British Empire."

What would those men think who lie in Flanders fields? What would those who fell at Dieppe feel? What do those who hold their memory dear feel? What of those who fought and returned to vote?

Do these men, who speak for us, represent Canada? For, if they do, her future as a sovereign state is in grave doubt, when Mr. Pearson, of whom we thought so highly, ignores the Statute of Westminster and prefers the American pretense that we fought because we had to.

Like the Americans, this government takes refuge in protestations of devotion to the U.S. dominated U.N. And it cries that it wished to "save" the Commonwealth by condemning and undermining it and lending itself to the economic blackmail of that great-hearted country to the south.

May future Canadians — if any — forgive those of us who voted for such men as my forebears had voted for over 100 years for this party, with its now bloated, sub-

CHRONICLE OF THE 20TH CDENTURY
Villages were left in ruins by British and French bombing as the two countries retaliated for Egypt's nationalization of the Suez Canal. One letter-writer wondered how to reconcile two direct and adamant opposites when the issue at stake is world peace.

servient majority, who may regard with complacency the delight their leaders' words will give in the U.S. and the U.S.S.R. with whom they have acted in such happy unanimity.

H. Mowat Biggar,
Guelph, Ont.

BRITAIN'S FINANCIAL POSITION
DECEMBER 10, 1956

Chancellor of the Exchequer Harold Macmillan told the House of Commons in London that "the reserves — shared by all sterling area countries — fell by $270,000,000 last month." Later on in his address to the House he declares: "Since the losses have arisen primarily from the international situation they should not be permanent. The trend will reverse itself as the position improves."

Those declarations were made at the occasion of the appeal by Britain to the U.S. and Canada to waive interest on the post-war dollar loans due this month. This British appeal, if granted, will cost the U.S. and Canada the insignificant sum of $104,000,000.

As I see it, Britain organizes a fruitless hunting trip in Egypt. Back from her trip she realizes that it is impossible for her to pay the expenses. The normal procedure in such instances is to send the bill to those blooming Canadians and Americans.

And those are the people who tell us in their press that the U.S. and Canada are wrong when they repudiate those unnecessary, expensive hunting trips. They even go as far as to tell us: if you people there don't stop criticizing us we will sever our friendly relations with you.

That might be quite a profitable, welcomed happening on our part if Britain doesn't stop organizing such revelries in the future.

Alice Perrier, Ottawa

BRITAIN'S HISTORY
DECEMBER 26, 1956

Strange indeed it seems to me how many people there are who are saying the most contemptible things about Britain and the British people: "Let her fight her own battles."

Read Britain's history. How many times has she fought against fearful odds, always when the battle was going against her?

Let Mr. Nasser and some of the others beware. Others have tried and failed. The Kaiser scoffed at Britain's contemptible little army, to his sorrow.

(Mrs.) C. Clark, Ottawa

1957

Local: Construction of Carleton University begins along the Rideau River in South Ottawa (June); Work starts on the Queensway, most ambitious engineering project in Ottawa since the building of the Rideau Canal (August); Council approves installation of 1,000 parking meters (December)

National: Led by John Diefenbaker, the Conservatives end 22 years of Liberal rule by winning minority government (June); CBC broadcasts *Front Page Challenge* for the first time (July); Lester Pearson awarded Nobel Peace Prize for his solution to the Suez crisis (October)

World: Ten European nations sign treaty creating European Common Market (March); Soviet leader Nikita Krushchev foils coup attempt by other members of Politburo (July); Soviets launch first satellite into orbit around Earth. A second launch a few weeks later carries a dog into space (October)

Births: Princess Caroline of Monaco; skier Steve Podborski; wheelchair athlete Rick Hansen; B.C. premier Glen Clark; TV journalist Wendy Mesley

Deaths: Actor Humphrey Bogart; U.S. senator Joseph McCarthy; Canadian diplomat Herbert Norman; U.S. polar explorer Richard Byrd; designer Christian Dior; comedian Oliver Hardy; FBI agent Eliot Ness; Harry Westwick, member of Ottawa Silver Seven; Finnish composer Jean Sibelius; governor general Alexander Cambridge (Earl of Athlone)

DRINK BILL
JANUARY 30, 1957

The Canadian Temperance Federation, I believe, is responsible for the Liquor Control Board raising the price of hard liquor. Do they really think it will curb drinking?

A man as a rule drinks just as much between pay cheques and will continue doing so no matter what they make the price. Even if the price were doubled it means he will keep just that much more of his pay that should normally go to his family.

So if someone can show me proof that the temperance people are doing any good I will gladly apologize for this letter. I think it is high time the government turned a deaf ear to them and stood on their own feet instead of being dictated to by these teetotallers.

Frank Huttington, Ottawa

THE 'CRIME' OF WALKING
FEBRUARY 6, 1957

I disagree strongly with the sentiments expressed in the letter from your correspondent, R.B. Maybury, who seems to think that we, in this country of progress and prosperity, should revert to a primitive way of life.

As one who holds an executive position, I like to think my responsibility is to give a lead to others in their choice of material possessions, their social habits, and even to some extent their spiritual life.

I should like to say that these people who just want to be different are nothing but exhibitionists. By their envy of the more solid citizens among us, I should even go so far as to say they exhibit Communistic tendencies, which should be eliminated from our way of life.

Regarding your correspondent's eccentric habit of walking to work in the morning, it should be made clear to him that he is a menace on the streets of our city, with or without sidewalks. The finish of many an expensive automobile has been marred as a result of contact with such as he. Further, sidewalks are intended primarily to provide a safe place to alight from your car; and a means of passage from automobile to front door.

Your correspondent's jibes against that great philanthropic institution, the Ottawa Transportation Commission, are another symptom of his deplorable state of mind. The authorities, in their magnanimity, have provided a means of transportation for the weaker and less fortunate members of our community. They are doing great service by keeping these people off the streets.

It is unfortunate that the buses and streetcars occasionally impede the progress of the more personalized automobile, but that is something we have to tolerate and we can only look forward to the day when not only jay-walking, but the act of walking itself, will be regarded as a crime against progress and conformity.

Earl C. Jones, Ottawa

WRESTLING GLADIATORS
FEBRUARY 7, 1957

Who said burlesque was dead? It has merely changed its sphere of activity from the stage to the arena. The old chorus line of buxom pulchitrude has been replaced by the strutting pachyderms who are billed as professional wrestlers.

Let's be downright generous and say that about 20 per cent of the bouts are exhibitions of speed, strength and skill. But the other 80 per cent is sheer farce, with perhaps a little *bona fide* mayhem thrown in now and then when they can't agree whose turn it is to win.

Of course, the big drawing card is the most convincing actor, the one who seems to be the roughest, toughest and dirtiest, and who time after time emerges the winner, usually over an opponent 30 to 60 pounds lighter. The rabid fan will come back again and again in the hopes of seeing him get clobbered.

Sure, the public is gullible, and old Barnum probably wasn't far wrong when he said there's one born every minute. But after a while even the glamour of these gladiators will wear off and wrestling could put an illegal stranglehold on itself.

C.J. Stewart, Ottawa

TRADING STAMPS AND HIGHER PRICES
FEBRUARY 14, 1957

It would seem that Ottawa housewives are being taken for the biggest ride ever. Not only do we have the opportunity of obtaining stamps for "free gifts," but we have the privilege of paying for them, too.

In spite of the protestations of Mr. Bertram Loeb [who brought IGA stores to Canada], the budget-wise housewife feels it more than mere coincidence that food costs jumped just as trading stamps appeared.

We have no proof, unfortunately, but neither can the stamp supporters prove the contrary.

Last week, a "no-stamp" downtown store was selling ground round steak at 69 cents a pound, and blade roast at 49 cents a pound, as compared with 79 cents and 56 cents at the large chain stores using stamps.

We are told that the large stores are giving stamps as a token of appreciation to the customer. All right, then, let them redeem the stamps in foodstuffs.

May I suggest that your columnist, Miss Charlotte Whitton, investigate the whole stamp business and report the facts to the people?

Isabelle Petrie, Ottawa

THE NEXT GOVERNOR GENERAL
FEBRUARY 28, 1957

I have recently been reading suggestions in the paper that the next Governor-General be a French-speaking Canadian. I would like to put forward what I consider an even better solution to the problem.

Why not abolish the position entirely, since it has just become a political plum? (No reflection on our French-speaking friends, or on the present Governor-General.) After all, it would be unthinkable for a Liberal government to have a Conservative Governor-General, or a Conservative government to have a Liberal Governor-General.

Abolition would prevent a lot of friction, hard feelings, and save the taxpayer thousands of wasted dollars. Why

not have the decision put to the general public at the next election? Also the question of abolition of the Senate at the same time.

David C. Myles

Editor's note: Canada's next governor general, Georges Vanier, appointed in 1959, was a French-Canadian. As for the matter of partisan appointments, Mr. Myles' prediction was wrong in two instances — long-time Conservative Roland Michener was named governor general in 1967 by Liberal prime minister Lester Pearson, and New Democrat Ed Schreyer by Pierre Trudeau, another Liberal PM, in 1979.

WELCOME TO ELVIS
APRIL 3, 1957

In view of Mr. Elvis Presley's upcoming visit to Ottawa, I would like to wish him a grand welcome. I know he will get a big crowd of people, and I would like him to do me a great favour by singing either at the beginning or the end of his recital *Faith, Hope and Charity,* or another song wherein he mentions his Maker.

I am sure then that when he goes to his Church at Easter, his Easter will be an everlasting success, because he used the talent that Lord gave him to work for him.

(Mrs.) Elisabeth Drayson, Ottawa

Editor's note: Elvis Presley's 1957 visit created a bit of a row in Ottawa when eight girls were expelled from Notre Dame Convent School after it was learned they had defied a convent edict against attending the concert. In the days leading up to the show, students at the all-girls school were made to sign a pledge they would not attend. But the eight girls, with the blessing of their parents, went to the concert anyway, arguing the convent's nuns had no authority over their lives outside school. After a week of heated public debate, the convent's Rev. Mother Superior rescinded the expulsions "due to certain extenuating circumstances." She never elaborated. But by then, the parents of at least four of the girls had decided to send their children to other schools. Three letters on the incident follow:

PARENTS' RESPONSIBILITY
APRIL 12, 1957

In the recent incident involving convent girls, nuns and Elvis Presley, a few elementary facts have been forgotten:

1. Children are their parents' responsibility; therefore, the parents have authority over the children.

2. When the children are in school, part of the parents' authority is delegated to the teachers.

3. When the children return home they revert to the authority of their parents.

How sadly mixed-up and confused those poor nuns are! They seem to think that, not only do they have authority over the children when the children are home, but that even at home, the teachers' authority has precedence over the parents' authority. Or, in other words, that the teachers' authority extends not only over the children at home, but over the parents as well.

When nuns at Notre Dame Convent School expelled eight girls for attending an Elvis Presley concert, reader reaction was divided.

If we tolerate that, what right have we to condemn totalitarian practices in other countries?

P.E. Libert, Ottawa

THE CONVENT'S CORRECT DECISION
APRIL 12, 1957

Elvis Presley comes to town with a vulgar and sexy show. He twisted, wiggled and jiggled, transforming the Auditorium into a juvenile hell, as 9,000 teenagers turned out to be but an hysterical mob.

Now no editorial came from *The Citizen* condemning the exhibition. But when the sisters in authority at Notre Dame Convent School, conscious of their responsibilities in preparing young mothers of tomorrow, aware of God's requisites as found in the Bible and of the seriousness of disobedience, decided to expel a few girls having deliberately defied its prohibition, out comes an editorial putting in doubt the wisdom of the penalty. It seems to me that the editors might be in need of Billy Graham's revivals.

The rightful decision taken by the authority of the Convent proves that the nuns wanted to protect their stu-

dents from immorality or at least not permitting to approve by their presence the public exhibition of unChristian and impure contortions.

Wilfrid Lefebvre, Ottawa

THE PRESLEY INFLUENCE
APRIL 15, 1957

Considerable ink has been spilled within the last few days regarding the expulsion of a number of students from Notre Dame Convent for attending the Elvis Presley show.

To put in my two cents worth, I would like to say that having signed pledges not to attend, they did so, some on the advice of their parents. This constitutes a wilful disregard for authority and a very bad example on the part of the parents who advised their children to attend. The expulsions, therefore, were in order and the nuns are to be congratulated.

I have noted within recent months the hold the Presley influence has taken on teen-agers. It is phenomenal to watch the gyrations of the children when one turns on the radio and Presley music is being played. It seems to stir the lowest instincts to make them act in the way they do.

I am only a layman but it is plain to see that the action of the nuns in forbidding the students to attend this performance with its sexual underlay, was entirely justified as Presley's performances are decidedly not in the interests of our teen-agers and the nuns are in a position to judge this much better than we are — don't you think?

K.N. Fairfield, Ottawa

THE GOOD SAMARITAN
APRIL 15, 1957

We would like to thank Mrs. Aurore Dascenso of Aylmer for saving our three-year-old daughter's life last Sunday night. Our little girl had swallowed a coin from my purse, while our car was stuck.

This lady brought my little girl back to consciousness, took us to her home, returned with a little truck and pulled out our car. She did all this for strangers, then let us rest before continuing on our way to Toronto.

Mr. and Mrs. Leslie Corby, Toronto

CONSCIENCE MONEY
APRIL 22, 1957

The Department of Finance acknowledges receipt of the sum of $9.00 conscience money received in an envelope addressed to "Receiver General of Canada, Dept. of Finance, Ottawa," post-marked Ottawa, Ontario, April 15, 9 p.m., 1957.

J.S. Sutherland, A/Chief Accountant,
Department of Finance, Ottawa

DOMESTIC DECOR
JUNE 8, 1957

"Rumpled look new in home furnishings," exclaimed a recent *Citizen* headline. Man, are they behind the times in New York. Why, here in Deep River (pop. 4,000), we've furnished our house that way for years.

To would-be do-it-yourself home decorators who would

like to redecorate in this increasingly popular style, the following suggestions are offered:

It doesn't matter what type of furniture you start out with — just keep changing styles each time you buy a new piece.

The most important items are ornaments or accessories. Strategically placed, these can add just the right degree of casualness. Mounds of unanswered mail, circulars, photos, yesterday's newspaper, empty glasses, full ashtrays — all these give a pleasantly "busy" look to a room.

Today many families combine the living room with the hobby room. Informal seating arrangements can be made around Mother's quilting frame, Dad's lathe, junior's shrunken head collection and sister's Elvis Presley records.

Just this morning, while standing in the middle of our living-room surveying the mound of broken toys in one corner, the baby carriage blocking the front door, three dozen diapers in a heap on the sofa waiting to be folded, the scatter rugs well scattered, two half-eaten apples, three trucks of assorted sizes, a yo-yo and a half empty nursing bottle tastefully arranged on the coffee table, I thought, with perhaps just a little pride, that even a professional decorator could not have achieved a more rumpled look.

Barbara Ditmar, Deep River, Ont.

CIVIC UGLINESS

JUNE 28, 1957

With reference to your recent editorial, "Placing Wires Underground," these Hydro and telephone poles and consequent overhead wires are the epitome of ugliness in our country and cities. However, in my travels I have never seen a city where this defacement is more deplorable than Ottawa. Ottawa is one of the last cities to run outmoded street cars, and the Hydro and telephone wires are augmented by a low overhead network of streetcar wires.

It was encouraging to note that Mr. Vincent Massey recently spoke of the mess of signs that splash the surface of our buildings and stores. The city should clamp down on the commercial interests that are reducing our streets to such agonizing ugliness. And the business firms should have enough civic pride to vie with one another in negating such a hodge podge of advertising.

Alice Gaman, Ottawa

RACING DEATHS

AUGUST 12, 1957

As I assisted at the funeral of Mr. Allan Wilson, who met his death recently while driving in the stock car races, I was stirred as I thought of that fine young man who lost his life making sport for the public, and I was greatly stirred as I witnessed the six pallbearers, all friends of his who are at the same work, wondering which boy will be next.

My letter is directed to we the public. Are we becoming more and more a barbarous type of people, fast adopting to the policy of the Romans years ago when they raced the chariots, held bull fights, etc.

Many a boxer and wrestler has been injured, some maimed for life and some dead. Yes, I know money is dangled before our boys, but where does it come from? None other than the public gate receipts. If we the public would adopt the policy of attending only the many good clean safe sports, our boys would no longer die in these places where lives are risked to give people a so-called thrill.

Rev. R. H. James, Metcalfe, Ont.

EXTROVERT AND INTROVERTS

AUGUST 19, 1957

If I'm ever shipwrecked on a desert island with one person, give me a good introvert, not an extrovert. The latter is scared to be alone, whereas the introvert loves it. While the extrovert would be moaning for company, the introvert would be busy, and would, as a result, himself be good company.

An introvert (at least one who is not a neurotic) is simply a person largely occupied with jobs which start inside his own head. An extrovert can see jobs only when they start outside his own head. The introvert is the healthy state. It's the extroverts who need the sympathy.

D. F. Stedman, Ottawa

ANIMALS AND RESEARCH

NOVEMBER 6, 1957

If all these frenzied characters babbling inanities about the poor little doggie in the Russian satellite would only return to their teacups and Pekingese, then we might be able to hear the whisper of the worried Western scientists as they beg for a stepped-up scientific program and a pooling of Western resources to enable us to equalize the achievements of Russia.

The Slavs are not such a sentimental race as the Western peoples — which is probably one of the reasons why they are now so far ahead of us. They have no time to waste on maudlin sentimentality — they know that before a man can be shot into space, the first step is to test the reactions of other living creatures.

A.N. Stankiewicz, Ottawa

COLONIAL FOOTBALL REFEREES

NOVEMBER 8, 1957

A great furor apparently exists about the quality of the refereeing in the Big Four Football League which culminated recently in the rather absurd suggestion that we should import American referees. How colonial can you get?

Granted, since the end of the war the caliber of the football played in the Big Four has improved faster than the overall standard of refereeing, but this condition is not the fault of the referees.

The qualities that make for a good referee in any sport are four in number: He must possess a high order of intelligence, a strong character, unimpeachable integrity and a thorough knowledge of the game, preferably derived from coaching or playing it. We have, in the Big Four, referees who qualify on these counts.

Any improvement of refereeing in the Big Four is a job for the executive of that league. Eastern Canada has plenty of men with the four essential qualifications. Only one slight difficulty exists — to locate and detect men with these qualities, the seekers must themselves possess them.

Francis J. MacNamara

1958

Local: Ex-mayor Charlotte Whitton runs for Conservatives in Ottawa West, but loses to Liberal George McIlraith despite PC landslide across Canada (March); New city hall opens on Green Island on Sussex Drive (August); Several injuries, but no deaths, as gas explosion levels office building in Centretown (October)

National: Regarded as the most advanced fighter aircraft of its day, the Canadian-built Avro CF-105 Arrow flies for first time (March); Seventy-four miners die when they are trapped in a coal mining explosion at Springhill, N.S. (October); Blanche Meagher becomes first female Canadian ambassador with her appointment to Israel (October)

World: Four months after Soviet launch of Sputnik, U.S. sends its first satellite into space (February); Cold War tensions rise as Nikita Khrushchev solidifies Soviet ties with Red China at a meeting with Mao Tse-tung (August); Fidel Castro begins final guerrilla offensive against troops of Cuba's Batista government (September)

Births: Terry Fox; pop singer Michael Jackson; Quebec politician Jean Charest; actress Sonja Smits; Canadian writer Anne Michaels

Deaths: Poet Robert Service; composer-musician W.C. Handy; Pope Pius XII; actor Tyrone Power

TIMELY HELP

JANUARY 7, 1958

I would like to thank the two gentlemen — and also obtain their names — who so kindly went out of their way to assist my aged husband, who was overcome with a weak turn on his way to the barber shop.

Between them they managed to get him home, after first trying a place of business to get him a cup of coffee, only to be told that was no place for a sick man. The Christmas spirit has gone so soon.

Mrs. Richmond Scharf, Ottawa

CBC ADVERTISING

JANUARY 9, 1958

On CBC radio stations there has been an increasing number of obnoxious advertisements. The usual reply to criticism is that the Royal Commission on Broadcasting, the Fowler Commission, recommended that more revenue be derived from commercial advertising and that therefore we must accept this offence to our ears.

However, there is a way in which the listener can make objection — to inform the advertiser that his products will not be bought until he treats his audience as adult. Any business concerns will think twice about a pitch which repels people from its products, rather than attracts them.

W.N. Roberts, Ottawa

Editor's note: The ads continued until April 1974, when the Canadian Radio-television Commission ordered the CBC to eliminate radio advertising by year's end. The CRTC argued that ad revenues were already low because of the essentially non-commercial nature of CBC radio's mandate, and they probably would only go lower.

THE POWER OF SONG

JANUARY 20, 1958

In a recent TV play, *The Other Place*, by J.B. Priestley, one of the characters says, "But I haven't sung a note since I was 10" — which gave me the fleeting thought, quite out of context with the story, "Why, that's right, people don't sing anymore."

I wonder if that sad fact isn't partly to blame for a lot of tension on all levels of society today. Goethe, that wise old bird, said "*Boese Menschen haben keine Lieder,*" or, loosely translated, "Nasty people don't sing." Now I certainly don't want to imply that we're all nasty people, but I do suggest that we seem to have lost the ability to express ourselves in song spontaneously, as easily as breathing, and have lost the relaxed frame of mind that goes with it as well.

It explains to me, at least, the sorry state of popular music today. Just listen, if you can stand it, to the unceasing parade of incoherent and vulgar lyrics set to a series of hiccups and caterwaulings known as "hit tunes." Is this the natural expression of a people who like to sing?

M. McDonald, Edwards, Ont.

FLUORINE POISONING

JANUARY 30, 1958

A radio address not long ago by Dr. Waldbott has revealed a new kind of illness which is spreading throughout the land.

Dr. Waldbott based his results on a study of 18 patients inflicted with this disease. The symptoms are "severe pain and stiffness of the spine, brain damage, lack of control of arms and legs, certain stomach disturbances and failing eyesight."

Leading specialists failed to find any reason for these facts, yet in each case the elimination of fluoridated water completely cured those infected. Foreign medical experts describe similar symptoms and see it only as the beginning of fluorine poisoning.

Unless something is done soon this problem may be ours. Our city fathers are being fast-talked into fluoridation and we have nothing to say about it.

Those who haven't got a well on their property had better start digging unless they want to end up with semi-paralysis or softening of the brain.

B.J. Langill, Ottawa

Editor's note: After years of debate, Ottawa followed the lead of most other major Canadian cities and added fluoride to its water supply in 1965.

HICK TOWN OTTAWA

JANUARY 30, 1958

Emily G. M. Brandon is either a Canadian, and therefore biased, or has never been to Ottawa. To suggest that Queen Elizabeth and Prince Philip should spend nine months of the year here because of Canada's setting as a geographic centre of the Commonwealth, as her recent letter suggests, is almost unthinkable.

Britain may not be the centre of the Commonwealth, but it cannot be equalled for its culture, and only there can the royal couple enjoy the society of men and women who excel in learning and achievement. The Queen enjoys horsemanship, whether it be racing, horse shows, polo, or just riding with her family. Excellent entertainment is also to be had for the asking, and the Queen enjoys it.

Where in Ottawa could these things be provided? I have been here only three months and I miss so many things I accepted as normal at home in England. Although to Canadians, Canada — and Ottawa in particular — is a wonderful place, to me, with its dirty potholed roads, its second-rate TV, its appalling radio, its horrible street-cars and rude conductors, its absence of the words "please" and "thank you" and common good manners, make it a hick town compared with London.

Before thinking of inviting our hard working Queen to uproot herself, may I quote your dreadful radio announcer and say, "Wake up, Ottawa."

Ellen L. Barton, Ottawa

HICK TOWN COMPARISON
FEBRUARY 3, 1958

The views of Ellen L. Barton against a country in which she has been only three months merit retort. Certainly Ottawa could fit into London many times. By the same token Britain could fit into Canada many times. Certainly, Ottawa has potholed roads, and, possibly, horrible street-cars.

But I would much sooner listen to the cheerful tones of the radio-announcers here than to the Oxford tones used by the London radio announcers. One would almost imagine they were favouring you by giving the news. Ottawa's streets may be dirty, especially at this time of the year, but they have nothing to equal Soho, nor its immorality, which is right in the centre of London.

Has Ellen L. Barton ever shopped, say, in a butcher's shop in London in June? Has she ever felt nauseated at the way uncovered bacon and meats are handled in London shops? Has she ever, in London, looked at the tenements and squalor of the East End where thousands of people look forward to an annual excursion to the sea-side, to get away, just for a day, from their surroundings?

May I suggest that Ellen L. Barton have an honest look at England's standard of living before she criticizes further.

J.A. Jones, Hull

WORKING MOTHERS
FEBRUARY 14, 1958

Has no one figured out that the main reason for so much unemployment is because so many married women are working and earning a man's wage? This makes two incomes in one family, while another has none.

Meanwhile, anyone can care for the family. Without the influence and moral support of a mother, the character of the youngsters deteriorates. It must do, when she is only home at weekends and is then too busy doing the things which the sitter has left undone.

It is useless to compare the number of unemployed of a few years ago with the number today. The mothers were at home in those days, as they should be today, rearing their families and using their brains to cook good nourishing meals for their offspring.

The man who does not let his wife work outside the home will have a healthier, better living family than any babysitter can give him. No matter how good a sitter and worker she may be, the children are absorbing her ideas, her moral standards and her religious convictions, instead of those of their own parents.

Margaret A. Roper, Ottawa

PROVING GROUNDS
MARCH 11, 1958

All the city fathers have to do is offer Ottawa streets to General Motors for a proving ground for new vehicles. I'll bet they would really be surprised at the amount of revenue they would get.

This plan should meet with the taxpayers' approval since their taxes would be greatly reduced by not falling in the potholes. Think, too, of the tourist attraction; they would swarm in to see the daily trials of Ottawa drivers competing against General Motors' best test drivers.

W.A. Johnston, Ottawa

'HAUTE COUTURE'
MARCH 24, 1958

It would appear that Canadian women have become slaves to the dictates of Paris fashion. The most startling example of this is the way slim, graceful women have adopted the ugly, baggy chemise dress because it has been described as the "subtle look."

Had this been just a Canadian idea no one would consider it anything but the visual results of a nightmare. There is nothing very subtle about a "sack" which adds about 30 pounds to a wasp-like waistline.

Audrey Hepburn is considered one of the 10 best dressed women in the world. Yet she delights to intrigue her husband by wearing "slim-jims" in red and white stripes to accentuate her slenderness.

In Paris, I discovered that many well-dressed Parisiennes could not afford an original turned out by "haute couture." Instead, they jealousy guarded the name of a Madame X, who lives in the Paris suburbs and can create a Dior or Maggy Rouff for a mere fraction of the cost of the original.

Surely in our large cities of Montreal, Toronto, Winnipeg or Vancouver, we have some bold and brave designers who could create distinctive Canadian fashions of grace and beauty. The materials are all there — both the cloth and the pulchritude.

Here is a challenge to some enterprising Canadian designer to make Canada the centre of fashion!

Rosemary Kirk,
Ottawa

MR. DIEFENBAKER'S NECK

APRIL 2, 1958

I fully realize the question I am about to ask is not at all pertinent and could almost be classed as frivolous. However, there is a need within me that must be satisfied.

At first I considered sending this note to your "Ask Andy" column, but upon further consideration decided that you, Mr. Editor, would be best qualified to provide the information.

For several months now I have been observing Mr. John Diefenbaker in his various capacities and have watched with some admiration mingled with a certain amount of concern the head and neck movements of the above-mentioned gentleman, and I have reached the conclusion that it is some sort of exercise to increase the size of the neck muscles.

Now the question is: what size shirt does Mr. Diefenbaker wear? If any member of your staff could supply the answer to this pressing problem it would be deeply appreciated.

A.B. Wells, Ottawa

Editor's note: The Citizen of 1958 did not reply to the letter-writer's question, but a 1999 call to the Diefenbaker Canada Centre at the University of Saskatchewan revealed that the former prime minister wore a size 15½-16 shirt. For those who are interested, Mr. Diefenbaker never cared much for fashion, and bought his shirts off the rack.

HAIRCUTS

APRIL 10, 1958

With the possible advent of a $1.25 haircut, may I suggest that a series of brush-up courses be initiated by the barbers' union for the enlightenment and pride of skill for quite a few of its members. Special attention could be given to the execution of children's haircutting and to tapering and shaping — or has this now become a lost art, like shaving?

Most of the tonsorial artists in this fair city of ours seem to be obsessed with the idea of speed: they chop it off, paste it down and shout, "Next."

Tis no little wonder that the home haircutting sets are becoming so popular.

J. Cappelic, Ottawa

FUNERAL FLOWERS

MAY 6, 1958

In a news report appearing in your paper, Mayor Nelms requested the oil companies to plant flowers around their service stations.

What does this man want now? He has already killed our business by forcing through a by-law on early closing, and now, apparently, he wants us to decorate the graves by planting flowers.

John K. McManus, Ottawa

AIR RAID SHELTERS

JUNE 9, 1958

For the sake of human safety, I would like to know

THE CANADIAN PRESS

Admitting his question could be termed frivolous, a reader wanted to know the shirt size of Progressive Conservative leader John Diefenbaker, seen with his wife Olive, during a 1950s stopover among the blossoms in Wallaceburg, Ont.

what action our civil defence authorities have taken to provide community air raid shelters for Ottawa. If there are any I have never heard of them and do not know where they are.

One trusts that we will never have a nuclear war — but it is a possibility. In view of international tension a "volcano" might explode any time and anywhere. It was evident from the last war that capitals were the chief targets — evidence London, Berlin, and others. Thus Ottawa would be vulnerable.

In a great many American cities I have seen signs pointing to the air raid shelter and, if it is not needed, so much the better. One is proud that the government has and is erecting so many beautiful buildings in Ottawa but it is my humble opinion that the personal safety of citizens has been sadly neglected.

In this scientific age, if Canada were attacked it would no doubt be with lightning speed and perhaps people would not have time to evacuate their homes; but if shelters were available they might be able to save themselves until they got their breath.

Charles E. Compton, Ottawa

STREET CARS

JULY 25, 1958

The worst thing that could happen to Ottawa would be to take the streetcars off and replace them with buses. Buses are a boon where there are no streetcar tracks, but to put buses where there are now street cars, is in my opinion a crime against the underprivileged public.

Are there not enough buses, trucks, etc., congesting our streets and poisoning the atmosphere? I've been in packed buses where six teenagers were smoking. The bus driver couldn't see them so they got away with it. Another thing, what about mothers who have to take their babies in baby carriages? Is consideration given to the blind and crippled? Think it over, these agitators for the removal of street cars.

E. Earl, Ottawa

Editor's note: Streetcar service continued through most of the 1950s, but by 1958, with ridership dropping, operation costs rising and the need to service the expanding suburbs, the Ottawa Transportation Commission decided to go to an all-bus system. Streetcar service ended May 1, 1959 when Britannia car 831 rumbled into the Cobourg Street transit barn at 3:25 a.m.

DOG HIT

JULY 28, 1958

Last Wednesday at Wakefield Lake my nine-year-old daughter accompanied by our family dog went down the road for the mail. A station wagon, driven by a woman, tore past at high speed, hit the dog and did not stop. The dog took about five minutes to die and the child, by the time her mother got there, was on the verge of hysterics.

It is hard to believe that a woman can be so callous as not to stop and see if she could help the child, or at least call the parents.

If by chance the driver reads this, I want her to know that I am thankful that it was not my daughter who was the victim of her high-speed driving. "Just a dog" can become all too readily "just a child" when a moron gets behind the wheel of a high-powered car.

F.J. Rapp, St. Sylvestre, Que.

LESS SPIRIT

AUGUST 6, 1958

Why don't we whistle and sing more, or even hum? I notice that out of 10 persons living in a house or apartment only one, it often happens, utters any sound at all as they work or play or just sit. Have we less spirit these days or have we gravitated to mere shadows like the oldtime movies? In many homes people walk on tiptoe like burglars or congregations entering a church.

As for playing a musical instrument, that's a crime. There is actually a city by-law prohibiting music being played even outside in free air. Are we oppressed or suppressed? Dictatorship is very infectious. We must be very careful to avoid an automatic drift into Russian hypnosis.

Let's whistle and sing more everywhere. Let us stay free.

Charles P. Stokes, Ottawa

NATIVE DRESS

SEPTEMBER 11, 1958

I would like to suggest that the Indians on all reservations in Canada dress in their native costumes — soft white fringed leather costume for the women and children and the men in a natural shade of leather. I have a feeling that the maidens would be married off in no time at all.

The money brought in by tourists would increase the present allowance for Indians.

(Mrs.) H. Cameo, Ottawa

OTTAWA'S GIFT TO SPRINGHILL

NOVEMBER 4, 1958

I'm one of many people terribly disappointed in our city fathers where the city's donation to the Springhill mine disaster fund is concerned. One's imagination does not have to go far to see and feel the grief of the people who lost their loved ones in a shocking disaster.

Ottawa especially, however, should be understanding in its donations in the light of our own experience in the downtown blast last week, where had it been a few hours of difference in time, the death list could easily have exceeded that of Springhill.

I guess our city fathers did not see it this way, though. They sent $1,000 as the capital's donation. Toronto voted $25,000 to the fund; the Ontario government $50,000; the new pontiff $5,000; Ontario school children $3,000. Surely we could do a little better than $1,000. I strongly believe Ottawa had better send no money at all rather than make a poor show. The city may not have a budget like the city of Toronto to work with, but $1,000 is just a little too cheap for a city this size.

A.D. Boudewyn, Sr., Ottawa

Editor's note: City council did not increase its $1,000 donation to Springhill, N.S.

1959

Local: Streetcar service ends, transit system now buses-only (May); Changing of the Guard ceremony begins on Parliament Hill (July); City councillors visit Toledo to view pedestrian mall that could serve as model for proposed Sparks Street mall (September)

National: 14,000 lose jobs when government cancels Avro Arrow jet fighter project, citing spiralling costs (February); First ship enters St. Lawrence Seaway (April)

World: Fidel Castro's Cuban revolutionaries overthrow Batista government (January); Alaska becomes 49th U.S. state (January); Hawaii becomes 50th state (August); Admitting the car was a failure, Ford Motor Co. drops the Edsel (November)

Births: Olympic speed-skater Gaetan Boucher; pop star Bryan Adams; Reform politician Stephen Harper; Canadian women's rights activist Joan Grant-Cummings

Deaths: Quebec premier Maurice Duplessis; jazz singer Billie Holiday; architect Frank Lloyd Wright; rock 'n' rollers Buddy Holly, J.P. (Big Bopper) Richardson and Richie Valens; film director Cecil B. De Mille; actors Ethel Barrymore and Errol Flynn

CANADA: FLAG AND ANTHEM

JANUARY 2, 1959

Why this talk about Canada having its "own" flag and its "own" national anthem? Ever since the day Wolfe defeated Montcalm on the Plains of Abraham, we have flown the Union Jack, and with rightful pride have sung *God Save the Queen*.

Are we so soon to forget that we owe our freedom — indeed, our very existence — to England, the greatest nation in the world?

Let us not disgrace ourselves by flying some hideous banner bedecked with maple leaves, fleurs de lis, beavers, mounted policemen, hockey players, polar bears, or whatever else is believed to be distinctively Canadian. Let us fly instead the Union Jack, the flag of England, of Canada, of the British Empire.

O Canada is an extremely beautiful song, but should not take the place of our national anthem, *God Save the Queen*. I fail to see why *God Save the Queen* is not widely accepted as our anthem, for the Queen of England is also officially the Queen of Canada.

I also believe the adoption of a distinctive flag and anthem would only serve to draw us farther away from England and closer to the United States. The qualities of shallowness, materialism and arrogance inherent in the American character can only have a bad effect on us.

R.W. Allan, Ottawa

RESERVE FOR ENGLISHMEN

JANUARY 6, 1959

The lonely, heartrendering outcry which Mr. R.W. Allan inserted in your columns has profoundly touched me. I, too, realize the deep debt of gratitude we owe our imperial British friends for the magnificent job of colonizing, educating, and developing they have carried out in Canada.

To dare think of trying to change the noble flag and anthem we now have, would not only be an act of the grossest sacrilege, but a sign of blatant ingratitude. Therefore, as a noble gesture of goodwill, I respectfully suggest we submit the following plan to our Prime Minister, Mr. Diefenbaker:

That a certain area of Canada be developed and set aside in perpetuity, as a home away from home for all Englishmen resident in Canada (ex-mineral rights, of course.) A suitable area that comes naturally to mind is the magnificent island park of Victoria Island, District of Franklin, N.W.T. Here, in a wild and rugged all-year-round play-

ground the imperial soul will be able to roam, ruminate, and enjoy the company of other kindred spirits from the fair isle across the ditch.

To assist in the establishment of this haven, our government could construct living accommodations and other facilities all wired to hear such rousing national songs as *Rule Britannia, God Save The Queen, White Cliffs of Dover, Hearts of Oak*, etc. In such ways the residents will be kept in a suitably happy frame of mind.

Once inaugurated, the island could be turned over to Great Britain for maintenance with funds for this purpose obtained by giving all comers the honour of paying the British level of taxes while there.

A further small item — the construction of a flag pole on every square mile flying the Union Jack — would assist the Eskimo unemployed at the same time. Thus, each and every holidaymaker would be reminded, wherever he gazed, of his glorious heritage.

I expect the real benefit that will be derived by Mr. Allan and others from this retreat will be the pleasant remoteness from the "shallowness, materialism, and arrogance" of our large neighbour to the South. The great project could, with little difficulty, be built up as our achievement of the century.

E. P. McLoughlin, Ottawa

UNSUITABLE GARB

JANUARY 21, 1959

Love makes the world go round, and round, as the song goes. Seemingly, the producers of the popular TV musical program *Showtime* think that tight jeans and black leather jackets are also a requirement of love for both sexes.

I am sure any adults who happened to be watching the above program must have been thoroughly disgusted as were the members of my household. How can any individual or organization that is interested in combatting juvenile delinquency make any impression when the young people are confronted with this sort of entertainment?

This attire which has come to denote gangs has been banned at our community centres as well as in school and other organizations. I was therefore surprised to find this type of dress presented on a program such as *Showtime*.

Claude Bennett, Ottawa

Editor's note: Mr. Bennett, 22 when he wrote this letter, later became a prominent Ottawa politician, serving on city coun-

cil, board of control, regional council and, as MPP for Ottawa South, in the Conservative cabinets of premiers Bill Davis and Frank Miller. In January 2000, Mr. Bennett was put in charge of the group established to oversee the transition of Ottawa-Carleton's 11 municipalities into one large city.

SENATE ACTION
FEBRUARY 9, 1959

A few days ago Senator Ralph Horner laid much of the blame for unemployment on unemployment insurance. How a man in any walk of life can make such a wild assertion I'll never know.

As a Senator, you would expect him to know at least that one has to be fully qualified to draw unemployment insurance, and it being part of a government department, it is his duty to know at least that much about it. But obviously he prefers to make the labouring classes look like scroungers, and the unemployed look like tramps.

It is small wonder that public opinion is for the abolition of the Senate, that is costing the taxpayers $2 million annually for salaries to people who have either become unco-operative MPs and are sent there, or are sent to make room for someone else, and whose only function is to sign any bill that suits their friends.

Charles E. Roe, Maxville, Ont.

DOG PROBLEM
FEBRUARY 23, 1959

I hope that I will see the day coming when no one will be allowed to keep a dog, since according to my observation many dog owners care more for a dog than for helping one of their less fortunate fellow men in distress.

T. Viau, Ottawa

TORY VISION GROWING DIM
MARCH 2, 1959

If the present government budgeted a million dollars a day for the Arrow, which they knew was going to be scrapped, why was not that million a day put into a research unit, built by Canadian scientists for Canadian defence weapons?

Why do we continue to buy second-hand mistakes? If the answer is that we must have a defensive weapon and such a plan would take too much time, just what are our defensive weapons now? The Arrow is dead and the obsolete Bomarc missile has not yet arrived to take its place. It may be years before we receive it, if ever. Why is our government so lacking in the vision and faith in Canada and Canadians that our pioneer forefathers had?

We will never achieve national greatness limping along in the shadow of another great country. Greatness comes from within and the time is long past when we should look to ourselves for our own salvation.

P.M. Hipkin, Manotick

Editor's note: The Diefenbaker government cancelled development of the Avro CF-105 Arrow, an advanced jet fighter, in February 1959, when it became clear sluggish sales of the supersonic aircraft to the U.S. and other western countries would not cover costs. More than 14,000 employees lost their jobs, the government ordered the destruction of all Avro plans and prototypes, and many of the project's top engineers and scientists left for jobs in the U.S. or Britain, taking with them the hopes for a vibrant Canadian aerospace industry. In the meantime, the government ceded to U.S. requests to deploy in Canada two squadrons of American Bomarc missiles to replace the scrapped CF-105s.

MORE NURSES ARE REQUIRED
MAY 5, 1959

A national crisis in the nursing profession has arisen, partly due to the erroneous impression that all salaried "grass roots" nurses (the ones who do the work, not those who sit behind a desk all day), are adequately paid.

Nursing today is a means of livelihood, as well as a vocation. Younger women are increasingly breadwinners, and have dependents, the same as other voters and taxpayers. These family responsibilities are of primary concern, and their financial needs must come before any vocation's demands, if that profession remains an ill-paid one.

The result is that, in alarming numbers, "grass roots" nurses are leaving Canada for the United States because of the higher salaries they can command there. Similarly, many public health nurses are turning to the teaching profession, where they can earn $1,200 a year more with attractive annual increments.

Therefore, as some very concerned "grass roots" nurses across Canada want positive action in the matter, all registered nurses who are discouraged and angry at the present situation are invited to write their views to the undersigned, for further discussion and more constructive channeling of effort.

Those nurses who are planning to leave for the U.S. or change to another line of work, please state reasons in detail. Our aim is, "to keep nurses in nursing, and nurses in Canada."

(Miss) Cecilia Pope, RN,
1668 Eglinton Ave. W., Toronto

IN DEFENCE OF PARENTS
MAY 7, 1959

The Citizen heralded Dr. Chisholm's visit here with the quote, "The worst tragedy that could befall tomorrow's children would be to be like today's parents." Doesn't the eminent doctor know that parents are human beings, some good, some not so good, and that to lump them all together in this fashion is pure foolishness?

As a teacher of little children may I say that never have there been better parents than those of today. I find them intelligent, conscientious, self-sacrificing and so very, very anxious for their children — all that in spite of the false psychology that has been directed at the parent in the last couple of decades, re the disciplining, or shall we say non-disciplining, of children.

As for Dr. Chisholm's nasty slam at the family of eight, is it not a well-known fact that to be born of a large family, blessed with brothers and sisters, is to have had a great advantage over, say, the only child?

Further, this continent is bulging with over-production; our agriculturalists could produce 10 times as much any time they wish, so Dr. Chisholm should have no fear about over-population. It is not less children, it is more Christian charity that is needed, with a better distribution of food and a greater sharing of agricultural know-how.

Irene Bradley, Ottawa

Editor's note: Controversy seemed to follow Dr. G. Brock Chisholm wherever he went. A psychiatrist and medical administrator, he first came to national notice as chief of medical services for the Canadian army during the Second World War. In the mid-'50s, he became front page news for his attacks on the use of superstition and myth in education. His opposition to teaching children to believe in Santa Claus triggered a national debate, and his warnings about the dangers of pollution, over-population and the nuclear arms race ensured he remained a much-discussed figure until his death in 1971.

LOST OPPORTUNITY
JULY 31, 1959

Since school was let out in June, I have watched from my Civic Hospital bed two and sometimes three small boys gather up the odd empty pop bottle from the grass between the hospital and the nurses' residence.

We appreciated that those boys were smart enough to take advantage of opportunity as it knocked, probably to turn the bottles in for cash and thereby supplement their allowances, or possibly to help out at home with the few pennies per day that 20 or 30 bottles would bring.

It did our hearts good to see these little lads ambitious enough to take an interest, day after day. Besides their own profit they were doing a good job of ridding the lawn at no cost to the Civic.

Lo and behold about a week ago, our bubble burst when I looked out to see an employee of the hospital chasing these young lads. Ever since then, he chases them away daily and gathers the bottles for himself in a gunny-sack.

I think this man should be given a "meanness" medal of some kind.

David Potter,
Ottawa

THE RED MENACE
AUGUST 27, 1959

The red menace marches on. Not satisfied with having grabbed North Vietnam, the Communist Chinese are annexing Laos.

What steps are the western democracies taking to stop this outrage? History repeats itself, and the ghost of Hitler grabbing his European neighbours should be clearly before us all.

We will have to fight these Chinese fiends very soon in a to-the-finish conflict unless those bandits are shown that not one square inch of free soil can forcefully become the property of Mao Tse-tung.

Lawrence J. Segal,
Ottawa

FOOTBALL SHORTCOMINGS
SEPTEMBER 11, 1959

It seems characteristic of the football mentality in Ottawa to focus on incidentals when something serious is at stake. With the Rough Riders' 0-4 record, headlines on the front page of *The Citizen* dealt with Ottawa football executives' concern in losing footballs to over-enthusiastic youngsters. The solution should be no more than an administrative detail. The real problem, fielding a team worthy of Ottawa's faithful football public, is being treated as secondary.

It is amazing that the shortcomings of the Ottawa Rough Riders have to be pointed out by an out-of-town newspaper. On Sept. 2, the *Montreal Gazette* carried a story which stated "the Ottawa management can't take any bows for its scouting to build up a pass receiving corps. The Riders haven't recruited an outstanding import offensive end in years."

Last year's offensive backfield, which held its own in annual accumulated yardage, would have been second to none (as this year's could be) if the Rough Riders had an aerial attack. It seems elementary that a ground attack could double in effectiveness if the opposition had to divide its defence to guard against both a ground and an aerial attack. But for the last three years, the Riders' aerial attack failed time and again because of ineffective receivers.

Let us hope, next year, when the management is put on a professional basis, the Ottawa football club will be supplied with an executive that will do more than fiddle while the Ottawa football public burns.

Joe A. Gatner, Ottawa

Editor's note: Mr. Gatner got his wish. The next year, the Riders finished with a 9-5 record, and after beating Montreal and Toronto in the Eastern playoffs, defeated Edmonton 16-6 to win the 1960 Grey Cup.

RACE RELATIONS
SEPTEMBER 14, 1959

I see by *The Citizen* that the CBC is in hot water again because a guest on one of their panel programs spoke out against equality between the white man and the Negro.

Like any decent person, I become indignant when I see another person deprived of his basic rights, and it is distressing to think that the world may be deprived of a great statesman, doctor or teacher because there is prejudice against his race or the colour of his skin.

However, every human problem has two sides, and this one is no exception — there is also the woman's point of view. The simple fact is that if the Negro is considered the equal of the white man, he then becomes the superior of the white woman (I am not taking into consideration the myth about "equality of the sexes," because I am talking about what actually exists).

When I visited England two years ago, I noted flashily dressed young Negroes on London street corners looking over the white girls as though those girls were so many cuts of meat in a butcher shop window, and I thought there would be trouble one day.

I doubt that there is anyone who wishes to see the same situation prevail in Canada.

(Mrs.) C.J. Richards, Ottawa

PARLIAMENT HILL LIGHTING
OCTOBER 7, 1959

I wonder whether you agree with me, and many of my Ottawa friends, that your beautiful Parliament Buildings are ruined by the red and green flood-lighting at night.

Ottawa is beautiful and well cared for, and a joy to visit, but one is shocked by the vulgarity of the appearance of the seat of government lighted like a circus, when the dignity of the buildings in the daylight is such a delight.

Lucile W. Hupman, New York

ERROL FLYNN STORY
OCTOBER 21, 1959

Recently I read your front page death "tribute" to Errol Flynn, of which I think "exposé" would be a better word for the story gave the impression his whole world revolved around sex and liquor.

The former I feel was his own affair and the latter a fault or not depending on the opinion you hold. Even a casual reader of this coverage (which I wasn't) would notice no mention was made of his numerous movies, acting ability or anything of this nature.

In death, indeed as in life, the press just couldn't resist the temptation for sensationalism. Isn't it about time this hounding of our entertainment folk is slowed down? For a man who gave me and millions of others so many moments of pleasure this is just not a fitting obituary.

(Mrs.) Joan Bennetts,
Cardinal Heights

SINK OR SWIM
NOVEMBER 18, 1959

Ottawa's darkest hour came last Saturday afternoon at half time at Lansdowne Park. At first glance it appeared to be a large-sized bubble gum wrapper floating across the playing field, but after asking a few sober fans what "it" was I was told "it" was our Grey Cup float.

Well, sir, I have seen better floats on the end of a 10-cent fishing line. We (football fans) all know that the interest shown toward sports by the city of Ottawa is almost negligible, and it has not improved any since Charlotte Whitton left the scene.

Our football team deserves a better representation than what we are prepared to give them. If that monstrosity gets to Toronto for the Grey Cup parade on Nov. 28 I am sure the sanitation department will pull it in before it reaches the football stadium.

I think that our Miss Ottawa Rough Rider riding a bicycle would get more attention and cause less embarrassment — and it would not cost the city a cent.

R. Daniels,
Ottawa

THE OTTAWA CITIZEN

Errol Flynn, seen with Olivia de Havilland in the movie Robin Hood, gave pleasure to millions, said a reader, who objected to the sensationalism in the Citizen's death 'tribute' to the actor.

CANADA'S FLAG
DECEMBER 2, 1959

If a new Canadian flag is necessary should it not honour our patron saints?

The patron of Canada's football awards — Whiskey.

A patron of Grey Cup broadcasts — Cigarets.

The patron of arts in Canada — Sir Liquor.

The Saviour of Ottawa's Community Chest — Saint Bingo.

So Canada's flag might be designed to show a whiskey flask, top left; a cigaret, top right; a bingo card, bottom left; and a monkey, bottom right.

For pleasure, fun and health, these are our patrons.

David S. Christie,
Ottawa

"Canada is in trouble. Those of us who will celebrate
Confederation in 1967 will celebrate not unity
but growing disunity. If we allow these differences
to continue growing, we may end up
with five separate Canadas."

— March 12, 1966

1960-1969

Local: Ottawa's Anne Heggtveit wins gold in Olympics slalom skiing (March); Pedestrian mall tested as summer experiment on Sparks Street (May); Charlotte Whitton wins mayoralty in her return to municipal politics (December)
National: PM John Diefenbaker opens new National Gallery on Elgin Street (February); Maurice (Rocket) Richard retires after 18 seasons with Montreal Canadiens (September)
World: Fifty blacks killed by police gunfire in protests at Sharpeville, South Africa (March); Soviets sentence American U-2 pilot Gary Powers to 10 years for spying (August); John Kennedy narrowly defeats Richard Nixon in U.S. presidential election (November)
Births: Canadian film director Atom Egoyan; country singer George Fox; journalists Kenneth Whyte and David Frum
Deaths: Writers Albert Camus, Boris Pasternak and Richard Wright; Quebec painter Paul-Emile Borduas; Canadian public servant Brooke Claxton; movie star Clark Gable; U.S. tycoon John D. Rockefeller Jr.; composer Oscar Hammerstein; Emily Post, arbiter of etiquette

MASS MEDICATION

JANUARY 20, 1960

The proponents of fluoridation have two things in common: (a) they are experts on the subject or they quote others as being experts; (b) they imply that in advocating fluoridation they are benefactors of mankind, and of children in particular.

Yet it is safe to say that not one of them has any personal scientific knowledge of the matter — beyond the common knowledge that sodium fluorides are in general use as a rat poison.

They say that dental and medical associations endorse mass fluoridation. If they do, and I doubt if the majority of dentists and doctors recommend fluoridation from any personal knowledge, they are accepting the loud claims of others.

Whereas any one can fluoridate their own drinking water, these experts (?) would enforce their will on the entire population — and they would do this in the name of good. Perhaps it is kindly to say that they may be unconscious of the fact they are advocating mass medication.

David S. Christie, Ottawa

Editor's note: Ottawa began to fluoridate its water in 1965, but not before the issue had been put through a vigorous public debate, including two referendums — one which rejected the idea in 1962 and one which approved it in 1964. Here's another letter on the subject.

FLUORIDATION

JANUARY 23, 1960

The fluoridation sales promotion meetings say to keep pushing the subject and your editorials which appear in regular monotony confirm that you are following this to the letter.

Your latest attempt, however, would indicate that you could be more enlightened on the subject than previously, by your remark that there is an "absence of danger if the addition of fluorides is carefully controlled." The sales promotionists would never commend you for that statement, however, as they never use the term "adding fluorides." They say, they "adjust the quantity." I trust you'll remember this the next time you write.

As for the Eskimo being fortunate (according to you) in having fluoridation, my head hangs in shame that I am even a member of the race that forced this 20th Century

hogwash on these unsuspecting citizens under the guise of benefiting their health.

(Mrs.) M. Lefebvre, Ottawa

GROCERY STORE CLOSING HOURS

JANUARY 24, 1960

With our ever-changing world, and the many improvements constantly being brought before us to make life easier, I can't understand why our City Council must stick to some old out-dated laws that are not flexible to our modern day living.

All around us, in Montreal, Toronto, Hull, Eastview and even City View, officials have become aware of how greatly grocery shopping practices have changed in the past 10 years, and have altered their closing laws accordingly.

A few years ago, there was no such thing as a supermarket, and nearly all of us did our grocery shopping at a corner store, either in person or by telephone, and most of the time the groceries were delivered. But now, Friday has proven to be the most suitable day for shopping with most of us, and instead of phoning or going to a little corner store, it is the common procedure to visit a supermarket. And if there are small children in the family, and the husband takes the family car to business, and in the case of working supplies, it means the shopping can't be done until after 5 p.m.

With our stores being permitted by an old bylaw to remain open only until 7 p.m., there is a mad stampede to get to the store, without dinner, in most cases, to get the shopping done before 7 p.m. For an hour or more you push your way though crowded aisles, selecting the groceries, then nearly always have to stand in line for a further 15 minutes or more, waiting to have your groceries checked. Quite a frustrating experience!

It is ridiculous for council not to allow the grocery stores of Ottawa to remain open one night a week, until 9 p.m. as is the custom everywhere else. The people of these other cities and towns are to be congratulated; they must have some women members on their council — it seems to take men so much longer to see the need for change in life.

(Mrs.) G.M. McKay, Ottawa

Editor's note: City council extended Friday night shopping hours to 9 p.m. in October 1962.

QUESTIONS ABOUT KILLING
JANUARY 26, 1960

During the war I agreed with a statement I had once heard that one could not simultaneously be a Christian and an effective soldier in offensive battle. But I quickly came to understand that such an attitude was unpatriotic and treasonable.

It was rationalized that the attacking soldier was shielding his loved ones from the ugly, untrusted enemy, and so I affected to agree that under certain circumstances it was quite right to creep up on a man and blast his head to eternity.

Consequently, I now find myself agreeing with those who are not disturbed by the irrevocable removal from society of a man guilty of child-murder.

But I am quickly coming to understand that such an attitude is sadistic and revengeful, that in fact I cannot claim to be a Christian and simultaneously hold this view, and so I affect to agree that under no circumstances is it right to obliterate the life of a man.

Thus I am confused. Was I right then, during the war? Is it possible for me to be wrong in both instances?

Nina Green, Ottawa

Editor's note: Capital punishment, the source of lively public debate since Canada's earliest days, was not abolished outright for civilian crime until 1976. It remains in use under the National Defence Act for cowardice, desertion, unlawful surrender and spying for the enemy. The last execution in Canada occurred in 1962.

ADVANTAGES OF UNDERGROUND WIRING
FEBRUARY 20, 1960

I feel that any argument or discussion involving a public utility should be principally concerned with utility and service rather than beauty. If these points are considered, it will be clear that beauty will be achieved, one might say painlessly, certainly automatically, and without great expense.

To restore the service in Southern Ontario after this winter's ice storm cost a tremendous sum of money. In addition, there was great inconvenience and possible financial loss to consumers. Electricity is such a part of our lives today that we fail sometimes to see that from being a new gadget and luxury it has become, in most communities, as necessary as the air we breathe.

I would like to ask how long the exposed lines would last in an ordinary bomb blast, leave alone a nuclear attack? Going back again to personal experience during the blitz in London, houses fell all around and blast damage was severe, but we still had electricity because for years the local lines had been underground.

It has been reported that an Ontario Hydro spokesman said that it would be difficult to locate and repair an underground break. This is true; however, if inspection pits are provided at strategic points, it should be relatively easy. Buried wires were also mentioned as a danger to power shovels. I find it difficult to believe that this spokesman really thinks that there is less hazard using a pole on streets heavily travelled by trucks, buses and fairly powerful cars.

To achieve the minimum disruption of traffic while these hydro lines were laid, they should run under sidewalks and preferably on the inside edge. Transformers which are now poised on poles could very well be placed in steel cabinets as they are in Europe on the sidewalk.

D.B. Price, Ottawa

TAXES AND HANGING
MARCH 2, 1960

Since January, there has been a great concentration of articles, news reports and letters concerning the abolition of capital punishment. All of these, whether they were for the abolition or retention of the death penalty, were written with respect, consideration and regard to our method of democratic procedure.

One, however, I am sorry to say, lacked this dignity and resorted to undemocratic methods in the expression of his views. In a front page news story, Mr. Peter Churchill, a CBC news editor, was reported to have said that he has written to Prime Minister Diefenbaker, Justice Minister Fulton and Finance Minister Fleming saying that he will not file an income tax return until capital punishment is abolished. He was, furthermore, reported to have said in his letters that he plans "to incite others to follow by example."

Should we all, both abolitionists and retentionists of the death penalty, follow his example, I shudder to think of the utter chaos which would prevail in our courts and our economy. I commend Mr. Churchill on his enthusiastic public spirit, but I must vehemently object to the conduct he is using in trying to influence the convictions of our MPs.

Rodney E. Riley, Ottawa

ANNE'S HIGH GOAL
MARCH 19, 1960

A recent letter referred to the tribute given by the city of Ottawa to slalom skier Anne Heggtveit on her triumph in the 1960 Olympics and went on to ask this question: "How can we encourage our children to go to school and study when winners in sport are given greater recognition?"

On the contrary, I believe that our children can draw inspiration from Anne's example. She chose her field of endeavour at an early age, set her sights high and was willing to work hard for many years (without financial reward) in order to reach her goal.

Are these not the qualities which will help our young people to excel, whether in sport or scholarship?

(Mrs.) Israel Button, Ottawa

THANKS FROM ANNE
MARCH 29, 1960

Through the medium of your newspaper, I should like to thank everyone who contributed to the purchase of the lovely sports car that was presented to me on Friday.

I wish also to thank all of those who organized the pro-

OTTAWA SPORTS BOOK

Slalom skier Anne Heggtveit exhibited qualities that inspired children to excel, said writer.

ject and worked so hard to reach their objective in a very short time. I shall never forget how wonderful everyone has been.

Anne Heggtveit, Ottawa

CBC DANCERS

APRIL 6, 1960

The Talent Caravan show on March 31 was generally a good show. But I wish to protest against such a performance as the ballet dancers who appeared on the program.

It is a shame to permit a young girl of 14 and boy of 18 to show themselves in such an open way. I cannot say too much about the girl, but let me tell you that the young man who was dancing with her was something to look at. I think the CBC should take proper steps in the future and make sure that what was shown on TV will not be repeated.

Raymond Hardy, Hull

LEGALIZED LOTTERIES

APRIL 9, 1960

With hundreds of prospective patients in many of the chief cities across the country awaiting admittance to our overcrowded hospitals, surely it would be pertinent at this time for the government to consider the sponsorship of legalized lotteries on a par with the Irish hospitals sweepstakes, and the proceeds therefrom utilized to finance the enlargement of existing hospitals or the building of new ones.

Thousands of dollars, now going out of the country, would, without doubt, be "invested" here at home if some such scheme existed. Then again, it is hard to find enough money to finance normal, let alone advanced, education. Even the most bigoted opponents of gambling, both church and state, must realize what a terrific contribution this potential revenue would make toward the successful achievement of both projects.

Gambling will persist wherever an outlet presents itself, and as the stock market and the race track are legalized media for the "better lined" gambler, let's at least be consistent and include a government-controlled lottery in which all can participate.

H.R. Allen, Ottawa

Editor's note: A provincial lottery organized in Quebec in 1968 was the first such government-sponsored scheme in Canada used to raise money for public works, in this case Expo '67. The western provinces followed in 1974 and Ontario in 1975. The federal government got into the lottery business the next year with Loto-Canada, a Crown corporation created to raise money to help pay for the 1976 Montreal Olympics.

DISCOUNTED MONEY

APRIL 20, 1960

The other evening over a CBOT news edition, the Ontario Minister of Travel and Publicity mentioned something would have to be done regarding the discounting of American coin from American tourists visiting in Canada, but nothing was said about Canadian coin in the United States.

From past experiences, many of us have had the insulting experience of having our money thrown back at us by our contemptuous American hosts disdaining to accept our legal tender. I recollect an occasion in Boston when stores took off 18 per cent and the glee on the clerks' faces was most insulting.

My beef — what about Canadian coin in the United States? Will it be taken at par?

Myrtle Roxborough, Ottawa

Editor's note: The Canadian dollar was worth roughly 0.97 U.S. throughout most of 1960.

SPARKS MALL

MAY 26, 1960

The amazing mall of Sparks Street draws my criticism, but I doubt that my unprofessional thoughts will prove valuable to anybody. The first thing to hit my well-known sensitivities was the lack of hideous noise. I thought I had hit a stone wall or had become deaf from an excess of black dust from 20 years of Ottawa roads. I rattled my ear holes in vain.

Then my emotions became rattled at the way I had to meander to get along the mall. First to the right, then to the left, then a circle or half-circle, then a colliding with an obstruction because I stroll always with my nose in the air. Next to puzzle me were the Metcalfe and O'Connor cross-

ings. When the signal denoted "Walk," the north and
south traffic stopped me.

When traffic stopped, the signal said: "Don't Walk."
And the light was green. Then suddenly everybody started running six different ways. I was nearly knocked down.
I had to dodge people, not traffic. But I got across. I guess
that's the main thing.

Ambling along, I said to myself: "We need a little music.
We need more flags." Suddenly I barged up against small
shrubs. I lost my balance and became mixed up with vegetable soup, macaroni, steaks and a big man puffing a big
Cuban cigar. One of my hands went in soup, one went in
hot coffee. I saw a waiter coming.

I thought of Charlie Chaplin, and I ran. The screams
and laughter faded. I wasn't followed.

Are they sidewalk cafes or road cafes? Should they have
red and green lights on the shrub barricades of cafes?

Charles P. Stokes, Ottawa

ALFRED SCHOOL
JUNE 22, 1960

Whoever came up with the headline "Police Mix with
Prisoners at Training School Fun Day," should really be
proud.

At the Alfred school is a Christian order of brothers
who dedicate their lives to help wayward and abandoned
boys find a place for themselves in this life and you have
to come up with one of your sensational headlines that
brand the boys as "prisoners."

That's a below-the-belt blow to a wonderful Christian
organization.

Don M. Lake, Ottawa

Editor's note: In the early 1990s, 11 Roman Catholic broth-
ers were convicted of more than 100 charges of sexual abuse
connected to the assaults of dozens of boys at the St.
Joseph's Training School in Alfred. The abuse took place for
more than 30 years beginning in the 1950s.

RADIO SNATCHED
AUGUST 3, 1960

On Friday, a retarded boy whom I am taking care of
went to the park near St. Patrick's Bridge, with his radio
under his arm, which he had just received for his birthday.
Along came some persons — I don't know whether to call
them hoodlums or teenagers — and snatched his radio
from him and ran away.

I think this is very mean. Would they please return it
and make a boy happy who is not able to enjoy life like
them as he is a sick boy.

(Mrs.) F. Laroque, Ottawa

TRAFFIC ACCIDENTS
NOVEMBER 5, 1960

I write regarding the large number of tragic traffic accidents. Much advice for avoidance of these has been given
by press and radio.

I suggest all drivers use prayer to the Great Pilot for direction and guidance and that sincere thanks be given up-

on safe return. If all drivers did that a great improvement
would soon take place.

Colin M. Keill, Ottawa

'SWAN LAKE'
NOVEMBER 9, 1960

I was delighted to see so many entranced little girls at
the National Ballet's "Swan Lake" the other night. Their
presence transported me back to the early years of the
century when I was taken to see Anna Pavlowa at the old
Russell Theatre.

I don't remember if I saw the whole ballet, or if the great
dancer was doing various roles. But I will never forget her
interpretation of "The Death of The Swan" (which never
seems to be done these days). As the lovely creature died
of a broken heart on the stage, my seven-or-eight-year-old
heart broke, too, and I, howling, was hustled up the aisle
by my embarrassed parents. I can only hope that the in-
comparable Pavlowa accepted the wails as a tribute.

(Mrs.) Jennifer Harris, Ottawa

PUBLIC MEETS OTTAWA TEAM
NOVEMBER 23, 1960

Ottawa Rough Riders won the [Eastern Conference] final game in Toronto but they didn't win too many fans at
the Uplands Terminal on Sunday night. It was the most
poorly organized show I ever had the misfortune to see —
the fans saw plenty of Ottawa's civic officials but not
much of the players.

Coach [Frank] Clair attempted to introduce the players
and we saw seven or eight of them. They had from 4 p.m.
to get the public address system up and at 8 p.m. it still
wasn't ready. When it was ready you could barely hear
what was said. The majority of the players didn't even approach the railing so you could see them, and those who
did didn't even have the decency to wave their hats or
hands.

I left home at 6:30 p.m. and fought traffic all the way. I
stood from 7:15 to 8:30 to catch a glimpse of the players. I
sat in my motionless car from 8:30 to 9:45. I went to the
coffee shop and had a watery coke at 10:30 when I finally
got served. I got back to the car at 11 p.m. and service police got me out a back road or I'm sure I'd still be there.

James A. Gauthier, Ottawa

POLITICAL DIFFERENCE?
DECEMBER 17, 1960

Do you know what is the difference between the Liberals and the Conservatives in Canada? I have been asking
this question since I arrived in Ottawa two months ago
and I had not obtained a satisfactory answer until yesterday, when Mr. Lester Pearson gave me his clever response.

"The only difference between the Conservative Party of
Canada and the Liberal Party of Canada," he said smiling,
"is that the Conservative Party is in power for the time being and the Liberal Party is not."

F. Habashi,
Ottawa

Local: Study finds Dutch Elm disease ravaging hundreds of trees in Ottawa's core (May); New parkway improves public access to Gatineau Park (September)
National: Controversial new Columbia River Treaty gives Canada half the electricity from dams built on Canadian section of B.C. river (January); U.S. president Kennedy, on visit to Ottawa, hurts back planting tree at Rideau Hall (May); Bank of Canada governor James Coyne forced to resign over fiscal disagreement with government (June)
World: Anti-Castro exiles botch invasion of their Cuban homeland at Bay of Pigs (April); Soviet cosmonaut Yuri Gagarin first man in space (April); Berlin cut in half by Communist wall (August); Nazi SS chief Adolf Eichmann sentenced to death in Israel (December)
Births: Hockey great Wayne Gretzky; singer k.d. lang; actor Michael J. Fox; figure skater Brian Orser; Canadian race horse Northern Dancer; U.S. track star Carl Lewis
Deaths: Writers Ernest Hemingway and James Thurber; psychoanalyst Carl Jung; baseball legend Ty Cobb; actor Gary Cooper; Ottawa sports impresario T.P. Gorman; UN secretary general Dag Hammarskjold; detective writer Dashiell Hammett; British conductor Thomas Beecham

FREE BUT JOBLESS
JANUARY 28, 1961

In your editorial on Mr. Kruschev, you make a statement which will probably go unnoticed by many readers: "In Russia, the working class has less voice in its country's affairs than does the working class in the United States, Britain or Canada."

This may be so, but it is hard to understand that with all these so-called freedoms why Canada should maintain a regular force of unemployed workers far in excess of the countries whose workers have no voice. It would suggest that the voice of the working class in Canada is either weak or non-existent.

Perhaps it's not freedom the unemployed most need, because they are certainly free to roam the cities and towns of our country. What they need is the dignity of honest work, honest reward, and security for our future generations.

B. Elsworthy, Ottawa

SPACE HOAX
APRIL 26, 1961

Now that Russia claims the first astronaut there seems to be popular acceptance of this information as fact and I have heard few doubts and criticisms of Russia's recent achievement.

The British Interplanetary Society is one of the most authoritative and reputable sources of astronautic information in the world. If the Russians have information to divulge about Yuri Gagarin's flight it should show no reluctance to present it to the British Interplanetary Society. Until I hear of publication of a reasonable amount of detail about Gagarin's flight in the *Journal of the British Interplanetary Society* I would not discount the possibility of a hoax.

H. Verdier, Ottawa

NATIONAL THEATRE NEEDED
MAY 13, 1961

A national capital should be more than a mere seat of government — it should also be the fount of national culture. It is therefore deplorable that the city fathers of Ottawa, including Big Sister Charlotte, have allowed the federal government to continually outshine them in provi-

ding whatever cultural features Ottawa has. Even the Ottawa library is the result of an endowment while the art gallery and the museum are both creatures of the national government.

There is an opportunity, however, for the city fathers to redeem themselves. There is a crying need for a national theatre in Ottawa, a theatre that could house a national professional company and also be a proper forum for visiting artists and touring companies. The city of Ottawa owns a large plot of ground in its very heart, an ideal location for such a theatre. In view of the rapidly onrushing centennial, surely it would be most fitting that a national theatre should be built and operating in time for that event.

I am sure that if the city made the handsome and generous gesture of dedicating the land which now supports the old car barns on Albert Street to such a project, it would be the spark for a nation-wide campaign to raise necessary funds to complete and equip the building itself.

There are citizens of Ottawa who have worked unselfishly for many years to stimulate such a program and they would be only too glad to spearhead this drive. As this location also suits the overall development program of the National Capital Commission, undoubtedly funds would also be forthcoming.

It would be a great pity to see such a perfect site for this project disappear. In the years to come it will be a matter of great pride to the members of this year's City Council to realize that they had the vision and the public spirit to get this project under way. A national theatre — gift of the city of Ottawa to the people of Canada.

Melville M. Goldberg, Ottawa

Editor's note: In the end, it was federal funds that built the National Arts Centre, which opened in 1969 on Elgin Street at Confederation Square. As for the city-owned land on Albert Street, it became the site for Tower A of Place de Ville, the first office highrise built by developer Robert Campeau in downtown Ottawa in the 1960s.

MR. KENNEDY'S VISIT
MAY 23, 1961

President Kennedy's recent visit to Canada appears to have been masterfully designed to bring Canadians to their senses, and specifically to make them realize that

THE CANADIAN PRESS

Jacqueline Kennedy helps plant a tree at Rideau Hall watched by the U.S. president, John F. Kennedy, and prime minister John Diefenbaker, during a visit to Ottawa in May 1961. Farley Mowat saw the visit as a way to bring Canadians to their senses.

Manifest Destiny has marked Canada out to be the United States' "closest friend."

It was clear from Mr. Kennedy's remarks at Ottawa that the Americans are willing to overlook our carping criticisms of increasing U.S. domination of Canada, providing that we are willing to desist from such injurious actions in the future and will demonstrate that we are prepared to accept the role envisaged for us by Washington without further nonsense.

To make the point even clearer, the U.S. Strategic Air Command chose Wednesday, May 17, while Mr. Kennedy was preparing to confer with Mr. Diefenbaker, to provide us with a most impressive demonstration of U.S. goodwill over Canadian soil.

B-52 multi-jet hydrogen-bombers crossed the undefended border in force. Between 8:00 and 9:30 a.m., six of these mighty aircraft, flying at intervals of 10 to 15 minutes, passed over the Palgrave area just north of Toronto on a course which would appear to have taken them near Ottawa. This particular group, which I observed, flew at about half the normal altitude for either training or operational flights — presumably so that visual effectiveness from the ground would not be too greatly reduced by distance.

It is, of course, not known whether this or any other group carried their ordained weapons. Nevertheless it was an extremely sobering display of Old Glory in the most modern manner of "showing the flag."

Farley Mowat, Palgrave, Ont.

Editor's note: By the time he wrote this letter, Mr. Mowat was already the popular author of such best-selling books as People of the Deer, Never Cry Wolf *and* The Dog Who Wouldn't Be. *And as his letter shows, Mr. Mowat had al-*

ready developed the nationalist sentiments he became better known for in the 1970s and '80s. The letter was written one month after the bungled U.S.-sponsored Bay of Pigs invasion of Cuba.

THE MAYOR ON THE NUMBERS GAME
JUNE 10, 1961

I want to thank your organization for the warm resurgence of courage and devotion to office given to me by the well integrated misrepresentations — or rather, mathematically erroneous circulations — published in your Tuesday edition.

It is tragic that at a time when the government is appealing for every one in the country to "Help Canada Count" that the oldest paper in the nation's capital can't.

Apparently the deadline did not allow the headline to be changed on one streamer, to the effect that the majority wished the Mayor to quit. For you published 11 street "shots" of which six wanted the Mayor "to stay." This is a most heartening increase in popular support, being nearly treble the majority by which I was elected and over 55 per cent of the poll when I barely made it in December.

But how you — in your story — ascribe as the "overwhelming" number of aldermen wanting me to resign as eight in a field of 24 in Council, I, and those I have consulted in the Dominion Bureau of Statistics and Honour Maths, cannot figure. I could have saved you all this trouble, for seven aldermen worked against my election [and] have consistently, directly and indirectly, attempted to frustrate much of what is advanced in policy or estimates. I could have provided you with the list with one name added — and given you your total of eight. This however, is not one-third of Council and consequently two-thirds — the vote required for major contested decisions — are still the solid majority core of Council.

So, thanks again for your invigorating proof of increasing public support and my understanding sympathy in *The Citizen's* inability to calculate correctly.

Charlotte Whitton,
Mayor of Ottawa

A CHAMPIONSHIP STADIUM
AUGUST 8, 1961

Ottawa has finally made the "big time." At Saturday's football game I saw a sight for sore eyes. How many times have I heard people squawk about the state of the football stands; well, there is no reason for complaint now. It seems only fitting that a championship city such as Ottawa should have such a fine stadium.

Along with the new stadium we have new uniforms, new players, and greater heights to attain.

Our Rough Riders Majorettes also have a new look and no longer give that amateurish feeling. It certainly is a pleasure to see them perform with such grace and ease. Our half-time show is second to none.

M.A. Lachapelle, Ottawa

Editor's note: After the Rough Riders won the Grey Cup in

1960, city council rewarded the team by adding permanent seating along the south side of the field at Lansdowne Park. Until then, six or eight rows of temporary seating were set up for each game, and taken down once play ended. The permanent seats installed in 1961 remain today as the lower deck of the two-tier southside grandstand.

SUNDAY LAWS
AUGUST 23, 1961

I must confess that I am rather confused by the restrictions now slapped on motion picture and field sport operations on Sunday. "Restriction," of course is rather a euphemistic word; perhaps one should substitute "ban." And this ban seems to run drastically counter to even elementary logic.

Apologists for the ban justify their stand by pointing out that it was ratified by a majority vote at the recent election. These people forget that there are some things which cannot be passed upon by a majority.

The people voting against Sunday entertainment — movies, for example — are voting (I will give them the benefit of the doubt) purely on principle. Therefore, they would refuse to attend Sunday movies even if they were in operation. And, therefore, the process is entirely meddlesome, an example of somebody who is willing to do without something firmly decreeing that everybody else must do without, too.

The majority is not infallible, because no individual is infallible. As a matter of fact, a popular majority is rarely even right. It does not operate logically, and its morals are 60 years out of date. And this particular majority is not only denying a liberty to those who want a liberal Sunday, but also to those whose only day off is Sunday.

William L. Cameron, Ottawa

Editor's note: The majority finally overcame its "infallibility" and voted to relax Sunday sports and entertainment laws in 1965.

HOT DOGS AT THE 'EX'
AUGUST 23, 1961

People are talking about the exorbitant prices of hot dogs (30 cents each) currently being sold at the Exhibition by some scalpers.

This may seem like a minor item to some people, but because so many parents and their children are affected by the ridiculous prices being charged for hamburgers, potato chips, etc., it is suggested that those people operating on a limited budget patronize their respective church booths, where such food stuffs can be obtained at reasonably fair and just prices.

Francis G. Heggtveit, Ottawa

OTTAWA'S CLUSTER LIGHTS
AUGUST 30, 1961

Coming up Rideau Street with my husband and children the other day, I glanced up at a vestige of old Ottawa life and thought how charming the antique clusters of street lights were. It crossed my mind that someone "up there" had feeling for the past and was retaining at least one of the furnishings which lend character to what has not always been considered a beautiful street.

So I was startled to hear that not only Rideau Street, but Parliament Hill, are to be stripped bare of these garlands of light and studded, instead, with those harsh fluorescent installations. (They give you a headache and make you look 10 years older, too.)

Please, before we allow the sausage-machine mentality to take over, consider keeping this lovely touch on our streets, even if we have to make up a special supply of globes.

Helen Gougeon Schull,
Rosemere, Que.

MEETING THE THREAT OF NUCLEAR WAR
SEPTEMBER 30, 1961

The other day my nine-year-old son, after listening to the news on the radio concerning Russian bomb tests and threats of nuclear war, remarked somewhat fatalistically, "I guess I'll never know what it's like to be big."

His words struck home when I realized that I didn't have an answer to them. All the pat reassuring clichés that we so aptly use to salve our children's problems seemed terribly inadequate.

How do you explain to a child after trying to instill in him concepts of truth, love, kindness equality, etc., that world powers are seemingly quite prepared to liquidate in as foul a means as has ever been devised, many millions of their fellow human beings for the sake of an ideology, or political system, and even in the name of freedom?

To my mind an atomic destruction committed with with the intention of preserving freedom is very much like the comic strip character Fearless Fosdick who ran around shooting large holes in people's heads to protect them from eating cans of poisoned beans. This kind of freedom we can do without.

Now we have some of our citizens rushing to build fallout shelters. This could be the most dangerous philosophy of all. Isn't it very much like the person with a loaded gun pointing at his head, who looks around for something to hold the blood? These people are not only burrowing into the ground physically but mentally, too.

Fight we must, but it must be a fight for peace by all of us.

James J. Clarke, Ottawa

COMIC STRIPS ARE ANALYZED
OCTOBER 14, 1961

A new comic strip entitled "The Flintstones" is now appearing in *The Citizen*. The environment is a "wacky" combination of contemporary with stone age domestic.

I have been following the comic strip trend fairly closely of late and comparing it with my juvenile reading of the same genre. It seems clear that a great change of tone has occurred over the past two decades. The laugh-a-day, "just folks," wacky and facetious schools are now in ascendancy and working hard at presenting their diminishing image of man. An increasing sense of the inanity of human life has moved in step with increasing affluence, and the man-the-microcosm has been replaced by man-the-microbe.

An inquiry along these lines discloses the widespread belief that to laugh at ourselves (collectively) is a great need of our age, lest we succumb to pride. To speak of a flight from human dignity is not much of an exaggeration in the present cultural context.

In this connection, it is worth noting that one of the characters in the "Alley Oop" strip (a carry-over from a healthier era), when challenged by the incredulous remark "This is the 20th century!" replied: "That's right, so let's not sell it short!" Oop doesn't sell us short, and he deserves credit accordingly. It's entirely fitting therefore that he has been banished to a separate page of *The Citizen.*

Philip Belgrave, Ottawa

Editor's note: This is among the first letters to the editor from Philip Belgrave, arguably the most prolific letter-writer in the Citizen's past. Nearly 40 years later, Mr. Belgrave is still sending in his controversial views on a wide range of topics.

VERSION OF 'AVANT GARDE' ART IS UNDER QUESTION
OCTOBER 25, 1961

By the tone of his letter, I doubt very much if Bill Boss heard my recent talk entitled "The Avant Garde, 1961," at the National Museum. Perhaps he drew his conclusions from the rather sketchy reports in the local press — in any case, he is a bit too anxious to sound profound and "arty" without knowing the facts.

I did not condemn true progressive revolutionary or avant garde painting, and spoke at length on the validity of much of it. The main topic of my talk was about the "Dadaism" of 25 years ago and similar anti-art fads so much in vogue today, including the "Art of Assemblage" now on view at the Museum of Modern Art in New York, which is a farce, and taken as such by most serious critics, not to mention the public.

If Bill Boss enjoys a certain Paris artist's "creations" (?)

which consist of piling rubbish between two sheets of glass, or another artist (?) who smears paint on a nude and rolls the nude on a canvas (to mention only two examples), he is, of course, free to call such nonsense progressive. I call them ridiculous, and certainly not art.

It is naive to accuse anyone who condemns trash of being a reactionary — it has become a game for too many arty intellectuals who acclaim anything novel, crude or facile as avant garde art.

Bill Boss should have a good hard look at much of the tripe being produced by phonies and exhibited now by too many museums (mostly in the United States) as progressive art — if he did, he would perhaps be less inclined to rush into print and keep a sense of values.

Henri Masson, Ottawa

Editor's note: Although he travelled extensively and his works were exhibited nationally and internationally for decades beginning in the 1930s, Belgian-born painter Henri Masson lived in Ottawa for most of his adult life. Largely self-taught, Masson employed a loose, vigourous brush style in his depictions of choir boys, monks, hockey games, musicians, parades and Hull streetscapes from the 1930s and '40s. Many of his works hang today in the National Gallery. He died in 1996 at 89.

FOOTBALL ON TV
NOVEMBER 1, 1961

Obviously the three television stations servicing the Ottawa area consider it inconceivable that many of their viewers do not care for football. Amazing and unbelievable as it may seem there are some people who would prefer a good movie on Sunday afternoon.

It is therefore regrettable that one station out of three cannot see its way clear to featuring something other than football. After all, football fans cannot watch the three channels at once.

I have often heard the comment that Ottawa is not sportsminded and wonder if this exhibition of so much football is supposed to promote more interest in the game. I'm afraid that it will only create the same feeling experienced when too much food is eaten.

L.J. Rallard, Ottawa

Local: National Capital Commission announces expropriation of 154-acre LeBreton Flats (April); City council extends Friday shopping from 7 p.m. to 9 p.m. (October); Charlotte Whitton wins re-election as mayor (December)

National: Canada's first medicare program introduced in Saskatchewan (July); Trans-Canada Highway completed with stretch of highway in Roger's Pass, Alberta (August); Canada's first orbiting satellite, *Alouette I*, launched from California (August)

World: U.S. military strengthens its presence in South Vietnam to combat increasing guerrilla activity from Communist North (January); France grants independence to Algeria, ending protracted civil unrest (July); U.S., Russia on brink of nuclear war over Cuban missile showdown (October)

Births: Pop singer Sheryl Crow; Canadian singer Sue Medley; CFL quarterback Matt Dunigan; French pianist Philippe Cassard

Deaths: Marilyn Monroe; writer William Faulkner; Eleanor Roosevelt; Niels Bohr, A-bomb designer; Nazi war criminal Adolf Eichmann; TV comic Ernie Kovacs; Canadian Arctic explorer Vihjalmur Stefansson; poet e.e. cummings; actor Charles Laughton

FALLOUT SHELTERS

JANUARY 20, 1962

I am writing this in the hope that it will discourage at least some people from building private fallout shelters. In fact, I feel sorry for any person building these units, as they offer no protection from the type of bomb that will be used, should another war come upon us.

Hydrogen bombs will be used in very limited quantity in another war. Neutron bombs will be used in almost all operations, as they do no damage to the area the enemy wish to take but will kill every person within miles of the target, even if their shelter contains one foot or more of concrete, or several feet of earth as protection.

There is only one solution that would provide almost complete protection in the event of a war lasting a year or more, and that is community shelters 300 or more feet underground. These shelters would be less expensive than the cost of our defence program over a period of time, and would contain concentrated canned food for the entire city and rural population.

Small steam electric atomic units would supply electricity for all needs, and would turn water into a superheated gas, which would be used for heating and breathing purposes. Water would be provided by underground springs channelled into a man-made underground lake.

T.J. O'Meara, Ottawa

TREATMENT OF NON-WHITES

FEBRUARY 3, 1962

The removal of many restrictions in the new Immigration Act will prove of small advantage to non-whites entering Canada unless provision is inserted in the Act to make it an indictable offence to refuse them accommodation, if it can be proved that said accommodation is still available or has been advertised as being vacant at time of application, provided their credentials and ability to pay are satisfying.

Similarly, with the refusal to serve non-whites in restaurants, barber shops or any establishment available to the general public.

This practice of discrimination, especially against Negroes, is far more prevalent than is generally supposed, and with so many new Asian and African diplomats visiting Canada from the United Nations, serious embarrassment could confront the federal government if this discrimination is permitted to continue.

H.R. Allen, Ottawa

Editor's note: The Diefenbaker government made non-white immigration to Canada somewhat easier in 1962 by relaxing long-standing rules favouring applicants from Britain and some Commonwealth countries. However, it wasn't until 1967 that the law was changed to eliminate ethnicity and geography as factors in the selection of immigrants. Even so, because immigration offices are not set up in many Third World states, it remains more difficult for applicants from these countries to find their way to Canada as official immigrants.

NEW FACADE OF CHATEAU

MARCH 14, 1962

To most people the name Château Laurier is synonymous with Ottawa at her best, gracious and conservative. It is in the gloaming, the last hour of the day that the Château seems at its loveliest and finest, a mixture of fairy-like improbability and reality. Straight out of a picture book, the pearl-grey stone lifts the emerald-tinted tiles and many dreaming turrets into the twilight, sheer to the waiting stars. Splendidly sited, ordered and contained, an expression of architecture in its highest moment and of our national pride.

And now, what have we done? Superimposed upon the once regally gilded legend, straight across the unadorned façade above the ever-open doors is now another sign, extruded ribbons of compelling, titillating light, a credit-jeweller's concept, spelling it all out — the writing on the wall — to catch the eye of the stranger, lest tired and uncertain, he fail to know it from any other hotel in town.

Nothing but the best for the Château, the very latest thing, at any price, the price of good taste.

G.H. Dickinson,
Ottawa

SPEED LIMIT ON CONSUMPTION

MARCH 17, 1962

Serenely, I consider why we have so much garbage. Has quantity increased because progress has increased? Garbage has been multiplied by the system of fast multiple selling of the increased things invented — the insane way of making the public buy more and more at breakneck speed. Business needs a speed limit applied at once.

Charles P. Stokes,
Ottawa

TRUE DEMOCRACY
APRIL 18, 1962

Capitalism, in this day and age, has brought our world to a point where there is no longer any security. There is chaos on the international level, on the national level, there is a lack of employment, want and hunger for the masses even in the "have" countries. Let us go back to true democracy under the guiding hand of God.

Today, free countries are facing Communism and socialism, the seeds of which have been sown by exploitation of the working classes. Since this segment of the population is by far the largest group in any land, it will eventually determine the fate of a country. Are Communism and socialism the solution to which they will turn? Can free enterprise and work not be more evenly distributed and the abundance shared by all without such sacrifice?

Yes! A better monetary system; statesmen instead of politicians; true equal privilege for all races, creeds, and classes; a better distribution of the wealth to all, could ward off the eventual bondage or destruction which, at present, is our destiny.

Joe Metail, Ottawa

MOTHER'S DAY
MAY 12, 1962

Tomorrow is to be observed as "Mother's Day," or what many now like to call "Christian Family Day."

Our organization would like to appeal to the leaders of all religious faiths and the members of their congregations to devote part of their worship period toward thoughts of their responsibility for the creation of a saner world and prayers for guidance for purposeful activities in which they can engage toward easing world tensions and turning men's minds from war.

As Dr. Margaret Mead has told us, "The people of each nation have become responsible for the people of each other nation on the face of the earth, however hostile its government." Our children can no longer be safe without the safety of all children.

Charlotte McEwen, Chairman,
Voice of Women, Ottawa

Editor's note: Created in 1960, and most effective during the decade that followed, the Voice of Women is a non-partisan organization of women that promotes peace and disarmament.

BIRTH CONTROL VIEWS
MAY 30, 1962

In reply to my letter, D. Williams states, "While some people believe that all birth control is contrary to God's will, many churches support the alleviation of suffering wherever possible, even when this involves the use of some method of birth control."

It is important that a distinction be made not only between artificial and natural birth control, but also between motives when using the "natural" method.

The providence of God reveals to mankind, through sci-ence, saving phenomena such as the "rhythm" system for when mankind is really in need of them.

However, the evil nature of the motive of the deed by Onan, who was slain by an act of God (Gen. 38: 8-10), is not lessened an iota when used by those who can now take advantage of the scientific discovery of a natural phenomenon.

While it is true that the Catholic Church supports research for improving the "rhythm" system because it desires the alleviation of suffering, it is vigourously opposed to the distribution of "artificial" birth control information and equipment.

If birth control is necessary, and most agree it is, the means provided by God is the only morally permissible method.

H.W. Mason, Ottawa

BIRTH OF A CHILD
AUGUST 29, 1962

I am a woman about to have her first baby. As part of the Victoria Order of Nurses pre-natal course, I was invited to visit the hospital in which I would be confined, to give me an idea of what to expect. As I entered the hospital doors many thoughts passed through my mind, but there was one thing that really struck and has stayed with me since.

This baby has been conceived by choice out of love between two people. It is planned for and dreamed about for nine months as it develops within the body of woman, and yet when the time comes for the final fulfillment of this waiting and planning, the woman is taken by her husband and partner to the hospital entrance.

He fills out the necessary forms for admittance and is then told very politely to go home and wait for any news.

The woman is then taken to a room, which may or may not contain other patients, to finish her labour and deliver the baby among strangers, who for the most part are indifferent to her and her case as it is an everyday occurrence to them.

Is this then to be the ending of this chapter in life? The moment man and wife should most share together, at the time when woman most needs the reassurance of someone familiar and loved, they are separated! I realize that at present, hospital facilities are cramped, but I hope in the future much thought will be given to this and something can be done.

Mrs. P. DeVries, Ottawa

SUPPORT FOR PRESIDENT'S ACTION
OCTOBER 27, 1962

I was amazed to hear the CBC newscaster report that, in the present Cuban crisis, T.C. Douglas was the only "dissenting voice" among the parliamentarians.

This accusation was made on the basis that the New Democratic Party leader had been reported as saying "that we must remember that the Soviet Union has for years been surrounded by American misfits." How on earth can this be regarded as a dissenting voice?

Surely, it is the voice of sanity and objectivity. Mr. Douglas was stating fact.

CHRONICLE OF THE 20TH CENTURY

Cuban president Fidel Castro, left, meets Soviet leader Nikita Khruschev as the Cuban crisis escalates. Readers were divided on president John F. Kennedy's stand against the buildup of missiles in Cuba.

Perhaps if a few more of us would come out of our comfortable cocoons of complacency and would peruse such books as *The Ugly American* and *A Nation of Sheep* (both stinging indictments of American foreign policy), we might realize that the world is not divided into black and white, virtuous and immoral ("our" side being the virtuous side, of course).

David J. Weston, Ottawa

SUPPORT FOR MR. KENNEDY'S ACTION
OCTOBER 27, 1962

Your editorial condemning President Kennedy's stand against Cuba and Communism was quite disappointing.

It came at a time when people, fighting for a common cause, should be united. Your editorial motivated dissension.

Your criticism of the President's move was based on the fact that Mr. Kennedy had no legal right to act as such. Who are we to respect international laws against a country which uses these same laws as decoys to spread its germ throughout the world, a country which has no respect whatsoever for human rights or for any other moral law!

André Richard, Ottawa

ASSESSING FLUORIDE ARGUMENTS
NOVEMBER 3, 1962

The people of Ottawa should realize that most of the very vocal anti-fluoridationists are quacks and food fadists, while the strongest supporters of fluoridation are doctors and dentists.

One usually consults a garage mechanic when concerned with automobile maintenance; it follows that the advice of medical men should be accepted in matters of public and personal health.

Harvey Glatt,
Ottawa

THE BIRTH CONTROL ISSUE
NOVEMBER 3, 1962

Your correspondents, belabouring one another with Biblical quotations, have endeavoured to discuss birth control in a highly emotional manner, thereby documenting their intolerance, bigotry and slavish adherence to ecclesiastical pronouncements.

I suggest that logic cannot function within prescribed limits set by the various religious creeds in accordance with postulates, the applicability or veracity of which are not demonstrable.

It seems probable that the root of the controversy is the apparent Christian church philosophy that enjoyment of sex without a view to procreation is evil *per se*. I find it difficult to accept this view, since it would, therefore, appear that the Supreme Being has played a vast and perpetual joke upon mankind in creating a pleasurable experience, the end result of which is responsibility for individuals and a population explosion for mankind.

In other words, pleasure as an objective, unless it be asexual, is not desirable.

The Christian way of life has so much to offer mankind that it is a pity the enormous web of man-made rules is allowed to take precedence over the simple virtues of tolerance, understanding and brotherly love.

L.G. Shurben, Ottawa

MEDICARE BOGEYMEN
NOVEMBER 24, 1962

In raising the bogeyman of medicare, M.I. Wilson blames "labour" for this welfare measure. While "labour" may accept credit gladly for this, I feel it necessary to point out that all political parties, major church denominations, service clubs and practically all newspapers (including *The Ottawa Citizen*), support this measure just as sincerely. Would the above describe themselves as "labour"?

The medical profession (the highest income group in our nation again this year), are establishing themselves as the most reactionary group in the country. We all know what they oppose, but not what they favour. Did they not oppose government hospitalization insurance a few years ago?

B. Smith, Ottawa

BENEFITS OF PUBLICLY OWNED TV
NOVEMBER 24, 1962

The CBC renders Canadians a fine service despite a constant campaign against it. One only needs to travel south of the border for examples of how bad TV can become under private ownership. The sooner private interest and commercial advertising are removed from our television programming the better.

Unfortunately, there are influential vested business interests who would lose some of their profits if private TV were eliminated. These interests have succeeded in convincing Canadians of lower intelligence levels that private ownership and commercials result in cheaper TV. Even the simplest of minds should realize that soap, tobacco, brewing, and all companies, including CTV, are not benevolent societies.

Private TV cannot produce anything that public ownership cannot. Advertising reduces time available for the program. The public must pay the cost of the commercials. Many of these cost as much to produce as the fee paid for the canned program presented. In addition, profits for the pockets of the producers of the commercial, advertising agencies, and TV station owners must be added to the cost of goods and services used by the public.

G.W. Durham, Ottawa

FLUORIDE IN FOODS

DECEMBER 12, 1962

So fluoridation has been rejected and now, as you say in your editorial, "the campaign of education and persuasion in favour of fluoridation should continue."

I very much dislike the idea of having for the next two years this sort of brainwashing. If campaigning is to be done in favour of something which, some day, may be good for the teeth, I would like to know what is also going to be done right now to fight proven causes of tooth decay. For example, why not campaign against those horrible candies? They certainly do spoil children's teeth. It is also well known that malnutrition is another important cause of tooth decay.

Why not campaign to educate the public about health measures, such as the proper use of natural fresh food, to point out the importance of well balanced diets for all ages as well as the mistakes to be avoided when planning meals.

(Mrs.) A.F. Romanowski, Ottawa

Editor's note: In a December 1962 referendum, Ottawa voters rejected fluoridation. In another referendum two years later, they approved it. As a result, Ottawa's drinking water was fluoridated in 1965.

1963

Local: City council proposes annexation of all Nepean, Gloucester lands within the greenbelt (January); Plans unveiled for $100-million renovation of Confederation Square and Union Station (September); At $4,516 annually, Ottawa ranks ninth in Canada for average income (November)

National: Defence Minister George Harkness resigns when cabinet refuses to allow U.S. nuclear warheads on Canadian soil (February); Liberals led by Lester Pearson win minority government (April); Montreal bombings by separatist Front du libération de Québec damage buildings and mailboxes, and kill night watchman at army recruiting centre (April-May)

World: British war secretary John Profumo resigns amid scandal he had sex with prostitute with ties to Soviet attaché (June); Kim Philby, British journalist and former diplomat, is exposed as Soviet agent (July); President John Kennedy killed by assassin in Dallas; Lyndon Johnson takes over (November)

Births: Baseball slugger Mark McGwire; Canadian comedian Dave Foley; Quebec speed skater Nathalie Lambert; Canadian writers Linda Frum, Donna Laframboise and Lynn Crosbie

Deaths: Poets Robert Frost, William Carlos Williams and Theodore Roethke; chanteuse Edith Piaf; Pope John XXIII; U.S. black leader Medgar Evers; black scholar William E.B. Du Bois; jazz singer Dinah Washington; playwrights Clifford Odets and Jacques Cocteau

EMERGENCY DRILLS IN SCHOOLS

JANUARY 8, 1963

Your article concerning nuclear war drills in Ottawa schools was most illuminating and revealed both the stupidity and futility of such superficial precautions.

It is appalling that responsible bodies such as the school boards should participate in precautions that are, in effect, merely those used in Europe during the Second World War and illustrate the antiquated and ludicrous thinking of the Emergency Measures Organization in regard to civil defence in the nuclear age.

If a real civil defence system is demanded to defend the populace in the event of a nuclear war, then the financial burden must obviously lie with the federal government, since it would be far too expensive for provincial or local authorities. Each school would require its own shelter, food, water and medical supplies and so forth; very costly, it is true, but a high premium is demanded for a bad risk.

Let us stop these grand illusions at once and refuse to accept the possibility of a nuclear holocaust; without peace all is lost to mankind. The only possible defence is complete disarmament.

C. R. Barnes, Ottawa

NO ANNEXATION FEARS

JANUARY 16, 1963

Mayor Whitton's proposal to annex Gloucester and Nepean Townships out to the greenbelt has raised howls of protest from the officials of the two township councils concerned. I suggest this is merely the normal reaction of an official who sees his little kingdom overtaken by the march of progress.

As a 10-year inhabitant of Meadowlands, I can testify that as of right now we have nothing which does credit to the Nepean Township administration. For city level taxes we have the following "benefits:"

1) Mud roads.

2) Ditches cut in such manner as to leave water lying around for weeks in spring and after every rain in summer.

3) A sewer system put in at the lowest possible cost which will probably prove inadequate when all householders are connected. Its shortcomings already have hit the headlines.

4) Excessive hydro rates — $15-$25 per month.

5) No street lights.

6) No storm-sewers.

7) Schools constructed one room at a time and always six months late. (Last year I had five children in five different schools — this year in four schools — how's that for efficient planning?)

8) No bus service and no prospect of one.

What are we supposed to lose by annexation? Faults that Ottawa's administration may have? But at least it's organized and has some professional ability.

J. Male, Meadowlands

Editor's note: Nepean and Gloucester townships, outraged at Ottawa's bid to annex all the land within the greenbelt, took their case to the newly created Ontario Municipal Board. After extensive hearings, the OMB largely agreed with Nepean's case, but was less convinced when it came to Gloucester. As a result, Ottawa was granted only small portions of Nepean, but got enough of Gloucester to increase the city's land mass by 500 per cent and to completely enclose the communities of Rockcliffe Park and Eastview, now Vanier.

MARGARINE LAW
JANUARY 26, 1963

I know I am only one of countless busy Ontario homemakers who want the right to purchase yellow-coloured margarine. It is high time that this ridiculous law was changed, but just wishing won't make it so. Our provincial members of Parliament need to know our feelings on this subject.

If your readers agree, and take just a few short minutes to write their own members at Queen's Park, they might soon see less action in the kitchen and more in the provincial legislature. Down with squeeze bags and messy mixing bowls!

Mrs. E. Tanner, Ottawa

Editor's note: Within 15 years of margarine's invention in France in 1869, the Dominion government bowed to pressure from the powerful dairy industry and banned the butter substitute in Canada. Although the prohibition was lifted for a few years during the First World War because of food shortages, it took a 1948 Supreme Court ruling to finally make margarine permanently legal. However, the provinces — led by Quebec and its powerful dairy lobby — stepped in to disallow the colouring of margarine to make it less appealing. That prohibition was lifted at various times across Canada over the next five decades, but didn't end entirely until the mid-'90s when Quebec finally allowed the sale of coloured margarine. Here's a letter from the other side of the debate.

THE CASE AGAINST
MARGARINE COLOURING
JANUARY 29, 1963

Consumers find that applying a butter colour to the nutritious, pure, white, unpolysaturated, inexpensive fat called margarine is a time consuming nuisance, and this nuisance is agitating them again.

When propaganda leans on the wallet and health fears, tossing in disturbing rumours about heart attacks, hardening of the arteries, and layers of cholesterol rapidly building up (how remote lung cancer can be) the bedevilled consumer gulps it down.

So before creamy yellow is added to margarine, thus allowing everyone to play "let's pretend," let us consider a few figures: in the years 1926 to 1960 butter consumption per person in Canada has decreased by 57 per cent and consumption of margarine in the U. S. has increased 375 per cent. Figures for Canada are not at hand for so long a period but the trend is similar. How can animal fat be blamed for the increase of heart trouble? The American Medical Association says, "the anticholesterol food fad is a wasted and dangerous effort."

If milk prices keep pace with costs a quart should cost 40 cents, but a one-per-cent increase brings an anguished howl. Fine, we are trying to keep milk prices down, too, but this extremely well-fed country has long been subsidized by agricultural producers with their time and guaranteed quality of products.

The edible oils people are always chiseling at butter, "fresh churned," "country sweet," and now they want the colour. Let margarine stand on its own merit.

(Mrs.) J. Elliott, Renfrew

SKYSCRAPERS
FEBRUARY 20, 1963

Some builders are reported to object to regulations designed to control skyscraper building on the basis that they will "stifle the growth of the city."

This is exactly the purpose of such regulations — to stifle uncontrolled growth of the city, and anyone who feels this is "impractible" should take a trip to New York, Chicago or Los Angeles, on a windless day when there happens to be a temperature inversion. They stink.

A skyscraper city is a boil on the skin of the earth. The idea of cramming the most possible city into the least possible space is about the most asinine idea that man has ever come up with. The earth has some 100 million square miles; let's use a few of them to spread a green city for our children, not build an abscess for them. Let's have no skyscrapers at all.

D. F. Stedman, Ottawa

Editor's note: Although there has been some tinkering and a few exemptions over the years, a 1963 Ottawa bylaw set graduated height restrictions beginning at 90 feet on Wellington Street and rising to 250 feet on Gloucester Street. The idea was to protect the integrity of the parliamentary precinct by keeping the seat of government from being dwarfed by taller structures.

STREET NAMES
FEBRUARY 28, 1963

Let us hope that as little as possible of Hog's Back Road will be renamed Meadowlands Drive. There are too few colourful names surviving inside Canadian cities. Hog's Back and Tunney's Pasture have some character. Meadowlands Drive may be an attractive street but it is an uninteresting name.

Hog's Back Road may not quite be everyone's idea of poetry, but Meadowlands Drive is just prose.

James Brierley, Ottawa

A NEGRO IN OTTAWA
MARCH 20, 1963

I am a Negro recently arrived in Ottawa. Frankly, I came here because I have had offers of a job and to look over the housing situation, etc., before moving my family from Nova Scotia, where we have lived all our lives; for Negroes, a move of locality is a serious matter because there are many unknowns.

However, since reading the letters in your paper, I feel I can bring my family to Ottawa with confidence that they will meet with no discrimination on account of colour. Those letters speak of a high moral principle in your lovely city which convinces me that we will be welcomed with open arms.

I look forward to living in peace among you in one of your beautiful residential districts, or magnificent apartment buildings, and sending my children to one of your schools to make many friends. Thank you, Ottawa.

Paul Foster

PEARSON EQUALS LEADERSHIP
APRIL 24, 1963

May I suggest that your readers who have stated that Mr. Pearson, now Prime Minister Pearson, lacks qualities of leadership keep their eyes and ears open and they will learn that he is not only the right man in the right job at the right time, but will prove to be one of the greatest leaders this country has ever produced.

He is not a windbag nor a dramatic actor, but he is a man of parts who puts first things first, knows government, knows international affairs and has great common sense. If these are not the qualities of leadership, then let's change the dictionary; it has been done before.

D.E. Thompson, Ottawa

CROSSWALKS A HAZARD
MAY 8, 1963

Crosswalks for Ottawa — yes or no? To date, I have seen very little on this subject from the point of view of the motorist, who will have to contend with these innovations.

Metro Toronto's Traffic Director Sam Cass is of the opinion that the motorist disapproves of crosswalks because he is lazy. Lazy? He has to watch green lights, amber lights, red lights, turn lights, brake lights (if they're working), as well as a horde of miscellaneous signs and the traffic around him. He hasn't time to be lazy.

The point to remember is that the average motorist is just not enough of an expert to be able to cope satisfactorily with all the distractions which modern, high speed driving brings, and by introducing the new element of crosswalks there is greater likelihood of inducing driving error.

I believe that the best solution to the crossing problem would be the installation of regular traffic lights which

may be activated by the pedestrian. Such signals could be synchronized with existing lights, and, most important, all motorists know what they mean.

J.R. Post, Bells Corners

Editor's note: Like a lot of things, crosswalks are a controversial export from California. They were first introduced to Ottawa in the mid-'60s as an experiment, becoming a permanent fixture in municipalities throughout the region by 1970. At one time in the 1980s, there were nearly 100 crosswalks in the Ottawa-Carleton area and several dozen more in the Outaouais. But by 1990, after several fatalities and increased concerns about safety, municipalities began to remove crosswalks at the rate of about 10 a year so that today only about a dozen remain.

THE MORALITY OF TEENAGERS
JUNE 19, 1963

In *Maclean's* and *Chatelaine* of May, both published articles concerning teenage morality; one was written with cynical levity, the other regarded low standards as inevitable, and neither had any constructive ideas to offer. Both were very unpleasant.

If they were written as sensational verbiage, they do not deserve attention. If true, then a disastrous situation needs the attention and co-operation of every organization working for the ultimate good of the country. There are many such forces, and the more publicity they get the better.

Times may change, but it remains a fact that high moral standards are conducive to the prosperity of its people. Low moral standards, and license, lead to misery and degeneration.

I must say the teenagers I know are fine young people and give promise of becoming citizens of whom Canada can be proud. I have found that they respect and like firm discipline and that they respond well to high ideals of conduct.

Of course, I am well aware of many adverse influences around them. They have to mix with other indulged, undisciplined boys and girls. There is emphasis on dating and going steady. The teenager should be concentrating on preparing for the future by making the most of all the opportunities provided by costly education.

Marion J. Ord, Bells Corners

ARE SHORTS INDECENT?
JULY 10, 1963

Congratulations to Mrs. Joseph Charron for her "courageous" stand on the public display of people in shorts. One shudders to think of the effect on the poor, uneducated public if such paragons of virtue did not forever guard us from the sight of a, if you will pardon the expression, woman's legs.

Once again, decent people are standing up for our right to be regimented and pressured by bigots with an excess of prurience and a distinct lack of education in the facts of life.

I fail to see the logic of the position that shorts are "de-

Some will remember John F. Kennedy — seen with his wife Jacqueline in theDallas motorcade shortly before his assassination — to the end of their lives, a reader said of the U.S. president.

cent" in one location and "indecent" in another. Perhaps people undergo radical changes in emotional makeup when visiting shopping centers, and are more easily aroused.

May I inquire as to the nature of the indecency or shame of the human body, or to put it another way, is the human body shameful *per se*? Perhaps the degree of shame may be equated with the quantity of drapery worn.

L. G. Shurben, Ottawa

JOHN KENNEDY'S SACRIFICE
NOVEMBER 27, 1963

How long will we remember John F. Kennedy? Some of us will remember him to the end of our lives. Some of us will not remember him past tomorrow.

Today we have paid homage, shed tears, eulogized, because a precious gift has been snatched from a world that can ill afford it. Tomorrow when we pick up the threads of

our lives, will the world return to insanity and hatred?

For some it will. For some the world will never seem the same. The shame is not for Dallas, Texas, but for every human being. The shame is for me. Because I have been uncharitable, because I have allowed pettiness and prejudice to creep into my heart, was it necessary for John Kennedy to die? In the sad silence of this moment I cannot think of the faults of others, only of my own.

Somehow it always seems necessary for the good to suffer and die so that in some way goodness, love and truth will balance the evil and hatred in the world. Perhaps this is all that keeps us from falling over the precipice.

God alone knows whether this will be the last time such a sacrifice is given to us. It is time for each of us to look into his own heart and root out evil. Time for each man in this world to realize that we are bound together on this planet.

Barbara Woods, Hawkesbury, Ont.

1964

Local: Census finds 54,960 government workers in Ottawa area, 21,000 in private sector (July); E.B. Eddy agrees to cut air pollution at famously pungent Hull pulp mill on site of present day Museum of Civilization (October); Don Reid ends Charlotte Whitton's reign as mayor (December)

National: Quebec first province to lower voting age to 18 (January); Defence minister Paul Hellyer unveils controversial plan to integrate army, navy and air force (February); Federal government introduces social insurance numbers (April); Northern Dancer first Canadian horse to win Kentucky Derby (May); Parliament approves new Maple Leaf flag, which flies for first time on Feb. 15, 1965 (December)

World: Beatles make first tour of North America (February-March); Warren Commission dismisses conspiracy theories in Kennedy assassination (September); Nikita Krushchev ousted as Soviet premier, replaced by Leonid Brezhnev (October); Civil rights leader Martin Luther King Jr. wins Nobel Peace Prize (December)

Births: Canadian swimmer Alex Baumann; baseball pitcher Roger Clemens

Deaths: Newspaper baron Lord Beaverbrook (Max Aitken); Joseph-Armand Bombardier, Canadian inventor of the snowmobile; U.S. general Douglas MacArthur; Indian PM Jawaharlal Nehru; ecology writer Rachel Carson; James Bond creator Ian Fleming; entertainers Gracie Allen, Eddie Cantor and Harpo Marx; Irish playwright Sean O'Casey

NATURE OF THE COMPLAINTS WITHIN QUEBEC

JANUARY 15, 1964

Recently there has been much clamour from our French-Canadian countrymen concerning the lack of biculturalism and bilingualism in our country. Perhaps you could enlighten me as to the nature of these complaints and demands.

What I don't understand is why the people of Quebec are so discontented. As far as I can see, they have a high level of autonomy.

There constantly seems to be a squabble between Ottawa and Quebec concerning money. For 40 years it has seemed to me that Quebec has always demanded a preferred position, compared to the other provinces; when the rest of Canada wanted to take a certain course, Quebec always wanted things directly opposite. Perhaps it is only my imagination, but I really don't think the people of Quebec believe in Confederation.

Until recently, the Quebec standards of education were backward in the most charitable sense of the word. What there was seemed to be concerned mainly with the religious and philosophical aspects of life. Now we are being continually informed that theirs is the only native culture in Canada and that the rest of us are barbarians in danger of Americanization.

How completely ludicrous! And even if it were so, the vast majority of "English" Canada has far more in common with the United States than with Quebec. A thousand times over I would rather become part of that Republic than to be part of a Confederation increasingly dominated by an alien culture like that of Quebec.

J. Dickinson, Edmonton

DISGUSTED BY CBC THINKING

JANUARY 25, 1964

I always considered the CBC to be the best television network in Canada — until now. I had felt that the CBC had proved that government-owned television could work well and produce excellent viewing. The CBC had presented all types of programs — the doctor-lawyer melodrama for the simpleminded, the controversial public affairs programs such as *Quest* for people who liked to think.

However, when I read the report that the CBC might cancel *Quest*, presumably because of public opinion, I was disgusted. I am sure there are still some people in Canada who use their head for something more than an ornament; people who like using their intellect for 30 minutes every week; people who don't mind watching a program that pokes fun at them and the people around them.

In your paper I am continually reading letters from people complaining about *Quest*. What I don't understand is why they watch the program if they object to it. Are they the type of people who depend on television to entertain them all evening? Can they not stand watching something that makes them think? Are they too lazy simply to turn the television off?

Why should these people suppress what others enjoy?

Doug Hewitt-White, Ottawa

Editor's note: The often-satirical Quest *was eventually cancelled by the CBC, but replaced in the fall of 1964 with* This Hour Has Seven Days, *one of the most controversial public affairs shows in Canadian television history. After two years, it, too, was cancelled. A letter commending* This Hour *appears later in this section.*

WINTER OLYMPICS

FEBRUARY 8, 1964

The Austrian community in Ottawa has been hurt deeply by the unfair and mean way in which two of your sports columnists, Jack Kinsella and Red Smith, have chosen to report on the opening ceremonies at the Winter Olympics in Innsbruck, Austria, our native country.

We are a proud people, proud to be Canadians, but still proud of where we came from. Some of the things written by Messrs. Kinsella and Smith make us think they must have some kind of grudge against the Austrian people, who are world-renowned for their hospitality and good fellowship, as well as their sportsmanship.

Surely the lack of snow was not the main story; rather, the resourceful manner in which snow was "imported" to Innsbruck to make the Games a success speaks volumes in favour of our resourceful countrymen's efforts. That was a real accomplishment.

Ed Sullivan is flanked by the Beatles, viewed by a reader as an idiotic-looking foursome when they appeared on his television show in February 1964. The reader felt they had absolutely no talent.

As for criticizing the condition of the roads as being of 1500 BC vintage, surely Mr. Kinsella has driven a car in Ottawa! Might this experience not have mellowed his views of Innsbruck thoroughfares?

In general, it was the small, nasty wisecracks at the expense of the Austrian people that I and many of my friends and associates resent, and which we were surprised to see reproduced on the sports pages of *The Citizen.*

Kurt Ortner, Ottawa

THE BEATLES: PATHETIC AND IDIOTIC

MARCH 15, 1964

The four, greasy-haired individualists who call themselves the Beatles are about the most pathetic, idiotic-looking foursome I have ever seen. They have absolutely no talent in either vocal or instrumental fields.

A lot of people, mostly teenagers, may think I'm nothing but an old-fashioned folk-song bug — and maybe I am — but if folk singing is past and the Beatles are present, then I hate to think of what's in store for the future.

K. R. Woodill, Ottawa

DREADING THE QUEENSWAY

APRIL 8, 1964

We are not surprised to learn that more accidents occur on Carling Avenue than any other street. Thirty-five mph, the speed limit there, is not much faster than 30 but when an Ottawan gets on Carling he gets a fever. He must go faster than anyone else.

When we first drove along that avenue it was like a nightmare to us, although we have driven in many large cities, including Los Angeles and Mexico City. The worst fault is changing lanes or direction without signalling. You'd be fined heavily in Los Angeles for that. Signalling turns is a habit we should all have, whether in traffic or not.

We are waiting for the time when a driver from the inside and a driver on the outside will collide in front of us,

without signalling, of course. That would be our fault, wouldn't it? Dead or alive.

So, as you can imagine, we are dreading the time when the Queensway will be completed and everyone will be going at 60 miles per hour, changing lanes and cutting in, all without signalling. Perhaps the top speed could be held under 60 mph until Ottawans learn how to drive with more consideration.

D. Anderson, Ottawa

WELFARE PROGRAM HELPFUL TO WEAK

MAY 13, 1964

You ran a news story the other day on the Canada Pension Plan, quoting E. R. Alexander, vice-president of finance, Sun Life Assurance Co., as saying that Canada appears to be "preoccupied with redistributing income from the productive to the non-productive elements in the community." He also compared welfare measures to the giving out of the "free bread and circuses which contributed importantly to the decline and fall of the Roman Empire."

I've had the feeling for many years now that the closer one gets to Finance the further one gets from Humanity. Mr. Alexander prefers nice, cool impersonal terms — for example, when he refers to the "non-productive elements in the community." When you say it that way, it sounds evil. It sounds like a blight on society; something that should be exterminated promptly.

But when you stop to examine what he has said, you realize that he is speaking of children and old people, the weak, the crippled, the blind and other unfortunates in our midst who count on the love and generosity of their fellow human beings for their very survival.

Then we come to the bit about bread and circuses. Do you see what has happened to Mr. Alexander? He is so close to Finance that he has completely lost touch with history as well! If I recall correctly, much of the bloodshed and revolution of the past was largely caused by too little bread and too few circuses.

I don't think we should mind sharing our bread with the hungry, whether we think they are deserving or not. No man could ever know enough about another man to judge whether he was deserving or not.

And as for circuses — no one in their old age wants circuses! Too much excitement! All old age wants is a little dignity, a little comfort, and a little calm just before death.

Jack E. Nugent, Ottawa

ON A NEW FLAG FOR CANADA
MAY 20, 1964

On this national Victoria Day holiday, I was upset by reading in the morning paper about the so-called "Canadian" Legion's shameful and unpatriotic reaction to Prime Minister Pearson's proposals for a purely Canadian flag.

It is important to let it be known that here is at least one British-bred, Canadian-born citizen of Canada (who does not ordinarily vote for Mr. Pearson's party) who does most definitely welcome the idea of a flag that will be unashamedly Canadian, rather than simply a reflection of the origins of some part or other of our population.

I feel that there must be millions, like me, who are proud of some of the British traditions we inherit, but who are even more proud of the purely Canadian traditions we are creating together with our fellow citizens of non-British ancestry.

Vernon H. K. Lang, Toronto

Editor's note: In December 1964, after closure was used to end a raucous Commons debate, Parliament passed an act giving Canada its new maple leaf flag. Royal assent was given in January 1965 and the flag was flown for the first time on Parliament Hill on Feb. 15. Here are two letters opposing a new flag.

DEMAND FOR NEW FLAG 'PROVINCIALISM'
MAY 23, 1964

The Red Ensign has served us nobly. It is our only truly Canadian battle standard, as it is the flag of the Canadian army. It represents to the world our pride in a divided heritage united in one nation.

The fact that it includes the Union Jack further emphasizes unity — the unity of free nations into one Commonwealth. This surely is a virtue in a world so otherwise divided. The demand for a new "distinctively Canadian" flag is a provincialism at best, and a denial of our belief in peaceful co-existence of nations.

Patricia Kempffer, Ottawa

SURRENDER TO CATHOLICS
JUNE 6, 1964

If the maple leaf flag is adopted it certainly will be a surrender to the French Catholics of Quebec. It is not a case of superiority over the French-Canadians as there are French Protestants that are working very hard to retain the Canadian Red Ensign and that is not racial bigotry, or superiority.

Alice Pugh, Chatham, Ont.

TV COMMERCIALS
SEPTEMBER 26, 1964

How much longer are we going to have to listen to these awful TV commercials? Surely there is a limit to everything.

I will refer to just one program on Channel 13 on Tuesday night at 7:30 p.m. — *Let's Sing Out*, a program which I think is very popular but only lasts half an hour. So what do we get? — one commercial to start, four more during the half hour and one more for good luck to finish it off.

I just can't take any more. There must be others who think as I do. Isn't there something we can do to end this awful mess that TV programs have fallen into?

G. MacDonald, Ottawa

SUPERSONIC JET AIRLINERS
JULY 11, 1964

Perhaps the most outrageous example of keeping-up-with-technology-at-any-cost is being set by the major airlines. Now that the supersonic jet passenger airline is almost technically feasible, the airlines are in a hysterical competition to be the first to install one in service.

Observing this mad scramble, one is led to believe that the supersonic airliner will be a wonderful thing indeed. Obviously, it will be faster than the conventional airliners of today, but that could hardly be the sole reason why the airlines covet it so, considering that the longest part of the trip in any case is between the airport and downtown.

At a glimpse, one might speculate that it will be more economical, perhaps safer, and that it will allow longer range flights. Actually, none of this is true. The supersonic airliner will cost more per passenger-mile, it will have a more limited range than the conventional aircraft, it will have to fly at heights at which solar flare radiation is a real danger. Because it must be safe to handle on take-off and landing and yet be capable of supersonic speeds, such an aircraft is necessarily a compromise in design, which cannot achieve the efficiencies of an aircraft designed solely for supersonic speeds.

S.W.P. Wyszkowski, Ottawa

MISS WHITTON'S BROOM
OCTOBER 31, 1964

At this time of year, I think Miss Whitton's choice of a symbol for her campaign — a broom — is wonderful! She not only will be able to "sweep the city clean," but also to travel on it from one end to the other to do the job!

Peter Wertheim, Ottawa

Editor's note: Even witchcraft was not enough for Miss Whitton this time. She lost the mayoralty to Don Reid, and never again held the job she filled with so much colour for the first half of two decades — the '50s and '60s.

CBC PROGRAM WORTHY OF PRAISE
NOVEMBER 3, 1964

The CBC deserves much praise for its impartial, intelligent and forthright presentations of its public affairs programs. I cite the program *This Hour Has Seven Days* as an example, and in particular the edition of Oct. 25, in which an interview with the leader of the American Nazi party was presented.

Material of this nature, while not pleasant viewing, nevertheless represents a very necessary part of constructive and mature television programming; it serves to focus public attention on issues which, while appearing relatively harmless superficially, present a very real threat if ignored too long.

Nazism and all its vicious abhorrent manifestations will not disappear simply because the majority do not care to discuss it; only by exposing it can the problems relating to extremism of this kind be successfully overcome. The program in question attempted to present the Nazi party as realistically as possible by interviewing its leader.

Such thought-provoking, dynamic, diverse and balanced programs are all too rare in television today. Let's hope *This Hour Has Seven Days* is here to stay.

B.W. Rangham, Ottawa

FLUORIDATION AFTERMATH

DECEMBER 12, 1964

A clever and well-financed campaign of brainwashing has proved very successful in the fluoridation referendum by appealing to the people who are always seeking panaceas. The crash ending with full-page advertisements in the daily press really burned the scale. Its effectiveness is indeed disturbing.

Nevertheless there are at least three insuperable objections to fluoridation of the whole water supply.

1. To compel a person to take medicine with every glass of water is a gross infringement of his basic rights. This is a point of paramount importance.

2. Fluoridation of the whole water supply is an inexcusable waste of public funds. Over 99 per cent of the water is used for other than drinking purposes. However, it must be admitted that it is a highly profitable method of disposing of a useless byproduct.

3. The dosage is uncontrolled, whereas exact amounts of a chemically pure substance can be administered to children in the form of drops or tablets. The cost would be a mere pittance.

W. Burrows, Ottawa

Editor's note: In the second referendum on the issue in two years, fluoridation was approved by a vote of roughly 58,000 to 38,000 in the December 1964 municipal elections. Fluoride was introduced to the water supply in October 1965.

1965

Local: Consultants recommend Lansdowne Park as site for new civic sports arena (February); Design unveiled for 2,300-seat concert hall and 900-seat theatre, later to be known as National Arts Centre (March); Just five years after its last expansion, Civic Hospital to get 200 new beds (February)

National: Canada-U.S. auto pact eliminates all tariffs on new cars and parts made in either country (January); Canada's new Maple Leaf flag raised for first time on Parliament Hill (February); Provinces and federal government end years of wrangling with agreement on Canada Pension Plan (April); Federal budget includes 10-per-cent reduction in personal income tax (April); Liberals retain power in federal election, but fail for second time to win majority (November)

World: Black activist Malcolm X assassinated in front of 400 in New York theatre (February); Protests mount as U.S. increases its combat role in Vietnam (July); Dozens killed, thousands injured in bloody race riots in Watts section of Los Angeles (August)

Births: Country singer Shania Twain; Canadian cellist Ofra Harnoy; Canadian cyclists Brian Walton and Curt Harnett

Deaths: Sir Winston Churchill; poet T.S. Eliot; singer Nat (King) Cole; philosopher Dr. Albert Schweitzer; writers Somerset Maugham and Lorraine Hansberry; comedian Stan Laurel; news broadcasting pioneer Edward Murrow; Hollywood producer David Selznick

BEATLEMANIAC

JANUARY 2, 1965

This is just a reminder to all the adults and Beatle-haters in Ottawa and area.

Do the words, "These moppots won't last another month!" sound familiar to any of you?

You made this snide remark last February after witnessing the hysteria on *The Ed Sullivan Show* caused by Paul, Ringo, George and John.

Now we have entered into 1965 — almost one year later. And are the Beatles dead? No! they are ALIVE, ALIVE, ALIVE.

As a devoted Beatlemaniac, one who has seen them on stage and in their movie and loved every minute of them, and as one who has a room dedicated to them, my last words are, BEATLES FOREVER!

Cathy Manion,
Ottawa

Editor's note: It seems nobody loved the Beatles more than Canadians. According to a 1965 study by the London-based Beatle Fan Clubs International, Canada boasted nearly 55,000 official fan club members, more per capita than any other country.

WHY NOT A CANADIAN HOLIDAY?

JANUARY 20, 1965

Your paper has been carrying stories concerning politicians who have been holidaying in the southern states and various parts of the Caribbean.

While I agree that these men need a holiday, wouldn't it be better to "See Canada First"? Canada offers a great deal for the winter vacationer. There is nothing nicer than sitting by a pot-bellied stove in Cornerbrook singing salty folksongs, or spending a weekend in an igloo in the N.W.T. If they crave excitement they could go to Toronto and ride the streetcars and subway trains . . .

It is my opinion that these politicians deserve a severe tongue-in-cheek lashing.

John R. Wylie, Ottawa

REMEMBERING SIR WINSTON
JANUARY 27, 1965

As one of the younger generation who shared those darkest days with the millions of Britons who are this day mourning the passing of the man who to us symbolized the one flicker of hope in a dark, confused and frightened world beyond our comprehension, may I pay tribute.

How can one explain our deep sense of loss to those people who never heard the reassuring voice of this truly great man carried through the silence of damp air-raid shelters which literally became our homes?

It was because of his "voice in the darkness" that the spark of freedom remained alive in all of us and gave us the will to endure worse yet to come. That he touched upon my life personally he was never aware, but I am sure many, as I did, learned through him that when you may be down, you are not necessarily out.

D.A. Staff, Cumberland

CRITICISM OF BIRTH-CONTROL SERVICES
FEBRUARY 8, 1965

It is not encouraging to note there is a slowly-but-steadily-developing trend in the United States to provide birth-control services to welfare recipients at public expense. Anyone subscribing to an alternate belief must not realize that partaking of such methods is contrary to the will of God.

Birth control is opposed to the natural dictates of morality. For instance, no decent man would eat food merely for the sake of eating and vomit so he might eat again. Our appetite for food is an instinct ordained to the preservation of our race; so then the sex appetite is ordained to the preservation of our race.

The pleasure that surrounds this sacred sexual act is but a secondary purpose, the primary purpose being the begetting of children. One who practices birth control is selfishly satisfying passion for the sake of passion, a trait common to lower forms of animal life. Such a man violates the moral law of God.

Many support birth control clinics blind to the problems that may result from this action. It may lead to injustice being practiced without the consent of one party. It will destroy marriage, for it makes women but toys used for sensual pleasures. The divorce courts are full of couples who have based their marriage on sensuality and have

tired of one another. One can only consider such marriages as being legalized prostitution.

More than often when birth control is practiced in early married life, sterility results and no children may be born when they are wanted. The health of the woman may be jeopardized with neurosis, bad cases of fibroid tumors and the like. It logically leads to the destruction of the human race. If you imply that all may indulge in the art of procreation for pleasure, you ignore God's purpose in granting us this gift.

John Cardill, Ottawa

BIGOTED MALES AND BIRTH CONTROL
FEBRUARY 12, 1965

I am fed up with the slander and insults thrown at our morality by every half-baked male who gets his facts wrong. Do men really believe that birth control will turn us women into a horde of wantons? There are thousands of mothers with four to 20 children who welcome birth control in any form or shape, by whatever name bigoted males choose to call it and by whoever supplies it, from priest to witch doctor.

We will not be called selfish under any circumstance. Where would you find a worker willing to work as hard and as long as we mothers do?

We will not have our marriages called legal prostitution. As every woman knows, prostitution has been rampant since civilization began, aided and abetted by men.

Birth control is not going to make this profession any more attractive to us mothers.

Surely this is a private matter for each individual family and not to be bandied-around by every John, Dick or Harry with nothing better to do but stir trouble.

Georgiana Langford, Ottawa

OUR NEW FLAG
FEBRUARY 13, 1965

I should like to express my deep disappointment at the lacklustre, diminutive ceremonies which will accompany the raising of our new flag.

Surely the government is missing a golden opportunity to make a positive step for unity in this country of ours by not declaring this day a national holiday. After having initiated and guided this project through Parliament, is the government now going to say that the birthday of Queen Victoria ranks higher in importance than the birthday of our own flag?

Leo J. O'Byrne

CHIEF: MAN OF COURAGE
FEBRUARY 17, 1965

John Diefenbaker — the man of courage; the man of wisdom; the man of tenacity! No wonder he draws bitterness from his foes, and breeds fears and doubts among the less colourful of his party!

He has been fearless in his defence of the rights and freedoms of every Canadian citizen.

THE CANDIAN PRESS

RCMP Const. Joseph Secours raises Canada's new flag on Parliament Hill on Feb. 15, 1965. One reader was disappointed the day was not declared a holiday.

He has sown terror in the hearts of those who would filch from us our heritage.

In a word, he is a leader of his people in their greatest time of need.

The greater the man, the stronger the criticism. The late Sir Winston Churchill had similar troubles. On the other hand, the present prime minister, in his handling of party and national affairs, has lost the confidence of the country.

He will go down in history as Canada's greatest and most pitiful mistake.

H.C. McCorkell, Ottawa

Editor's note: This letter was likely written in response to the efforts of a group of Conservatives, led by new party president Dalton Camp, to remove Mr. Diefenbaker as Tory leader. Ever stubborn, though, the Chief held on to the job until a leadership convention elected Robert Stanfield in 1967.

HOCKEY FANS

FEBRUARY 20, 1965

What happened to all sports-minded people in Ottawa? Are they so engrossed in getting rich that they'll let them take our senior Montagnards from us, or are they going to get up and fight?

Surely I am not the only supporter of this team, but last year my husband and I travelled up to 100 miles per game.

I don't believe we missed more than one or two games, and we believe we are not alone in this fight.

I remember what happened to the Ottawa Senators and how hockey has suffered, right here in the capital, from lack of players and support.

Mrs. D. Monette, Ottawa

Editor's note: In the seven decades after its formation in 1908, the Montagnard Amateur Athletic Association sponsored sports teams and leagues as well as providing equipment and support to poor athletes across the city. Among the activities it organized were bowling leagues, men's and women's softball and hockey teams and a well-known senior baseball team in the 1920s. For many years, the association sponsored a senior men's hockey team that was among the most feared in Eastern Canada. Although that team folded in 1965, largely because it could not find a league in which to play, a Montagnard-sponsored junior hockey team played into the 1970s. The club eventually folded in the late '70s, but it didn't die altogether. Many of its members formed the core of the Ottawa Nepean Canadians Sports Club founded in the early '80s.

SPARKS STREET MALL

MARCH 20, 1965

It surprises me that no one has objected to the city spending $600,000 to build a shopping mall for the Sparks Street merchants. The news release of March 9 says that there is to be $248,000 for street surface improvements, sidewalks and storm sewers, and $352,000 for special embellishments to convert Sparks Street to a mall.

Why are we spending money to try to put life into this backward, obsolete inefficient shopping district? If the merchants think it can be made into a paying proposition, let them build it.

Why should the general taxpayer be required to perpetuate their capital equity for another generation?

A.E. Winn, Ottawa

The Citizen replied: The actual cost of the mall will be $600,000, including $10,000 in architect's fees. The city is issuing the debentures necessary to finance the project. However, the city will recover an estimated $325,000 of this amount from abutting property owners over a set period of time.

PLEA FOR 'CABLEVISION'

APRIL 21, 1965

Concerning the question of whether cablevision should be allowed in Ottawa, I would like to make the following statements:

First, hundreds of cities in the U.S. and Canada already have cablevision; secondly, if people are willing to pay for the increased entertainment it provides, there is no reason why they should be deprived of it.

Hull has a cablevision system in operation. Why shouldn't Ottawa be allowed to have one, too?

If local TV stations are afraid of competition, they should not be in business. Would these stations want to deprive others of added enjoyment from a greater variety of programs that cablevision would provide?

I don't see why Ottawa should always be a "have-not" city.

Richard L. Smith, Ottawa

Editor's note: Ottawa TV viewers finally got cable service in mid-1966.

MOSQUITO SPRAY
MAY 29, 1965

The other day, a machine passed through our district in west Ottawa, belching two streams of foul-smelling smoky mist out of its rear. "Mosquito control," they called it.

The children of the neighbourhood thought this machine was great fun, and were following on their bikes and trikes as close as 15 feet, getting right into the mixture, which is supposed to kill mosquitoes on bushes 100 feet away.

To make things worse the "gun" operators were sitting there, waving their hands like two pea-brained Pied Pipers, while the neighbourhood children were getting their dose of insecticide, which is already dangerously high in their bodies.

It's time more people read Rachel Carson's *Silent Spring*.

Arthur Read, Ottawa

SAVING OUR TEEN-AGERS
JUNE 9, 1965

Instead of paying millions of dollars for art centres, cultural institutions, national and international defence, we could be spending those millions to eliminate the teenage problem. What useful purpose will art, culture and defence serve when the future mainstay of our society, the teen-agers, are perishing morally, physically and physiologically?

Are we to content ourselves with pride and appearances? If so, we are a very shallow-minded society. If not, then let's do something useful for our future generation of adults; only then may we rest on our laurels and truly enjoy culture, art and security from within and without.

J.R.R. Hudon, Ottawa

RESPONSIBILITY OF WIFE TO FAMILY
AUGUST 7, 1965

Ruth Millett's article "Wife must put family ahead of pay cheque" is most timely, but I feel it should have been given more prominence and not put on the women's page.

There are, I am sure, a legion of women who are deeply aware of the unfair division of labour today. This is a problem which is deeply affecting our society and seems to be almost completely ignored.

While shopping this summer, I particularly noticed how many disagreeable mothers there were. Everywhere I went children were being yanked off their feet, having their faces slapped or being given shrill admonitions. All these women wore the signs of weariness and fatigue.

How can a mother be close to a child and lavish loving care and devotion when worn out by being both a career woman and wife? Society is still able to sell the young girl that marriage is an enviable state but for how long?

Frances Montgomery, Ottawa

HOCKEY OVER INDIANS
DECEMBER 1, 1965

On Sunday evening, the people of Ontario received a "slap in the face" when CBC radio cut short a lively "open-line" discussion about Indians on *Cross Country Check-Up* in favour of the hockey game in New York.

We had listened to Miss Kahn-Tineta Horn argue about everything from the United Nations to outhouses, then along came Foster Hewitt with the first face-off.

The CBC must feel either that we benefit more from listening to hockey, or that we would rather do this than concern ourselves with interesting, controversial, and relevant issues. The first suggestion is preposterous; the second is a miscalculation and an insult, unworthy of the CBC.

It should realize that in the future we will be prepared to forego the first part of the Sunday hockey game, and not be deprived of *Check-Up*.

Jim Peterson, Ottawa

RELIGION OR SPACE ON TV
DECEMBER 15, 1965

On Sunday Dec. 12, hundreds — and possibly thousands — of Ottawans watched while science defeated religion in their age-old conflict, with the help of CBOT — and on the Lord's Day, too!

I am referring to the scrubbing of the telecast of the church service from St. John's Anglican Church. This was to have been a first in Ottawa. The service of Holy Communion was to take the form of a folk mass, led by the Rev. D. Bolton, assistant curate of All Saints Anglican Church, Westboro, with music by the Glory Singers.

We often read and hear that the Christian church is not modern enough to appeal to today's younger generation.

It seems to me that this telecast would have done much to demonstrate to Ottawans of all faiths — churchgoers and non-churchgoers — that the church is not sticking rigidly to antiquated ritual.

I admit that the launching of the Gemini 6 space craft is of vast importance to humanity everywhere. I believe, however, that the content of that telecast after 11 a.m. was of little value to most viewers.

I can see no valid reason why CBOT did not at that time break away from the CBC network and show the scheduled program.

Mrs. F. McCartney, Ottawa

1966

Local: Plans approved for children's hospital for Ottawa area (April); Old Union Station closed as new passenger rail terminal opens in Alta Vista (July); Nine workmen die when Heron Road bridge over Rideau River collapses (August); Ottawa television stations begin broadcasting in colour (October)

National: Man killed in washroom of Parliament Buildings by bomb it was believed he intended to throw into House of Commons (May); National Hockey League announces six-team U.S. expansion, with Toronto and Montreal remaining the only Canadian teams (June); Provincial premiers reject federal plan for national medicare scheme (July)

World: India's Indira Gandhi becomes first woman to head a major world state (January); Mao Tse-tung launches Chinese "cultural revolution" by purging enemies of communism (April); Unmanned U.S. spacecraft *Surveyor I* lands on moon, sends back detailed film (June); Ronald Reagan elected governor of California (November)

Births: Canadian speedskater Susan Auch; Canadian cyclist Alison Sydor

Deaths: Comic actor Buster Keaton; U.S. satirist Lenny Bruce; Andrew McNaughton, commander of Canadian army in Second World War; singer Sophie Tucker; British writers Evelyn Waugh and C.S. Forester; actor Montgomery Clift

THOREAU ON TYRANNY

JANUARY 5, 1966

"How does it become a man to behave toward this American government today? I answer, that he cannot, without disgrace, be associated with it.

"All men recognize the right to refuse allegiance and resist the government, when its tyranny or inefficiency are great and unendurable. All machines have their friction, and it is evil to make a stir about it. But when friction comes to have its machine, and oppression and robbery are organized — when a whole country is unjustly overrun by a foreign army and subjected to military law, I think it is not too soon for honest men to rebel.

"What makes this duty the more urgent is the fact that the country so overrun is not our own — but ours is the invading army.

No, these are not my own words, but those of Henry David Thoreau, a truly great American whose words 100 years ago are becoming even more fresh and vivid today. The war he spoke about at that time has almost been forgotten in the obscurity of passing time, but the message is relevant and clear with today's Viet Nam.

Mrs. Walter Josephy, Ottawa

RENÉ LÉVESQUE

FEBRUARY 12, 1966

It is the opinion of this writer that Mr. René Lévesque is being over publicized. He is beefing now about "big business" charitable contributions (English speaking division) in the Montreal area, wherein he states, "The situation will have to change and big business will have to accept its role as 'a good citizen' and think in terms of the majority and not just the minority."

Mr. Lévesque, how about applying this thinking in relation to all of Canada where you will find lots of good people of European and diverse origin that can and do speak many languages and are not so boastful about lingualism, bi, tri, multi, or what have you?

I suggest that you practice what you preach and not just locally or provincially, but Canada wide.

J. A. Whittaker
Plantaganet Station, Ont.

Editor's note: Although René Lévesque was still a cabinet minister in the Liberal government of Jean Lesage in 1966, he had already established himself as Quebec's most visible nationalist voice. In September 1967, with the Quebec Liberals' rejection of separatism for Quebec, Lévesque resigned from the party and began to lay the groundwork for the separatist Parti Québécois, the party he eventually led to power in 1976.

BILINGUALISM BONUS

FEBRUARY 19, 1966

I am very disturbed over the proposed extra pay for bilingualism in the civil service.

It seems I have chosen badly in supporting the Ottawa Public School Board and in sending my children to these schools. For if they wish to enter the city's main industry after graduation and have something to offer the federal government in whatever field they choose, they will be discriminated against. Although they have taken French since Grade 2 (they are now in Grades 7, 9 and 11), they cannot carry on a conversation with French-speaking children their own ages in the French language.

The only ways that this can be accomplished is to send one's children, beginning at nursery school, to a French-language school for the first three of four years; or to hire a French-speaking maid to speak French only in the home.

But why should this be necessary? With implementation of these proposals in the civil service, the federal government will automatically cut itself off from the products of the public school system, and it follows, therefore, that only those being educated in the French-speaking separate schools will be attracted to the civil service — and this without regard to whatever other ability anyone possesses.

Mrs. Eleanor G. Cope, Ottawa

Editor's note: The interim report of the Royal Commission on Bilingualism and Biculturalism recommended in 1966 that French, along with English, become a normal language of work and correspondence in the federal civil service. To overcome the dominance of English speakers in the civil service at the time, the government proposed, and eventually implemented, bonuses for employees who could speak both languages. To varying degrees, the bonuses are still used today.

Famous British model Twiggy wears a miniskirt, a style which a reader found 'awkward-looking' and 'fault revealing.'

THE ESTHETICS
OF THE SHORT SKIRT

MARCH 5, 1966

There are few less esthetic sights than a joint. A hem line just above one — be it ankle or knee — focuses attention on it and emphasizes its gaucherie.

It would be much better to dispense with skirts altogether, except for a frill around the hips, than to wear the awkward-looking, fault-revealing "shorts" of today.

How nice it would be to have some of these bow-legs, knock-knees, skinny pins and piano legs removed from our view.

Riding in buses is trying enough without having to watch girls tugging at a short, tight piece of cloth in the vain attempt to keep portions of their anatomy from view. Fabric manufacturers should try and do something about this.

P. Meadows, Ottawa

VIET NAM: A STAND
FOR DEMOCRACY

MARCH 9, 1966

Most young Canadians are troubled by the events which daily plunge the United States ever deeper into war. This perplexity, no doubt, stems from a realization that sufferings and slayings are being perpetuated by a nation which we have become accustomed to regard as the stronghold of democracy.

It is a moral compulsion, a feeling that something in this war is contradictory to all that a democratic nation should stand for that inspires most students who take part in demonstrations, such as the recent on Parliament Hill.

Have we not, however, failed to grasp the real necessity for the war in Viet Nam? Once reason has become obscured by feelings it is difficult to appreciate that what is at stake is far more valuable than a thousand deaths — the life of democracy and all that it stands for.

Regardless of how good their intentions may be, students who permit their feelings on the Viet Nam issue to be their only guide to action are especially liable to exploitation by Communist sympathizers who know how to employ these feelings for the attainment of their own evil ends.

The right to free speech should indeed be exercised by every democratic citizen; but let him use it wisely, lest he undermine the very system which protects it.

J. E. Petzold, Ottawa

ONE CANADA

MARCH 12, 1966

Canada is in trouble. Those of us who will celebrate Confederation in 1967 will celebrate not the unity but the growing disunity — British Columbia talks separatism and Quebec talks sovereign state, the Maritimes have their economic problems and the West its isolation.

Canada has Social Credit provinces and socialist provinces. This so-called nation has two, sometimes three flags and at least three anthems. Enter one province from any other and you've entered a foreign country. Education is different: so are traditions, laws, licensing regulations, taxes, even road signs.

If we allow these differences to continue growing, we may end up with five very separate and wholly monolithic Canadas.

Provincial governments and their autonomy create these differences. I say, abolish provinces or set up an administration with only the federal government having any say in education, roads, natural resources, taxes, laws, etc., leaving the provinces the right to enforce federal rulings without being allowed to destroy our unity by creating nations of their own.

Let the educators and the sociologists and the political scientists shape one Canada from coast to coast.

Vic Chabot, Ottawa

EVILS OF PREMARITAL SEX

APRIL 20, 1966

An official of the Alcoholism and Drug Addiction Foundation of Toronto recently told about 300 young people at a youth panel discussion that "premarital sex is good if it involves responsible persons." He arrived at this conclusion by methods of "logic" — that being young and unmarried is good and sex is good; therefore sex activity between the young and unmarried is "good."

This is totally false logic. It is equivalent to saying that fire is good (it keeps people warm) and money is good (it feeds them) so burning money is good.

Unwed sex is an unadvertised act, essentially clandestine, carefully avoiding public knowledge, with its natural consequences carefully nullified, either by some form of separation, the pill, or other methods, because if these precautions are neglected an illegitimate child can, and often does result.

To the girl — and others — who asked what is meant by "new morality," might I add that sex has been around for hundred of millions of years, there has been no change in its immense beauties when properly used, and equally no change in its dirt when improperly used. The term "new morality," is simply a statement that many men are totally promiscuous if they can get away with it.

Burning money may make a fire blaze, so no doubt does unwed sex. And both are totally destructive.

D. F. Stedman

POLICE CHASE AT 100 MPH
AUGUST 6, 1966

I was infuriated by an article headed "Two held after 100 mph chase" which told of two Ottawa men being chased by the police along Highway 7 between Stittsville and Bells Corners at speeds in excess of 100 mph.

In what kind of a society do we live which allows public servants to indulge in actions of this nature? Surely safer methods can be employed in the apprehension of reckless drivers.

I don't care about the lives of the culprits, nor am I particularly interested in those of the policemen. But I am concerned with the safety of my wife and family and myself.

A police car travelling in excess of 100 mph is nothing more than an unguided missile and a potential killer, which could snuff out the life of some innocent victim should he be unfortunate enough to cross its path.

W.B. Fay, Ottawa

BILINGUALISM AT EXPO 67
SEPTEMBER 14, 1966

Is 1967 to be Canada's centennial celebration, or that of the province of Quebec? Is Expo 67 to be Canada's world's fair or that of Montreal alone?

It is surely an undoubted fact that English is the language most generally understood in the modern world, yet the recent experience of an overseas visitor to the preparations at the Expo site causes doubt as to the wisdom of the officials.

For one unable to understand French but with a full command of English, it must be frustrating in the extreme to be guided by a tour bus driver addressing his remarks entirely in French, apart from the very occasional sentence in unintelligible English, and to turn in desperate reference to printed signs to find a vast majority of these in French with no English equivalent.

While provision has undoubtedly been made in many areas to overcome language difficulties of Expo next year,

something should be done immediately to assist the thousands of non-francophones who will visit the site between now and then.

Jean Woodfield, Ottawa

REMEMBRANCE DAY DEMONSTRATION
NOVEMBER 16, 1966

I would like to comment on the demonstration by Carleton University students at the Cenotaph. Of course we must remember with sorrow, on Nov. 11, the young men so tragically dead in two world wars, but we must also remember the young children and young mothers and the old men and women killed by bombs.

The Second World War pointed the way; babies were in the front line in the streets of London and of Berlin and other cities. The forces are no longer the main target, and when World War III begins and the missiles start flying, they will not be aimed at soldiers but at people.

This is why the students were there, to remind people that yesterday's sorrow is nothing to what the future may hold if the present course of military escalation continues. And they particularly wanted to remind us all that even during this two minutes of silence, what U Thant calls, "the most barbarous war in history" still rages on.

The last figure I read on U.S. military deaths was 5,000, while a conservative estimate of civilian dead in North and South Viet Nam in the 18-month period ending last June was 200,000. For the first time in modern war civilian deaths exceeded those of the military.

Pamela Lee MacRae, Ottawa

DISGRACING MR. DIEFENBAKER
NOVEMBER 23, 1966

If Mr. Dalton Camp and his followers set out to disgrace Mr. John Diefenbaker they didn't succeed. What they have managed to do is thoroughly disgust most intelligent Canadians. To a good number of people I have spoken to, they have simply disgraced the party.

The result is that many people will refuse to support the Conservative party now, regardless of who the leader is. To them, a party that will knife a leader, is not a party to be completely trusted.

Mr. Diefenbaker should have been allowed to leave gracefully. Instead they knock him down, boo him, step on him and tell him to get out. Some way to treat a former prime minister.

And before someone thinks that I am one of the "over-50" crew that is supporting the "old" leader, let me reassure them that I am far, far from the age of 50.

I resent all we Young Conservatives being lumped into one group known as "Camp's punks" or "Camp supporters." A good number of us are not, and what's more we deplore Mr. Camp's actions.

What he has said about Mr. Diefenbaker should be said in private, not in front of millions of TV viewers.

L. Brown,
Ottawa

Editor's note: As national president of the Progressive Conservative party from 1964 to '69, Dalton Camp helped to engineer the removal of John Diefenbaker as party leader, eventually succeeding, after years of bitter rancour, in 1967 when Robert Stanfield replaced the Chief at a convention in Ottawa.

A NECESSARY WAR
DECEMBER 10, 1966

If I may, I would like to express myself on a subject which makes my blood boil, namely, these anti-Viet Nam War groups and U.S. draft dodgers who come to Canada.

I respect an individual's own philosophy of life, and I agree it would be marvelous if all the people in the world had a pacifistic sort of philosophy. But we don't. Some day this might be achieved but in my opinion, it won't be for a very, very long time, and when I say that I mean hundreds of years.

When these people say the Viet Nam War is insane, do they mean that it is insane for us to be fighting for the right of free people the world over to do what they want to do?

These draft dodgers say that if it is a free country, why should we be told what to do? If we were not in Viet Nam now, it wouldn't be long before none of us the world over would have the right to do as we wanted.

Harry B. Foster,
Ottawa

Local: Ottawa Technical School first in region to get a computer (February); First homes go for sale in subdivision known as Kanata (April); Store owners fight to keep singers off Sparks Street mall (June); New National Archives and Library building opens in June; new Science and Technology Museum opens in October; Ottawa Civic Centre begins operation (December)
National: Centennial Train, a travelling heritage museum, begins its 85-stop cross-Canada tour in B.C. (January); Expo '67 opens in Montreal in April. Before the World's Fair closes in October, it is seen by 50 million visitors; Parliament approves unification of armed forces (April); French president Charles de Gaulle sent packing after notorious *Vive le Québec libre* speech in Montreal (July)
World: Three astronauts killed in flash fire that engulfs *Apollo I* spacecraft (January); Israel smashes Arabs in Six Day War (June); Race riots ravage several U.S. cities, including Detroit and Newark (July); Louis Washkansky, world's first heart transplant recipient, dies in South Africa after living 18 days with heart of 25-year-old woman (December)
Births: Canadian sprinters Donovan Bailey and Bruny Surin; Olympic swimmer Sylvie Fréchette
Deaths: Governor general Georges Vanie;, Jack Ruby, killer of Lee Harvey Oswald; jazz saxman John Coltrane; actors Spencer Tracy, Vivien Leigh and Basil Rathbone; writer and wit Dorothy Parker; folksinger Woody Guthrie; magazine magnate Henry Luce; A-bomb pioneer Robert Oppenheimer; German chancellor Konrad Adenauer; starlet Jayne Mansfield

U.S. MISUNDERSTOOD
FEBRUARY 8, 1967

The large "L" Liberals under the Peace Tower and on Capitol Hill, and their counterparts in North American academia, are getting nowhere in their criticism of President Lyndon Johnson's Vietnam policy because they fail to appreciate its objective.

The critics claim not to see how the bombing of northern Vietnam renders any easier Washington's avowed diplomatic efforts to initiate negotiations — they are distressed by the constant rebuff of negotiation feelers from the North.

Evidently, it has not occurred to these Liberals that the Johnson administration doesn't seem to be promoting negotiations because it doesn't want negotiations. After all, any non-martial settlement of the Vietnam conflict that will leave the United States looking even vaguely like a supporter of democracy will have to provide for elections, as does the 1954 Geneva accord — free, internationally supervised elections throughout the entire country to decide not whether Vietnam is to be re-united (it was never divided), but to decide under what regime it is to be governed.

And such elections in the view of those making current U.S. policy, would spell sure disaster: the end of American military occupation and the confutation of that old saw about Communist governments never being freely brought to power.

Stephen Wohl, Montreal

SHE'S OUR QUEEN TOO
FEBRUARY 22, 1967

It is high time more publicity was given to the fact that Canada is a monarchy. With all this publicity about Expo, very little is said about our Queen.

Yet if you took the trouble to read a word-for-word account of her coronation, you would see that Queen Elizabeth II was crowned Queen of Canada. Why else do we have Governor General Georges Vanier here, if not to act in her place?

It seems the present Prime Minister and his government do their very best to make as little mention of our Queen as they can get away with. Our rightful flag was taken from us without our consent. Our armed forces are being stripped of their identity, and our Queen is kept in the background. Print a protest, do!

(Mrs.) Nellie G. Maxwell, Errington, B.C.

WE'RE BEING ABSORBED
MARCH 4, 1967

Donald Duncan, a veteran of the Green Berets, a crack U.S. special combat force, hit the nail squarely on the head when he told 600 students at the University of B.C. that "the United States has become a near-perfect corporate military state with only the trappings of democracy," and that a large standing army has been maintained since the end of the Second World War to protect worldwide interests of large American corporations.

It is time Canadians started seeing things as they really are. When the foreign policy of any country is based on the theory that "might is right," then it is time for the rest of the world to condemn such a policy.

American investors have established ownership and control of over 60 per cent of Canadian industry. Our most subtle danger is the economic, cultural and eventual political absorption of Canada by the United States.

Thomas A. Murphy, Ottawa

IS DE GAULLE PLOTTING QUEBEC TAKEOVER?
MARCH 8, 1967

General de Gaulle publicly referred to Montreal as the second city of France. The Canadian government did not protest. Thus encouraged, he gave another speech in which he referred to the people of Quebec as French and part of the soul of France. Again silence from the Canadian government.

The next move was to beat the propaganda drums to make Quebec a nation. More silence from the Canadian government. Another was for Quebec to be the key in forming a French Commonwealth of Nations, and to take "a leading part" in that Commonwealth.

Now the French nationalists in Quebec, aware that Lester Pearson's government is not going to stand up and fight, are pushing ahead with a planned program to make Quebec a nation. They will give Canadians another slap in the face by dealing directly with foreign governments. It seems there is not one member of the Canadian Parliament prepared to make a stand.

THE OTTAWA CITIZEN
The welcome given to Gen. Charles de Gaulle in Quebec, seen giving his famous 'Vive le Québec libre' speech in Montreal, was another insult to the people of Canada, a writer said.

There is only one answer to the Quebec problem. Let Canada retain all land south of the St. Lawrence and let the rest of Quebec go. Unless this is done Canada will break up, with many areas going over to the United States.

Victor W. Forster, Toronto

Editor's note: French president Charles de Gaulle went even farther in July with his infamous "Vive le Québec Libre" speech, a diplomatic intrusion so serious that it prompted prime minister Pearson to cancel the rest of the French president's state visit and to strongly suggest he was no longer welcome in Canada. More letters commenting on de Gaulle and Quebec are ahead in this section.

THIS IS PROGRESS?
APRIL 5, 1967

It looks as though the powers-that-be are going to make divorce a little easier, and legalize artificial birth control, abortion — the whole works.

Well, what a nice Centennial project that will be!

Since birth control and abortion were introduced in the more so-called advanced countries in Europe, their birth rate has dropped to an alarming degree, and their suicides have increased. This is progress?

Mrs. V. Dalton,
Burlington, Ont.

A LAW FOR BEATNIKS
APRIL 12, 1967

As I look out the window I see groups upon groups of young teenagers marching past — for Oxfam. They have now walked 25 miles. I see them wearily plod on — for Oxfam. Each mile means that much more money for the cause.

And, as I watch these people, I notice the absence of the unkempt, unshaven Parliament Hill demonstrator types. It comes to mind that a law should be passed requiring that demonstrators march 40 miles around the city before marching on Parliament Hill: thereby supporting their cause materially — not just drawing attention to it and themselves.

D. McLeay, Ottawa

DR. KING AND VIETNAM
MAY 3, 1967

There is no incompatibility in Dr. Martin Luther King's stand for civil rights at home and against the war in Vietnam abroad — both have as their basis strong opposition against the exploitation of peoples.

Whether the victim of such exploitation is a Negro lynched in Mississippi or a Vietnamese child burned to death with napalm, a true humanitarian such as Dr. King sees a common ground for protest.

Your columnist, by talking of "intrigue" and "mystery," and giving credence to an FBI report that "a man" (unidentified) is manipulating King for sinister purposes, has fallen into the old McCarthyist trap.

The FBI is notorious for its stand on civil rights in particular and progressive actions generally: J. Edgar Hoover has praised the racist governor of Mississippi for doing "a fine job."

John Baglow, Rothwell Heights

INFORMATION WANTED
MAY 3, 1967

My liaison work with the Ontario Archives involves contacting persons in and out of the province of Ontario regarding the locating and acquiring of private manuscript material pertaining to Ontario's history.

Some time ago we acquired a large collection of private papers belonging to the late Simon Dawson, engineer-surveyor who opened up the Dawson Road from Fort William through the Red River.

Simon Dawson had two brothers, William Macdonell Dawson, who at one time was crown timber agent in Bytown, and Father Aneas Macdonnell Dawson, a well-known priest and lecturer at St. Patrick's College in Ottawa. They also had a sister who I believe was the only member of the family to marry. This sister had a daughter, Mrs. W.H. Fuller, who was living in Ottawa in 1911.

We would be most interested in getting any information about descendants of Mrs. Fuller who might be living.

Hugh P. MacMillan, Archives Liaison Officer,
Parliament Buildings, Toronto

Editor's note: No one any longer seems sure whether the Ontario Archives got a response to this letter, although its Dawson family records today are extensive.

CARRY ON, JOHN
MAY 17, 1967

It has become quite plain that our British heritage is being slowly but surely taken away and if this process continues we will be reduced to the status of second-class citizens, and our Italian and other ethnic friends will be cast aside and forgotten in order to please a certain section of the country.

The Conservatives who are competing for the leadership of the party have no regard as to what is happening to the nation. All they want is votes from a certain French-speaking province and to hell with Canada no matter what concessions they make as long as they get the necessary votes.

The Conservative party needs the leadership of John Diefenbaker, that great fighter, who can hold Canada together under majority rule where all citizens are assured equal status.

Help us make "John carry on." Address your letters to: Carry on John Club, 45 Second Avenue, Ottawa.

G. Hughes, Ottawa

Editor's note: Mr. Diefenbaker lost the leadership of the Conservative party to Robert Stanfield at a September convention in Ottawa.

WHEN THE WRONG MAN WAS HANGED
MAY 20, 1967

Back in the 19th century around Kingston, Upper Cana-

da had its first legal hanging. The unfortunate victim was some obscure indigent accused of stealing a watch. Though he maintained his innocence and held that he purchased the watch from a wandering salesman, it did him no good.

Two months after his hanging the salesman he spoke of returned, and, as it turned out, the watch's real thief was indeed that salesman. The first man legally hanged in Canada was innocent.

Regardless of the pap we were fed in public school about the so-called sanctity of our honourable courts, where, amid much pomp and splendour, justice with a capital J is always seen to be done, any school child can see Canada has not progressed one iota since that first unfortunate innocent was murdered by so pious and self-righteous a society.

In Huron County, a 14-year-old child is sentenced to death on the basis of not one piece of direct evidence, only one piece of extremely suspicious circumstantial evidence, and pound after pound of inflammatory pap. And in Ottawa, a man who did in fact kill somebody, is acquitted. Good Lord, deliver us!

R.L. Whitmore, Ottawa

HALT CBC SPENDING
JUNE 10, 1967

If the government considers its citizens, it will refuse the CBC application to expand. Although facing constantly increasing living costs swollen by excessive taxation, Canadians are forced to pay $144,000,000 this year so the CBC can continue its extravagant spending spree.

It's time to say NO! There's a point in family and government spending where the desires for unneeded extras must be balanced against incomes and abilities to pay. Taxation caused by unnecessary spending deprives people of this choice. The money is taken before the cost of necessities can be considered.

The lack of financial responsibility within the CBC is secondary. Immediate relief from excessive taxation is needed more. Choosing between $25,000 to $40,000 a year executives, $700 an hour newscasters, dozens of $800 TV sets for well paid public officials — and having more take-home pay — well, it's easy.

By forbidding the CBC to expand the government can best help people cope with taxation and living costs.

Stanley A. Ward, Moose Jaw, Sask.

Editor's note: The government did give CBC money to expand its operations, but only about half the $26 million originally requested by the public broadcaster for the expansion.

A DEEPLY DISTURBED CANADIAN
JULY 26, 1967

I am a Canadian. As such I am deeply disturbed and disgusted with the French residents of Quebec. I am referring, of course, to the happenings of the past few weeks in "La belle province."

I have never felt prejudice against any race or culture before, in my life, and find what I am now feeling for French Canada is a most disagreeable emotion.

I have many acquaintances of French origin, and I must

say of them, that they do not resemble in any way, other than in language, the French residents of Quebec.

First there was the lack of any type of celebration to mark our nation's 100th birthday. Every provincial capital in the country celebrated July 1 except Quebec City. The best that could be done there was a 101-gun salute.

Queen Elizabeth received a tumultuous welcome at Expo '67, but probably from visitors from other parts of Canada and from the U.S. What would have happened had she gone to Quebec City? Undoubtedly, she would have been ignored.

The latest Quebec insult to the people of Canada is the way they have welcomed President de Gaulle to "their country." The provincial government has indeed sided with the separatists, for among all the flags flown in his honour and to welcome him, the Canadian flag was conspicuous by its absence.

Our present flag was adopted mainly to make the French-Canadians happy. I, along with many Canadians, have accepted proudly our new flag, but the French in Quebec won't even acknowledge it.

These people can no longer call themselves French-Canadians, for it is evident that they are pro-French and anti-Canadian. As far as I am concerned, let the French have Quebec. Quebec needs Canada far more than Canada needs Quebec.

A shame it is that the cultural differences between French, English and the many other ethnic groups in our land could be our great strength, but have turned out, thanks to French Quebec, to be tearing us apart.

Mrs. H. Wilson, Ottawa

THE GALL OF DE GAULLE'S CALL

JULY 29, 1967

Charles de Gaulle has "de gall" alright.

Certainly those of us who were once partially sympathetic to the Quebec cause are now able to realize that drastic measures must be taken to keep this, our country Canada, the great country it now is — and is destined to be.

Carol N. Hiscox, Ottawa

THOSE MALL HIPPIES

AUGUST 16, 1967

Hippies? "Hippos" better describe those grey-faced creatures wallowing away the long, hot summer on our Sparks Street Mall. These anti-work, anti-wash waifs, having "rejected society," even have the nerve to ask for special consideration from the very society they reject. Curiously flexible, their ethics!

I too feel strongly about social and political injustices. So I work for that political party which I believe has the most constructive internal and external policies. Strong views demand positive action; ergo, the do-nothing citizens of Dismaland-on-the-Mall have none. The very monotony of their existence demonstrates that they are lazy, mindless or both.

They do no harm sitting there: if a group wants to bore itself to death — it's a free country. But I wish people would stop wasting time paying attention to them.

Leave them alone and — ultimately — they'll go home.

Mrs. Audrey Stankiewicz, Ottawa

THE HIPPIES' CODE

SEPTEMBER 27, 1967

While some people ask at parties: "What do you do?" I ask: "What do you do besides your job? Do you in fact do? Do you paint, or write, or draw, or grow things, or even think new thoughts, or sit on the Mall?"

Don't knock the hippies, don't knock pot; don't knock LSD — unless you've tried it and found it wanting. I haven't tried it. I don't think I need it. I live a quiet full life: of the senses, of the mind, of ideas, of doing — writing, painting, walking, looking, feeling, tasting, sunning, running, making love, trying to understand someone else's new ideas.

I don't have time to knock anybody — not even the most popular whipping boy at the moment: LBJ.

Jon Makai, Ottawa

ON PAYING TO KEEP KILLERS

NOVEMBER 22, 1967

I maintain anyone who advocates abolition of the death penalty should have his or her head examined.

Just one year before I was married, my father and sister were murdered in cold blood because they refused to hand over what money was in the house.

That murderer is now serving out a life sentence in the penitentiary, and I am paying to keep him there. I pay taxes in both Ontario and Alberta and I dread to think that one penny of my money is going to keep the man who murdered my father and sister alive.

I understand that the cost of maintaining our penitentiaries in Canada represents a stupendous sum. Now I ask you why should the Canadian people be asked to pay for keeping alive any person who has proven that he is no good to himself or his family and is a menace to society?

Is that what we call British justice?

Mrs. Dorothy Marion, Kingston

TIME TO MAKE OTTAWA A FUN CITY

DECEMBER 20, 1967

Bully for architect John Leaning! More people like him could turn Ottawa into a fun city instead of the smug, regulated and rather dull image now presented.

Visitors complain there is little to intrigue them in this, our capital. The views are wonderful, the food only fair, glimpses of the East Block, West Block and Centre Block boys in their identical homburgs rare and fleeting, and who wants to spend a vacation on Wellington Street?

It is high time Ottawa kicked up her heels. It was a swinging town back when grandpa used to smoke a corncob pipe. Sure we have the Tulip Festival and we did have the guards but what about every day? A large beer hall underneath the rumble of the Plaza with a loud German band would be the perfect complement for the new holy of holies, the National Arts Centre.

Culture could then mingle with the proletariat and who knows some of it might rub off — both ways.

Gladys Blair, Ottawa

1968

Local: Adult bus fare rises to 25 cents, sparking public outcry (February); Ottawa-born Nancy Greene wins gold in giant slalom at Grenoble Olympics (February); Ottawa wins the Grey Cup 17-14 over Calgary Stampeders (November)

National: New federal law allows divorce solely on grounds of marriage breakdown (April); Tallest building in Canada, 56-storey Toronto-Dominion Bank tower, opens in Toronto (May); Montreal becomes first non-U.S. city to be granted major league baseball franchise (May); PM Pierre Trudeau showered with rocks and bottles, 290 arrested in St. Jean Baptiste Day riots in Montreal (June); Driven by Trudeaumania, Liberals win majority government (June);

World: Martin Luther King shot to death on Memphis motel balcony (April); Workers and students paralyse France with strikes and mass demonstrations (May-June); Senator Robert Kennedy killed by gunman in kitchen of California hotel (June); Soviet tanks roll into Prague to squash Czech program of reforms (August); Richard Nixon elected U.S. president (November)

Births: Canadian pop diva Céline Dion; Ottawa sprinter Glenroy Gilbert

Deaths: Beat writer Neal Cassady; Yuri Gagarin, first man in space; Helen Keller; American writer Upton Sinclair

GOUGING AT HOCKEY GAMES

JANUARY 3, 1968

Congratulations to the City of Ottawa for its efforts with the new Civic Centre which provides our community with much-needed arena facilities. It is a centre to be proud of, as is our Ottawa 67's Hockey Club, which has the makings of a very effective team.

However, I do take exception to the prices charged by the concessions. It is especially hard on a man who, after paying for tickets to a hockey game for himself and perhaps two sons, finds it costing him 25 cents for one soft drink, two-thirds of which is ice, and 30 cents for a hot dog. At this rate, each evening spent with his family at a game costs him approximately $7.

I can see no plausible reason for these concessions charging more than 15 cents a drink — the popular price at most restaurants . . . even more so when one considers that these concessions have little overhead and staff to maintain.

J. Hill, Ottawa

FALSE PROMISES

JANUARY 13, 1968

Our governments have spent large sums of taxpayers' money to lure thousands of people to Canada from many parts of the world. In their propaganda they have made people think this was a veritable paradise, and that there were jobs and good livings for anyone who wanted to come.

But they did not tell the whole story. They did not warn prospective immigrants that 20 per cent of the carpenters in B.C. are unemployed, and have very little hope of steady jobs for some months.

They did not warn many other tradesmen that they may have to be idle for a long time during the winter months, but only stressed that there was a shortage of help during the summer.

Possibly we do need more people here in Canada, but not before we have leaders who do some-year-round planning.

Instead of tolerating an increase in mortgage rates that will impede much needed housing, they should be in the forefront making funds available to overcome this shortage. Instead of shipping our natural resources out of Canada, they should be promoting enterprises that would pro-

duce the finished products and put many more of our people to work.

Carl Erickson, North Burnaby, B.C.

JACKIE HELPS US DREAM

MARCH 16, 1968

In the sob magazines we read about Jackie Kennedy's heartbreaks — real or otherwise. For the very simple reason that money doesn't buy peace of mind or any kind of real happiness, Jackie has, without doubt, heartache and quite possibly her private heart-breaks are different from the published ones.

Nevertheless, in public she is glamourous, and who doesn't want to be glamourous? A passing glimpse of Jackie leaves every woman filled with daydreams of plush beauty parlours or, more likely, a personal beautician; of French boutiques, and dazzling lights, and private rendezvous.

And as long as there is a woman left who daydreams, Jackie will be publicized to make us daydream. The rest of us belong to the great crowd who don't inspire daydreams, so what editor needs us?

Winifred Paris, Hull

Editor's note: Seven months after this letter was published, Jacqueline Bouvier Kennedy, the 39-year-old widow of slain president John Kennedy, stunned the world by marrying Greek shipping tycoon Aristotle Onassis, 68, in a secret ceremony on the Greek island of Skorpios.

HE'S NOT PM YET, BUT TRUDEAU HAS FAILED

MARCH 20, 1968

Most of us who were crying, praying and pleading for a new look in Canadian politics thought for a few happy days that the ex-NDP supporter, Pierre Elliott Trudeau, might provide the change.

It seems we were wrong. Like the handsome John Turner, another of the "younger candidates" for the Liberal party leadership, Trudeau has recently proven that his "youth" is purely physical.

On the thorny issue of Quebec separatism, "young" Mr. Turner is as old politically as any member twice his age. The same goes for Eric Kierans. By his seeming willingness to slough off all of Canada's unity problems onto the shoul-

After winning the Liberal leadership, Pierre Trudeau is mobbed by young fans as Trudeaumania sweeps the party to a majority government on June 25.

ders of the wicked "anglais," Kierans has lost the confidence of many in and outside Quebec.

As for Justice Minister Trudeau, questioned at a press conference about his earlier attacks on Pearson and the Liberals (whom he called a bunch of idiots before he joined them), he said he had some regrets.

He admitted he should not have called "all the Liberals" idiots. Later he went further, and conceded that in politics it was "sometimes necessary to accommodate beliefs to the facts of the moment."

So much for Pierre Elliott Trudeau.

It seems that all members of Lester Pearson's orchestra, be they member of the wind, brass, or tinkling cymbal section, know only one form of composition. The Pearson musicians obviously intend to strum the same old arrangement, no matter who is conducting the state band.

Edmond Bayard, Ottawa

Editor's note: Mr. Trudeau won the Liberal leadership, and assumed the prime minister's job, at a party convention in Ottawa in April. On June 25, swept along by a tidal wave of Trudeaumania, the Liberals won a majority government, taking 155 seats to 72 for the Conservatives, 22 for the New Democrats and 14 for the Créditistes.

COSTS THE REAL ISSUE
MAY 22, 1968

Little of any constructive value is being said by our politicians about the high cost of living — no speeches are being aired about controls on food prices, rents or education.

We are constantly being told, on the other hand, that we have one of the highest standards of living in the world, and

that we should be grateful for being part of this continent. And for all this, what a price we have to pay.

Hospitals are growing in number and size, medical plans and benefits are emerging at a rapid pace and more people are dying of heart attacks. Wives are required to work and husbands are required to take on a second job.

It is sadly and truly a land where the rich get richer and the poor get poorer.

Our politicians have their work cut out for them if they can stop quibbling over changing the constitution, bilingualism and high-rise buildings in the capital.

J. N. Sorrenti, Ottawa

BILINGUAL POLICY HOAX ON VOTERS
JUNE 5, 1968

The federal government must be stopped from using the civil servant as a tool for political experimentation. I refer to plans being laid to legislate bilingualism!

This has started to be one of the greatest hoaxes perpetrated on the Canadian people — using their own money. The federal treasury is empty again and yet the Liberal Party is laying plans to introduce one of the most wasteful exercises ever undertaken, and one which does not have the approval of the Canadian people.

English-speaking and French-speaking Canadians had come a long way in the last 15 years in improving their communications, until the costly B and B commission undid all the good work by getting people's backs up — for no one wants to have something shoved down his throat!

Harry Splett, Bells Corners

Editor's note: The Royal Commission on Bilingualism and Biculturalism, in a series of studies issued from 1967 to 1970, reported that the place of francophones in the decision-making structure of the federal civil service did not nearly equal the status warranted by their numbers. To rectify the situation, the government in 1969 implemented an official bilingualism policy which, among other things, declared the equality of French and English in Parliament, the Canadian public service and all federal agencies and Crown corporations. The practical outcome was that many francophones were added to the public service, and, more crucially, that francophones — who were more likely to speak both languages than anglophones — began to receive a disproportionate number of promotions in the effort to alleviate the historic domination of English speakers. Not surprisingly, the idea was far from popular with anglophones, especially in the capital.

RFK AND THE GUILTY ONES
JUNE 19, 1968

All the people of America did not kill Robert Kennedy, but many contributed to the climate of violence that induces this kind of tragedy. They include:

Everyone who condones or abets the Vietnamese war, a war that forces strong young men to kill men, women and children, mothers and babies, and to burn with napalm the living bodies of little children, permanently disfigure people, destroy homes and send families into concentration camps.

All who promote the kind of setup that permits some to seek war for financial gain, and causes others to shun peace for fear of unemployment.

Officials who deal unjustly with any other country.

Everyone who goads Negroes into violence by denying them rights that white men take for granted.

All who stand in the way of a prosperous life for everyone.

Those who peddle violence through literature, television, or movies.

All who cling to old prejudices or give place to bigotry and the suppression of new ideas, or who seek to punish in any way those holding minority views.

All who seek in any way to close legitimate avenues of expression or dissent.

Those who concede the right of the rich and powerful to express their opinions, but who would deny that right to the humble.

Anne Johanson,
Powell River, B.C.

EXPO VISIT
JULY 31, 1968

I was glad to see travel editor Dick Statham's article entitled "Man and His World needs your support." He's perfectly right — and if we want to have this wonderful, changing show within reach every summer, we're going to have to support it right now. Lack of crowding and line-ups are an attraction, too.

I plan two or three more visits before it closes Oct. 14 and expect to enjoy them just as much as the first, when I saw the two delightful new national pavilions — Ireland and Poland — and paid my third visit to the fascinating 15-nation Africa Place.

I still haven't seen Biosphere or the ancient autos and only the ground floor of the Humour building with its marvelous collection of cartoons from around the world.

I'm also anxious to see again the five brilliant "Man and His World" shows ("Man the Explorer" etc.) held over from Expo; Tunisia, Ethiopia, Burma, Korea, the great collection of brass in Ceylon, the beautiful rugs in Iran — and of course the Canadian Indian and Christian pavilions.

Paul A. Gardner, Ottawa

Editor's note: To help pay for the debts incurred by Expo '67, and to capitalize on the enormous popularity of the World's Fair, an annual exposition known as Man and His World was established the next year on the Expo '67 site. It operated into the 1980s.

SUMMER'S DONE
SEPTEMBER 14, 1968

Contributors to your letters column have written of the Soviet invasion of Czechoslovakia, the rumoured romance of Pierre Elliott Trudeau, the military rape of Viet Nam and many other newsworthy topics.

Not one has written about the tragedy that is about to descend upon us.

Surely there must be an awareness that as the summer grows late, bird song has ceased. Those that have not already left us gather in groups and whisper excitedly about the trip south.

The honeysuckle is gone. Rose petals fall like teardrops and like the late September frost football fever spreads across our land.

Kids are talking about new text books and old teachers. Out in the garden just back of the other summer vegetables the Halloween pumpkin has taken shape.

Yes, September morn is here. For us it is a last opportunity for one more brief embrace with a Canadian summertime.

Lew Hill, Ottawa

WHO CARES ABOUT THE HIPPIES?
SEPTEMBER 28, 1968

The United Appeal is getting a bit carried away with its program of help for the unfortunate. Its principle of helping those who honestly need help is an honourable one, but I question its definition of "help" when it includes the support of a local hippie drop-in hangout.

Why should I, a responsible, working and paying member of society, help to support unproductive and irresponsible individuals, who openly claim to reject the institutions and accepted social mores of this society?

Indeed, why should anyone?

Whatever philosophy the hippies have, if in fact they have anything to which the term could properly be applied, whatever their reasons for "opting out" from society, whether they be valid or not, they are no more than feeble excuses to cover up their own self-inflicted inadequacies. In brief, they are lazy!

It is a flagrant contradiction to reject a society with one breath, then seek its support with the next. They have not rejected society: but society will reject them.

C. W. Allan, Ottawa

WHAT DO WOMEN WANT?
OCTOBER 9, 1968

Wendy Day says in her column in Saturday's *Citizen* that few men attended last week's hearings of the Royal Commission of the Status of Women. And only three presented briefs.

Too bad, she says. But, after all, the commission was designed chiefly for the bringing forth of the problems of women, not men. And personally, I can see nothing worthwhile coming out of any recommendations made by this inquiry so far.

It was mainly women talk, and there is plenty of that on radio and television and in the newspaper, and to no avail insofar as concrete action is concerned.

Besides, governments at any level are carefully eyeing their finances before implementing any recommendations involving public expenditures.

What are women clamouring about, anyway? They hold all the leading cards and advantages over the male population in most of the vital areas of life, such as birth rate.

They hold more than 85 per cent of the wealth of the country, control trust funds, home and school meetings, papers and magazines, they have a longer life than men, and greater opportunity for enjoyment than most workingmen. It's easier for them to get positions in many areas where economically they are in demand.

What women want are equal rights but not equal treatment!

J. O. Thibault, Ottawa

Editor's note: In response to the increasingly vocal concerns of the women's movement, the Pearson government appointed a royal commission in 1967 with a broad mandate to "make recommendations to improve the condition of women in Canada." After six months of public hearings in 1968, the commission — headed by Ottawa broadcaster Florence Bird — made 167 recommendations on matters such as equal pay for work of equal value, daycare, maternity leave, birth control, family law and pensions. The commission report laid the groundwork for many changes in the law made over the next two decades.

A MOST DISGUSTING FILM
NOVEMBER 9, 1968

Last Sunday I looked at the TV program *The Way It Is*, a CBC production. It was the most disgusting broadcast I have ever seen, another anti-U.S. show, showing the police and soldiers as brutal men who seem to enjoy beating the crowd up, white and black Americans giving stupid comments, and to top off this gem, naked hippies dancing about full of dope and covered with flowers.

Now isn't that great? As if there was not enough hate and maniacs in our world today.

Is it just to extract only the bad side of the U.S. and present it on television? How would we like it if the United States showed films of our riots, our separatist strikes, and our hippies?

Surely there must be some producers who can think of better programs.

M. Jacqueline Auger, Ottawa

1969

Local: Vanier the new name for Eastview (January); In an effort to rescue Hull's sagging economy, government proposes large federal office complex for waterfront (May); National Arts Centre opens (June); Government austerity program could cost 25,000 federal jobs in next two years (August)

National: 90 arrested as anti-racist protesters destroy computer at Sir George Williams (now Concordia) University in Montreal (January); Separatist tensions rise with dozens of bombings in Montreal area (February-March); CBC bans tobacco ads from its TV and radio outlets (May); Criminal Code amendments relax laws on homosexuality and abortion (May); French and English declared the official languages of Canada (July)

World: Disaster looms in Biafra as millions face starvation (February); Concorde makes its first flight, a 30-minute test run over France (March); Neil Armstrong first man to walk on moon (July); Protests mount over Vietnam war with the news U.S. troops massacred 567 South Vietnamese civilians at Mylai (November); Charles Manson and four followers charged in cult murders of actress Sharon Tate and four others (December)

Births: Tennis great Steffi Graf; jazz saxman Joshua Redman; Canadian actor Matthew Perry

Deaths: Actress-singer Judy Garland; U.S. president Dwight Eisenhower; Rolling Stones guitarist Brian Jones; actor Boris Karloff; Supreme Court justice Ivan Rand; jazz musician Coleman Hawkins; boxing great Rocky Marciano; German-American architect Mies van der Rohe; North Vietnamese president Ho Chi Minh; governor general Harold George (Alexander of Tunis)

SPACE EXPLORATION IS THE FUTURE
JANUARY 15, 1969

Many people have dismissed man's space exploration as a total waste of money which could better be spent helping the world's poor.

These people fail to realize that the space program takes up less than one half of one per cent of America's gross national product, while 10 to 20 times as much is spent on war, and that we receive more immediate benefits from space than just the satisfaction of our curiosity and our sense of adventure.

Do these people realize that temperature control of spacecraft has led to better and cheaper ways of heating and cooling homes; that tiny mercury batteries, designed for use in space, are now running wrist watches; solar cells are now powering portable radios and cordless shavers: infra-red gadgets for satellites are opening garage doors and switching TV channels automatically?

A stainless steel parachute cloth for spaceships will make inexpensive inflatable houses in the near future. Do you housewives realize that those dishes you use for cooking that can be switched from frigid to torrid temperatures without cracking resulted from experimentation with nose cones? One of the drugs used to treat tuberculosis and mental illness was derived from a rocket propellant. New sensing and measuring gadgetry has revolutionized diagnostic techniques in medicines.

Research into new foods and food synthetics for astronauts will lead to more inexpensive good-tasting and nutritious food and edible food containers. The result will be food for the millions of underfed on earth.

The cure for cancer may be lying on the surface of Venus or on the way there. On Mars, we might discover how to synthesize all the food we could use. Space exploration will make Earth a much better place to live.

Earl Schultz, Ottawa

USE POLITICIANS INSTEAD
FEBRUARY 22, 1969

The plan of the Ontario government to enforce the handing over of stray cats and dogs to medical researchers is nauseous.

As a more suitable and eminently more appealing solution to the guinea pig problem, why not politicians for medical research? The supply is inexhaustible and certainly the disposal of 10 or more thousand politicians would have naught but the most salubrious effect on our beleaguered Canadian society.

C.S. Puxley, Ottawa

RESPECT FOR FRENCH
FEBRUARY 26, 1969

In spite of substantial progress, there are still many areas of Canadian life where the French language does not enjoy respect. It is therefore heart-warming to see the large number of English-speaking parents who want bilingual children so badly that they are ready to send them to French schools.

To believe so strongly in a new Canada is admirable indeed. But the method proposed is wrong.

The idea of sending children to a school where the language of instruction is not their mother tongue is an educational monstrosity. In 89 per cent of the cases it will do irreparable damage to the personality and language skills of the student.

The attempt to have citizens who are equally proficient in both languages can only result in poorer quality and weaker citizens.

Canada must be made up of Canadians who are strongly and firmly English-speaking and other Canadians who are strongly and firmly French-speaking. They should live together in a country which respects the presence of two languages in its institutions, in its way of life, in its attitudes.

To make this a working arrangement, many citizens would have to acquire some knowledge of the other second language. The amount of proficiency would vary according to the level of education and the type of employment.

Pierre Lesage, Ottawa

KEEP DON MESSER
APRIL 19, 1969

The decision by the CBC to discontinue *Don Messer's Jubilee* will be a serious blow to thousands of Canadians. Messer, along with *Hockey Night in Canada* and *Festival*, presented viewers with a truly Canadian phenomenon, in this case "down east music."

The excuse given in the Commons by the government that the replacement program, *Singalong Jubilee*, would "inject new life" and "add a young look and orientation" to the time slot is a poor one and shows a surprising ignorance on the part of the CBC of the musical tastes of the young people of Canada.

The vast number of *Singalong Jubilee* fans probably range from at least 30 years of age; hardly the "young look" people referred to by the government.

I am not a country music fan, nor do I watch *Don Messer's Jubilee*; however, according to the ratings a significantly large proportion of the Canadian viewing audience does and the CBC should consider them.

David Flemming, Ottawa

Editor's note: Although he was born in New Brunswick, the music of Don Messer will forever be associated with Prince Edward Island. For nearly four decades, Messer and his band — known as the Islanders after their move to Charlottetown in 1936 — were synonymous with "old-time,

CBC PHOTO

CBC's cancellation of Don Messer's Jubilee — the group seen here in 1936 with Charlie Chamberlain, far left, Messer, far right and Marg Osburne, centre — was a serious blow to thousands, a reader said.

down home Maritime music." In 1959, Messer, along with his popular singers Charlie Chamberlain and Marg Osburne, began a 10-year run on CBC-TV on Saturday nights, where in most of the country they were seen just before Hockey Night in Canada. The cancellation of the show in 1969 brought howls of protest from across the country. In response, CHCH-TV in Hamilton syndicated the show nationally — including many CBC affiliates — until Messer's death in 1973.

DRAFT DODGER'S VIEW

JUNE 4, 1969

One of your readers recently advocated that U.S. deserters should be barred from Canada on the grounds that they will break any pledges of allegiance to Canada after they tire of politics.

Being a draft dodger perhaps gives me the right to speak on this subject.

It seems to me that deserters fall into two main groups.

The first consists of religious persons and former students who felt that due to their educational background, they would not be sent to Vietnam.

In reality, these are the most useless people to the American military, which is why almost all of them are ordered to Vietnam.

The second class consists of people who were not, at first, particularly opposed to the South Vietnamese Nazis but were unable to stomach the methods of modern warfare.

Canada, by her attitudes to China and NATO , has shown herself to be one of the very few countries in the world dedicated to peaceful co-existence, rather than an armed co-existence where the two sides are simply too terrified to attack one another.

Your reader's charge that deserters will soon become tired of Canada's policies of internal freedom and external peace seems rather unfounded in view of the fact that most of them came here in search of these exact same policies.

Charles F. Sudduth, Ottawa

Editor's note: Although officially Canada was an impartial observer and later an objective peacekeeper in the Vietnam war, Canadian aid during the war was heavily directed to South Vietnam. Still, prime ministers Lester Pearson and Pierre Trudeau were queasy about U.S. involvement in the conflict, and Canada gave refuge to more than 20,000 American draft dodgers and 12,000 military deserters between 1966 and 1975. The majority of them stayed in Canada after the war.

NEW ARTS CENTRE IS UGLY MESS

JUNE 10, 1969

Canada's new trainless subway station, the National Arts Centre, is simply the ugliest building I've ever seen.

I hate the sordid grey low ceilings with orange light shining down on red carpet.

I thought the chandelier and fountain looked like reconstructed junk from a car dump, and the mess of paint on the wall of one area lacked only a circus "barker" and the smell of hot dogs.

I sat on a purple seat and looked at the red carpet, and thinking the shades were not quite right, remarked that it wasn't "very pretty" and got a dirty look from another person who obviously thought I'd said the wrong thing.

The one thing I did like, the metal doors, I expected to open to reveal something magnificent, but had to peek through a crack only to see three people doing nothing in an unattractive dismal studio.

Will that crumbling (they were patching it up as I walked in) mass of cement last for 100 years, or is it a monument to a decaying civilization, and as it crumbles so will we?

If in criticizing Canada's new sacred cow I step on any toes, let it be with hobnailed boots because it was built with the Canadian taxpayer's money.

Barbara Jackson,
McDonald's Corners, Ont.

PM'S CONDUCT BRINGS BRICK AND BOUQUET

AUGUST 13, 1969

It's just about time Pierre Elliot Trudeau took a tumble and conducted himself in public with the decorum and dignity one would expect from Canada's prime minister.

His recent behaviour out West must have reduced his prestige to a minimum. His actions in dragging a poster from a young girl and bashing a demonstrator's hat over his eyes was more the action of an irresponsible kid than Canada's mature leader entering his 50th year. It's time he realized that such actions would be ridiculed by the representatives of other nations' diplomatic corps.

During his election campaign, these childish actions were to be accepted as part of gaining publicity. But having succeeded in attaining his high office he should at least show the dignity expected from a prime minister, especially our own!

H.R. Allen, Ottawa

WHO NEEDS US?

AUGUST 15, 1969

I have just returned from my first visit to Ottawa. After years of hearing about the stately and venerable house of Parliament, I was disgusted to see what an old, dirty and disgusting building it was.

But perhaps a fit setting for the dirty laws which have been passed there recently on abortion, divorce and homosexuality.

Perhaps we should have a new building to house the government in Winnipeg, Regina or Calgary. It is high time the four Western provinces separated from the Upper and Lower Canada mess.

Who needs the East anyhow?

M.O. Robinson, Calgary

WHY WORRY?

SEPTEMBER 6, 1969

Why worry if our younger generation is interested only in sex and drugs?

Why worry if our 25 to 30-year-old slovenly-looking ninnies are taking over our universities?

Why worry if our 18-year-olds are acting like 12-year-old adolescents?

Why worry if there is no discipline and respect, because 10 years from now we will probably be dead and forgotten?

Why worry because we, the older generation, allowed it all to happen?

Why worry because we permitted our infants' self-expression to develop their own wonderful personalities?

Why worry because we didn't tell the youth what would happen if they used drugs and were caught by police?

Why didn't we tell them about the dangers of venereal diseases, the decaying flesh and the insane?

Why worry the little darlings, just give them all they ask, and, a depression and war will rectify the situation for a while, as in the past.

But the hell of it is I do worry, because responsibility is a worry — and a duty.

E. A. Ritza, Ottawa

PATRONS CLIPPED

SEPTEMBER 10, 1969

What justification have barbers for raising their prices to $2 a haircut? Have there been any new developments in the field of "tonsorial artistry?" No! Has service improved? no!

I think I'll have my tonsors out.

Christopher McLeod, Ottawa

MARIJUANA HERE TO STAY

OCTOBER 25, 1969

Unless you are a teenager today, there is no way you can understand the drug scene in Ottawa or any other town. It is everywhere, in every school hall, at every small restaurant.

And face it, it is here to stay. If people were really upset over this problem, they would use some common sense.

The penalty for a harmless drug like marijuana is just as stiff as for a more dangerous one such as methedrine. If marijuana were legal, people would use that, instead of the more potent, but smaller drugs, such as LSD.

How can the law be respected when just about any teenager you talk to will tell you how unfair this law is? The people who carry out these laws, the RCMP who make arrests are, on the average, cruel and sadistic beasts. Yet how can the word of a "dope fiend" stand up against that of a supposedly responsible member of the law?

Please, please do something about it. If it keeps on this way, every young person in Canada will be in jail for grass, which is definitely no major crime.

D.E. McGee, Ottawa

A PEOPLE'S PARK

NOVEMBER 19, 1969

If LeBreton Flats cannot be dedicated to defence, why not dedicate it to fun? A Tivoli park or fun fairs *à la* Expo would be an attraction for visitors — and provide a great deal of employment for the jobless. The upper and middle class of Ottawa have had their share of the government slush funds in the sacred name of "culture" — the National Arts Centre.

Can't the "others" have equal time and money to create a people's park?

Jim Lotz, Ottawa

Editor's note: Until the late 1950s, LeBreton Flats was home to 2,000 residents, several schools and dozens of businesses. That's when prime minister John Diefenbaker decided to expropriate the Flats and clear away the buildings to make way for a huge national defence complex dubbed Pentagon North. The complex was never built, and although politicians have had dozens of ideas for the area since, it remains open fields today.

MAKE IT A RINK

DECEMBER 24, 1969

While driving along Colonel By Drive, my wife and I have often thought that if the city officials could turn the Rideau Canal from the Château Laurier to Dow's Lake into a skating rink for young and old alike it would be a great addition to Ottawa winter sports activities.

The canal could be used all winter for skating parties, hockey games and winter weekend festivities.

Surely a few trips up and down the centre of the canal by a city snowblower wouldn't cost that much in return for the added enjoyment it would bring to thousands of Ottawans.

Wayne Wilson, Ottawa

Editor's note: Although it's difficult to imagine today, several attempts in the 1960s by the City of Ottawa to develop the Rideau Canal into a community skating rink were failures, mostly because the efforts were conducted half-heartedly. That changed with National Capital Commission chairman Douglas Fullerton, whose single-minded vision for a well-maintained ice sheet from the National Arts Centre to Dow's Lake became reality in January 1971.

THIS IS ART?

DECEMBER 30, 1969

While visiting the National Gallery I was amused by Andy Warhol's "Brillo," a group of eight cubes with advertisements stencilled on them — then horrified to notice that in these times of government austerity the gallery had actually purchased this exhibit.

Could somebody please inform me what contribution to art this exhibit makes? How much did the gallery pay for the eight cubes and who was responsible for the purchase?

(Mrs.) Brenda Winchester, Ottawa

Editor's note: The question of what Andy Warhol's pop art really means will likely never be answered to everyone's satisfaction. However, the answer to Mrs. Winchester's second question is easier. The National Gallery paid less than $1,000 for the Brillo boxes exhibit in the late 1960s — a bargain basement price considering some of Mr. Warhol's art has sold for more than $1 million since his death in 1987.

"They bully, bash, bruise and bleed their opponents. They hack, harm, harass and create havoc. They pummel, punch, injure and intimidate. They are vicious and filled with violence. In Canada we call it hockey. Shame."

— July 10, 1976

1970-1979

1970

Local: Police set up first drunk-driving roadblocks using breathalyzers (January); Snowmobiles banned from Gatineau Park after study reveals extensive ecological damage (October); Queensway completed to Kanata in west end, to Gloucester in east (November)
National: Liberian-registered tanker *Arrow* runs aground off Nova Scotia, spilling 15,500 tonnes of oil on water and beaches (February); Montreal awarded 1976 Summer Olympics (May); Federal voting age lowered to 18 from 21 (May); Government invokes War Measures Act to deal with separatist unrest in Quebec, including kidnappings of British trade commissioner James Cross and Quebec labour minister Pierre Laporte, who is murdered (October); Royal Commission on Status of Women urges equal pay for work of equal value, universal day care, abortion on demand and relaxation of birth control rules (December)
World: Vietnam War expands as U.S. president Richard Nixon sends troops into Cambodia to destroy communist military sanctuaries (April); National Guard kills four student anti-war protesters at Kent State University (May); Paul McCartney leaves the Beatles, disbanding the most successful pop group of all time (April); Palestine Liberation Organization extremists hijack five planes, blow up three, in Jordanian desert (September)
Births: Tennis star Andre Agassi; actors Uma Thurman, Matt Damon, Minnie Driver and Ethan Hawke; pop singer Beck Hansen; models Naomi Campbell and Heather Graham; rapper Queen Latifah
Deaths: Philosopher Bertrand Russell; French president Charles de Gaulle; rock stars Jimi Hendrix and Janis Joplin; Abraham Zapruder, who filmed John Kennedy's assassination; British writer E.M. Forster; Egyptian leader Gamal Abdel Nasser; Canadian human rights activist Francis Shofield; painter Mark Rothko; burlesque queen Gypsy Rose Lee; legendary NFL coach Vince Lombardi

NOT RELEVANT

JANUARY 14, 1970

Come on. Do we really care whether Nancy Greene breastfeeds her newborn twins or not?

For goodness sakes, let's have some reporting we can think about.

P. Render, Ottawa

FRENCH WILL BE DEAD BY YEAR 2000

JANUARY 16, 1970

Why should we English-speaking Ottawans have to finance, build, support and maintain costly French-speaking schools? For that matter, why should we English-speaking Canadians be obliged and coerced into the bilingualism bit at all?

History and basic logic are there to prove that the French are a vanishing breed, and by the year 2000 even the majority of Quebeckers will have seen the light and will be speaking English, the language of progress, finance, business, technology, science and anything else you can imagine.

We are currently spending our hard-earned tax dollars in promoting an agonizing, not to say moribund, language.

Does the Bilingualism and Biculturalism Commission's report not show that Quebec is fast becoming English-speaking? And a good thing, too. Only then will it become really and truly the 10th province of Canada.

R.D. Smythe, Ottawa

PM TOO POWERFUL

JANUARY 21, 1970

Since the last federal election, the parliamentary system has slowly, but definitely, deteriorated to make way for what seems to be a republican-type government headed by a president.

Pierre Trudeau, the person in the position of prime minister, has seen it justifiable and necessary to erode the duties of the MP to the point of almost complete irrelevance in the everyday decisions of the country.

A complete contempt for the parliamentary system and the duties and privileges of the opposition parties was evident in the introduction of closure as a feasible tool of a majority government in making Parliament more relevant to the needs of the Canadian people.

In his bids to increase parliamentary efficiency, the prime minister has increased his own personal power while failing to submit himself to the various checks and limits characteristically surrounding the president in a republican system.

It is possible, of course, that our prime minister has, in his concern for the country, overlooked these essential means of control over the "first among equals."

If such is the case, then Mr. Trudeau, as an intelligent man, will now introduce legislation which will ensure that these new powers will not be abused.

Maureen A. McTeer,
Cumberland, Ont.

Editor's note: When Maureen McTeer wrote this letter, she was a 19-year-old student working her way through the University of Ottawa. Two years later, she took a part-time job as constituency assistant to a rookie MP from Alberta. Within a year, Ms. McTeer married the MP, Joe Clark, and the rest, as they say, is history.

WHAT PARLIAMENTARY DIGNITY?

MAY 23, 1970

Justice Minister John Turner's reaction to the women's demonstration seeking more liberal abortion laws is the reason many people get fed up with the democratic process. Instead of going off in high dudgeon and yelling blackmail, etc., couldn't he have accepted the women's "demands" as rhetoric?

These women were fed up because the amendments to the abortion law actually made it more difficult to get an abortion.

Some progress!

A woman should be able to have control over her own body. No one suggests that anyone should be forced to undergo an abortion, so why should the reverse be true? Why should any of them be prevented from having one?

Instead of being so concerned about the "dignity" of Parliament, why not more concern for the dignity of the individual? When you sit in the gallery and see what goes on in the House of Commons, the childish debates, members reading newspapers and writing letters, the dull speeches, you'd wonder how the "business" of the House could be that much disturbed by the occasional demonstration.

Personally, I think this demonstration brought a breath of fresh air to proceedings in the House.

H.M. DeForest, Ottawa

AN APPRECIATION
JULY 13, 1970

This is a note of appreciation for *The Citizen* over a period of many years.

Over the years I did not want to be without it, and learned of the larger quality of character that animated the publishing and editing of this paper, its aiding of great causes and its lack of fear in expressing support of such causes.

I scanned it from front to back — even the funnies. I guess *Gasoline Alley* is the strip longest in existence.

Since retirement, I've been gratified to have it delivered by a variety of boys, sometimes just over from Italy or Germany, and one little girl from India, also French or English-Canadians.

So, I say a prayer for the continuance of this fine paper that over the years has been such a good friend.

(Miss) Erica Selfridge, Ottawa

ABOUT THE SNOW — SHHHH
SEPTEMBER 16, 1970

Various administrators in Washington have been noted for concealing the truth and practising deceptions and our former president, Lyndon B. Johnson, achieved fame by telling whoppers that exceeded those of Ananias.

On a visit to your city, I see that the Ottawa authorities are more subtle. Not one shop in the city purveys postcards of winter scenes in your very attractive city. Why not? Everyone should know that now and then numerous snowflakes descend upon the earth here.

Does the government here insist that all postcards omit snow scenes?

P.S. I'm leaving town tonight on the Super Continental to avoid the vigilantes of your local Chamber of Commerce!

Charles W. Swenson,
Fallbrook, Calif.

WE'RE SUCKERS
OCTOBER 14, 1970

The waiter in my favourite pub gave me the cold shoulder yesterday. A belated glance at the price list was all the explanation needed. What I thought to be a tip had now become part of the price of beer. It's gone up again.

This time the hike is only indirectly due to the govern-

ment. Supposedly the recent change in Ontario's minimum-wage legislation made it absolutely unprofitable to dispense suds at prevailing prices. That's a lot of swill.

The extra intake at five cents a drink will be several times the expense incurred through additional wages. This is precisely what the Prices and Incomes Commission said must be avoided.

But it's highly unlikely for that body to interfere on behalf of the drinking public. The lushes of this fair land have yet to find a champion. Boozers are suckers.

W.W. Stanzar, Ottawa

TROOPS ARE WELCOME
IN THE STREETS
OCTOBER 17, 1970

I find completely incomprehensible the strangely hostile attitude of many people to the stationing of armed troops in Ottawa. If people had wakened up one morning to find the streets patrolled by armed FLQ terrorists, they would have had real reason for alarm and horror.

If we are guarding lives from terrorists armed with automatic weapons, it is only reasonable to use trained soldiers similarly armed. Why be affronted by the sight of helmets and weapons?

Let's be thankful for their help in performing their very useful duties which free the police from the impossible task of guard duty, retaining our criticism only for those responsible for the frightening circumstances which require their presence.

Mrs. L.W.G. Hayes, Ottawa

Editor's note: The Oct. 5, 1970, kidnapping of British trade commissioner James Cross by FLQ terrorists began one of the tensest, most discussed periods in Canadian history. When the government refused to negotiate the FLQ demands for a ransom of $500,000 in gold and safe passage out of Canada for 23 jailed FLQ members, the terrorist group responded by kidnapping Quebec labour minister Pierre Laporte. Within days, the government invoked the War Measures Act, allowing authorities to overrule civil rights and marking the first time such powers had been used in peacetime. Using the act, nearly 500 people were arrested, most of them in Quebec, although only 18 were ever convicted of any crime. After Mr. Laporte's strangled body was found in the trunk of a car, the government offered a $75,000 reward for information on the kidnappings. In early December, police surrounded the house where Mr. Cross was being held. In exchange for his release, the kidnappers and their families were given safe passage to Cuba. Needless to say, the events of the October Crisis triggered a heated debate across the country. Here are some other letters reflecting the tone of the discussion.

CIVIL LIBERTIES ARE FRAGILE
OCTOBER 28, 1970

Democracy and civil liberties now seem to be fragile things and the events of the last few weeks have underlined how shallow is some Canadians' belief in them.

At a time when law and justice are being challenged by

Ottawans should be grateful that armed soldiers are available to perform guard duty during the October Crisis, a reader argued.

a few, our government demonstrates its lack of confidence in our democratic institutions by invoking the War Measures Act and, by repeated calls for "unity," implies that anything less than uncritical support of its actions will aid the criminals.

On the contrary, nothing will encourage terrorists more than the claim, implicit in the government's action, that our institutions are unequal to the challenge of terrorism.

W. Burgess, Ottawa

STANFIELD DOESN'T UNDERSTAND

OCTOBER 30, 1970

The murder of Pierre Laporte horrifies me, but it does not affect me personally as do the comments of two men who presume to govern me.

Conservative leader Robert Stanfield is reported to have commented on the murders, "I can't understand how their minds work," and Newfoundland premier Joey Smallwood, "I didn't believe men could do that."

Such innocence (?) makes me uneasy. By the fact that these gentlemen ran for office they are implying the authority to protect us all. By what authority do they protect us from what they do not understand or even recognize exists?

Nina Green, Ottawa

WE HAVE THE AGONY OF CHOICE

NOVEMBER 2, 1970

Since the Magna Carta, English people have progressed to a generous system of justice. Canada has even managed to achieve its own sovereignty without resorting to revolution and the assassination of kings. Surely this is a symbol of pure democracy.

Yet today we are faced with the knowledge that this justice can no longer accommodate the type of deranged person in our midst. The dilemma of whether we have been too lenient in the past, and the sad alternative of going backward instead of forward, is upon us.

Government is not God — only men; for the most part dedicated, courageous men, who stand out in full view of us all. Democratic government is not easy — it has the agony of choice. Violence and chaos have no beginning or end. We may never find our way back.

D. Warren, Ottawa

NO SEX BAR FOR MUSICIANS

NOVEMBER 11, 1970

Many of the National Arts Centre Orchestra's most experienced, most hard-working, most co-operative, most talented, best-trained (and best-looking) members are women.

As a result, some of the most important, and therefore best-paid, positions in the orchestra (including assistant concertmaster and leader of the second violins) are occupied by women. In addition, two sections of the orchestra (the violins and cellos) are predominantly female and, overall, more than 30 per cent of the musicians in the orchestra are women.

I don't know what orchestras Nina Falk [a NACO viola player] had in mind when she charged that women musicians are discriminated against, but it can't have been ours.

I have been present at almost all auditions for the orchestra, and I have never heard our conductor, Mario Bernardi, even mention the sex of a candidate as something to be considered. He has only one criterion: ability.

Thus, it sometimes happens that a woman candidate will win out over a group of male candidates. This is what happened in the case of Miss Falk, who, incidentally, earns more than several of her male colleagues.

Kenneth S. Murphy, Ottawa,
Manager, National Arts Centre Orchestra

TV IS TO BLAME

NOVEMBER 25, 1970

If parents wonder why their children are not responding to discipline at home and at school, they need look no further than the television set.

I have seen numerous commercials which emphasize a definite lack of respect for parents:

• Two children who eat all the chicken before they get it home, and mummy just smiles benevolently. No word of recrimination.

• A teenaged boy who rushes into the kitchen and ignores a delicious breakfast his mother has prepared. Again, no word of scolding at all.

• The worst of all, a mother saying that she was "in trouble with her son" because he couldn't keep track of his belongings.

Children are watching and absorbing this garbage, and the sooner it is taken off the screen, the better.

Gwyneth C. Ledsham, Ottawa

1971

Local: Plans announced for two big west end shopping malls — Bayshore and Lincoln Fields (March); First stages of bikepath system opens (May); *Ottawa Citizen* sells Queen Street building to parking firm, paving the way to move to western suburbs by 1972 (June)

National: Post Office begins "assured mail-delivery program," guaranteeing next-day delivery of letters posted before 11 a.m. in major cities (February); Pierre Trudeau surprises nation by marrying 22-year-old Margaret Sinclair (March); Cigarette advertising ends on TV and radio (September); Canadian recognition of Red China formalized with exchange of ambassadors (September); Ottawa researcher Gerhard Herzberg wins Nobel Prize in chemistry for work on molecular spectroscopy (November)

World: Violence rocks Northern Ireland after government invokes emergency powers to detain IRA leaders (August-September); After years of debate, Britain votes to join the European Common Market (October); China gets seat at United Nations after U.S. lifts its 20-year veto (November); *Mariner 9,* a 300-pound U.S. spacecraft launched in June, slides into orbit around Mars (November)

Births: Stock car driver Jeff Gordon; rapper Tupac Shakur; actors Ewan McGregor and Winona Ryder; supermodels Claudia Schiffer and Nadja Avermann

Deaths: Soviet premier Nikita Krushchev; jazz pioneer Louis Armstrong; Russian composer Igor Stravinsky; rock stars Jim Morrison and Duane Allman; fashion designer Gabrielle (Coco) Chanel; George Lukacs, Hungarian philosopher and literary critic; retail legend J.C. Penney; Haitian strongman François (Papa Doc) Duvalier; New York mobster Joseph Colombo; U.S. publisher Bennett Cerf

PROTECTING OUR PROTECTORS
JANUARY 6, 1971

The Canadian cabinet has commuted another death sentence for the killing of a police officer. It seems a strange approach to supporting that most necessary of all our citizens — the policeman.

The criminal or terrorist who is trapped by the police can surrender and possibly receive 10 years for his crime and be paroled after seven years. The other choice is to shoot the arresting officer and possibly escape. This might be a chance worth taking because, if he is apprehended, he will receive life imprisonment, which means after six or seven years of good behaviour he will be paroled.

Really, what does he have to lose?

Policemen are expected to maintain law and order, but they can only be expected to do this if they know that Parliament and the courts are behind them. When you play with the law the way the cabinet does, then you cannot expected the policeman, whose life is in jeopardy, to be overly conscientious about his duty.

Your newspaper and your columnists write a great deal about the total abolition of the death sentence. It must be very easy to do; after all, you are not the people who must face a killer.

Gerald Reidy, Ottawa

Editor's note: In a five-year experiment started in 1967, Parliament abolished capital punishment for murder — unless the victim was an on-duty police officer or prison guard — and replaced it with mandatory life prison sentences. The experiment was renewed in 1973. In 1976, Parliament officially banned hanging for all civilian crimes, including murder of police officers and prison guards.

'ALL WE ASK IS TO BE EQUAL'
FEBRUARY 3, 1971

Once more, Canadians of French origin in this "just society" are being treated like the white Negroes of America. We are being made to feel guilty because someone, somewhere, has decided that it is time to stop talking and to act.

Specifically, $2 million is (or was) to be set aside to provide francophone university graduates with jobs in the public service. And suddenly, as one voice, members of Parliament, journalists and people everywhere are crying "discrimination."

What a confusing situation. Anglophones are a majority in this country. Anglophones are the highest-paid, best-educated, best-housed people in this country. Anglophones control the economy, they control the industry and they control the politics of this country.

For over 100 years, francophones have survived because we have accepted to be subjected to this majority. Those of us who treasured our identity and fought to preserve it realized full well that we would pay the price. Those for whom the price was too high, and to whom money and position were more important, became assimilated.

Times are changing. All over the world there is a stirring of fresh air — air that carries words like equality, liberation, social justice, freedom. We are beginning to understand what it means that all men are born equal. Words like love and respect are becoming more important and meaningful to many of us.

Canadians probably have a unique possibility of allowing this atmosphere to permeate their country. We have a large country, a small population, a high economic level.

Francophones in Canada have lived with discrimination all their lives. We don't need journalists and members of Parliament to tell us what it is all about. We know what it can do to people inside. We don't like it. But we can't deny what we are.

What do francophones want? We want to be equal — not the same. Equal. We want the same choices as anglophones, in job opportunities, in educational opportunities, in developing our culture, in enjoying the quality of Canadian life.

We do not believe that we are penalizing other Canadians in expecting them to recognize and respect this right.

Adèle Lavoie, Ottawa

PM'S STYLE SINGES BARBERS

FEBRUARY 6, 1971

In our time there are changing styles for clothing, cars and industrial products to keep up the consumer's interest in buying. These changes keep the economy rolling.

Lately, though, our economy has been rolling downward. I see it going from bad to worse.

The barbering trade, for instance, is suffering badly. The longer hair styles have come to suit many people as an excuse not to visit the barber shop. Quite a number of these are excusable because they may lack the money because of high unemployment.

But our prime minister could contribute something to the diminishing barber trade by setting an example with a proper (shorter) hair style. My own son produces a picture of Mr. Trudeau with long hair in answer to my continued attempts to keep his hair to a proper length.

If the prime minister would set an example and get his hair cut, we barbers might get some badly needed customers back into our shops.

John Monnich,
Ottawa

SORRY, NO DRINKS — YOU'RE WOMEN

MARCH 10, 1971

My sister and I recently arrived in Canada from New Zealand. Naturally, when we arrived in Canada one of the first places we wanted to visit was Ottawa.

In all fairness, I must say that our tour of the city was quite enjoyable overall.

But when we went to the bar of the Ottawa House, we were coldly informed when we ordered that since we were not escorted by men, they would not serve us. We were not embarrassed but decided to stand our ground and refused to leave. Some gentlemen, noticing our dilemma, asked if they could be of assistance. When one of them went to the bar to order drinks for us, their orders were also refused.

My sister and I have always been quite happy in our role of femininity, and have never wanted to be part of the bra-burning crowd. However, if we women are treated as third-class citizens in this way, we will have no recourse but to take up the cause.

In our travels to many parts of the world, my sister and I have never been subjected to such indignity. Ottawa-Hull, is this the way you treat your visitors?

C. Pellell,
Toronto

Editor's note: In the belief that unescorted women and alcohol inevitably lead to loose behaviour, Ontario liquor laws for many decades prohibited women from entering drinking establishments without a male companion. Even with a male partner, women were only allowed into special rooms labelled 'Ladies and Escorts.' The laws also limited a woman to two male escorts — if there was a third, he had to sit in a separate room labelled 'Men's Only.' After several years of promises, the law was dropped in 1975.

WOMEN'S RIGHT TO A NAME

JUNE 26, 1971

Every time I glance through the women's pages of *The Citizen* — and other papers, too — it makes my blood boil, and I can almost see the point of view of the fanatics of the women's lib set.

Mrs. Norman X, Mrs. William Y, Mrs. Trevor Z. Who are these nameless creatures hiding behind their husbands' names?

Do they not have the right to at least their own Christian names? Or are they the true self-effacing "handmaids" of their lords and masters?

The tradition is all very well, but carried to extremes it makes a laughing stock of everyone, including their "lords and masters."

R. M. Pronski, Ottawa

HIDEOUS, HORRIBLE SIGHT

JULY 10, 1971

I couldn't agree more with your editorial condemning the appearance of that new Department of National Defence headquarters building.

Every time I see it, which is almost every day, I think how absolutely hideous it is. It's horrible, an eyesore. It absolutely ruins the view from both sides of the Rideau Canal and I think it's a crime it was allowed to be put up in that spot, or any place else for that matter.

And, of course, there's nothing we can do about it now, unfortunately.

Mrs. J. W. Stalker, Ottawa

A FRENCH TAKEOVER

JULY 14, 1971

English Canada should wake up and realize that the Quebec power group is not interested in a fair deal for the whole of Canada but desires a complete reversal of the last 100 years.

A quick look will show any Canadian how much of our culture and media now come under French-language domination.

The festivities July 1, supposed to be representative of all ethnic groups in Canada, ended with a rousing chorus of *O Canada* sung completely in French. As I stood there patriotically belting out English to be heard, I distinctly felt the stupidity of two opposing forces.

Should we English-Canadians acquiesce and become French-Canadians, or resist this ironical idiocy?

Mary Anne Rutherford, Aylmer

MURKY SUNSET

JULY 21, 1971

Some friends and I recently went to Parliament Hill to watch the sunset behind Hull and over the Gatineau Hills.

It could have been an exquisite sunset; the hills silhouetted against the multicoloured sky. Even E.B. Eddy's neon swans and super roll of toilet paper have a strange beauty. People in the Ottawa-Hull area know this scene well.

Sadly, we also know this picture with a large black cloud

across it, a cloud produced by the E. B. Eddy Co. and Canada Cement.

Will we ever see a sunset without a dirty black cloud?

Francis Budden, Ottawa

Editor's note: From Ottawa's earliest days as a lumber town, industrial pollution along the Ottawa River has been part of public debate in the capital. While many of the large mills and factories along the Hull waterfront have been closed or scaled back, the century-old E.B. Eddy complex on and around Chaudière Island continues to operate, although in a much cleaner way than it once did. For decades lasting into the 1970s, the odour from the Eddy mill was as much a part of the capital as the Parliament Buildings. In 1972, the company agreed to sell its entire Chaudière operation to the federal government for $62 million and phase out its operation over the next 15 years. But by 1977, Eddy had backed away from the deal and convinced the government to provide $25 million to help modernize the mill and reduce water and air pollution. These days, Eddy runs a much cleaner operation, although it was fined $85,000 as recently as 1992 for an acidic water spill.

EASY DIVORCE?

AUGUST 7, 1971

In recent years the grounds for divorce have been widened. While this is a step "out of the dark ages" in the handling of divorce, other elements are in urgent need of updating.

The intelligence of the average Canadian cannot help but be insulted by the law which sets a waiting period of three years before separated couples can even apply for divorce.

Surely those who formulated such a law could not have believed that the decision to sue for divorce is a "spur of the moment" one on the part of married couples. It should be recognized that it is usually a slow, painful process, resulting from years of inability to get along, reached because the couple can see no other way out of the problem with which they are faced.

Surely a waiting period of one year should be more than ample.

Robert Ramsay,
Marathon, Ont.

Editor's note: Until the 1968 Divorce Act, divorce in Canada could only be obtained on the basis of infidelity. The new law, the child of Justice Minister Pierre Trudeau, expanded the parameters to permit divorce in the event of a marital breakdown, although a couple had to live apart for at least three years first. That condition was a compromise designed to reduce opposition to relaxed divorce laws from the Catholic Church in Quebec. In 1986, the waiting period was shortened to a year.

HYPOCRISY AND RED CHINA

AUGUST 21, 1971

Negotiations on recognition of Red China did not represent such a major breakthrough as your correspondent believes. Forty-five countries recognized Mao's regime before us.

The real Western breakthrough was achieved by the French. However, de Gaulle was honest about it and at the same time withdrew recognition of the government on Taiwan.

We, on the other hand, trumpeted our virtue and our stand on principles, and pushed the Chinese nationalist government envoys from Taiwan quietly out of the back door of Rideau Hall, and are in the process of doing so at the United Nations.

Indeed, we gave new life to a cliché by demonstrating that we, too, are not above sacrificing our principles on the altar of political expediency.

Perhaps in our discussion and concern over the feelings of the envoy from the Peoples' Republic of China, we should think back a few short years to the crest of the Chinese "cultural revolution," when Western diplomats and their families were assaulted, spat and urinated upon by the mobs in the streets of Peking, when Western embassies were being sacked and burned while the government Ambassador Huang represents did nothing to stop these outrages and preserve the time-honoured immunity of foreign envoys, and Chairman Mao went swimming.

Mao Tse-tung once wrote that political power grows out of the barrel of a gun. Let us accept our newly re-established relations with a government of mainland China for what they are, without attempting to drape the cloak of virtue over the still warm muzzle.

Luanna M. Blackmore, Ottawa

TIME FOR ONE-PARTY SYSTEM

SEPTEMBER 4, 1971

As I religiously agree with every word that comes out of the mouth of the *Ottawa Citizen*, I rejoice at its desire that all our children be educated under one unified system. As any kook knows, religion separates people and when they are separated they are very, very naughty.

Now, the way to unify the education system is, of course, to unify the political system. Away with parties; they only separate people into competitive Conservatives, Liberals and socialists. The U.S.S.R. has achieved the one-party system, and only the insane dispute that the U.S.S.R. is unity personified.

So let's stop being stuffy about differences. Just cease being different. Just be like me.

Nina Green, Ottawa

HIDEOUS INTESTINE

SEPTEMBER 8, 1971

Who is responsible for placing in the park opposite the Lord Elgin Hotel that hideous representation of the large intestine? And who is paying for it, and how much?

Eugene Forsey, Ottawa

Editor's note: Traffic, the formal name for the infamous fibreglass sculpture condemned by Senator Forsey, was set up in Confederation Park in 1971 by the National Gallery, which had commissioned the work from British artist Ed Ze-

Who is responsible for the hideous large intestine in Ottawa's Confederation Park? asked Eugene Forsey.

lenak. For years, the $27,000 sculpture was the subject of derision — it was variously dubbed the Horror, the Thing, the Intestine and most popularly, the Worm. But over time, it seemed to grow on Ottawans, and eventually came to be viewed with a sort of affection. In 1993, it was moved to a site outside the new Gallery building on Sussex Drive. Four years later, it was removed for restoration and remains in storage with no plans for reinstallation. Here's another letter on the subject.

SO THAT'S IT
SEPTEMBER 14, 1971

Further to Senator Forsey's letter of Sept. 8 complaining about the sculpture across from the Lord Elgin Hotel, he may be amused to know that it is an artistic representation of the Senate. It goes up and down, around and around, performing no specific function at great expense.

K.C. Stein, Ottawa

BILLING PET?
NOVEMBER 13, 1971

Elimination of the Queen from our $10 bill (just a proposal, but obviously in accordance with government poli-

cy of eradication of all traces of our English heritage) will unfortunately not make it worth a damn cent more.

Can we now anticipate seeing all Canadian prime ministers depicted on our money?

I seriously question the future value of a "Hairy Hippie" dollar.

M. R. Martin,
Ottawa

FORCED TRANSFERS TO HULL
DECEMBER 1, 1971

As one of several thousand civil servants who have been or are scheduled to be moved to Hull within the next two years, I would point out at least 70 per cent are English-speaking residents of Ottawa who are strongly opposed to the move.

A few of these displaced civil servants may eventually decide to live in Hull rather than fight the bridge traffic twice a day, but the majority have children whom they wish to educate in Ontario. In addition, the combination of the language problem and Quebec nationalism produces the kind of environment that most English-speaking Canadians will not accept.

The government urges business and industry to consult with their employees on major employment matters affecting them but ignores this good advice when its own employees are involved.

Once again the civil servant is being made the scapegoat in the appeasement of Quebec's insatiable demands.

W. H. Hansen, Ottawa

Editor's note: To undermine arguments from separatists that Quebec was not a full partner in Canada, the federal government undertook a program to increase its presence in the province. As part of the process, the federal workforce in Hull, Aylmer and Gatineau grew from about 1,200 in the early 1970s to more than 15,000 by the mid-'80s, the large majority from Ontario. Although exact numbers are hard to get, the letter-writer was correct when predicting very few of those Ontarians would decide to live on the Quebec side.

1972

Local: Le Hibou, Ottawa's legendary folk music coffeehouse, closes (March); Rideau Street Convent dismantled and stored by NCC, resurrected in late 1980s inside new National Gallery (April); Pollution closes city beaches on Ottawa and Rideau rivers (July-August); Ald. Charlotte Whitton, weakened by a fall that broke her hip, decides to end her career in municipal politics (November)
National: LeDain Commission recommends abolition of penalties for possession of marijuana and hashish, but stops short of urging legalization (May); Maple Leaf Gardens president Harold Ballard jailed for three years for fraud and theft (August); Canada defeats Soviet Union four games to three, with one tie, in historic hockey series (August-September); Liberals hang on to power in federal election, edging Conservatives 109-107 seats, with NDP holding balance (October)
World: U.S. president Richard Nixon makes historic visit to China (February); Viet Cong launch major offensive into South Vietnam (April); Five burglars caught in Democratic party offices at Watergate apartment complex (June); Arab terrorists massacre 11 Israeli athletes at Munich Olympics (September); Nixon re-elected in landslide over Democrat George McGovern (November)
Births: Figure skater Elvis Stojko; actors Gwyneth Paltrow, Ben Affleck and Cameron Diaz; basketball star Shaquille O'Neal; rapper Snoop Doggy Dog
Deaths: Prime minister Lester Pearson; poet Ezra Pound; Duke of Windsor (formerly King Edward VIII); baseball greats Jackie Robinson and Roberto Clemente; gospel singer Mahalia Jackson; U.S. president Harry Truman; chanteur Maurice Chevalier; U.S. historian and critic Edmund Wilson

SICK SOCIETY
JANUARY 8, 1972

The resumption of the moronic and inhuman bombing of North Vietnam is just one more symptom of the disease of militarism in U.S. foreign policy.

That one man, the president, should have such dictatorial power and authority in a so-called democracy is beyond belief. Thankfully, this could never happen in Canada.

The reasons given by the secretary of defence for the resumption of bombing are ludicrous. Melvin Laird is the inventor and merchandiser of imaginary fears. A more misguided use of a hypothetical situation to frighten conventionally minded people could hardly be imagined.

May God forbid that Canada should ever be forced to submit to the machinations of such an incredibly sick society.

Thomas A. Murphy, Ottawa

ALICE COOPER: A SHALLOW VIEW
JANUARY 19, 1972

The article by your reviewer, Bill Provick, on the recent Ottawa performance by the Alice Cooper group, refers to the music as "electric din."

This statement not only cuts down the sounds we evolve ourselves around, but the entire younger generation whose music plays an important, if not essential, role in everyday life.

Alice's compositions are ones of deep meaning. The obvious allusion projected to the people by his appearance and stage performance, is not the true depth of his thoughts.

Only those of shallow minds and biased opinions could take Alice's music as "sinister," "evil" or "din."

Donna Milks and Wendy Milne, Ottawa

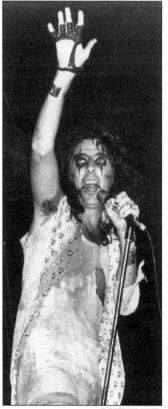
Alice Cooper's music is much more than a "din," says a reader.
THE OTTAWA CITIZEN

PROTESTS SAVED SEALS
JANUARY 26, 1972

Humanitarians around the world will rejoice at the news that the seal hunt in the Gulf of St. Lawrence is to be stopped. Credit for triggering world-wide protests against this brutal slaughter must go to the International Fund for Animal Welfare.

Environment Minister [Jack] Davis's insistence that pressure from many sources had no bearing on the decision seems barely credible. Without these protests, the hunt would have gone on down to the very last seal pup.

H. Mackey, Ottawa

SAVE THE PAST FOR THE FUTURE
APRIL 8, 1972

Every community needs a history, but we are fast losing ours.

The old hotel near the General Hospital, the elegant stone registry building that stood where the "Kulturbunker" (NAC) is now, and the picturesque Bytown Inn have all vanished. The Billings home is still only on a temporary reprieve, as is the Church of Notre Dame in Hull; the Convent on Rideau Street has just lost its cause.

These fine buildings say something of our past and give depth to our existence. When they are gone, it will be too late. In their place, we may have to look at some horrid boxes like the new National Defence Headquarters that looms over the canal.

What is lacking? Not only some historical and esthetic consciousness in our population. We also need some laws: In all civilized countries it has been found necessary to develop means to protect those buildings which an impartial commission has declared to be of historical or national importance.

Why don't Ottawa and the NCC press for some common-sense legislation?

Paul de Bellefeuille, Ottawa

Editor's note: Provincial legislation to protect heritage buildings arrived in the late 1970s, but whether the laws are common sense is open to interpretation. Pro-heritage advocates believe the Ontario Heritage Act is not tough enough to guarantee the protection of important historical buildings or areas. Developers and property owners, however, say the act is a draconian measure that allows municipalities to take control of property without having to pay for it. (In 1998, there were about 3,000 provincially designated heritage buildings in Ontario.) The federal government also has the power to protect buildings important to Canadian history. Although those rules are considered tougher than Ontario's, they generally apply to properties already owned by the government.

SUNDAY REST
JULY 26, 1972

It should be quite evident to everyone, including those who choose to cut their lawns on Sunday, that many people make a point of not doing so — a commitment to one noiseless day of rest in the week.

It's an easy act to follow.

John A. Kavanagh, Ottawa

SATURDAY MAIL DELIVERY
AUGUST 12, 1972

I'm so disgusted with the disruption caused by cancellation of Saturday delivery of mail that if the Conservative party promises to restore Saturday delivery I'll vote Conservative — no matter what other promises it makes, or does not make.

The people did not want it cancelled, nor did the postmen. Only Trudeau and his so-called experts, including the vice president of IT & T who was "loaned" to the post office department, wanted it.

Here I am on a Thursday night, having just written a letter that is important to a company, and knowing it will not be delivered until Monday or Tuesday, although its office is open Saturdays.

Don't Trudeau and his bunch of experts in Ottawa realize they are there to serve our convenience and not the other way around?

Calbron Mandala, Don Mills, Ont.

Editor's note: Postmaster-general Eric Kierans ended Saturday mail delivery and post office service in 1968 to save money. Although Saturday delivery was never reinstated, some post office branches, especially in rural areas, were reopened on Saturday mornings, a practice that continues today.

KEEP OTTAWA SMALL
SEPTEMBER 7, 1972

The master planners for the Ottawa-Carleton region have developed a plan based on a future population of one million people. Why, in view of all that is known or suspected about the effects of over-population, do they plan for 1,000,000?

If such forward-looking plans make any pretense at planning for the health, happiness and welfare of people, they will show how NOT to let the population of this area grow to 1,000,000.

Ottawa-Carleton's growth should be stopped where it is. It still has the potential for a pleasant environment and some hope of curing the pollution that has already occurred.

At 1,000,000 people, there will be no such hope.

We have everything to lose — twice as much traffic on the streets (or twice as many noisy throughways), more raw sewage in the river, more general degradation of the quality of living.

Every large city I have visited in this country and Europe produces more misery than happiness, more dehumanization than opportunities for fulfillment.

R. K. Brown, Ottawa

Editor's note: Although the population of the greater Ottawa-Hull area, including the Outaouais, passed a million in 1996, the population of the Region of Ottawa-Carleton — soon to be the enlarged City of Ottawa — is still less than 750,000 today.

LET PUNISHMENT
MATCH THE CRIME
SEPTEMBER 9, 1972

Following the massacre at the Munich Olympics, plus the heinous deed of last week when close to 40 persons lost their lives in a Montreal fire, is it not right to ask the question: What punishment will these criminals receive if apprehended, tried and convicted?

With the death penalty a thing of the past, the persons responsible know that the most they can expect is life imprisonment. This in Canada means approximately 10 to 12 years.

During that period society will allow them to:

1) Further their education;
2) Wear civilian clothes;
3) Watch TV — most likely coloured;
4) Wear the long hair currently in vogue;
5) Receive pay while serving;
6) Have weekend "private" visits from girlfriends and wives.

And what of the victims? Snatched from this life by tormented souls who after being convicted complain about conditions, being treated fairly, etc. while in prison.

With the killings mounting yearly, and the laxness in our penal system, there is little deterrent to the would-be murderer. For pre-meditated killings (and throwing gasoline bombs in a stairwell knowing many persons are in an area above) the killer(s) should meet their end on the gallows.

Nothing less will satisfy.

Kenneth S. Vowles,
Ottawa

WE'RE NO BETTER
THAN THE SOVIETS

SEPTEMBER 30, 1972

Anyone who watched the final Soviet-Canada hockey game in Moscow would agree the game was a very close and hard-fought one. And despite Canada's victory, I do not think that the Canadian players are necessarily better than the Russians.

In fact, the Russians seem better in team play, puck control and physical conditioning, but I don't think we should use these facts as excuses to explain Team Canada's three bad losses, especially since so many Canadians had predicted a Canadian eight-game sweep of the series.

With this series having been so close (the Russians actually outscored the Canadians 32-31), I think another series might end with a Soviet victory, and no one should be too surprised.

Shirley Eng, Ottawa

NEXT TIME, LET'S WIN
WITHOUT BEING BULLIES

OCTOBER 4, 1972

Since Team Canada won, congratulations are in order. However, we didn't have to tarnish our win by attacking the referees, holding up fuddle duddle fingers and heaving benches on the ice.

When Team Canada next plays the U.S.S.R., we should win decisively without the traumas of the past series and without the tactics of a spoiled bully.

Stephen Pallavicini, Ottawa

HOORAY, WE'RE THE CHAMPS
— FOR NOW

OCTOBER 4, 1972

The reception that Team Canada received in Montreal and Toronto was just fantastic. To think that 80,000 came to Nathan Phillips Square to honour the players is just terrific.

Even though the Canadians won the series, I would not be too surprised if one day, if and when a rematch is held, the Russian team is victorious. The power plays and the precision shots are two really strong points of the Russian team.

The historic series between Russia and Canada is now over, but the excitement and pride will remain. Congratulations to Team Canada!

Judy Obereander, Ottawa

IT'S TIME FOR MORE TALK
ON HIJACKINGS

NOVEMBER 18, 1972

U.S. Secretary of State William Rogers has submitted to the United Nations General Assembly a draft treaty aimed at bringing a halt to international terrorism. The treaty would guarantee that all offenders would be extradited to the country in which their crime was committed, or they would be prosecuted in the country that harboured them.

In 1972, 25 airliners from 13 countries were skyjacked; another 26 were unsuccessful in their attempts; a total of 237 persons were either wounded or killed in acts of terrorism concerning air piracy. In the last five years, 27 diplomats from 11 countries have been kidnapped — three were murdered in cold blood. (It is frightening to think that my father, who is a diplomat, could be transferred to one of those countries which harbours terrorists).

Andrei Gromyko, Soviet foreign minister, termed the murder of innocent Israeli athletes in Munich, "a tragic event and impossible to condone."

Mitchell Sharp, whom we all know so well, called on the General Assembly to take a firm stand with regard to terrorism. He drew parallels between slavery, piracy, and terrorism — of which the former two have been outlawed. He felt terrorism should also be outlawed.

My point is that all the leaders of "concerned" countries are calling on the assembly and making speeches about the situation — without doing a blessed thing!

Can we not do anything else but talk?

Ingrid Smith, Ottawa

Editor's note: Although the International Civil Aviation Organization (ICAA), an agency of the United Nations, got the signatures of more than 100 nations on anti-terrorist conventions as early as 1970, the accords were weakened by the non-participation of several of countries where skyjackers often sought asylum. It wasn't until 1986-87 that conventions with real teeth were put in place, and considerable progress was made to end air terrorism.

WHERE ARE OUR HOCKEY FANS?

DECEMBER 16, 1972

Either the citizens of Ottawa have not noticed they have a professional hockey team here, or they are showing their usual studied indifference toward anything new and exciting.

The average attendance at World Hockey Association games in Ottawa has been about 1,200 through the Grey Cup playoffs, and before that and since, between 2,000 and 3,000.

The Ottawa Nationals are an excellent, well-coached, spirited team. The lack of interest therefore reflects not on the team, but on the Ottawan, who is exhibiting his typical apathetic outlook toward the diversification of his community.

L. Klusendorf, Ottawa

Editor's note: When the World Hockey Association's Ottawa Nationals arrived in the capital in 1972, they promised a credible alternative to the NHL. Ottawa fans never bought it. In fact, interest was so low — only 400 season's tickets, just one sellout in 40 games (to see Bobby Hull's Winnipeg Jets) — the Nationals never finished their first season in Ottawa, fleeing secretly overnight to Toronto just 48 hours before their first playoff game.

TIME TO SHARE THE GLORY

DECEMBER 18, 1972

We provided the cannon fodder for the massacre at

Dieppe and the peacekeeping force in the Gaza strip. We are still in Cyprus and now we are going to Vietnam [as peacekeepers].

All we get is a pat on the head from Britain and the United States and a load of grief for the Canadian taxpayer.

So, Canadians all — mothers, fathers, sweethearts and wives, etc. — voice your protest to Mitchell Sharp or the prime minister. Let us stay home and let some other small nation get the glory.

To start, here are a few suggestions: Norway, Sweden, Spain, Portugal, Scotland.

John Monahan,
Toronto

IT'S TIME MPS WERE 'SOMEBODIES' AGAIN

DECEMBER 30, 1972

In a few days, we shall have a new Parliament, and one that has cost this nation a great deal of money and hard work to elect. It is our right to demand it be spared the usual contemptuous treatment by the Trudeau government, and not be turned into a mockery, as was the shameful fate of its predecessor!

There was a time when Parliament was accorded the re-spect which is so necessary for the preservation of our freedoms. Do Canadians remember:

1) When closure was a bad word and not used regularly to ram government bills, such as Rule 75-C and the tax bill, through a protesting House?

2) When the rules were equitable enough to allow free debate?

3) When the Queen was still listed as our sovereign and head of state in the publication entitled *Organization of the Government of Canada*?

4) When backbenchers provided a useful means of contact between their constituents and the government?

5) When the prime minister and the government members remained in their seats to listen when an important member of the opposition addressed the House?

6) When questions were answered properly by the prime minister and most cabinet members were present during question period?

7) When MPs were somebodies?

If so, Canadians will recall a Parliament that was vital and alive, and not (as in the words of an eminent member of the House of Commons) "a Parliament like a cemetery in which only the dead have been left to guard it!"

Marjorie Le Lacheur, Ottawa

1973

Local: Ontario approves new hospital for west end, to be called Queensway-Carleton (March); 3,000 striking rail workers storm inside Parliament, smashing 20 windows (August); Artificial turf approved for field at Lansdowne Park (November)

National: Canada sends peacekeepers to Vietnam as observers of truce (January); Dr. Henry Morgentaler acquitted of having performed illegal abortions (November)

World: American Indians seize hostages, beginning 37-day standoff at Wounded Knee, South Dakota (February-March); Four top aides to president Richard Nixon resign amidst growing Watergate scandal (April) Leftist president Salvadore Allende killed in army coup in Chile (September); Israel repels surprise attack from Syria, Egypt during Yom Kippur religious holiday (October); U.S. vice-president Spiro Agnew resigns over tax evasion charge; Gerald Ford takes job (October)

Births: Ottawa Senators centre Alexei Yashin; White House intern Monica Lewinsky; model Tyra Banks; actress Neve Campbell; comic Chris Tucker

Deaths: Painter Pablo Picasso; prime minister Louis St. Laurent; U.S. president Lyndon Johnson; David Ben Gurion, first prime minister of Israel; poets W.H. Auden and Pablo Neruda; writer J.R.R. Tolkien; playwright Noel Coward; film director John Ford; actors Edward G. Robinson and Lon Chaney, Jr.; drummer Gene Krupa

AMERICAN DEFENDS BOMBING

JANUARY 3, 1973

As a U.S. citizen, temporarily living and working in Canada, I must protest the many letters submitted to your paper condemning the bombing in Vietnam. Too few people see the present U.S. frustration in the light of the entire history of Vietnam.

A decade ago, China was licking her lips over the prospect of an easy victory in India, after having swallowed Tibet.

China had also stated that Thailand "was next." Communist expansionism in Indonesia and the Philippines was rampant, China was investing huge sums in Africa and South America, and Russia was freely expanding into the West Indies and Mediterranean. The expansionist plans of Russia and China have probably not been stopped, but they certainly have been impeded by the resolve shown by the U.S. in Vietnam.

I believe, as an American citizen, that my government (over three administrations) has exhibited super-human restraint in not administering the "extreme unction" of a 20-kilotonne yield bomb right over Hanoi.

M.R. Mesnard, Ottawa

A WAY TO HONOUR PEARSON

JANUARY 4, 1973

One of Lester Pearson's achievements of which he was most proud was the new Canadian flag. It was officially raised on Feb. 15, 1965.

Canadians have no holiday in the long period between Jan. 1 and Easter, probably the dreariest period of the Canadian winter. Why don't we now declare a national holiday in mid-February as "Flag Day," or "Pearson Day?"

It would be a welcome and permanent tribute to one of Canada's greatest statesmen and to his vision of one Canada.

John Dawson, Vancouver

Editor's note: Almost from the moment Mr. Pearson died in 1972, there were suggestions for a flag-related winter holiday in his honour. Twenty-eight years later, it still hasn't happened.

KEEP US SAFE
JANUARY 15, 1973

Deep down, the reason we anti-abolitionists don't agree with the morally superior people who think the death penalty is just ghastly is that we don't want our loved ones killed for giggles by psychotics, who can escape from our prisons (or con some expert masquerading as a psychiatrist).

If the bleeding hearts would suggest a way of keeping these persons from my daughter, son, wife, or myself, I'll join their cause.

Don Smith, Cumberland

OLYMPIAN EGO TRIP?
JANUARY 16, 1973

The Olympic Games for Canada? Are we ready for such extravagant spending? What's in it for Canadian people and how long after the Games are over will we continue to pay for what would appear to be nothing more than an ego "trip" for Mayor Jean Drapeau?

Perhaps one day the athletic ability of this country will become such that the Games will be welcomed by the Canadian people, but until then let's remain spectators to such events and spend the money to help Canada grow.

Roslyn Ritza, Ottawa

Editor's note: In May 1970, the International Olympic Committee awarded the 1976 Summer Games to Montreal. Although Drapeau insisted the Olympics had as much chance of going over budget as a man having a baby, the Games' final cost was $1.3 billion, more than four times the $310 million initially promised by the mayor. As it turned out, Canada became the first country to play host to an Olympics and not win a gold medal (although Canadian athletes earned five silver and six bronze). At the 1988 Winter Games in Calgary, Canada again came away without gold but did win two silver and three bronze.

BUSES FOR MPS PROTESTED
JANUARY 23, 1973

I strongly protest the use at taxpayers' expense of a fleet of mini-buses to transport MPs the 500 yards from the Confederation Building to the Centre Block.

MPs piously refer to themselves as public servants devoted to serving Canada. A goodly portion of an MP's salary is tax free, they get postage privileges, travel privileges, parliamentary restaurant facilities, even bargain-

rate haircuts and shoeshines, all of which are subsidized by Canadian taxpayers.

Getting elected as an MP, regardless of party affiliation, appears to be a licence to gouge the taxpayer and become a pampered egotistical parasite.

To me, these buses are the last straw. It is unfortunate the general public is so helpless and can be bled perpetually by its public servants.

C.J. Porteous, Ottawa

Editor's note: The fleet of green mini-buses is still used to ferry MPs to and from various points on the Hill — but to be fair, the service is not just available to politicians. The staffs of MPs and Senators, as well as bureaucrats and members of the Parliamentary Press Gallery, are all eligible to ride.

CFRA'S TACTICS OFFEND
JANUARY 24, 1973

I am writing to deplore the promotional tactics employed by radio station CFRA. This station offers $500-plus to anyone who, when called by the station, answers the telephone by saying "I listen to CFRA."

Consider what is happening. The people of Ottawa are being tempted to say something which, when repeated often enough, will eventually become so deeply embedded on the subconscious mind that they will be compelled to believe it. This is very close to Pavlov's experimentation in which dogs were conditioned to expect food every time a bell rang, but there is one important difference: the participants in this experiment are real people!

I believe a private company should not be allowed to use the public telephone system to brainwash its customers in this manner and therefore I advocate that the practice be stopped, immediately.

Doug Watson, Ottawa

LEAVE BIBLE OUT OF DEBATE
FEBRUARY 4, 1973

The use of quotations from the Bible, particularly from the Old Testament, for retention or abolition of the death penalty is an illegitimate use of the Bible.

Each biblical text must be studied in the light of its historical context and weighed against many passages in the New Testament where Jesus rejects the normal human tendency to redress injury by violence and invited, instead, generosity.

To a Christian, as for all people, the starting point should be reverence for life. The death penalty, then, can surely be only a desperate resort. The question is whether it is an absolutely necessary deterrent required for good order in Canada today.

G. Nolan, Ottawa

DO MDS EARN THEIR HIGH PAY?
FEBRUARY 6, 1973

The high earnings of the medical profession cannot be justified. It is not right for a young graduate to obtain $24,000 to $30,000 when his education was largely supported by the public, and his academic capability is likely no greater than that of students from other faculties.

While he will stay in the educational stream longer than the engineer or architect, this is solely because the protected medical profession so elects it.

Let the medical professional open its doors to the thousands of young well-qualified kids anxious to get a bite at medical school. I suspect there is still too much of the "Who's Who" game in the selection process.

As for the public, it should block an exploiting system by talking about controlled wages, and by demanding that its political representatives intervene on its behalf and not be intimidated by the profession's powerful pressure groups.

L.A. Swick, Ottawa

WOMEN'S RIGHTS NO JOKING MATTER

FEBRUARY 25, 1973

Your editorial, "Women's (ouch) Lib," hit a new low in the kind of tasteless journalism we are coming to expect of *The Citizen*.

The right to equal pay for equal work is a serious and important one that women have been fighting for far too long. Your tone of condescension and superior amusement helps explain why the battle is not yet won.

If you had made a tasteless ethnic joke on your editorial page, an apology would be demanded. An apology should be made at once to women everywhere who are mocked and damaged by such an attitude.

Carol Kirby, Ottawa

NO SUBSTITUTE FOR 'CHEZ HÉLÈNE'

MARCH 9, 1973

I was horrified and then saddened to read that the CBC intends to drop *Chez Hélène*. The pathetic excuse offered by CBC executive Knowlton Nash was that *Sesame Street* now presents five minutes of French to an audience twice as large as that which watches the 15-minute program, *Chez Hélène*.

If child-hours of exposure to French are counted, this action of the CBC would result in the reduction of two-thirds.

Of greater importance is the fact that *Chez Hélène* is an excellent program. It presents French by a natural, indirect method that commands the attention of young children. The machine-gun approach of *Sesame Street* may have some merit, but it is not a substitute for *Chez Hélène*.

J.G. Hollins, Ottawa

Editor's note: CBC-TV's cancellation of Chez Hélène, a fixture from 1959 to 1973, sparked an outcry from parents and children across Canada, and even triggered a few angry exchanges in Parliament. But the CBC held to its view that the show was "losing its vibrancy" and its popular host, Hélène Baillargeon-Côté, was a bit old-fashioned. A well-known folksinger in Quebec, Ms. Baillargeon-Côté first received national exposure in 1955 as co-host of CBC's Songs de Chez Nous. Her acclaimed children's series, featuring a temperamental puppet mouse named Susie, began four

OTTAWA CITIZEN

Readers were horrified when the CBC dropped the bilingual children's program, Chez Hélène, starring Hélène Baillargeon-Côté and Susie.

years later. Ms. Baillargeon-Côté never understood why Chez Hélène was dropped: "The ratings were still high ... if I had been too old or too fat, I could understand. I was very angry," she once said. In 1976, she was named a citizenship court judge by prime minister Trudeau, a job she held until '85. She died at age 81 in 1997.

DOWNTOWN PLAN DISAPPOINTING

MARCH 24, 1973

I was very disappointed to read in the *Citizen* of the proposals for new building in downtown Ottawa.

Are we trying to construct yet another (shudder) Toronto? Must Ottawa develop just like dozens of other cities on this continent and inherit the same problems? Is it already too late to do anything about building a distinctive capital city?

What a beautiful capital city we could have if all the buildings north of Albert Street were razed (not raised) and a broad avenue of trees surrounded by grassy parkland were to extend up to Parliament Hill. This open area could be bounded on the east by the National Arts Centre and the Rideau Canal with an extension southward along the canal created by the restoration of Cartier Square. The western border of parkland would extend to LeBreton Flats, which has already been suggested as a suitable site for a zoo or botanical garden.

Government buildings could be constructed on the south side of Albert Street which would provide a fortress against commercial encroachment. We would then have a capital area of which all Canadians could be proud.

It would seem, however, that our present regime at City Hall is more interested in taxable development than in national dreams.

Robert F. Nelson, Ottawa

SO NEAR, YET . . .
APRIL 4, 1973

I have been living in Canada for a number of years and I have always been bewildered by the fact that I could be here, for I am an American deserter.

It is a difficult concept I wish to communicate — I am so close yet so far away. The invisible boundary between the United States and Canada has allowed me to remain here, unmolested and understood for what I am.

In spite of my cynicism of politics, ideologies, and nationalism, I find myself being thankful to the government and people of Canada for allowing me to enter a relative sphere of sanity.

Frederick W. Beinhauer, Ottawa

BAD BAIT
MAY 11, 1973

Members of the National Arts Centre Orchestra chose plastic rain hats as souvenirs of Canada to give to people they meet in Europe, and then we hear Air Canada say Europeans just don't think of Canada as a place that swings. I wonder if there is any connection?

Jo. M. Haythornthwaite, Ottawa

TRIP TO SCHOOL
MAY 26, 1973

Students (and others) are so keen on their rights these days that scant attention is paid to the essential responsibilities on which all rights depend. Maybe students should have a bill of responsibilities to complement their bill of rights, something like this:

Students will appear punctually, tripping like fawns most willingly to school. Students will be clean and neatly dressed with shining morning face, and none of that lank greasy hair, and straggly whiskers.

Students will work hard all day and pay strict attention to what the teacher says, even if the old crab is a bore. Students will behave well in public and especially on the roads where they will be most courteous to motorists.

This will promote a good public image, which is a matter about which students worry a lot.

Such a bill would, I am sure, be very popular with students.

L.G. Wilson, Ottawa

TIME FOR A COVER-UP
SEPTEMBER 5, 1973

If you have ever strolled in the streets of Ottawa, you must certainly have noticed how pathetic the women look with their bouncing breasts and bare thighs. Not many years ago there were municipal laws governing dress, and the police saw to it that these laws were enforced.

It is the duty of the men in office to legislate, and their failure to do so can only result in social confusion. If on the other hand, the necessary measures were adopted, other municipalities would undoubtedly follow suit.

Mrs. R.S. Calta, Ottawa

SLIPPED UP
DECEMBER 8, 1973

I was somewhat surprised to discover a letter in the "new" Citizen commenting on an article which I wrote for the Ottawa Journal. But I wasn't half as surprised as my mother, my managing editor and (no doubt) your own city editor.

It shows, I suppose, that the public finds it difficult to distinguish between the two papers in spite of the exaggerated claims of both our advertising departments. But surely The Citizen's editorial department should know the difference?

Susan Riley, Ottawa

The Citizen replied: We apologize and compliment Miss Riley for producing an article worthy of our reader's attention.

Editor's note: In 1984, Ms. Riley joined the Citizen, where she is still a columnist.

1974

Local: 25-cent cup of coffee predicted for Ottawa restaurants (January); New Ottawa Public Library opens at Metcalfe and Laurier (May); At $12,100, Ottawa-Hull has highest average family income in Canada (June); New satellite city of Orléans approved for east end (July)

National: Global, third Canadian TV network, launched in southern Ontario (January); Canada suspends nuclear shipments to India after New Dehli detonates nuclear device using Canadian technology (May); To placate growing separatist sentiments, the Quebec government passes Bill 22, making French the province's official language (July); Liberals regain majority, winning 141 seats to 95 for PCs, in federal election (July); First female RCMP recruits begin training in Saskatchewan (August)

World: Newspaper heiress Patty Hearst is kidnapped, later joins abductors in bank robbery (February-April); Hank Aaron eclipses Babe Ruth to become baseball's all-time home-run king (April); Watergate scandal forces Richard Nixon from U.S. presidency (August)

Births: Pop singers Alanis Morissette, Jewel Kilcher and Victoria Adams (Posh Spice); actor Leonardo DiCaprio

Deaths: Aviator Charles Lindbergh; TV host Ed Sullivan; journalist Walter Lippman; comedian Jack Benny; anti-nuclear activist Karen Silkwood; UN secretary general U Thant; movie pioneer Samuel Goldwyn; Argentine president Juan Peron; U.S. Supreme Court chief justice Earl Warren; baseball great Dizzy Dean; novelist Jacqueline Susann

LEARNING HOW TO MAKE BOMB

JANUARY 17, 1974

Assume, for argument's sake, you are a terrorist. Would it not be the ultimate in terrorism to threaten the world with an atom bomb?

Of course, it takes an immense amount of knowledge, money and well-equipped research and manufacturing facilities to build such a device. Not to mention the nuclear material which only governments have access to.

So if you are a terrorist better forget about the A-bomb and stick to conventional explosives. Right?

Wrong! CTV's program *W5* showed it all. A nuclear scientist explained in detail how to go about building such a bomb. He suggested where to get the theoretical basics, how much and what kind of fission material one needs, where to get it and how easy it really is to make such a bomb right in your basement!

We think it is irresponsible of CTV's management to let such a program go on the air. Telling potential maniacs how to make an atom bomb is disgusting.

D. and R. Wegmann, Ottawa

CHAUDIÈRE A BETTER NAME

FEBRUARY 2, 1974

Last week you had an article about Hull and its name that should have been labeled "Popular myths."

Philemon Wright did not come from Hull, England, nor did his family. He descended from Sir John Wright (1488-1551) of Kelvedon, Sussex, which is about 150 miles south of Hull.

Deacon John Wright left his farm in Kent and came to Massachusetts in 1630, and in 1640 he was a founding settler of the town of Woburn, Mass. Philemon was his great-great-grandson. He brought the settlers from New England to the Ottawa River in 1800.

It is probable that "Hull Township" was a random name attached to a wilderness town-site by some government clerk in Quebec City, before Wright ever got there.

In any event, Hull is not an historically meaningful name. The Indians called the place Asticou — the boiling cauldron.

The French translated that as "chaudière." By this beautiful word the place was known to Champlain, to the voyageurs and the fur brigades for 200 years. And this is what Philemon Wright called it.

Why don't we go back to this historic name of La Chaudière?

R.B. Hale, Low, Que.

FOOD CRITIC IS UNFAIR

FEBRUARY 6, 1974

I've had it right up to here (hand at chin, face glowering) with the pseudo-sophisticated journalism represented in Tom Ford's "Eating out" column.

With all the witty venom and snobbery of a grade school socialite, he knocks the Ponderosa Steak House and its patrons for its and their "summer camp" informality.

His profound indignation at having to dine with common people, no doubt at the insistence of his editors, lacking ties, cocktails and Irish linen napkins, may well cause him to question the value of the employment which his temporary financial situation has forced him to pursue. This fellow's shallow elitism must render him nothing but daily discomfort in this most ordinary of worlds in which he had the misfortune to be born.

Ah well, Mr. Ford, better days ahead once you've put in enough time recovering your proper situation in life.

In all seriousness, I want to object vehemently to the misuse of the privileged position of the "Fourth Estate" in inflicting twisted notions of what constitutes socially unacceptable decorum and conduct on an all-too-malleable generation of young people trying to come to terms with what's really important in life.

Not only has *The Citizen* a responsibility to refrain from scrambling the heads of another generation, it has also the duty to allow a fledgling local business to have a few hours flight before letting it have it with both barrels.

John M. A. McKay, Ottawa

BOO TO BUCKLING UP

MARCH 16, 1974

"Compulsory seatbelt use" was the message from a meeting of federal and provincial ministers of health and from the Ontario speech from the throne. Surely this takes the cake among all recent moves that needlessly chop at our little remaining freedom.

With the idea of freedom lightly cast aside, what arguments does Big Government offer in support of this? Fewer casualties, lower medical costs, an Australian law, and Health Minister Marc Lalonde's personal roll-over testimony make up the list.

As to fewer casualties, where is the evidence? Is there not a story of a life saved? If this becomes law, will government pay damages with our tax dollars for any case of death, injury or damage due to seatbelts being used? Our car insurance companies might keep this in mind.

As to lower medical costs which would depend on the relative number of injuries prevented by, or caused by, seatbelt use, how much of a triumph would be a 15 per cent reduction (as claimed) in a five per cent sector (guessed) of medical costs? Far greater savings surely, would be possible by removing abortions from medicare.

Let Mr. Lalonde and all Canadians who choose to do so, use their seatbelts. Let me and all Canadians who choose to do so ignore ours.

John Krocker, Ottawa

Editor's note: Using statistics suggesting people who wear seat-belts were 21 times more likely to survive a serious car crash, the Ontario government made seat-belts mandatory for drivers and front-seat passengers in 1975. Over the years, the laws were strengthened to include back-seat passengers and stiff rules were introduced for infants and children. While seat-belt use is no longer a major public issue, a significant portion of drivers still refuse to buckle up. According to a 1998 Ministry of Transportation survey, about one in five Ontario drivers does not use belts.

SEX NOT IMPORTANT TO JOB SEARCH
MARCH 20, 1974

I am writing to protest the flagrant discrimination against women practised in job interviews by some federal government departments.

Recently I was interviewed by representatives of Statistics Canada and I found questions asked very offensive. A male official asked me to justify why he should hire me, since in two years nature will probably take its course and I would have to leave temporarily or permanently for motherhood.

What does the possibility of my quitting a job in the future have to do with my being hired now? People resign every day. If employers worried about potential employees quitting their job they would not do much hiring. And if employers ruled out all applicants who might some day become pregnant, there would not be many females in the work force.

I spent three years in college because I'm interested in a long-term career; it would be self defeating to end these plans abruptly. The interviewer may have asked the question as a test of my character. Would he ask a male applicant if he planned to get his wife pregnant in the near future? Both questions are equally irrelevant.

When are women no longer going to have to prove they are equally as competent as men? Sex should play no part in the elimination of job applicants.

Joan Van Dusen, Russell, Ont.

BAN THE STRAP
MARCH 20, 1974

If parents remain silent on the Ottawa Board of Education's decision to retain the use of the strap, then they are inviting more sadists to seek office as school trustees. And if nine out of 10 school principals favour retention of the strap, I am horrified at the kinds of people entering the teaching profession.

As a children's caseworker a few years ago, I once had to plead with a school principal not to strap an 8-year-old girl for running to hide in the washroom when it was time for an immunization shot.

(Mrs.) Barbara Murphy, Ottawa

Editor's note: Although all Ottawa-area school boards prohibited teachers from using the strap by 1987, the Criminal Code of Canada still allows the "reasonable" use of corporal punishment to discipline students. In the early 1990s, for instance, an Ottawa teacher was given back his job after a court agreed he had not exceeded his authority by strapping a student. Still, the practice is uncommon in Ontario schools, and as recently as 1999, attempts were made to change the Criminal Code so that corporal punishment would be no longer permitted.

CRITIQUE OF ANNE ANTI-CANADIAN
MAY 11, 1974

Is Dave Mulholland anti-Canadian as far as talent is concerned, or is he just not an Anne Murray fan?

His review of Anne's performance in Ottawa was terrible. No wonder Canadian talent leaves for the United States.

My wife and I have attended several of Anne Murray's performances, and as far as we are concerned there is no one better.

The excitement and happiness she gave the people of Ottawa was something only a person who was there could feel.

Glen and Ann Allen, Ottawa

LOUSY DRIVERS
JULY 31, 1974

I have returned to Ottawa after living in a small town for three years and I must say that it is still a fantastic city: I love its lights, gardens, entertainment — but I hate its drivers.

The turn signal on most cars must be as good as when it was new, and I would bet that on the new cars the magnifying glass could not turn up a single fingerprint on that annoying stick. As I am still commuting 100 miles a day, I tend to see a great deal of cars, and it burns me to watch them cut in and out of traffic, some skillfully, some not, and never indicate their intended move.

Then there are the times when the offensive driver decides that this is the moment to turn; on go the brakes, the turn is completed and still there is no wink for the poor cars behind.

Hugh Nelson, Ottawa

Prime minister Trudeau's silence on Quebec's language law, while English-speaking Quebecers protested, was no surprise, a writer noted.

BILL 22 MOCKERY OF BILINGUAL POLICY

AUGUST 7, 1974

Prime Minister Trudeau's decision to remain silent on the constitutional legality of Bill 22, Quebec's recently-enacted language act, comes as no surprise to me, but that does not make that decision any less questionable.

Here we have the man who espoused bilingualism — guaranteeing the rights of the people to be allowed to carry on any dealings in the two major languages — allowing his home province to make a mockery of the word bilingual.

That the French-speaking people of Quebec be guaranteed the right to be educated and carry out their work in their mother tongue is not questioned.

What is questionable is the fact that the Bourassa government, in doing so, has placed the rights of the non-French-speaking population in jeopardy.

The prime minister should have spoken out immediately against Bill 22 and the manner in which it was passed into law.

He chose instead to keep silent, reasoning first that it would be better first to let the experts study the legislation.

Poppycock.

I wonder how long it would have taken Mr. Trudeau to get off the starting blocks had Ontario or any other province enacted legislation which would have thrown into jeopardy the rights of the French-speaking people in those provinces?

Paul Gragg, Ottawa

CRAZY CANADIAN LAWS

AUGUST 16, 1974

So your travel editor thinks the British have some odd licensing laws. As an Englishman I agree. But if ours are odd, yours are crazy.

On Saturday evening I was taken to the Gatineau Hills by some young Canadian friends for a barbeque. All was peace and delight. The smell of the pork chops was idly wafting across my nostrils, stirring my gastronomic juices. To pass the time before getting my teeth into this succulent Canadian meat, I was amusedly reading a Canadian article mildly "taking the micky" out of our strange British habits and innocently (as I thought) sipping a glass of ice-cold Canadian beer. Delicious. No criminal offence this in Britain.

Suddenly the peace, the innocence, was shattered. Through the leafy glade came the sound of tramping feet. The Mounties had arrived! Our beer confiscated and our friend booked for breaking your oh-so-sane licensing laws. All the joy, the fun, the delight, the innocence completely ruined, and for me, worst of all, one of my oldest dreams gone.

The Mounties, the intrepid Mounties who always get their man — visions of red-coated heroes pounding through the snow and ice, trailing the mad trapper who had murdered the prospector, the banished son of an English earl! The Mounties reduced to sniffing round idyllic picnics and carrying off a few miserable bottles of beer being drunk in a public place.

Oh Canada! How can you so shatter the dreams of a simple Briton? The shame of it to so degrade our childhood heroes.

Donald S. Burt, Templecombe, Somerset, England

PARENTHETICAL (COLUMNIST)

AUGUST 31, 1974

I agree with your readers that local sports editors almost totally ignore amateur sport. Professional sport is another matter with pages of drivel and acres of ungrammatical copy.

One improvement would be to remove certain keys from Mr. Koffman's typewriter because he scatters parentheses like snowflakes in February until they have absolutely no grammatical relation to the sentence in which they are inserted. For example:

Rick (Cassata) told the team (Ottawa) that he (Rico) would not play against the (B.C.) Lions at the (Empire) Stadium in Vancouver (B.C.) next month (September) where Barry (the Pup) Ardern is now located. Later (last week) the team (the Riders) coach (Jocko) Gotta said that (Soupy) Campbell would play but Jerry (Campbell) declined comment at that time (then).

Somebody (please) stop (Jack) Koffman.

M.A. Moffat, Ottawa

The Citizen replied: Jack (Koffman) says thanks (a lot). He also notes that he (Koffman) takes no responsibility for reader's (Moffat's) inspired paragraph.

NEEDED: A NATIONAL NEWSPAPER

AUGUST 31, 1974

Charles Gordon, in his column entitled "Canadians aren't always best," makes a good point. If Canadians are the best in journalism (as some Canadian editors and publishers seem to believe) how come Canada does not have a national newspaper?

Some Ottawa newspapers published from the nation's capital often turn out editorials on such subjects as the proposed Bank Street promenade and publish stories on the beer gardens in Ottawa while giving lesser prominence to national and international stories.

Ottawa represents a large and diverse country. It surely deserves a good newspaper serving the entire country — not just the Valley.

Raghav Santana, Vanier

YANKEE WORSHIP
SEPTEMBER 16, 1974

Ever since I was 12, I have been puzzled by the way English Canadians behave. It was then that I became aware of their worship of American culture. This was first apparent to me, and still is, in our own news broadcasts.

Tell me, when is it that Canadian issues make it first, that is, have priority over American happenings? Very seldom indeed. Yes, Canadians are forever under Uncle Sam's spell, and all too often put aside regional and even national events as secondary issues.

This confounded situation is known to everyone (though nobody seems to mind it). There is no denying the fact that we turn to Americans for actors, comedians, singers, musicians, etc.

Canada has talent, copiously so. However, what it lacks is interest in its own creations. This is what inevitably triggers the defection of our artists. French Canadians certainly stand out when it comes to having homespun stars and having an identity.

If Canada really wants to; if we, the Canadians wish to see a more culturally independent nation, we must seriously pursue and increase whatever self-exploitation we have so far undertaken. We definitely can shut off some American influence by consolidating a stronger identity, which means kissing Yankee adoration goodbye.

R.A. Bégin, Ottawa

TIME TO ACT AGAINST U.S. MAGAZINES
OCTOBER 11, 1974

Why, in God's name, should there be any doubt about applying restrictions on the publishers of *Time* and *Reader's Digest* magazines?

For years, we have been pointing the finger at American-controlled companies producing automobiles, oil, chemicals, etc., as the culprits in Americanizing our way

of life and undermining the heritage we have belatedly come to appreciate.

All the while *Time* and *Reader's Digest* have been feeding the Canadian public American policies, American accomplishments and American sports. No other media extant have been, and are, so dedicated in conveying American views and aspirations to gullible Canadians.

And what do they do about conveying Canadian views and aspirations to the American public? Not a damned thing. Some years ago a group of 10 members of the House of Representatives in the U.S. expressed themselves as appalled at the ignorance of Americans about Canada and Canadians.

Many articles published in the Montreal editions of both *Time* and *Reader's Digest*, if printed in the American editions, would go far toward educating our southern neighbours.

Unfortunately, it seems to be the policy of the publishers to avoid printing for American readers anything which would enhance the Canadian image.

If the government does not cancel the benefits now favouring these magazines at the expense of Canadian industry, the whole country should rise up in protest.

E.L. O'Leary, Ottawa

HELMET LAW
OCT. 25, 1974

The Ontario government decided against passing a law making seatbelt use compulsory because "the public would rebel" against such a law, because the belts are "uncomfortable" and such a law would "infringe on individual freedom."

I must agree on all counts. However, some time ago a similar bill did become law — the compulsory wearing of helmets by motorcycle riders and passengers.

No one who has ever worn one would argue the fact that motorcycle helmets are uncomfortable and the law requiring their use is just as much an infringement on personal freedom.

Furthermore, there is some indication that the very nature of a motorcycle helmet renders it unsafe for it prevents the wearer from hearing approaching traffic until it may be too late.

Why is one law passed but not the other? I would expect that it is because some people's individual freedom is more important than others'. Besides, how many cabinet ministers ride a motorcycle?

David F. Blackburn,
Ottawa

1975

Local: Charlotte Whitton, Ottawa's most colourful and controversial mayor, dies at 79 (January); General Hospital gets first brain scan machine in region (July); St. Pius X High student Robert Poulin goes on rampage, killing two, before shooting himself (October); Timber era ends in Outaouais as logging discontinued on Gatineau River (November); Queensway completed from Orléans to Carp (November)

National: Parliament makes beaver the official symbol of Canada (March); Metric era arrives as government begins plan to convert Canada from imperial measure by 1980 (April); PM Trudeau announces three-year program of wage and price controls to combat inflation (October); Ontario lowers highway speed limits to 55 mph and makes seat-belts mandatory for driver and front-seat passengers (November)

World: Saigon surrenders to Viet Cong, Americans vacate Vietnam (April); Suez Canal reopens eight years after 1967 Arab-Israeli war (June); Civil war erupts in Lebanon (September); U.S. president Gerald Ford escapes two attempts on his life in 17 days (September); PLO terrorists abduct 11 OPEC oil ministers in Vienna, surrender after flight to Algiers (December)

Births: Golfer Tiger Woods, actresses Kate Winslet and Drew Barrymore; singer Lauryn Hill

Deaths: Spanish dictator Francisco Franco; baseball legend Casey Stengel; Greek tycoon Aristotle Onassis; U.S. labour leader Jimmy Hoffa; Ethiopian emperor Haile Selassie; Chiang Kai-shek, president of nationalist China (Taiwan); Saudi King Faisal; International Olympic Committee president Avery Brundage; actress Susan Hayward; Muslim leader Elijah Muhammad; historian Arnold Toynbee; torch singer Josephine Baker; bluesman T-Bone Walker

CANAL CREATURES A JOY TO WATCH

FEBRUARY 5, 1975

You may well be the most elegant patron at the National Arts Centre, the shyest flower on the Mall, the most dedicated bargain-hunter in the supermarket, the best organized home manager on the block, the best executive in the building or the most talented actor in the cast — but from December to March, if there's one place to be an individual, it's on the Rideau Canal.

The one and only common denominator is the skates. For the rest, we're every one of us free and zany souls, each doing his own thing with as many styles of performance, getups and queer quirks as there are participants.

Here comes those two nuns again — they're really getting good! Arms intertwined, white veils and layers of skirts flying out like sails, propelling them on, incongruous black ski jackets sealing their uniqueness.

And here is the youth tribe, authentic in costumes of ragged jeans whipping around their ankles, no hats, no gloves, no sign of awareness except for that imaginary puck just out of reach, their speed only outdone by the determination on their faces.

The old couple, giggling like young lovers, each supporting the other on skates as ancient as their legs, long coats and stiff knees impeding their progress, yet every bit as pleased with themselves as the college couple across the ice, skating so close and in unison they could be one, quite alone among the thousands.

And the wee ones, packed stiff in too many woollens, like marionettes, each hand held firmly by a preserving parent chanting rhythmically "Glide, glide, glide . . . oops!"

The solitary man head bowed in concentration, hands clasped expertly behind his back, elegant long blades shining like a European postcard in motion, speed, wind, frost, people, bumps, oblivion . . . heaven!

If you truly can't or won't get out and join us, you do owe it to yourself to grab a bench next sunny Sunday and catch a show no television producer has yet devised.

Thank you, Douglas Fullerton, thank you, Mayor Greenberg, thank you whoever — it's great to be here!

Penny Couture, Ottawa

CELSIUS BY DECREE

APRIL 12, 1975

I for one deeply resent the government's lack of prior consultation on the Celsius matter.

Policy by fist or decree, especially without a detailed rationale in an adequate time frame, is no substitute for public input.

Nowhere have briefs on the metric issue yet appeared, either from the private or public sector.

It is my opinion that the transition will not be as smooth as the policy-makers think, and that the Canadian people may yet voice their misgivings.

Paul Harwood, Ottawa

Editor's note: In 1971, the Liberal government created the Metric Commission to guide Canada's full-scale — and mandatory — conversion away from imperial measure to metric by 1980. The idea was to bring Canada in line with the system used in most of the world, although, notably, not by two of Canada's main trading partners, the U.S. and Britain. Metric's implementation, which began in 1975 with conversion to Celsius measure for temperature, went much slower than anticipated so that by 1985 only 80 per cent of the economy had switched. That year, the Mulroney government decided the mandatory use of metric alone would no longer be required and retailers would be allowed to use imperial measure alongside metric. That arrangement is still in place, although the generation or two of Canadians taught metric in schools have little familiarity with the imperial system.

OOPS! THIS TIME CITIZEN FUMBLED

JUNE 7, 1975

Last June we had the celebrated picture of Robert Stanfield fumbling a football. Conveniently forgotten were the half dozen or so good catches he made.

Now we have the Opposition leader appearing to fumble a softball.

Perhaps it would be wise to inform your readers just how this picture came to be taken.

Stanfield is not fumbling a softball. Instead, a foul tip is going past him — as they go past major leaguers like Johnny Bench and Steve Yeager.

The point is not that Stanfield, at 61 years of age, played with a tolerable degree of skill and enthusiasm in a game between his office and the Parliamentary Press Gallery, but rather that he did play, despite a crowded schedule.

The prime minister will not be playing: He cut that stuff out right after Stanfield was victimized with the football photo.

And so . . . I agree with your caption: Oops — again. But it is the *Citizen*, not Stanfield, which has fumbled.

Ken Colby,
Parliamentary Press Gallery, Ottawa

Editor's note: CBC reporter Colby, who played in that press-versus-politicians softball game, was one of a half-dozen journalists who wrote to the Citizen to complain about the photo caption. Like Mr. Colby, the other writers argued that the Citizen was too quick to stereotype Mr. Stanfield as clumsy and unathletic because of an infamous photo published the previous year showing him dropping a football. In response to the complaints, Citizen news editor Nelson Skuce wrote a column defending the newspaper and suggesting that the public's view of Mr. Stanfield was actually enhanced by the photo, which "depicted him as a damn good sport . . . not too proud to risk being photographed in an awkward, but human, situation." As for Mr. Stanfield, he shrugged off the incident in his usual self-effacing manner.

COURT CORRECT
TO OVERRULE MORGENTALER

JUNE 25, 1975

Some people are appalled that Dr. Henry Morgentaler's second acquittal might be reversed by an appeal court, and feel that his first acquittal never should have been appealed.

I, on the other hand, am appalled that Morgentaler was acquitted in either instance, as no doubt is the majority of over one million Canadians who signed the recent petition to Parliament for better legal protection of the conceived but unborn child.

When I asked my husband, who is a lawyer, how a jury could render a verdict of "not guilty" concerning a man who has boasted about having performed 6,000 illegal abortions and has openly defied the law, he answered that the man on the street, typified by members of the jury, has lost his perspective.

They were, without doubt, influenced by the media's portrayal of Dr. Morgentaler as a great humanitarian and a martyr.

What obviously disturbs some people is the prospect of a jury being overruled a second time. The jury system has indeed served us well, but it is no guarantee of justice. For decades, Negroes of the southern United States have been denied justice through an abuse of the jury system.

The jury's verdict was reversed because it was in conflict with the law, i.e., the provisions of the Criminal Code concerning abortion.

Because of the media's sympathetic attitude toward

Dr. Henry Morgentaler ended up in prison after the Quebec Appeal Court overturned his second acquittal by a jury of performing an illegal abortion. A reader was appalled by the acquittals.

Morgentaler, there is a great deal that is not being said, and many have been seriously misinformed and misled.

Is it too much to hope that the media will face up to their responsibilities to the public and put things into proper perspective?

Elizabeth Wickham,
Lucerne, Que.

Editor's note: In November 1973, one of the most controversial legal cases in Canadian history moved into the spotlight when Dr. Henry Morgentaler was acquitted by a Montreal jury of having performed an illegal abortion — despite his admission that he had carried out at least 6,000 other abortions. In a highly unusual move, the jury verdict was overturned by the Quebec Appeal Court, a decision which was supported by the Supreme Court of Canada in March 1974. As a result, Morgentaler was sentenced to 18 months in jail. But after 10 months, a retrial was ordered and on Sept. 18, 1976 he was again acquitted. A few months later, the Quebec government dropped any further charges against the doctor. As a result of the case, the Criminal Code was amended to prevent appeals courts from reversing jury acquittals.

SMOKING BOORS

SEPTEMBER 10, 1975

How can those inhumane locomotives, those smoking boors, attempt to whitewash their disorder by claiming it is their right to smoke wherever and whenever they please, thus forcing members of the non-smoking majority to become co-smokers against their will?

Would our elected officials, to show their hospitality and consideration for other human beings, invite and crowd people into their faulty fireplace to spew smoke and poisons into the faces of their guests, and for good measure let loose a few skunks to add their perfume to the noxious fumes already in the air!

This is done to the non-smokers who are suffering paying guests in our universities, health-care facilities and doctors' office waiting rooms, cafeterias, restaurants, retail stores, enclosed shopping malls, places of employment, public transportation and facilities.

Our elected officials should take steps to give sanctuaries to all non-smokers in all places accessible to the public, where there are no separately designated smoking areas.

Rebecca Liff, Ottawa

MEDIA POLLUTION

NOVEMBER 12, 1975

There are many kinds of pollution plaguing our society today and one of the worst is the reporting of violent news in the media. Do these stories have to be headlined and sensationalized?

Your continuing reports on the tragedy at St. Pius High School are a glaring example. Can the press not leave the coroner to do his work without fanfare, and allow these families to mourn their dead in peace? Must you continue to report every development and recap this tragedy over and over?

This sort of violence pollution will soon claim another victim of our sick society and we will be responsible for yet another tragedy.

Rivers are being polluted by garbage and mercury; the air polluted by unfiltered factory smoke and car exhaust; our land polluted by our throwaway society and our minds are being polluted by the news media.

We are gradually killing ourselves.

Rosemary Pugliese, Ottawa

Editor's note: In October 1975, 18-year-old Robert Poulin went on a shooting rampage at St. Pius X High School, killing one and wounding five others before taking his own life. Earlier that day, he had raped and stabbed to death a 17-year-old female friend in the basement of his parents' home, which he then set on fire. In a diary found later, Poulin had recorded — seven months earlier — a detailed plan to rape a girl, set fire to his parents' home and commit suicide. Two psychiatrists who testified at a coroner's inquest said Poulin had become "almost two people" and had gradually lost control over his "sadistic and sexually perverse fantasies." The coroner's jury recommended a total ban on handguns and tough licensing rules for all firearms. The jurors also attacked the media for sensational coverage of the case. Another letter on the Poulin tragedy appears later in this section.

SECOND-HAND SMOKE

NOVEMBER 22, 1975

I wonder if the people of Ottawa are aware of the situation at the Children's Hospital of Eastern Ontario. This hospital is "dedicated to the preservation and mainte-

nance of health," yet smoking is permitted in the admitting waiting room, foyer waiting area, and the x-ray waiting room where very young children gasping for breath are waiting for chest x-rays to be taken.

I question the logic of the opinion of the board of trustees "that although the hospital would prefer people not to smoke in the emergency waiting room, it must be realized that many of these people are under stress and it would be more upsetting to forbid smoking in such a situation."

Why is there such concern for the inconsiderate smoker? Why don't the members of the board of trustees obtain from the Christmas Seal Campaign headquarters the free pamphlet, *Second-Hand Smoke: Take a Look at the Facts,* and read about the eye irritation, nasal symptoms, headaches, coughing, wheezing, sore throat, nausea and dizziness which are caused to the non-smoker whether he or she is allergic or non-allergic to tobacco smoke?

JoAnne Morrissey, Nepean

A CHRISTMAS TRAUMA

DECEMBER 6, 1975

Picture a crowded shopping centre. You are three years old and your kind Mummy is telling you she is taking you to see Santa. There sits this strange-looking person, dressed like no one you have ever seen before; you can't see his face, as it is covered in white stuff; you feel uncomfortable.

Suddenly he reaches out and gets hold of you; your Mummy pushes you. "Go," she says. You don't want to go, you don't know what is going on; you want to get down and be with your kind Mummy, not with this strange person. Your little mind cannot absorb it all and you begin to cry; you are afraid, you struggle to get down but he holds you tighter, telling you, "Don't be afraid, little one."

Why won't she help you; why are all those people standing around laughing and no one helping you?

Why is your Mummy doing this to you, your kind Mummy who does so much to ensure you grow up healthy and would protect you against all ills? Why?

I would guess the only reason Mummy could come up with if asked would be: "I was taken when I was little," and "It's fun." Fun for whom? Yes — for Mummy!

In case you didn't know, mothers, it's possible you will have marked your child for life by putting her or him through such trauma. A child is not ready psychologically for this sort of thing until approximately her or his fifth year.

Please wait until they ask or show interest and let them back out at the last minute if they want to. Imagine yourself that small and see it through their eyes.

(Mrs.) B.V. Hunt, Ottawa

FRIGHTENING WORLD

DECEMBER 17, 1975

I'm amazed at the seemingly universal condemnation by your readers for the *Citizen's* coverage of the recent inquest in the Robert Poulin shootings.

The subject of the inquest was bizarre, sordid and shocking. But when a seemingly normal high school student kills three people including himself, this is, whether we like it or not, a public event.

The purpose of an inquest is to give the public as much information as possible, so that the community may learn from the experience. Had the reporting of the events been watered down, as many of your readers seem to wish, I wonder if there would be the heightened increase in parental seminars which you reported on your front page recently?

We live in an increasingly crowded and frightening world. We do ourselves no service in learning to cope with that world by blotting out of our newspapers the details of events that we wish hadn't happened.

Hugh G. Doyle, Ottawa

1976

Local: *Wall Street Journal* creates a fuss by saying Ottawa is a backwater with few good restaurants, little nightlife and no good newspaper (January); Gloucester proposes region be divided into three cities — west, central and east (March); Unionized workers locked out at *Ottawa Journal*, beginning protracted and often ugly labour dispute (October); Thrilling pass from Tom Clements to Tony Gabriel helps Rough Riders beat Saskatchewan for the Grey Cup (November)

National: An era ends as Eaton's closes its catalogue operation (January); Joe Clark surprise winner of Conservative leadership race (February); Canada declares 200-mile coastal zone to protect fishery and coastline against pollution (June); Queen opens 21st Olympic Games in Montreal (July); More than a million Canadian Labour Congress members participate in one-day national strike against wage-and-price controls (October); Country thrown into turmoil as separatist Parti Québécois elected (November)
World: Argentine military overthrows prime minister Isabel Peron (March); Mao-Tse-tung dies, triggering political chaos and purges in China (September); Democrats return to White House with election of Jimmy Carter (November)
Births: Ottawa Senators forward Radek Bonk; actresses Alicia Silverstone and Melissa Joan Hart
Deaths: Billionaires Howard Hughes and J. Paul Getty; black singer and activist Paul Robeson; bluesman Howling Wolf; mystery writer Dame Agatha Christie; British war hero Field Marshal Bernard Montgomery; songwriter Johnny Mercer; French writer-politician André Malraux

CANADIANS SHOULD LOOK SOUTHWARD

JANUARY 9, 1976

Yes, Santa Claus, there *is* a Virginia! And a North Carolina, a South Carolina, and particularly a Florida — all of which seem to have a cost of living about a third less than that of Canada.

A drive to Florida and back for Christmas and New Year holidays is made most interesting by the everyday things, like prices.

Motel rates for double rooms start at $10; kids eat free at many of the chains, such as Holiday Inns. Helpings at meal-time are huge and there is always a *pot* of coffee on the table and more offered.

Prices are low: luncheon buffet at many motels started at $1.65 for all you can eat. Canadian restaurants are niggardly in comparison.

In the stores most goods are about 20-per-cent less than in Canada, and whole chickens only 45 cents a pound — we haven't seen meat prices like that in three years here.

Housing, too, is less expensive, with condominiums and bungalows still available from about $18,000 and up — and no price-hiking rent controls in sight.

And the man in the street still considers himself responsible for his own destiny with minimal reliance on government programs.

We need to look more to the U.S. than we do, rather than less. They still have the produce-more-and-lower-the-price outlook that originally brought different types of consumer goods within the reach of the average person. We appear to have lost that vision in Canada.

Eon Fraser, Ottawa

ICY RECEPTION

JANUARY 16, 1976

I was quite pleased to see *Citizen* sports columnist Bob Mellor's affirmative attitude towards our new hockey franchise. With support like this, we have a much better chance of keeping them here.

But why is it that there is always a loudmouth whose pessimism spoils everything? Such is the case with [CFRA sportscaster] Ernie Calcutt. When the Ottawa Nationals were here, he criticized them to such an extent that crowd support was negligible.

The Nats' style was to come sweeping in like a [World Football League] franchise. The Civics have done exactly the opposite. The odds against them are above board and known to everybody, yet Mr. Calcutt continues to berate the club owners, prospective buyers and potential fans.

Even city hall's reception has been lukewarm. Think of the free promotion the Civics will give to Ottawa's name. Perhaps they could drop the parking fee for all Civics and 67's home games.

Peter Hadwen, Ottawa

Editor's note: In 1976, less than three years after the Ottawa Nationals of the World Hockey Association abandoned the city, the Denver Spurs of the WHA moved to Ottawa. The newly minted Ottawa Civics played only two home games — both sellouts at the Civic Centre — before the team owner dissolved the franchise. In 1978, efforts were made to bring the Colorado Rockies, a struggling NHL franchise coached by Don Cherry, to Ottawa, but the team was eventually shifted in 1980 to New Jersey, where it became the Devils.

PARLIAMENT CAN'T CHANGE OTTAWA'S NAME

FEBRUARY 6, 1976

There is no question of "changing the name of Ottawa." Only an act of the legislature of Ontario can do that.

Section 16 of the British North America Act, 1867, makes Ottawa "the seat of government . . . until the Queen otherwise directs." The Queen, acting of course, on the advice of her Canadian ministers, could change "the seat of government" to anywhere in Canada, from Seldom Come By to Aklavik.

The Queen could personally sign the necessary documents. But they could equally well be signed by the governor general, since the 1947 letters patent empowers him to exercise all or any of the Queen's functions and powers in Canada.

Any change in "the seat of government" would not legally require an act of Parliament, or any resolution of either House, though of course either house could pass a motion against it (which would, however, have no legal effect).

Even without any change in "the seat of government," the executive government of Canada can be, and has been, carried on outside Ottawa at various times over the last 100 years and more. Rideau Hall is not in the city of Ottawa, for instance. Formal meetings of the Queen's Privy Council for Canada, with the governor general present, have been held in Halifax, Quebec, Montreal, Tadoussac and Prescott. Meetings of the cabinet have been held in a variety of places. Parliament itself could meet outside Ottawa (indeed, in case of nuclear or other disasters, it might have to).

Any government of Canada which proposed to change our "seat of government" would be very foolish to do so without consulting Parliament, especially when there is a joint committee of both Houses actually studying the future of the national capital region. Clearly, Michael Pitfield was merely asking the Department of Justice, confidentially, for a legal opinion, without which no government would dare to formulate any policy in the matter.

The "leak" of the department's confidential reply is reprehensible, and has stirred up a great deal of unnecessary dust.

Eugene Forsey, The Senate, Ottawa

Editor's note: The fuss over a name change for Ottawa began in 1974 when NCC chairman Douglas Fullerton, in his push for a national capital district encompassing West Quebec and Ottawa-Carleton, mused that the new megacapital could be called Algonquin or Asticou. While his proposal for a single city, with or without a new name, received little support, a Commons-Senate committee was asked to study the idea. Mr. Pitfield, clerk of the Privy Council, sought guidance on a name change in response to a request from a Liberal member of that committee. However, there was never any serious intention of changing the name, nor of following Mr. Fullerton's suggestion for a capital district straddling both sides of the Ottawa River. Nevertheless, the idea sparked a spirited, if short-lived, public debate, as the next letters shows.

OTTAWA IS OUR NAME

FEBRUARY 10, 1976

Can you imagine the screams of outrage that would be heard from the Channel to the Mediterranean if anyone suggested that the capital of France should be called anything but Paris? Washington, the capital of the U.S., would be unthinkable under another name to an American.

The capital of England could never be called anything but London by an Englishman.

Ottawa was designated the capital of Canada in 1857, and I have yet to hear any really good reason for any changes. You can't rewrite history.

How can we sustain any feeling of national pride or any sense of heritage when we have politicians in power who would even consider changing the name of our capital?

N.E. Burns, Ottawa

PLEASE, NO MORE MARGARET

FEBRUARY 18, 1976

Applause, applause to your television columnist Keith Ashford for saying what had to be said about Mrs. Trudeau.

Of late she seems unable to realize that the identity she is so anxious to forge for herself is not likely to gain any substance through her petulant breaches of protocol, or her tedious exhibition of a flower child's limited vocabulary.

Perhaps, at some point, we may all have been sympathetic to Margaret's desire not to stay barefoot, pollinated and in the mansion. But she was presuming a great deal by bringing her cliché festival to dinner-hour television.

In the immortal words of Tallulah Bankhead: Darling, please, people are eating.

Randall Stanton, Ottawa

Editor's note: Although it would be another year before her infamous escapades with the Rolling Stones in Toronto, and 15 months before her marital separation from the prime minister, Margaret Trudeau was already a figure of considerable controversy in early 1975. Among other things, her constant statements on the restrictiveness of her life as the PM's wife, her song for Fidel Castro in Cuba and her unfocused crusade to bring clean water to the Third World, had begun to turn public opinion against her. Here's another letter on the media and Mrs. Trudeau.

LEAVE MARGARET ALONE

FEBRUARY 18, 1976

Recently the media have paid considerable attention to Margaret Trudeau. The public has followed suit, often perceiving her behaviour in relation to Women's Liberation issues.

Regrettably, neither the media nor the public are well-informed regarding the nature of her emotional disorder.

Margaret Trudeau is currently a troubled person, and likely could use professional help in resolving her personal and professional dilemmas. What she does not need is reinforcement by the media of her publicity-seeking behaviour.

Mary Valentich, Ottawa

HATS OFF TO MR. MULRONEY

FEBRUARY 25, 1976

As a non-Conservative who watched the party's leadership convention with great interest, I wish to make the following observation: Brian Mulroney, the man supposedly snubbed by the party for lack of parliamentary experience, was the only suitable candidate who, after being dropped from the ballot, didn't rush to jump on somebody else's bandwagon in the hope of gaining future favours.

Mr. Mulroney, and he deserves to be called *Mister* Mulroney, was the only one with enough class and courage to free his delegates to vote as they wished.

I say hats off to Brian Mulroney, a credit to Canada and his party.

Wayne Perrin, Aylmer, Que.

SPELLING LESSON

MARCH 13, 1976

Philip L. Cooper's appeal for Canadian independence from Britain in spelling is based on a rather petulant nationalism and on a misunderstanding of the nature of language.

Language is not a mechanical tool serving expression — it is expression. When the Latin *color, labor, honor* were absorbed into English they underwent quite natural changes to bring them within the ambit of English as it then existed. Each language has a distinctive quality or "feel."

Governour is a little too stately and definitely quaint now. *Colour,* however, is not quaint; the added vowel subdues and rolls the end of the word slightly and obviates a second-syllable stress. Similarly *programme* could probably be beneficially shortened — it fits the present-day clipped pronunciation with strong initial stress, to leave out the last two letters.

The esthetic element in spelling is more important than eliminating vowels at the slightest excuse, on the plea of rationalizing or nationalizing the language. (I prefer *aesthetic* because the "e" alone is too thin and it may also suggest a chemical compound.)

Philip Belgrave, Ottawa

GOOD FOR MAUREEN

MARCH 20, 1976

I disagree with comments that Maureen McTeer's outspokenness on controversial issues has raised the public's ire. Rather, she has gained much admiration for being a person in her own right.

I think your humourless cartoon was a "cheap shot" and a senseless male chauvinistic put-down. If a woman stands out as a total human being with opinions of her own, she then becomes domineering.

I hope more women like Maureen McTeer gain the spotlight to show that wives of newsworthy men are not mere appendages to them.

K. Archer, Ottawa

Editor's note: As hard as it is to imagine today, the news

THE OTTAWA CITIZEN

Maureen McTeer, seen with husband, Joe Clark, and new baby, Catherine, was admired by a reader for being a person in her own right.

that Maureen McTeer, the wife of newly elected Conservative leader Joe Clark, had not taken her husband's name — and had opinions of her own — triggered a national debate characterized by attacks on Mr. Clark for being weak and unassertive and Ms. McTeer for being shrill and bossy.

OUR OWN WORST ENEMY

APRIL 30, 1976

It's unfortunate that your columnist, Charles King, has to indulge in the favourite Canadian pastime, namely panning Canadian shows.

His remarks concerning Peter Gzowski's new late-night talk show on the CBC network were extraordinarily rash and typically Canadian. We always put down our own whether they are bad or not.

I'm not saying that Gzowski's *90 Minutes Live* is the best thing on the tube. But I find it welcome relief from the tired artificiality of Carson, Griffin and company.

With all its flaws and defects, Gzowski's show manages to bring a rare informality, a pleasant casualness to television. His guests aren't phony, rehearsed glamour stars patting themselves on the back or second-rate bozos acting as if they were Hollywood's gift to mankind.

Certainly Gzowski needs to improve his interviewing style. He's no Patrick Watson, but I wish him all the luck in the world. Knowing Canadian audiences and critics, he's going to need it.

Michael Carroll, Ottawa

Editor's note: Despite mixed reviews and decent ratings, Peter Gzowski's 90 Minutes Live is usually remembered as a television disaster. Two years in planning, the talk show — it debuted in spring 1976 — was saddled from the start with the host's folksy, almost bumbling interviewing style, an approach that worked wonderfully on radio but made Gzows-

ki appear uncertain and ill-prepared on TV. After two seasons, it was cancelled. Although letters to the Citizen were split over the show, many readers were most unhappy that its 11:35 p.m.-1 a.m. time slot affected the late local news. Here's another letter on the program.

GZOWSKI SECOND RATE

APRIL 30, 1976

This is just to thank Charles King for his remarks on Mr. Gzowski, which I have cut out and sent to the CBC. My beef is the 30-minute delay before the local news and I begrudge sitting up that much later for such a second-rate performance.

Charles E. Nash, Ottawa

SENATOR NEEDS GOOD, SWIFT KICK

JUNE 12, 1976

After 16 years of dabbling in Canada's Parliamentary Old Age Home, the Senate, that great socialist, Hazen Argue (CCF-er turned Liberal) has spoken again.

In return for all the goodies he's received from the Canadian taxpayer during these years, one would expect that at least once in a blue moon he'd have something constructive to say. Not on your life!

Senator Argue apparently doesn't argue for the better Canada — Argue argues for Argue. Now he has opened his mouth to criticize the Parliamentary tailor for not pressing his two suits.

Never mind the country's near bankruptcy, the heck with unemployment or inflation. Come hell or high water, Hazen Argue's pants should be pressed regularly at no charge. How sickening.

I suggest that Canadians again take a hard look at this preposterous institution called the Senate. We don't need it. We should start with a firm kick in the pants for Hazen Argue.

Jacob Moerman, Ottawa

THIS IS SPORT?

JULY 10, 1976

They bully, bash, bruise and bleed their opponents. They hook, harm and harass, creating havoc and delight in sending their opponents to the hospital.

They pummel, punch, slash, injure and intimidate. They are vicious and filled with violence.

In Canada we call it hockey and the courts seem to agree. SHAME!

Ron Reid, Perth, Ont.

1977

Local: Mayo report on municipal restructuring recommends three cities for region — Gloucester-Vanier-Rockcliffe in the east, Ottawa in centre, Nepean-Kanata in west (March); Ancient aboriginal cemetery discovered during Sparks Street excavation (March)
National: Blue Jays defeat Chicago 9-5 in Toronto's first regular season major league baseball game (April); PM Trudeau and wife, Margaret, announce marital separation; PM retains custody of three sons (May); PM Trudeau creates national unity task force co-chaired by Jean-Luc Pépin and John Robarts (July); Highway speed signs converted to metric (September); Canada severs economic ties with South Africa to protest racial policies (December)
World: *Roots* mini-series draws record North American TV audience of 80 million (February); 574 die in crash of two jumbo jets on Canary Islands (March); Elvis Presley found dead in Memphis mansion (August); Egyptian president Anwar Sadat makes historic visit to Tel Aviv (November)
Births: Ottawa Senators defenceman Wade Redden; Ukrainian figure skater Oksana Baiul; actresses Sarah Michelle Gellar and Liv Tyler; golfer Se Ri Pak; classical trumpeter Sergei Nakariakov
Deaths: Comic genius Charlie Chaplin; opera diva Maria Callas; actress Joan Crawford; crooner Bing Crosby; writer Vladimir Nabokov; comedian Groucho Marx; Canadian-born bandleader Guy Lombardo; Lady Spencer Churchill, widow of Winston Churchill; Canadian aboriginal artist Benjamin Chee Chee; British actor Peter Finch; gum and baseball tycoon Philip Wrigley

RIDEAU STREET PROPOSAL IS FOOLISH

FEBRUARY 12, 1977

I feel compelled to protest the foolishness of turning Rideau Street into a mall. Whereas normal planning would have as its aim the removal of any kinks in the east-west flow of traffic, here we have the introduction of a kink.

Why do city planners have to fight the natural development which has already occurred?

Rideau Street has always been an east-west "artery" and the residential areas in Lower Town East have grown with this fact in mind.

The natural place to put a mall would be George Street. Or is it that the Rideau Street merchants pack more clout than those in the Byward Market?

M. Blundell,
Ottawa

Editor's note: Although this letter was written six years before an enclosed bus mall was built on Rideau Street, the writer showed great prescience. For a two-block stretch from Sussex Drive to Dalhousie Street, the mall limited Rideau Street traffic to buses and taxis, and caused such chaos in the area that it drove shoppers to suburban malls. But traffic wasn't the only problem associated with the mall. Its enclosed sidewalks became dank, smelly tunnels that were havens for street people — most of them harmless, but a few of them menacing — and a graveyard for businesses. After a decade, it was demolished.

Margaret Trudeau must have been an inspiration to husband, Pierre, when he addressed the U.S. Congress, according to a reader.

CANADA NEEDS TRUDEAU

MARCH 2, 1977

Please grant me space in your paper to add my contribution of heartiest congratulations to Prime Minister Trudeau for his wonderful performance in Washington, on the historic occasion of his address to the American Congress.

His address was of the highest order and combined with his general deportment in Washington, his academic brilliance, his sharp wit, his dignity and statesmanlike dedication, he has created for Canada an image favourable to us for generations to come.

I am sure Margaret Trudeau supplied most of the inspiration to the prime minister, she was particularly charming. I watched the perfect pair, on television with much delight, during this memorable Washington episode, and it certainly made me feel proud to be a Canadian.

Canada needs Prime Minister Trudeau for many more years. We are now approaching what may be well described as the most critical stage in our history, and with the increasing difficulties on the international scene we need a man at the helm, who apart from being scholarly, is strong and humane, and is capable of making tough and even unpopular decisions in the interest of the country as a whole.

We may be mad at Trudeau at times, but Canada would be in real trouble if we lost him at this stage.

V.L. Reid-Hibbert, Ottawa

Editor's note: Mr. Trudeau's visit to Washington came on the heels of Quebec premier René Lévesque's now famous

trip to Wall Street to calm the investment community's concerns about the election of his separatist government the previous November. Mr. Lévesque didn't have a lot of luck, and Mr. Trudeau seized the opportunity to assure U.S. politicians Canada would stand tough against the separatists, and the country would remain stable for investors. As for Mrs. Trudeau, the Washington trip turned out to be her last major official function as the prime minister's wife. Although the formal announcement of their separation did not come until May, the couple had pretty much decided to go their own ways by the time they went to Washington.*

ACT OF TREASON

APRIL 6, 1977

The Quebec minister of education's order to abolish the singing of the Canadian national anthem and to remove Canadian flags from French classrooms is a travesty of our national heritage and a traitorous act.

Until further notice, Canada is *still* one nation and no provincial minister has the right to order such action. This not only adds to the fire against keeping Quebec in Confederation, but is an insult to the rest of Canada.

Paul Taillon, Ottawa

HUMILIATING INDIGNITY

APRIL 16, 1977

Because I am confined to a wheelchair, I have encountered many architectural obstacles in my life — but one of the worst experiences I have ever had came last month when I had to go to Riverside Hospital for an X-ray.

I certainly didn't anticipate any problems in getting around in my wheelchair in a hospital. After all, hospitals are designed and built for the sick.

However, I found out to my utter dismay that the X-ray department at Riverside Hospital has no facilities for a patient in a wheelchair. I was taken by a hospital attendant down a narrow corridor with small cubicles on one side and two washrooms on the other and she asked me to remove my clothing and put on a white gown.

My wheelchair would not fit into any of the cubicles nor would it go through either one of the narrow washroom doors. I asked if they would give me a larger room to change in privacy and was told, No, they didn't have any, so I had to undress in the corridor without any privacy.

We hear so much today about dying with dignity. Will the day ever come when a person with a physical handicap can live with some dignity?

Barbara Forrest, Ottawa

BILINGUALISM WAS A WASTE

MAY 13, 1977

For the past dozen years or so, the various Liberal governments have pumped millions upon millions of dollars into a program of bilingualism that has, in my opinion, been unfair and unrealistic.

But whatever the past consequences of the program, and whatever the views on it, any arguments for its continuation have now been shot to hell.

With the Parti Québécois' introduction of its white paper on language, we can no longer pretend that this is a bilingual country. With the government of Quebec calling for unilingual French throughout the province, why should the federal government continue to pursue a policy of bilingualism for the rest of the country?

Can you imagine the outcry if Ontario, Alberta, Nova Scotia or any of the other provinces declared a policy of unilingual English?

With one move, René Lévesque and his boys have put to waste every dollar spent on the bilingual effort over the past years.

It appears the experiment of bilingualism has been a damned expensive waste of time.

John Gilmour, Ottawa

VANIER'S MESSAGE WORTH REMEMBERING
JUNE 1, 1977

With all the controversy over Canadian unity, it might be of interest to your readers to note the words of the late Gen. Georges P. Vanier, governor-general of Canada from 1959 to 1967, who said:

"We Canadians of every origin, irrespective of race or creed, must go forward hand-in-hand to ensure the greatness of our country. If Canada is to attain the greatness worthy of it, each one of us must say, 'I only ask to serve.'

"In Canada, because of its immense area and different cultures, unity is essential. We cannot get on without one another. We must find a basis of mutual understanding."

What keen foresight this concerned and distinguished French-Canadian patriot must have had to foresee the danger that even then threatened a united Canada. His solemn words are as pertinent today as the day they were uttered 15 years ago.

F.R. Inglis, Ottawa

CONVICTED MUST PAY FOR THEIR CRIMES
JUNE 18, 1977

"The Senseless Death of Mario Hamelin," which appeared in last weekend's *Canadian Magazine*, raises basic questions concerning the justice system in this country. This story revolved around the shooting death of 3-year-old Mario Hamelin caused by a passenger in a moving car attempting to shoot at a road sign.

There appeared to be no malice but rather a very unfortunate and improbable coincidence of events which caused this random shot to kill the boy. However, it is the stupidity which surrounded these events which requires comment.

It was senseless and thoughtless stupidity that prompted the killer, Peter Peer, to shoot at a sign from a moving vehicle. Stupidity, fear and ignorance prompted those involved to remain silent and cause a long, expensive investigation.

It was stupidity in the political reaction of the Ontario attorney-general who felt a more severe sentence on the guilty individual would somehow better rectify a tragic situation.

However, the greatest stupidity lies with our socio-legal system which appears intent only on seeking out the guilty and sentencing them to a jail term at the taxpayers' expense. The system is predicated on the belief that these actions will somehow "pay" for the crime, carelessness or stupidity.

Peer and friends were not made liable for the cost of the investigation because of their decision not to report the incident.

Meanwhile, the father of the child is unemployed, saddled with debt and carrying a puzzling grief which he cannot control. The child lies in a grave without a headstone and was put in that grave by a funeral not yet paid for.

The judge, in sentencing Peer, took pains to ensure he continued to be employed and, in fact, all participants continue to hold good jobs. Could they not then at least pay for the headstone and funeral of the boy whose death they had caused? Could not someone ensure that the grief-stricken father regains employment?

Our legal system feels that justice is served when the guilty are apprehended and "punished." Would it not be better for the guilty to assume some of the responsibilities for their actions?

Allan Porter, Ottawa

CROWD'S ACTIONS AT SHOOTING APPALLING
JULY 16, 1977

This letter concerns the recent shooting incident at Gladstone and Bronson avenues. I'm greatly appalled that citizens of Ottawa, our nation's capital, would be happy and cheer when a police officer is shot.

I was angry that people who the police officers asked to stay back for their own safety laughed at them and ran in the range of fire. I'm sorry that people don't have more respect for our police officers who risk their lives every day to protect ours.

I understand the officer who was killed was only 21 — the suspect 22. The people did cheer when the suspect was caught and then started to race forward.

It's a wonder people weren't trampled, especially children who should have been in bed anyway, since it was between 11 p.m. and midnight.

My condolences go to the young officer's family and I hope and trust in God the other officers will be all right. Ottawa's finest. They are the best.

Sue Weller, Ottawa

Editor's note: After the fatal shooting of 21-year-old police recruit David Kirkwood, Ottawa police surrounded the suspected gunman, Fred Koepke, in a house at Gladstone and Bronson avenues. A large crowd gathered at the scene, and as Koepke took potshots at the police, some of the onlookers moved into the line of fire. According to 1977 news accounts, each time the police risked their lives to move these people to safety, they were jeered and taunted with lines like, "It's a barbecue, who's got the wieners?" — a reference to the fire ignited by the tear-gas shot into the house by police. After a three-hour standoff, Koepke shouted that he was coming out, and was arrested as he began walking backwards from the house with his hands up. He was sentenced to life in prison.

STAR WARS VS. STAR TREK
AUGUST 10, 1977

Upon reading your recent article on *Star Wars,* I noticed a small passage indicating that we Trekkers should be nervous about the possibility of being wiped out by *Star Wars* fans. This is complete nonsense.

It is obvious that you do not understand *Star Trek* fans. We are basically science fiction lovers and most of us love *Star Wars* and *2001: A Space Odyssey* just as much as *Star Trek.*

Similarly, I think you'll find that most *Star Wars* fans are also science fiction (and therefore *Star Trek*) fans. There is not —nor will there ever be — any conflict between these two great productions.

Sandeep Sehdev, Ottawa

ONE-WAY ROAD, TWO-CLASS COUNTRY
SEPTEMBER 21, 1977

Prime Minister Trudeau has finally put his cards on the table and offered Quebec some form of special status by not opposing René Lévesque's law making French the only official language in the province.

What it seems to mean is that the federal government has all but abandoned the English-speaking people in Quebec, and the Quebec government will be given special status when it comes to language rights in that province.

Does this mean that there will be two kinds of Canadians, ordinary Canadians (all those outside Quebec) and preferred Canadians (all those in Quebec)? Perhaps it would even be fair to say that Quebecers who oppose the government would be called ordinary Canadians, since the Quebec government would frown on them.

Is Canada so far down the road of disunity that she must have two classes of people? Shouldn't all people of Canada be equal no matter where they live?

Once the federal government gives in to Quebec on any matter, it has placed itself on a one-way road with no return. It will be like it always has been — once you give in there is nothing left to do but give in more and then more again.

I am sure all Canadians still remember the prime minister's remark back in 1970, when he declared the War Measures Act. He called all those who opposed the introduction of the War Measures Act weak-kneed and that his government would not give in to blackmail or to any person or organization out to destroy Canada.

Where are all the prime minister's big words now?

Larry Charlebois, Ottawa

CANADA IS A BEAUTIFUL PAINTING
OCTOBER 5, 1977

As a 12-year-old girl, I am really concerned about the future of our country and I am tired of hearing about the separation of Quebec.

I would just hate to think how John Cabot, Samuel de Champlain, Father Brébeuf and all our other famous founders would feel if they knew what the country they died for was coming to.

Ever since I was a really small child I have travelled and lived in many countries, so I appreciate being a member of the second-largest country in the world. Some say, "Let Quebec go," but if it does, so does a great deal of our culture and history.

I would like to know why people aren't more concerned. I guess sometimes it's easier to watch a hockey game than go to a history lecture.

All politicians should remember that they are taking care of our country for the children who will have to take over the responsibility one day.

Is this country not strong enough to stay together? Canada is like a beautiful painting done by our founders, both French and English. Are we going to tear it up into little pieces?

Geneviève Rickman, Ottawa

FRANCE'S PRO-QUEBEC STAND TREACHERY
NOVEMBER 9, 1977

Each year at this time, Canadians pause to remember their fellow countrymen who died fighting for freedom around the world. They fought, too, for the freedom of France, from the poppy fields of Flanders and the trenches of Verdun to the bloodied beaches of Dunkirk, Dieppe and Normandy.

My uncle lies there with his comrades in the corner of a quiet cemetery in northern France, his grave still tended by those who buried him, by Frenchmen who have not forgotten that he died for them.

Yet now, for the second time in recent years, a president of France has publicly supported the personal political ambitions of a small rabid group of Quebecers which seeks to tear apart this country — a country which has bled so unselfishly for France in the past, now only to be rewarded in return with all the treachery of Judas.

The actions of successive French presidents and governments are unworthy even of the contempt of civilized man.

Peter G. Keith, Ottawa

Editor's note: Beginning even before French president Charles de Gaulle's infamous "Vive le Québec libre" cry from the steps of Montreal city hall in 1967, and continuing well into the '90s, a succession of French politicians has flattered and encouraged Quebec separatism. In 1977, premier René Lévesque made his first official visit to France, where president Valéry Giscard d'Estaing, who had once disapproved of Mr. de Gaulle's call, chose to send a similar message himself. In a formal toast to Mr. Lévesque, he used the diplomatically loaded word "recognize" when speaking of Quebec, and talked of Quebec's right to determine "without interference" the course of its "nationhood." The remarks, widely reported in Canada, were greeted with dismay by the Trudeau government, which sent a formal protest to Mr. d'Estaing.

1978

Local: 16-month labour lockout ends at Ottawa Journal (February); No-name grocery products make their first appearance in Ottawa (March); Kanata holds first election as a city, Marianne Wilkinson wins mayoralty (November)

National: Sun Life Assurance Co. to move its head office to Toronto from Montreal because of Quebec political uncertainty (January); Nuclear-powered Soviet satellite crashes in Canadian North (January); PM Trudeau names long-time New Democrat Ed Schreyer governor general (December)

World: Ex-Italian PM Aldo Moro kidnapped, killed by Red Brigades terrorists (April-May); Louise Brown, world's first test-tube baby, born in London (July); Israel, Egypt sign Camp David accord, setting framework for Mideast peace (September); As Pope John Paul II, Poland's Karol Cardinal Wojtyla becomes first non-Italian pontiff in 455 years (October); More than 900 followers of cult leader Jim Jones die in mass suicide in Guyana (November)

Births: Ottawa Senators defenceman Chris Phillips; basketball star Kobe Bryant

Deaths: Painter Norman Rockwell; anthropologist Margaret Mead; Israeli prime minister Golda Meir; Pope Paul VI; Pope John Paul I; U.S. vice-president Hubert Humphrey; Kenyan leader Jomo Kenyatta; Belgian singer Jacques Brel

RADIO 'WOODPECKER'

JANUARY 7, 1978

For many months now, radio signals from Russia have deliberately interfered with radio services from most countries in the free world. To say these signals have been disruptive to both local and transatlantic services is an understatement.

Those of us who tune shortwave bands soon recognize the "pulsing" clicks of what is known in Europe as the "Russian helicopter," and in North America as the "woodpecker."

In late December, the "woodpecker" was up to its old tricks but on frequencies lower than previously used. The effect was unchanged.

Flagrant disregard for international agreements on the use of the frequency spectrum should not be condoned. Members of the International Telecommunications Union would be well advised to exclude Russia from participating in next year's conference.

Comrade, please feed your "bird."

Ralph Cameron, Ottawa

LET QUEBEC GO SO REST CAN JOIN U.S.

JANUARY 11, 1978

Pierre Trudeau says that regardless of how the people of Quebec vote in the referendum, they may not leave Canada without some sort of permission. In essence, Trudeau is threatening military rule over one-fourth of Canada's population against its will.

Does Canada really need its own Northern Ireland or Vietnam? Do English Canadians really want to send their sons to die in Quebec in order to deprive Quebecers of the right of self-determination?

And what happens to Canada's economy in the event of civil war? To keep Canada "united," Trudeau would destroy everything it stands for. Is not the rationale for Canada's very existence that Canada is a "noble experiment in tolerance, in unity with diversity?"

If French Canada should decide that diversity is more important than unity, Canada can resort to violence only by abandoning tolerance. And if there is no "noble experiment in tolerance," there is no Canada. So, then, what will Trudeau have "saved?"

René Lévesque offers English Canadians release from the "French fact" and all the problems that has brought.

Trudeau, by contrast, would turn a headache into a nightmare — in order to hold on to the headache!

Let Quebec go if it wishes to go. Indeed, welcome its departure as an opportunity to pursue your own best interests — in cultural, economic and political union with the United States.

L. Craig Schoonmaker, Chairman,
Expansionist Party of the U.S., New York

IT'S NOT THE 'FEDS'

JANUARY 11, 1978

All who treasure the unity of this land might usefully make one more New Year resolution — always to refer to our national government as the "Government of Canada."

I am not alone in being sick and tired of hearing it called, even by ministers of the Crown, the "federal government" (always in lower case) or, worse still, "the feds" — as though it were merely a co-ordinating committee for the powerful provincial administrations.

The Government of Canada faces awesome national unity problems in 1978. We can all help, a little bit, by at least using its rightful name.

Robert F. Legget, Ottawa

LIBERAL HYPOCRISY

JANUARY 21, 1978

The Liberal government is concerned about Sun Life Assurance Co. moving to Toronto. Where was its concern when it moved thousands of people from Ottawa?

More than 2,000 public servants have been transferred from one city block alone, causing layoffs in banks, retail outlets, restaurants, beauty salons, and vacancies in office space. Finance Minister Chrétien isn't doing anything to help that block survive.

Two thousand jobs are lost from the centre of Montreal against the total of 20,000 from Ottawa, and Chrétien is quoted as saying, "I didn't vote for the legislation that caused this problem."

Well, I'm not voting for the Liberals. More power to Sun Life. I am a policy holder, too.

G. Dolan,
Ottawa

WHY NOT A FEMALE MASCOT?
FEBRUARY 12, 1978

As numerous studies have illustrated the predominance of male over female animals in children's tales and mythology, reinforcing an unfair stereotype, it came as no surprise to hear the new ice hog mascot for our winter carnival would be called "Bytown Bert."

One does, however, regret the missed opportunity its creators had to display a spark of imagination and demonstrate their liberated consciousness by naming her Alberta.

Would we really like her any less?

Louise L. Nollet, Ottawa

THIS IS GOOD CHARACTER?
FEBRUARY 16, 1978

I would like to second the views of other letter writers concerning the former solicitor general Francis Fox.

A man of "good character" does not have an affair with a married woman, conspire to destroy a life and then forge another man's signature.

Teresa Middleton, Ottawa

Editor's note: Touted by many as a potential successor to Pierre Trudeau as Liberal leader, Francis Fox was forced to resign as solicitor general in early 1978 following the news he had forged another man's signature to obtain an abortion for his mistress. Although Mr. Fox eventually returned to cabinet, and to prominence in the Liberal party, the incident ruined his chances of becoming prime minister.

SAP SUPPER
MARCH 15, 1978

Solange Chaput-Rolland says that, apart from Quebec, we eat terribly in Canada, that is, "with rubber toast, frozen salads, and jam in little containers."

Next month, when the sap starts running I suggest she visit the sugar bush just a little north of Ste. Eustache were she can sit down to a typical French Canadian meal: two fat pork chops: a big pile of baked beans and a boiled potato, all smothered in maple syrup, served along with a quart of beer.

How's that for haute cuisine? Bon appetit, Solange.

Robert Haydon, Ottawa

Editor's note: Ms. Chaput-Rolland, a journalist, author of 15 books, politician, former senator and life-long defender of federalism, is among Quebec's most famous women of the past 50 years.

NO TRAUMA FROM BIKINI-CLAD GREETING
MARCH 29, 1978

I imagine your editorial office has been fairly inundated with mail spawned by your front page publication of the bikini-clad girl's picture and the ensuing affronted readers' letters.

May I, as the mother of two young *Citizen* carrier boys, reassure you that they have received no trauma from handling and delivering these issues of the newspaper.

Rather than lewd and provocative, that beautiful young lady in brilliant colour appeared as a true harbinger of balmy weather ahead!

Thank you for that cheering picture. It was a tremendous improvement over portrayals of accident and death.

Pat M. Stewart, Ottawa

HOLOCAUST IS OLD NEWS
APRIL 20, 1978

Regarding the TV production of the *Holocaust*: Who cares about 40-year-old news that we have all heard many times before when Israelis murdered more than 1,000 Lebanese only last month?

Give us less about the Gestapo and the SS and more about the Irgun and the Stern Gang.

What's happened to you Anglo-Saxons? Have you bartered your souls completely?

M. Ayoub, Ottawa

Editor's note: With a world-wide viewership estimated at more than 220 million, Holocaust, a powerful 9½-hour NBC-produced mini-series on the extermination of Jews in Nazi death camps, remains one of the most-watched TV programs in history. It also provoked an international controversy. In Germany, it was widely condemned by those who considered it an indictment of all Germans. Other critics said the series turned one of history's darkest episodes into cheap soap opera. But overall, it was hailed as a TV landmark that showed the reality of Nazi terror to the generations born after the war. Here's another letter.

HOLOCAUST: WE ALL MUST CARE
APRIL 25, 1978

Of the agony explored by *Holocaust*, your readers say that "the Germans have paid the price," and that "none other than Hitler was responsible," and even "Who cares?"

All have missed the point; moreover, their myopia shows just how necessary the telling of the tale of Holocaust was.

Neither the historical reality of the events, nor the fictionalized treatment provides justification for current Israeli policies, or for renewed and hypocritical censure of the Germans.

To the contrary, *Holocaust* dramatized two essential elements of the historical truth. First, that if a crime of such enormity could be committed in the country that gave us some of our civilization's finest music, art, theology, literature and philosophy, then the same could happen anywhere that persecution is allowed to exist.

Second, that Hitler's dependence on the common man's following orders shows both how culpable the common man was and how vulnerable we all could be to "leadership."

Holocaust, the TV series, was neither pro-Israeli nor anti-German. Its message was that such a catastrophe could happen anywhere with any of us as either victim or villain.

James Woods and Meryl Streep starred in Holocaust, one of the most-watched TV programs, even though one reader found it old news.

We all must pay the price; we all must take responsibility; we all must care. We can't afford not to.

C.L. MacGregor, Ottawa

PRETTY BABY IS VOYEURISM, NOT ART

APRIL 28, 1978

I marvel at the naiveté of your columnist Richard Labonté. In the film *Pretty Baby* he sees only the "joyous fantasy land whorehouse" free of illegitimacy, disease or dilemma. He extols "Molle's exploration of the film (as) chaste . . . because it is neither exploitive nor manipulative."

The profound irony is almost amusing except it is so sad. A 12-year-old child, Brooke Shields (who plays Violet) is seduced by adult monetary and moral standards to perform sex scenes as a prostitute. This is complete, unfeeling exploitation and manipulation of a minor.

"Violet is redeemed," writes Labonté. But, alas, there will be no redemption for the child-star. This is voyeurism, involving a real flesh and blood girl, not a fictional "Violet."

Please don't promote this film on the grounds that filming techniques are well-employed with "great tact . . . avoiding the shocking and sensationalistic." A girl is used. There is no way that we should reward this type of sham with our box office dollars.

C.P. Wilson, Ottawa

GOOD RIDDANCE TO DOCTOR

MAY 18, 1978

On May 11 The Citizen carried a story about Dr. Barry Thompson's decision to leave his Ottawa general practice and move his family to Crosset, Arkansas (pop. 8,000), where he ex- *pects a higher income and lower living costs. The story brought a flood of correspondence, one of which appears below:*

I am angry, very angry with Dr. Barry Thompson and his wife who are leaving this beautiful, civilized city to live in an Arkansas lumber town to make money.

They are gleeful that everyone else earns less. Maybe they don't know some of the unpleasant side effects resulting from large economic disparities. They will learn soon enough.

I am angry with doctors who want money so badly they move to a country where a 20-year-old friend of mine died from kidney failure because he had no money for dialysis. I have other friends who lost their home and business through illness. How can people who uphold the Hippocratic oath be so socially irresponsible?

Even more, I am angry with the *Citizen* for giving so much coverage to vocal malcontents. In times of economic uncertainty a lot depends on the confidence of the public in themselves, their economy and their country. The *Citizen* harms Canada's future by dramatizing dissatisfied minorities.

Be fair. On tomorrow's front page run a full colour picture and story about one of the people who recognize the problems of running away: Doctors working with OHIP to find a reasonable fee schedule or former Americans like myself who feel the greater quality of life in Canada outweighs the lesser economic standard of living.

Francis J. Ahern, Ottawa

BOOZE, THEN GAS?

JUNE 10, 1978

Now that we are allowed to buy a drink without a meal in Ottawa restaurants on Sundays, is it too much to hope that we'll soon be able to purchase gasoline without hassle in Ottawa on Sundays?

Scott Honeyman, Ottawa

BIRTHDAY GREETINGS, CANADA!

JUNE 30, 1978

From all the thought-stirring talk of Canada Week I have selected some of the nicer memories from my life as an Air Force kid stationed on bases across the country. Canada is:

• Six-horse teams at the Lachute Fair.
• Baked potatoes in Prince Edward Island.
• Horseback riding in the Rigaud hills and the Laurentian Mountains.
• Banff in fresh snow.
• The prime minister at a public gathering, well guarded, but in no danger.
• Horse-drawn carriages in old Montreal.
• Fastening the tire chains to go through Kicking Horse Pass in December.
• Parliament Hill at midnight.
• Sooty window sills in Halifax.
• 60 degrees below zero in a trailer rocked by the wind north of Moose Jaw.
• Frost on the tent by the Miramichi.

• Pigtailed Indians on the Kamloops foothills.
• Mission fields populated by prairie dogs and generous farmers.
• The Atlantic, the Pacific, their rocky shores and exploding waves.
• The Scots of Cape Breton.
• Frobisher Bay dogsled races.
• A foggy Port aux Basques sunrise.

Happy Birthday Canada, and may you remain one country from sea to shining sea.

Cheryl Dewar, Vankleek Hill, Ont.

CHEERS FOR ATHLETE

AUGUST 9, 1978

Congratulations to Rachelle Halpenny, the only Canadian entrant in the Fourth International Cerebral Palsy Games in Edinburgh. She copped three gold and two bronze medals and placed fourth and seventh in two other events.

As Halpenny asks in your story, "Three golds and nobody noticed," where were the sports reporters? This was an exciting sports story and should not have been included in a "Lifestyles" item.

Even so, as someone who suffered a stroke, I would like to thank Bozica Costigliola for her story on Halpenny. For any disabled person to enter a sporting event in another country on his/her own deserves the highest praise and commendation for showing such tenacity of spirit.

Bette Hay, Ottawa

KEEP WOMEN OUT

AUGUST 26, 1978

The retiring chief of Canadian Forces air command says it is only a matter of time before the Canadian Forces employ women in combat roles.

Well, the fact that there are precedents in other countries, going back to Boadicea in Roman times, does not make this right for Canada in the late 20th century.

One could hardly imagine anything more calculated to cheapen feminine virtue and destroy the remnants of chivalry that remain in our society. Surely this would diminish all of us.

If Canadians value Christian virtue, decency and the dignity of womanhood, they will not allow their armed forces to go through with such a morally reprehensible and crackpot idea.

Some things are too important to be left to the generals!

P. Webb, Ottawa

JOY OF FOOTBALL WORTH RISK OF INJURY

NOVEMBER 11, 1978

There has been much controversy recently in the media regarding injuries in high school and little league football. A lot of the publicity is unfavourable to the sport and I wish to take issue with the forecasters who are predicting lifelong disabilities as a result of injury.

As a mother of football-playing boys, I do not believe that this is the case. We all know that sports involve a certain amount of physical risk. Football is no exception, nor does it result in more serious injury.

Experts in sports and medicine have proven this, but the bad news bears seem to get all the publicity. Statistics can be manipulated to illustrate almost any point.

What the "gloom-and-doom" people have overlooked unfortunately, is the sheer enjoyment that is derived from playing the game. Football is a team sport that teaches discipline, conditioning, endurance, and sacrifice, and results in true comradeship amongst its players. The competition and physical contact does not appeal to all boys, but the option should remain for those who wish to participate.

Four of my sons have played little league and high school football, and I can vouch for their love of the game. They have played soccer and other sports, but football comes first. At the risk of sounding sacrificial, I would rather they be injured on the football field, than to be forever scarred by "smoking up" as a result of idleness and boredom.

What many critics of the game have overlooked is the sheer energy and exuberance of our youth. Some need an outlet for this vitality and football is the answer for them.

The Ottawa school boards should not allow themselves to be coerced into eliminating the foundation of one of the best games in the world of sport.

Mrs. M. J. Kennedy,
Ottawa

FORGET SEXY PM

DECEMBER 28, 1978

The letter by Angela Hefferman regarding the possibility of former solicitor general Francis Fox being prime minister is typical of the mentality of the voter who is responsible for the presence of our charismatic calamity of a leader.

Her suggested list of qualifications — "preferably good-looking and young" — are as ludicrous as her letter. She'd have probably thought Ronald Reagan would have made a fine U.S. president, or how about John Wayne?

Give me the substance of Winston Churchill, the decency of Bob Stanfield and the integrity of Dwight Eisenhower.

You can keep your Cosmetic Charlies such as are now running the government. Perhaps before the next election people like Hefferman will learn to judge a government by its results, not its fancy footwork and sex appeal.

Ray V. Ewbank, Toronto

1979

Local: Mayor Marion Dewar launches Project 4000 to bring 4,000 Vietnamese refugees to Ottawa (June); Small leak at Pembroke-area Rolphton nuclear plant, Canada's oldest, reveals safety problems (May); Historic Rideau Club destroyed by fire (October); City council makes first (unsuccessful) attempt to force non-smoking areas in restaurants (October)

National: Gasoline goes metric (January); PCs under Joe Clark win minority government in May, but lose power in non-confidence vote in December; 200,000 evacuated in Mississauga when train carrying deadly gases derails (November)

World: Shah of Iran forced into exile by Muslim insurgency inspired by Ayatollah Khomeini (January); Leak at Three Mile Island nuclear generating plant worst in U.S. history (March); Margaret Thatcher elected British prime minister (May); Sandinista rebels force General Somoza from power in Nicaragua (July); Iranian students seize 49 hostages at U.S. embassy in Tehran (November); Soviet Union invades Afghanistan (December)

Births: Ottawa Senators forward Marian Hossa; actresses Claire Daines and Jennifer Love Hewitt; singer Usher Raymond IV

Deaths: Prime minister John Diefenbaker; actor John Wayne; Canadian political theorist John Porter; actresses Mary Pickford, Merle Oberon and Jean Seberg; jazz great Charles Mingus; L'il Abner creator Al Capp; British war hero Lord Mountbatten; U.S. vice-president Nelson Rockefeller; punk rocker Sid Vicious; hotel magnate Conrad Hilton; Marxist philosopher Herbert Marcuse; composer Richard Rodgers; Boston Pops conductor Arthur Fiedler; baseball catcher Thurman Munson

A DOG DETERRENT

JANUARY 3, 1979

Recently *The Citizen* carried a story about deer being killed by domestic dogs running loose. It was pointed out that the penalty for any dog caught running loose was death by shooting (of the dog, not the owner).

The logic behind this, I assume, is to set an example for other dogs who might get it into their heads one day to go for a run. However, if we assume that dogs are not capable of rational thought, and are not capable of reading the obituary column for names of their dead friends caught while chasing deer, then it must follow that the killing of dogs caught running loose will not deter other dogs from doing the same thing. If we want to stop dogs from running loose and chasing deer, would it not be more logical to penalize the owners of the dogs that are running loose? Aren't they really to blame?

Meanwhile, the deer and moose are probably wondering what the fuss is all about.

After all, 70,000 human sport hunters "bagged" 9,000 moose last year (figures quoted from James Auld, minister of natural resources in *The Citizen*).

I understand the difference is that human sport hunters are conservationists harvesting a renewable resource and the dogs are nothing but bloodthirsty animals killing for the fun of it.

Michael Belec, Ottawa

SLOW DOWN!

MARCH 3, 1979

We are men over 65 looking out for the safety of your children at school crossings. We do this, four times a day, rain or shine, cold or hot — and for this we get cursed and sworn at, daily.

We are doing this for the safety of your children because we need this job to keep on living. So please, when you see an old man with a red cape and a sign saying "Stop!", bring down your speed, salute him with respect and have pity.

For we, the school brigade, are risking our lives for the protection of your children, every day.

J. Gariepy, Vanier

CANADA SHOULD HAVE WALKED OUT OF UN

MAY 30, 1979

Many Canadians deplore the action of the United Nations in refusing to accept the credentials of the South African delegates when a debate on South West Africa (Namibia) was on the agenda.

Our representatives should have walked out. Canada has been very generous in its aid to African nations. Some of us think we have been over-generous to those who have plenty of resources to slaughter their neighbours, but South Africa has provided aid of every kind that Namibia has needed to make it prosperous and keep it from becoming a fiefdom of Moscow.

It's time we embarked on a more realistic and just policy in respect to foreign affairs.

R. Keith Earls,
Renfrew

SMOKING MAD

JULY 7, 1979

Hooray for Imperial Tobacco in cancelling their ads while your non-smoking campaign is running. I only wish they would withdraw completely from your newspaper — for good.

It would seem you not only challenge their intelligence but also that of, I hope, most of your readers, whether they smoke or not.

Yes, I do smoke, whether it is good or bad, right or wrong, socially acceptable or not, because I choose to, and it makes me quite ill at your rally-around-the-flagpole crusade over quitting.

I wonder if you do-gooders realize the dollars and jobs which would be lost if the total smoking population quit. Where would this money and employment come from? Now that would make an informative article.

Tobacco is an industry which you or I could not afford to eliminate. The people, all 1,000 or more (most unimpressive response) who joined your campaign, disgust me. They show no individual control or strength if they need your "contest" to quit.

Why not a follow-up article on how many actually continued to refrain from the nasty weed? It would probably be unimpressive as well.

Within a group of my peers (the majority, by the way, are non-smokers who have some degree of intelligence), have come up with some other crusades for your newspaper:
• Crusade for all people to use deodorant.
• Crusade for all people to use mouthwash.
• Crusade for all people to refrain from profanity.
• Crusade for all people to donate to one charity.
• Crusade for all people to visit their parents once a month.
• Crusade for all people to take driver education classes.

I will be writing to Imperial Tobacco to tell them that because of their stand against your crusade, I will now switch to an Imperial brand cigarette.

Paul Williams, Ottawa

THE GOOD OL' DAYS
SEPTEMBER 22, 1979

You only have to look at the recent United Auto Workers wage settlement to see one of the major reasons why the North American economy is in such chaos. The vast majority of wage earners, both here and in the U.S., are grossly overpaid.

Thankfully I can look back on more pleasant years in this country, before it became a land of dog eat dog, and the devil took the hindmost.

R.A. Steele, Ottawa

POLICE OFFICERS
MUST SHOOT TO KILL
SEPTEMBER 29, 1979

Florence Berndt expressed her concern that police officers are shooting to kill more frequently than in the past.

A police officer draws his revolver only in situations where he feels his life is in danger. With a revolver or a shovel or a crowbar aimed at his head, a police officer who is forced to make a quick decision to fire would be foolish not to shoot to kill.

There are too many officers lying in their graves who failed to assess the potential viciousness of their executioners. Not to shoot to kill would be tantamount to poking a broom handle into a wasps' nest and then standing there waiting to be stung.

All police officers are required to file a detailed report when they fire their revolvers, and, in some forces, a report is required even if a revolver is removed from the holster while on duty.

Berndt may be sure that the administrators of the police who protect her life and her property would not hesitate, and do not hesitate, to charge any officer who cannot show just cause for firing his revolver.

Lynn Cummings, Nepean

CANADJUN, EH?
OCTOBER 13, 1979

Yer Arthur the lower don't seem to think much of the wee fellow Canadjuns judging from the article in the pa-

per last week. Maybe that's what's wrong with this country and not yer democritic self-governmint as Mr. lower thinks. I mean all these acadumics and exsperts putting us down all the time.

Yer Mr. lower says the Canadjun lectorate (I guess that's the most of us) gets by without having too much on the ball — a minimum of rationality and intelligence was the way he put it. And we elects the worst of us to Parliament. We ain't too proud either and spends all our time sittin' round waiting fer yer Yanks to tell us what to do next.

So what does Mr. lower think we should do instead? Take on the Yanks own kind of governmint, that's what...

Why he would want us low calibre people to vote in a senate and a prezzdent after what he said about us jest don't make any sense.

We got to admit though it's getting pretty hard these days ta tell yer liberalls from yer conservatiffs, but they'll soon straighten themselves out and if they don't there's always yer NDPers sitting on the sidelines waitin' ta get into the opposition's seats. And as fer our pollitics being like a game of hockey we don't too much see what's wrong with that.

Me and the boys take our backward sides down to the rink every Sunday and have to go at each other. But we're still friends after and we all come back every week year after year. But yer Mr. lower apparently don't much care for our hockey either.

We wus wonderin if the trouble with Mr. lower is that in his hole darn life nobody ever elected him to anything at all.

D. Turner, Perth

OFFENSIVE DECISION
OCTOBER 20, 1979

As a career public servant and happy resident of Ottawa for the past 12 years, I am saddened and offended by the recent decision of the department of public works to give one of the potentially most beautiful pieces of land in the heart of Ottawa to the Americans (for their embassy and military).

The Cartier Square site on Elgin Street is such a prominent piece of property that whatever goes there will become a symbol of Ottawa, and Americanism and militarism are not my ideas of the face Ottawa wants to present to the world.

There are so many things that could be done to transform Cartier Square into a showpiece for the rest of the world to admire. Tourism is a cleaner industry than war. Books rather than bombs. It's all possibly at a fraction of the cost of new warplanes purchased from the United States.

It would be so much more interesting to see the Cartier Square Normal School as a branch campus of the United Nations University, also housing Ottawa's first multicultural and community radio station.

Cartier International Society Square could be transformed into an image of international understanding with gardens from around the world, and international music playing softly in the background.

Bob Fancy, Ottawa

Editor's note: After the U.S. government offered Canada a prime piece of real estate in central Washington for a new embassy, the Canadian government felt it owed the Americans a site of equal prestige in Ottawa. Cartier Square was proposed, but was pulled off the table after a strong local protest echoing the sentiments of the letter above. That led to a long list of proposed sites — including Mile Circle in Rockcliffe Park and property at Sussex Drive and Murray Street — before a location on Sussex opposite York Street was approved in the mid-'90s. The embassy was opened there by President Bill Clinton in September 1999.

TAXES AND THE ABILITY TO PAY

NOVEMBER 7, 1979

The Citizen's news item, "Taxation changes explained," was a revelation! It revealed that Glebe resident Bob Keyserlingk was right and Mayor Marion Dewar and her administration were wrong in proposing to levy municipal taxes in such a way as to cause the taxpayer to have to pay higher taxes because the book value of his property has increased.

In the field of taxation it is almost universally the practice not to tax capital gains until after they are realized.

Because of inflation and other factors the book value of our homes and, in fact, of all our properties, increases year by year. Unfortunately for those Canadians on low or fixed incomes (44.7 per cent of us) the current inflated book values of their properties does not reflect their ability to bear inflated municipal taxes!

Proposition 13 in California was a landmark in the struggle to get people to realize that taxation for municipal needs must be collected on an ability-to-pay basis as reflected by the taxpayer's income. Therefore, about 80 per cent of taxes based on the book value of properties were cancelled. The needs of the municipalities that resulted from the cancellation were met from funds supplied by the State of California which were, for the most part, collected on the ability to pay as reflected by the taxpayers' incomes!

John H. McKay, Ottawa

YES, IT CAN HAPPEN HERE

NOVEMBER 10, 1979

An incident occurred the other day that disturbed me a great deal.

I was walking along Bank Street during lunch hour when a middle-aged woman walked up to me and started cursing me with words like, "What are you doing here? You animal! Get back to the zoo where you came from! You probably haven't done a thing in your life! Get the hell out of here! You are all animals!"

I was stunned. I couldn't understand what on earth was going on. Strange things have happened to me before in this same city, but this incident topped them all.

You see, I have slanted eyes, straight black hair and legs that are a bit bowed. I also happen to be from the Canadian North. I am an Inuk.

In the middle of the heated exchange, it began to occur to me why this woman was so angered. Since my physical features closely a resemble the Vietnamese boat people this woman was actually taking me for one of them.

There was no mistake about it. She hardly gave me a chance to respond because she was machine-gunning words out of her mouth so fast. The only reason I was not hurt by her words was because I am now quite used to this kind of abuse after living for more than an decade in the south.

This woman appeared very poor. The message she put across to me and others who gathered around us was that the boat people were being given almost everything for free for up to a year until they get settled in their new country, and here she was, deprived of such benefits.

I am saddened by this reality, and ask why this should happen in a country like Canada. It is a rich country in many ways compared to the Third World countries. Why can't we share this wealth? There seems to be enough for everyone.

Alootook Ipellie, Ottawa

NO FRILLS CARE

DECEMBER 29, 1979

My husband, a terminal cancer patient, died earlier this year. During his last months he suffered unspeakable horrors of pain. As a result of the Ontario government's cutbacks his condition was exacerbated by overcrowding, sub-standard care, shortages of supplies and breakdown of equipment.

Even though my husband had paid for hospitalization for 25 years and for group medical insurance, in his dying months he was unable to get a private room, even if we had offered payment. On his floor there was obvious need for twice the nursing staff.

My husband's dressings required frequent changing. Until I hired special nurses and bought protective pads from the nearest drugstore, he was left wet and cold most of the days and nights. Pads and specialized dressings to protect patients and linen were considered "frills."

The conditions resulting from Health Minister Dennis Timbrell's cutbacks have contributed to a decline in both patient and staff morale to the extent that there was a hopelessness throughout that hospital.

Personally, I saw and my husband experienced some of the effects — wrong diagnosis, both at the onset and after remission of his particular cancer, a six-hour wait in an emergency ward before being admitted to the intensive care unit, breakdown of communication between patients, family, and doctors.

Hospitals were never meant to be self-supporting. Why not turn over some lottery proceeds to hospital care and to medical research? I would sooner support hospitals, which are running into debt, and cancer research than the building of auditoriums and sportsplexes.

Muriel Harrison, Ottawa

Editor's note: It took another decade, but the Ontario Lottery Corp.'s mandate was eventually broadened in 1989 to allow a portion of lottery proceeds to be turned over to hospitals. By 1999, that amounted to roughly one-quarter of the $2.1-billion in revenue generated by the corporation.

"The polls lately have become more and more asinine. The latest absurdity is the Angus Reid poll that says the Liberals could win if Jean Chrétien came back. Why stop at Chrétien: why not Trudeau, Mackenzie King, Napoleon, Ghengis Khan or Snow White? It's little wonder we mount a Rhinoceros Party."

— August 29, 1987

1980-1989

1980

Local: *Ottawa Journal* folds, leaving *The Citizen* as the city's only English-language daily newspaper (August); General Hospital moves to new complex on Smyth Road (August)
National: Canadian ambassador Ken Taylor hides six Americans at Canadian Embassy in Tehran during Iran hostage crisis (January); Pierre Trudeau returns to power as Liberals topple PCs in federal election (February); By margin of 60 per cent to 40 per cent, Quebecers reject sovereignty association in referendum (May); Terry Fox forced to abandon his cross-Canada run when he learns cancer has spread to his lungs (September)
World: American bid to rescue hostages ends in disaster in Iranian desert (April); Volcanic eruption at Mt. St. Helen's in Washington State kills eight, darkens sky with tower of ash (May); U.S., Canada, Japan and West Germany among countries boycotting Moscow Olympics to protest Soviet invasion of Afghanistan (July); Ronald Reagan unseats Jimmy Carter in presidential election (November)
Births: Tennis star Martina Hingis; actress Christina Ricci; Canadian swim star Yannick Lupien
Deaths: Film director Alfred Hitchcock; Beatle John Lennon; Canadian media guru Marshall McLuhan; actors Peter Sellers and Mae West; governor general Jules Léger; writers Henry Miller and C.P. Snow; jazz pianist Bill Evans; U.S. labour leader George Meany; U.S. track legend Jesse Owens; comedian Jimmy Durante; psychoanalyst Erich Fromm; philosopher Jean-Paul Sartre; Yugoslavian strongman Joseph Tito; Soviet premier Alexei Kosygin

STARVE THE SOVIETS, ASSIST THE AFGHANS

JANUARY 23, 1980

An army, the saying goes, marches on its stomach. The huge Soviet force now occupying Afghanistan presumably devours a substantial amount of food each day. A portion of this is derived from Canadian grain exports. We would not have been assisting these Russian invaders any more had we supplied them machine-gun ammunition and napalm.

The Russian economy is notorious for its inability to meet its own food requirements. Nonetheless it is capable of maintaining an enormous military force. The world would be a better place today had these millions of armed men been engaged in the fields of food production.

Bruce Young,
North Vancouver, B.C.

RIGHTS SACRIFICED

FEBRUARY 2, 1980

The decision of the Conservative government to move the regional office of Parks Canada from Cornwall to Peterborough, although 30 per cent of the employees are francophone and Peterborough does not have facilities to accommodate French-language students, is a blatant example of the sacrifice of individual rights for political gain. Such a decision reinforces René Lévesque's view that francophones cannot expect justice outside Quebec.

Helen Sallmen, Ottawa

IMMIGRANTS MALIGNED

MARCH 19, 1980

The assertions in R. Keith Earls' letter are insupportable. Mr. Earls is in effect saying that a person whose skin differs from his own lacks, by definition, the intelligence and strength of character which is necessary to participate in the defence of our democratic freedoms.

Traditionally, many of the staunchest supporters of our democratic rights have been immigrants. They are blessed with that rare, realistic perspective which truly appreciates the preciousness of the freedom we take for granted. We Canadians are in the fortunate position that we can, through our immigrants, become acquainted with the meaning of the absence or loss of freedom without having to experience it for ourselves.

As a people, we need to encourage our continued enrichment by other cultures, colours and religions, for if we wish our nation to grow in maturity, that implies not contraction and insularity, but inclusion and expansion of our humanistic ideals.

Niela Peach, Ottawa

NO MORE NHL GAMES FOR ME

MARCH 29, 1980

I agree with *The Citizen's* editorial concerning the National Hockey League, whose body of "governors" unanimously felt it proper to assist Clarence Campbell during this time of pressure on his cash flow. They gave him $50,000.

The governors' attitudes and the action they have taken is an insult to sports fans everywhere, particularly those who have been ardent supporters of hockey and hockey clubs. I am most disgusted and certainly not content to "know that my tickets helped pay the expenses and fine of a man convicted of breaking the law," particularly since he was president of the NHL for a long time, "a lawyer and war crimes jurist," who suspended Maurice "the Rocket" Richard (after a brawl) at a crucial stage in his career.

As a fervent supporter of *Les Canadiens*, I will not attend any further games at the Montreal Forum.

Michel Renaud, Vanier

Editor's note: In 1980, NHL president Clarence Campbell and Bahamian businessman Gordon Brown were convicted of conspiracy for paying $95,000 to Liberal Senator Louis Giguere in a bid to persuade the government to extend the lease of duty-free Sky Shops Export Ltd. at Montreal's Dorval Airport. Mr. Campbell and Mr. Brown were each sentenced to a day in jail and a $25,000 fine. Senator Giguere was acquitted.

TEARING US APART

MARCH 29, 1980

For months I have been bombarded by the rhetoric of

men who would destroy this nation. Elected politicians East and West proudly proclaim that their goal is the destruction of my nation.

It is time they were called publicly what they are: traitors. Their destructive bent is fuelled not by the common good but by power — the power of ultimate control. It is time these self-seeking politicians understand that there are many of us who are proud of this diverse country and its peoples.

It is time those in power realized that many Canadians will never accept the peaceful destruction of Canada. I am afraid that as men died in the past for this nation, so shall men die for this nation in the near future.

D. Lenaghan, Nepean

FOOLISHLY TOUGH

APRIL 12, 1980

The captain of the Oshawa Generals Hockey Club should be commended. Ottawa native Jim Mellon, now off the team as a result of arriving late for a partial practice Tuesday after driving his father to Toronto Airport to visit a seriously injured second son, acted wisely and commendably.

Coach Paul Theriault should be taught a few of the principles of an intelligent team program. Tolerating Mellon's 20-minute-late arrival with such an excuse would likely have strengthened team unity, and most certainly have helped in the remainder of the series.

Paul Theriault owed it to the captain of his team, with draft time approaching, to accept and understand the difficult position Mellon found himself in, instead of foolishly trying to prove himself a tough disciplinarian.

Steven Winogron, Ottawa

'NON' TO UGLY GRAFFITI

MAY 17, 1980

Defacing the Ottawa cenotaph with the very word (Oui) that would break up Canada has riled me and numerous comrades in arms.

Born in Hull, I like many others said "Oui" gladly and freely when Canada needed me. We answered the call to arms promptly and defeated the enemy hordes. The cenotaph stands witness to the sacrifice of those who did not return, who gave so much of themselves so that Canada can be free.

To see this tribute to their effort defaced and splattered by the separatist horde's slogan is enough to make any Canadian's blood boil. I was voting "Non" before. I swear now that I shall be more active than ever in convincing other Quebecers to rid the province and the country of these shameless, prideless, honorless pieces of scum that have sprouted and developed amid our dearest and most honored political system.

I shall vote "Non" to René Lévesque and his power-hungry dreamers. I shall vote "Non" to a government that can only inspire its youth to deface monuments to the efforts of the past. I shall vote "Non."

Vince LaBelle,
Hull

GAY ARTICLES TOO 'SEAMY'

JUNE 21, 1980

Your articles on homosexuality and limited aspects of the gay community, combined with the front page article on the murder of a priest by a "queer basher," have once again reinforced the stereotype of the male homosexual as a furtive creature, solely in search of short-lived physical pleasure, and as a potential victim of an oppressive heterosexual majority.

Like the pop sociologists of the early '60s, ignorant heterosexual reporters are sent on a brief tour of the most visible aspects of the gay community and rush back to type out an "authoritative" report, in lurid prose worthy of *The National Enquirer*, on the "truth" of the gay lifestyle.

If *The Citizen* asked me, as a homosexual, to write an article on heterosexual lifestyles and I reported on bars where prostitution is overt, parking spots where heterosexual sex is constant, and made snide remarks about public heterosexual displays of affection, there would be an outraged cry from the heterosexual majority. If I recounted the frequency of rape and molestation of young girls by heterosexual men, described the dance of a man and woman as simulated coitus and referred leeringly to the flirtations of a waiter with a friend and customer, I would be accused of outright distortion.

Yet all these instances parallel the description of gays in the articles by Tom Van Dusen and Tim Harper. The responsibility for any murder or mugging of gay people that occurs as a result of your series lies on your heads. As gay people, we will continue to affirm our self-respect and teach younger gays the self-respect that is denied them by ignorant and bigoted heterosexual parents, teachers and media.

One day, I hope you will realize that what was described in the articles are the external manifestations of an oppressed minority. The essence of homosexuality is the courage to love another human being, to break free from confining sex roles and to have the guts to be one's self in a society terrified of anything that differs.

To borrow a phrase from the black movement, there is no homosexual problem — there is a heterosexual problem. Why is heterosexual society so afraid of homosexuality that it has to ostracize, segregate, outlaw and murder homosexuals? When is *The Citizen* going to report on that?

Charles C. Hill, Ottawa

GALLERY BUYS DUBIOUS ART

JULY 23, 1980

As a recent visitor to the National Gallery, I was completely disgusted with the absolute nonsense that is being foisted on the public as "contemporary art."

I refer to the almost empty rooms with charcoal smears by Poulin and a couple of hollow squares of some grey material which could pass for children's sand boxes but nothing else. Who selected this junk for display?

If we must get off the elevator on the 6th floor to be faced with six huge photos of a naked man knee-deep in ferns with everything God gave him hanging out, why not the young star of *The Blue Lagoon*?

It can well be argued that there is beauty and art in male nudity, but not in the grotesque, bearded, disgracefully posed exhibitionist in the ferns. This is merely an obscenity. Why the Canadian taxpayers' money is spent for such trash is beyond comprehension.

Strome Galloway, Ottawa

CALL IT A DAY
AUGUST 9, 1980

Regional Council will vote in a few days on chairman Andy Haydon's proposal to give $2,000 to the Miss World Canada pageant to be held shortly in Ottawa. Not long ago, this same fellow strongly opposed a grant to the Ottawa Women's Centre, which provides social services on a next-to-nothing budget. "Let's give them a dollar to buy badminton birds," he said, "and call it a day."

It is clear what he thinks of women, or rather what he thinks women are for. But as a taxpayer, I strongly object to his trying to impose his values on me at my expense. I don't want a human meat display in this city, and I most assuredly don't want to pay for one. Let regional council give Haydon a copy of *Penthouse*, and call it a day.

John Baglow, Ottawa

BEAUTIFUL PICTURE
AUGUST 23, 1980

Regarding your front page photo entitled "Relief is just a hydrant away." This is a beautiful picture. It clearly shows that Canada is a multi-cultural, multi-national society. It is a nation of people with different pasts living, playing and working together towards a common future of peace and harmony.

Our congratulations to the photographer and to *The Citizen*. We needed something like this in this troubled time of the "invasion" of the Ku Klux Klan. People of Canada must join forces to drive the Klan out of this country or we will end up having the same kind of racial riots that have recently occurred in the southern United States.

If men don't learn from the violence of today, will there be a tomorrow?

Andy Jacob, Andrew Huntington,
Kenneth Wong, Ottawa

PREMIERS REVEALED
AS OPPORTUNISTS
SEPTEMBER 24, 1980

The constitutional talks were not a failure, because they gave us a chance to see the provincial premiers for what they are — greedy, narrow-minded opportunists with little regard for individual rights, average Canadians and Canada as a nation.

The premiers hoped that by portraying themselves as champions of their own provincial "rights" they would prepare their way for certain re-election. They failed to recognize the intelligence of most Canadians. In the West we are also more Canadian than Albertan and are willing to share our resources with the rest of Canadians, but also know from experience that our rights are better protected by courts than politicians.

Canada did not achieve its greatness through honesty of politicians, but the generosity of its peoples and an uncorruptible judicial system. For us to survive as a free nation, our basic rights must and shall be entrenched in the constitution.

Sorry, Mr. Lougheed, but if the central government resorts to a referendum, our resentment of Eastern domination will not conquer our love for Canada.

Donald Alex Donovan,
Calgary

NO EXCUSE FOR RAPE
OCTOBER 22, 1980

I am disappointed in the recent court decision to sentence a convicted rapist to only "two years less a day." This means that a man with a documented history of violent crimes like common assault, and now rape, could be back on the streets in eight months.

I also deplore the apparent misguided notion that because the rape victim was a "woman of the world," supposedly a polite euphemism for "not a virgin," a lengthier sentence seemed out of place.

Our judicial system continues to exhibit a lack of appreciation toward current social trends of thought, particularly concerning acts of violence against women.

Dale Hodorek, Ottawa

JOHN LENNON, A SYMBOL OF HOPE
DECEMBER 13, 1980

I was shocked to learn of the death of John Lennon, former Beatle, former superstar, the symbol of a generation of hope. While his life may have been less than the standard of perfection set by modern-day society, his passing must certainly be regarded as symbolic, if not, proof, of the present sickness of North American society.

We have certainly passed on an era where good-intentioned politicians can offer the hope of security through vague promises of measures to be taken toward a law and order society. It is time that the citizenry, as a collective body, demanded that stiff punitive measures be enacted to demonstrate that such acts will no longer be accepted.

The tone of these remarks can only reflect a deep feeling of personal loss which I am sure is shared by many readers who are members of my generation, or those who genuinely appreciate the sentiment of the 1960s. Perhaps it is significant that the senselessness of such acts finally strikes home once they affect not our politicians, but the symbols of our generation.

Richard Stead, Ottawa

1981

Local: Mitel Corp. president Michael Cowpland buys Ottawa River mansion from developer Robert Campeau (February); Hundreds of homeowners in trouble as mortgage rate hits 20 per cent (July); G-7 leaders gather at Montebello for annual economic summit (July)

National: Census puts Canada's population at nearly 25 million (June); Terry Fox dies 10 months after abandoning his cross-Canada run for cancer (June); Clifford Olson charged in murders of nine children in B.C. (August); Public angered at the news a stamp for regular letter rising to 30 cents from 17 (September); Federal government, all provinces except Quebec reach constitutional agreement (November); Wayne Gretzky breaks NHL record by scoring 50th goal in 39th game of season (December)

World: Iran releases 52 American hostages (January); President Ronald Reagan survives shot in chest by assassin (March); Gunman wounds Pope John Paul II in St. Peter's Square (May); Prince Charles, Lady Diana Spencer wed at St. Paul's Cathedral (July); Doctors identify AIDS, a deadly disease without a cure (December)

Births: Video game character PacMan; actors Elijah Wood and Jonathan Taylor-Thomas

Deaths: Boxer Joe Louis; reggae star Bob Marley; rock pioneer Bill Haley; actress Natalie Wood; folksinger Harry Chapin; U.S. dramatist Paddy Chayefsky; Albert Speer, architect of Nazi death camps; Egyptian president Anwar Sadat; Israeli soldier-statesman Moshe Dayan; historian Will Durant

METRIC FRUSTRATES HOMEMAKERS

JANUARY 21, 1981

I don't want to go metric! I am surrounded by men and women who share these feelings, and the helplessness and frustration of knowing our policy-makers have taken a major decision without asking us how we feel.

The transition from imperial to metric will be very costly, involving many physical changes in scales and other instruments. Shopkeepers will pass these costs on to the consumer. For many (including me) who were not good at math in school, figuring out and converting things on a daily basis will be a nightmare.

Pity the poor homemaker all ready to prepare a Thanksgiving dinner with her measuring cups and spoons all laid out, only to notice suddenly that the recipe is in litres and kilograms. Why should she have to go through all that converting before she can sit down to a turkey dinner?

Even the weatherman now speaks in an alien tongue. All I hear on the radio is wind in kilometres, and rain and snow in centimetres.

If all those who feel as I do write their MP, or the Metric Commission, and make enough noise, perhaps our collective voices will be heard and we will gain a few inches of ground.

(Mrs.) Norma Ezri, Ottawa

Editor's note: In the early 1970s, the Liberal government created the Metric Commission to guide Canada's full-scale — and mandatory — conversion away from imperial measure to metric by 1980. Metric's implementation, which began in 1975 with conversion to Celsius measure for temperature, went much slower than anticipated, so that by 1981-82, metric measure was only arriving at grocery stores. Despite widespread protests from business and the public, the move to metric went ahead until early 1985, when the newly minted Mulroney government decided retailers would be allowed to use imperial measure alongside metric, an arrangement still used today.

WOMEN'S RIGHTS

MAY 6, 1981

Three cheers that Quebec women and men can now both be identified by their family names. This is a step toward equality. But we can't cheer the editorial, "You win some, you lose some." For women to use their family name is not a loss of freedom but an assertion of their identity.

And why not replace the term "maiden name" with "family name." Many people find "maiden name" offensive because of its sexual connotations. It trivializes an important development to suggest parents will not give their children manageable names. This law acknowledges that women now have the same right that men have always had to give their names to their children.

No one loses here. We all win.

Joan Sergeant (and five others), Ottawa

WHAT ARE CHARTER RIGHTS?

MAY 23, 1981

A recent Gallup poll says most Canadians want a charter of rights in the Constitution. But that doesn't necessarily mean that they want the particular charter proposed by the Trudeau government. There is no evidence, either, that those who do favor the Trudeau charter really know what they are supporting.

How many realize, for example, that Section 1 would allow Parliament to nullify practically any rights we might possess? And how could the courts presume to set aside a political decision to restrict them? The answer has already been given by Mr. Justice S. J. Robins in *Dehler v. Ottawa Civic Hospital et al.* "The court is not entitled . . . to substitute its judgement on the wisdom, policy or values underlying the legislation for that of Parliament."

It would be indecent to railroad the charter through the Canadian and British parliaments. If a charter of rights is really important, then it's also important to know what kind of charter we are getting.

Philip L. Cooper, Ottawa

COURT POWER

MAY 27, 1981

The proposed charter of rights will be the greatest tragedy to strike this freedom-loving land. It effectively gives the Supreme Court (appointed by one man — the PM) the right to final and irrevocable decisions in all matters of individual rights.

This is a frightening development and I am dismayed that more MPs on both sides of the House are not loudly voicing their concern.

Until now, our rights have been vested in the people through elected representation in the legislatures and Parliament. The common people do have wisdom and a deep desire for freedom with integrity, while those who sit in lofty halls of power, because of their very isolation, tend to be less concerned about the individual freedoms of the common man.

If I had a choice I would choose the electoral system. I hope our present Supreme Court judges rule likewise.

Ray J. Lewis, Ottawa

MATERNITY LEAVE A MORAL ISSUE
JULY 22, 1981

John Bulloch, president of the Canadian Federation of Independent Business, by being "vehemently opposed" to paid maternity leave, is revealing another of his out-dated and ultra-conservative approaches to modern social problems.

The issue is straightforward. In the first place, women have babies. That's how we procreate the human race; that's how Mr. Bulloch's organization is able to employ more than a million people.

Second, we have developed a society and an economy where women *have* to work — as single parents, as single families, as vitally needed income earners playing their role, along with men, in trying to cope with inflation and the other difficulties of day-to-day living.

Given these self-evident truths, is there any possible justification for financially penalizing women who physically bear children and thereby perpetuate the human species? CUPW and Treasury Board agree that paid maternity leave is not costly (about two cents per hour). Paid maternity leave should not have become a collective bargaining issue. It is a basic social and moral issue.

John L. Fryer, President,
National Union of Provincial
Government Employees,
Ottawa

BANKRUPT POLICY
AUGUST 5, 1981

Jimmy Carter was accused during his four years in the White House of failing to formulate a consistent and effective foreign policy.

After seven months with Ronald Reagan in office, U.S. foreign policy is in worse shape than ever. On the East-West conflict, his views are as simplistic and repetitive as any layman's. The whole strategy of his administration is arm now and talk later. This approach is dangerous to world stability.

Concerning the Middle East, his policies represent fully the contradictory and ambiguous lines in American thinking. The American reaction to the Israeli raid on Baghdad's nuclear research plant is a fresh example. On North-South negotiations, Reagan's policy, if he has one, is marked with negligence and inconsideration. His main

conviction is that all the developed countries can do for the less developed is help them help themselves.

Such an approach is wrong and ignorant. Reagan's attitude is isolationist. Unless the U.S. adopts some basic compassion and consideration for the needs and aspirations of other people, its image abroad will remain a symbol of imperialism and arrogance.

Elie M. Nasrallah,
Carleton University, Ottawa

TOO EXTRAVAGANT
SEPTEMBER 2, 1981

On the very day that Premier Bill Davis was telling the other nine premiers that Canadians must be told to practise restraint, his government announced the purchase of a $10.6-million executive jet. The government's present fleet of aircraft is better suited to service this vast province than this new luxury jet, which is unable to land at 222 of the province's airports.

The timing could not have been worse. The government will have to borrow to finance this plane. At current rates, the interest will total about $2.4 million this year, or $6,600 per day. What's more, the Montreal manufacturer of the jet estimates that it costs $1,150 per hour to fly.

At a time when Ontario schools are in dire need of funds and hospitals across the province are contemplating layoffs and bed closures, such extravagance by Mr. Davis's government is deplorable.

Karl Feige, Ottawa

A QUESTION
SEPTEMBER 9, 1981

Can readers advise me regarding the following: I am offered 18½-per-cent interest on my money if I invest with a group called Federal Government. It will net at least four per cent after inflation and taxation. But from what I have learned, I doubt whether the company is to be trusted. They are many billions in debt and are losing further billions each year, which they finance by writing IOUs.

Altogether it is not a reassuring situation. Any advice would be appreciated.

Barry Mather, Wakefield, Que.

FOX WAS A HERO
WHO WANTED ANSWERS
SEPTEMBER 12, 1981

I am a paraplegic and unable to take part in any activity on Terry Fox Day. I never met Terry Fox in person, only through the magic of television.

By the time he had reached Thunder Bay, I felt as though I had known him all his life, because in my mind, I had been right by his side, during each long, lonely mile that he ran.

My mother died of cancer, and her father before her. Neither death could be attributed to any of those vile habits that scientists say causes cancer. Terry needed the answer to what made cancer malignant: not just one type, all types. And he went about getting the answer the right way: not by talking but through research, and research

Marathon of Hope runner Terry Fox, shown with his mother, Betty, died June 28 from cancer.

costs money. At the cost of his own life, he succeeded.

To me, Terry was many people. A God-loving Christian, a giant among men, a standout in any crowd and a fighter all the way. But first and foremost, he was a Canadian, and proud of it. Vaya con Dios, Terry. We all miss you.

Robert P. Chase, Prescott, Ont.

Editor's note: Terry Fox died June 28, 1981. Since then, annual cross-country runs held in his honour have raised more than $150 million for cancer research.

CANDU DOES
SEPTEMBER 23, 1981

A recent *Citizen* article is typical of the sensationalism used today to sell newspapers.

Tritium, an isotope of hydrogen, combines with oxygen to form a compound chemically identical to water. This compound occurs naturally, as does H_2O or D_2O (heavy water). The amount of tritium which the Three Mile Island plant planned on releasing is equal to the amount that flows past the plant in Susquehanna River in a year. The release of tritium from the Rolphton Nuclear Generating Station is well within the Atomic Energy Control Board's monthly release limits (less than two per cent of the monthly limit).

The CANDU (Canadian Deuterium Uranium) reactor is the most efficient fission reactor in the world, outperforming the American pressurized water reactor and boiling water reactor. In fact in 1980, Unit 3 at Bruce Nuclear Generating Station was No. 1 in the world.

I didn't see that in the newspaper. Is it because it isn't sensational enough?

J.C. Boyle, Kincardine, Ont.

RUNNING A RISK
NOVEMBER 11, 1981

It is fine for Robert Eady to complain that too much attention is placed on the political actions of Poland's Solidarity movement, but Solidarity's "courage and determination" increasingly runs the risk of inviting Soviet intervention.

Only moderation and constant compromise will prevent this. Solidarity started as an ideological movement, and will probably be judged historically as such; but right now, its problems arise from real-world politics that require practical solutions, not political or ideological theory.

It is for this reason that I feel the current emphasis on the day-to-day activities in Poland is appropriate rather than premature kudos handed out to an organization that has the potential to get half of Poland killed, while trying not to be "cut to ribbons by mass arrests."

I wonder what option Mr. Eady would prefer?

Robert J. Carter, Ottawa

THE VIDEO KING
DECEMBER 23, 1981

The future of television holds little hope for the networks, for they will soon become obsolete. Dramas, comedies, sitcoms and talk shows (largely spiced with poor and redundant advertisements) will be totally phased out. Pay television and cable television companies will also die a quick and painless death, due directly to home video entertainment.

The video world will soon become king. Individuals now have the luxury of viewing whatever they wish (through video libraries) whenever they wish. The only basic large capital investment, besides the television, is the video cassette or video disc machine and as time progresses, they will become cheaper.

The only remnants of network television will most likely be a live sports and information network and a 24-hour news network. So let us now say goodbye to the "big three" U.S. television networks and our own government and private Canadian networks.

They have done us proud, but must make way for the future.

Ron Waserman, Ottawa

1982

Local: New Year's Day celebrated as 150th anniversary of Rideau Canal opening (January); Turkish ambassador murdered in car on Ottawa River Parkway (August); Marion Dewar wins third successive term as Ottawa mayor (November)

National: Queen proclaims new Canadian Constitution and Charter of Rights (April); Federal government limits salary increases of public servants to five per cent in 1983 and five per cent in '84 (June)

World: Britain sends troops to recapture Falklands Islands from Argentina (April-June); Israel launches major Lebanon offensive in bid to clear out terrorist camps (June); Tylenol removed from shelves after eighth death due to deliberate poisoning (October)

Births: Prince William; figure skater Tara Lipinski; singer LeAnn Rimes

Deaths: Piano giants Glenn Gould, Thelonius Monk and Arthur Rubinstein; Soviet defector Igor Gouzenko; writers Ayn Rand and John Cheever; baseball legend Satchel Paige; Soviet leader Leonid Brezhnev; actors Ingrid Bergman, Henry Fonda, Grace Kelly, John Belushi and Romy Schneider; Tom Swift Jr., author of Nancy Drew, Hardy Boys books; German film director Rainer Fassbinder

RIDICULOUS BUDGET

JANUARY 27, 1982

May we add our voices in protest to this ridiculous budget that has been imposed on the Canadian population.

This government that we are stuck with has bungled the country's finances to the tune of millions of dollars; its members speak from both sides of their mouths and hide behind this thing called "inflation."

We, the wage earners, are told to use restraint in our demands for salary increases, while our members at every level of government simply vote themselves a raise. We are told that the government is the people; yet the cries of discontent from the Canadian people go ignored.

Credit is rampant, unemployment is out of hand, uncertainty and fear is everywhere, interest rates are beyond any reason or common sense, but our government concerned itself only with bringing home the Constitution. (Nero fiddled while Rome burned.)

It is difficult to see the logic of such thinking as raising prices when there is a surplus — raising oil prices so that the poor cannot pay for it and then subsidize it; unemployment at an all-time high and support welfare recipients. The changes being made to this infamous budget will affect those who have money but the clause concerning the tax on employee benefits still remains. This will affect all wage earners. No doubt, our honourable members will still enjoy their tax-free benefits.

Marcel and Mary Lecuyer,
Cumberland

GORDON STONEHAM

FEBRUARY 24, 1982

I was shocked and saddened by the report of the death of your critic, Gordon Stoneham.

Working in television news for the past 25 years, I have seen reviewers come and go. Mr. Stoneham was a *rara avis.* As one who has become increasingly cynical of television and its role in society, I found his weekend look at film for TV a source of delightful reading and information on an intelligent level.

If he said it was junk, I just went to bed.

Larry MacDonald, Ottawa

TRUDEAU A DICTATOR

MARCH 16, 1982

Pierre Trudeau is a fitting dictator of the party that al-

most destroyed Parliament during the Pipeline Debate of 1956 with its repeated imposition of closure.

The Trudeau government is acting true to form when it presents to the House of Commons this monstrous omnibus energy bill, consisting of 15 separate acts, four of them new; a bill which enhances government power and is said to contain more unpleasant taxation surprises than even Machiavelli could devise — and apparently, is of such scope and complexity that responsible discussion is impossible.

This inherent distaste on the part of the Liberals for parliamentary discussion was exemplified years ago in their most powerful cabinet minister, the Hon. C.D. Howe, who during second reading of a money bill, arrogantly protested — "Mr. Speaker, I do not think this should be allowed to degenerate into a debate."

Marjorie Le Lacheur, Ottawa

Editor's note: To fight the Liberals' use of a single bill to amend or introduce 15 other pieces of energy legislation, the Opposition Conservatives employed a procedural bell-ringing trick to shut down the Commons for two weeks. Although the Liberals tried to paint the Tories as the bad guys by saying their filibuster was costing taxpayers $714,285 a day, the strategy didn't work and the government was eventually forced to split the omnibus into smaller chunks for debate and voting in the House. The omnibus contained several sections that were extremely unpopular in energy-rich Western Canada, including legislation giving state-owned Petro-Canada an automatic 25-per-cent share of all new offshore oil and gas discoveries. Here are two more letters on the bell-ringing affair.

CLARK PATHETIC AND PANICKY

MARCH 16, 1982

The latest of Joe Clark's choleric attempts (the bell hoopla) to divert everyone's attention from the fact that the governing party, after giving the country a beautiful flag and a proud national anthem, will soon give Canada a Constitution, is an act of a puny, pathetic and panicky man, who is not quite qualified to lead a cow to water, let alone a party to power.

M.R. Fajrajsl, Kanata

MICKEY MOUSE QUEEN

MARCH 16, 1982

The Governor General should summon the House leaders and inform them that Her Majesty is deeply disturbed over the crisis in her favorite Mickey Mouse club.

D.A. Armstrong, Manotick

TOO MUCH HIGH-TECH
APRIL 21, 1982

I still have not lost hope that one day soon I shall open *The Citizen* and not find one article related to high tech. Am I the eternal optimist?

[Early high-tech executive] Mr. Gordon Gow, among others, spent a great deal of time elaborating at the recent Infotech show, as reported in the *Citizen*, on how technology will permit us to have our coffee made, lights turned on, drapes drawn, play endless games and God knows what else, simply with the use of a home microcomputer.

In a society where many people cannot even afford to have coffee or drapes, let alone a computer, this is ridiculous. Even if everyone could afford this toy who, except the severely handicapped, would want it?

As a social worker, and a taxpayer, I find this mentality extremely alienating. We have now not only produced but in fact are being led by what the late C. Wright Mills referred to as the "Technological Idiots." The only direct result high-tech has had on me so far is to cause my bank teller to take twice as long to bring my chequebook up to date.

Bob Rickman, Renfrew

OUR SLOW MAIL
APRIL 24, 1982

I sent a letter to Family Allowance in Ottawa from Nepean Jan. 5. In February, I got a nasty letter asking why hadn't I replied to their letter. Sent a second letter immediately. On April 5, I received an acknowledgement, dated March 20, of my January letter.

What gives? I mailed a parcel first class mail March 18 to Calgary and the same day one to England. The one arrived well on time in England. The one to Calgary had not arrived by April 5. I should have sent it fourth class mail and saved money.

Next time I have something for Ottawa, I'll get someone else to deliver it.

Dorothy Cole, Kanata

SAVE SAN MARTIN
MAY 22, 1982

I like the statue of Jose de San Martin in Minto Park. I do hope we aren't becoming so narrowly nationalistic, or merely narrow, that we can't tolerate a long-dead and long-forgotten (at least in Canada) foreigner's statue in a tiny city park. I think he adds to the charm of the park in a city that isn't noted for its charm, despite its many wooded areas.

Let's keep Jose de San Martin in Minto Park. He's all paid for, is an interesting oddity, and makes a handy pigeon stand. Besides, if we want Canadian-hero statues we have a lot of other parks to put them in.

M. Lortie, Ottawa

Editor's note: Despite talk of transferring it to another site, the monument to San Martin, a 19th century hero of the South American independence movement, remains in Minto Park, at Elgin and Gilmour streets. In 1992, it was joined there by a monument honouring female victims of violence.

A DIFFERENT LOOK AT GALLUP RESULTS
JUNE 28, 1982

The reign of Prime Minister Trudeau and his henchmen has been the greatest catastrophe to strike Canada since Confederation. In a few short years they have squandered most of this country's wealth on projects no prudent person would touch.

Unfortunately, we are stuck with these extravagant clowns for at least two more years, by which time our dollar may be worth 50 cents. If we ever get this country back on the rails it will probably take the rest of this century to straighten out the mess.

Thanks, Pierre, you'll go down in history.

R.A. Steele, Ottawa

NEW CITY HALL
JUNE 30, 1982

It sure looks as though Mayor Marion Dewar has already forgotten that this year's mismanagement of Ottawa's affairs by city council has produced an unwelcome and considerable tax increase.

Not content with this year's failure, she now seems to be hard at work on future tax disasters. The first salvo of her campaign to "prepare" ratepayers was fired when she recently very casually mentioned on TV that the present city hall building on Sussex Drive was "too small" and a "presence" in the downtown core was desirable.

Blinded by her delusions of grandeur and totally oblivious to the fact that Canada's total government, corporate and personal debt is now about $500 billion, or about $200,000 for every Canadian, she wants to spend another $30 million on a new Dewar Monument, adding a considerable amount to our current tax load and deferring huge tax increases to the next generation of homeowners.

She should be satisfied with the construction of the new police building. If, in the future, there is a genuine need for more space for the already overstaffed city hall, an addition to the present building should suffice.

R.G. Chênevert, Ottawa

Editor's note: Three years after Marion Dewar retired as mayor, city council, under Mayor Jim Durrell, approved a $72-million glass-and-steel expansion of city hall designed by architect Moshe Safdie. It opened in 1993.

DALY BUILDING
JULY 17, 1982

The Daly building — which only an architect could love — has all the charisma of a parking garage and none of the utility. It hides and detracts from the Château Laurier and the Customs Building, both of which have a more pleasing appearance and a design more indigenous to Ottawa.

The "see-through" body of structural steel of this "Chicago school of architecture" monstrosity makes it an excellent conductor of heat and cold — at the expense of energy conservation.

The only solution is to level the Daly Building and use the space for a people park and to help solve the inevitable traffic problems that will be associated with the Rideau Centre.

Henry Verdier, Ottawa

Editor's note: The Daly Building was demolished in 1992.

SVETLANA GOUZENKO REPLIES

JULY 19, 1982

In reply to the ugly letter of A.P.C. Hopkinson, there is no use in discussion if he has any connection with "intelligence" work in Canada. Like most of them, he would resent any disclosures of espionage and treachery as proof of incompetence in western security.

However, there is a chance that he is just plain thoughtless, a quality in part responsible for successful Soviet penetration into British security in the 1950s. The same situation existed in Canada, the U.S. and all other western democracies, where only "coverups" seemed to be practised with any success.

Only the very simple-minded cannot comprehend that a Roman slave who escapes from the galley is not a "traitor" to the galley. Kim Philby and company, however, were people who, while enjoying the good life in the West and all the privileges, worked to destroy this very same democracy to which they owed so much.

Kim Philby and company were the ones evaluating information brought by my husband and it is they who set the negative mood toward intelligence officers who escaped from behind the Iron Curtain. Mr. Hopkinson's line of thinking greatly resembles the "appraisal" by Kim Philby of the events of September 1945.

No money was involved in the decision by Igor Gouzenko to escape and no financial remuneration was received for services to Canada (see royal commission of 1981, chaired by Mr. Justice D.C. McDonald, page 349, line 11 from the bottom).

In December 1946, he sold his life story for serialization, bought a house and lived with his family on a small personal income from books and the movie *Iron Curtain.* Only in 1962 were we granted a pension of $500 a month, for which we are forever grateful to the government of the Right Honourable John Diefenbaker.

My husband was partially disabled due to diabetes and this amount represented only $50 per month per person. (Welfare benefits at the time were larger.) Any information to the contrary is fraudulent.

As for "desecration of the Order of

THE OTTAWA CITIZEN

Svetlana Gouzenko defended her husband who defected to "our chosen country."

Canada," this has been done already. Some of those honoured by the order have their names on the list of Soviet espionage, and by their deeds have proven to be of great service to the Soviets. Sir Anthony Blunt of Britain is a classic example.

We love our chosen country and are petrified by the thought that it could crumble into enslavement. My husband was very much concerned about the security of Canada, the birthplace of all of our children.

Svetlana Gouzenko,
Mississauga

Editor's note: In 1943, Igor Sergeievich Gouzenko was named cipher clerk at the Soviet Embassy in Ottawa, where he became familiar with several spy networks operated by Soviet intelligence in Canada. Unhappy with the idea of returning to the Soviet Union, he stole documents from the embassy and defected in 1945. At first, he was not taken seriously, but eventually he and his family were given protective custody and the federal government arrested 12 spy suspects, several of whom were eventually convicted and jailed. Gouzenko and his family were given new identities, and for several decades remained under police protection. In 1946, he wrote a memoir and in 1954 a novel, The Fall of a Titan, *which won the Governor General's Award. The letter from his wife was written in response to articles which appeared after her husband's death in June 1982.*

FUN CITY

AUGUST 11, 1982

The 13th Jim Smith Fun Festival, held July 16-18 at the Talisman Motor Inn, was a highly enjoyable get-together for Jim Smiths and their families and friends. Thirty-eight Jim Smiths from 11 states and Canada took part.

We want to thank the people of Ottawa, the city officials, especially Nancy Smith, the alderman, and all those who helped make our event successful. Ottawa is a lovely city and its people are just super.

We are glad that James E. Smith of Ottawa, was persistent in his suggestions that we meet in your city. Ottawa — we tip the Jim Smith hat to you!

James H. Smith Jr., Founder-President,
The Jim Smith Society,
Camp Hill, Pa. U.S.A.

TRUDEAU'S GESTURE JUSTIFIED

AUGUST 28, 1982

Although the prime minister's one-fingered salute to a group of protesters in Salmon Arm occurred almost three weeks ago, columnists and prudish prigs across the country continue to shriek over a very minor incident.

I, for one, have had enough.

If my children were on a train and a bunch of strangers started to throw things at the windows close to where they were seated, I would — like any sensible parent — get very mad. I remain convinced that Trudeau's gesture was not only warranted, it was rather mild.

Ask yourself this question, parents: If they had been throwing things at the windows near your kids, what would you have done?

Warren Kinsella, Ottawa

CARTIER SQUARE
SEPTEMBER 1, 1982

The *Citizen* recently featured an article on the design of the provincial courthouse proposed for Cartier Square. Mayor Dewar was quoted as saying she'd rather see the National Art Gallery on Cartier Square, and the courthouse elsewhere.

Her comment reinforces the sentiment of citizens who met last year to protest the placement of the provincial courthouse on Cartier Square. Cartier Square, in the heart of Ottawa, is too valuable to use for a provincial purpose.

The courthouse would be more appropriately located on Wellington Street, beside the Supreme Court Building, with the judges' chambers overlooking the Ottawa River. That would leave Cartier Square available for the National Gallery, which badly needs a better home.

Robert L. Fancy, Ottawa

Editor's note: The courthouse went ahead on Cartier Square and the National Gallery was built on Sussex Drive at St. Patrick Street.

TAKING THE BIAS
OUT OF LANGUAGE
DECEMBER 4, 1982

Regarding the naming controversy for the Museum of Man/Humanity, the English language has changed quite a bit since Chaucer's day, and the modern electronic revolution is changing it even more.

Why is it that few "language purists" object loudly when words such as "interface" or "access" (as a verb) become common, but all hell breaks loose when 400 respected academics and concerned feminists suggest that "generic" titles such as "man" and "mankind" be changed to reflect reality?

A bias in language leads to biased research which in turn leads to policies (e.g. in pensions, housing, etc.) that may work for men but not for women. To improve the language is a beginning. What's so difficult (or threatening) about that?

B.M. Baird,
Ottawa

Editor's note: After considerable public debate, the Museum of Civilization was chosen as the name for the new museum, located in Hull.

1983

Local: Rideau Centre shopping complex opens (March); PM Trudeau canoes across Ottawa River to turn sod for new Museum of Civilization (May)

National: Statistics Canada reports jobless rate of 13.6 per cent (February); Ontario forms inquiry to investigate mysterious deaths at Toronto's Hospital for Sick Children (April); U.S. space shuttle's Canadarm first used to release and retrieve a satellite from space (June); Air Canada jet runs out of fuel but manages emergency landing at Gimli, Man. (July); PM Trudeau launches world peace initiative with six-nation European tour (November)

World: Ronald Reagan describes Soviet Union as evil empire, proposes Star Wars defence plan (March); 60-volume diary written by Adolf Hitler revealed as fraud (May); Soviets shoot down Korean jetliner, killing 269 (September); 216 marines killed in Beirut bombing (October); U.S. invades Grenada in bid to restore democracy (October)

Births: Junior hockey prospect Jason Spezza; the Teenage Mutant Ninja Turtles

Deaths: Quebec writer Gabrielle Roy; Canadian folksinger Stan Rogers; playwright Tennessee Williams; pop singer Karen Carpenter; pianist-composer Eubie Blake; boxer Jack Dempsey; TV-radio personality Arthur Godfrey; bluesman Muddy Waters; actors David Niven, Ralph Richardson and Gloria Swanson; inventor Buckminster Fuller; U.S. football legends George Halas and Bear Bryant

'BIG, BAD RUSSIANS'
JANUARY 22, 1983

In her recent letter, Meredith Van Beek wonders why we are afraid of the "Big Bad Ugly Russians. They too are people," she claims. She would like us to trust them and begin negotiating nuclear disarmament with them, beginning with a nuclear freeze now to show them we are serious.

I wonder whether Miss Van Beck knows of any Canadian or Americans who have been sent to the Northwest Territories or Alaska by their respective governments in the way that the Kremlin expels "dissidents" and "counter-revolutionaries" to Siberia?

Does she know of North Americans who are afraid of

being awakened at 3 a.m. by the RCMP or the CIA and never being heard of again? Many Russian citizens are afraid of exactly this from the KGB.

How many of her acquaintances vanished in purges when literally tens of thousands of Kulak peasants were slaughtered during the 1930s? If the Kremlin will act in this way to its own citizens, surely it would not stop any effort against its perceived enemy.

While the "capitalist imperialist" democracies of the West are far from incorruptible, they base their *raison d'être* on liberty and justice. The "people" in the Kremlin can in no way be trusted to keep their word on disarmament.

Certainly, let us not forget whom we are dealing with,

and let us not believe their propaganda about the benefits of a nuclear freeze.

Ron Resnick, Ottawa

SOVIETS ARE HUMAN TOO

FEBRUARY 2, 1983

On New Year's Eve in Montreal, Soviet goaltender Vladislav Tretiak received a standing ovation as he was recognized as the best goaltender in the world. While he was waving to the crowd, a thought hit me.

Would I like to vaporize his countrymen with nuclear bombs? The answer is a definite no. But if our country and the Soviets went to war, it would be my duty, and your duty, to press all the buttons. If Tretiak was guarding his goal in the middle of a nuclear holocaust it would be like destroying the artistic creative star of a Russian ballet.

Later in an interview, Tretiak revealed (as I suspected) that he was a normal humble athlete, a human being just like all the other NHL players or you and me. Maybe we should invite a Soviet to dinner. At least keep up the sport-cultural exchanges so we can get to know each other better.

On a New Year's Eve in the future, when Tretiak is taking his bows, I would like to cheer back, without having a black thought in my mind that some day we will have to meet, not on a hockey rink, but on a nuclear battlefield.

Wayne Toll, Nepean

WORKING GHETTOS

MARCH 9, 1983

In the recent *Citizen* article, "Study says most women trapped in job ghettos," it was revealed that more than 70 per cent of working women remain in clerical, sales, service and processing occupations. The significant part of this article was the fact that it is yet another study commissioned by the Canadian Advisory Council on the Status of Women.

I would like to see the same sort of study done on the status of men in our country. Most men are trapped in job ghettos also, only they perceive it not as a ghetto, but a reality of the working world. Most jobs are of the clerical, sales, service and processing nature.

Obviously, too, most men are not earning high salaries or most wives and mothers would not have to work. It is time the Status of Women stopped insinuating that men are to blame for our woes, and got on to the business of solving problems for both men and women.

Marian Kay, Ottawa

SOVIET INVADERS

MARCH 9, 1983

Thirty-five years ago, on Feb. 25, 1948, the Moscow-backed Communist Party of Czechoslovakia staged a *coup d'état* that brought Czechoslovakia into the Soviet orbit. In August, 1968, the Soviet Union invaded and occupied Czechoslovakia. An estimated 80,000 Soviet troops are still in Czechoslovakia, making a mockery of the Soviet-inspired world-wide movement for "peace and disarmament."

It is unprecedented irony, arrogance and hypocrisy that in the presence of these Soviet troops, a world peace conference will take place in Prague on June 15-19. It will host "representatives of the peace movement from the whole world," according to the Prague Communist daily, *Vaecerini Praha,* including some 3,000 delegates and hundreds of journalists.

The well-meaning, honest, sometimes idealistic or naive people, lulled and lured by Soviet-inspired propaganda for "peace and disarmament," should wake up. They should demand that the Soviets withdraw their troops from Czechoslovakia, Poland, Afghanistan (over 100,000 troops), East Germany, Hungary, etc. — from all 20 countries now under the Soviet oppression.

Ota Hora, Ottawa

TURF MANAGEMENT, NOT 2,4-D

APRIL 20, 1983

According to *The Citizen*, a few Ottawa aldermen seem determined to undermine the proposed turf management program and reinstate the spraying of the herbicide 2,4-D in parks.

They have obviously not grasped that if 2,4-D is used, those weeds strong enough to withstand the assault multiply rapidly. Each successive spraying contributes to greater resistance. Eventually, the parks contain weeds so tough and poison-resistant they can be eradicated only by digging them up. Continued spraying of 2,4-D therefore becomes senseless.

As for soil conditions in parks, a 1980 study by the U.S. Department of Agriculture revealed that most pesticides have the effect of either destroying or suppressing soil life. Weeds grow in poor soil; healthy turf does not. Clearly the use of 2,4-D in Ottawa parks has been a poor substitute for a well-planned, consistent program of turf management.

Neither Health and Welfare Canada nor Agriculture Canada can guarantee the safety of children in areas sprayed with 2,4-D.

It follows that these agencies will also not accept responsibility for injury. Is city council prepared to accept moral and financial liability if someone suffers the known symptoms of acute toxic poisoning from 2,4-D?

Obviously, a few aldermen would like to scuttle the turf management program under the guise of thrift. If council rejects it, the operations branch and these same aldermen will be back in two years insisting that the parks are in terrible shape and therefore we must spray 2,4-D again. It's high time council put a stop to this predictable and ridiculous cycle.

M.E. Wellar, Ottawa

PHILOSOPHY OF WORK

APRIL 27, 1983

The *Citizen* article "Genuine job seekers 'few and far between'" made me sad to think there might be a considerable number of people in Canada who have given up hope in work. I thought it would be appropriate to share some wisdom I have come across reading Joseph Conrad:

"'Work is the law. Like iron that lying idle degenerates into a mass of useless rust, like water that in an unruffled pool sickens into a stagnant and corrupt state, so without action the spirit of men turns to a dead thing, loses its force, ceases prompting us to leave some trace of ourselves on this earth.'

"The sense of the above lines does not belong to me. It may be found in the notebooks of one of the greatest artists that ever lived, Leonardo da Vinci. It has a simplicity and a truth which no amount of subtle comment can destroy."

Daniel Collison, Aylmer

BRING OUT CHILDREN — TO POISON
MAY 4, 1983

I am old. I live in a highrise. I am a statistic on a high shelf in this cement and steel filing cabinet. From my balcony I look down on the Ottawa River Parkway and bicycle path. I love the trees and birdsongs. But walking, I discovered wild flowers, stems distorted and curled in obscene death agony. There was a chemical stench.

I called the NCC: "2,4-D," they told me. "We have a mountain of the stuff. We only follow orders." It reminded me of the Nuremberg Trials.

There had been a young man down there, a new Canadian, sitting under a tree, shoes off, eating lunch from a paper bag. "Beautiful, this park," he said. "I'm bringing the kids to pick salad greens." I should have warned him but he'd gone.

I called Poison Control. "Wash all exposed skin," they told me, "including clothing and hair — immediately." For me it doesn't matter. What of the children? Now I no longer enjoy the view of children rolling and tumbling and lovers strolling.

I remember a young lad running — every step an agony, every breath sucking in air along sprayed highways, under sprayed forests — Terry Fox — a courageous innocent boy. A martyr to chemical pollution? Who knows?

Anyway, I'm tired of arguing with self-serving politicians. I'm sickened by lobbyists from giant chemical conglomerates, mouthing the same old threats — "Weeds will engulf us. Taxes will rise, parks will be destroyed."

If the young parents won't fight back — very well. It's a lovely spring day. Bring out the children, to poison.

Maggie Garrick, Ottawa

TRANSPO OFFER TOO GENEROUS
JUNE 4, 1983

I was shocked to read in *The Citizen* that OC Transpo had offered its 1,601 drivers and mechanics an 18.8-percent salary and benefit increase over two years.

Although the article went on to suggest that the settlement was reached after 12 hours of "hectic bargaining," I feel the management representatives of OC Transpo must have left the table and allowed the union to "hammer out" its own final offer.

No responsible management group could present such an extravagant offer to any group of employees when Canada is only now showing faint signs of economic recovery.

Possibly the classic summation of the whole event is the words of Rolly Jolicoeur, who was reported to have said, "I think the men will accept. If they don't they are crazy."

What right does OC Transpo have to offer such an inflationary contract when the majority of Canadians in the private and public sectors are subject to increases ranging from zero to six per cent?

And what about the many Canadian workers who have lost their jobs because they priced themselves out of world competition? Did general manager John Bonsall not wonder the effect of this settlement on the cost of bus fares and the effect on other public sector bargaining?

The Transit Commission has no choice but to accept John Bonsall's resignation.

Harry J. Martin, Ottawa

Editor's note: The negotiated agreement was rejected by the Transit Commission, which voted to reopen talks with the union, not so much because of the wage hike as the Transpo offer to pay the workers' disability insurance premiums. Eventually, the two sides agreed on a 17.5-cent-raise over two years (hiking the drivers' average pay to $12.65 an hour), with no company contribution to the insurance plan.

WHAT'S WRONG WITH ENGLISH SIGN?
AUGUST 8, 1983

Paul Boudreau sounds like an emissary of the Commission de Surveillance de la langue Française in Quebec when he condemns the Westin Hotel for using its own and proper name.

Franco-Ontarians have far more rights in Ontario than the English in Quebec. I have never heard of a Franco-Ontarian being fined for erecting a French sign on his store or front lawn. It is quite common in La Belle Province — when the sign is in English.

The Westin Hotel has provided many jobs in Ottawa and will do so for many years, which will bring revenue for both governments and the City of Ottawa. Surely it deserves commendation and not criticism!

J. Young, Ottawa

MIND-BOGGLING
AUGUST 8, 1983

Here we have another Franco-Ontarian complaining about an English-only sign in Ottawa!

The federal government wants us to believe that the nation's capital is Ottawa-Hull and that Ottawa should be bilingual. What is mind-boggling is that in half of our capital, namely Hull, English is virtually illegal.

Scott Voelzing, Ottawa

METRIC AND AIR CANADA CRASH
AUGUST 22, 1983

The editorial, "Measuring lives in metric," was to be expected. *The Citizen* has a record of triviality, incomprehension and misinformation in its treatment of Canada's change to metric measurement.

The Citizen says, in effect, that because a few incompe-

WINNIPEG FREE PRESS

Metric mix-up was the reason for a Boeing 767 jet running out of fuel and landing safely near Gimli, Man.

tents misused or misunderstood the metric gauges they were using to measure fuel in the Air Canada 767 that was forced into an emergency landing at Gimli, Manitoba, the metric system should be banned.

This logic is bizarre; should we also ban the use of prescription drugs and household chemicals because thousands of people, mostly children, are annually poisoned by them? Should we prohibit the study of physics because nuclear weapons could wipe us all out?

The editorial goes on to tell us that "all Canadians" are "confused" about metric measurement of temperature. Apparently "all Canadians" haven't been able to remember, since they were first told in April 1975, that 30°C is hot, 0°C is freezing, and -20°C is cold. After over eight years of grappling with these fearsomely difficult concepts, "all Canadians" remain "confused."

It is puzzling that during those same eight years Canadians managed to remember new telephone, car registration and bank account numbers; to remember new (and constantly changing) prices of everything from cars to hamburger, new wage scales, changing pension and unemployment benefit amounts, birth dates and bus route numbers; and how to operate complex new equipment such as video recorders, home computers, word processors and electronic cameras. Some of them can even work out their own income tax.

Yet, *The Citizen* asserts, they are still unable to grasp half-a-dozen figures related to temperature. To me this seems a gross libel on "all Canadians."

The editorial also informs us that the rationale for metric usage in trade has been undermined by what it calls the U.S. decision to "back away" from metric conversion. This assertion is demonstrably untrue: the U.S. is rapidly converting to metric, and a large proportion of Canadian exports to the U.S. are in metric.

The Citizen warns that changing to metric imperils Canadians when they fly. The inference is that if fuel was measured in imperial gallons or pounds, there would be no such risks. Is *The Citizen* seriously suggesting that no accidents have occurred as a result of the misuse of imperial measurements?

Aircraft types have changed dozens of times in the past; whole new technologies, practices, and equipment have been adopted in commercial aircraft. Where were the editorials advocating the scrapping of these innovations on the grounds of their potential hazards?

Lionel Loshak, Ottawa

BACK TO IMPERIAL?
AUGUST 24, 1983

Air Canada admits a metric mix-up was the reason why a Boeing 767 jet ran out of fuel, forcing it to a crash-land and risk the lives of 69 people aboard.

I wonder now if our federal government will reverse its drive to make Canada metric? The established world measurement for aviation is imperial, and the U.S. has now given the boot to metric in favor of the imperial foot in all sectors. Thus we can assume that the imperial system will be predominant in North America for a long time.

R.H. Luft, Guelph, Ont.

TERRIBLE MOVIES
OCTOBER 19, 1983

Movies are deteriorating to the point where many can be considered unacceptable gibberish. Producers must think the public has a very low expectation of films today; where has the quality of movies such as *Gone with the Wind* and *Casablanca* gone?

Before long the only worthwhile thing about going to the movies will be the popcorn!

Astrid Player, Ottawa

'EASY JOURNALISM'
NOVEMBER 2, 1983

A plethora of pundits feeds us "informed guesses" as to whether Prime Minister Trudeau will run in another general election.

We have had this type of "food" for months — or is it years? It has now become "easy journalism." When all else fails, return to the perennial subjects: Mr. Trudeau, the cruise missile; bilingualism, ethnic minorities; the rape of the North, etc.

Enough! Mr. Trudeau will not be re-elected. Just look at the recent Gallup figures!

Betty Irwin, Ottawa

Editor's note: Mr. Trudeau resigned the following year, and his successor, John Turner, was soundly defeated in the September 1984 election by Brian Mulroney's Conservatives.

COMMON CAUSE
NOVEMBER 9, 1983

I fought back feelings of self-conscious embarrassment when I walked down Bank Street to Parliament Hill to protest the testing of cruise missiles over Canada. My self-consciousness stemmed partly from the fact that I had no group with whom to walk.

I didn't come from Lanark, I didn't belong to the Marxist-Leninists, nor to the Gays of Ottawa, nor to Carleton

University. I was embarrassed by the simple-minded slogans like "Peace Now" and "No Nukes," shouted all around me by marchers who I assume were RCMP dressed in circus garb, and were there to discredit the march. Surely no serious protester would deliberately set out to alienate possible support.

But back to the groups and their banners. Is it really necessary for each group to identify itself? Isn't it possible, at such a time, to submerge special interests, to dispense with self-proclamation and to make common cause merely with other human beings? This might be one occasion when the whole is more important than its parts.

Helen Deachman, Ottawa

VIEWS ON NEPEAN
DECEMBER 7, 1983

Inspired by *The Citizen's* coast-to-coast survey of Canadian awareness of five-year-old Nepean, I conducted my own underground poll on the Bloor Street subway.

One man thought Nepean was a flavor of high-tech ice cream. Another said it was a place for OC Transpo buses to turn around. A young woman said it was a dormitory run by an American. She thought his name was Liberty Bell. A bright young student said it was a buffer to keep Ottawa from running into the real world. An old man said it was a giant sponge to soak up civil servants.

Orland French, Toronto

1984

Local: Regional council gives approval in principle to idea of a 911 emergency service (July); Would-be robbers shoot Nepean police officers Robin Easey and Ralph Erfle in Bayshore Shopping Centre parking garage (September)
National: U.S. cruise missile tested for first time over western Canada (March); Canada wins best-ever 44 medals, including 10 gold, at Los Angeles Olympics (August); PCs under Brian Mulroney win election landslide over Liberals and John Turner (September); 7,000 migrating caribou drown crossing Quebec rivers (October); Marc Garneau first Canadian in space (October)
World: Gunman kills 20 in rampage at McDonald's restaurant in California (July); Indian prime minister Indira Gandhi murdered by two of her own security guards (October); World rallies to help starving millions in Ethiopia (October); More than 2,000 die in toxic gas leak in Bhopal, India (December)
Births: Prince Harry; teen pop singer Britney Spears
Deaths: Bandleader Count Basie; Canadian broadcaster Gordon Sinclair; R&B singers Marvin Gaye and Willie Mae (Big Mama) Thornton; photographer Ansel Adams; film directors François Truffaut and Sam Peckinpah; writers Truman Capote, Lillian Hellman and J.P. Priestley; actors Richard Burton, James Mason, Jackie Coogan and Johnny Weismuller; McDonald's founder Ray Kroc; Soviet leader Yuri Andropov; jogging guru James Fixx; polling pioneer George Gallup

CLEAR INSANITY
JANUARY 4, 1984

A few weeks ago in these columns I asked rather rhetorically, referring to the arms race and risk of nuclear war, whether we all were mad.

Now I learn that at the recently held 40th reunion of the Los Alamos physicists — Rabi, Teller, Alvarez, and others — Dr. Victor Weisskopf described the arms race as "a virulent case of a collective mental disease." What else can it be?

Hundreds of millions of people are supinely letting themselves be referred to as not even identifiable statistics within the term "megadeaths" — as though all of us were grains of rice to be boiled.

This is what our leaders, our presidents and prime ministers and secretaries-general and generals — our Joneses! — are doing to us: Weren't we all shocked by the Jonestown suicides? And just what, other than size, is the difference between Jonestown and the promised nuclear war?

We all must be collectively diseased to agree to go so uncomplainingly into personal agony and universal extinction.

Charles Haines, Ottawa

NEPEAN BYLAW
JANUARY 7, 1984

Mayor Ben Franklin and the Council of Nepean the

Prurient have, somewhat deviously, arranged to stop the spread of topless dancers in that community.

Until now, people not interested in that sort of thing have always gone in terror of being stopped at gunpoint on streets and marched into the Silver Dollar (the only place currently involved). Armed thugs sit at their table while they order a meal they do not want and hold their eyelids open so that they cannot avoid seeing the unveiled mammary glands of the strippers.

Mayor Franklin "suspects" (hopes?) "the bylaw will be a model for other municipalities which have been unsuccessful in controlling this kind of activity." (In revolutionary France, there was an offence "suspected of being suspected" which Mayor Franklin might well include in another bylaw). It is extremely probable that, for example, the less-sanctimonious City Fathers of Hull know that if people do not wish to look at naked ladies in that city, no one will force them to do so.

It is understood that Nepean Council is also considering banning the underwear section of the Eaton and Simpson-Sears catalogues.

Cy Whiteley, Ottawa

Editor's note: Nepean's bylaw, still on the books, limits the number of strip bars and adult bookstores in the city to one each. The Silver Dollar remains in business on Merivale Road.

SLEEPY NO MORE

JANUARY 10, 1984

I saw in the Montreal *Gazette* recently that American TV newsman Dan Rather called Ottawa "a backwoods capital."

I grew up in Ottawa and that's what it was. What a charming little city. I think it was what the Fathers of Confederation intended. "Let's put the capital in a sleepy little lumber town out of the way where it won't interfere too much with the nation's business," I can hear them saying.

But alas, Dan Rather is wrong. Now the city is a gigantic circumlocution office, as Dickens would put it, where scores of thousands of public servants study "the art of perceiving — how not to do it."

There is nothing backwards about the scale of this operation.

John Brinckman, Way's Mills, Que.

PROPHETIC VOICE

JANUARY 18, 1984

A Department of Communications spokesman said on CBC Radio that, by the late 1980s, a new system of car telephones would be available, operating on 64 channels and, initially, costing around $1,200 a year.

Arthur C. Clarke, a well-known science fiction writer (*2001, A Space Odyssey*), addressed the United Nations on World Communications Day, May 17, 1983. He said: "Commencing in the 1990s, more and more businessmen, well-heeled tourists and virtually all newspersons will be carrying attaché case-sized transceiver units. These will permit direct communication with their homes or offices via the most convenient satellite. As the sets becomes cheaper, smaller and more universal, they will make travellers totally independent of national communications systems. No longer will news gatherers be at the mercy of censors or inefficient, sometimes non-existing, postal and telegraph services."

Clarke was the first to think of communications satellites, though he did not patent his idea. So what he says, however apparently far-fetched, should be taken seriously by people and companies it could affect.

Cy Whiteley, Ottawa

WOMEN LOSE PENSIONS

JANUARY 30, 1984

Reporter Peter Maser, in "Why [justice minister Mark] MacGuigan wants to ease the agony of divorce," says American studies have shown that, in the 12 months after a divorce, a woman's standard of living drops an average 73 per cent.

Indeed, the Canadian government is considering recognizing pensions under its jurisdiction as family assets to be divided equally when the marriage ends. But where a member of the Armed Forces or the federal public service has already retired, there should be no delay in recognizing pension income as a family asset to be divided equally when the marriage ends. At present:

• Women suffer indignity, loss of home and independence, sometimes after 40 years of marriage.

• Society has to support these demeaned women when courts are not directed to recognize their contribution to these pensions.

• Provinces vary in legislation pertaining to the splitting of family assets — Ontario lags far behind all western provinces in clinging to historical bias and social attitudes.

Thus in the matter of pension income under federal jurisdiction, the courts reflect the bias of the province in which a divorcee petition is heard.

I have been married for 40 years and raised and educated six children. From 1945, I moved the family from B.C. to the Yukon, to Ontario and Quebec as my husband served with the Armed Forces. He took his pension in 1965.

Over the next 16 years, my husband acquired a government of Canada public service pension and retired at age 60 in 1981. He was an alcoholic and in 1974 had left the family while four of the children were still dependent upon me.

I obtained a court order for support which remained in default most of the time. In 1981, my husband petitioned for divorce in Ontario. I now receive $400 per month. I am thousands of dollars in debt. Friends and relatives across the country have provided shelter but I have forfeited identity, privacy and independence.

I live from two suitcases, try to stay out of people's way and have sometimes lived out of my 1973 Toyota. I don't even have the use of the latter now. At 63 (the same age as my husband), I am unemployed (with no benefits). He is retired with two pensions under federal jurisdiction.

Women deserve better than this and the solution is available to the federal government.

Claudia Matheson Paton, Ottawa

MARKET CHANGED

FEBRUARY 13, 1984

The fuss over the rainbow design painted on the front of the Scarboro Fair building in the Byward Market is not about to lead to a pot of gold.

Who is offended by this flare of imagination? A friend who recently returned to Ottawa after a long absence asked what had become of the Byward Market as he remembered it. What were all those people doing hawking macramé tow ropes for Volvos and Indian cheesecloth where once there had been local people selling their produce?

And what was a multi-storey parking garage doing smack dab in the centre of the market? What had become of the stores that sold clothes for working people? What of the numerous pawn shops?

My friend remarked that the area now reminded him of the trendy areas in so many other Canadian cities: Gastown in Vancouver, the Historic Properties in Halifax etc. It was not at all as he recalled it during his childhood.

In his letter to *The Citizen*, John Carroll calls the Byward Market "a very sensitive historic design environment." But then why does the market reflect less and less of its history? Perhaps the answer lies in Mr. Carroll's remark about "the continued positive evolution of this irreplaceable heritage asset." This comment smacks of Orwell's Big Brother and the work of rewriting history performed by the Ministry of Truth.

When I showed my friend the inside of the striking market building that houses a Mexican restaurant, complete with a fake waterfall, he said it struck him as a caricature of the whole "new" Byward Market: all style and no substance.

Christopher Bain, Ottawa

SORRY TRUDEAU WENT
MARCH 23, 1984

I would like to express my sadness about Pierre Trudeau's decision to step down as leader of this country. He lifted Canada out of her provincialism and on to the world stage as a force for the good.

Cornelia Fuykschot, Gananoque

SINTARIO NEXT?
MARCH 24, 1984

Premier William Davis's devilish scheme for ridding Ontario of the Mafia gradually unfolds. Instead of simply talking about organized crime like the RCMP, his idea is to make sin a government monopoly, then outsell and out-advertise the crooks.

Can one imagine Frank Costello or Lucky Luciano trying to compete with Lotto 6/49? The Sintario move began years ago with the provincial cigarette tax addiction, followed naturally by a provincial monopoly on booze. Gambling wasn't far behind. By now, much of the population of Ontario is engaged in the sale and processing of Lotto 6/49 tickets.

"Rubtario is in the works," says Bill, with his shy but wicked smile, "we'll have the girls off the streets and into the civil service before you can say OPP." Asked about the possibility of Pornfario, Bill blushed with his shy but wicked blush. "Bette and I have been talking about something educational," he whispered.

Mafia boss Unlucky Luciferano, as he caught a plane for Quebec with his family, was heard to shout, "Curse you, Bill Davis." With Unlucky gone, the RCMP can now come out of hiding and begin barn-burning and commie-chasing once more.

James Harrington, Deep River

FALLING DOLLAR
APRIL 2, 1984

Bank of Canada Governor Gerald Bouey's fortitude in standing up to the facile arguments for an even more devalued Canadian dollar by Minister of Finance [Marc] Lalonde cannot receive enough commendation.

Debasement of the "coinage" has been the most popular recourse of irresponsible and/or bankrupt regimes. It discriminates against the thrifty while favoring the profligate — among them governments which repay their debts in funds worth a fractions of those they had borrowed.

If the government allows our dollar — already down around 30 per cent compared to $1.06 U.S. a few years ago — to go through the floor, our country's private sector bor-

rowers as well as the public ones will be saddled with higher (up to 40 per cent to make up for a 30-per-cent devaluation) interest and capital payments on loans contracted in the last decade or two in U.S., as well as hard European currencies or Japanese yen.

Against this long-term financial burden, the short-term (until the election?) gain in exports, at artificially reduced bargain prices for our commodities, will prove illusory. Our dollar's often vaunted relative strength against European currencies has also evaporated.

Our dollar has not only dropped in terms of U.S. funds but the mighty greenback itself, also facing an election nightmare, has dropped about nine per cent against European currencies and the yen this year.

M.L. De B. Backendorff, Ottawa

PERK FOR RICH
JUNE 13, 1984

The universal day-care system promoted in *The Citizen* by the Canadian Day Care Advocacy Association would only marginally improve the service for those who really need it, such as single parents and low-income families who need two incomes for life's necessities.

But it would be rather self-serving to those individuals who feel it is not only their God-given right to bear children, but then to have the government assume responsibility of looking after such children, while these same "parents" pursue lucrative careers, at taxpayer's expense. In my estimation this would be downright robbery.

The user-pay system already in place might need expanding and some modifications to help those who really need it. However, the user should continue to pay. Universality in this case is not the answer.

W.A. Moran, Kanata

HOUSEWIVES' PLIGHT
JUNE 20, 1984

Regarding Elizabeth Thompson's article, "Thousands of housewives turning to drugs for relief," one of the reasons for the "enormous amount of depression" in housewives is the terminology of her article. The word housewife is used four times in the first seven paragraphs to distinguish this type of person from a group referred to as "women who work." The implication is painfully clear: One group works and the other does not.

Sure, we all know that looking after children and a home is work, but it is not recognized as a legitimate job. If anyone disputes this, try to name any other job that requires a 12-16 hour day, a seven-day work week, and offers virtually no annual leave.

The lack of any real status is humiliating. Over time, work that has no glamour and no mystique, and is not even recognized as legitimate work, erodes one's feeling of self-worth. The void is filled with depression.

A second major reason for the distress of housewives and stay-at-home parents, not even mentioned in the article, is that full-time child-rearing has got to be one of the toughest jobs. I have experienced life in both camps: as a professional architect for 10 years and for the past two years as a professional housewife pursuing two pre-school children full-time, plus all the housework (well, most of it.)

Another twist is that I happen to be male, which makes it no easier. As a partner in an architectural firm, I used to put in many a long day, even the occasional 80-hour week. Now as a househusband (or whatever a male housewife is called), I find the average work week is 80 hours.

The stresses at home are different from those at the office; shorter in duration but much more intense emotionally.

As an architect I can't remember a single day when I got exasperated enough with my fellow workers to scream at them not just once but perhaps three or four times in a single day. Such is the life of the everyday housewife. Of course, this kind of tension dissipates quickly after the blow-up. You don't go around carrying a grudge against your toddler for the next five months.

Yet the incessant presence and charmingly unreasonable demands of young children must, in the long run, affect the parent exposed to this hazardous job condition. After only two years of exposure, I now am frequently troubled by feelings of "isolation and lack of support" and occasionally by feelings of "anxiety and depression."

I don't think it's possible to completely avoid these feelings when exposed to young unrelenting minds for 12 hours a day. But when I flop down at the end of a 12-hour shift, exhausted from forcing out more energy, patience and creativity than I readily possess, it would be some comfort to feel, instead of second class, that I am part of the elite of society which is doing one of the most important jobs that there is.

Stuart Kinmond, Ottawa

LIBERAL PATRONAGE
JULY 23, 1984

As expected, "the deal" between Mr. Trudeau and Mr. Turner has been made public. The list of appointments to the Senate and other lucrative spots has been announced. A lot of the hogs who have been feeding at the public trough will do so in perpetuity.

We all know the Liberals have been notorious for rewarding their faithful. Some of the most inept ministers in a completely inept government will continue to run this country from behind the scenes. Mr. Trudeau has left, thank heavens, but his pork barrel runneth over.

The only way to resolve this blatant abuse of public funds is to put the Liberals away for a long time. Mr. Turner has promised us nothing new, and has said that Mr. Lalonde's last two budgets were a step in the right direction. Canadians would be fools to renew the mandate of a government that has been a disaster for years. Let's give Brian Mulroney a chance to get us out of this mess. It may be our last chance!

Mrs. J. Kennedy, Ottawa

1985

Local: Security guard slain as three Armenians raid Turkish Embassy in Ottawa (March); Julie Elizabeth Lyon is Ottawa's first test-tube baby (June); 26 Ottawans among 329 killed when Air India jet explodes near Ireland (June)

National: Ontario inquiry exonerates nurse Susan Nelles in baby deaths at Toronto's Hospital for Sick Children (January); Defence Minister Robert Coates resigns after *Citizen* report that he visited a red-light bar during NATO tour of West Germany (February); One-legged runner Steve Fonyo, 19, completes 8,000-km, 14-month marathon across Canada (May); U.S. icebreaker *Polar Sea* enters Canadian Arctic without permission (August)

World: Mikhail Gorbachev becomes Soviet president (March); State of emergency declared amid escalating turmoil in South Africa (July); Earthquake kills thousands in Mexico City (September); Arab terrorists hijack Mediterranean luxury liner *Achille Lauro* (October)

Deaths: Writer E.B. White; painter Marc Chagall; actors Orson Welles, Yul Brenner, Rock Hudson and Ruth Gordon; Robert Welch, founder of John Birch Society; jazz saxman Zoot Simms; seismologist Charles Richter; poet Robert Graves; singer Ricky Nelson

COTTON BEST
JANUARY 16, 1985

I note with sadness another sign of the decaying bedding habits of our population: the impossibility of obtaining plain white 100-per-cent cotton sheets. At Christmas, I searched in vain for them through the Eaton's Centre in Toronto.

It has been suggested that pure cotton wrinkles and requires ironing, while polyester does not. Big deal! What are a few wrinkles compared to the oily smoothness of plastic? Doesn't anyone care that cotton is natural fibre, whereas polyester is made from chemicals? Do you want your children sleeping in beds lined with chemicals?

Ah, the thrill of fresh, new cotton sheets and pillowcases or the soft, reassuring comfort of older, more experienced ones. With time, polyester sheets form little roll-up balls, giving them a texture as if embossed in braille. No wonder people have insomnia and the divorce rate is skyrocketing. We note that the gradual displacement of pure 100-per-cent cotton by polyester coincided with 16 years of socialist rule by Pierre Trudeau and his clique. Perhaps Brian Mulroney will allow small business to restore our priceless heritage.

Roger Taguchi, Ottawa

LET THEM SUE
MARCH 18, 1985

The recent trial of Ernst Zundel has forced the press and the legal system to consider the moral and ethical issues of giving a crank the ability to disseminate his posi-

THE CANADIAN PRESS

The media should reconsider how much coverage they give to the messages of cranks such as Ernst Zundel, a letter-writer said.

tions to an audience far more massive than would ordinarily be possible. The issue is serious, for we all know, looking back to the Second World War, what propaganda is capable of.

Section 15 of the Canadian Charter of Rights and Freedoms comes into effect in about a month. It guarantees the rights of minorities under the law without discrimination by race, colour, creed, religion, and so on.

Perhaps for future cases, in order to give full meaning to this section, the government of Canada should consider a few reforms. Perhaps the best possible reform would be to the laws under which a disseminator of false news could be prosecuted. It is not hard to conclude the laws in their current state are not altogether effective against hate literature.

The Law Reform Commission should consider the possibility of group defamation. Should a group identifiable as a minority within the meaning of current legislation be defamed, where the defamation is known to be false through judicial notice or generally accepted knowledge, it should constitute a group libel and its disseminator should be subject to a civil lawsuit by representatives of the defamed group. Criminal action rarely provides adequate deterrence.

Russell Molot, Ottawa

Editor's note: In 1985, in a private charge laid by a Holocaust survivor, Toronto Nazi sympathizer Ernst Zundel was tried and convicted of "wilfully spreading false news" for publishing a pamphlet in which he claimed the mass extermination of Jews by the Nazis was a hoax created by Zionists to obtain financial compensation from Germany. Two years later, the Ontario Court of Appeal ordered a new trial because of legal errors by the trial judge. But Zundel was convicted a second time in 1988 and sentenced to nine months in jail. He appealed again, and in 1992 the Supreme Court of Canada ruled the obscure law used to convict him was unconstitutional and an unacceptable violation of free speech. In essence, the court decided more harm is done to society by keeping "false news" laws on the books than by allowing Nazi apologists to reach their tiny audience.

WAKE UP TO REAGAN DANGER

APRIL 25, 1985

If at this late date Canadians are not frightened by President Ronald Reagan, they have not been listening to him. Like Senator Joseph McCarthy 30 years ago, Mr. Reagan has found a soft spot in the American self-image, the hunger to regain self-respect and to be Number One again, after a series of reverses and humiliations at home and abroad. He is clearly very successful in this exploitation.

One of Mr. Reagan's more bizarre utterances lately has been the comparison of the murderous Contras in Nicaragua, led by ex-Somoza military aide Enrique Bermudez, to the Founding Fathers of the United States. Such a statement could be a sick joke; but the president means it.

And now Star Wars! Not a single reputable scientist and very few military analysts think such a scheme has the slightest chance of averting a nuclear catastrophe, supposing that one doesn't happen by miscalculation any day now. But the Canadian government, apparently locked into some Second World War mental time warp and hypnotized by the Reagan charm, bids fair to sneak us into this crazy scenario.

Eminent scientists such as Carl Sagan and our own David Suzuki remind us that we are in an exponentially more destructive era than that of Dresden or Hiroshima. Will lethargic Canadians ever wake up to such danger?

Derek McDermot, Richmond, B.C.

TORTURING THE SICK

APRIL 25, 1985

I read your article "Civic Hospital rejects smoking ban" with disbelief. They would permit not only patients but selfish, inconsiderate and insensitive visitors to smoke in so-called designated areas that are not properly ventilated and sometimes wedged between patients' rooms.

Recently in the cancer treatment ward, I had to offer to shove a foul-smelling cigar up a visitor's nose to get him to move out of the corridor and into the smoking area. He didn't have the decency to put it out and others in the vicinity jumped to his defence. There is a sunroom about 240 feet away with windows that can be opened and a door that can be closed to keep smoke from spreading through the ward. It has been designated a non-smoking area.

I hope that none of those who have the power to implement this ban have ever had to sit in a hospital room and watch a loved one retch and vomit due to their sensitivity to acrid clouds of cigar and cigarette smoke drifting into the room, especially on treatment day.

How much more proof do we need to gather about the

harmful effects of smoking, not only on the ones who exercise the right to smoke, but on the innocent non-smokers, before a "healing" institution has the guts to stand up and be counted?

R.B. Watts, Nepean

Editor's note: The Civic, now part of the merged Ottawa Hospital, banned all smoking from its buildings in the early '90s. The General was the first to outlaw smoking for visitors in 1985, but still allows patients to smoke in two specially ventilated rooms.

SENIORS PROTEST
JUNE 17, 1985

Regarding the federal budget proposal to partially de-index seniors' pensions, this writer cannot recall any time during the 1984 election campaign when Brian Mulroney had a deep concern that Canada has an acute shortage of rich people.

Nor do I recall him promising that if elected he would use pensioners, the poor and those on fixed incomes as stepping stones to improve the lot of the rich and provide the investor, the profiteer and the affluent with a $500,000 lifetime capital gains exemption. Bus fares, telephone, hydro, insurance rates, rents, food prices, fruit and vegetables, sales tax on the necessities of life, etc. continue to rise; yet the Mulroney government has the audacity to further reduce the incomes of those least able to afford it.

The Mulroney government should be long remembered by us as the government that deigned that the middle class be reduced to the poor class, the poor class reduced to poverty or below the poverty level and the rich be made richer.

A.D. Campbell, Ottawa

BOGUS ISSUE
JULY 10, 1985

I know the dog days of summer often lead to over-emphasis of the frivolous in the newspaper business, but all the attention to the bogus "issue" of Old Coke vs. New Coke really takes the cake. Did any of you newspaper people ever stop to think that while you were concentrating on such rubbish, real issues were being ignored?

You know what I mean. You know the story you're all afraid to touch. When one newspaper in this country works up the courage to go after Seagram's for taking the purple velvet marbles bag off Crown Royal, I'll know the fourth estate has regained its concern for the human condition.

Dan Turner, Ottawa

A MONSTROSITY
JULY 29, 1985

I find it difficult to understand how people can get all worked up about the preservation of a monstrosity like the Daly building. Perhaps if it were called the "Acme Enterprises Building" it would disappear without a whimper — except maybe from a few heritage zealots.

So, out of respect for those who want to preserve histor-ical names, why can't we agree to remove this eyesore and name its replacement the "Daly Building?" Or, how about "Daly Park?" Or, looking down the road, the "Daly subway station?"

J. Paul Maisonneuve, Ottawa

A VIEW FROM THE PUBLIC SCHOOLS
SEPTEMBER 9, 1985

To the continuing debate on school funding, I offer this view from the public school classroom: During the past school year, the 26 of us met at nine every morning. Two were Vietnamese, one Malaysian. Three were Lebanese Christians, another Palestinian. One young woman was an Egyptian Muslim, and a young man an Iranian Baha'i whose father is imprisoned in Tehran, a victim of religious intolerance. Another was a Rastafarian from Jamaica. Three others were, in part, North American Indians. The remaining dozen were of mixed and varied European extraction. I was their teacher, an Irish Catholic.

Together we were a Grade 11 English class at Rideau High School in Ottawa. This was not a group hand-picked to reflect a particularly rich piece of the Canadian cultural mosaic. This class just happened; this is public education. The separate school may also offer a varied ethnic mix, but it is by its very nature much less diverse in the religious sense.

Many of these students were Catholic, and I don't think their faith was shaken or weakened by the experience. In fact, I think they may have learned a tolerance, an understanding, even a love for the others.

They, and the young woman who was New Apostolic, and the young man who was Pentecostal, indeed all of them, may have found in others a touchstone for their own faith. We certainly found that most faiths are based on common values, and there were many more things that drew us together than ever drove us apart.

Don McCormick, Gloucester

ON LATE PARENTING
SEPTEMBER 12, 1985

Of late there has been a glut of articles in the newspapers and magazines attesting to the joys of late parenting. Your article, "Rejuvenated dad enthuses over joys of late blooming fatherhood," provided another dreary testimony.

Though we are aware of this burgeoning trend, it hardly seems worthy of so much media hype. Fatherhood is indeed a joy, but many of us in the same age bracket as the Mr. Winfrey featured in your article can remember when we were in our 20s experiencing parenthood.

Then, the Mr. Winfreys of society would not allow child-rearing into the realms of acceptable social conversation. Even to allude to the fact that we had children was a definite invitation to social ostracism.

Now, it seems, Mr. Winfrey and his friends have proceeded to reinvent parenthood.

Parenting at any age is likely to have its best of times and worst of times and to suggest that older fathers give and receive more within the relationship is a self-satisfied naive assumption.

Perhaps it is more relaxed to father without the stress of lean finances, but children can learn and grow from the realization that financial resources are not unlimited, that their parents have needs too, and that they are each but one person in a family, not mini-gods.

Holly Kritsch, Nepean

MIRABEL FOLLY
OCTOBER 9, 1985

After reading the article on the continuing saga of Mirabel Airport, I have a suggestion that not only finds an appropriate use for the site but also addresses the long-standing dispute with surrounding farmers, poor ground access from Montreal and Ottawa, and perhaps also some of the country's fiscal problems — conversion of at least half of the building into a world-class casino.

Instead of trekking to Las Vegas, northeastern Americans could simply jump on a budget flight, land at Mirabel, check into the existing CP hotel, and spend their sinking American dollars on Canadian-built roulette tables and slot machines (accepting only Canadian gold Maple Leaf coins, of course). European travellers would be strongly tempted to land first at Mirabel, spend their sterling, francs, lira and marks, and reap their earnings before trekking on to Tahrahna and its $4 cappuccinos.

I suspect that enough income would soon be generated to finance a privatized high-speed bullet train to Montreal (Bombardier, of course), Ottawa (UTDC please) and maybe even Toronto (thereby obviating the need for expansion of Pearson Airport or resurrection of Pickering).

Although all Canadians would benefit from this idea — even if they are not allowed into the casino — the area farmers should be offered free equity in the operation. Within months, they would have the money to buy back their farms, open the restaurants and nightclubs the area so badly needs, and maybe even franchise the operation to Expo '86 in '87.

Cargo handling as Mirabel's solution? It is such a typically Canadian, lame-duck response to a unique opportunity to have a whole lot of fun.

Edward Leman, Ottawa

Editor's note: Needless to say, Mr. Leman's idea was ignored by the authorities, who eventually converted the $1.5-billion Mirabel complex from an international airport to a terminal for cargo and charter flights in 1997.

MR. ROBBER, GIVE BACK OUR VCR
NOVEMBER 11, 1985

I'm a nine-year-old boy. Friday, Oct. 18, at two in the morning, you cut my locked door. You entered my apartment. You put a knife on my throat to keep me silent. My parents were sleeping. Then you took away our VCR machine. I was not hurt but I was terrified. I was shaking and could not speak to my parents for a while.

Dear sir, my parents work very hard daily. With minimum salary, they saved money for 19 months. They bought the machine for me and for my four sisters, from two to 12 years old, so we can watch some children's movies.

Sir, you are a man, you can work. You can save money. You can put aside $1,000 to buy the recorder or anything you want. My father does not make big money, but he can make big things for us. Why can't you do what he did? Why did you take away our machine?

Sir, the snow time is coming. We cannot play outside all day. It is very cold out there. In our apartment, we have nothing left. Only sadness and sorrow. Only some pencils and comic books on the floor.

We suffered much in our former land. Why should we suffer again in this lovely city? The city of a giant country where children can have real happiness.

Dear sir, you may keep the machine and enjoy it for a while. Then please give it back to us. Christmas is coming. We do not know when my parents will be able to afford to buy it again. Maybe never, maybe in four years. My older sister will then be 16. She then may be able to go to work. But that will take so long.

Sir, we are waiting for you. We imagine that you are approaching our door. You put the machine on the doorstep and just leave. We do not know you but you know us. We do not know where you live. But you know where we are living. It will be very easy for you to give us back our machine.

Dear sir, we will forgive you for what you have done to us, knife-on-throat. Christ and Buddha will forgive you the day you bring back the machine. For us, you still are a gentleman. Thank you for reading these lines. Please give us back our machine.

Nguyen Cung, Ottawa

ON SACRIFICE IN WAR
NOVEMBER 18, 1985

I am not normally given to flag-waving, but I watched the TV coverage of the colorful Remembrance Day ceremonies at the Cenotaph in Ottawa.

Through jumbled emotions, the memory reverts to England, 1939. They were Royal Navy boy recruits, one named Tom East, the other Tom West. HMS St. Vincent, a Royal Navy barracks in Gosport just across the harbour from Portsmouth, took raw recruits 15 to 16 years old and, after one year of intensive training, graduated well-skilled, all-purpose seamen regarded as the elite of the Royal Navy's lower deck. The training was demanding, the discipline physically brutal. The food was atrocious, the entire environment a massive culture shock.

Into all of this came East and West, selected to the same class of 40 boys. T. East and T. West, it was so convenient for the military mind. "Need two volunteers to clean the latrines." No response. "East and West, front and centre," would bark the petty officer. An object accidentally dropped overboard, "East and West, over you go."

Then came the semantic nicknames T. East and T. West. It was inevitable, they became "Teast and Twest." Oddly enough, they didn't resent the torment or each other. They became good friends. They were inseparable.

War was declared on Sept. 3, 1939. Tom East and Tom West were assigned to *HMS Barham*, one of the mightiest battleships in the British fleet. East and West, numbers one and two respectively, on the same gun crew. East and West assigned to the same watch.

HMS Barham wreaked havoc with the Italian fleet, captured merchant shipping, took part in massive bombardments and shore landings. Tom East and Tom West grew up fast. They were a proud, integral part of an awesome fighting unit. Then one day, some time in 1940, *HMS Barham* was cruising the Mediterranean off the coast of Libya. An Italian submarine lurking submerged nearby fired a string of torpedoes.

HMS Barham erupted from the water, torn asunder by the violent explosions in her ammunition holds. Within minutes she sank, gurgling in her death throes and taking over 900 of her devoted crew with her. Today her remains lie on the bottom of the Mediterranean. Somewhere deep within her, rest two fine, young seamen, Tom East and Tom West. Teast and Twest, the inseparables. Both gave up their life at the ripe old age of 16 years.

Time passes, carefree cruise ships now crisscross that Mediterranean water. But the memory of East and West remains strong, as does the enormity of their sacrifices.

At least for me it does because I was one of the 38 others in Class No. 72 back there in 1939 and "I shall remember them."

Dennis McDermott,
Ottawa

1986

Local: Mitel Corp. purchased by British Telecommunications Ltd. for $320 million (January); Closing of Rideau Hall grounds to public sparks outcry (May); Ottawa surgeon Wilbert Keon makes Canadian medical history by implanting artificial heart into 41-year-old Orléans woman (May); Record 300,000 turn out for Canada Day celebrations on Parliament Hill (July)

National: Dollar sinks below 70 cents US for first time (January); Prince Charles and Princess Diana open Expo '86 in Vancouver (May); Ontario doctors end 25-day strike, longest in Canadian history, conceding that they underestimated public anger (July); Lifeboats carrying 155 Tamil refugees come ashore in Newfoundland (August)

World: Space shuttle *Challenger* explodes after takeoff, killing all seven astronauts (January); Ferdinand Marcos flees Philippines; Corazon Aquino elected PM (February); Jean-Claude (Baby Doc) Duvalier flees Haiti (February); Accident at Chernobyl nuclear plant in Ukraine releases deadly radiation across eastern Europe (April)

Births: Twin actresses Mary-Kate and Ashley Olsen

Deaths: NDP leader Tommy Douglas; actors Cary Grant and James Cagney; sculptor Henry Moore; writers Simone de Beauvoir, Jorge Luis Borges, Bernard Malamud and Theodore H. White; jazzmen Teddy Wilson and Benny Goodman; Scientology founder L. Ron Hubbard; Swedish prime minister Olaf Palme; painter Georgia O'Keefe; (Poppa) Joe Brown, patriarch of singing Family Brown; film director Otto Preminger; French playwright Jean Genet

THE INS AND OUTS OF OUR TIMES
FEBRUARY 4, 1986

I recently picked up my copy of *The Citizen* on the doorstep, walked past my cat, opened the front door, and entered my hallway. This meant that I was in and the cat was out. In my favourite easy chair, I read, "What's hot, What's not" in the People section. I learned that panels of experts are in and many pushy individuals are out.

Suddenly there was scratching at my door. In my haste to finish the article, I carried the paper with me and opened the door. Imagine my chagrin when I realized the cat had darted past me and somehow the door had locked on its own! This meant that now the cat was in and both I and *The Citizen* were out.

I ran next door and tried phoning some of the panel's losers: Cyndi Lauper, Madonna, agents for bulk food, acupuncture, running, and anyone dealing in sequin tops or stirrup pants. There were no replies. All were, in fact, out.

I then tried phoning some of the "in crowd:" Princess Diana, Flora MacDonald and folks in charge of non-surgical facelifts, Volvo 760s, winking jewels, Thinsulate, massages, flying cheap (?), blue margaritas, mesquite barbecues, dhurri rugs, faux finishes and faux paws . . . er . . . pauses. There were no replies, although, technically, they were in.

And so I still have a problem as I live with my neighbours. The questions remain: Am I out? Forever? Is my cat in? Is *The Citizen* out? Are ins out and are outings in? Are extra-inning games out? And what is to become of my cat, Indearah?

Dan Doyle, Nepean

MEIGHEN STATUE OVERDUE
FEBRUARY 11, 1986

The passing last year (at age 103) of Isabel Meighen, widow of Arthur Meighen, twice prime minister of Canada in the '20s, should act as a reminder to the government.

A previous government commissioned statues of those implacable foes, W. L. Mackenzie King and Arthur Meighen, for erection on Parliament Hill. The King statue is now in place. The Meighen statue, according to press reports quoting those who have seen it, is "completely unacceptable" and will never be erected. It is hidden away somewhere.

Recently Public Works announced the commission of a statue of the Right Honourable John Diefenbaker to be erected on the west lawn of the Hill. Not a mention of Mr. Meighen. Is this some kind of an under-the-table trade-off?

A new statue of Mr. Meighen should be commissioned now. Though a failed politician, Mr. Meighen was considered by many of those who knew him and heard him to be the most brilliant mind ever to grace Parliament Hill. He deserves his place on the Hill.

Garrett J. O'Neill, Ottawa

Editor's note: A statue of Arthur Meighen, briefly prime minister twice in the 1920s, was sculpted in 1967 to celebrate Canada's centennial. But it was never unveiled on Parliament Hill. Politicians of the day considered it too "avant-garde" — former prime minister John Diefenbaker described it as "the greatest monstrosity ever produced, a mixture of Ichabod Crane and Daddy Longlegs." As a result, the statue spent 20 years in storage before being adopted by St. Marys, a town near the rural southwestern Ontario hamlet where Mr. Meighen was born. It stands in the town's main park, where it has become something of a conversation piece.

NO AID FOR HURT MAN

FEBRUARY 13, 1986

Recently I fractured my leg when I slipped on ice while walking on Voyageur Avenue in the Convent Glen area. I attempted to flag down a passing car. Many vehicles passed me, and some drivers obviously saw me and slowed down, but no one stopped to offer assistance. I crawled approximately 40 metres to a house where I managed to obtain help.

One wonders if humanity has gone the way of low gas prices or an efficient postal system. To those who were merely reluctant to become involved, I fervently hope that if you have an accident or serious problems, you encounter someone who does not share your outlook. If the reluctance to render assistance was generated by fear, I suggest our elected officials should look more closely at public attitudes towards law, order and personal security.

Just prior to my accident, there were eight armed robberies, four in the eastern Ottawa area. Odds are that if you work in a convenience store or gas bar, sooner or later you will obtain first-hand experience of an armed holdup. Canadians are always prepared to engage in U.S.-bashing and frequently point towards the fear generated by violent street crime in major cities in that country. In my case, if fear outweighed what should have been a simple act of charity, perhaps we had better take a closer look at ourselves.

S. Sutherland, Ottawa

GIVE BUSES PRIORITY
IN TRAFFIC PLANNING

MARCH 4, 1986

Regarding your article "Even parkways can help move people:" I'm steaming! The opening paragraph said in effect that the National Capital Commission has always viewed buses on its parkways as a violation of divine law. My God, it

A new sculpture of Arthur Meighen should replace this "avant-garde" version hidden in a Hill basement, a reader recommended.

was we at the NCC in the early 1970s who proposed using the parkways for this purpose, pushed it, and overcame objections.

I wish the city and region had shown as much concern about giving the buses more priority on our busy streets. Why do they not give buses turning out from bus stops right-of-way over cars? Why did they take away the bus priority on Bank Street in favour of the demands of local merchants and the car drivers?

We have a good bus system in the capital, but it could be a lot better — at lower costs in capital spending. Buses must come first in our traffic planning, instead of forcing OC Transpo to lay out hundreds of millions of dollars to let the privileged cars, with their usual single passenger, whiz by.

Douglas H. Fullerton, Ottawa

Editor's note: Douglas Fullerton was chairman of the National Capital Commission from 1969 to 1973.

WELFARE ABUSE

MARCH 21, 1986

My mother became a welfare recipient when my parents separated. She was responsible, raising four children, and welfare accomplished what it was meant to.

But hundreds of welfare recipients would laugh at my mother's conscientiousness. These people rely on their right to be supported and know exactly where to turn if this right is threatened. There are many categories of bleeding hearts: MPs, churches, public support groups and, most effectively, the press.

We only hear complaints about how the less fortunate are neglected. If the general public knew about the extent of this abuse, there would be a second outcry. With rights come responsibilities. Responsible parents consider what they have to offer children, not what larger families will bring in increased welfare benefits. Responsible people pay their rent to keep a roof over their head. Others know they will never be put out on the street: A bleeding heart will come to their rescue.

Responsible people respect their property. They don't destroy it and then cry for better living conditions. The poor lower-income people can't afford to feed their children but they have VCRs, the latest in telephones and beer delivery by taxi. I am definitely not against welfare use: I am against welfare abuse.

Sharon Ogilvie, Ottawa

AIR CANADA'S LETHAL ARMORY

JUNE 16, 1986

Among other knick-knacks, a folding pocket knife resides in my business briefcase. It has but one blade, total effective length seven centimetres (2¾"). It produces excellent chisel shapes on HB pencil leads, is useful in removing wire staples to separate agglomerated papers, and is an incredibly efficient uncoverer of those intriguing bonus secrets embedded under the metallic paint of Wintario tickets.

It serves as a makeshift screwdriver and has been known to assist in the excision of persistent warts. I keep hoping it might one day be employed as a temporary, if blunt, scalpel in the performance of some kind of heroic emergency surgery. Its versatility is nowhere near exhausted.

Unfortunately, I temporarily lost it during a recent mandatory security check at Ottawa airport. This decision was no doubt prompted by an Act, such as the Defence of the Realm or perhaps the War Measures. It was effected with dignity. No one suggested I was a potential hijacker.

But Air Canada's early morning Toronto flights can be highly recommended, principally because of their tasty and substantial breakfasts, accompanied by three gleaming pieces of stainless steel Korean cutlery. The fork has three needle-sharp tines and the business end of the knife possesses vicious-looking serrations. This blade was superior in quality, a good three centimetres (1-3/16") longer, infinitely stronger and eminently more lethal than the puny toy that awaited my return to Ottawa.

My Toronto meeting was a disaster. The chairman greeted my late arrival with a cutting remark, stabbing the air with a dirk-like finger; the boss glared daggers at me; others mumbled obscenities with an edge to their voices; and while the meeting progressed it was obvious that we had merely scratched the surface of our concerns; my planned presentation was axed. I failed to summon a rapier riposte of razor wit to such an unexpected decapitation.

But I had the last laugh. No one had anticipated how the several miles of red tape surrounding our problem could be cut. The solution lay in a sealed brown envelope within a securely locked drawer at Ottawa airport.

W. Pullen, Ottawa

DEBATE, NOT DECORUM
JUNE 27, 1986

Far be it from me to gainsay 200 British Columbians and the Speaker of the Commons, John Bosley, in their attempts to "tame" the House of Commons. But it should be pointed out that the "name-calling, sarcastic putdowns and judgmental language" are very much a part of the British parliamentary system.

Debate, not speed or decorum, should be the first consideration in any democratic legislative body. In the rough and tumble of parliamentary debate, sometimes a great deal of sound and fury is generated, but at least all aspects of a question are examined from a variety of viewpoints.

The American Congress, at times so decorous as to rival a Molière farce, is famous as a body where the most inane drivel is read into the *Congressional Record* with nary a word of protest and dangerous laws (such as the Tonkin Gulf resolution, which led to the Indochina war) are regularly passed almost without debate.

Debate in Britain's "Mother of Parliaments" is much rougher than anything in the Canadian House, but most Britons rest secure in the knowledge that democracy is safe in this rugby match. Or, as one partisan of rough debate, Harry S. Truman, put it, "If you can't stand the heat, stay out of the kitchen."

Randall Barnhart, Ottawa

LANSDOWNE EMBASSY
JULY 7, 1986

I suggest that my neighbourhood park, Lansdowne Park, become the site of the new U.S. Embassy. Mile Circle could be formally declared a city park and the present facilities from Lansdowne, notably the football stadium, the hockey arena, the fairgrounds and the animal display barns, could be relocated there.

This will be a real sacrifice on my part. No longer will I enjoy free concerts by Tina Turner from my bedroom. The supplementary income I enjoy, from the occasional thrown beer bottle which fails to break in my front yard — 10 cents each — will disappear. I know the flapping of the halyard against the embassy's flagstaff might cause me sleepless nights and the whir of teleprinters and word processors might disturb my morning calm. I would be willing to put up with such disadvantages to relieve the distress of the residents of Rockcliffe and Manor Park.

J. R. Brocklebank, Ottawa

DON'T MOVE
JULY 17, 1986

Don't move, change your address or relocate even one mile away; you may never receive mail again.

Case in point: Resided at old address eight years, an Ottawa box and RR number. Notified post office two weeks before moving date of new address — also an Ottawa box and RR number, four miles away, and paid them $9.50 to reroute mail, for a period of three months until all concerned persons notified by us.

No mail was received 10 days after move. Became suspicious and called post office (Alta Vista); yes, they had change of address — couldn't understand what had happened to mail, mail carrier gone home, would check with him in a.m. and call us. No call. Waited two days, checking both boxes. No mail.

Called in at Alta Vista Post Office, explained situation again and was told to use grey phone at end of counter and call 114 for mail carriers. Did, and explained the situation again. Sorry, but office locked, they had no key and the responsible person had gone for the day.

Asked to see manager. Information desk personnel advised me someone named Bob was manager. Went back to the counter and yelled that I wanted to see Bob. One person condescended to come over and, although Bob was not there, listened to my story and stated I was wrong about office being locked — only registered mail got locked up. Would investigate and call me. Said the carrier at our old address was responsible. I went home.

Next day drove to old address to wait at box — just missed carrier — left note with new address. Fourteen days after move, still no mail. Oh yes, received one letter marked "return to sender — unknown."

I would like to apply for a job with the Post Office, to be

in charge of rerouting mail. They could fire about 100 people — it would be a start.

June Collins, Manotick

SHE'S NOT GUILTY
JULY 22, 1986

I am saddened by the sentencing of the Campbell's Bay 15-year-old girl found guilty of murdering her father. She should have been found innocent and her actions understood as necessary for survival. Society should have intervened before she felt driven to such a drastic action.

She and her mother lived in a reign of terror for 15 years, and we ignored their pleas for help. We should be helping the daughter and mother with emotional support, counselling and even financial compensation. Instead, we call her guilty of murder.

The message other beaten daughters and mothers will get from this verdict is, suffer in silence, no one will help you. It's time all women joined together and demanded justice and equality.

Rose Mary Murphy, Ottawa

A GOOD SOLDIER
JULY 30, 1986

Recently, in the middle of your paper, you reported the death of a very fine and gallant Canadian, Lt.-Col. David Currie, VC. I wonder if you would have mentioned it at all had he not been a former Sergeant-at-Arms in the Commons. David Currie was one of a very small number of remaining winners of the most respected of decorations, the Victoria Cross. There are now only six in Canada.

David Currie proved he was a good soldier just 12 days after "D" Day in 1944 as a tank commander in Normandy, when his "gallant conduct and contempt for danger set a magnificent example" and plugged an escape route of the German army. During the last few years, he proved he was a good vice-chairman of the Victoria Cross and George Cross Association, helping his fellow VC-holders whenever the need arose.

I last saw him in Latchford, Ont., when that town honoured its only VC winner, Sgt. Aubrey Cossens, by naming a bridge after him. Col. Currie and I took a walk around the town that evening and I asked how he felt about all the attention he received that day. His answer was simple and typical: "I'm proud to wear the VC but I don't just wear it for me. I wear it for all the boys I served with, especially those who didn't come home!"

He was a good soldier, a good Canadian and a good friend. By your lack of interest, you ignored not only David Currie, VC, but all our fighting men, "especially those who didn't come home." I miss him, and "at the going down of the sun, will remember."

Robert G. Little, Gloucester

IS CANADA A COLONY?
SEPTEMBER 18, 1986

My attempt to purchase a recently published Canadian book in a downtown Montreal bookstore was not only frustrating but also a humiliating. A friend had the same thing happen in Ottawa. Patricia Morley's biography of the Ukrainian-Canadian painter William Kurelek was not in Coles, Classic Books or the main branch of W. H. Smith, nor was I able to discover whether it was coming.

With the exception of Alice Munro's new collection of stories and Pierre Berton's *Vimy*, Canadian books are not prominent in the chains. Where are those great promises we heard when a British bookseller purchased a Canadian book chain — to feature Canadian rather than British or American books? Thank God for the four booksellers in Canada who really specialize in Canadian books.

I came away with a bit of well-meant advice from a clerk: "Try the Double Hook. They specialize in Canadiana." Ironic? Remember, this conversation took place in Canada. The effort to buy a Canadian book was like trying to find ancient coins or variations of Sanskrit. My taste was exotic, if not perverse, and I needed a specialist supplier.

Is Canada a country or a colony?

Milly Charon, Montreal

WHY PAY FOR SLIME?
DECEMBER 23, 1986

My favourite hardware and department stores left some colourful Christmas toy flyers at the door: suggestions for "exciting play combat" and "survival of the fittest is the name of the game!" toys. (Nowhere do they mention war toys.) Cleverly simulated toys of missile-carrying tactical and supersonic jets, assorted nuclear weapons, helicopters, all-terrain vehicles to waste the enemy, etc.

But these toys don't go far enough in simulation, and what about the girls (sorry, persons)? What are REAL little women going to play with? Tarted up bird-leg Barbie or sex-pistol Rambo dolls?

Never fear. I have the answer. You don't want to be afraid to show your kids you love them. You want to give them what every kid on the block is saying he's going to get, don't you? At the same time, toys should have some educational value, without being boring, right?

The answer is in your kitchen, or nearest grocery shelf, butcher shop, abattoir, or, if you are lucky and live in the country, nearest farm: simulated wounds and fractures, blood and gore. It teaches the little darlings cause and effect, and it's creative, too. As it is now, when your little one fires his laser-photon-galactic-nuke-whatever gun, his victim's sensor beeps. They've taken away the fun of yelling, "pow-pow-zapp-zapp-bang-bang you're dead." There is nothing creative for the kids to do now.

This is where sister comes in. The REAL little woman must be trained in sharing, caring and cleaning up after you know who. So she grabs a handful of spaghetti and meat sauce (to simulate brains), or braising rib bones, or pig's intestines, or cow's eyes and pig's intestines, and splatters the loser wherever she or he has been hit. Hours of fun, and educational too. Cause and effect, get it?

I mean why pay $10.98 plus tax for the "Evil horde slime pit?" This is described as "Fearsome claw traps victim as skull head opens to disgorge deadly slime." Why pay for slime? Look around the house, or visit my kitchen.

Muriel MacDonald, Ottawa

1987

Local: Zuri, Kiza, Anya, Rhys and Matthew Forgie, the Ottawa area's first quintuplets, are born (September); OPP suspect serial killer responsible for six slayings of reclusive Ottawa Valley residents (September)

National: Federal, provincial governments reach tentative agreement on constitutional accord at Meech Lake (July); 174 illegal Sikh immigrants come ashore at Nova Scotia fishing village (July); Ontario voters elect Liberal government for first time in four decades (September); Canada, U.S. agree in principle to free trade pact (October)

World: U.S. president Reagan, Soviet leader Gorbachev reach historic missile reduction accord (December); Iran and Iraq enter eighth year of war which has claimed nearly one million lives (December)

Deaths: Quebec premier René Lévesque; actor-broadcaster Lorne Greene; writers James Baldwin and George Ryga; violinist Jascha Heifetz; hockey coach George (Punch) Imlach; Canadian feminist Kay Macpherson; cookbook author Jehane Benoît; actors Mary Astor and Lee Marvin; bandleader Woody Herman; director Bob Fosse; Tory MPP Paul Yakabuski; Vic Chapman, Buckingham Palace press secretary and former CFL player

JUNIOR HOCKEY BRAWL

JANUARY 10, 1987

I was pleased to read that Bert Templeton, coach of the Canadian Junior Hockey Team, accepted the blame for the conduct of his players during the bench-clearing brawl at the World Junior Hockey Championships.

That is exactly where the blame belongs. The players were drawn into this incident; they responded as they have been coached to respond, not necessarily at the world championships, but ever since they watched their first hockey game and played on an organized team.

Coaches at all levels have to start eradicating this senseless violence in hockey. As any player, fan or "hockey parent" knows, this penchant for butt ending, slashing, elbowing, high sticking or other means to intentionally harm another player is, at the moment, an accepted part of the Canadian game from professional through junior to competitive and even house-league levels.

When the coaches and advocates of goon hockey, such as Don Cherry, are finally given no voice (why does the CBC continue to employ this mouthpiece of thuggery?), we will be able to take more pride in this sport.

David Kendall, Ottawa

MASS DISCRIMINATION

MARCH 3, 1987

I am an Inuk (singular for Inuit) living in Ontario for eight years, in a farming community where the majority are of Scottish ancestry. I came to live here for my children's education.

My bond and connection is in the Arctic where I come from. My family live in Broughton Island, N.W.T., relocated by the government from Paalakvik in 1965. I grew up in a traditional manner until I left home, at 13, to attend boarding school. My generation experienced boarding schools away from home — entering school wearing sealskin boots and coming out of it in a miniskirt.

It has been a traumatic experience going through a period where I have been brought up to value and respect strongly the land, only to find out that the land of my family and ancestors does not belong to us, according to the government of Canada.

Twenty years ago when I first found out about this, I thought it was one of those myths that the white man often connected the Arctic and Inuit with. Until recently, I

buried it along with the pain of it all. I don't possess enough of a thick skin to regard it as a thing of the past, so I am dealing with anger and pain and trying hard to learn to live with the pain.

I felt suspended in a void of uncertainty, a feeling oddly justified by the loss of four young people who, within the space of nine months, chose to take their own lives — in a community of only 400. Growing up in a traditional manner, there was no guarantee of sustaining life. There were times when my father was late from his hunting trips, and my family and I were left with uncertainty to a point where we feared saying and reacting too much too soon. This uncertainty was sure to be answered one way or the other and we were prepared to overcome the situation — coming out of it with a positive result.

The uncertainty regarding the land comes with the same feelings and emotions — the only difference is that it is prolonged. Although I am trying hard to live within the frame of the next day, I catch myself thinking, am I acting too happy for someone who is about to lose something I was strongly brought up to value? Am I unnecessarily dwelling on the anticipated sadness of loss?

Discrimination, I can and have tolerated when it is committed by an individual, knowing that it is a result of ignorance; but mass discrimination I can neither tolerate nor understand. A Canadian government handed out "free" concessions of land to Scottish soldiers to persuade them to stay in the country and a Canadian government is now taking away ancestral land from Inuit who were in the country before a Canadian government ever existed. Is this insensitive, stupid or discrimination?

The investment that my family and ancestors made is not the kind that is put in banks to collect interest and tax dollars. The investment they made was knowledge to ensure our existence, based on ecological and other conditions of each particular place. No one outside the family and ancestory line has the same respect and bond to the land; therefore the land is vulnerable to abuse.

Just like any other society, Inuit have had different classes of people: settlers and others. Settlers established areas where they would move within a boundary from time to time. The others sustained their living going from place to place, never establishing much of a connection except through marriage. Since relocation and centralization took place, the settlers and others have become one class of people, experiencing struggles and poverty more than ever.

It is ironic that the others, not the settlers, have been the ones who are more apt and have more willingness to go along with what happened. During the beginning of the transition period of acculturation, the others were also an easy target to act as puppets for the government agents to promote an ideal lifestyle of centralized community life. Why not? They had only to gain.

I am trying to come to terms with the pain and irony of it all!

Jeela Alikatuktuk, Balderson, Ont.

CANADA AS A MODEL
MAY 7, 1987

People who form themselves into different camps over policy on South Africa tend to forget that they are all chiefly interested in the same goal — an Africa of free countries ruled democratically by all of its peoples, including the whites.

We reject South African criticism of how we have treated the native people in this country. But we have not done well enough. No Canadian can be proud of the conditions that exist on many of the reserves and among native people in the slums of our major cities. South Africans might be more interested in hearing how we intend to improve things in our country than how we think they should change theirs.

It would be nice if we could just tell the rest of the world how to behave and have them accept our advice. But we know it won't happen, just as we wouldn't pay any heed to the dictates of any other self-righteous nation.

The world is watching to see what we do with this young, rich, democratic nation. It may be a slow way to bring about change in the world, but it is the only way that will work.

Henry F. Heald, Nepean

DON'T SPOIL TURKS AND CAICOS
MAY 12, 1987

Are we really considering colonizing the Turks and Caicos Islands again? If they become part of Canada, entrepreneurs will embark, carrying briefcases. They will build jet ports, malls and cruise ship facilities. They will build hotel towers, craft markets for the distribution of Taiwan carvings, free port shops for the laundering of Japanese "seconds," and schools of "traditional" dance run by Montreal fine arts majors.

Fast food will materialize. There will be McDonalds Turk Burgers, Caico-Tacos and Arby's Beach Buns. There will be colour cable TV offering *ET* and *Canada AM* in simulated Palm Springs motel rooms. The clear waters will cloud. Trendy people will arrive. They will come for the sun, sit in the shade, wear sunglasses and discuss the latest gossip from Bay Street.

I am a Canadian, born in Vancouver and bred from the age of five in the West Indies, son of a tourist board public relations director. I saw Kingston metropolize. I have seen the Americanization of San Juan, the Caribbean Honolulu.

I have watched the Bahamas consume itself in North American-inspired materialism. I have eaten of the vinyl Virgin Island pizza. I have stumbled on the beer cans of Negril. I have sniffed the silk hibiscus. I have seen the proliferation of prostitution answer the call of monetary example and emulation, manifested in "Cadillac-envy." I have seen the busboys spit in the salad dressing in the frustration of "good life" exemplified but not realized. I have seen the children grow hungry after the bankers arrive with new concepts of gala proprietorship.

Yes, I know. It will happen to the Turks and Caicos eventually anyway. But why collaborate? Let those emeralds degenerate in their own time. Ever since Columbus was discovered wading malevolently out of the surf by the Lucayans, the Antilles have suffered from cultural, social, religious, economic (and always Caucasian) interference. It's the kind that avariciously imposes the "infrastructures" that are supposed to make the world suitable for "civilized" habitation, i.e. "developed" (a Euro-concept that regards Mother Nature as inadequate for the provision of beauty, peace and tranquility, and therefore requiring the intervention of developers to build hotdog stands, subdivisions, concrete pathways, information booths and metered parking for enjoyment and profit.)

By all means, let us help. A long-term aid package, perhaps. We could build trade schools, offer scholarships, install sewage, water, and power systems, send equipment and make soft loans, since these are proud and responsible people obviously genuinely interested in the betterment of their citizenry.

But for pity's sake, leave them be. They will "develop" themselves.

Greg Wilmot, Pitt Meadows, B.C.

EXEMPLARY CITIZEN
JUNE 4, 1987

I was furious to hear that a Vietnamese mother of nine children, all brilliant students, was refused Canadian citizenship because she could not speak English. Twice she applied but was refused. Her husband has been employed since they arrived in Canada 10 years ago. All her children are Canadians.

I've been in Canada for 73 years, born and raised in Ottawa. I've never been inside the Parliament Buildings. I've never met a prime minister. I never knew the words for our national anthem, either French or English — and I am a real Canadian.

This beautiful devoted mother never got to attend school because she attended to the welfare of her children. Her home, her family is her life. What more does one ask for in a model parent? Because this refined lady can't hack the English language, can't pronounce the letter "L," is an exemplary citizen to be refused her Canadian citizenship?

Elaine D. Lewis, Ottawa

AN APPLE FOR HISTORY BOOKS
JULY 8, 1987

I was awed by your full, in-depth coverage of the Meech-

Langevin accord. The blow-by-blow, minute-by-minute report by Neil Macdonald was palpitatingly exciting, and one realized he was witnessing history in the making as he recorded that "shortly before 2 a.m. Mulroney called a 15-minute coffee break. A secret service agent fetched an apple for the PM from the trunk of his RCMP car."

As significant as the moment was, I regret that I must take exception to your reporter leaving us unworldly readers ever pondering as to whether the apple was an English speaker from an Okanagan orchard or was it of French-Acadian heritage from the Annapolis Valley? The possibility that it was a southern spy sent to gain insight into our free trade posture should also not be overlooked. Perhaps the apple was a magnificent McIntosh, in which case it is rightly just and lawful for the Scottish-Canadians to be recognized in the accord as a distinct society within Canada.

Fortunately, the accord did not receive the immediate finalization hoped for by the prime minister, thus allowing sufficient time to appoint his apple-bearer to the Senate before such privileged powers are passed to the provincial premiers.

Whatever the future may hold, generations of Canadian schoolchildren should be able to readily recollect the Meech-Langevin Accord by committing to memory their piece of doggerel — an apple that day allowed the provincial premiers their own way.

Ken Eccles, Ottawa

ILLEGAL IMMIGRANTS
JULY 25, 1987

Immigration Minister Benoit Bouchard and this weak, lacklustre cabinet are learning that to err once is human but to make the same mistake twice brands them as fools.

Prime Minister Mulroney's capitulation to the deceit of the Tamil boat people informed the world that Canada, with its unprotected coastline and weak jello-spined marshmallow government, was an easy mark. It was a green light to those who engage in this profitable illegal trade to dump these opportunists on our shores.

The Sikhs who landed this month are not political refugees. Like the Tamils, they paid good money to gain access to German and European ports and again, to illegal traffickers, for the opportunity to bypass our immigration system. With 10-per-cent unemployment, who needs that kind of immigration or drain on our social and welfare programs for those who have paid their dues to this country?

Despite advance warning, the costly legal and social process is to be repeated again because Immigration Minister Bouchard does not know the difference between an illegal immigrant and a real political refugee.

Frank H. Shipp, Hull

Editor's note: A year after a boatload of Tamils waded ashore in Newfoundland, the arrival in a Nova Scotia village of 174 Sikh refugee claimants triggered national calls for tougher laws that would tell the world Canada was not

an easy target. In response, the Mulroney government branded the situation a national emergency and recalled Parliament to introduce legislation to deter and punish abusers of Canada's refugee system. For a time, the Sikhs were detained at a Maritime military base, guarded by soldiers and denied access to lawyers. Eventually, the tough new rules were passed, but most of the Sikhs were allowed to stay. The Swedish captain of the ship that brought them was fined $5,000 and sentenced to a year in jail.

ABSURD POLLS
AUGUST 29, 1987

The polls lately have become more and more asinine in the quest to make the pollsters more money. The latest absurdity is the Angus Reid poll that says the Liberals could win if Jean Chrétien came back. Why stop at Chrétien; why not Trudeau, Mackenzie King, Napoleon, Ghengis Khan or Snow White?

It's little wonder we mount a Rhinoceros Party!

Ron Fraser, Ottawa

ROUGH RIDE FOR OC TRANSPO
SEPTEMBER 15, 1987

One can sense immediately the outrage among Ottawa's cultural organizations upon learning that sports fans will now get free bus rides to football games.

I think that a coalition of all such local arts groups should be formed and they should go to OC Transpo and insist that all buses travelling to football games must carry a minimum of six paintings by local artists. As well, poets could be engaged to read from their work while the buses are en route; local musicians of the acoustic variety could perform, too.

The NAC Orchestra or Le Groupe de la Place Royale dance company could perform at half-time. Perhaps Ottawa's poet laureate could be persuaded to write an ode to the third down. The possibilities are endless.

If these possibilities seem absurd, reflect for a moment on the prospect of a bus company sponsoring something called the Rough Riders.

Randall Ware, Ottawa

A BEAUTIFUL DREAM
NOVEMBER 2, 1987

Now that my Man in Motion World Tour is over and I have completed most of the commitments and responsibilities during the wind-down phase, I have had an opportunity to reflect on some of the experiences and highlights of the tour.

One thing that consistently comes to mind, and has inspired me to write this letter to you, is the incredible support generated in each community as we travelled home across Canada. It was because of this team effort that we were able to accomplish, beyond our wildest dreams, the objectives of the Man in Motion World Tour. I thank everyone in Ottawa who participated and helped fulfil my dream.

Your friendship, love and support has meant more to me than words can ever express. I encourage everyone in this

THE CANADIAN PRESS

Rick Hansen crossed the wide-open spaces of Saskatchewan during his 40,000-kilometre trek to raise funds for the disabled and awareness of their plight. He was awarded the Order of Canada.

country to remember that the dream of one day seeing all disabled persons having the opportunity to reach their full potential has still not been accomplished. With your continued support, we will ultimately achieve that goal.

Rick Hansen,
Man in Motion World Tour, Vancouver, B.C.

Editor's note: Rick Hansen, a 30-year-old paraplegic con-

fined to a wheelchair, raised more than $20 million for spinal cord research in a gruelling 26-month, 34-country tour in which he travelled more than 40,000 kilometres. For his efforts, the B.C.-born Mr. Hansen was awarded the Order of Canada and voted Canadian newsmaker of the year in 1986 and '87.

FINAL 'CURE'

NOVEMBER 21, 1987

In reading *The Citizen's* column of apology for and correction of purported printing errors, I was struck by one dealing with a misprint in an earlier Dear Abby column.

A certain ambiguity exists as to whether she recommends carbon dioxide or carbon monoxide as a cure for unstoppable hiccups. For permanency, there is no doubt in my mind as to which is the more effective for terminating hiccups or any other frustrating ailments.

Glen S. Morley,
Ottawa

ONE NAME, TWO MEN, TWO VIEWS

DECEMBER 19, 1987

You published an anti-free trade letter by Duncan Campbell, Ottawa. He and I have several things in common: a name, prior residence in the United States, and current residence in Ottawa. We also have several differences. I am an economist, a former senior policy adviser to Simon Reisman in the Trade Negotiations Office and I believe the new agreement will have a favourable economic impact on Canada.

While I am concerned lest any of your readers believe I disagree with myself, I would be even more concerned if they believed I agreed with Duncan Campbell of Ottawa.

Duncan Campbell, Ottawa

1988

Local: National Gallery opens in spectacular building on Sussex Drive (May); After 25 years of delay, 911 service begins in Ottawa-Carleton (June); Ottawa host for Grey Cup, won 22-21 by Winnipeg over B.C. (November)

National: Canada bans all forms of tobacco advertising (June); Edmonton Oilers shock nation by trading Wayne Gretzky to Los Angeles Kings (August); After testing positive for steroids, Canadian Ben Johnson is stripped of the gold medal won in 100-metre sprint at Seoul Olympics (September); Brian Mulroney's PCs returned to power in bitter election fought over free trade agreement with U.S. (November)

World: Iran, Iraq sign truce to end bloody eight-year war (April); Earthquake kills 70,000 in Soviet Armenia (September); Soviet Union begins final withdrawal of troops from Afghanistan (October); PanAm 747 blown up over over Lockerbie, Scotland, killing all 258 on board (December)

Births: Sandrine Craig, girl killed in tragic 1999 school bus crash near Dunrobin

Deaths: Canadian philosopher George Grant; naturalist filmmaker Bill Mason; Father David Bauer, founder of Canadian national hockey program; writer Raymond Carver; Quebec nationalist chansonnier Félix Leclerc; singer Roy Orbison; poet B.P. Nichol; actors John Carradine and John Houseman; film director Hal Ashby; hockey star Babe Pratt; baseball legend Carl Hubbell; shipping heiress Christina Onassis; U.S. attorney general John Mitchell; CBC president Alphonse Ouimet

A GENEROUS, LOONIE OFFER

JANUARY 4, 1988

Friends in Ottawa have sent me "for luck" a coin which I think is very attractive, but in Canada it has been named the "loonie." My Canadian correspondent tells me that "nobody wants to take them as change."

In Britain we had a similar problem when the "round pound" coin was minted to replace the pound banknote. (The Scots, having their own ways, still print and use their own Scottish banknotes for the pound.)

Few people like the pound coin, but I think if it had been as attractive as your dollar coin, it would have been more acceptable.

However, because I am by birth a canny Scot (and a generous one, if I say so myself) I shall be delighted if your readers who dislike your "loonies" gather as many as they can and send them to me. Perhaps I can relieve them of having to carry in pockets and purses a coin they would prefer not to have.

Frank Curtis, London, England

WORLD'S TALLEST
TINY PERFECT TYRANT

JANUARY 9, 1988

Your columnist Ilya Gerol is surprised to discover North Korean President Kim Il Sung, who stands five foot five, is taller than anyone appearing in photographs with him.

Upon reading of Mr. Gerol's perplexity, I sauntered over to my bookshelf to consult the well-worn first volume of the life of Kim Il Sung. (In fact, I am perplexed as well. Surely this very readable three-volume work by Baik Bong, entitled simply *Kim Il Sung: Biography*, has an honoured place in Mr. Gerol's library. Perhaps he has loaned his to a friend.)

In the first volume, subtitled "From Birth to Triumphant Return to Homeland," Kim is indeed taller than all his compatriots. But a quick perusal reveals that this is the very least of the leader's accomplishments. It pales when compared to the fact that Kim had achieved a distinguished military rank by the time he was in primary school: "In the spring of 1925 the general was enrolled at the Fusing First Primary School."

While Baik Bong is silent on the question, it would appear Kim was the only general in the class at the time. In order to achieve such a high rank by such a tender age, one might imagine Kim had to give up most if not all of the delights of childhood. Not so. "As a child, like all others playing at horseriding on a stick, riding a sledge or playing kick-ball with a straw and rag ball, he was rough on his clothes." Amazing.

I would be pleased to lend Mr. Gerol my copy of Kim Il Sung's biography should he wish to expand his knowledge of this giant of our time.

John P. Crump, Ottawa
(6-2, but still shorter than Kim.)

CITIZEN ASSESSED

JANUARY 16, 1988

Do you really edit over there at Baxter Road? I learned that Douglas Dewar was led to the chemical source of a shellfish toxic. Then I saw that a rescued sailor was en route home. In the item on the million-dollar fire in Kingston, during which firefighters were hampered by biting cold (Jan. 8), Caroline Rundle reportedly said: "It was pretty horrible. I couldn't bare to watch . . ." I can hardly blame her.

A. M. MacKenzie, Ottawa

AN OFF-COLOUR JOKE

JANUARY 16, 1988

Apparently a Windsor housewife fought legally enforced colouring of margarine in the Ontario Supreme Court, on the basis that restricting the colour of the spread violates the freedom of expression under our Charter of Rights.

Many people in the world would be very glad to have olive green margarine to spread on their bread (which they don't have much of either). And although its economic impact on Ontario's dairy industry makes the Oleomargarine Act somewhat important, the inches of prime space you devoted to it would have been better used to publicize real infringements of our rights to freedom of expression.

Alana Boltwood,
Stittsville

TRUST FUN

JANUARY 30, 1988

I don't trust anyone who prints "Who do you trust."

F. M. Barnes, Ottawa

AN EAGLE EYE FOR SYMBOLISM

JANUARY 30, 1988

After seeing the picture on the front page of *The Citizen* of the huge bald "American" eagle grasping Brian Mulroney's head in its talons, I was left with a few questions.

Was it a deliberate attempt on the part of your photographer to wait until our PM made an "I surrender" gesture to shoot, or was it just a coincidence? Does this mean the editorial staff of your paper is now officially renouncing its stand on free trade? Would it be correct to say the prime minister found himself in a very "untenable" or "tenable" position?

Finally, are you going to be selling just the 8 x 10 glossies, or will you be bringing out the poster-sized version? Put me down for a couple if you are.

Dan Millar, Orléans

FINE CANADIAN

FEBRUARY 27, 1988

Your entertainment writer, Jamie Portman, talks of Disney's "nine old men" — ex-animators of the studio that produced the early cartoon classics — who "are gone now." I wonder if Mr. Portman was aware that these old men — in their 90s now — have been working for the past 15 years or so for a young Toronto-born animator named Dick Williams.

A couple of us living in Ottawa knew Dick in high school, and have kept in touch. His career has been amazing, yet most Canadians have never heard of him. His work won a Cannes Film Festival award some 30 years ago, followed by an Oscar for his animated Dickens' *Christmas Carol*. The animation in *Charge of the Light Brigade* was his, as was the introductory cartoon work in a couple of the *Pink Panther* movies. *Raggedy Ann and Andy* was his — and last year he left his studio in Soho, London, to do a film with Steven Spielberg.

These old Disney animators have been working for years on Dick's dream — a full-length movie — almost completed, but never quite, because of the lack of funds. He's a Canadian success who's been one of the better kept secrets, and it's a shame. He is, after all, one of our own.

D. Simpson, Ottawa

MULRONEY'S PAL

APRIL 16, 1988

I sympathize with the Mulroney government's new secretary of state, Lucien Bouchard. Bygones are bygones. When trying to explain his work with the "yes" section of the Quebec referendum a few years back, he did declare his long-standing allegiance to his country and to his home province. The poor man was forced to practically drape himself in his beloved maple leaf and then he revealed to us that his Canadianship extends way, way back, to the 1600s.

Now, I admit, Canada as a political entity hasn't existed quite that long. But we know all about the fine distinctions between colony and nation, independence and dependence and all that. And hey, it's not his fault.

Remember, he's only a little guy out of Laval University who happened to know the prime minister as a buddy.

He was made an ambassador and then he was yanked all the way back to Canada without so much as an "excuse me, please," and made a minister, without even being elected a member of Parliament.

It's enough to unsettle even the most self-righteous of patriots.

Robin Collins, Vanier

CREDIBILITY LOST

APRIL 23, 1988

The decision to sell Air Canada is another treacherous move by the government to disenfranchise the Canadian people. For now, it's 45 per cent of the company that is to be sacrificed. In the future it will be total ownership by private interests.

It is conceivable that Air Canada, like Dome Petroleum, might fall into the hands of foreign interests, despite Mulroney's promise that the company will remain our national airline. Did he not also promise at one time that Air Canada was not for sale, as he once stated that free trade with the U.S. was not in Canada's best interests?

Mr. Mulroney's latest about-face should strengthen the belief that he cannot be trusted.

Frank Donovan, Gloucester

Editor's note: Air Canada was eventually entirely sold to private interests, but remains in Canadian hands.

UNFAIR SITUATION

MAY 7, 1988

I've been reading about young people on welfare in Ottawa. As a small general contractor, I would like to hire such people.

But people from Quebec underbid us on small jobs. They carry no liability insurance and are not registered in Ontario. We can't work in their province without a permit, but they work in Ontario without one.

I hope that the Ontario labour authorities wake up and do something. It is really unfair.

Claude Lalonde, Vanier

Editor's note: Ontario and Quebec did not resolve their long-simmering construction industry dispute until late 1999, when the two provinces agreed to a deal giving Ontario workers full access to Quebec jobs for the first time in 30 years.

MEANING OF WAR MEMORIAL

MAY 13, 1988

Passing by the war memorial recently, I stopped to admire the scene. For me, its message has never been clearer.

Above, I saw the familiar faces, still struggling with sadness and war, pulling their load through the arch. On the steps below, free, happy, healthy Canadian youths played.

As children, we were all taught by parents and teachers about the great sacrifices more than one million Canadians made for freedom in Europe and the world.

We collectively remember every Nov. 11. We have museums, monuments, films and books to remind us. Ask the children playing on the steps of the war memorial if they know why the memorial is there and, depending on age, they will be able to tell you.

We will always remember our heroes and be grateful to them.

Does this mean that we should stop our children from playing in the shadow of the war memorial? Is this not an appropriate place for them to enjoy our hard-won freedom?

Robert Craig Myers, Ottawa

Editor's note: This letter was written in response to complaints from some veterans that skateboarders and other youths should be stopped from hanging out at the war memorial.

MUST IT GET WORSE?

MAY 20, 1988

I know that Sparks Street will never be the same, but must it get worse? Are the pink fake paving stones, squat lamp-posts and ugly green things that house telephones not enough?

I dread the day when the new furniture will make its appearance. What will we be subjected to then? Orange paisley chairs with mirrored backs and rhinestone-studded legs? I have one word for the "new and improved" Sparks Street Mall — eyesore!

N. Singhal, Ottawa

INSPIRING WEDDING

AUGUST 4, 1988

Your articles, "Canada's royal wedding" and "Disability no barrier for this happy couple" are in sharp contrast.

So Wayne Gretzky can skate and shoot a puck and this equates to royalty? Your article discusses in the usual mundane, speculative detail, the size and expense of the wedding rings for the happy couple, the bride's $40,000 wedding dress and the fact that she arrived with nine large boxes containing dresses and had her very own dress designer. Along with this was the usual analysis by psychics who feel they'll be happy, though one numerologist said the future bride needs to control obsessions such as food and sex.

In sharp contrast is the article, "Disability no barrier for this happy couple." They are Paul Legault, a quadriplegic, and Janet Graham, who is not disabled. They are the true winners in a society of badly misdirected values. They are attempting to accomplish what almost seems impossible and they must be commended for their strength and courage. Here is a couple trying to wipe away some of the prejudices and misconceptions about marriage between a disabled person and someone who's not. The article says that while they're happy and are working hard to dispel

THE CANADIAN PRESS

Wayne and Janet Gretzky's wedding certainly was expensive, but the marriage of a city couple was more inspiring, a reader argued.

myths about paraplegics, Legault and Graham say they had to enter marriage with more than a handful of realism.

I wonder how much realism Canadians have. It's sad that we must idolize and admire the superficiality of the rich and glamorous.

Vivian Menzies, Orléans

THE MACHINE NATURE MADE

AUGUST 19, 1988

These days in the media, citizens generally are being alerted by genetic scientists to a new era approaching in dairying, for example, with the development of a super cow. Such an animal would be capable of producing quantities of milk greatly in excess of totals available under present-day circumstances. High-technology is apparently making such a revolution possible.

We already know, from major agricultural authorities on this continent, that the cow we have is a mobile, animated machine acting within a coating of unprocessed leather.

One end, we understand, is equipped with a mower, a grinder and other standard equipment, including bumpers, horn and headlights.

At the other end is a milk dispenser and insect repellant.

To this impressive assortment may be added a centrally located storage tank and fermentation vat plus three converters in a series along with appropriate conveyer tubes. Other useful equipment includes a central heating plant, pumping system and air conditioner. Current output per unit ranges up to 21 tons of milk per year.

Do geneticists really believe they can vastly improve upon nature's super-efficient plant, let alone the quality of the product? When they finally realize the odds against accomplishing this, they should be thoroughly cowed.

Don W. Thomson, Ottawa

MULTICULTURALISM ENRICHED CANADA

AUGUST 27, 1988

I beg to differ with "Let us be just Canadians," by D.C. McCaffrey. Culture is the way of life. It is about people and is as alive as people. Ours is a living culture, growing, changing and continuously enriching itself.

Canada is not threatened but enriched by multiculturalism. Multiculturalism in Canada is a reality like bilingualism. Neither a public debate nor a referendum can change it. In fact, we should be proud of it.

When it is enshrined in Canadian law, let us rejoice, not be afraid. Multiculturalism makes our country more lively, competitive and enviable among the family of nations. Our culture is young but also as rich as any old cultures.

I adopted Canada 25 years ago. I learned English and French, but I have not forgotten my mother tongue, Chinese. It did not take five generations for me to become a Canadian through and through. I don't consider myself a visitor from another culture in a "boarding house."

Canada is my home, and Ottawa, my home town. One of my children married a hyphenated French-Canadian from Buckingham, and another recently married an Irish-Canadian from Halifax.

My daughter has just given birth to a boy who has black Chinese hair and dark-blue French eyes. He is a beautiful Canadian baby, and everyone adores him.

When he grows up, I hope that in addition to English and French, he will speak Chinese. He does not have to sever completely the Chinese culture ties to be a valuable Canadian.

Canadianism is not a narrow and radical nationalism that calls for crystalization and purification. To me, Canadianism is a field of beautiful flowers that grow on a vast land, out of a soil of diversity and cultivated by a people of greatness — great enough to accept different colours and shapes.

Yes, I was enticed by Canada when I decided to immigrate to Canada, and I have never lost faith in Canada ever since.

S. Tsai, Ottawa

STRUGGLING ARTIST DESERVES A RAISE

NOVEMBER 27, 1988

The Canada Council has been central to the growth and excellence of the arts in Canada for more than 30 years. My career as a dancer would have been impossible without its support.

The National Ballet School would be beyond the reach of most promising dancers but for the funds it receives from the council. It provides the largest amount of government funding for The National Ballet of Canada.

In recent years funding from the Canada Council has not kept pace with inflation, let alone with the recent exciting growth in the arts. Operating grants to the National Ballet of Canada and many other fine arts organizations have not increased for more than four years. Grants to training institutions — the lifeblood of the arts — are now insufficient to assure their continued very high quality.

The council is seeking an increase, over three years, of $47 million in its annual appropriation from Parliament, equal to $1.62 for each Canadian.

Currently, many artists live below the poverty line. My fellow dancers who freelance or work in small companies often have annual earnings of $5,000 to $10,000.

Add to this the fact that dancers' careers are very short — often ended prematurely through injury — and one can see that it is love for the art that motivates them.

Surely artists have the right to enjoy the benefits and respect accorded other professionals. Additional funding for the Canada Council can help.

Karen Kain, Toronto

CLUMSY DAN

DECEMBER 10, 1988

I read Dan Turner's recent column about afflicted left-handers. It is nonsense. My left-handed daughter, a ballet-dancer, is beauty in motion, every action of her body a manifestation of the poetry of perfect co-ordination.

I lived in Zimbabwe for some of the time that Turner did. I came to dread opening the house door to him and seeing what newest part of him was bandaged, bruised, bumped, banged.

Turner is not clumsy because he is left-handed. He is clumsy. Clumsiness is a recognized physical syndrome, a fact which Turner should accept. He is, however, a good tennis player.

Michael Valpy, Toronto

1989

Local: Hijacked bus driven from Montreal to Parliament Hill, where gunman eventually surrenders (April)

National: Free trade deal with United States takes effect (January); Finance Minister Michael Wilson unveils details of proposed new goods and services tax (August); Marc Lépine kills 14 women at Montreal polytechnical school (December)

World: Oil tanker *Exxon Valdez* spills 43 million litres of oil after running aground off Alaska (March); Chinese army kills student protesters in purge of demonstration at Tiananmen Square (May); Earthquake rattles San Francisco-Oakland, killing 67 and causing $2 billion damage (October); Berlin Wall comes down, signalling the beginning of the end for the Communist hold over Eastern Europe (November)

Deaths: Iranian spiritual leader Ayatollah Khomeini; composer Irving Berlin; pianist Vladimir Horowitz; Irish playwright Samuel Beckett; actress Bette Davis; hockey legend Doug Harvey; Canadian historian C.P. Stacey; Maryon Pearson, widow of Lester Pearson; Philippines strongman Ferdinand Marcos; Japanese Emperor Hirohito; physicist and human rights advocate Andrei Sakharov; baseball player-manager Billy Martin

OUR JUSTICE SYSTEM FAVOURS THE GUILTY

APRIL 20, 1989

A few weeks ago, my family became victims of a "system of justice." Two and a half years after my brother's death, the man charged with impaired driving causing death, and dangerous driving causing death, walked out of the courtroom. A fine of $300 and a two-year licence suspension is the only penalty in our country for causing death.

I have a dead brother; but the accused has rights. How can my dead brother defend his rights? What kind of justice system is that? One thing that I have learned from this tragedy is that you can trust no one. If you have enough money for influence and a "hot shot" lawyer, you're ahead of the game. We are the victims because we were ignorant of what justice really means in our society.

Of course, the accused has to live with his actions for the rest of his life. However, I question the conscience of a man who can hit a pedestrian and keep on driving. He did not turn himself in until the next day. When are our laws going to protect the innocent?

Joan Gruttner, Carleton Place

RURAL LIFE

JUNE 11, 1989

Ahhh, country life: Tree-lined dirt roads, rolling hills, babbling brooks, apple trees, quaint farms. Sounds wonderful doesn't it?

More and more people are deciding to leave the hustle and bustle of city living to find their own little "peace and quiet" corner of the world. Of course, they are entitled and even welcome to do so.

However, please allow us to offer a little advice. When looking at a piece of property, make sure you know what's around. If you find the smell of manure offensive, don't like the roar of a tractor, the lowing (actually bawling) of cattle, the sound of cow bells in the night, or a farmer calling the cows home at 5 p.m., then living anywhere near an active farm is not for you.

Please remember that many farm families have been there a very long time and it is not only their home but their business as well.

Most people who move out are wonderful, while most farmers are good neighbours. Unfortunately, the odd person who moves out expects to find Utopia. If you are one of those people, may I politely suggest that you move back to the city and enjoy the never-ceasing sound of traffic and the ever-present exhaust fumes.

To the majority who are realistic and only want to slow down and enjoy life a little more, welcome neighbour!

Paul and Debbie Yuck, Kinburn

EMPTY TAXIS

JUNE 14, 1989

On June 5, at 5 p.m., 20, maybe 30, people were waiting at the Ottawa airport, tired, hot, anxious to get home. Taxis arrived, deposited passengers and rolled away empty.

A security guard, with the grandiose title "Ground Transportation Inspector," bustled to and fro making sure none of the cabs stopped. They were west-end cabs, forbidden to rescue anyone, even west-end passengers, from this dreary queue. Airport cabs, the only ones licensed to pick up at that stand, were few and far between.

And so I, greying and past 40, became a rebel for the first time in my life. As the next Kanata taxi was hustled past the swelling queue, I leapt from the curb, yelled in my loudest voice that I was going to Kanata and wanted the cab to take me there.

The "inspector" attempted to physically restrain me. When he found me determined, he threatened legal action. My driver defused the situation by calling my request in to her dispatcher and obtaining RCMP clearance for us to proceed.

So I rode home comfortably, conveniently and quickly. We must end restrictive taxi licensing policies in Ottawa-Carleton.

D. B. Bell, Kanata

LANGUAGE GESTAPO

JULY 28, 1989

What in the name of all that's sane has become of our Canada? You are living in a small rural community in the (so-far) peaceful Gatineau Valley. You are a respected, respectful, hard-working, tolerant, helpful sixth-generation Canadian of Irish descent. Today you are doing what you have been doing for years — taking care of business.

But, hark! Who goes there?

It's Quebec's tongue troopers, here because you have committed a dastardly crime, a deed deserving of the harshest punishment. You have dared to use, on a sign, an English word such as "Store," or "Open Monday" or "Market" or "Closed."

How audacious. Whatever gave you the idea you could legally use the language of the vast majority of Canadians? Could it be the fact that your forefathers carved a civilization out of rock — in this very spot? Could it be that you believed that there were sacred freedoms in Canada? Could you have suffered from momentary insanity and assumed that Quebec respected such a basic right?

How can our national leaders allow this to happen in a democratic country? (Notwithstanding the notwithstanding clause.) They are probably too busy. It takes time and energy to ensure that illegal immigrants from illegal boats are provided with interpreters so that they can communicate in the language of their choice.

We have the God-given luck to live in the most wonderful country in the world. It boggles the mind, frazzles the brain, that any Canadian who watched students being gunned down in Tiananmen Square in China could then look at Canada and say: "Something is terribly wrong here. Let's send the troops out to find an English word on a sign somewhere in Canada. Let's prosecute!" Canadians, awaken, please.

Eva Henry Desormeaux, Ottawa

PUSH ROUGH RIDERS
INTO 21ST CENTURY
JULY 29, 1989

It is hard to find words to describe my disappointment with your newspaper's campaign against the Rough Riders.

While your editorial was supportive, your headlines, including front page negative stories, are terrible. If some alderman is stupid enough to destroy a 100-year-old institution because he received 10 phone calls, then so be it. Instead, you give credibility to this foolishness by running front-page headlines saying "ratepayers don't want to bail out the team."

One recent night, I watched more than 21,000 men, women and children enjoy a wonderful night of entertainment — and we lost! I saw public servants, businessmen, college students, senior citizens, high school kids and tourists enjoying themselves. I saw rich and poor and every imaginable ethnic and religious group sitting side by side, cheering on their team and having fun. I saw more than 21,000 people show Toronto that we too had a domed stadium by putting umbrellas over our heads.

Foolish? Of course, and God bless them for forgetting in a political city the nonsense on Parliament Hill, and elsewhere for the moment, and just being citizens in a well-rounded, well-balanced beautiful city.

Your coverage is not worthy of a newspaper in a city on the move. Shame on you. I will do everything in my power to see that the Ottawa Rough Riders move proudly into the 21st century, in spite of your paper's attitude.

James A. Durrell, Mayor, City of Ottawa

Editor's note: Mr. Durrell was true to his word — he fought tooth and nail to keep the Riders in Ottawa, even be-
coming team president in 1996 in a last-ditch attempt to save the franchise. In the end, however, the Riders folded after the 1996 season and, although hopes remain the team will return some day, Ottawa entered the new century without a CFL franchise.

NEPEAN BIRD CONTROL
SEPTEMBER 14, 1989

We understand that Nepean is considering a "Bird Management and Protection" bylaw after it was brought to council's attention that irresponsible persons are harboring birds by feeding and providing birdhouses for them.

The authorities have been alarmed to discover that these birds are carriers of toxoplasmosis as well as lice and some 27 different varieties of other parasites.

The presence of these birds on the lawns of people who do not wish to be exposed to these health hazards is directly traceable to irresponsible bird fanciers attracting them with food and shelter. The raucous noises these birds make, often at unreasonably early hours, are also interfering with the peace and quiet of non-bird fanciers and can no longer be tolerated in a city as health conscious and supportive of property rights as Nepean.

The problem of stray and unwanted songbirds should be solved by the elimination of the offending creatures as is being done with other household pets in Nepean. The "Bird Management and Protection" bylaw will deal with avian trespassers first by warning the offending neighbours whose birds are trespassing on others' properties, and after that by netting, trapping and impounding the offending birds.

If the birds can be identified as having been harbored by a particular neighbour, that person will be subject to a heavy fine and costs to obtain the release of the birds. If the birds are not claimed within four days, they will be considered strays and destroyed.

This aspect of the bylaw may considerably reduce the cost of feeding all the cats impounded under another of Nepean's carefully considered and humanitarian bylaws. This is an almost perfect example of complementary bylaws and Nepean is to be complimented on such clear thinking and common sense.

J. D. Corbett, Nepean

Editor's note: This satirical letter was written in response to a proposed bylaw limiting the number of cats per Nepean household to three.

HAS AUTUMN PEAKED?
OCTOBER 8, 1989

Regarding the article "Colour-blind tree watcher keeps eye out for peak fall peeks," when did we decide we had to know whether autumn leaves were at their "peak" before we could tell whether we could have a good time going for a walk in the woods?

Heaven forbid that tourists should come the weekend before or after the "peak." I can hear them now: "We went for a walk in Gatineau Park, and the leaves weren't

at their peak. We were so disappointed we're never going back." And what does this "peak" business mean,
anyway? Exactly what percentage of leaves have to be
turned for us to have a really good time? Twenty? Fifty,
Fifty-five?

What if 60 per cent have turned but 20 per cent have already fallen? Can we have fun then, or have we waited too
long and passed the peak? What if we simply went out to
enjoy the crisp autumn air and the smell of the forest, regardless of what colour the leaves are?

Must we always feel we've missed something if we don't
maximize each and every experience? Life can pass us by
if we'll only walk in the woods when things are at their
peak.

Tunde Nemeth, Ottawa

IT'S NOT 'JACKSON'
OCTOBER 22, 1989

I think Ray Hnatyshyn is an excellent choice as the
Queen's representative in Canada. His appointment has
certainly made my life easier. No longer do I have to explain that my wife's family name, Jacyszyn, does not
rhyme with "action." It rhymes, of course, with
Hnatyshyn.

There always will be doubters, though. When I phoned
my mother-in-law (the one whose name is not Jackson) to
ask her what she thought about a Ukrainian governor general, she was not as impressed as I.

"I wait for Ukrainian Queen," she said.

Rudi Aksim, Carp

NEW MUSEUM
SHOCKING DISAPPOINTMENT
NOVEMBER 15, 1989

Help! Stop the museum, I want to get out! The Museum
of Civilization reminds me of a low-budget movie with
paper sets, a discordant sound track and a random cut-
and-paste editing process.

For nearly two years we had looked forward to getting
inside the extravagant but very interesting new building.
Recently we did — but then could not wait to get out.

We had travelled more than 3,000 miles to see some of
the old buildings of Eastern Canada and our national museum. We wanted to see the real things that people made
and used in previous generations. We found an assortment of cheap movie props and recent art works but very
few "real things" which museums should show and explain.

Where are our national treasures? In some damp ware-
house — never to be seen by taxpayers and students? We
got a better sense of our history from the old National
Film Board movies we used to see in school. A small museum at Wakefield provided us with a more satisfying experience, even though it was closed for the season and we
could only peek through the windows. The McLaren
Grist Mill and Miller's House mean more to us than all
the "pretending artifacts" of the air-conditioned comfort
of the new Museum of What.

Ginny and Wayne Jenkins, Prince George, B.C.

ALARMING INCREASE
IN INTOLERANCE
NOVEMBER 16, 1989

Archie Bunkerism, that is, cultural, ethnic and linguistic
intolerance, is on the rise across Canada. Traditional Eng-
lish-French tensions are not at issue here, but the rise of
overtly anti-ethnic sentiment in the guise of protecting
certain institutions that are considered quintessentially
"Canadian."

I refer, of course, to the primarily Western Canada-
based movement to prohibit Sikh RCMP officers from
wearing turbans.

For a country peopled by immigrants from around the
globe, with each new group bringing a different language
and faith, this reaction should be alarming. Of course,
these reactionaries will argue that they are not anti-any-
thing but are only seeking to protect Canadian culture
and its visual exemplification in the red RCMP uniform
topped with the American-inspired and, in the early days,
manufactured, Stetson. The problem here isn't that Canadian culture isn't worth protecting but rather how it is defined. These anti-turban crusaders equate Canada's culture with white, anglo-Protestant characteristics that no
longer reflect our reality. Maybe in the '30s, but no longer.
In addition, let us remember that not all RCMP officers
will be sporting this head gear, if it is authorized, but only
a few members whose religion prescribes this. Let's not
exaggerate.

Tolerance and a willingness to accept new arrivals to
our shores was once a great virtue of Canadian society. I
only hope that this welcome was not meant solely for
white Europeans. As for these anti-turban crusaders, I
suggest that their time, money and effort would be better
spent planting trees and recycling so as to save an essential part of this country — its environment.

Michael O'Neill, Hull

*Editor's note: Despite polls showing two-thirds of Canadi-
ans favoured prohibiting turbans in the RCMP, the government decided such a ban would violate the Charter of
Rights and permitted Sikh officers to wear turbans while on
duty. In 1990, the government expanded the policy to allow
aboriginals to wear braids.*

WALKING TIME BOMBS AMONG US
DECEMBER 18, 1989

Because Marc Lépine was obsessed with "feminism,"
the media have left the impression that anti-feminism is
the villain here.

It is not. The villain here is Marc Lépine's psychosis —
and our scandalous neglect of the chronically mentally ill.
On this occasion, the violence focused on women. On
other occasions, it has victimized children, blacks, homosexuals, political leaders, McDonald's customers, and so
on.

Our society fails to distinguish the "mentally handicapped" from the "mentally ill" (which Marc Lépine surely was). What we cannot see, we cannot fix. So the Marc
Lépines will continue their sporadic violence, aimed

senselessly now at women, now at children, now at any other particular target whispered by their latest voices in the air.

And this will continue if we interpret each outburst as proof only of endemic anti-feminism, child abuse, political extremism, or what have you.

Thirty years ago, when medication became available to manage the behaviour of people with chronic mental illness, the "deinstitutionalization" saga began. These people were released from their asylums into the community, but then cheated of the continuing treatment facilities promised to them and their families.

This, combined with a trend toward protecting patients' civil liberties, has given us a growing population of tortured, often unstable, sometimes dangerous people.

They wander our streets, shopping malls, and other public places, suffering without hope. (Count "the homeless" among them.) Every mental health professional knows some of these "walking time bombs" personally.

In a democracy, only an informed public can create political will. The media bear a grave responsibility. Their depiction of the Montreal massacre mainly in "feminist" terms insults and blurs the valid cause of women's rights.

It also robs society of a rare chance to mobilize public opinion in favour of attacking the real problem: the 30 years' record of broken promises to our fellow citizens who suffer chronic mental illness.

Arthur S. Gillman, Winnipeg

MAGIC OF CHRISTMAS
FOR CHILDREN
DECEMBER 19, 1989

Four years ago, my two children, aged three and five, missed the visit to the fire station that was arranged by their school.

I took them the following week and, as we were getting out of our car, who did we see but The Jolly Old Elf Himself — Yes, Santa Claus.

He informed my children that he was very pleased to see them and that they were the first children he had seen since he arrived from the North Pole that year.

He took them into the fire station and spent an hour touring around and answering their questions about the magic of Christmas. He shared with them the information about his magic key to get into houses without chimneys.

DREW GRAGG, THE OTTAWA CITIZEN
Santa, with a young admirer at Bayshore, made Christmas special for a Nepean family.

After that, we watched and waved as he drove off in the fire truck to Bayshore.

Two weeks later we arrived at his workshop at Bayshore and I was surprised to hear that not only did he remember us but he shared our adventure with the crowd.

I left his workshop that day in tears of happiness.

Last year, we had to return to Santa the collar from one of his reindeer as it fell on our back step. He was so thankful to have it back.

Now my son is nine and my daughter is seven and they both believe in the magic of Christmas. They both realize that Santa sends his elves to help out in the cities and dress up as him but they are never sure which one was Santa and which one was an elf until now. Now they are sure that the Santa at Bayshore is the real man from the North Pole.

Well, we'll never know which is Santa and which is an elf but let me tell you that the Jolly Old Elf at Bayshore really brings out the spirit of Christmas.

He not only makes a real effort on his attire but he makes an extra special effort for the kids. And that's what Christmas is all about — kids.

Thank you, Santa, for making all our Christmases full of Christmas magic.

Roberta Farrell, Nepean

"Yes, Virginia, there is a Canada. You will not find it by gazing at coloured areas on a map that can be carved and divided among small minds. You will find it in your heart and in the heart of your neighbour."

— December 23, 1991

1990-1999

1990

Local: Paul Newman and Joanne Woodward spend a few days shooting *Mr. and Mrs. Bridge* in Rockcliffe Park (February); Soviet president Mikhail Gorbachev given hero's welcome in Ottawa (May); Ottawa Board Of Education elementary teachers stage 26-day strike (May-June); Ottawa awarded NHL franchise (December)

National: Meech Lake constitutional accord fails to get necessary provincial approval (June) 50 Mohawk warriors, women and children keep police and army at bay for 11 weeks at Oka, Que. (July-September); NDP wins majority in Ontario election (September)

World: Nelson Mandela freed after 27 years in South African prison (February); Tunnel collapse kills 1,426 Muslim pilgrims in Mecca (July); Germany merges into one country of 78 million after 40 years of division (July); Saddam Hussein sends Iraqi troops into Kuwait (August)

Deaths: Canadian writers Hugh MacLennan and Morley Callaghan; actress Greta Garbo; Muppets creator Jim Henson; conductor-composer Leonard Bernstein; entertainer Sammy Davis, Jr.; Maple Leaf Gardens president Harold Ballard; racehorse Northern Dancer; comedian Johnny Wayne

TAMPERING WITH CANADA'S HISTORY

JANUARY 3, 1990

The Museum of Civilization announces a special exhibition, "The Maple Leaf Forever," to "relive the post-Confederation struggle for independence."

What "struggle?" This travesty of Canadian history goes even beyond what Donald Creighton used to call "the Authorized, or Grit, Version." The exhibition includes, we are told, "vintage photographs" (of what?), "rare documents" (they must be rare indeed), "and an overwhelming selection of flags" (what flags?).

This brazen attempt to rewrite our history to make it more like the U.S. model may sit well with the Free Trade Agreement, and with the government's approval of the American invasion of Panama (an object lesson of what membership in the Organization of American States may mean). But it is likely to give viewers a biased impression. The Americans won their freedom by force. Ours "slowly broadened down. From precedent to precedent." Britain was not its foe, but its "imperial fountain." Our Parliament is the lineal descendant of the Parliament of England. Responsible government we took from Britain. Our judicial system and our criminal law are English. So is our civil law, except in Quebec.

Americans had a violent revolution. We had unsuccessful rebellions in Upper and Lower Canada before Confederation and on the Prairies after, but none in the Atlantic provinces, and no revolution anywhere. Will the museum provide Sir John A. Macdonald with a cherry tree and a hatchet, and New Brunswick a Saint John Tea Party? Who was our Paul Revere? Where is our Bunker Hill? Where are our Minute Men? Will the "vintage photographs" give us all these?

"O say, can you see?" I can't.

Eugene Forsey, Ottawa

WAIT, THE DECADE HASN'T ENDED YET

JANUARY 16, 1990

The media have inundated us with a plethora of reviews and assessments of "the decade: just ended — 10 consecutive years" apparently chosen because of the convenience of labelling that time period "the eighties."

Would it not have made more sense to have waited a year, and then given the same massive treatment to the ninth decade of the 19th century — the period from Jan. 1, 1981, to Dec. 31, 1990? Those people probably think that at the end of the countdown during the darkness of last Dec. 31-Jan. 1, there were 10 years left in the century. Wrong. There were 11.

And if, their thinking uncorrected, they are still around, they will embarrass themselves by greeting Dec. 31, 1999, as the end of the 10th decade, the 20th century and the second millennium. It happened in 1899, when the result was widespread and angry confusion. Something similar occurred in 1949 when reporters and commentators short-changed the first half century of the 20th century by allotting it only 49 years.

In the orderly consideration of the *anno domini* years using the Gregorian calendar, every decade, century and millennium begins January 1 of a year ending in 1. Every decade, century and millennium ends Dec. 31 of a year ending in 0.

Wilfred Kesterton, Ottawa

INJUSTICE SYSTEM

FEBRUARY 3, 1990

A Nova Scotia commission studying the Donald Marshall case has found that there is one law for the rich and influential, and another for the poor and minorities.

Two-tier justice is unfortunately practised in Ontario, too. New Democrat MP Lorne Nystrom was judged to be "forgetful" and was acquitted of shoplifting, while thousands of low-income people who are equally "forgetful" are convicted. A few weeks later, Dr. Selwyn Smith, a renowned Ottawa psychiatrist, was given a nine-month sentence for a $600,000 fraud, to be served at nights and on weekends, so as not to interfere with his practice.

These verdicts justify the contempt cynics have for our justice system. One of the measures of a civilized and orderly society is its ability to equitably dispense justice for all. Many prominent lawyers refuse to handle legal-aid cases, despite the fact that their higher education was heavily subsidized by the public.

A two-tier system of justice represents a crisis of credibility for our legal community that must be resolved as soon as possible before the public loses all faith in the justice system.

Wayne Mannion, Ottawa

INVISIBLE NATIVES
FEBRUARY 16, 1990

Why does Canada keep cheating the Indians? I am the chief of a small isolated community on the coast of James Bay (Eastmain, population 450) that is not connected to the rest of Canada by a road or a powerline.

Our hunting, fishing and trapping, our normal source of food, were seriously curtailed by Hydro-Québec's massive 1975 La Grande hydro-electric project. We have been forced more and more to rely on southern sources for our groceries and our basic nutrition.

In 1975, we were promised a road that would connect us with Canada. We still don't have it. Eastmain, like other northern native communities, has been cheated by Canada.

We do not have the roads, playgrounds, telecommunications, power supplies, streets, sidewalks, public libraries and other infrastructure that other Canadians take for granted. We are the invisible people. You won't see us on your way to work in the morning.

Milk in my community costs $2.05 a litre, bread is $1.89 a loaf, apples are $0.65 each and 10 kilos of flour is $23.85. These are the prices before the upcoming postal rate increase.

You could not afford these prices. Yet you live in the south where there are good prospects for work and adequate income to purchase nutritious food. We don't have these things.

There are no jobs and there is no way to stimulate employment because there are no roads, we have poor communications and our power still comes from worn-out diesel generating equipment.

Should not the people of Canada bear some expense to assure that our isolated native communities have equal access to nutrition and medicine?

Ted Moses, Chief,
Eastmain Band, Eastmain, Que.

OH DEAR!?!
MARCH 4, 1990

I was shocked last Saturday to see Mary Worth saying peevishly to a television news announcer: "It certainly takes forever to get to the point!" Can this be the same woman who once took three weeks to complete a local phone call? Is this the woman whose ability to suspend all signs of life for days on end has been an inspiration to me for longer than I care to remember?

If this marks some sort of permanent personality change, I can't say I like it. I have no desire whatsoever to be thrown back into the hurly-burly of the everyday world. If she doesn't get a grip on herself before, say the end of June, I vote we dump her.

G.W. Green, Ottawa

Editor's note: In 1994, after nearly four decades as a regular feature on the comics page, The Citizen *did dump Mary Worth, saying the strip's faithful, almost cult-like following was no longer big enough to justify keeping more popular contemporary strips off the comics page.*

SELFISH ACTS
MARCH 23, 1990

I am angry. Nay, not angry, but hostile. I am sick, sore and tired of watching selfish, uncaring, unfeeling, inconsiderate, imbecilic, able-bodied idiots parking in disabled parking spaces. In the space of one hour recently I saw one park at the Bank of Montreal on Greenbank (a frequent spot), two at Loblaws' at Barrhaven and one at the cleaners at Barrhaven (both frequently abused as well).

The ones that really burn me up are the hockey players and other jocks at the Walter Baker Arena and Nepean Sportsplex who park and get out with their skates, sticks and duffle bags and jog into the arenas. It's frustrating to watch disabled people having to hobble to a store because of some selfish, uncaring, unfeeling individuals.

There doesn't seem to be anything one can do about it. The sentence ought to be to confine these people to wheelchairs for 30 days in January or February for the first offence, double it for the second, etc.

C.E. Massey, Nepean

PRESIDENT'S CHOICE
APRIL 1, 1990

So President George Bush won't eat broccoli. That should surprise no one. He is merely following the honourable trail blazed by Ogden Nash who said: "Parsley is gharsley."

Garrett J. O'Neill, Ottawa

PROUD BUT SAD
APRIL 5, 1990

It is a sad day for me. I am 66 years old and have seen and been through a lot, but nothing like what is going on in "our" country now. I saw on TV a bunch of people (instigators, I guess) declaring with hate and disdain their feelings about the French and saying that they did not want them in Canada and that the Queen had won the war.

It reminded me of 50 years ago when I did my training in Toronto. I remember a little old lady hitting a young serviceman over the head with her purse (in a bus) because he spoke French. I also remember dance halls for Armed Forces people with signs that said, "No French."

Where are the Christian principles of love and tolerance that people constantly claim to believe in? I am proud of my French heritage, and will remain so till my last moment. I am a Canadian and proudly so.

If this thing is to increase, I hope that I won't be around to witness it. But I pity our young people.

Paul Lepage, Ottawa

BOOZY MOTHER'S DAY
MAY 4, 1990

If any of your readers have been affected, directly or indirectly, by alcoholic family abuse, your local liquor store may give you a shock.

"Mother's Day" is coming, and booze is suggested as the perfect gift. As the son of an alcoholic mother, I am deeply offended. The display at the LCBO flooded me with bad memories I thought I'd forgotten or at least forgiven.

Then I thought of all the thousands of children of alcoholics who still live at home. Suddenly a day to do something special for your mother is given LCBO reality — just another excuse to drink, leading to one more drunken nightmare of physical, verbal or emotional abuse. And you can bet that a kind friend of your mom's will buy her a bottle as an "appreciation" for being such a nice friend and a "perfect" mother.

People drink, of course, and discreet signs near champagne bottles or special dinner wines might be acceptable. But if these larger-than-life signs stay up, you can be sure there will be more drunken moms on this May 13 than ever, at least in trend-setting Ontario.

Booze shouldn't be an important part of this celebration.

Christan Nicholson, Ottawa

AMERICAN FEARS FOR CANADA
MAY 5, 1990

The Meech Lake deadline of late June is becoming front-page news in the United States, accompanied by talk of the breakup of Canada and absorption of the pieces by the U.S. As an American friend of Canada, I urge you: don't let it happen. Canadians seem to be near-sighted about their country, perhaps because of their overpowering neighbour to the south.

But your population is greater than that of Sweden, Norway, Israel and Switzerland combined, your per capita income one of the highest, your natural resources as rich as those of any country on the planet. Canadian science and technology have been top rank for many decades.

Canada has helped win two world wars, fought under the UN flag in Korea, and supplied peace-keeping troops for decades. You helped found the United Nations and NATO.

A fragmented Canada would undoubtedly be welcomed as an addition to the U.S., should it come to that. But the loss would be greater than the gain, to the world, to the Commonwealth, and especially to Canada. So grit your teeth, make the right decision in time, and keep your magnificent country together.

Paul D. Lowman,
Bowie, Maryland, U.S.A.

Editor's note: Reached in 1987, the Meech Lake accord was an effort to bring Quebec back into the Canadian "constitutional family" after the province's rejection of the 1981 constitutional patriation package. To become law, the accord, which recognized Quebec as a distinct society within Canada and formalized the federal-provincial constitutional amending process, had to be ratified by Parliament and all 10 provinces by June 23, 1990. The deal fell apart when the deadline passed without the consent of Manitoba and Newfoundland.

DYING IN PEACE
MAY 26, 1990

When we returned from Portugal on Sept. 1, 1987, it was clear that my wife Margery was very ill. Her condition had been diagnosed as sarcoidosis (triggered by a pneumonia bout in 1982), which had been controlled by the drug prednisone.

After a short stay in hospital, she was given the bad news in my presence. "You have an advanced case of fibrosis of the lungs, and will need oxygen continuously for the rest of your life."

"How much time do I have?" she asked. "Hopefully, three years." She accepted her sentence of death with composure, and thanked the doctor.

At first she required three litres of oxygen per minute, which could be applied by a light portable tank. We bought a station wagon, in which a larger tank could be securely fastened. This permitted us, in 1988, to visit her girlhood home in Dunnville, and relatives in Toronto and Hamilton.

Slowly, she weakened, and the rate of oxygen was stepped up to four, then five, five-and-a-half, six, six-and-a-half, and finally seven litres per minute.

In May 1988, after a visit to our daughter's home, she said she did not wish to go in the car any more. After three short hospital admissions in 1987 and 1988 for stabilizing medication and the insulin she now needed because the prednisone had rendered her diabetic, we had decided she would spend the rest of her days at home.

I cannot say enough about the wonderful, sensitive care of the Victorian Order of Nurses, and the help we received from home care programs. With their help, I was able to cope with Margery at home. Fortunately I am retired and still in good health. By September 1989 she was confined to bed, and incontinent. Her mind was clear and she never cried (but I did!).

She did, however, ask every day to be allowed to die. I could not bring myself to grant her request, nor could our attending physician. Canadian law is clear on the subject. Helping anyone to die is an offence.

Margery would have liked to call in her family and her friends to say her goodbyes, and then to terminate her life. Instead, she was condemned to three months of agony, suffering and lack of human dignity before she died in December.

Could not our laws be changed to avoid these last painful moments?

I am aware that this is a difficult decision, and permission for euthanasia can be abused, but no one should have to suffer as she did.

Lloyd Francis, Ottawa

Editor's note: Mr. Francis, a long-time municipal politician and Ottawa-area Liberal MP, is also a former Speaker of the House of Commons and ambassador to Portugal.

NATIONAL GALLERY SHOULD BE FREE
JULY 4, 1990

Canadians can be justifiably proud of their National Gallery. The building itself is a work of art and it houses a fine, growing collection — not least the "happening" titled *Voice of Fire.*

But ordinary Canadians are getting a raw deal: They have

to pay $4 to see their national collection or go on Thursday when it is free but there are twice as many people.

The National Gallery is not so "national" after all — it is mainly for the rich and privileged.

Other great galleries have a different attitude. The National Gallery in London, England, is free to the public every day. Any day of the week you can see pensioners and students, waitresses and cab drivers, moms, little kids and entire families. It is a fun place to be, and so-called "great" art is not only for the privileged; capital C Culture is for everyone to enjoy.

The real reason for cutting free Thursdays is not overcrowding or lineups. It comes to us at the end of a *Citizen* article. "We are expected to make money at the box office," says gallery spokesman Helen Murphy.

Aha, now we understand. A national gallery is not for the enjoyment or enrichment of a nation; rather, art is a commodity, a money-making proposition, only appreciated by those who can afford it. Lesser peons should be grateful for July 1 (if this plan goes through, our one remaining free day a year).

Ordinary citizens of Canada, and especially of Ottawa, need to make some noise, to stand up and be counted.

Suellen Seguin, Ottawa

Editor's note: Free Thursdays were never cut. In fact, the idea was expanded in the mid-'90s when the Gallery decided to drop the admission fee for its permanent collection every day of the week. Admission is still charged for special exhibits.

SUNDAY SHOPPING BAD
JULY 15, 1990

If retailers are required to open their stores for an additional day, the expenses will be paid for by the retailer. These expenses include, but are not limited to, salaries, hydro, taxes, and advertising. Consumers will not have increased spending power during the additional hours of retail, unless they increase their personal borrowing power or the government reduces the personal tax rate — both of which are unlikely.

Remaining open for one more day each week will not result in increased sales: It will simply take seven days to accomplish the same amount of business retailers now do in six. The result will be reduced profit margins.

There will be additional costs: public transit, law enforcement, road maintenance, and day care. Subsidies for these services come from municipal taxes. Employee concerns are being raised by the various unions involved. Their main concerns are: job security; termination of employment; denied promotions; denied bonuses and pay increases; replacement by part-time staff hired at lower pay rates and receiving reduced benefits.

Although an employee may not be terminated for refusing to work on Sunday, it is common knowledge that an employer can find many excuses to release an employee who refuses such work. Retail employees are entitled to

THE OTTAWA CITIZEN

While those opposed to Sunday shopping held a protest rally, a store manager said community-oriented stores would suffer by having to open seven days a week.

one common pause day per week — which may be spent with families, offspring, spouses, or sweethearts. They do not want Sunday shopping.

The hours now faced by retail operations make it difficult to find experienced professionals. Increasing these hours will make it even more difficult to find qualified help. There will be no stopping point until a full seven-day work week exists for all. Mall landlords can force tenants to open against their will. With the gradual erosion of the viability of the independent retailer, consumer traffic patterns will be altered in favour of the larger chains.

Small, community-oriented stores will suffer. As they disappear, everyone will feel their loss. Once Sundays are open to shopping, other statutory holidays will be jeopardized. If asked, most consumers would agree to Sunday shopping, as a child would say "yes" if offered candy. The question is: would you work on Sunday?

Elaine Vacher, General Manager,
Tallmire's Fashions,
Co-founder of the Coalition
Against Open Sunday Shopping

DON'T BLAME CHICAGO
AUGUST 19, 1990

I am currently visiting my fiancé in Ottawa and I couldn't help but notice that hideous square building next to the Château Laurier. As a Chicagoan, imagine my horror when I was told that this building has not been torn down because it represents "Chicago" style architecture.

While Chicago is known for its beautiful buildings, this is clearly not one of them. If, for some reason, you do decide to let this building stand, please don't blame Chicago.

Donna Krejc,
Mount Prospect, Illinois

1991

Local: Under public pressure, Jim Durrell resigns as Ottawa mayor to devote all his time to presidency of Ottawa Senators (February); Public service strike paralyses region for 10 days (September); Outbreak of meningitis-related infection sparks massive region-wide inoculation program (December)

National: Calgary-based Reform party announces it will run candidates in all provinces except Quebec in next federal election (June); Keith Spicer's Citizen's Forum calls for national referendum on constitutional change (June); Federal government releases wide-ranging package of constitutional reforms (September)

World: U.S.-led allies bomb Iraq, forcing Saddam Hussein to retreat from Kuwait (January-March); South African government announces plans to scrap apartheid (February); Typhoon kills 125,000 in Bangladesh (April); Soviet Union ceases to exist (December)

Deaths: Senator and constitutional expert Eugene Forsey; Newfoundland premier Joey Smallwood; theorist Northrop Frye; *Star Trek* creator Gene Roddenberry; jazz musicians Miles Davis and Stan Getz; film directors Frank Capra and David Lean; writers Graham Greene, Isaac Bashevis Singer and Jerzy Kosinski; New Brunswick premier Richard Hatfield; governor general Roland Michener; actresses Lee Remick and Jean Arthur; actors Fred MacMurray and Yves Montand; dancers Martha Graham and Margot Fonteyn; Canadian journalists Marjorie Nichols, Warner Troyer and Dick Beddoes; baseball legend Leo Durocher; Theodor (Dr. Suess) Geisel

NATION OF TAX WIMPS

FEBRUARY 21, 1991

An American in Washington told me recently about visiting a store in London, England, and asking if some tea could be shipped back to him in the United States. When he inquired in all innocence about shipping and taxes, the tea-store lady declared frostily that Britain did not tax tea sent to the U.S.

What inspired this wonderful story was the way Canadians roll over and die when hit with outrageous taxes (our best and bravest fighters against the GST, for God's sake, were doddery old senators armed with kazoos).

A recent letter to *The Citizen* demanded an end to complaints about the GST; it's here, said the writer, so pay up and shut up. A similarly wimpy editorial appeared in my local weekly not long ago. Far from shutting up, we should be screaming blue murder and demanding changes in the name of fairness and sanity. The GST is ill-conceived, stupid and inhumane.

Ill-conceived? The cost of administering it will eat up most if not all the "profits." It's like having to run 100 miles to get to the starting line for a marathon.

Stupid? I bought 10 one-cent stamps to add to 39-cent stamps when the price went up, and was charged one cent GST. To start with that's 10 per cent, not seven. As a business expense, it's eligible for an "input credit," what people in the real world would call a refund. Think of the paperwork.

Inhumane? I registered for a CPR course and could hardly believe my eyes when I learned I had to pay GST on it.

Only Brian Mulroney could give the kiss of life the kiss of death.

Geoff Johnson, Manotick

NICE TRY, KID

MARCH 30, 1991

I was very touched by the recent article on Corey Smart of Bradford, who handed over $168 from the sale of his toys to Finance Minister Michael Wilson to help the government reduce the federal deficit. But the government has just undertaken to provide $80,000 to East European army officers so they may attend a seminar on the role of the military in a democratic society.

It was a nice idea, Corey, but I'm afraid they're gaining on you.

G. W. Green, Ottawa

MEAT IS THE ISSUE

MARCH 30, 1991

Again this year the National Gallery cannot attract enough people during the winter months and it has to resort to shocking the public into visiting it.

I am disgusted and ashamed by the choice of contemporary art at the gallery. Besides exposing a urinal, a sink, a shovel, some rocks, plywood boxes, shelves, soap boxes, black, yellow, grey and red frames we are now paying a so-called artist for a dress made of meat (while people down the street are lining up at the soup kitchen).

Something must be done. Our government is paying for garbage art. It must be made clear to the curator that it is no longer acceptable. Most Canadians want art that embodies beautiful and sensuous forms either in painting, photography, statues, music, or speech.

Write your MP or minister, now. Don't wait for another *Voice of Fire* or dress of meat. Don't encourage this, boycott the gallery.

Maxine Robert Bédard, Gatineau

WRONG HEADED

JULY 31, 1991

I read with interest the article, "Pretty Cool Training in Hot Weather." But I would like to correct the statement that "80 per cent of your body heat escapes through your head."

The original research on heat loss from the head was done by Dr. Alan C. Burton at the University of Western Ontario and published in the *Journal of Applied Physiology* in 1957. Burton measured the heat loss from the head at temperatures from about -8 C to +32 C. His test subjects added clothing as the temperature decreased so they remained comfortable.

Burton found that at high temperatures, very little of the heat produced by the body was lost through the head. However, as the temperature decreased, such heat loss increased, so that at -4 C, about half the heat production of the resting subject was lost through his head.

Thus, the statement that "80 per cent of your body heat escapes through your head" might be true for a very well-insulated person at very cold temperatures, but certainly not for lightly clad people at warm temperatures.

R.M. Crow, Stittsville

PRESUMED INNOCENT?
NOT IN ONTARIO

AUGUST 16, 1991

During a period of three weeks, the government agrees to compensate nurse Susan Nelles on the one hand and then announces its intention to recommend immediate 90-day licence suspensions for drivers who fail breathalyser tests before trial.

In paying Ms. Nelles, the government obviously recognized the unfairness she endured because she was treated as if she was guilty long before any trial into the deaths of the babies at Sick Children's Hospital took place. But now, once again, proposed treatment of the individual violates the presumption of innocence.

Not surprisingly, a government spokesperson claims that "the general public will accept this kind of measure." That may well be the case, but should the government score cheap political points by pandering to the public's sympathy for anything that might (or might not) further reduce drinking and driving? A very large proportion of working individuals depend upon their ability to drive a motor vehicle. A suspension might have disastrous consequences for an individual who is later found not guilty.

It is not only civil libertarians who are concerned about the constantly moving line between an individual's rights and freedoms and that which society collectively sanctions. The first step was random stopping through RIDE-type programs — as long as the programs were widely publicized in advance. Then the need for publicity was eliminated, and random stops were sanctioned in the name of decreasing the carnage on the highway.

The present proposal would mean that any driver could be stopped anywhere, any time, by the police without any evidence of impaired driving, required to take a breathalyser test, which if failed would result in an immediate 90-day licence suspension.

The government had best be prepared to deal with many more Susan Nelleses in the future.

Lawrence Greenspon, Ottawa

Editor's note: Mr. Greenspon is a well-known Ottawa criminal lawyer.

WARHOL MEETS PAVLOV

AUGUST 30, 1991

While strolling through the National Gallery recently, I noticed a very disturbing thing: In the Contemporary Art wing, we came upon a room with a 20-by-20 foot square of raised tiles on the floor, right in the middle of our path. Concerned, we avoided the tiles, and I searched the walls for an explanation.

A member of the Gallery staff smiled and tried to show some tourists behind us that the tiles were not art. He

walked on the tiles, and beckoned the Japanese family forward. Everyone laughed.

We were struck. We watched for 15 minutes, and of the 42 people who entered the room, every one walked around the tiles. I'd like to find the poor guy who laid those tiles for an average Canadian wage, and tell him that if only he wore different clothes and gave his work a vague title, he could make a whole lot more money.

He already has a big following.

Allisen Gibson, Ottawa

THE CANADIAN PRESS

Ovide Mercredi, national chief of the Assembly of First Nations, was said to be right to demand self-government for aboriginal people.

HISTORY ON NATIVES' SIDE

OCTOBER 3, 1991

Ovide Mercredi, national chief of the Assembly of First Nations, is right in demanding that the federal government's latest constitutional proposals recognize the aboriginal people's inherent right to self-government.

History is on his side when he points out that, as original inhabitants, they organized themselves into sophisticated political organizations. They never agreed to forfeit their rights to those institutions. Granted, under duress they lived according to other systems.

But this no more stamped out their religious, cultural and institutional rights than the fact that Christians in the Soviet Union, forced under duress to close churches, thereby gave up the right to live as Christians.

Mercredi's assertion that the first people are by nature reasonable and generous has been borne out through my own experience with Micmac, Cree, Ojibway, Mohawk, Dene, Inuit, Métis and other aboriginal peoples. They have taught me a great deal about what it means to be a decent, sharing, human being.

Many in Canada view our country as generous and compassionate. If we exemplify generosity toward the first people today, they might, in turn, teach us to better become who we say we are.

Vern Redekop, Gloucester

DISTINCT QUESTIONS

OCTOBER 8, 1991

As an anglophone grandmother living in Quebec, I have some questions for your readers.

If the distinct society clause is included in the Constitution, who exactly will become distinct? Will all Quebecers become distinct, including immigrants and anglophones? What about children of an English-speaking mother and French-speaking father? Will they become half-distinct? How can I identify these distinct people? Will the distinct people wear identifying symbols? Or, will those not distinct be required to wear identifying symbols? Since all non-French-speaking Quebecers are referred to as English, should I start knitting Union Jacks?

J. A. Donovan, Luskville

ARROGANT ELITE

OCTOBER 22, 1991

Each time the term "redneck" is used (as in your recent editorial on gun control), the user contributes to disunity and hatred in Canada.

Rural Albertans have the right to their opinions, and to their way of life, which is not that of Montreal, Toronto or Ottawa. We rural Canadians are tired of the arrogance and name-calling of the self-appointed urban élite.

Marion MacMaster, Alexandria

HARD TIMES AND RAW NERVES

NOVEMBER 29, 1991

As a fifth generation, 33-year-old Canadian farmer, your article, "A circle dance for dinosaurs," touched a raw nerve.

The fear, paralysing uncertainty and the proud men and women whose nerves have snapped due to farm financial pressures, are prevalent coast to coast. Urban dwellers, including the "urbaniks" who have bought farms, due to manipulative government indifference and just plain ignorance, do not understand the farm crisis because they are not one of "us."

The gutless manipulative scum who run our marketing boards, wheat boards and other farm organizations are on a par with the politicians that they slither to, and a large part of this mess can be laid on all their shoulders. The 7,000 who jammed that hall in Regina signified that we have had enough. That is why the family farm will survive.

Being one of us is hard to explain but it's having a dad who went to school in a horse and buggy and today punches a computer on his farm; a dad who worked his guts out to help set up all his boys in farming — considering it a sacred duty. When an "important" man proclaimed "the family farm is almost finished," Dad scorned him. "Us" is having neighbours who, when your wife is in the hospital, move into a corn field at 4 p.m. with a combine and when you wake up at 5:30 a.m., the field is not only combined but plowed.

"Us" is having a wife who slaves her guts out and does without holidays, money, nice clothes, and a decent car, yet goes through life with a quiet dignity and total sacrifice to her children and the farm's welfare. When a woman who is one of "us" dies, people stand in the cold November wind for three hours outside a nursing home to pay their respects.

Being one of "us" is living one mile from a small graveyard that has two sets of great-grandparents, one set of grandparents and a 19-year-old brother buried there. Being one of "us" means going to a church that is over 200 years old. Being one of "us" is being tough, yet sobbing for the first time in years over the three farmers in Lambton County who killed themselves in the space of a week.

Alan Cumming, Glengarry Farms,
Williamstown, Ont.

ADJECTIVAL IDEA

DECEMBER 2, 1991

In an effort to assist the constitutional committee with one of its many problems, I suggest this possible antidote to the designation of Quebec as a "distinct society."

The assigned adjectives would serve to describe each of the provinces and the territories in the Constitution:

Newfoundland — Disadvantaged
Nova Scotia — Disgruntled
New Brunswick — Disenchanted
Prince Edward Island — Disabled
Ontario — Disorganized
Quebec — Distinct (or Extinct)
Manitoba — Distressed
Saskatchewan — Disturbed
Alberta — Disillusioned
British Columbia — Disjointed
Yukon and N.W.T. — Disinherited

Orval F. Bush, Stittsville

FOR VIRGINIA/POUR VIRGINIE

DECEMBER 23, 1991

"I am greatly troubled by the world around me. My friends tell me that there is no such thing as Canada and that I am a fool for believing in such childish fantasies. I am very confused. My father tells me that if I read it in the *Citizen*, it must be so. Oh tell me, kind persons, is there a Canada?

Sincerely, Virginia"

Ma chère Virginie

These times are very trying for young hearts. There will always be some among us who seek to tear apart the dreams and visions of wiser men and women, as if they derived an immense satisfaction from the act of tearing down what could simply be renovated. Their small minds and dark souls lack the imagination that has built a nation and created a soul.

The childhood of our great grandparents was filled

with Canada and they laboured for it proudly and nurtured it lovingly. Without a Canada this continent would be a large island of stripes and stars and its people would be struggling with greater dilemmas than we can imagine.

As insanity struggles to find a home in this land and some find new ways of sowing seeds of division, you must remember that we are all distinct and that no single group of people can claim safe refuge from those who would impose their culture and their values upon us because of their sheer immensity.

You are blessed because your native friends can share their rich culture with you, your English-speaking friends can entertain you, and your French-speaking friends can sing songs for you, if only you will let them and you, dear Virginia, after tasting the sweet diversity that surrounds you, will be richest of all.

Yes, Virginia, there is a Canada. You will not find it by gazing at coloured areas on a map that can be carved and divided among small minds. You will find it in your heart and in the heart of your neighbour.

Edmond Hétu,
Aylmer

1992

Local: Newly minted Ottawa Senators defeat Montreal Canadiens 5-3 in their first regular season game (October); Graeme Kirby's report on municipal restructuring urges larger role for regional government (November)

National: Atlantic fishery crisis results in two-year shutdown of cod fishery (July); Details of North American Free Trade Agreement unveiled in August; PM Mulroney signs deal in December; Toronto Blue Jays win first of two successive World Series (October); Canadians reject Charlottetown Accord constitutional reforms in national referendum (October)

World: Russia's first experiments with free market economy trigger soaring inflation and severe shortages (May); 42 killed in Los Angeles rioting related to verdict in Rodney King case (May); 100 world leaders gather to discuss worldwide environmental strategy at Earth Summit in Rio (June); Fighting over Bosnia escalates amid charges of ethnic cleansing and other atrocities (July)

Births: Avery Brown, fictitious out-of-wedlock child of television's Murphy Brown

Deaths: New Brunswick tycoon K.C. Irving; Senator and Liberal politician Paul Martin, Sr.; singer-actress Marlene Dietrich; feminist politician Pauline Jewett; journalist Bruce Hutchison; science fiction writer Isaac Asimov; singer-songwriter Roger Miller; composer John Cage; bandleader Lawrence Welk; CFL executive Sam Berger; hockey legend Irwin (Ace) Bailey; Rough Riders coach Wally Masters; country singer Roy Acuff; Czech president Alexander Dubcek, father of 1968 Prague Spring reforms; baseball broadcaster Red Barber

CANADIANS STILL FOGGY ABOUT CANADA

JANUARY 4, 1992

So "Canadians know quite a bit about their country." The *Citizen* must be joking.

The Angus Reid-Southam News Quiz on Canada to which you so glowingly referred on Dec. 29 says, plain as a pikestaff, that 54 per cent of your sample failed. At least when most of us went to school a score of 44 per cent or less was a failure.

The questions were based on those posed to applicants for Canadian citizenship, you say. So the abysmal fact is that half, yes half of us, simply don't qualify. Put us in front of a citizenship court judge and we'd be told to come back when we know enough to, well, vote.

We have no national educational policy and it may be too late to develop one. But here, surely, is something for all those school trustees in Ottawa-Carleton and their elected counterparts across the nation to get their teeth into. Here is something for voters at municipal and provincial levels to speak out on.

We can restructure our Constitution until we're blue in the face but unless we insist on teaching our children in school what Canada is and why (along with seeing they're adequately versed in at least one language and have the essential mathematical skills for a decent working career), we'll never have a country worthy of the name.

Tony German, Kingsmere

FAIR DEAL WANTED

JANUARY 17, 1992

I work in a factory, making $7.20 an hour. I just found out I'm getting a zero-per-cent raise this year. My taxes will probably be going up to support the welfare increase. Bus fare has gone up, food prices, hydro have gone up — everything has gone up. I'm not in this boat alone.

Last night on the television news, I listened to a young healthy woman crying because her free glasses may no longer be available due to welfare budget cuts and how she and others in her situation may have to turn to illegal activities to supplement their incomes; not get jobs mind you, but turn to illegal activities.

Well, all I want is a fair deal. No one helps us, the working poor. We get nothing, not even a raise. Does anybody know we're out here? Does anybody care?

Hazel Martin, Ottawa

DON GETTY APPALLING

JANUARY 18, 1992

I am appalled at Alberta Premier Don Getty's statements on bilingualism and multiculturalism. Are Canadians of British ancestry the only ones to be allowed to feel at home in Canada? Bilingualism in Canada should by now be beyond question.

Multiculturalism has three main functions: 1. To fight racism; 2. To increase one's understanding of other cultural groups in Canada; and 3. To foster cultural expression in Canada.

Many seem to object to this third objective. It is said that the government should end any sort of support for Chinese, Ukrainian, or Sikh, etc., cultural activities.

Where will this policy end? Is not ballet nothing but stylized French folk dancing? What of the theatre, which stages Shakespeare, i.e., ethnic British literature? Will the Calgary Stampede be shut down as an ethnic festival celebrating the heritage of Albertans of American descent? What about tax money spent on football stadiums (American-dominated) or curling rinks and golf courses (both "ethnic" Scottish cultural activities)?

Could it be that Mr. Getty foresees a Canada where everyone studies aboriginal languages between hockey games? Not a bad idea in itself but certainly it should not become the extent of cultural activity in Canada.

Havrylo Onutsky, Ottawa

BLAME THE ADULTS

FEBRUARY 1, 1992

A typical day outside the Rideau Centre. The evening rush hour is almost over; latecomers are waiting to catch a bus home. A 13-year-old boy is harassed by a gang of six teenagers, clearly out to steal his skateboard. They boast loudly of what they are about to do.

And the adults sit by and watch the events unfold. "Swarming" is the latest media fad. A more newsworthy approach would have been corrective: Instead of depicting a teen as a victim of a swarming, why not show the teen as a victim of adult apathy, of those too afraid or intimidated to help?

Anyone who has ever turned a blind eye to such activities is as guilty as those who commit the crime. It is time adults stopped behaving like a pathetic herd of bleating sheep, and started taking leadership and action in encouraging social change.

Britta Santowski, Hull

VALOUR AND HORROR

FEBRUARY 8, 1992

The real horror is that the CBC and NFB, with our tax money, produced that televised pack of lies and anti-Canadian, anti-British, and pro-Nazi propaganda in the first place.

I landed on the beaches in Normandy as a member of the Stormont, Dundas and Glengarry Highlanders with the Third Canadian Infantry Division under Maj.-Gen. R.F.O. Keller. We did not have drunken, bumbling idiots commanding us, as the "peaceniks" who obviously produced the TV series monstrosity try to make our young people believe. The producers failed to explain the strategic plan, and why it was vital for the Canadians and British to keep up unrelenting pressure on Nazi armour in the Caen sector. It was to permit the Americans to break out in the west, and we did it. We then pushed on to Falaise and Trun, still against the stiff opposition of an outsmarted enemy.

Of course, we were dog-tired, from our commanders down. But we knew we had a job to do — to liberate Europe and the world from Nazi terror. The bomber raids on British cities had taken place, and indiscriminate V1 flying bomb and V2 attacks on Britain were taking place, with Hitler promising worse to come. (He was working on the atomic bomb. The film said nothing about that.) One of the Canadian Army's tasks was to eliminate the V1 launching sites.

We were at war. People get killed. Of course there was horror. The Nazis of the SS units were killers, trained since youth. We were, for the most part, just young Canadians who valued our way of life and our home enough to fight for them in spite of our shortcomings, mainly through lack of trained reinforcements because Prime Minister Mackenzie King catered to Quebec over conscription.

The CBC and NFB, in airing such a horrible production, have done an enormous disservice to the men and women who served Canada and their families. I wonder now, whether I, too, should have stayed home in comfort, and let the Nazis eventually take Canada.

What kind of people have snatched the torch we hoped to pass to young Canadians?

R. R. Dixon, Ottawa

SCHOOL BUS DEATHS

MARCH 14, 1992

Another death of a child, the third run over by a school bus in less than a year, is a call for parents and taxpayers to consider doing away with busing children to schools outside their own district.

Children should have the privilege of walking, each morning, to their own school where they would meet the neighbour's children.

Thelma Wasteneys, Ottawa

TREES FALL IN FOREST

MARCH 28, 1992

I recently watched from my front porch as an old friend was killed just a few feet down the street. In broad daylight this friend was swarmed by a gang of vandals and cut to pieces.

The victim of this chainsaw massacre was not a person but an important survivor of a vanishing, endangered species. It was a giant elm tree, one of the last in the Ottawa Valley and the only one of its kind left in our concrete jungle. It was 150-feet tall and was estimated to be 150-250 years old. It was healthy and without structural flaw or weakness.

It had cast its shadow over this land long before Canada was a country, it was here before Colonel By completed the Rideau Canal. In the summer, when we looked at its regal spread of branches and its dense, lush foliage it was our link to the past.

We will now have to wait until at least the year 2142 for something its equal to stand over our neighbourhood. Will Canada be around then? The giant elm survived the ravages of Dutch elm disease but it could not survive an Ottawa council determined to bring it down.

Christopher J. Dodd, Ottawa

MILA MULRONEY: ENOUGH, ALREADY

MAY 2, 1992

If *The Citizen's* intent was to attract attention, it did. If the intent was to mislead, it did. I don't know anyone in my work environment, circle of friends or acquaintances, or my age group (mid-30s), who is "adoring of Mila," except maybe Mila herself, Sally Armstrong, the author-groupie, and one or two would-be clones.

This journalistic lightweight would have the public believe that the average Canadian woman identifies or even admires Mrs. PM, hence we will buy the book. The book will sell, largely because most people are curious about the private life of anyone with notoriety, i.e. any piece on Imelda Marcos or Elena Ceaucescu. Even Margaret Trudeau's tell-all accounts went into paperback edition.

So please, enough bombarding us with Mila *ad nauseam*. Isn't it all only election propaganda, and not true journalism?

Margaret Nowland, Ottawa

MOVE OVER, BOYS!

MAY 28, 1992

Could we please suggest to the wonderful Constitutional Affairs Minister, Joe Clark, that the quickest way to get "the boys" to settle their arguments over the Senate is to remind them that at least half the seats should be available to women?

We have many who are waiting to be invited — people of ability, idealism and proven achievement, not just party hacks and other rejects.

Janet Parry, Ottawa

ABORTION/ADOPTION

JUNE 13, 1992

Pro-lifers who are so determined to save lives and believe that abortions are a mortal sin, should back up their views with action. Each one should sign a legally binding document that they will personally adopt or undertake to financially support each and every child whom they have saved from being aborted. In my opinion, then and only then should they have a right to challenge any woman's right to have an abortion.

Albert Rivers, Ottawa

NOISE OVER BYWARD

JUNE 26, 1992

We have murders in this city, wife beaters, child molesters, rapists, poverty . . . the list goes on. But our councillors worry about noise in Byward Market. Give us a break!

Cathy Parsons, Ottawa

TOPLESS PROTEST

JULY 25, 1992

How are women to be taken seriously on such issues as abortion rights and the rape crisis when these issues are being represented by women baring their chests?

It is obvious whose attention was aroused and why. The pursuing crowd was predominantly camera-bearing men. What a joke!

Laurie Bloom, Gloucester

DON'T CLOSE MINDS

JULY 31, 1992

The article on book censorship in some Canadian schools left me concerned. While in high school I read *Catcher in the Rye*, but I did not become a deranged sex maniac. I read *Lord of the Flies*, but do not practise satanic rituals. I read *To Kill a Mockingbird*, but am definitely not a racist.

The themes and words for which these books were banned are no different from what children are exposed to on the streets, in movies, or on television. They are no different from the words which they sometimes overhear their parents or older siblings speak.

What comes next? Should schools ban Shakespeare's *Macbeth* because the hero is a criminal; or Robertson Davies' *Fifth Business* because it deals, in part, with vengeance and death? And what about *Romeo and Juliet*, and *Death of a Salesman*?

It is much worse to ignore such important issues than to confront them. Books should be used as teaching tools to educate kids about things such as racism, and to formally discuss them as a group, allowing children to discover what is right and what is wrong.

It is truly time that parents find confidence in their parenting skills, and learn to trust their children's judgment.

M.J. Roy, Ottawa

IS CANADA SORRY FOR AIDING HANOI?

OCTOBER 30, 1992

I have been watching with interest the outrage of Canadian citizens with respect to the Canadian flag being displayed upside-down at the Atlanta Braves-Toronto Blue Jays game.

As a retired U.S. naval officer, I have long wondered how the average Canadian feels about his country's support of the Hanoi regime in the 1960s and early 1970s. This involved not only the delivery of supplies to Haiphong, but the policy of giving sanctuary to our draft-dodgers and deserters.

Vietnam veterans like me would welcome Canadian views regarding how they feel about their nation's actions in the historical light of what North Vietnam has done to South Vietnam, Laos, and Cambodia since 1975.

James P. Brown, Jr., Cmdr. USN (ret), Bethesda, Maryland

KIM AS PLAYGIRL OF THE MONTH?

NOVEMBER 7, 1992

Where is equity, meaning fairness and recourse to principles of justice?

The picture of Kim Campbell, minister of justice and attorney general of Canada in the Nov. 1 *Citizen*, was rather revealing with bare shoulders, and with the appearance of being braless, behind a judge's robe.

This photograph of Kim Campbell drew the wrath of a reader who said it depicted her as "playgirl of the month."

Premier Bob Rae fired his minister Peter Kormos for appearing fully dressed as the Sunshine Boy. Is Kim Campbell one of the distinct cabinet members or will she too be history?

Equality and justice for all should be the cabinet watchwords. Why not the Hon. Kim Campbell, Distinct Canadian, Playgirl of the Month?

Joy MacGregor, Ottawa

BAN RUDOLPH SONG
NOVEMBER 17, 1992

The song *Rudolph The Red-Nosed Reindeer* is blatantly racist and should be purged from Christmas lore.

Rudolph was humiliated by his peers; "all of the other reindeer, used to laugh and call him names." Why? Because of his shiny nose. He was a visible minority. (Almond eyes, dark skin, red nose, choose your own identifying feature.) Rudolph was socially ostracized; "they never let poor Rudolph play in any reindeer games." Why? Only because he looked different from those of the dominant culture in which he lived.

What happened next? On his own merit Rudolph became a hero. (He guided Santa's sleigh, scored the winning touchdown, graduated at the top of his class; again, choose your own achievement.) "Then how the reindeer loved him ..."

Is this what we want to teach our children? Love those who attain distinction, but otherwise, it's OK to scorn those who are different?

Let us, rather, concentrate on the true meaning of Christmas — peace on earth and goodwill among people and their substitute creatures of every colour and creed. Ban the Rudolph song.

D. Desmond Nolan, Nepean

RUDOLPH FANS SEE RED
NOVEMBER 21, 1992

Awwwww ... c'mon. Rudolph the red-nosed reindeer started as a department store promotion jingle, became a much-loved worldwide Christmas song, enjoyed by kids to grampas from all walks of life.

Why, when Rudolph joined Santa's sleigh, he proved that Lewis Carol's poem *The Night before Christmas* was really true, as NORAD started picking up Rudolph's dazzling red shnoz on the DEWLINE radar system as Santa left the North Pole on Christmas Eve.

But now poor Rudolph's being accused of being racist. Hmmph. Just hope some of Scrooge's ghosts start haunting Rudolph's accuser; better still that Santa leaves him nuthin' in the sock he hangs on the mantle.

Ken Waplington, Ottawa

BERNIE AND LONIE, TURN OUT THE LIGHTS
NOVEMBER 21, 1992

My message to Bernie and Lonie Glieberman is please don't forget to turn out the lights on your way out. Goodbye and good luck.

Rough Riders fans, new and old, have had enough of your extortion attempts. In as much as the business deal with the city hasn't changed since you bought the team in 1991, why should it be renegotiated? Did you buy the team with the thought that your good works would be rewarded by a dim-witted council? The concessions at Lansdowne are not even the question at this point, are they? Honestly, isn't this just a smoke screen to justify moving the team?

May our civic mothers and fathers stick to their guns and call the bluff of the Gliebermans. Who knows, maybe a real Canadian Football League will resurface, with a roster full of Canadian kids playing for the love of the game and pocket money.

Hey, maybe Lonie and Co. will rescue the game after all!

Rick Oliver, Ottawa

LION WRONG MASCOT
NOVEMBER 28, 1992

I am writing in response to a contest *The Citizen* is conducting in conjunction with the Ottawa Senators hockey club — a contest to name the Senators' mascot. While I congratulate the Senators on their entrance to major-league hockey, and support *The Citizen's* support of the club, I am somewhat distressed at the Senators' choice of mascot — a lion.

While lions are truly majestic creatures, the only connection that lions have to the Roman Senate and Roman Empire — the symbolism alluded to by the Senators' logo — is that lions were used in Rome's arenas for the sole purpose of barbaric entertainment. Lions were pitted against gladiators, criminals and Christians — expendable and unwanted people.

I doubt, for instance, that the German Olympic hockey team would ever consider having a Nazi concentration camp "doctor" as their team mascot.

I see little difference between that unsavoury image and what the Senators are asking us to accept as their "mascot."

Rev. Whitman Strong,
City View United Church,
Nepean

Editor's note: For the record, the winning name was Spartacat.

1993

Local: Ottawa's new city hall expansion, the work of architect Moshe Safde, opens on Sussex Drive (January); Ottawa Senators select junior sensation Alexandre Daigle first in the NHL draft, then sign him to a $12.5-million contract (June); The city's first Triple-A baseball team in four decades sets league attendance record in opening season (September)

National: Four members of Canadian Airborne Regiment, in Somalia as part of UN contingent, charged in death of Somali teen in their custody (April); St. Catharines accountant Paul Bernardo charged with murder in the deaths of teens Kristen French and Leslie Mahaffy. Police say they are also talking to a woman in connection with the murders (April); Kim Campbell becomes Canada's first female PM by winning PC leadership vacated by Brian Mulroney (June); PCs reduced to two seats — and Ms. Campbell's role as PM limited to 123 days — as Liberals win majority in election (October)

World: Both sides in Bosnia-Herzegovina conflict reject peace plans to settle their ethnic bloodshed (February); Standoff in Waco, Texas ends in tragedy when authorities storm cult compound (April); PLO leader Yasser Arafat and Israeli PM Yitzhak Rabin sign historic peace accord secretly negotiated in Norway (September); Agreement reached paving way for all-race elections in South Africa (September)

Deaths: Governor general Jeanne Sauvé; hockey broadcaster Danny Gallivan; writers Anthony Burgess and William Shirer; jazz trumpeter Dizzy Gillespie; musicians Frank Zappa and Carlos Montoya; tennis star Arthur Ashe; Ottawa lawyer Gordon Henderson; actresses Audrey Hepburn, Kate Reid, Lillian Gish and Myrna Loy; actor Raymond Burr; Pat Nixon, wife of Richard Nixon; baseball pitchers Don Drysdale and Tim Crews; dancers Rudolf Nureyev and Ruby Keeler; lecturer-author Norman Vincent Peale; singer Conway Twitty

TRIPLE-A FOOTBALL
JANUARY 9, 1993

The woes of the Canadian Football League will not be solved by expansion into the United States. Competition with the National Football League has produced most of our current problems. The CFL competes openly for new players from the U.S. with ever increasing salaries. Fans choose between going to the CFL games or watching NFL telecasts.

The answer lies in "Triple-A Football," in which each CFL team would have a partnership with an NFL team. The NFL teams would each provide five or six players to their Canadian associate, under contract to and paid by the NFL team. Each Canadian team would have a maximum of about 15 such players.

With 15 associate players at a salary of $67,000, each CFL team would save over a million dollars a year. Ticket prices could be stabilized or reduced. The league would have a better product. NFL teams would have a proving ground.

Glen D.G. Driedger, Osgoode

Editor's note: The CFL didn't pay much attention to people like Mr. Driedger and later that year began a game of American musical chairs that ended four seasons later in failure — and almost sunk the league in the process. Things started in 1993 with Sacramento's addition to the Western division.

The next year, Shreveport and Baltimore joined the Eastern division and Las Vegas was added to the West. In '95, Sacramento moved to San Antonio, Memphis and Birmingham were added and Las Vegas folded. The league split into Northern and Southern divisions and Baltimore became the first U.S. team to win the Grey Cup. But by the end of the '96 season, the experiment was over, and all the U.S. teams folded except Baltimore, which moved to Montreal.

WHO'S LAUGHING NOW?
JANUARY 23, 1993

Yes, well, I guess the chickens have come home to roost. For many a year, the Ottawa sports fan and especially the Ottawa sports media have joked and hee-hawed about those poor Toronto Maple Leafs.

Well, the Toronto sports fans must be holding their sides with laughter watching the Ottawa Senators. Their ice performance, I would suggest, equals the performance of their namesakes in the "Red Chamber."

It all goes to add credence to that old adage, "He who laughs last, laughs the best."

J.C. McLean, Nepean

BEWARE THE PARENTS
JANUARY 23, 1993

I have attended one too many minor hockey games to let this pass any longer without commenting. At each of these games, I hear hockey parents berate game officials, scream commands to players, and name-call the opposing team members.

Whose game is it anyway? Why do we put in all the hours that a child's hockey commitment requires? For ourselves? No, for the players. My son plays hockey for the love of the game, for the skill development, and for the comradeship he builds as a team member.

As a parent, my role is to support him, not by screaming instructions and hollering rude comments during the game. Criticism comes into play at times, but through proper channels. Don't pollute the hockey atmosphere with your offensive behaviour.

Be proud, cheer loud, but above all maintain your dignity and set a good example for those young people watching from the ice.

V. J. Hynes, Ottawa

SISTER HARASSED
BY ANTI-FUR ADVOCATES
JANUARY 30, 1993

I am writing out of a sense of helplessness and anger over a recent incident in the Ottawa area involving my sister. She was harassed and physically threatened at a bus stop on her way to work by anti-fur advocates who live in her apartment building.

The harassment continued while she was on the bus, with no one, the bus driver included, moving to help. The harasser was a man, accompanied by a male friend. I myself am a non-fur wearer and a vegetarian. I feel strongly about stopping the exploitation of animals, but I believe that people should lead by example and rational discussion, not hysterical attacks.

Women who wear fur are private citizens who are not breaking any laws. They should not have to walk in fear of one more type of assailant when there are already so many out there for us to worry about.

I have a mother and a sister who do wear fur and frankly their physical safety is more important to me than the self-righteous rantings of people who might be offended by their choice of clothes.

Virginia Hughes, Ottawa

BASEBALL AND MONEY
FEBRUARY 3, 1993

Does anyone play baseball simply for love and enjoyment of the sport anymore? Or is it only to make the almighty buck?

Whatever happened to the 18-year-old whose dream was to make it to the majors, just so he could say that he played in the same league as his heroes Jackie Robinson, Willie Mays, and Hank Aaron? Is he just temporarily lost? Or is he sadly gone forever?

The worst part is when you see a little kid who wants to make it to the majors, not because of the love of the game, but because he heard that his "hero" just signed a contract for $40 million. Whatever happened to make baseball so jaded, so cold, and so heartless? Money, that's what.

Alexis Cragg, Orléans

TEEN SELF-PITY
FEBRUARY 9, 1993

Puleese. Last fall we got a full page write-up about how rough life was for teens in Kanata. Today, it's teens in Barrhaven who feel hard done by.

Imagine those poor kids actually have to take a 30-minute bus ride to go see a movie or shop, or even take up to an hour to get to Bells Corners for a Big Mac. The greenbelt cuts them off physically and psychologically from the rest of Nepean. They have only about five video stores, two or three pizza houses, a fully equipped sports centre, a public library, a youth centre, numerous public parks and a great community association.

When we hear of the desolate life for the people of Davis Inlet, who have no way out except charter plane or suicide, it is hard to have empathy for the teens of Barrhaven. They should reflect on what they have rather than dwell on what they want.

Barbara Hill, Ashton, Ont.

FAVOURITISM TO ELITES
FEBRUARY 27, 1993

Brian Mulroney's tenure as leader of this country has been a disaster from beginning to end. His preoccupation with his place in history and his obvious favouritism toward the rich and the powerful elites have not served the rest of us well.

My only regret at seeing him go is that there is no one waiting in the wings, in any political party, who appears to offer a real new beginning. We have only to look to our neighbor to the south, where such a new beginning seems to be taking shape with Bill Clinton, to see how bereft of leadership we have become.

Barry McLarnon, Ottawa

BAD PRESS UNFAIR
FEBRUARY 27, 1993

Brian Mulroney has had a lot of bad press in the last couple of years, largely because of the poor economy, high unemployment, and the GST.

Much of this criticism is undeserved. Mr. Mulroney was a champion of free trade, without which Canada would be well on its way to self-destructive protectionism. The infamous GST has significantly helped our export industries, as recent export data from Statistics Canada show.

As for the economy, we are ignorant of the facts if we think that it's Mulroney's fault. We are pulling out of a global recession. Brian Mulroney took us from adolescence to adulthood in world trade. He is to be commended.

John Noguera,
J.G. Noguera & Associates, Kanata

A BURNING ISSUE
MARCH 15, 1993

In Grade 2, one of my classmates set his desk on fire. I remember vividly how the teacher reached into the fire for the flaming books, threw them on the floor and stomped on them.

In Grade 3 one of my classmates stole some colourful

pills from the local drugstore and passed them around as candy to the boys in the class. There were only girls present for the afternoon class; the boys were in the hospital emergency ward.

In Grade 8, two of my classmates were arrested for armed robbery. There was the young teenager from our school charged with raping a four-year-old child who lived in the neighbourhood. At one point during my adolescence, I carried a long hat pin up my sleeve when I went to the movies, "just in case." We lived in fear, fear of being beaten up, fear of the knives some of the kids carried, fear of having some of our prized possessions stolen.

Weapons and violence in schools are not a new phenomenon. My memories go back 35 years to a beautiful middle-sized city in Western Canada. In our rapidly changing society, one thing has not changed: There will always be lonely, angry children who take out their hostilities on those around them.

I would suggest that the problem would be better defined, and more meaningful approaches suggested, by the people who live with the situation every day: the students.

Diane Skulstad, Ottawa

IN A GREY AREA
MARCH 20, 1993

Thank goodness someone is finally getting rid of these insulting dictionaries. I am a woman of "a certain age." Have you seen what these awful books say about me?

Elderly: past middle age and getting old. Old: dating from a long time ago. Grey: old, ancient. Feminine: effeminate. Mother: an old or elderly woman. Matron: a staid woman of middle age or older.

Heaven forbid you should cast your eye on the likes of "womanish" or "stout" or "overweight."

Loretta Craig-Taylor, Ottawa

HAVING YOUR CAKE
MAY 1, 1993

The Citizen just carried a full page advertisement in support of a local food bank. Simultaneously there was news of a "farewell tour of European capitals" by our prime minister, presumably at taxpayers' expense.

This leads one to believe that a genealogical search just might reveal that Mr. Mulroney is a direct descendant of Marie "Let them eat cake" Antoinette.

Jean M. Siddons, Ottawa

MOST SOLDIERS GOOD
MAY 15, 1993

My husband left Canada in December for Somalia as a proud member of the Canadian Airborne Regiment. He was elated to finally put his many years of training to use.

The first month I spent wondering if he had even arrived in Somalia and if he was safe. There was no mail system, telephone lines were still being established and media coverage of the Canadian effort was practically nonexistent. It was over a month before we finally had a chance to hear each other's voices, for five minutes. Support for the troops was widespread then. It helped ease

the pain of separation when positive reports began to filter out on the regiment's efforts.

Unfortunately, this has changed. Because of the actions of the few, I am constantly bombarded with insults and hateful comments from the media and politicians about my husband's regiment. My husband has worked very hard to call himself a paratrooper. He is *not* a neo-Nazi, white supremacist or a murderer. His only crime is that he always wanted to be a soldier — and a part of the elite group that call themselves the Canadian Airborne Regiment.

Unfortunately, the comments have reached him in that far corner of the world. Fortunately, through co-workers and friends from major centres across Canada, I am informed that the Canadian population still supports our husbands so far from home.

Jennifer Young, Pembroke

Editor's note: The Airborne regiment, an elite military unit formed in 1968 and based at CFB Petawawa, was disbanded in disgrace in 1995 amid a flurry of tragedies, scandals and embarrassing rituals. The most serious involved allegations of a coverup of a March 1993 killing of a Somali man by Airborne members, and the torture and murder two weeks later of Somali teenager Shidane Arone, who was in the Airborne's custody when he died. The incidents led to criminal charges and a soldier's conviction for manslaughter in Shidane's death, a federal inquiry that condemned military brass of incompetence and the disbandment of the regiment.

INSULT TO PIGS
JUNE 26, 1993

You don't have to be an animal rights activist to ask that your editorial cartoonist and writers stop insulting pigs by showing them as Tories.

Len Gelfand, Ottawa

SENATE'S LOSS
MAY BE SENATORS' GAIN
JULY 7, 1993

It is ironic that the same people who are horrified by the Senate's proposed $6,000-expense-allowance increase are very pleased about the $12 million (plus benefits) going to new Senator Alexandre Daigle.

While I don't know why a senator needs $6,000 more, I understand much less why any teenager, even an athletic one, needs two thousand times as much, or about twice as much as the entire Senate earns in a year.

According to some, the real source of the mega-salary is gaping tax loopholes that allow corporations to deduct expenses for "sport." The real paymaster, in other words, is the taxpayer. In any event, I am withdrawing my application for a seat in the Senate, and bringing it directly to the hockey Senators.

David Rudman, Ottawa

DAIGLE NOT MESSIAH
JULY 10, 1993

Having duly noted the amount of press and media coverage afforded Mr. Daigle, I can't help but be forced to remind you and your colleagues that the man is, first and foremost, a hockey player. That's spelled H-O-C-K-E-Y P-L-A-Y-E-R, and not T-H-E M-E-S-S-I-A-H. One wonders whether cancer might not have been beaten years ago if we were willing to pay our researchers $12 million for a few years' work.

Jim Harris, Ottawa

COUNTING BLESSINGS

SEPTEMBER 1, 1993

Every day I count my blessing that I am able to stay at home on welfare, as opposed to having to pay taxes on a $41,000-a-year income. As I walk into my local grocery store, the one where I cannot cash a personal cheque because I'm on welfare, I am so grateful not to be burdened with a corporate pension plan.

As I see the expression on my child's teachers' faces when they find out his mother is single and on welfare, I thank my lucky stars I don't have to deal with tax-deductible child care of my choice.

As those soliciting credit cards to just "anyone" turn me down because I'm on mother's allowance, I am thrilled not to have to decide which RRSP suits me best. As I avoid the dentist office's phone calls reminding me how long it's been since my teeth were cleaned, I fully appreciate not having the hassle of a dental plan.

The list goes on of the many ways in which I'm truly grateful not to have to deal with the terrible life I would have if I had a $41,000-a-year job.

Helen Berry, Ottawa

Editor's note: Helen Berry, 28, the single mother of a 10-year-old boy, wrote this letter in response to news stories about Helle Halgaard, a Toronto woman who quit her $41,000-a-year job to protest high taxes. When she quit, Ms. Halgaard said she'd be better off on welfare than to keep her job.

MISSED THE TRAIN

OCTOBER 2, 1993

The other night on the news Kim Campbell said she would jump in front of a speeding train if necessary to protect Canada's health care system.

With the Conservative cuts to Via Rail in the past few years, she might have difficulty finding any kind of moving train, but I would like to know who or what she is protecting our health care from? The only one attacking it is the government.

Kathi Stewart Boucher, Aylmer

GRINCHES STOLE PRESENTS, NOT SPIRIT

DECEMBER 18, 1993

On December 11, our home was robbed. The thieves smashed through our back door, and took a lot of our things, between 2 and 4:30 in the afternoon, in broad daylight, on a busy bus route, and no one saw it.

As I write this letter, I think of my all-time favourite Christmas tale — *How The Grinch Stole Christmas*. It has a happy ending, with the Grinch returning all the trappings of Christmas to the town and being honoured as a guest at the town dinner.

Our story will also have a happy ending and has changed our lives, too, but not for the same reasons. You see, they took our TV, our video camera, a few cassettes, VHS tapes and CDs, and *all* our Christmas presents.

The thieves made their way through the house, turning things over and generally upsetting the place.

Then they knocked over our tree, and made away with the goods. I have often heard it said that being robbed is a violent personal invasion, some compare it to rape.

Having experienced each once now, in my 38 years, I can say unequivocally — they do not compare. A rape is truly personal, they take something our society generally regards as very private — your body. No insurance policy can replace or compensate for what is taken, and no amount of soap, water or kind words can erase what has been done.

A property theft in comparison is impersonal. All they take are the things you have collected in your lifetime. Sometimes these articles hold a special personal attachment, inspire nostalgia or help to keep a piece of your past intact.

When counted and measured, they are still just things.

The parallel that can be drawn between robbery and rape is that when the initial shock and hurt wear off, self-doubt and reassessment of your life begin. We will not be made bitter or jaded. We will not bar our windows and doors and retreat into the safety of a fortress, either. We have lost a collection of material things that can be replaced.

What it will make us, though, is more conscious of those who have less than we do at Christmas. We may have less at Christmas than we expected, but we still have riches beyond evaluation in our friendships, good neighbours and each other.

Perhaps we overlook these "gifts" because there are no ribbons attached. Merry Christmas.

Carol Lewis, Gloucester

1994

Local: British-born high-tech worker Nicholas Battersby killed in drive-by shooting on Elgin Street (March); After years of arranging finances, work finally begins on the Palladium, a new 18,500-seat Kanata arena for Ottawa Senators (June); Kanata teen Shayne Norris killed on bicycle by OPP officer who left the scene saying he thought he struck a deer (August)

National: Federal government, joined by several provinces, slashes tobacco taxes to counter increase in cigarette smuggling (February); Federal-provincial meeting results in agreement to reduce inter-provincial trade barriers (May); Labour dispute ends major league baseball season with Montreal Expos in first place (August); NHL lockout delays start of season until December

World: Zapatista rebellion for land reforms in Chiapas province sets stage for turbulent year in Mexico (January); Tens of thousands of Tutsis die at the hands of rival Hutus as Rwanda dissolves into ethnic bloodbath (February); Nelson Mandela wins presidency in South Africa's first all-race election (April); U.S.-led forces land in Haiti to pave way for return of president-in-exile Jean-Bertrand Aristide (September)

Deaths: U.S. president Richard Nixon; Jacqueline Kennedy Onassis; actors Jessica Tandy, Burt Lancaster, John Candy and Joseph Cotten; activist-actress Melina Mercouri; rock star Kurt Cobain; playwright Eugene Ionesco; journalist Charles Lynch; scientist Linus Pauling; anti-war radical Jerry Rubin; composer Henry Mancini; Ottawa contractor Thomas Fuller; singers Dinah Shore and Cab Calloway; separatist politician Gerald Godin; writer James Clavell; hockey legends J.C. Tremblay and Rudy Pilous

LONELINESS OF AIDS

JANUARY 3, 1994

I am hospitalized in my two-year fight with AIDS. I consider myself lucky that my health is still reasonable, physically and mentally. This is probably due to the number of good friends, family and medical support that I get constantly.

While in National Defence Medical Centre, I searched through *The Citizen* every day and I noticed that no messages of kindness were published for the holidays in regards to people living with HIV/AIDS.

I am lucky to have family and friends who think of me. But what about those with HIV/AIDS who are not so fortunate? They live in isolation because of indifference or misunderstanding. I cannot stop thinking about Bruce House, the AIDS Committee of Ottawa, the AIDS Committee of Ottawa-Carleton, the Living Room, the Bureau Régional D'Action SIDA (BRAS) and especially those who share moments every day with individuals like myself.

God in his boundless love will recognize their infinite kindness and reward them accordingly. Especially in these times, so many are giving up because of the rejection of family, partners and friends. It is very cruel. In our society today so much selfishness renders us almost indifferent to our brothers and sisters who are less fortunate.

I am not asking anything for myself because I have everything I need to pass the days. But I wish we could offer a little hope in this time of hardship to my friends living with HIV/AIDS and their partners, because we are all from the same family — the family of God.

Your newspaper can bring a little smile to a lot of people and remind us to touch someone and express our considerations. If you know someone living with HIV/AIDS, just call and say: "I'm thinking of you today."

Mario Genereux, Ottawa

A GAY SON FINDS HAPPINESS

JUNE 9, 1994

Being gay or being lesbian is not necessarily a chosen lifestyle. My son spent a childhood and early adulthood trying to avoid what his inner soul was telling him. Those years were such an unhappy time for him and for our fami-

ly, he spent his waking hours reacting to life as a "bee in a hornet's nest," we were prone to say.

Finally, in his late 20s, when he accepted what he knew must be, he found a partner we have come to love as our own son. My son is a changed, happy, productive, caring human being. His most unhappy time comes when he and his partner dwell on the fact that they will never have a family, though they can well afford to look after one.

Many homosexuals hide their sexuality and marry so they can have a family — what a terrible disservice they do to their wives. In business, because of bigots, my son must hide his lifestyle. One in every 10 persons is either gay or lesbian.

Canadians should wake up to the reality of the situation, not by judging their fellow human based on their own misunderstanding and bigoted judgment but by love and enlightened acceptance. Please try to understand.

Cynthia Miller, Ottawa

ROCK STRIKES OUT

JUNE 21, 1994

My husband and I recently went with another couple to an Ottawa Lynx game. We were looking forward to an enjoyable evening of good conversation and good baseball. However, it seems that attending sports events and having a conversation with your seatmates is no longer possible in Ottawa.

Someone has determined that rock music is essential to baseball, football and hockey games. The music must be loud, without a noticeable melody, and played until a split second before the game is under way and then at any break in the action. You cannot talk. What would be the point? Your friends cannot hear you and you cannot hear your friends.

We looked forward with great anticipation to the arrival of the Lynx, and we bought four season tickets. We looked forward to the ambiance and tradition that go with baseball. That tradition does not include rock music blaring at a volume sufficient to jolt the unwary fan out of his or her seat into centre field.

Our family has had Ottawa Rough Rider season tickets for four generations and we have bought season tickets this year. The season starts in a couple of weeks so please, Mr. Firestone, temper the music.

I do understand and appreciate the trend to turn major sporting events into entertainment packages. But surely there are options to loud, ugly music that offends a large portion of the crowd.

Marilyn Shouldice, Nepean

DAVE CHAN, THE OTTAWA CITIZEN

How can anyone be such a musclehead to complain about youngsters cheering too loudly at a Lynx ball game?

FANS TOO LOUD?

JUNE 21, 1994

I took in a Lynx baseball game. Score was tied in the ninth. As the drama unfolded, I saw a member of the stadium security staff climb to the top of the stands where he proceeded to tell a group of exuberant youngsters to pipe down.

I was stunned. The scoreboard was exhorting us to make noise, and here was this musclehead telling fans to shut up. True, they were noisy, but they weren't abusive or violent. They were having fun — too much fun as it turns out.

On my way out of the park, I stopped at the security office to speak my mind. The gent behind the desk replied with a straight face that the security people had probably received a complaint. A complaint about cheering too much and too often? This was a baseball game, not Bach.

I left shaking my head. This is a town where the House of Commons is often a free-for-all, yet the ballyard has rules about cheering too passionately.

So, hey kids, ignore the stooges and keep cheering.

Oh, and for those patrons miffed by the noise — get over it, or stay home. Remember, the word fan is derived from fanatic.

Kevin McKendrick, Ottawa

COWPLAND BUILDS WRONG HISTORY

JULY 11, 1994

In a recent column, reporter Alana Kainz says Corel Corporation's Michael Cowpland is building history by

lavishly spending $10 million on a palace for himself. To hold him up as a role model for today's youth will be disastrous for them and for the country.

This master of information has somehow not received the information that many of his neighbours are suffering. Some are starving. Perhaps he gives a lot of money to help those in need. But to keep that much wealth for one's own pleasure is not what "history" needs today.

Why not a $300,000 house for himself, and a $10-million home for battered women? Or a research centre at the children's hospital? Or a school for handicapped children? The $10 million would also keep our four orphanages in India and Nepal (230 destitute children and women) going for the next 50 years. Those would be much better history than emulating Nero.

There was a parable told 2,000 years ago: "The land of a rich man brought forth plentifully; and he thought to himself, What shall I do, for I have nowhere to store my crops? And he said, 'I will . . . pull down my barns and build larger ones . . . And I will say to my soul, 'Soul, . . . take your ease, eat, drink, and be merry.' But God said to him . . . This night your soul is required of you."

Michael Cowpland is building a $10-million prison for his soul.

Fred and Bonnie Cappuccino,
Directors, Child Haven International,
Maxville, Ont.

BRUSHING UP ON ART

AUGUST 18, 1994

Often, the people who eagerly enrol in a music appreciation course, admitting their need to learn to hear how Bach elaborated his themes, feel no necessity to learn to look at art. While they accept the complexity of Bach's vocabulary, they deny the complexity of Poussin's or Newman's.

For more than 20 years the National Gallery has been my visual university. Pictures I ignored years ago have become my favourites; the more I looked, the more I learned. Although I have two university degrees, they are in non-art subjects, and the hours I've spent learning to appreciate the gallery's collection have been the most rewarding scholarship of my life.

In the past year, large crowds have filled the galleries for the curatorial lectures. We learned about Gandolfi from an enthusiastic curator, Mimi Cazort, about the vocabulary of Baroque art from curator Catherine Johnston, and we benefited from the knowledge that associate curators Douglas Schoenherr and Michael Pantazzi shared at the National Portrait Gallery Show and at Egyptomania.

And lucky Ottawans, we have attracted another scholar-teacher to join the gallery's gifted staff. Colin Bailey's gracious remarks, quoted in *The Citizen*, showed that he is aware of the scholarship and expertise of his colleagues in the department of Canadian art, and is looking forward to learning from them (good scholars never stop learning, even when they are hired as administrators).

Particularly well-mannered was his expressed pleasure at working "in one of the most beautiful museums built in the past decade," considering he is coming to us from Fort Worth's Kimball Museum, acknowledged as one of the most beautiful museum buildings in the world. I have confidence that most Ottawans will welcome Mr. Bailey cordially.

At 72, I am not too old to learn and I have found the more knowledgeable my teachers, the more rewarding it is for me. There's nothing "insulting" about getting educated; it's a trip and it will keep you young.

Nan Sussmann, Ottawa

SPORTS FAN STRIKE
SEPTEMBER 15, 1994

A Sports Fans Union. Does the idea sound preposterous now, after all we are going through with the players' strikes? How many people have we heard say, "Nobody is worth $4 million or $5 million a year?" or "If the owners pay these guys this, they must have the money?"

What about the fan? Every business depends on entrepreneurs, workers, a good product and a user of the product. What the owners and players are overlooking here is the customer.

What if those customers — the fans — formed a union? This union could single out a wealthy team and boycott their games until a reasonable ticket price was negotiated. The owners and players would have to go back to the negotiating table to split up the pie.

Does this sound crazy? Look only as far as our own back yard where football tickets have plummeted in face of fan revolt.

Sports was once a pastime from the rigors of everyday life. Now it has become big business involving millions of dollars. If professional sports were banished tomorrow, life would go on, and maybe then, we all would realize the true meaning of sports in the lives of our children and ourselves. We could go back to a pastime that exercised our bodies and our minds and forget about how much so and so is making for the Leafs and if so and so is holding out for more money.

Will it take a Sports Fan Union to bring this about or will the parties involved come to their senses? I think not.

Serge Beaubien, Waltham, Que.

RESTAURANT NO PLACE
FOR BREASTFEEDING
OCTOBER 17, 1994

Health Canada proclaims in a TV commercial that breastfeeding in public is a normal and perfectly acceptable form of behavior. I do not agree and would be very surprised if the majority of Canadians did.

I would like to know on what basis the department arrived at this moral judgment and what authority it has to spend $90,000 in tax dollars trying to force it on Canadians.

Breastfeeding should be encouraged as a highly desirable method of properly nourishing babies. But please not at the table next to mine in a restaurant where I am trying to enjoy a quiet meal. Breastfeeding is a natural body function, the same as urinating and defecating, but we don't engage in those activities in public.

If breastfeeding is going to take place in a public restaurant as the department suggests, then I trust there will be non-breastfeeding areas provided, the same as non-smoking areas.

Gordon Ford, Clayton

HUNTERS TURN YARD
INTO WAR ZONE
OCTOBER 18, 1994

I've been reading about all these people protesting the imposition of stronger gun control laws. They tell us how responsible they are and how they shouldn't be punished for the sins of a few. I find the timing ironic, because, for two weeks starting the end of this month, my life will be turned upside down and I will be living in fear for the safety of my animals and myself.

This is because I live in the Gatineau Hills and deer-hunting season is about to start. I live a few kilometres north of Wakefield and, during that period, our whole region will be crawling with pseudo-hunters, mainly from town, who have no regard for anyone living in the area.

I cannot walk safely on my own property; neither can I let my dogs out to exercise or go to the bathroom. I constantly have to keep an eye on my horses to make sure they are not being shot by some hunter who's annoyed because he missed a deer. It even becomes dangerous to drive on the back roads because, despite laws to the contrary, many of these characters hunt close to the roads.

If I were to enter the backyard of someone living in the city carrying a loaded gun, I would be arrested. But in the country, it becomes my responsibility to keep these so-called responsible gun owners off my property and from killing or wounding myself and my animals.

I am not saying all hunters are irresponsible, but the number we see in this area during hunting season who clearly are makes one wonder about the crowds demonstrating on Parliament Hill, all claiming to be responsible gun owners.

People say, "I don't care as long as they are not in my backyard." But I do care, because they leave their own backyard and turn mine into a war zone.

Andrea C. Simmons,
Farrellton, Que.

BOY, WE'RE IN TROUBLE
OCTOBER 28, 1994

I read the newspaper, and I disagree with what you wrote. Boys are very smart, too. Boys and girls are equal. It matters if you try hard. You are making a dangerous statement to boys. Boys are now saying boys are better than girls! It is not fair to say that boys are not as good as girls, when it comes to reading and writing.

P.S. Je peux lire en anglais et en français.

Jonathan Smithers, Age 7, Ottawa

LESSON ON BONKING

DECEMBER 3, 1994

In his film review of *Golden Balls*, Noel Taylor refers to a car crash in the film as providing "a break from the regular alternation of business deals and bonking ... "

"Bonking," as any seven year-old can attest, happens in a Saturday morning cartoon when one character strikes another, usually over the head, with a hard, blunt object to gain attention, usually to peculiar sound effects.

It most often provides cheap laughs and is considered by aficionados, broadly humorous.

"Boinking," on the other hand, while it may involve certain indiscreet similarities of weapon, goal, and even sound effects, rarely occurs on Saturday morning TV. Whether it involves cheap laughs and broad humour is a matter of personal taste and individual peccadillo of the participants. I trust Mr. Taylor will revert to his usual vocabularic precision.

Tim Thibeault,
Ottawa

PUTTING THE BOOT TO SEXISM

DECEMBER 7, 1994

The letter, "Your daughter wears army boots," angered me. The writer's claim that "willowy, delicate, doe-eyed teenaged girls" who sported combat boots were disgracing the Canadian Armed Forces was not only extremely petty, but highly sexist.

I am an 18-year-old woman who has worn combat-style boots for five years and find them advantageous in two ways. First for their comfort. I can walk all day and my feet will not be blistered or sore. Second for their function. I can wear my boots through the winter and summer.

I know of no other footwear with the same versatility. I would like to ask the writer if he feels that these "delicate" teenage girls should be wearing delicate and uncomfortable footwear simply to please him or if he feels he can dictate what all women should be wearing on their feet. I also wonder why he feels that young women wearing army boots strips away dignity from the Forces and is somehow linked to the cuts in government funding to the military. The Armed Forces need no help from teenagers in disgracing themselves when they participate in torture and murder in Somalia.

However, it is sexist to assume that young women should not be wearing combat boots. We can wear anything we choose. If the writer is offended, maybe he would be happier blindfolded or perhaps wearing a narrow, uncomfortable yet delicate pair of pumps.

Anne Clarke,
Ottawa

SO LITTLE PENSION, SUCH HARD WORK

DECEMBER 9, 1994

We came to Canada from Holland in 1952. In 12 years I had six children and my husband had two jobs to keep everything rolling. We always made it with the money, sometimes with a bit of a fight, but we had a decent life.

I made all the kids' clothes, even winter coats from old coats I got from church bazaars. I was into recycling before anybody else. I mostly stayed home with the kids, took some foster children in, did babysitting and worked in some stores part time, always working around my family, the most important thing in my life.

I brought up our children mostly by myself. My husband's two jobs kept him away a lot of nights. I always had a clean house; the joke in the neighborhood was that you could eat from my floors. The kids had every pet they could think up, they volunteered my cookies for every party in school and I made costumes for plays.

Recently I heard from my doctor that I have arthritis in my joints. When I asked why, he said: "You had a hard life and worked hard."

So why am I telling you my life's story? A couple of days ago I became 65, and you know what the government is going to pay me per month, besides the old age pension? The sum of $29.69. Why so little? Answer: I have never "worked."

So stay-at-home moms out there, be smart and have somebody pay into the Canada Pension Plan for you. I never thought about it but maybe my problem can help others.

Christine Vann, Kanata

FATHER'S GRAVE ROBBED OF ITS SPRUCE

DECEMBER 21, 1994

Three weeks ago my father was buried beside a blue spruce in Beechwood Cemetery. There was a lot of emotional stress on our family in deciding where his final resting place would be. Because of his love of nature we decided the grave by the blue spruce would be the perfect place.

Every weekend since the funeral we have visited the grave but last week could not find it because the tree had been cut down on the evening of Dec. 10, probably to be used as someone's Christmas tree.

This was to be father's Christmas tree and his grandchildren had bought decorations for him and they were going to hang them on his tree on Christmas Eve.

It is unbelievable that someone can stoop so low as to rob someone of a little dignity to satisfy their own needs. They have added more heartache and pain to one family. I think they are sick.

Linda Baggs, Orléans

1995

Local: TV sportscaster Brian Smith killed by gunman outside CJOH studio (August); Ottawa Senators star Alexei Yashin holds out and is suspended by team over contract dispute (September-December)

National: Canadian Airborne Regiment is disbanded after new scandal compounds damage done by Somalia affair (January); Canada ignites world-wide protest against European Union overfishing when it seizes Spanish trawler in Grand Banks, Nlfd. (March); Mike Harris's Conservatives win Ontario election (June); After months of horrific testimony, Paul Bernardo sentenced to life in prison for killings of teens Leslie Mahaffy and Kristen French (September); Federalists narrowly win referendum on separatism in Quebec (October)

World: Mexico grapples with severe financial crisis as peso falls to record low (January); Bomb blast in federal building kills 180, injures 400 in Oklahoma City (April); Israeli PM Yitzak Rabin killed by militant Jewish student unhappy over peace deal with Palestinians (November)

Deaths: Canadian writers Robertson Davies, Earle Birney and Ted Allan; jurist Emmett Hall; actors Lana Turner and Bruno Gerussi; sports broadcaster Howard Cosell; Canadian diplomat Charles Ritchie; hockey great Hector (Toe) Blake; dancer-actress Ginger Rogers; polio vaccine inventor Jonas Salk; rock legends Jerry Garcia and Wolfman Jack; singers Dean Martin and Burl Ives; regional chair Denis Coolican; British writer Kingsley Amis; filmmaker Louis Malle; figure skater Sergei Grinkov

PEACEKEEPING WHERE KIDS RARELY SMILE

JANUARY 20, 1995

Many Canadians question whether it is worthwhile to continue spending large sums of their tax dollars on peacekeeping operations in foreign countries. Why do we bother when the opposing sides seem hell bent on destroying each other despite our best efforts? Why not let them settle their own affairs, in their own way, without risking Canadian lives?

In the past, I have wondered these things myself. But I have been here in Croatia one and a half months now, and the answer has become clear. Around me is the devastation of war, a very tentative peace between two sides filled with hatred. But there are more than soldiers here. There are the elderly, their often anguished looks giving testimony to the fact that they have seen this all before, many, many years ago.

And there are children, scruffy and unkempt. They rarely laugh or smile and their eyes have lost that sparkle of innocent youth. Their toys are sticks and rocks, or sometimes a hand grenade. There are few dolls or teddy bears, even at Christmas. There are no sand-boxes or swings in the schoolyard, only occasional shell crates and a basketball net erected by Canadian soldiers. The classrooms have no windows except some replaced with plastic. Bullet holes mark the classroom walls instead of pictures. The few desks have no pencils, crayons or paper and there are no books.

I have a beautiful daughter at home, now almost two years old, whom I miss dearly. As I look at her picture I see her smile and that magical sparkle in her eye. She will never have to worry about not having food to eat, a coat for winter or toys at Christmas. Her opportunities for education are limitless.

Should Canadians continue to play a role in peacekeeping? How could we not?

Lt.-Cmdr. J.E. Scott Taylor, Rastevic, Croatia

BOOMERS MAKE POOR EXAMPLE

JANUARY 28, 1995

It's too late to say anything to the boomers. But to Generation X, I say: We who were born in the '30s were born into a Depression. There was no silver spoon, just a ration card. There was no social safely net so we built it. I was born at home, as most people were, because we couldn't afford a hospital. We had no high schools, let alone universities; so we built them for the boomers (who promptly began destroying them in the '60s.)

Now we're grandfathers and we understand only too well, because we've been there. We have a lot in common with the Generation X who are faced with a mess similar to that created by the war. We inherited a debt, too. But we paid it off and ran surpluses until 1970.

We were outvoted from about 1972 onwards by the boomers who promptly began to run up the debt. We were trying to warn them of the disaster they were creating and they didn't want to hear it. Now it's coming home to roost. We're not saying we made it by working hard, we're saying we didn't have any other choice.

It's useless to point the finger of blame but let me caution you against taking history lessons or advice from boomers.

John Dugan, Gloucester

ART FOR CHILDREN

FEBRUARY 24, 1995

"Why are you taking five-year-olds to the National Gallery?" asked a parent.

Because an expert guide will unfold for them all the treasures within the gallery's walls. We can lie on the plate floor of the Great Hall and feel the cool glow of its stone. We can examine the architectural structure of entwining glass and metal. We will squeeze between the columns of its descending walkway, and march along the depths of the Roman steps. We will throw a penny into some magical waters and make a secret wish. We will examine the geometrics and colours of abstract art and see one of life's lessons portrayed in a sombre painting depicting the sale of the family farm to a wealthy land baron.

We will be marble statues while standing frozen on the pedestals surrounding the flourishing triangular gardens. We will marvel at the pristine beauty of the church, moved from the city and replaced inside the gallery. And each time we return to this gallery there will be some new experience awaiting us.

"We must visit the National Gallery," replied the teacher. "It may be the chance of a lifetime. It could open the door to some child's bright future."

Jane Conley,
W.E. Gowling School, Ottawa

REWRITING HISTORY
FEBRUARY 25, 1995

Charles Lewis's article refers to the *SS St Louis* carrying Jewish immigrants seeking asylum in Canada before the war. Prime Minister Mackenzie King refused them entry and they were returned to Nazi Germany and ultimately the death camps.

The article in turn reminded me of a curious pageant staged at the Mackenzie King Estate in August 1994. Heritage Canada actually hired actors to portray Mackenzie King as a benign kindly man, welcoming Jewish immigrants from central Europe into Canada.

Aside from his turning back the *St. Louis*, we should also remember that Mackenzie King professed a profound pre-war admiration for Hitler and confided his anti-Semitism to his diaries. This was later reflected in Canadian policies that permitted post-war Jewish refugees (and other destitutes) entry on condition that they worked in menial capacities for a time. No such conditions were imposed on known war criminals admitted as part of an agreement with Britain and the U.S. in 1948.

In George Orwell's *1984*, the Ministry of Truth was responsible for rewriting history. In a dimension not too far removed, it's called Heritage Canada.

Brian Jewitt, Cantley

AIRBORNE WON'T GO WITHOUT A FIGHT
MARCH 4, 1995

I am the wife of a soldier serving in the Canadian Airborne Regiment. My husband has taken great pride in serving his country, for 13 years. His dream was always to join the elite, to join the ranks of the Airborne. Through hard work and dedication his dream was realized. Now a year and half after we arrived, it has fallen in shattered pieces around us.

In all my life I have never seen a group of men who work harder, train so intensively, with so much solidarity, pride and determination. Most were shocked and upset by the videos the media exploited, videos that dated back almost three years, and involved only a handful of the 700 men in the Airborne.

Many of the individuals shown in these tapes have been discharged, reassigned or dealt with internally. Yet for reasons that I and so many others can't comprehend, Defence Minister David Collenette disbanded the regiment.

The disbandment has devastated lives. It has caused men to question whether they can continue to serve their country with the dedication and determination they once did. It has caused children to ask if daddy is bad. These tough commandos are also some of the best husbands, fathers and and, in some cases, grandfathers anyone could aspire to be.

Their families feel the effects almost as deeply. We have to leave family and friends years before we thought we would. We have to leave jobs and careers that have been painstakingly built. The hardest task of all is trying to be a strong support for our husbands. I am not minimizing the effects on the single men. They are the ones I feel for the most; they don't have the loving support of a wife and family.

I, for one, would be better able to swallow this bitter pill if I knew I had done everything in my power to try to save the Airborne. The Airborne is made up of 700 voters, with families and friends. If every one of these people were to write a letter, send a fax or make a phone call, along with every other Canadian who feels this is wrong, the prime minister could not help but hear our voices.

Julie Rheaume, president,
Save the Airborne Campaign, Petawawa

I HUG MY DAUGHTER
APRIL 7, 1995

A man exposes himself to an innocent young girl at the school near my home. He jumps into a car where a woman waits and they race away.

I look into the huge blue eyes of my four-year-old daughter and think: "What kind of man can do this?" I try to dismiss these thoughts — the world is full of weirdos. I hold my daughter and kiss her head and pray she never encounters such a man.

And then my thoughts turn to the woman in the car. Did she know what he was doing in there? Did he say, "Wait here, honey, while I go molest a child?" Will we some day know your name as we know Karla Homolka's?

At the trial of Paul Bernardo, a videotape filled with the horrors inflicted upon two young women will be played. I want to weep for the parents who must relive the horrible events that must be replayed for justice to be served. I weep for the young women.

I hold my four-year-old and I hug her tightly and try to think of what to say when she looks in shocked wonder and asks: "Why are you crying, Daddy?" I want to say, "Because I love you so much and I'll always be there to protect you." I weep for the fathers of Kristen French and Leslie Mahaffy. They probably thought that, too.

I also weep for the jury of 12 who will be required — on our behalf — to witness events that will doubtlessly haunt them for the rest of their lives. And I want to weep for the media lawyers who try to justify having these horrors revisited in open view of the public. I weep for the mothers and fathers who are forced again to fight to protect their children.

God forbid that I should ever find myself in the position of Mr. French and Mr. Mahaffy. But if I should, I pray the public and the media, which claim to serve them, will have some compassion, for I would be forever tortured by the fact that, this time, I could not protect someone so very, very dear to me.

So I hug my daughter, and cover her beautiful, innocent head with kisses, and I tell her: "I'm sad for all the people who don't know what it's like to love someone as much as I love you."

Perhaps she didn't believe me, but it seemed to satisfy her. I hope she never really knows what made me weep.

Trevor John, Ottawa

KEY TO COURAGE
APRIL 8, 1995

It was studying *Science and Health with key to the Scriptures*, by Mary Baker Eddy, that gave me the strength and courage to fight to free my son David Milgaard from prison.

This Christian Science book was the key that opened up the Bible to me in such a way that my daily needs were always met. In a time of great stress and strain, I did not have to resort to tranquillizers or medication. Truth was my medicine.

Currently, I am the first reader at the Second Church of Christ, Scientist, in Nepean and also work as the Christian Science visiting nurse for Eastern Ontario. The best part of my job is seeing the wonderful healing that takes place. It is also having the children, who are not themselves Scientists, tell me how grateful they are to see their Christian parents not having to suffer and to see them live long lives with joy.

Joyce Milgaard, Kanata

Editor's note: In 1970, Ms. Milgaard's son David, then a 17-year-old drifter, was convicted of killing Gail Miller, a 20-year-old nursing aide, and leaving her in a Saskatoon snowbank. His mother never believed he was guilty and after years of tirelessly fighting on his behalf eventually won his release in 1992 following a review of the case by the Supreme Court of Canada. Five years later, he was fully exonerated when DNA tests showed he couldn't have been the killer. He was later given $10 million by the federal and Saskatchewan governments in the largest wrongful conviction settlement in Canadian history. Ms. Milgaard published the details of her crusade in a 1999 best-selling book, A Mother's Story. The final chapter of the tragedy was written in November 1999, when a jury convicted Larry Fisher of the 29-year-old murder.

FALL GUY
APRIL 15, 1995

I suggest that Jacques Parizeau is being unfairly maligned for saying the referendum is delayed until the fall, and that he was actually misquoted.

He actually said: "The referendum may be delayed until the fall of federalism."

Andrew Fraser, Ottawa

FRUSTRATED DOCTOR
READS U.S. OFFERS
APRIL 17, 1995

I became a family physician some 17 years ago because I love my work, and believe strongly in the role the family physician plays in promoting and maintaining the health of his/her patients. I believe strongly that an educated patient is a healthier patient.

To follow this philosophy has not come without cost. I see about 25 patients per day. I do not double book. I do a lot of psychotherapy and rarely refer my patients to a psychiatrist. I have a large geriatric and pediatric practice. I do house calls, nursing home visits and palliative care.

Every year I maintain my certification in the Canadian College of Family Physicians with 50 hours of extra educational seminars and try to keep up with the 20 or more journals a week which cross my desk.

Unfortunately, like most Ontario physicians, the more patients I see and the faster I see them, the more money I receive from OHIP. If I triple booked them, saw them only in a state of undress, left before they could think of another question and gave up trying to educate them about their condition I would financially be much better off.

I am not a "fat cat doctor" and am content not to be. I accept having just bought my first new car in 10 years. A Porsche or BMW? No, a Ford Escort.

When the Ontario government decided on a utilization cap to decrease doctor's billings to OHIP, it seemed reasonable to set a cap for each doctor so that everyone would work on reducing their own utilization. The Ontario Ministry of Health refused the Ontario Medical Association's request to do this, opting instead for an across-the-board cut. So in addition to cutting my own use of the system, I must now pay for those physicians who have not voluntarily decreased their utilization.

Each week I receive letters of enticement from health care organizations from across the U.S. They offer twice the income, a complete range of paid benefits and, perhaps most importantly, a sense that they really appreciate the value of my expertise. Those letters used to go right into the recycle box. Lately, they get opened.

Get your act together, Ontario government. Your present policies are penalizing and alienating the very doctors who are delivering high quality, cost-effective health care.

Karen L. McIntosh, MD,
Ottawa

FARLEY'S END WRONG
APRIL 25, 1995

I have always enjoyed the *For Better or Worse* comic strip because of its sensitive handling of difficult circumstances we all face. Aging parents, children leaving home, health problems, divorce and separation are just some of the issues dealt with in the strip over the years, always in a way that left me with a positive feeling.

However, I found the entire "April in the water" episode troubling. When she first fell in, I had to reread the strip a few times to make sure I understood what had happened. The technique Johnston employed for a few days, letting the images speak for themselves, was very powerful. I could not wait to read my newspaper each day to see what was happening to April and was cheering Farley on from the beginning.

There is obviously a very soft spot in my heart for many animals, particularly domesticated cats and dogs who

For Better or for Worse

'Goodbye, Farley, we will miss you' was a typical response from readers to the 'April in the Water' story.

have never asked for anything from anyone except love, food and shelter. The way Johnston handled Farley's death was honorable, although to have him perform such an extraordinary act one day and die the next leaves me cold.

Johnston had been introducing signs of Farley's advancing years over the past months and Edgar was a welcome addition to the family. Though I do not condone suffering or pain, had we been able to see Farley's age progress to the point, difficult for pet owners to accept, when it is better for the animal to be put to rest, perhaps his passing could be viewed as more of a blessing than a shock.

I felt compelled to write this letter as a tribute to him, and as a catharsis for some of us who have suffered the loss of a family pet.

Goodbye Farley, we will miss you.

Joanne Rae, Nepean

DIARY OF A GLAD DAY
SEPTEMBER 6, 1995

My father, C.B. (Bert) Elgar joined the 11th Canadian Field Ambulance (RCAMC) in Guelph when war was declared in September 1939, and by Christmas of that year he had gone overseas. We did not see him again until July 1945.

I was nine when he left and 15 when he returned. My father saw service at Dieppe and was in Holland at the time of its liberation. Needless to say, my diary brings back many sweet memories of the day 50 years ago when "Dad Came Home From War."

From the diary of Marilyn Elgar, July 26, 1945:

Dear Diary, I've sure had lots of wonderful things happen to me but none as wonderful as today. Daddy came home, after so long, and I thank God for being so good to us and sending him home. I worked until 2:30 and then went down to the CPR (station). Mom and Barbie were there with Auntie Vera and

Uncle Bill Roffey. We were all shaky. Everybody was there, all Daddy's friends, and they had the band out.

Then the train was late, but at last the old "Toonerville Trolley" pulled in. We rushed forward to the tracks and looked at those on board but there was no sign of Daddy. Mum and Barbie rushed to one entrance but Auntie was holding me back so I got there last.

I saw him get off the train and Mom and Barbie kissing him. I remember me yelling "Daddy" at the top of my voice and then I was in his arms and we were all crying, tears of joy. Gee, it was wonderful! People were coming up to him and shaking his hand and then we were in the car.

When I first saw Daddy, I didn't think it was him, he looked so different, and his voice was strange, but after, when we got home, he was the same dear old Daddy, not changed a bit except that he is minus four teeth but heck, who cares? It seemed so funny to be eating supper and setting the table for four but oh, it was wonderful. He had such a lot to talk about and we all have a lot to say to each other.

He brought home some of the loveliest silver-plated china, china from England too, and a whole menagerie of elephants. He brought Barbie a tiny gold bangle, Mom a pretty gold locket with the medical crest and our pictures inside. He brought me a present from Auntie Edie (my father's aunt in England). It is a gold engraved bracelet which is fastened with a little heart. The key to the heart is lost though, so we have to get one at the jewellers. It has been in the family for a long time and I'm so proud to have it. Well, I'm too thrilled to write more, so Goodnight for now, Dear Diary.

Marilyn Elgar Wagg, Ottawa

1996

Local: The Palladium — renamed the Corel Centre in March — opens with rocker Bryan Adams (January); The region's first big-time casino begins operation in Hull (March); After a century as an Ottawa sports institution, the Rough Riders fold (December)

National: Flooding kills 10, leaves thousands homeless in Saguenay region of Quebec (July); Gen. Jean Boyle resigns as head of Armed Forces after controversial evidence unveiled at Somalia inquiry (October); Quebec Lt.-Gov. Jean-Louis Roux resigns after apologizing for participating in anti-semitic rally in 1942 (November); Plans unveiled to merge Toronto and five surrounding centres into megacity (December)

World: Gunman kills 16 kindergarten children in Dunblane, Scotland (March); Christmas party at Japanese envoy's home in Lima invaded by Tupac Amaru guerrillas, who hold hostages for three months (December)

Births: Dolly, the first sheep cloned by scientists

Deaths: Quebec premier Robert Bourassa; French president François Mitterrand; Alberta premier Ernest Manning; singers Colleen Peterson, Tupac Shakur and Wilf Carter; LSD guru Timothy Leary; scientist Carl Sagan; hockey broadcaster Bill Hewitt; NFL commissioner Pete Rozelle; baseball owner Charlie Finley; actors Marcel Mastroianni, Greer Garson, Audrey Meadows and Margaux Hemingway; U.S. vice-president Spiro Agnew; dancers Gene Kelly and Juliet Prowse; jazzman Gerry Mulligan; anthropologist Mary Leakey; ornithologist Roger Tory Peterson

CHRISTMAS SAVED 30 YEARS AGO

JANUARY 4, 1996

Dear Person,

I'm sorry it took me so long to write this thank-you note. Thirty years is a long time to wait, but I hope you will understand. You see, when you gave me those Christmas gifts, I was a child. I didn't understand a thank you was in order.

All I knew was that Christmas was saved, somehow, by a basket. A toy, some food, some treats. A new snowsuit. I only vaguely understood where it came from. Christmas would have been unspeakably sad with nothing. I know that that's not the point of Christmas. But materialism is for those who have. To a nine-year-old, having nothing is not a philosophical coup. Christmas would have been like every other bad day, only worse, if it weren't for you.

I don't know who you are, and you don't know me. I am grown now, with a family, our own home (almost), a successful professional. Your neighbour. You might be in the Lions club, or the Salvation Army. You may have put a toy on Toy Mountain, donated to the food bank, or bought lots of Kiwanis fruit cakes.

You have been giving for years, for the good feeling in your heart. I can share in that now. But it would still be nice to know that what you are doing has an effect and is appreciated. To have someone thank you.

Santa does exist. You are Santa, one of the few heroes we have left, if you gave a toy to a tree angel, put a ham in a food hamper or a fiver in the Sally Ann collection plate. As surely as if you lived at the North Pole and flew a reindeer-pulled sleigh, you are Santa for them. As you were for me. Thank you Santa.

Peter Zorzella, Manotick

A FINE SUBMARINER

JANUARY 6, 1996

The revelations of the "Somalia Affair" were the result of an inquisitive and persistent media and it was media pressure that led to charges being laid against Lt.-Cmdr. Dean Marsaw, formerly commanding officer of *HMCS Ojibwa*. Media pressure — not senior officers' displeasure with his performance or sailors' complaints — led to the court martial of one of the best submariners ever produced by this country.

Throughout his career, Lt.-Cmdr. Marsaw's conduct, performance and leadership style had been lauded by his superiors. The vitriol emanating from the Halifax media portrayed someone completely different: a tyrant bent on crushing his subordinates by verbal and physical abuse.

Through its repeated references to a vulgar act involving a cigar tube, the media conditioned the public into associating Lt.-Cmdr. Marsaw with perversion. In such an atmosphere, the court martial could safely utter that old service phrase, "March the guilty bastard in!"

Roy Marsaw, Ottawa

Editor's note: The writer is the brother of Dean Marsaw.

THE OTTAWA CITIZEN

Ottawa's swans are a joy and a delight, a reader said.

SWANS SYMBOL OF CANADA'S CAPITAL

JANUARY 6, 1996

The suggestion from some city councillors that those who support keeping Ottawa's swans care less for people than for animals, entirely misses the point.

The swans are there for the pleasure of people — for us. During the summer months they are a joy and delight for both residents and visitors. Not only that, but with their beauty, grace and strength they are a living symbol of Canada and its fine capital city.

Anne Paterson, Ottawa

Editor's note: After city council voted to donate the swans to zoos in a budget-trimming exercise later in 1996, software company Cognos stepped in to pick up the $30,000-$40,000 annual tab for their upkeep.

MACABRE MURDER PUTS TOWN ON MAP

JANUARY 8, 1996

The small town of Constance Bay has recently made its mark on the map in a distinctively gruesome fashion: the recent arrests in a murder mystery involving body parts strewn along Stonecrest Road in nearby Woodlawn.

It appears that when a community contributes its share of good, it is rarely noticed; but for a macabre killing, you get a mark on the map. Does anyone care that the community has donated some 10 bags of winter coats to help the homeless? Is anyone aware that we have one of the best emergency response teams in the region and have set up our own community policing unit to protect our own? Does it matter that the haves look after the have-nots during the often bleak Christmas season?

Something sinister and dark indeed has transpired in this good small town. Down in this small town, good things happen all the time — just ask the people here.

Colleen Gray, Constance Bay

SPLINTERLUDE

JANUARY 17, 1996

Regarding the broken hip suffered by an Ottawa resident who was "bodychecked" by another canal skater, Steve Estabrooks, chief of canal operations for the NCC, said this was a rare occurrence and that "between three and six people" per day might require treatment from injuries sustained on the canal.

I worked for nine years in the emergency department of an Ottawa hospital, and although we were too rushed off our feet to record exact numbers, we had many times Estabrook's estimates come in with fractures, sprains and lacerations sustained on the canal.

I don't wish to diminish the efforts of the hardworking individuals who run the canal, and I cannot argue with thousands of happy users, nor the welcome tourist dollars. But the canal does present another picture, not one you'll see on a glossy wall calendar.

Sorry, Mr. Estabrooks. We called it "Splinterlude" — with good reason.

Karyn Curtis, Orléans

SLEAZIEST ROUTE

JANUARY 25, 1996

Two separate incidents, same day, Saturday, Jan. 20. Thirtyish lady with two children walks out of the Hard Rock Cafe at the Palladium without paying. Who suffers? My college-age son, the waiter, who had the misfortune to serve her. This woman wipes out a sizable portion of his income after he worked three consecutive, 14-hour days. And what of the example she has set for her children?

Perhaps they will grow up to be like the Carleton University student (an assumption) who stole my other son's ghetto blaster when he stepped out of the fourth-year architectural studio for five minutes.

John Said, Ottawa

DON'T USE THAT WORD

FEBRUARY 10, 1996

I have never noticed the use of the word in question in the *Citizen* before (and hope I never do again), because I am deeply offended that a well-respected journal would use such a vulgar term.

To me, the morning paper is associated with adulthood, in the sense of sitting down with a cup of hot coffee, and reading the paper before going to work. It is enough that, as an 18-year-old I hear this word hundreds of times a day at school, but to read it in the newspaper encourages a lack of respect for, and a feeling of disappointment in, those adults who should be setting an example, not following one.

Brian M. Kirk,
Bell High School, Nepean

YOUR SON, YOUR FAULT

FEBRUARY 17, 1996

When Ida Henderson said the system let her son down (Rubens Henderson was convicted Thursday of second-degree murder in the drive-by killing of Nicholas Battersby) she was employing a cop-out too common in today's society to shift blame to others.

Society and the system are not to blame. It is she who accepted the responsibility of rearing her adopted son, not society. She is not the only parent who has had troubles with 12- and 13-year-olds, nor will she be the last.

Many of these parents grasp the situation by keeping their children busy, by imposing rules which both can accept, by enrolling the child into one of the military cadet corps, by having him/her join the school band, cross-country running team, Little League sports — the list is long.

It is unfortunate she did not look into one or more of the alternatives.

Ted Meyers, Ottawa

CANAL CLOSING ONE MORE DOWNER

MARCH 4, 1996

Alas, the friendly voice on the recording told me that the Rideau Canal was closed for the season. Normally such an announcement would fill my heart with joy as I wait eagerly for the sights and sounds of spring. Not this year, as I wished for a few more days of skating pleasure on our city's contribution to the *Guinness Book of Records*.

Having grown up in countries where ice formations are encouraged only in freezers, I have always regarded ice with considerable suspicion. It was with some trepidation in the winter of 1994-95 that I first stepped on to a hockey rink in my brand new skates. Within a few seconds, a feeling of helplessness and fear overwhelmed me as I realized that I was at the complete mercy of this white sheet of ice, which soon greeted me with a painful slap on my bum.

I can still hear the howls and jeers from the eight- to 10-year-olds who had decided to hang around after their pee-wee hockey practice.

My practice usually started and ended with a bone-crushing fall, followed quickly by a frantic hobble to the

boards for sanctuary. We become too afraid to venture into the dangers of centre ice. But venture I did, not just to
centre ice, but out to the wilderness of the Rideau Canal.

In the midst the skaters gliding effortlessly across the
ice, there I was, clumsily clawing at the air, struggling to
stand and barely able to balance. I was never scared because there was always someone willing to help.

An elderly gentleman, with a kind smile, told me to
"keep at it," a college student remarked that I was "doing
just fine," and a mother, coaching her little son, encouraged me by saying that "it is difficult at first."

After numerous falls and near collisions, I am finally
getting it. I long for the day when I can glide effortlessly
from Dow's Lake to the National Arts Centre, and (accidentally) bump into those chuckling kids.

Winter has never seemed more enjoyable — there is a
certain exhilaration in finally being able to do something
so distinctly Canadian and so dreadfully difficult.

Chirantan Basu, Ottawa

RIDER SAYS THANKS
MARCH 16, 1996

For the past seven years I have had the privilege and honour to have been an Ottawa Rough Rider. Now, due to
circumstances beyond my control, I will no longer be a
part of the organization. But I want to thank all the people
of Ottawa. You accepted me and made me feel like a native son. You have been most gracious and hospitable. Ottawa will forever be my second home.

I have been very fortunate to have played with so many
talented and dedicated teammates. The friendships and
memories we share will never be forgotten. To the loyal
fans, my heartfelt thanks for your support, confidence
and encouraging words.

I encourage you to continue to support the CFL, especially your Rough Riders. I will always be proud to have
been one.

John R. Kropke, Addison, Illinois

*Editor's note: Mr. Kropke, a popular defensive tackle,
wrote this letter after he was traded to the Winnipeg Blue
Bombers.*

HONEST PORTRAIT OF THE QUEEN
MAY 11, 1996

The controversy concerning the portrait of the Queen
speaks volumes about the western world's obsession with
youth. Not too long ago, one had to be 65 to be a senior
citizen. Now, it's 55 and before long, no doubt, 50 will be
over the hill.

My 18-year-old son considers a kiss between his father
and me to be "unnatural at your age." I am 39, my husband
48. So, it would seem that a lady who has reached 70
should be locked away from public view, lest all those
wrinkles and lines cause discomfort.

Antony Williams is to be commended for his honesty in
producing a realistic portrait that does not negate the images of the shy 25-year-old who ascended the throne, the
young mother, or the dignified grandmother who shared a

THE CANADIAN PRESS

**Antony Williams's portrait of the Queen, which sparked a
controversy, was a realistic work, said a reader, that
celebrates a new phase in the life of a remarkable woman.**

nation's grief at Dunblane. It celebrates another phase in
the life of a remarkable woman.

Karen Sinclair, Kanata

ATHEIST COURT OATH
MAY 25, 1996

Raminder Singh is right that people should not have to
take an oath on the holy book of another's religion. But his
article falls short by not taking into account that the census of 1991 shows 3.4 million (12.4 per cent) of Canadians as
non-believers.

This is the fastest-growing group in Canada, at the rate
of 90 per cent in 10 years. Apart from some far smaller fun-
damentalist groups, it is actually the second-largest identified category in the census after Catholics, because the
United Church and Anglicans have fallen below 12 per
cent. While Singh, as a Sikh, would be quite comfortable
with taking an oath on his holy book, how does he think
humanists and atheists feel about having to swear on a
holy book of any faith?

There is no evidence that the elimination of the word God
in a courtroom would further undermine truthfulness in the
judicial system. In a pluralistic society, the only fair and tolerant way to accommodate all believers and non-believers
is to have a neutral oath of a solemn promise to tell the truth

with the understanding that perjury is likely to result in a jail sentence.

Sheila Ayala,
Humanist Association of Canada, Ottawa

CARIBBEAN GLORY
AUGUST 10, 1996

Two of our gold medals at the Atlanta Olympics were won by men whose roots are in the Carribean. Donovan Bailey, Bruny Surin, Robert Esmie, Glenroy Gilbert and Carleton Chambers represented Canada with pride and dignity. They gave us clout and glory. They made us the envy of many nations.

They showed dedication and determination, strength and courage, all the values and qualities for which Canada is known and wants to be known. Our golden men are well-read, clever, articulate and intelligent professionals. We couldn't ask for a better team to honour the maple leaf.

So let us not lose sight of this, because when we hear of violence at Toronto's Carabana, when the media highlight a brutal incident, aren't we quick with the "those people" remarks, pointing the finger at black Caribbean men in particular.

I do not have Caribbean roots, but I represented Canada in Jamaica for a number of years, and learned so much, mostly because my host country accepted me for who I was and what I had to contribute. Jamaica has an inspiring motto; it is: "Out of Many, One People." Perhaps we should borrow it and make it our national goal.

Louise E. Valle, Orléans

A GRAVE VIEW OF BILINGUAL SIGNS
OCTOBER 11, 1996

Crews, cranes and trucks converged on Aylmer's St. Paul's Cemetery the other day. They weren't there to fix the dozen tombstones toppled by vandals or age. Instead, they replaced the black iron bilingual archway at the entrance.

The cemetery has been there since 1872, as "Cimetière St-Paul Cemetery." The crews hauled large concrete monstrosities to each side of the entrance. On one is carved St-Paul and on the other *Les Jardins du Souvenir*. On the back of one side is carved "*Je suis la resurrection et la vie.*"

No English. Nearby was a broken tombstone. The crews ignored it. It lay against its base in the middle of four other markers, of two men who died in the First World War and two who died in the Second so Canada would be free and crews could come and eliminate the English from a cemetery sign to fit in with the new French-only Quebec.

What would they think of this? What of the others around them? The Brennans, McKeowns, Devlins, Finns, Mullarkey, Roneys, Kealeys and Murphys? Dad won't like it. I can see that special sneer developing. He and Olive's father, Eric, now here near each other, made it well into their 90s in two languages. You couldn't print what they called Quebec's language laws — in either language.

Over a row, on the tombstone of our granddaughter, Ashley, who died very young of a heart condition, is an epitaph that sadly may speak to the future of this wonderful young country being torn apart by racist separatists: "Rainbows don't last forever."

Jack Van Dusen, Aylmer

MOVE THE STATUE
OCTOBER 26, 1996

The placement of the Terry Fox statue is a civic embarrassment and should be moved by the NCC. Then, could you please rotate the War Memorial to face the Château Laurier? I believe the soldiers are tired of looking at the Lord Elgin.

Tom Fedorchuk,
Nepean

LOST IN TIME
DECEMBER 7, 1996

The arguments as to whether the Jan. 1, 2000 or Jan. 1, 2001 is the start of a new millennium are based on shaky premises.

In ancient times the new year was celebrated at one of the equinoxes or the winter solstice. The Romans chose March and the early Christians used March 25. In 1582 the new Gregorian calendar was introduced and New Year's Day was fixed at Jan. 1. This was not accepted in England until 1752 when 10 days were lost. The Jewish New Year falls in September-October and the Chinese use the period Jan. 10-Feb. 19.

The counting of the years is from an arbitrary event selected by a monk many years after. The counting could have been done from a number of events — for example, the birth of Adam, set by Bishop Berkely at 4004 BC, or even the time of the Big Bang if it could be accurately fixed.

Muslims use 570 AD as their start, and so have many years to 2000. I don't know how the Chinese count as their years are named after animals.

I do not expect things to be very different, or anything special to happen when we reach 2000 or 2001. I support 2001 as the start of the so-called millennium but what does it matter? Happy New Year anyway.

Arthur F. Powell, Westport, Ont.

1997

Local: Ottawa Senators reach playoffs, but lose opening round 4-3 to Buffalo (April); Schools closed as teachers stage province-wide strike to protest changes to education system (October-November); 100 nations represented in Ottawa to sign landmines treaty (December)
National: Federal government agrees to out-of-court settlement with Brian Mulroney in his libel suit over Airbus probe (January); Thousands displaced as flooding ravages Manitoba's Red River Valley (April); Bridge linking Prince Edward Island to mainland opens (May); Probe into tainted blood scandal says Red Cross negligent (October)
World: 18 years of Conservative rule in Britain ends with election of Tony Blair's Labour government (May); British colony of Hong Kong returned to China at end of 99-year lease (July); Princess Diana killed in high-speed crash in Paris (August); Saddam Hussein provokes confrontation with U.S. by barring UN weapons inspection team (November)
Deaths: Supreme Court justices John Sopinka and Ronald Martland; media baron Pierre Péladeau; politician Jack Pickersgill; Chez Hélène host Hélène Baillargeau-Côté; comedians Red Skelton, Pat Paulsen and Chris Farley; jazzmen Tony Williams and Stephane Grappelli; Elvis Presley's manager Col. Tom Parker; hockey legend William (Legs) Fraser; baseball greats Buck Leonard and Richie Ashburn; jockey Eddie Arcaro; writers Williams Burroughs, V.S. Pritchett, Matt Christopher and Harold Robbins; painter Willem de Kooning

DRACONIAN MEASURES IN ARENBURG CASE

FEBRUARY 20, 1997

The headline screamed, "Arenburg ruled unfit for trial." Having lived through the shock of sportscaster Brian Smith's murder in August 1995 in our usually safe city, I wonder why a man who is unfit for trial was considered fit enough to do the things that ultimately resulted in the shooting.

• Why was society unable to force Jeffrey Arenburg into treatment, for his own and others' protection, when he displayed bizarre and destructive behaviour, and was diagnosed as a paranoid schizophrenic and acutely psychotic?

• Why was he able to check himself out of hospital on several occasions, against medical advice?

• Why were police unable to force him into medical treatment or confinement, despite several violent episodes and threats?

• Why was he able to obtain a weapon and ammunition, with his history of mental problems?

• And why does it take an act of violence such as a killing before someone is considered ill enough to be forced into treatment?

Arenburg has an identifiable and serious mental illness. If he had been hospitalized and receiving the treatment he needs, then this crime might never have happened. Instead, he was out on the street. If doctors and hospitals had the resources and the right to put people who are seriously mentally ill into treatment, if the police had the right to confine individuals like this and force them into treatment, and if gun laws were more strict or guns were banned this crime would likely never have happened.

What would result from such draconian measures? A selfless and community-minded individual would still be alive. People with illnesses would be getting the treatment they need. And this city and others like it would feel a lot safer.

Shawn Leclaire, Ottawa

TOTO, WE'RE NOT IN PLAYBOY ANY MORE

MAY 24, 1997

Well, Mabel, we're at it again. We've just banned bare-breasted women from our indoor pools because we have to protect family values.

What hypocrisy! Since the advent of the bikini many women have been wearing what amounts to a G-string and pasties, and all kinds of clothing that exposes everything but nipples. I guess that's more alluring than bare breasts with nipples. Maybe it's because nipples remind us that breasts are biologically utilitarian.

Do you think that the people who oppose bare-breasted women in public also oppose the use of women's bodies to sell everything from toothpaste to cars and would rally to put girlie magazines out of business? When it comes right down to it, Mabel, those posed, airbrushed bodies are much more stimulating than the real thing with all its imperfections.

You want to bet that a few years of bare-breasted women in public places would reduce the sexual stimulus? Breasts come in all sizes and shapes, not many of them looking like the girlie pics.

If I were a man I'd be pretty ticked at being portrayed as so weak-willed that I need help controlling my sexual urges. Do you have any information about how much sexual harassment there actually is in countries where bare breasts are common?

Maybe if we were able to see how many of us have had breast surgery we'd put the pressure on for breast cancer research, and we could stop pretending it isn't affecting thousands of us every year.

As for little kids, do you remember how we had to wrestle with our little kids to get them to keep their clothes on because being naked seemed to be the most natural thing? Remember trying to explain to your little girls why they had to keep their tops on while their brothers dashed around bare-breasted in the breeze? I think it ended something like, "Because I say so." Even the little boys had trouble understanding that one.

Anyway, kids only cover up what adults tell them to, and then they spend a lot of time looking for opportunities to peek at what everybody had to cover up. Honestly, Mabel, I have to agree with the Catholic doctor who in the 1970s used to say to couples preparing for marriage, "Seems like a lot of fuss over five pounds of fat!"

Marlene Campbell, Nepean

GZOWSKI A SOLACE FOR 15 YEARS

MAY 31, 1997

I believe the only constant in life, besides death and taxes, is change. Intellectually, I accept the retirement of CBC broadcaster Peter Gzowski. Emotionally, I feel a deep sense of loss and I grieve.

Peter, for the past 15 years I have shared my life with you. You have been a constant comfort zone for me. There have been times in my life journey when I have taken refuge and solace in your warm familiar voice, and your wonderful sense of humour.

I felt I could go to you for inspiration, for motivation, to stretch my mind. I travelled the country and lived vicariously through your experiences and those of your guests. I have shared so many valuable experiences, cultures, values, etc., from people I probably would never have had the chance to relate to in any other way, given the restrictions in my life. You have enriched my life.

Someone recently wrote to the *Citizen* from Alberta to say Canadians simply cannot afford a government-funded, national radio network anymore. I feel sorry for that person. He has missed an exceptional opportunity to relate to the rest of Canada, through the wide variety of guests you have interviewed over the years. I wish you well Peter Gzowski.

Rosalie Reber, Nepean

A SOLEMN VOW TO PRINCESS DIANA

SEPTEMBER 3, 1997

Dear Princess Diana:

I feel so guilty for having read those tabloids, and I now want to burn all those tabloids that I have ever laid hands on that featured you in them.

I promise I won't ever read another tabloid ever again. If only this promise could bring you back. We will always miss you and you will always be the queen of our hearts.

Love,

Freeya Bajwa, Ottawa

PHOTO APPALLING

SEPTEMBER 5, 1997

Since the accident that claimed the life of Diana, Princess of Wales, there has been much written about the role of the paparazzi in her life and those of other famous people.

So, I was shocked when I opened your paper on Sept. 1 to see a photograph of Prince Charles and his children going either to or from church the day following the accident.

On the heels of such condemnation of the photographers who may have been responsible for the accident, I find it appalling that the *Citizen*, an allegedly respectable newspaper, would see fit to run a photo that is so intimate, so personal. This seems to me to be exactly the kind of muck-raking photography Princess Diana may have been trying to avoid — exactly the kind of muck-raking photography that may have had a hand in the deaths of these three people.

One would have hoped that a lesson could have been learned, but unfortunately the opportunity to rise above such invasive and intrusive "photojournalism" seems to have passed your newspaper by.

Once can only hope that in the future you will exercise more discretion and tact than was shown the other day.

Denise Corbett, Ottawa

FEMININE QUALITIES

SEPTEMBER 5, 1997

As a non-feminist and mother of two boys, I took the deaths of Mother Teresa and Princess Diana particularly hard. To me they represented the wonderful traditional qualities of nurturing, warmth, caring, softness and beauty. These qualities are so sadly missing in today's society.

Unfortunately, there is no one to take their places. I guess we're stuck with the likes of Hillary Rodham Clinton, Gloria Steinem and Madonna. What a sad state of affairs.

Nikki Kidson, Kingston

BLOC MP'S RUDENESS BELIES ANY CULTURE

SEPTEMBER 30, 1997

I was flabbergasted after reading the article, "Bloc mocks Ottawa MP for losing French identity," and started immediately pounding away at my keyboard to respond.

I believe I am as guilty as Liberal MP Hec Clouthier for having allowed myself to become assimilated to the "other side." My parents are French Canadian. They went to live in Brantford, Ont., so my father could work in the foundry at Massey-Ferguson. It was dirty, hard work. We had boarders.

This is what my parents chose to do in order to save money and get a good headstart. My sister, brother, and myself were all born in Brantford. We were enrolled in an English school, made friends and ultimately (to Bloc MP Ghislain Lebel's utter horror no doubt) preferred speaking English.

We returned to Ottawa a few years later and, sad to say, my spoken French had suffered.

I continued going to English schools. Later, I married a man who could barely speak a word of English at the time. When I had children, I sent them to French schools so they would be bilingual. My son is getting married next February to (heaven forbid!) an English girl.

I do not feel I have "totally lost the French culture." At get-togethers with my husband's family or my parents' families, I am immersed in French culture. I do not plan my life to fall into cultural categories. Let the chips fall where they may.

I have never belittled anyone for speaking in the language they choose. If someone addresses me in French, I will respond in French. I know it is obvious when I speak French that my first language is English, but that does not impede me. If my spoken French is not perfect and this bothers a Blockhead such as Ms. Lebel, so be it. It made me sick when I read the comment she made to Mr. Clouthier that he "represents exactly what I would never want to be." That comment could just as easily have been directed to me.

Well Ms. Lebel, let me tell you this. I am what I am and I am very content. I do not want or need your approval. I can also tell you that you are "exactly what I would never want to be!"

Gisele Lavictoire, Orléans

BILL PHIPPS SHOULD RESIGN

OCTOBER 26, 1997

Rev. Bill Phipps should do the honourable thing and resign, not only as new moderator of the United Church, but as a Christian.

He says in an interview with your newspaper that he does not believe in heaven, hell, the incarnation, or the bodily resurrection of Jesus, all of which are dogmatically stated truths found in the New Testament.

Jesus Christ's claim to be God was made so clearly that the "Jews took up stones again to stone Him." Jesus asked why they were trying to kill Him. They answered "for blasphemy, and because You, being a man, make Yourself God" (John 10:31-33).

If Jesus was not who He claimed to be, He should have spoken up and made it clear to these religious leaders that they were misinterpreting what He had just said. Instead He made His claim to be God and the only way to God so abundantly clear that they killed Him. If Jesus were alive today certain religious leaders would do the same.

The remarks of Mr. Phipps should not surprise anyone. The church he moderates ordains homosexuals in spite of what their Bible explicitly states.

Mr. Phipps, the honourable thing to do, as you reject clear biblical statements, is resign, write your own "bible" and start your own religion. Do not destroy the meaning of "Christian" for those who accept the Bible as historic and Jesus as God.

Rev. William Oosterman,
Westboro Baptist Church, Ottawa

REV. PHIPPS HOLDS ENLIGHTENING VIEWS

OCTOBER 29, 1997

When I read Rev. Bill Phipps's interview I was pleased and surprised to find that a member of the clergy has some enlightening views about Jesus, the church and Christianity.

These views do not affect his ability to lead the United Church of Canada. Whether Jesus physically or spiritually rose from the grave, was God in flesh, a representation of God, or just a prophet, does not affect the importance of His teachings.

Mr. Phipps's views that mending our broken world and

JOHN MAJOR, THE OTTAWA CITIZEN
Marlen Cowpland in her unusual dress stands behind husband Michael.

striving to live ethically are the main goals of the church.

Sara Gordon, Ottawa

WHAT MESSAGE IS PHOTO SENDING?

OCTOBER 31, 1997

By putting Marlen Cowpland on the front page not only wearing next to nothing but also being fondled in a lecherous manner, the *Citizen* does a disservice to itself and to all of its readers who purchase the paper believing it to be a cut above this sort of trash.

What message is the *Citizen* sending to women vis-à-vis their roles in the high-technology sector when the article gave more space for readers to ogle Mrs. Cowpland than for discussion of the performance of Corel Corp.?

What message is the *Citizen* sending to men vis-à-vis the role of women in society and the business world? The *Citizen* might have thought that the article and pictures were harmless but I think that they reflect, and certainly support, the sexual exploitation malaise that affects our society today.

Duncan Hill, Gloucester

TWO PHOTOS, TWO CHOICES

OCTOBER 31, 1997

Ottawa is blessed with two daily newspapers: one a respectable broadsheet, the other a racy tabloid.

On Tuesday, one of these newspapers used its front cover to run a very topical photo of a rally by teachers against Bill 160.

The other paper ran a photo of Marlen Cowpland, half-naked, with her husband's hands clamped firmly on her ass.

Guess which paper ran which of the photos? Be careful now, it's a trick question.

David Alexander, Nepean

HAVE FUN, MARLEN

OCTOBER 31, 1997

Shine on, shine on, Marlen.

The gown design is creative, sexy and fun. The woman is radiant with confidence and charm — what's the problem with this?

And remember that the Cowplands, in their business dealings, have placed substantial international focus on this area, enhancing our high-tech reputation as well as our employment situation . . . now, a fashion statement. Can you handle it all, Ottawa?

I am not a personal friend or well-paid employee of the Cowplands, just a person who would not hesitate for one minute, if given the opportunity, to jet to New York in search of the perfect Gucci. How exciting and what a hoot that would be!

Have fun, Marlen, and to all those insecure and critical people out there: Get a life. The Cowplands obviously have.

Colleen Maloney-Giard, Manotick

WHY I WAS PICTURED WEARING RIVERS HAT

NOVEMBER 8, 1997

If I may, I would like to add to the warm column by Dave Brown about Irving Rivers. I'm sure others have said the market will not be quite the same without him. I agree. I also gather from the very large turnout at his funeral that many of us have lost a real friend, and in my case a mentor.

In all the years I have lived away from Ottawa, a trip home without a visit to Irving was unthinkable. I never dared buy white wool work socks anywhere else, and in his memory I have vastly more than I shall ever need. My teenage children were devastated by the news. They were introduced to Irving as infants, and he followed their progress avidly.

I'm sure you have heard countless stories about him. My favourite is how the famous, very expensive Tilley hat became the very affordable Rivers hat. Irving knew an opportunity when he saw one. Just before the Gulf War, he had the Tilley hat copied (he had a China connection of course) and the word was he donated a large number of "Rivers" hats to Canadian troops on their way to the Middle East. He prevailed upon me to have my picture taken, wearing one in Saudi Arabia. How could I refuse, my journalistic standards notwithstanding?

To my eternal embarrassment he hung that picture over the cash register.

I can't complain. I'm sure he made up for it over the years in the little discounts my children and I got on all sorts of things we bought in the store. Some things we probably even needed.

I will miss his wisdom on any number of subjects. I will miss his passion about those things he cared for most deeply: Israel (I was working there when he died), family values, whether I was doing OK in the outside world, and above all, the Byward Market.

Peter Jennings,
ABC News, New York

1998

Local: Homes, businesses and farms held in paralysing grip of ice storm (January); Former Parti Québécois candidate David Levine appointed head of merged General and Civic hospitals (May) **National:** Hockey agent Alan Eagleson jailed for defrauding hockey players and corporate sponsors (January); Bank of Montreal, Royal Bank unveil plan for merger (January); Canadian dollar plunges to record low 64.02 cents U.S. (August); Swissair Flight 111 crashes off Peggy's Cove, N.S., killing all 229 on board (September); Supreme Court rules negotiations must take place if clear majority of Quebecers votes Yes on unequivocal question on separation (August)
World: Simmering ethnic turmoil explodes in Kosovo, the Albanian-dominated southern province of Yugoslavia (September); U.S. Congress prepares for impeachment trial of president Bill Clinton over his affair with White House intern Monica Lewinsky (December)
Deaths: Singer Frank Sinatra; writers W.O. Mitchell, Sheila Watson and Eric Ambler; "baby doctor" Benjamin Spock; Gabrielle Léger, widow of governor general Jules Léger; "Mr. Canada" Bobby Gimby; singer-photographer Linda McCartney; journalists Eric Malling, Eddie MacCabe, Jim Murray and Nick auf der Maur; baseball broadcaster Harry Caray; Khmer Rouge leader Pol Pot; Supreme Court justice Brian Dickson, U.S. politicians Barry Goldwater and George Wallace; black radical Eldridge Cleaver; athlete Florence Griffith Joyner; astronaut Alan Shepard, Bre-X founder David Walsh

THANKS FOR KINDNESS

JANUARY 15, 1998

It has been a full week since my family has had power. We live in St. Pascal [near Rockland] and my husband and I have physical disabilities. Our three children, 9, 12 and 15, have helped this past week in bailing water from the sump pump to avoid a basement flood.

On day five, we were so exhausted and cold despite having a wood furnace (which heated very little) that we decided to seek help at our local fire station in Clarence Creek. We were told that Barry Flood and his wife, Brenda, have generously donated their generator and their services to help individuals in the community empty their sump wells.

Barry works from early morning until very late at night. We know because he comes by around 11:30 p.m. and is back around 9 a.m. He goes from house to house

helping others in need, on his own time and in his own vehicle.

On day six his car lost its muffler, but he kept going. He also brought us some lamp oil and a heater which he plugs in to his generator. He has invited the whole family to take a shower or do our washing and has kindly invited us to dinner.

A big special thanks to the Flood family for all their help in this community's time of need. A special thank you also to the officials at Clarence Creek Arena, all volunteers and the companies that have donated food and time to help shelter and feed so many families.

We once asked Barry what his last name was. He said, "Guess." Here he is trying to help others avoid exactly what his last name is . . . Flood. We all had a good laugh. His kindness and generosity will be remembered always.

The Martel Family, St. Pascal

The Great Ice Storm of '98 will be remembered for more than its fierceness; it also brought out the best in people. Here, neighbours Carolyn Babcock and John Spratley clear branches from Kingston Avenue in Ottawa.

HYDRO WORKERS DESERVE MEDALS

JANUARY 16, 1998

In 1954, Hurricane Hazel travelled up through the U.S. from the Gulf of Mexico to Ottawa. This was my baptism of fire as a junior distribution engineer with Ottawa Hydro. The devastation in all of Ottawa was extreme.

Since then I have witnessed destruction by other storms: Tornados in Florida, a hurricane in North Carolina, a forest fire at Palm Coast, Florida, in which 132 homes were destroyed.

But none of these calamities compares with Ice Storm '98, from Kingston and Brockville to Smiths Falls to Kanata, Nepean and Ottawa, Gloucester and the surrounding townships to Cumberland, Vankleek Hill, Plantagenet and Alexandria. In Quebec, Montreal and the South Shore were and still are seriously affected. In the U.S., Vermont, New Hampshire and Maine got their fair share of wreckage. The area described is about 1,000 kilometres long by 200 kilometres wide. That's 200,000 square kilometres.

I worked in engineering and management at Ottawa Hydro for 30 years and my point is: The staff of Ottawa Hydro must be given the greatest credit for their handling of Ice Storm '98. The men and women who answered the phones at the service desk for long hours without losing their cool; the people in the operation centre who saw circuit after circuit trip and restored them only to watch them open again day after day; the linemen out in the cold working on 15,000 volt lines for long hours courageously and safely; management who foresaw early the extent of the devastation and corralled at least 20 extra crews from out of town. Every one of them should get a medal.

Those from utilities and contractors who came from areas unaffected by the storm to help should also receive

recognition. Great kudos should be showered on the customers who suffered loss of power for days on end and who co-operated with the authorities and with each other with little complaint. The news media, too, I thought, did a valiant job of reporting the facts and informing the public.

Edward J. Murphy, Ottawa

PEERS KEY TO AVERT TEEN SUICIDE

JANUARY 31, 1998

I am very impressed with the frank and informative discussion in this newspaper and other media regarding teen suicide. However, there is one more group that must be included in this discussion — teens themselves.

As we know, a teen will confide in their peers before talking to their parents or counselling services. The school system can help a great deal. If told of suicidal thoughts by a friend, a teen should be able to go the school counselling office and inform them. The school would call a taxi to take the teen and the friend, and possibly a guidance counsellor, to a hospital. The cost of the trip will be covered by the hospital, which has a budget for such emergencies.

The psychiatric department would be notified and be prepared to bring the patient in right away, as with any other life-threatening emergency. This would bring the patient immediately into medical care and the friend could give the true story, as the patient will often deny or minimize any problems. The hospital would perform a complete psychiatric evaluation, including interviews with friends and family. Medical treatment should start immediately with counselling, peer support groups and any other treatment deemed necessary.

The medical profession must treat any potential suicide warning seriously, not minimize the problem and send the patient home with a suggestion to come back if things get worse. This will cause the victim to hide their feelings deeper until it is too late.

I am glad the Children's Hospital of Eastern Ontario is changing its policy to reflect some of the above. Depression is a terrible illness that affects not only the victims, but their families and friends. When a suicide does occur, the toll on all involved is terrible.

The following poem, written by my daughter, Natalie, shortly before her death, illustrates the pain and despair she suffered.

> The darkness is around me, everywhere at once.
> It is suffocating, I can't breathe.
> I can't escape it, it's everywhere I go.
> I try to leave.
> I try to push it away and run, just run until
> I can run no more, but it is still there, right behind me.
> It wants me, and will not let me go until it has sucked every ounce of breath, hope, and joy out of me.
> This is what it wants, this it will get, for it will not leave until it has received this;
> this which is the ESSENCE of me!

Please do not allow anyone to take this route. You may lose a friend for a while by forcing them to expose their depression, but that is infinitely preferable to losing a friend *forever*.

A grieving dad,
Paul Schanzer, Kanata

CHAREST TRUE LEADER

FEBRUARY 19, 1998

Jean Charest leads a party that has members in Parliament from seven of our 10 provinces. That is a national party. It is the party of Confederation itself, led by the individual best suited to keep the country together.

The Supreme Court may very well rule that Quebec's separation is illegal and unconstitutional. When South Carolina seceded, president Abraham Lincoln declared the action unconstitutional. The Civil War followed.

Mr. Charest, as leader of the Conservatives, is saying the Supreme Court reference is not the best way to go to prevent secession. If a strong majority of Quebecers votes "yes" to a clear question, other Canadians will respect their democratic right to secede. We would not do to Quebec what the American North did to the American South. There would be no March by "Sherman" Manning to the sea.

Mr. Charest's policy is to prevent secession by respecting democratic rights. He follows in the footsteps of Sir John A. Macdonald who said: "Treat the French as a faction and they become factious. Treat them as a free people and they will respond as free people always do, generously."

It is not the Supreme Court that will keep Canada together, but leadership like Mr. Charest's that will bring a resounding "yes" to Canada and "no" to secession by people of Quebec. This is a prime minister.

Janet Morchain, Nepean

Editor's note: In April 1998, Mr. Charest left the federal Conservatives to lead the Quebec Liberals.

SERIOUSLY, CITIZEN

MARCH 28, 1998

When Conrad Black assumed control of the *Citizen* he indicated his desire that it become a sufficiently serious newspaper to be worthy of the capital city of a G7 country. A front page almost wholly taken up with a story about the search for Eric Clapton's father causes me to wonder how Mr. Black would assess progress toward his stated objective.

Michael Harrop, Kanata

GREED OUT OF NHL

APRIL 26, 1998

U.S. Ambassador Gordon Giffin is correct that if Ottawa wants to keep the Senators' franchise it must be prepared to compete with other National Hockey League cities in the benefits it offers the team.

There is little doubt that a major league franchise, in any sport, is valuable for the exposure it gives the community and is a prime factor in the decision of businesses to locate there.

In the rest of Canada Ottawa has too long been seen as the place where tax dollars are spent unwisely. The Senators help combat this negative image. Whatever it takes to keep them here has to be done, but no one can criticize taxpayers for not wanting to put money into a league unable to enforce reasonable financial restraint on its owners.

The NHL is a virtual hockey monopoly. Anti-trust laws in both Canada and the U.S. were developed to stop virtual monopoly operations from taking unfair advantage of their employees. Free agency is a result. We can't blame players for choosing free agency over loyalty to a team and its community. But greedy owners, anxious to produce winners, are paying out much more than is required.

Going back to the end of the Second World War, the New York Rangers have consistently paid to attract stars but have seldom been able to build a team. The Montreal Canadiens, on the other hand, have become one of the strongest franchises in all sport by developing their own stars through a strong farm team and scouting system. New Jersey, managed by ex-Canadiens, has gone the same way. Montreal and Ottawa seem to be headed in the right direction.

Why can't NHL owners with large financial resources learn from experience and understand that strong franchises are built, not bought? It's only a matter of time before fans and municipalities learn that they are unwise to subsidize the salaries of multimillionaires with tax dollars.

Ambassador Giffin should tell his friends in Atlanta that any new franchise there will share the fate of the old Flames if the operators must continually ask the community for subsidization from tax revenues. Sooner or later, the well will run dry.

Someone must show the NHL the error of its ways and demand the institution of a fair salary cap. The complaint by the players' association and agents that hockey players can only count on a career of about 10 years is bogus. A marginal player earning about $600,000 a year makes $3 million over five years. Over 40 years in regular business that would necessitate an annual salary of $75,000. If the players want more from their teams, let them invest some of their income back in the franchise and profit from ownership.

It's time the NHL operated on sound business principles rather than owner ego. If salary caps are instituted, where else are the players going to go for employment? Fair wages for a good day's work have always been the formula for a sound business with good employee relations. If it works in conventional business, it will work in the NHL.

Get the greed out and the profit and real fans back in!

Thomas Kent, Ottawa

OUTRAGEOUS LOGIC

MAY 16, 1998

There are, I am certain, a significant number of Ottawa citizens prepared to allow David Levine to prove that faith in him as the new administrator of the merged General and Civic hospitals has been well-placed by the board.

The logic of the position expressed by "outraged donors"

would suggest that admissions policy be changed to exclude treatment for "PQ candidates," and "separatists." Should we allow our hospitals to spend their resources to care for and to preserve the health and life of those who have different political views, so they may continue to fight for Quebec and by definition against Canada?

Are these "outraged donors" convinced there is a plot afoot, in the office of the devious Lucien Bouchard, to plant PQ operatives as agents in hospital systems in the ROC [Rest of Canada], to root out federalists by ensuring their eventual extinction through transfusions of *pur laine* separatist blood? We can't be too careful!

But what if David Levine is indeed the best hospital administrator in the field and proves it? Would he then say "I told you so" and require that we produce our paid-up PQ membership cards to gain admission to the hospital? Who knows, we may even be granted dual citizenship on discharge!

Blood is thicker than water.

Albert Tunis, Ottawa

NCC VISION: MAJESTIC OR MORONIC?

JUNE 12, 1998

Regarding the National Capital Commission's plans to widen Metcalfe Street in a Parliamentary Boulevard, the unsightly, chaotic jumble of buildings and streets to the south of the parliamentary precinct is a city. Some of us actually live there.

The NCC probably doesn't realize this is what a city is, given that for decades it and its predecessors have been bent on ripping apart every shred of its fabric. The NCC has come to worship in the twin cults of "green space" and "open space," without realizing that it is the buildings, and not the spaces between them, that make a city.

The most horrific part of their latest flashback to the 1930s is the proposal to rip out most of what remains of the heart of Ottawa in favour of (surprise, surprise) trees and underground parking lots.

I am half-surprised they didn't consider tearing down Centre Block during the upcoming renovations, and shift it a notch to the east, to better align it with their boulevard. Now that I have suggested it, I am half worried that they might.

For anyone who likes the look of the architectural drawings, the acid test is: Erase the drafter's standard-issue trees and pedestrians.

Does the proposal still have any charm? Or is it revealed as the barren, sterile, windswept monument to a bureaucrat it would undoubtedly become? If anything, further enclosing the Wellington Street side of Parliament Hill would do better justice to the Peace Tower and Parliament Buildings.

A good start would be to fill in the gap-toothed appearance of the block opposite the Centennial Flame, and redevelop the former Rideau Club site and the soon-to-be-vacated American Embassy. Then restore the line of mature trees that disease and previous generations of "improvements" stole from Wellington Street.

There are plenty of vistas that highlight the views of the Parliament Buildings, from the cenotaph, Major's Hill, Nepean Point, the Supreme Court, the bridges, or Hull. Is the NCC so bereft of new ideas to justify its continued existence that Metcalfe Boulevard is the best it can come up with? If so, it is not time to demolish Metcalfe. Instead, let's rip down all of the downtown, starting with the useless, outdated, unaccountable, and arrogant NCC. If a southern vista is truly what Ottawa wants, let's not stop at Metcalfe Street.

Wallace McLean, Ottawa

ECONOMIC TERRORISM

NOVEMBER 28, 1998

I congratulate the *Citizen* for publishing quotations from Jacques Parizeau's speech to students at Hull's Collège de l'Outaouais. Now we can see how truly despicable this man really is.

With quotes like, "As long as we're in Canada, we'll go get our booty" and "Sovereigntist premiers have better success than federalist premiers in grabbing money from Ottawa," how can Canadians feel anything but contempt for Quebec?

Clearly, as far as Mr. Parizeau is concerned, the only thing Canada is good for is filling his province's coffers with our money, and as soon as that runs out it's *au revoir*. If this isn't extortion I don't know what is.

If I were to threaten an individual in this manner, I would surely be charged with a criminal offence, but Quebec routinely does this to Canada and we accept it as an obligatory placation.

As an immigrant to this country from war-torn Northern Ireland, I am acutely aware of the benefits of being a Canadian, and as such have made an effort to do my best to give back to a country that has been so generous to me and my family.

In the rhetoric of Parti Québécois leaders, past and present, there is no humility, only arrogance, greed, disdain and contempt for the rest of Canada.

Where will we draw the line? How long will we allow the separatists to help themselves to all the benefits of being Canadian while spitting in our faces?

When will we stop the economic terrorism that the threat of Quebec independence wages on our dollar? Who will force them to call a "final" referendum on separation and finally allow us to either embrace Quebec as a permanent member of Canada, or bid them once and for all goodbye.

D. A. Russell, Ottawa

1999

Local: After one payment of $200,000, Ottawa Senators' star Alexei Yashin withdraws his pledge to donate $1 million to the National Arts Centre over five years (January); Four OC Transpo workers slain by ex-colleague who then kills himself (April); Province orders Ottawa-Carleton's 11 municipalities to merge into one large city by Jan. 1, 2001 (December); Looking for federal tax breaks, Ottawa Senators' owner Rod Bryden threatens to sell team to U.S. buyer (December); Prominent surgeon Wilbert Keon resigns in December as head of Ottawa Heart Institute after an encounter with policewoman posing as a prostitute. Board rejects resignation in January 2000 and Dr. Keon agrees to stay

National: Supreme Court rules same-sex couples deserve same benefits as heterosexual couples (May); B.C. court says possession of child pornography is protected under the Constitution (June); Adrienne Clarkson appointed governor general (September); Chrétien government spells out conditions under which federal government would negotiate Quebec secession (December)

World: U.S. president Bill Clinton survives impeachment bid over his affair with Monica Lewinsky (January); NATO bombs Belgrade to force Serbs out of Kosovo and allow the return of thousands of refugees (March-April); Two teenage gunmen kill 13 students in suburban Denver high school (April)

Deaths: Writers Brian Moore, Iris Murdoch and Matt Cohen; film-maker Stanley Kubrick; baseball legend Joe DiMaggio; race-car driver Greg Moore; basketball star Wilt Chamberlain; equine show-jumper Big Ben; golfer Payne Stewart; NFL star Walter Payton; Jordanian King Hussein; chemist Gerhard Herzberg; singers Hank Snow, Dusty Springfield and Curtis Mayfield; diplomat Saul Rae; Tanzanian president Julius Nyerere; Croatian president Franjo Tudjman; broadcasters Jack Webster and Alan Maitland

MAKES NO SENSE

JANUARY 4, 1999

The latest manifestation of this year's silly season is the anti-scent campaign currently being waged on bus placards by OC Transpo and some obscure organization identified only by its initials. If they have their way, those of us who use deodorant, shampoo or hair spray (not to mention cologne, aftershave or perfume) will be banned from public transit.

I suspect most of these zealots have never travelled in a crowded bus on a hot summer day, or they would be agitating to make wearing deodorant mandatory.

They claim to be motivated by medical considerations. Fortunately, OC Transpo already provides a Communibus service to accommodate those suffering from genuine disabilities. It is far more likely that their motivation is ideological — yet another example of the fruitcake fringe bent on setting the social agenda for the overwhelming majority.

Anyone care to join me in a "Common Scents Counter-revolution?"

Rick Power, Orléans

NAKED BREAKFAST

FEBRUARY 1, 1999

While reading the *Citizen* and enjoying a cinnamon bagel and coffee at breakfast, I turned to the letters page only to be confronted by a photo of the spread-eagled, mostly naked, mangled and apparently dismembered body of a man accompanying a letter by one Sue Adams, plaintively titled, "My art is not indecent."

I was holding the bagel in my teeth as I turned to this horror and I practically asphyxiated on it. I live alone. How I survived this without the Heimlich manoeuvre, I'll never know. You people could have killed me.

As for the "artist" responsible for this monstrosity, once my vision had cleared, I noticed that he or she had seen fit to dress the poor creature in a tiny tank-top and what appears to be a sweatband. Why a pair of trousers couldn't also have been provided is beyond me. Having reached

this point in the creative process, perhaps the artist was interrupted by a knock at the door and simply forgot. And what is that object piercing the victim's right thigh? There appears to have been a misadventure with something like a coffee table.

Ms. Adams goes on about the "physical and emotional power" of this piece of work and asserts that it deals with the "internal and external forces that battle constantly with a human's struggle with survival." In my view, this sculpture represents nothing so noble. It looks like road kill, or something you might find on the ground after a car crash.

Perhaps I'm an artistic neanderthal, devoid of appreciation and insight. On the other hand, maybe I just know what I like and what I don't like.

I used to like cinnamon bagels.

Paul Warburton, Ottawa

DEPORT FIRE-BOMBERS

FEBRUARY 20, 1999

Throwing Molotov cocktails at the RCMP is despicable and cowardly. Kurdish spokeswoman Christina Hernandez said it was more important for Canadians to understand the level of Kurdish pain and frustration. There is, however, no justification for terrorizing and setting innocent Canadians on fire. The people who threw the gasoline bombs should be deported.

Jennie Michelle Berkeley, Ottawa

VIAGRA MARKDOWN

MARCH 11, 1999

Congratulations to Arnprior on becoming the Viagra Capital of Canada. As a thrifty shopper, my question is: Will there be a factory outlet store at Pfizer's plant?

W. R. Kehoe, Ottawa

QUEEN OF CRASS

APRIL 10, 1999

I heard Marlen Cowpland's statement on television that people in Ottawa need to get a life. Perhaps it is Mrs. Cowpland who should get a life.

In the past, when I saw her in one of her tasteless outfits, I would think: "Boy, does this woman have issues she needs to deal with." But I always kept that opinion to myself, as I believe in: "Live and let live." I figured if she wanted to humiliate herself and her husband and tarnish the Corel name, that was her business.

But when she insults the entire City of Ottawa, I want to express my opinion.

She said if she had worn that same raunchy outfit in New York City, people wouldn't have even noticed. As a 28-year-old woman born and raised in Ottawa who has lived in London, England, Zurich, Switzerland and for three years in New York City, I can tell you that tacky is tacky whether it's in Ottawa or New York City, and her outfit would be noticed for its lack of taste there, just as it was here. The only place where she might fit in is Las Vegas.

What she does with her money is, of course, her business. She is an attractive woman, especially for her age (in a plastic sort of way), yet she doesn't seem to realize she can have style and flair without being the queen of crass. I salute anyone who is an individual, which she certainly is. But her comment about us getting a life insults the people of Ottawa and shows how little couth this woman has. At a time when there are hundreds of thousands of people being torn from their country, and at a time when so many people with much less than the Cowplands are donating money or offering their homes to aid the refugees of Kosovo, her $1-million outfit seems quite inappropriate.

It would appear by her statement that the golden armour she wore is worth more than her character. Someone should have told her that class is something one cannot buy.

Tammy Jeanveaux, Ottawa

MY FATHER'S LOVE
APRIL 23, 1999

It's over. Wayne Gretzky has called it quits. One had to expect it. Why then, do I still become teary-eyed when I think about it? After all, hockey is just big business and Gretzky is just a hockey player, albeit the most successful one who's ever played.

I think what most people find appealing about Gretzky is his decency. I admire the mutual love and respect that Wayne has for his father, Walter Gretzky. Everyone of us wants to know that we're loved and respected by our parents. And I think we all wish we could tell our father that we love him and appreciate everything he has done for us. Sadly, not all of us can do that. The great things that once brought us joy we inexplicably take for granted. Suddenly, almost without warning, the greatness is taken away and we wish that we could have done more to honour it. I'm not

TOM HANSON, CANADIAN PRESS
Wayne Gretzky played his last NHL game in Canada in Ottawa.

sure if there's a heaven or whether my dad can hear me, but Gretzky's retirement has made me think about you.

Dad, on my team, you and mom are the true Great Ones.

C. James McGuire, Manotick

DUCT TAPE HIS MOUTH
APRIL 24, 1999

Some executives have big mouths. Sometimes they don't have the guts to say negative things about Canada to our faces, they hide in places like Cleveland and berate us. This is just what Clive Allen, Nortel's executive vice-president and chief legal officer, has done. With his disparaging and threatening comments about Canadian taxes, he brands himself a 19th-century valueless capitalist. If he took the time to compare our record of taxation against all the G-8 countries, he would find us favourably in the middle. Some greedy people love to bellyache.

The damage done to Northern Telecom's image is terrible. Were I placing a project out for tenders, Northern Telecom's bid would have to be incredibly good for me to choose it over other more loyal Canadians. And that's good business. (But, of course, they are global and according to Mr. Allen couldn't care less about Canada.) Shrill, antiquated businesspeople could learn something from 21st century CEOs. This is an unfair comparison because the vice-president is not a CEO and may never get to be one. If I were this vice-president's boss, I'd fire him for making those statements — or at least require him to walk around with duct tape on his mouth for three weeks.

Rev. Brian S. Kopke, Ottawa

PINK-HAIRED VIRTUE IS ABSURD
MAY 1, 1999

With all due respect, John Robson, gimme a break. To equate pink hair with swastikas and murder videos is absurd. And to suggest that "good" grooming is a prerequisite to good citizenship suggests a pretty narrow view of civic virtue. The Nazis, as I recall, were impeccably well-groomed. So were the Canadian authorities who herded Japanese-Canadians into internment camps during the Second World War. So are those nice anti-abortion people who shoot doctors and bomb clinics.

When I was in high school, I grew my hair long and scruffy, wore jeans with holes in them and wore (horror of horrors!) a trenchcoat. But I also sat on the student's council, got top grades and treated adults with respect. My parents understood as long as I did that, my personal appearance was of minimal importance.

Kids are smart. And when you make simplistic statements like "neat good, sloppy bad," they're likely to just write you off and not take seriously anything else you have to say.

Tim Moerman, Orléans

ONLY A BARON

JUNE 23, 1999

A newspaper baron who strove to be a knight,
Found it not easy just to be black and white.
Though accepted in Britain as Sir Conrad Black,
With Jean Chrétien's denial, he was taken aback.
With that peerage denied, we know how you feel,
And advise you to consort with Lady Barbara
    Amiel,
And if to call you Sir Conrad is what you want
    most,
Then beware what you print in the National Post.

Michael Cronin, Ottawa

SADLY, IT'S NO JOKE

JULY 7, 1999

Three cheers for the people of Shawville for running the language cop out of town. The concept of language inspectors is ridiculous; it makes a mockery of human rights and it's embarrassing to the entire country. I was born in Montreal and raised in Ottawa. All my life this Anglo-Franco grappling has been going on and I'm sick of it.

It's about time the rest of Canada, along with anglophones and (rationally thinking) francophones from Quebec, joined the people of Shawville and said, "No more!" Give Mr. Bouchard a message that says loudly and boldly in English, Italian, Greek or Bantu that we aren't going to take it anymore. Let's stop being the wimps of the world and show some backbone for a change.

Ross Wilson, Ottawa

WE LOSE IF SENS GO

JULY 7, 1999

Opponents just don't seem to get it. Senators owner Rod Bryden is not asking the government to give him money, he just wants the government to take less out of his pocket.

The Ottawa Senators pay about $20 million in taxes every year. Mr. Bryden wants that sum reduced. He's still going to pay more than $10 million a year in taxes, which is $10 million more than he'll pay if he's in the U.S.

The main argument anti-hockey people have is that players' salaries are out of control. Even I can't argue that, however the Senators have the second lowest payroll in the NHL: at $22 million.

Considering they were the second best team in the league last season, management has been doing a fantastic job.

The current Stanley Cup champions, the Dallas Stars, had a payroll of more than $45 million, twice as much as the Senators. But Dallas and the other U.S. teams can afford it because their government doesn't tax them to death. They realize that sport teams bring spirit to their cities and spirit is something you can't put a price tag on.

This is what will happen if the Senators leave: local charities will lose millions because the Senators raise and give millions to them.

Thousands of people are going to lose their jobs because they are affiliated with the team (having an NHL team creates thousands of spin-off jobs).

This will put more people out of work and on welfare at the taxpayers' expense. The government loses the $10 million a year Rod Bryden will still pay if he's here and the city and country loses more of its heritage.

If Nike or McDonald's pays to have an ad put in the Corel Centre, that's a few thousand dollars coming to Ottawa. The Senators make millions in TV and advertising revenue. If the Senators leave, we lose that.

Do you really want to get rid of our heritage that badly?

Chris Swann, Ottawa

NOT MURDEROUS

JULY 18, 1999

I am a hunter. Yes, I've been known to dress in camouflage, or wear the gaudy orange hat. I even own more than one gun, and I have shot and eaten wild animals. But when I don my gear and grab my bow or gun, I don't become a murderous villain. I have no fantasies of slaughtering anything that moves in a volley of flying bullets.

My idea of hunting involves frost-covered fields, sunrises and mist-covered ponds with the sound of honking Canada geese in the background. Hokey maybe, but true. I've spent many hours in tree stands watching almost every animal from the Ottawa Valley in its natural environment.

The ultimate goal is to get an opportunity to harvest the animal you're hunting. Most times you're unsuccessful and you end up depending on the local grocery store for dinner. But if you are fortunate enough to harvest an animal, you gain a feeling of being part of nature and not just a spectator.

Contrary to popular belief, hunting has always been a valuable tool in helping control animal populations. If an area has 12 deer but food only for 10, it doesn't mean two deer will die. All the deer end up malnourished, causing the herd to suffer a higher death rate. Throughout Ontario, fish and game clubs volunteer to open trails through the snow and cut browse for the deer to eat. Other hunting organizations, such as Ducks Unlimited and the Federation of Anglers and Hunters, sponsor fundraising events and volunteer programs for habitat improvement or cleanup. All people and animals benefit from these initiatives. Because of the love hunters have for their pastime, we take responsibility for our environment.

Yes, I am a hunter and proud of it.

Brian McDonald, Ashton

IS PECA AVAILABLE?

JULY 30, 1999

Looking for a quick score, but won't work for it. Lacks commitment, and disappears when the pressure is on. To which situation do the above statements apply?

1. Alexei Yashin in the NHL playoffs?
2. Alexei Yashin and the NAC?
3. Alexei Yashin and his contract?

The correct answer, of course, is all of the above. The playoffs showed that no NHL team will ever prosper with Mr. Yashin in its lineup. The National Arts Centre fiasco showed that no city will ever gain from Mr. Yashin in its community. And Mr. Yashin's refusal to honour his contract shows that his presence in an NHL uniform will only further shame a shameful league. For the good of everyone, the Senators should simply ignore his ridiculous demands. Take the money saved, and spend it on players with courage and integrity. Is Mike Peca available?

Nicholas Stow, Ottawa

PAY HIM IN RUBLES

JULY 30, 1999

At the risk of antagonizing Senators' hockey fans and people of good sense, I suggest renegotiating Alexei Yashin's contract and paying him the $8 million to $10 million he appears to require. Yashin would, of course, have to agree to be paid in rubles.

Bruce Sach, Ottawa

CLEAN UP YOUR ACT

SEPTEMBER 11, 1999

To everyone who enjoys having sex outdoors: I'm glad you're wearing a condom to reduce teenage pregnancy and sexually transmitted diseases, but would you mind discarding your condoms in a clean and discreet way?

I love taking my two-year-old on nature walks and to parks, but in the past two days he managed to find a used condom at the park behind my house and another at Hog's Back. He gleefully displayed his trophy to my wife by wearing the thing on his hand like a mitten. This is nothing short of repugnant and a horrifying sight for a parent. Please be more responsible.

Steve Albert, Nepean

PULL A BOUCHARD

OCTOBER 5, 1999

While playing solitaire games on my computer, I discovered how to pull a "Lucien Bouchard." I look at a new game of solitaire and figure out that if there are two or more aces in the front row, I am likely to win. If they are not there, I scroll to a new game and do not lose any points by doing so. Hence, I have set up "winning conditions" and pulled a "Lucien Bouchard."

Mai-yu Chan, Ottawa

BIG MAC, MAYBE

OCTOBER 13, 1999

With respect to the Central Experimental Farm's decision not to give cows "offensive" female names in future, may I be among the first to suggest a bold pattern of New Age names for the coming millennium?

What about "Big Mac," "Quarter Pounder" and "Whopper Junior?"

Michael J. DiCola, Ottawa

Editor's note: The Central Experimental Farm drew an avalanche of hostile comment for its (quickly retracted) policy of not giving cows women's names.

STICKHANDLERS OR PANHANDLERS?

NOVEMBER 26, 1999

I'd like to see more action, and fast, to stomp on swarming and aggressive panhandling. Especially in Kanata.

I'm thinking of all those Kanata businesspeople who swarmed Kanata Council Tuesday night to wring a tax concession out of cowed municipal politicians for their pal, the chief tenant of the Corel Centre.

I'm also thinking about Senators owner Rod Bryden and his offensive and highly aggressive panhandling for what now seems like years. The next time they all show up at Kanata city hall, don't call in the fire marshal to clear out the surplus crowd, call the police to arrest the whole lot.

Just like what we'd do if the swarming and panhandling happened downtown on a cold street corner.

Frank Howard, Ottawa